PENGUIN C

SIDNEY'S 'THE DEFENCE OF POESY' AND SELECTED RENAISSANCE LITERARY CRITICISM

GAVIN ALEXANDER was educated at Leeds Grammar School and Gonville and Caius College, Cambridge, where he was subsequently a Research Fellow. He is currently a Lecturer in the Faculty of English, University of Cambridge, and a Fellow and Director of Studies in English at Christ's College. He has published on various literary and musical topics, and is completing a book on the literary response to Sir Philip Sidney.

 PENGUIN CLASSICS

SIDNEY'S THE DEFENCE OF POESY
AND SELECTED RENAISSANCE
LITERARY CRITICISM

DAVID ALEXANDER was educated at Leeds Grammar School and Downville and Caius College, Cambridge where he was subsequently a Research Fellow. He is currently a Lecturer in the Faculty of English, University of Cambridge, and a Fellow and Director of Studies in English at Christ's College. He has published on numerous literary and musical topics, and is completing a book on the literary response to Sir Philip Sidney.

Sidney's 'The Defence of Poesy' and Selected Renaissance Literary Criticism

Edited and with an Introduction and Notes by
GAVIN ALEXANDER

PENGUIN BOOKS

PENGUIN BOOKS

Published by the Penguin Group
Penguin Books Ltd, 80 Strand, London WC2R ORL, England
Penguin Group (USA) Inc., 375 Hudson Street, New York, New York 10014, USA
Penguin Books Australia Ltd, 250 Camberwell Road, Camberwell, Victoria 3124, Australia
Penguin Books Canada Ltd, 10 Alcorn Avenue, Toronto, Ontario, Canada M4V 3B2
Penguin Books India (P) Ltd, 11, Community Centre, Panchsheel Park, New Delhi – 110 017, India
Penguin Books (NZ) Ltd, Cnr Rosedale and Airborne Roads, Albany, Auckland, New Zealand
Penguin Books (South Africa) (Pty) Ltd, 24 Sturdee Avenue, Rosebank 2196, South Africa

Penguin Books Ltd, Registered Offices: 80 Strand, London WC2R ORL, England

www.penguin.com

First published 2004
5

Introduction and editorial matter copyright © Gavin Alexander, 2004
All rights reserved

The moral right of the editor has been asserted

Set in 10.25/12.25 pt PostScript Adobe Sabon
Typeset by Rowland Phototypesetting Ltd, Bury St Edmunds, Suffolk
Printed in Great Britain by Clays Ltd, St Ives plc

ISBN 978-0-141-43938-9

www.greenpenguin.co.uk

Contents

Chronology

GREECE AND ROME

Historical events	Authors
BC	
c. 1250–800 Greek Dark Age	
c. 800– Period of colonization; emergence of city-states	
c. 750– Greek colonization of Sicily	*c.* 750–700 Homer, Hesiod
c. 600– Beginnings of democracy in Athens	*c.* 600 Sappho, Alcaeus
509 Rome expels the king and Republic founded, according to tradition	
490–479 Persian wars	Aeschylus (525–456), Pindar (*c.* 522–443)
478–429 Athenian ascendancy	Sophocles (496–406), Euripides (480–406)
431–404 Peloponnesian war between Athens and Sparta, ending with surrender of Athens	Socrates (469–399)
	427 Gorgias brings formal rhetoric to Athens
	Aristophanes (*c.* 448–380)
404–371 Spartan ascendancy	Isocrates (436–338), Plato (*c.* 428–*c.* 348)
359–336 Rule of Philip II of Macedon	Demosthenes (*c.* 383–322)

336–323 Rule of Alexander the Great	Aristotle (384–322)
323– 'Hellenistic Age'; Ptolemaic rule in Egypt	Menander (c. 342–292)
c. 300 Museum and Library at Alexandria founded	Theocritus (c. 308–c. 240)
246–146 Republican Rome successful in wars with Macedon, Syria and Carthage, and in conquest of Sicily	Plautus (c. 254–184), Ennius (239–169), Terence (c. 190–159) second or first century BC 'Demetrius', On Style
60–42 First triumvirate (60); Caesar defeats Pompey (48); Caesar murdered (44); Republicans defeated at Philippi (42) by Octavian and Antony	Cicero (106–43)
31 Octavian defeats Antony and Cleopatra at Actium; end of Hellenistic Age	Virgil (70–19); Aeneid published posthumously Horace (65–8)
31 BC–14 AD Rule of Octavian as Augustus	Ovid (43 BC–18 AD)
AD	
14–37 Tiberius; 37–41 Caligula; 41–54 Claudius; 54–68 Nero; 69 Year of the four emperors	Seneca (c. 4 BC–65 AD) Lucan (39–65)
69–79 Vespasian; 79–81 Titus; 81–96 Domitian; 96–98 Nerva; 98–117 Trajan; 117–38 Hadrian	First century AD 'Longinus', On the Sublime Quintilian (c. 35–c. 100) Plutarch (c. 50–c. 125)

ENGLAND AND EUROPE

Historical events	*Authors*
	Dante (1265–1321); Petrarch (1304–74); Boccaccio (1313–75)

1337–1453 Hundred Years War between England and France

Gower (?1330–1408), Chaucer (c. 1343–1400), Lydgate (?1370–1449)

1455–85 Wars of the Roses
1509–47 Rule of Henry VIII (born 1491)

1511–12 Erasmus, *De ratione studii* ('On the Method of Study', 1511), *De copia* ('On Copiousness', 1512)

1516 Birth of Princess Mary

1516 Ariosto, *Orlando furioso*; More, *Utopia*; Colet and Erasmus devise model humanist curriculum at St Paul's School

1517 Luther posts his Wittenberg theses
1520 Henry VIII given title *Fidei Defensor* by Pope Leo X

1526 Tyndale, *New Testament* in English
1528 Castiglione, *The Courtier* Death of Skelton (?1460–1529)

1530 Henry VIII Supreme Head of the Church in England

1531 Elyot, *The Governor*
1535 Coverdale, *Bible* in English; execution of More (?1477–1535)

1532–33 Henry VIII divorces Catherine of Aragon, is excommunicated, and marries Anne Boleyn; birth of Princess Elizabeth
1536 Anne Boleyn executed; Henry VIII marries Jane Seymour; smaller abbeys suppressed

1536 Latin translation of Aristotle, *Poetics*

1537 Birth of Prince Edward
1538 Breaking of images in churches

1538 Elyot, Latin–English Dictionary

1539 Dissolution of the monasteries

1541 Henry VIII assumes titles of King of Ireland and Head of Church in Ireland

1542 Birth and accession of Mary, Queen of Scots

1544 War with France; capture of Boulogne

1547 Death of Henry VIII; accession of Edward VI

1549 War with France; Act of Uniformity

1553 Death of Edward VI; accession of Mary

1554 Wyatt's rebellion; execution of Lady Jane Grey; Mary marries Philip of Spain

1555–56 Latimer, Ridley, Cranmer burned

1557 War with France

1558 Loss of Calais; death of Mary

1558–1603 Rule of Elizabeth I

1559 Mary, Queen of Scots marries French Dauphin; Acts of Uniformity

1539 *'Great' Bible* in English

c. 1541 Susenbrotus, *Epitome troporum ac schematum* ('Outline of Schemes and Tropes')
Death of Wyatt (1503–42)

1546 Puttenham matriculates at Christ's College, Cambridge
Death of Surrey (1517–47)

1549 *Book of Common Prayer*; Du Bellay, *Defence et illustration de la langue Françoise* ('Defence and Illustration of the French Language')

1553 Wilson, *Art of Rhetoric*

1554 Philip Sidney born; first edition of 'Longinus', *On the Sublime*

1555 First instalment of Phaer's translation of Virgil's *Aeneid*

1556 Puttenham admitted to Middle Temple

1557 *Songs and Sonnets* ('Tottel's Miscellany')

1559 *Mirror for Magistrates* (after suppressed edition of 1555; enlarged edition 1563)
1560 *Geneva Bible*

1577 Drake's voyage around the world begins; Curtain Theatre and Blackfriars Theatre open

1579 Sidney writes against Elizabeth's projected marriage to the French Duke of Alençon

1581 Execution of Edmund Campion

1583 Irish rebellion defeated
1584 Assassination of William of Orange; failure of Ralegh in Virginia
1585 English intervention in Low Countries
1586 Babington plot; trial of Mary, Queen of Scots

1587 Execution of Mary, Queen of Scots; Sidney's funeral; Pope proclaims crusade against England
1588 Defeat of Spanish Armada

1577 Peacham, *Garden of Eloquence*; death of Gascoigne (c. 1534–77)
1578 Lyly, *Euphues*
1579 Gosson, *School of Abuse*, Spenser, *Shepheardes Calender* (both dedicated to Sidney); North's translation of Plutarch's *Lives*
c. 1580 Sidney writing *Arcadia*, *Defence of Poesy*, *Astrophil and Stella*
1580–81 Tasso, *Gerusalemme liberata* ('Jerusalem Delivered')
1581 Newton's translation of Seneca's *Tragedies*; Daniel matriculates at Magdalen Hall, Oxford
1582 Gosson, *Plays Confuted*; Hakluyt, *Voyages*

1586 Webbe, *Discourse of English Poetry*; Death of Sidney (1554–86) after Battle of Zutphen

1587 Kyd, *The Spanish Tragedy*; Marlowe, *Tamburlaine* first performed

1589 Puttenham, *Art of English Poesy*

	1590 Sidney, *Arcadia*; Spenser, *The Faerie Queene*, 1–3; Marlowe and Shakespeare both active
1591 Increased measures against recusants	1591 Sidney, *Astrophil and Stella*; Harington's translation of Ariosto, *Orlando Furioso* (prefaced by 'A Brief Apology of Poetry'); ?death of Puttenham (*c.* 1529–1590 or 1591)
1592 Rose Theatre opens	1592 Daniel, *Delia*
	1593 Sidney, *Arcadia* (composite edition); Daniel, *Cleopatra*; Drayton, *Idea*; Peacham, *Garden of Eloquence*, 2nd edition; death of Marlowe (1564–1593)
1594 Swan Theatre built	1594 Nashe, *The Unfortunate Traveller*; Daniel, *Cleopatra*
1595 Execution of Robert Southwell (Catholic poet)	1595 Sidney, *Defence of Poesy* published; Daniel, *The Civil Wars*, 1–4
1596 Essex storms Cadiz	1596 Spenser, *The Faerie Queene*, 4–6
	1598 Sidney's other works printed with *Arcadia*; first instalment of Chapman's Homer
1599 Essex imprisoned; Globe Theatre opened	1599 Daniel, *Poetical Essays* (including *Musophilus*); death of Spenser (1552–99)
1600 Fortune Theatre built; birth of Prince Charles, future King Charles I	
1601 Execution of Essex	1601–02 *The Works of Samuel Daniel*; death of Nashe (1567–1601)

1602 Campion, *Observations in the Art of English Poesy*

1603 Death of Elizabeth I
1603–25 Rule of James I
1604 Hampton Court
conference

1603 Daniel, *Defence of Rhyme*

1605 Gunpowder Plot

1605 Bacon, *Advancement of Learning*
1611 Authorized Version of the Bible
Death of Harington
(*c.* 1561–1612)

1614 'Addled' Parliament
(procedural chaos caused by
rift within Privy Council)

1616 Jonson, *Works*; death of
Shakespeare (1564–1616);
Chapman's complete
translation of Homer's *Iliad*
and *Odyssey*
Death of Ralegh (?1554–1618)

1618 Rebellion of Bohemia
against Holy Roman Empire;
start of Thirty Years War

Death of Daniel (1562/3–1619)
Death of Campion (1567–
1620)

1623 Failure of Spanish match
project for Prince Charles

1623 Shakespeare, *Comedies,
Histories and Tragedies* ('First
Folio'); *The Whole Works of
Samuel Daniel*

1625 Death of James I
1625–1649 Rule of Charles I;
his wife Henrietta Maria
of France a practising
Catholic
1625; 1626; 1628–29 Abortive
Parliaments dominated by
Puritan opposition

Death of Bacon (1561–1626)

1627 Drayton, *Battle of Agincourt* (including the 'Epistle to Reynolds')

1628 Assassination of Duke of Buckingham
1629–40 Personal rule of Charles I (no Parliaments)
1630 Birth of future Charles II

Death of Donne (1572–1631) and Drayton (1563–1631); birth of Dryden (1631–1700)

1633 Laud made Archbishop of Canterbury

1633 Publication of Donne's *Poems*; death of Herbert (1593–1633); publication of Herbert's *The Temple*
1634 Performance of Milton's *Comus*; death of Chapman (?1559–1634)

1637 Attempts to impose Anglican Prayer Book and episcopacy on Scotland
1638 National Covenant (pledge to resist innovations in religion) signed by Scottish presbyterians
1639–40 Bishops' Wars in Scotland
1640 Short Parliament; Long Parliament

1637 Publication of Milton's *Lycidas*; death of Jonson (1572/3–1637)

1640 Jonson, *Works* (including *Horace, his Art of Poetry*, and 'A Fit of Rhyme against Rhyme'); death of Alexander (?1567–1640)

1642 Beginning of English Civil War

Introduction

> 'Nevertheless, let it be said that if poetic imitation designed
> for pleasure has any arguments to show that she should have
> a place in a well-governed city, we would gladly receive her
> back from exile, for we are very conscious of her spell . . . So
> it would be right for poetry to return from exile if she could
> defend herself in lyric or in some other metre?'
>   'Certainly.'
>   'And we might allow her patrons . . . to speak on her behalf
> in prose to show that she is not only a source of pleasure, but
> also a benefit to societies and human life. And we shall listen
> favourably, since it will be our gain if she turns out to be not
> only pleasing, but also useful.'
>
>   Plato, *Republic*, 10.607[1]

The imagination has always had its critics. When Plato's
Socrates outlines his ideal state he is forced to make the tough
decision to exclude all poetry (that is, all imaginative literature),
with the exception of hymns to the gods and poems in honour
of great men. Poetry corrupts because it peddles fictions, either
poor copies of reality or dangerous phantasms; it tells stories
which glorify vice, wantonness and depravity; engaging the
mind with fiction is a bad habit to get into for those who would
be morally good in fact. If subsequent literary criticism can be
thought of as a response to Plato's kindly gesture of leaving
the door ever so slightly open at the conclusion of what remains
the most cogent and challenging critique of the arts, then we
notice several things. First, that poetry might make her defence
in verse, as Horace was to do in his *Ars poetica* ('The Art of
Poetry'). Second, that this will be a defence, a speech on behalf
of poetry before a judge and jury of philosophers. Third, that
the only admissible defence will be that poetry is a force for
social good, that it is intimately connected with politics, with

public and private morals, that it has social responsibilities and can discharge them well.

Sir Philip Sidney's *Defence of Poesy* meets Plato's specifications perfectly, both in its form – a speech for the defence – and in its content – an argument that literature is a force for moral and social good. It is edited here with other texts of the period 1575–1640, in verse and in prose, which share a pressing need to define literature, to defend it against its critics, and to generate the rules and standards needed by English literature in what was felt to be its fledgling state. Fiction involves the making of imaginary worlds. Its theorization, and the generation of artificial rules for its organization and verbal expression, coincided with the making and legislation of new worlds in reality. The English Renaissance was a period of religious reform, of colonization, of nation building and the resistance of foreign invasion. It was the job of literature to comprehend the changing world of its readers, to offer fictions which could help them make sense of their lives. And it is no coincidence that the criticism which attempted to make sense of that literature is full of the language of military conquest and defence, of colonization and international trade, of architecture, nation building, reformation, revolution, and legislation. When Samuel Daniel defends the role of poetic form in framing poetic fictions, he echoes God's role as creator: 'For the body of our imagination being as an unformed chaos without fashion, without day, if by the divine power of the spirit it be wrought into an orb of order and form, is it not more pleasing to nature . . . ?' (p. 216). For Sidney, likewise, the poet, by which he means the writer of imaginative literature in verse or prose, 'doth grow in effect into another nature, in making things either better than nature bringeth forth or, quite anew . . . : her world is brazen, the poets only deliver a golden' (pp. 8–9). The making of fictions, narrative structures, and poetic forms has much in common both with the philosophical imagining of the ideal state and with attempts to imagine and create England's political future. These analogies were acknowledged and exploited by Renaissance critics. But many also found that the activities overlapped not only metaphorically but actually: Sidney, for one, was intensely engaged in European politics and in new world exploration and colonization.

We cannot expect to find in Renaissance literary criticism a careful guide to how we should read Renaissance literature. Nor can we expect always to recognize early versions of the concerns of more recent literary critics and theorists. It is much more interesting than that. Sidney, Daniel, George Puttenham and the other writers represented here show both a larger philosophical and ethical scope than we might expect, and a greater concern for details of language, genre, and poetic form than we might care for. To understand why they chose to write at all, and to write in the way they did, we need to try to look at their world as they did.

THE ENGLISH RENAISSANCE

The period spanned by this edition – 1575–1640 – is bounded at either end by momentous changes. At its start, reformation, counter-reformation, and the establishment of a national Protestant church. At its end, civil war, regicide and a short-lived republic. The term 'Renaissance' is applied to the phase of English cultural development coinciding with the Reformation and extending into the seventeenth century. Our Renaissance was in many ways a delayed reaction to an impulse which began in fourteenth-century Italy. The rebirth which 'renaissance' signifies was of classical literature and culture. Learning had already begun to move out of the monasteries of medieval Europe into the newly established universities; under the enlightened patronage of princes and grandees it took an equally firm root in the Renaissance court. Central to the redefinition of culture which this power shift marked was the rediscovery and reappraisal of the ancient world, its history, philosophy and literature. To give a few relevant examples. Aristotle's *Poetics*, by and large neglected in the Middle Ages, was looked at with fresh eyes, and by the middle of the sixteenth century had begun a domination of literary criticism which was to last two centuries. Quintilian's *Institutio oratoria* ('The Education of the

Orator'), the most comprehensive classical treatise on rhetoric, survived only in parts until complete manuscripts were unearthed in the fifteenth century. And many speeches by Cicero were similarly recovered from the lumber rooms of neglected monastic libraries, including a speech in defence of the Greek poet Archias – facing deportation by Cicero's political enemies – which offered Renaissance critics many of the arguments they needed to defend their own poets. The canon of classical wisdom, always the foundation of modern learning, was re-appraised, revised, and extended. Hence the feeling, as evident in the minds of most Renaissance scholars as it is in the minds of many modern scholars, that a great gulf separates the Renaissance and medieval mentalities, and that the Renaissance scholar could rightly feel that he had more in common with Plato, Cicero and Horace than with Aquinas, Duns Scotus or Chaucer.

Two symptoms of the English Renaissance concern us in particular. One was the newly devised school curricula which put the study of rhetoric and of literature at their centre. The other was the translation and imitation of classical models. By the end of our period, many of the major classical authors had been translated into English for the first time, and some more than once: Virgil, Ovid, Seneca, Tacitus, Livy, Pliny, and Suetonius from Latin; Homer, some Aristotle, Plutarch and various prose romances from Greek (though often via French or Latin). Other authors were accorded the close attention of imitation, Horace and Catullus offering especially popular material for English lyric poets to revisit and give their own versions of. The new classics of French, Spanish and Italian literature were also brought into English: Du Bartas, Montaigne, Montemayor, Ariosto, Tasso. And those Continental authors who seemed most to embody the new way of looking and writing were imitated closely – Petrarch's lyric poems being perhaps the best-known example. By the end of the Elizabethan period, the new classics of English literature – works like Sidney's *Arcadia* (1590) and Edmund Spenser's *The Faerie Queene* (1590–96) – were being published. They were works of complex texture, woven from the threads of Greek, Latin, and modern European classics, and yet all the more original for that.

The writing of literary criticism was one other area where English authors were stimulated by classical and Continental examples. But their work was no mere rehash. What was at stake for English writers and theorists of literature? The Renaissance in England started to bear fruit as England broke from Rome. Before the 1530s, England had been one among many nations, all members of one Roman Church, their princes constantly squabbling over issues of dynastic succession, marrying each other's daughters, fighting wars sometimes with, sometimes against, each other. What Henry VIII did in rejecting the supremacy of Rome set England apart, its island status now a clear sign that it was unique in Europe, different from the rest, sovereign and self-sufficient. Its culture had always been measured against that of the Continent, and its authors had been happy to take inspiration, especially from French and Italian sources. But the Reformation gave an edge to questions about rivalry and dependence. England now had much more to prove. The same was to some extent true of its Continental rivals, for the counter-reformation led to some reconsideration and readjustment of the practices and ideologies of Rome. And the rivalry became a matter of which country was the most like ancient Greece and Rome in its language and literature, of which could be the most authentically classical. Parallel movements can be seen in each major European country. These include the study of the vernacular, to vindicate it as a vehicle of scholarship and poetry worthy of comparison to the classical languages; the theorization of vernacular versification and experiments with classical systems of versification, again to put the modern language on a footing with Greek and Latin; and the defence of vernacular literature, together with the generation of the rules needed to give it more confidence. In Protestant England the stakes were high: the self-confidence of English literature, its sovereignty, its right to claim authentic descent from the classics – these concerns seem to move in parallel to questions of national sovereignty, as the England of Elizabeth I, so recently delivered from a Catholic monarch and her husband, the King of Spain, encountered the threats of the Catholic Mary Queen of Scots, of Catholic rebels and plotters, of a plan to marry Elizabeth to a

Catholic French prince, and of an uncertain succession. Literary and political nationalism worked hand in hand.

For William Webbe, 'reformation' is naturally the right word to use for his plan to remodel the rules of English versification: like the reformed Church, English poetry should free itself from the superstitions and customs of the Dark Ages and rebuild itself to accord with the authentic, ancient model. For Daniel, 'reformation' should signify not an abrupt change in poetic doctrine, but rather an enlightened process of revision and improvement. It is 'the whole state of rhyme in this kingdom' which Thomas Campion's proposed system threatens 'to over-throw'; where the naturalization of new words is concerned, Daniel protests that some writers introduce foreign words and give them 'without a parliament, without any consent or allow-ance' the rights of 'free-denizens [naturalized citizens] in our language'. Faced with the 'alarum' of his 'adversary' and the threat of 'fealty' to a 'foreign' literary power, Daniel makes it very clear that this is war (pp. 208, 233, 229, 227).

Much work was to be done to establish the state of letters on firm foundations. There were too few vernacular classics – big, ambitious works on classical lines which could offer inspiration and encouragement to future generations of writers. And the rules needed by all artists were in a muddle. The English and Scottish could always boast Latin authors in prose and verse with international reputations. But when it came to vernacular literature, English prose lacked elegance and its verse regulation. English, after all, was a minor language, spoken only on a small island at the edge of the world. Why anyone would therefore bother writing English literature is a question debated in Daniel's *Musophilus*. When we look back via the prose of Dr Johnson or the verse of Dryden, it is too easy to view the history of the English language and its literature as a gentle, inevitable evolution towards regularity and refinement, and the idea of English as a world language as a foregone conclusion. But we must not forget what Dryden and Johnson knew well – that the Renaissance achievement had been sudden and substantial, and that the story of the language and literature they wrote, as of the nascent British Empire, really began in the sixteenth century.

To some, English literature seemed resolutely parochial. Many writers, as Michael Drayton observes (ll. 187–95), preferred not to have their works printed and instead kept them close or allowed them to circulate only in manuscript. Sidney was in this category; had he not died prematurely, perhaps the writings which had such a great impact on English literature in the 1590s would not have made it to the press for many more years. And although the printing presses were busy before this time, most printed literature was, as far as the learned and progressive were concerned, popular or old-fashioned. Webbe prefaces his *Discourse of English Poetry* by surveying 'the innumerable sorts of English books and infinite fardles of printed pamphlets wherewith this country is pestered, all shops stuffed, and every study furnished'. He hopes that by a thorough scrutiny of modern English poetry 'we may not only get the means, which we yet want, to discern between good writers and bad, but perhaps also challenge from the rude multitude of rustical rhymers, who will be called poets, the right practice and orderly course of true poetry'.[2] Although both drama and prose fiction remain peripheral to literary criticism in the period (except when included in discussions of 'poetry' broadly defined), the same aim of taking a popular kind of literature and elevating it to a more correct form is squarely that of Jonson as dramatist or Sidney as author of prose romance.

English Renaissance literary criticism comes in various forms. Because Horace's *Ars poetica* was itself a poem, the versified art was attempted by some on the Continent; Jonson's translation of Horace represents this kind. Others wrote extended treatises, not so much on the model of Aristotle's brief *Poetics* as on that of such rhetoric books as Quintilian's *Institutio oratoria*: Puttenham's *Art of English Poesy* is an example of this kind. Another kind is modelled on the classical oration, and may be a speech in praise of or in defence of literature in general, as we get par excellence in Sidney's *Defence of Poesy*. Other works address a particular issue and have a narrower scope, as Daniel's *Defence of Rhyme* at least appears to. And from these basic options all sorts of combinations were possible: Drayton, for example, takes the topos of surveying the national literature (exemplified by the final section of Sidney's *Defence* and the last chapter of Puttenham's Book I) and makes a poem out of it. Comment on literature was also to be found in rhetoric manuals (Henry Peacham's *Garden of Eloquence*) and works on learning in general (Daniel's *Musophilus*; Francis Bacon's *Advancement of Learning*).

Certain characteristics distance Renaissance literary criticism from the normal procedures of modern criticism. First, we see the predominance of the discussion of first principles rather than the detailed appraisal of specific works and authors: Renaissance critics prefer to deal in ideas and ideals rather than in actualities, and in many cases might better be called literary theorists. Second, classical rhetoric dominates these works in two fundamental ways: they are rhetorical through and through, directed at winning a particular argument on a particular occasion; and they view literature as a sort of rhetoric, aimed, in the most important common formulation, at instructing and delighting the reader, and not to be thought of as the self-expression of the author. Third, where we value originality and consider it as diametrically opposed to the imitation of previous authors and texts, Renaissance critics seem to value imitation above originality, or rather as a route to originality. Fourth, and relatedly, rules of all kinds are seen not as an encumbrance or even a necessary evil, but as a fundamental condition of any writing – without clear rules and conventions art is impossible. Most importantly, where we now tend to see the scholarly study of literature and literary theory as inhabiting a different world from the writing of literature, and expect there to be little communication between the two, Renaissance literary criticism is usually the work of writers of literature, and is aimed at readers and authors alike: it shows how to write, and how writing ought to be read.

HUMANISM AND LITERATURE

Before we proceed further, we need to look more closely at the intellectual background of those readers and authors, and at the movement known now as humanism. Humanism is a nineteenth-century name for an intellectual position central to the Renaissance. It values engagement with the classics, but within the civic framework out of which those classics came. The humanist author or reader will not simply accept that all modern writing must bow before the ancients and derive from them, but will be intensely interested in the relations and tensions between past and present texts. The humanist will also see intellectual activity as connected to civic activity, will wish authors to influence political life and politicians to be scholars. As Ben Jonson argues in *Discoveries* (published posthumously in 1640), the humanist reader was to be critical rather than slavish:

> I know nothing can conduce more to letters than to examine the writings of the ancients, and not to rest in their sole authority, or take all upon trust from them . . . For to all the observations of the ancients, we have our own experience; which if we will use and apply, we have better means to pronounce. It is true they opened the gates and made the way that went before us, but as guides, not commanders . . . Truth lies open to all; it is no man's several.[3]

The training of critical humanist readers was a serious business, leading to a boom in the foundation of schools, and a complete reappraisal of the system of elementary education. Desiderius Erasmus, the single most influential of the sixteenth-century humanists, divided knowledge into that of words (*verba*) and that of things (*res*). Words came first, and so elementary education – an education in Latin rather than the vernacular – was about mastering the arts of language: that is, grammar and rhetoric. After this, students could start to think about things – abstract concepts, types of argument. In teaching younger schoolboys to recognize rhetorical features, literary texts were preferred precisely because they made learning more fun. In *De ratione studii* ('On the Method of Study', 1511) Erasmus describes the new method. After learning grammatical rules and the rules of versification, the student should:

have at your fingertips the chief points of rhetoric, namely prop-
ositions, the grounds of proof, figures of speech, amplifications,
and the rules governing transitions. For these are conducive not
only to criticism but also to imitation. Informed then by all this
you will carefully observe when reading writers whether any
striking word occurs, if diction is archaic or novel, if some argument shows brilliant invention or has been skilfully adapted from
elsewhere, if there is any brilliance in the style, if there is any
adage, historical parallel, or maxim worth committing to
memory.

Erasmus in fact recommends that literary texts should be studied
as literature:

> Now in approaching each work the teacher should indicate the
> nature of the argument in the particular genre, and what should
> be most closely observed in it. For instance, the essence of the
> epigram lies in its pointed brevity . . . In tragedy, he will point out
> that particular attention should be paid to the emotions aroused,
> and especially, indeed, to the more profound. He will show briefly
> how these effects are achieved. Then he will deal with the argu-
> ments of the speakers as if they were set pieces of rhetoric. Finally,
> he should deal with the representation of place, time, and some-
> times action, and the occurrence of heated exchanges [*stichomy-
> thia*], which may be worked out in couplets, single lines, or
> half-lines.[4]

Dramatic dialogue is here to be studied as if it is formal rhetoric.
And students would go on to practise the writing and performing
of certain literary kinds as part of their rhetorical training.
Features of rhetoric given special emphasis included *prosopopoeia* (the representation of imaginary or absent speakers),
topographia (the representation of places real or imaginary),
ethos (the credible persona of the speaker), and *pathos* (the
stirring of the reader's or audience's emotions). One favourite
exercise was to make the student compose an oration in the
person of one character from literature or history addressing
another: poets and dramatists had learned many of their

skills by the time they left school. The literature they studied and imitated was used not only as a store of good speeches and illustrations of rhetorical figures. It also furnished many of the so-called commonplaces – adages, maxims, examples from stories – of which the orator needed to have an ample store so that he could always find the right arguments and illustrate them appropriately. Good commonplaces encountered in this way were to be entered throughout a man's life in a common-place book, with alphabetical headings under moral topics like bravery, foolhardiness, piety and generosity. The rhetorical education thus gave its students a skill and a resource which would be put to work when the perfect young humanists became poets and dramatists instead of politicians, diplomats or churchmen.

For the humanists rhetoric was the master discipline, the most fundamental and important form of learning. As Thomas Nashe puts it in 1589: 'Amongst all the ornaments of arts, rhetoric is to be had in highest reputation, without the which all the rest are naked'.[5] And literature was central to the rhetorical curriculum. But both arts were open to criticism. Rhetoric was first recognized as an art which could be taught in the later fifth century BC, when Socrates was revolutionizing philosophy, and other new approaches to knowledge and argument were competing in the Athenian educational marketplace. Already in these early days philosophers, most notably Plato, were keen to dent rhetoric's prestige, either out of professional rivalry (because it encroached on what philosophy regarded as its turf – dialectical argument), or out of a more sincere worry about rhetoric's apparent indifference to the truth and its ability to inveigle reason by appealing to the emotions. Plato's arguments against rhetoric – notably in the dialogues *Gorgias* and *Phaedrus* – were related to his arguments against poetry, and both arts responded by forming their own similar myths. For the orators, rhetoric is the cause of society, as the fourth-century orator Isocrates spells out in a passage echoed in this edition by Peacham in his *Garden of Eloquence* (see pp. 248–9, and note 2 on that text):

because there has been implanted in us the power to persuade
each other and to make clear to each other whatever we desire,
not only have we escaped the life of wild beasts, but we have
come together and founded cities and made laws and invented
arts; and, generally speaking, there is no institution devised by
man which the power of speech has not helped us to establish.
(*Nicocles*, 6–9)

For the poets, as Horace argues in the *Ars poetica*, the myths
about Orpheus taming wild beasts and Amphion building
Thebes with their song tell us that we have poets to thank for
the beginnings of human society. As Thomas Lodge summarizes
the argument: 'poets were the first raisers of cities, prescribers
of good laws, maintainers of religion, disturbers of the wicked,
advancers of the well-disposed, inventors of laws, and lastly the
very footpaths to knowledge and understanding'.[6] These mythic
defences were used to argue that rhetoric and imaginative literature were forces for good in society, teaching the right and the
good, inculcating morals, and, far from being either specious
distractions from the truth or peddlers of immorality, essential
to human progress.

But the moral authority of both rhetoric and imaginative
literature remained open to attack: it was still possible for
rhetoric to be used to prosecute an innocent man, or recommend
a bad course of action; literature was mostly about sex and
violence and tended to excite rather than to educate its readers.
One answer to this last objection was that only bad readers use
literature to bad ends: good readers (with the help of good
teachers) will emulate the good they see and treat representations of immorality as warnings of what is to be shunned.
Another answer was that one morally bad poet doesn't make
poetry bad. Writers on literature and rhetoric gravitate towards
ideals, because the stronger arguments are to be made about
what literature and rhetoric can be rather than what they have
been. Cicero defines the ideal orator, an idea 'which we can
have in our minds even if we do not see it' (*Orator* ['The
Orator'], 101), just as Sidney speaks 'of the art and not of the
artificer' (p. 20). The ideal orator had to be 'a good man, skilled

in speaking' (Quintilian, *Institutio oratoria*, 12.1.1), a broad remit:

> The art of speaking well, that is to say, of speaking with know-
> ledge, skill and elegance, has no delimited territory, within whose
> borders it is enclosed and confined. All things whatsoever, that can
> fall under the discussion of human beings, must be aptly dealt with
> by him who professes to have this power, or he must abandon the
> name of eloquent. (Cicero, *De oratore* ['On the Orator'], 2.2.5)

The Greek historian Strabo adjusted the arguments to define the ideal poet:

> Can one believe that a poet who can introduce characters
> delivering speeches, commanding armies, and performing other
> virtuous actions, is himself a humbug and a mountebank, capable
> only of bewitching and cajoling his audience without doing them
> good? . . . One cannot be a good poet without first being a good
> man. (*Geography*, 1.2.5)[7]

And Ben Jonson echoes Cicero:

> I could never think the study of wisdom confined only to the
> philosopher, or of piety to the divine, or of state to the politic.
> But that he which can feign a commonwealth (which is the poet),
> can govern it with counsels, strengthen it with laws, correct it
> with judgements, inform it with religion and morals, is all these.
> We do not require in him mere elocution [style], or an excellent
> faculty in verse, but the exact knowledge of all virtues and their
> contraries, with ability to render the one loved, the other hated,
> by his proper embattling them.[8]

It is easy to see how the Renaissance writer of imaginative literature becomes a composite figure, an ideal orator-poet: a good man, with broad knowledge and experience, skilled in the arts of language, and writing fiction which benefits his country and its people. What Sir John Harington says of poetry is at the heart of the humanist position:

this I say of it, and I think I say truly, that there are many good
lessons to be learned out of it, many good examples to be found
in it, many good uses to be had of it, and that therefore it is not,
nor ought not to be, despised by the wiser sort, but so to be
studied and employed as was intended by the first writers and
devisers thereof, which is to soften and polish the hard and rough
dispositions of men, and make them capable of virtue and good
discipline. (p. 263)

This may seem a curious view, but just as old arguments about
the moral perils of literature are repeated in current debates
about sex and violence in film and television, so the old answer
may still apply to what is best in our literary culture and in
contemporary novels or films or plays: that it can indeed 'soften
and polish the harsh and rough dispositions of men', that it is
what makes us civilized.

IDEAS OF IMITATION

Renaissance writers are for the most part little interested in
exploring their own hearts, or in laying them bare to their
readers. To read their work appropriately we need to leave
behind our post-Romantic prejudices, and most importantly the
assumption that literature is self-expression. Even when a poet
writes in the first person, the 'I' is a character, a rhetorical
construction intended to provide the reader with something he
or she wants to read about. It is a representation or imitation of
life rather than life itself, and it is often imitative in a further
respect, copying the scenario, method or style of a previous
writer. The hero of Sidney's amorous sonnet sequence *Astrophil
and Stella* (c.1581, printed 1591) bears many similarities to his
author, and their biographies overlap playfully. But he is not
Sidney because this is literature and not life, and he cannot be
Sidney because he is also composed of elements drawn from
previous sonnet sequences, notably Petrarch's. One word crops
up repeatedly in the efforts of Renaissance critics to explain
how literature works in this regard, and that word – imitation

– has several meanings. We encounter one meaning when Sidney tells us that 'Poesy, therefore, is an art of imitation, for so Aristotle termeth it in the word *mimēsis*, that is to say, a representing, counterfeiting or figuring forth' (p. 10). And we encounter another when he tells us that the three things needed by the writer are 'art, imitation and exercise' (p. 43). Elizabethan authors were alive to the distinction, and could find the two meanings contrasted in the important discussion of imitation in Roger Ascham's *The Schoolmaster* (1570); but their roots run deeper still.

Discussion of literary *mimesis* begins with Plato. In Plato's philosophy the world we live in is composed of imperfect versions of the perfect ideas of things which exist in a realm beyond the visible universe. There is one idea or Platonic form of a chair in this realm of true ideas; every chair in the world is just a flawed copy of that idea. Art imitates the world. The painter or sculptor or poet copies things observed in the world, and so his art is at two removes from the truth – offering imitations of imitations. Where the philosopher may hope to come close to the idea of beauty, the painter can only try to represent a particularly beautiful person, and that person is hardly the same thing as beauty itself. Aristotle circumvents this argument by ignoring Plato's theory of ideas and redefining *mimesis*. The artist does not simply offer poor simulacra of things observable in the world, people who exist, events which happened. He represents things which could be, according to rules of verisimilitude rather than fact: the test is credibility and not accuracy; the artist imitates possibilities. *Mimesis* becomes the representation of universals – characters in archetypal scenarios behaving in ways which tell us about human nature, for better or worse. Imitation comes close to creation.

These two versions of *mimesis* stand behind the discussions of Renaissance critics, but they come filtered through subsequent classical treatments. One successful remodelling of Plato by Cicero, Seneca, and the Neoplatonist Plotinus reintroduced the Platonic *idea* as something in the artist's mind – if we wish to represent Venus in sculpture or words we imitate an idea of beauty and not a particular woman. Just as, in Plato's creation myth *Timaeus*, the world is formed by the mimetic art of a divine craftsman, so the worlds of fiction are formed by the mimetic art of artists who become, in some Renaissance criticism, gods who preside over a 'second nature'. On the other hand, Aristotle's redefinition of *mimesis* as the representation of the universal and the possible was debased into a theory of character types, especially evident in comic drama.

Running parallel to these philosophical theories of imitation is the rhetorical practice of imitation, related insofar as it believed that art must proceed by copying the finest observable examples, in this case literary and stylistic models. Aristotle had observed that it is through *mimesis* that we learn (hence the child's love of play-acting), and the educators in Rome and the Hellenistic world made imitation the keystone of the rhetorical education. By copying approved models students learned how to write and speak well themselves. Again, different versions of this ideology were inherited by Renaissance humanists. A particular sixteenth-century controversy concerned the slavish imitation of Cicero's admired prose style; objectors to this practice include Sidney. Appropriately enough, it was Cicero who had suggested that the teacher must 'show the student whom to copy, and to copy in such a way as to strive with all possible care to attain the most excellent qualities of his model' (*De oratore*, 2.22.90). Quintilian stressed, on the other hand, that a number of model authors should collectively give us 'our stock of words, the variety of our figures, and our methods of composition' (*Institutio oratoria*, 10.2.1). He used Plato's arguments to criticize the imitation of a single model, for 'whatever is like another object, must necessarily be inferior to the object of its imitation, just as the shadow is inferior to the substance, the portrait to the features which it portrays, and the acting of the player to the feelings he endeavours to reproduce' (10.2.11): 'the mere follower must always lag behind' (10.2.10). And Seneca developed what became the most popular images for this more eclectic approach: we should copy the bees 'and sift whatever we have gathered from a varied course of reading' before using our natural gifts to 'so blend those several flavours into one delicious compound that, even though it betrays its origin, yet it nevertheless is clearly a different thing from that whence it came'. Even if one particular author has captured your imagination and is the object of your imitation, 'I would have you resemble him as a child resembles his father, and not as a picture resembles its original; for a picture is a lifeless thing' (*Epistulae morales* ['Moral Letters'], 84.5–8). It was not until the second half of the eighteenth century that the doctrine of literary imitation was overturned, although Daniel offers an important precursor: 'all our understandings are not to be built by the square of Greece and Italy. We are the children of nature as well as they; we are not so placed out of the way of judgement but that the same sun of discretion shineth upon us' (p. 217). For the most part, though, originality was not seen as requiring an avoidance of imitation, but rather imitation of a more sophisticated nature.

A third type of imitation came at the other end of the writing process, when the reader came to judge the work and the events it portrayed. Since we learn through imitation, our behaviour will to an extent be modelled on what we read. The negative version of this theory saw readers and theatregoers as under threat from the representations of immoral behaviour in poems, stories, and plays. The Elizabethan theatre controversy, led by Puritans like Stephen Gosson, was an argument over whether theatre was a danger to society in this respect; the issue never went away, and when the Puritans took over London in the Civil War the theatres were actually closed down. Indeed, this theory of imitation survives in our current fears that cinematic representations of murderers and rapists lead to murder and rape. Plutarch advised caution: 'The young student must . . . be taught that we praise not the action represented by the imitation but the art shown in the appropriate reproduction of the subject. Since poetry often narrates by imitation wicked actions and bad emotions or traits of character, the young man must not necessarily accept admirable or successful work of this kind as true, or label it beautiful, but simply commend it as suitable and appropriate to the subject'.[9] And many advanced the somewhat lame argument that 'the wantonest poets of all, in their most lascivious works . . . sought rather by that means to withdraw men's minds ... from such foul vices than to allure them to embrace such beastly follies as they detected'.[10]

But critics preferred the positive version of readerly imitation, inspired by Cicero's account of his own moral formation in his speech in defence of Archias the poet. His virtue and resolve would be nothing 'had I not persuaded myself from my youth up, thanks to the moral lessons derived from a wide reading, that nothing is to be greatly sought after in this life save glory and honour' (*Pro Archia poeta* ['In Defence of Archias the Poet'], 6.14):

> All literature, all philosophy, all history, abounds with incentives to noble action, incentives which would be buried in black darkness were the light of the written word not flashed upon them. How many pictures of high endeavour the great authors of Greece and Rome have drawn for our use, and bequeathed to us, not only for our contemplation, but for our emulation! These I have held ever before my vision throughout my public career, and have guided the workings of my brain and my soul by meditating upon patterns of excellence. (ibid.)

The language is again Platonic. The ideas we find in fiction are the patterns for our own imitations in life. These three ideas of imitation, then, are connected in complex ways and share top billing in a literary culture which places a high value on copying. The three ideas are often distinguished nowadays: imitation as representation is labelled *mimesis*, the Greek term; imitation of literary and stylistic models is labelled by the Latin term *imitatio*; and the readerly behavioural imitation may be called emulation. But when Renaissance critics label literature 'an art of imitation', they intend some overlap.

POETICS AND RHETORIC

We have already seen that rhetoric took up a position at the centre of Renaissance intellectual culture. And that it was a social, ethical and intellectual ideal, and not just a successful trick. We need now to look at how intertwined rhetoric and poetics were in this period, for unless we recognize rhetoric as the discursive system which contained both literature and poetics, Renaissance literary criticism makes little sense. Already in the classical period, it was recognized that poetry and rhetoric had a great deal of common ground. The poets were often credited with originating the art of language which rhetoric systematized, analogies between the orator and the poet or the play-actor were common, and quotations from the poets were commonly used in illustrations of rhetorical figures. As Cicero put it: 'The truth is that the poet is a very near kinsman of the orator, rather more heavily fettered as regards rhythm, but with ampler freedom in his choice of words, while in the use of many sorts of ornament he is his ally and almost his counterpart' (*De oratore*, 1.16.70). The success of rhetoric in the Hellenistic period had eclipsed what attempts at literary criticism and poetics had been made. For this reason Aristotle's *Poetics* lay neglected, most discussion of literature was offered in passing in works of rhetorical theory, and authors were happy to adapt the theory of rhetorical composition and performance to their literary writings.

The ideas about literature inherited by Renaissance humanists were intrinsically rhetorical. Not, at least at first, the formalism of Aristotle, but the reader- and audience-centred model of Horace. The most conspicuous sign of the rhetorical cast of literary theory is the ubiquity of a formula which is central to Sidney's case in the *Defence*: that poetry, by which he means all fiction, must delight, move, and teach. This formula belongs to rhetoric, and describes the job of the orator: 'For the best orator is the one who by his oratory instructs, pleases, and moves the minds of his audience. To instruct is a debt to be paid, to give pleasure a gratuity to confer, to rouse emotion a sheer necessity' (Cicero, *De optimo genere oratorum* ['On the Best Type of Orator'], 3). So common is the triadic formula *docere, delectare, movere* (to teach, to delight, to move) that it lies almost unnoticed behind many passages in this edition, as when Daniel talks of the 'offices of motion' of rhyming verse: 'delighting the ear, stirring the heart, and satisfying the judgement' (p. 212).

Horace had adapted it famously in the passage from the *Ars poetica* in which he tells us that 'Poets aim either to profit, or to delight, or to utter words at once both pleasing and helpful to life' (333–4).

The need to understand literature as rhetoric led to some problems. Rhetoric was traditionally divided into three kinds: (i) the deliberative rhetoric of political debate, a matter of recommending or dissuading from a particular policy or course of action; (ii) the judicial or forensic rhetoric of the law courts, speeches either for the prosecution or the defence; and (iii) ceremonial or demonstrative rhetoric (known as epideictic), the rhetoric of praise or blame. As Aristotle explains in the *Rhetoric*, the first two require a judgement about the future and the past respectively, whereas the only judgement in the third case is of the skill of the speaker (1358b). And as Thomas Wilson put it in *The Art of Rhetoric* (1553; second edition 1560), one of the first English rhetoric manuals: 'Nothing can be handled by this art but the same is contained within one of these three causes'.[11] If literature was in any way rhetorical, to which kind did it belong? The awkward answer was to the third kind, the rather inert epideictic. This seemed to work for the odes of praise which formed the bulk of the canon of the early Greek lyric poet Pindar, and it could be made to work for such a genre as satire. As long as drama was to be understood as commending virtues and exposing vices, a play too could be seen as an instance of epideictic rhetoric. But when it came to sonnets, long prose narratives or epic poems, it seemed less to be a case of rhetoric containing literature than of literature containing rhetoric.

Literary works, indeed, were fond of representations of rhetorical occasions. Sidney's *Arcadia* ends with a lengthy judicial scene; Shakespeare's *Troilus and Cressida* (written *c.*1602, printed 1609) contains an extended deliberative debate; praise of the mistress was a staple of love poetry. But the similarities did not end there. Rhetoric divided itself into five parts, and these corresponded to the five successive stages of any rhetorical performance. These were *inventio* (the finding of materials), *dispositio* (the arrangement of those materials), *elocutio* (the translation of ideas into words and the deployment of rhetorical figures), *memoria* (the memorization of the outline of the oration), and *actio* or *pronuntiatio* (its performance). Any piece of writing seemed to proceed in this way. A writer first generates a basic scenario or conceit; he then arranges the argument or plot; and he then puts the plan into words. The final two stages only applied in the case of a play, but the parallel remained important: actors had to memorize, and their performances were always compared to those of orators, with both deploying a common arsenal of gesture and vocal effect.

One important remodelling of learning, by the French philosopher and logician Petrus Ramus, assigned *inventio*, *dispositio* and *memoria*, as concerned with *res* (matter), to logic, and reduced rhetoric to a concern only with *verba* (words), which meant *elocutio* and *pronuntiatio*. Furthermore, *elocutio* was always the area of rhetoric which most naturally shared common ground with literature. It seemed natural, then, that efforts to adapt rhetoric to literature emphasized *elocutio*. Readers with a rhetorical education were always able to read poems and see plays in all sorts of other rhetorical ways, but insofar as literary criticism absorbed rhetorical theory, it was the theory of *elocutio*, or style. The third book of Puttenham's *Art of English Poesy* is substantially a treatment of poetic *elocutio*. Under *elocutio* rhetorical theory distinguished at least three kinds of style (high/grand, middle/mixed, low/plain), and it is these same kinds that are still invoked when we talk of Milton's grand style or Herbert's plain style. The theory also codified the kinds of choice any writer faces in the expression of ideas and the patterning of words, distinguishing innumerable rhetorical figures. These would be either schemes – arrangements of words other than the ordinary – or tropes, which were concerned with changes of meaning. *Anaphora*, by which consecutive clauses commence with the same word or phrase, is a scheme. Metaphor is a trope. Often thought of now as mere embellishment, rhetorical figures were tools of thought and expression, and were expected to work hard to delight, instruct, and move. As Puttenham puts it: 'a figure is ever used to a purpose, either of beauty or of efficacy' (p. 169). Schemes and tropes construct the language of Renaissance poets and prose writers. They were taught

carefully in schools, so that young students would have a repertoire of hundreds of figures, which they had been trained to
recognize in texts, and had practised in their own compositions.
Books from the period show the evidence of this rhetorical
training, their margins cluttered with the reader's efforts to label
the schemes and tropes used in the text. If we remember this,
the rhetorical figures employed in plays, poems, and stories must
be thought of not only as aimed at affecting audience and
reader, but as intended to be recognized and analysed, enjoyed
as evidence of impressive technique.

But things are even more complicated than this. Quintilian
puts it very clearly: 'It was, then, nature that created speech,
and observation that originated the art of speaking' (*Institutio
oratoria*, 3.2.3). People all the time use patterns of speech which
are found in the rhetoric textbooks, without realizing they are
doing so. This is why figures of speech do not seem artificial,
unless used clumsily. Longinus looks at uses of the figure *hyperbaton*, in which syntax is deliberately disordered, in just this
way:

> These consist in the arrangement of words or ideas out of their
> normal sequence, and they carry, so to speak, the genuine stamp
> of powerful emotion. People who really are angry or frightened
> or indignant or carried away by jealousy or any other feeling –
> for there are innumerable forms of emotion, and indeed no one
> would be able to say just how many – often, after they have
> brought forward one point, will rush off on a different tack,
> dropping in other points without rhyme or reason, and then,
> under the stress of their agitation, they will come right round to
> their original position. Dragged rapidly in every direction as if by
> a veering wind, they will keep altering the arrangement of their
> words and ideas, losing their natural sequence and introducing
> all sorts of variations. In the same way the best authors will use
> *hyperbaton* in such a way that imitation approaches the effects of
> nature. For art is perfect only when it looks like nature, and
> again, nature hits the mark only when she conceals the art that is
> within her.[12]

What all this means is that poets and dramatists who have had a rhetorical training may use a figure of speech which is taken to denote a certain emotion in order to signify that emotion in the character who is speaking instinctively. Not all literary rhetoric, therefore, is oratory.

Rhetoric is all about persuading a particular audience by appeals to reason and emotion, and with care taken to consider well who they are, and also what they think of the speaker. It is a contingent art, ready to adapt its resources to changing discourses and occasions. Renaissance literary rhetoric is equally flexible, adapting to the different readers and audiences who transform text into meaning. There were occasional challenges to the predominance of the rhetorical model. The Italian critic Ludovico Castelvetro, in his important edition of Aristotle's *Poetics* (1570; second edition 1576), is one who insists that pleasure, and not utility, is the main, even the sole, aim of poetry. The abiding criticisms of rhetoric were echoed by others who nevertheless accepted the validity of the rhetorical model. In Book 1 of *The Advancement of Learning*, Bacon had observed the tendency of words to engross authors in all areas of learning at the expense of subject matter, and Sir William Alexander insists on looking at the substance of literary works and not only 'that external gorgeousness, consisting in the choice or placing of words, as if it would bribe the ear to corrupt the judgement' (p. 298).

But most were happy to align rhetoric with moral utility, as the humanist education had trained them to do. Ann Moss comments:

> The underlying assumption that most of literature is to be classed as epideictic rhetoric and, therefore, by definition, devoted to praise or censure, together with the mentality produced by the commonplace book and its morally based classification system, ensured that pupils trained to read rhetorically would be programmed to read morally. The art of combining rhetoric and rectitude could be seen as integral to the range of expertise which literary critics were beginning to claim as theirs alone.[13]

In striving to produce orators, the humanist education presented its students with many ways in which they could conceive of literature as rhetorical. Literature could be rhetoric: a poem of praise was pure epideictic. Literature could also contain rhetoric on the large scale – a set-piece oration in a play, for instance – and on the smallest – a good example of a figure of speech. Literary theorists since Horace had taken over the tripartite aim of rhetoric – to teach, delight, and move – and applied it to imaginative literature. So the aims of a work of poetry, drama or prose fiction could be conceived of rhetorically, as the persuasion of an audience to change its view or outlook. In light of the prevalence of rhetorical ways of thinking about and analysing language and literature, it is no surprise that when someone who had been through the humanist curriculum came to write imaginative literature, the result should admit of rhetorical analysis and engage with the idea of rhetoric in many ways and on many levels. And it is no surprise that Renaissance literary criticism should be so dominated by the rhetorical model, both in its theories and in its methods of argument.

MATTER AND WORDS: GENRE, DECORUM, RHETORIC, VERSIFICATION

When Sidney digresses to discuss the state of literature in England he complains about the low levels of attainment on two fronts, and divides his subsequent treatment according to these same 'two principal parts, matter to be expressed by words and words to express the matter' (p. 44). The distinction between matter (*res*) and words (*verba*) may seem artificial – it is especially the case in poetic language that what is said cannot always be separated from how it is said. But it is a distinction which imparts clarity to the theory of literary composition, and allows Sidney successively to consider, as we will here, genre and decorum under *matter*, and rhetorical *elocutio* and versification under *words*.

Genre and Decorum

The classification of literature by kind is another example of the primacy of Plato's ideal forms in Western thought. Plato made a simple distinction on the basis of the method of representation: either the voice of the actor or narrator merges with that of the character, as in plays and direct speech, or the voice of the author is the only one represented directly, as in narrative and reported speech; a mixture of these two sorts of representation gave a third kind, part narrative, part direct speech, instanced by Homer. In the *Poetics* Aristotle combined these factors with others – including the metre or metres used and the kinds of things represented – in order to define tragedy and epic generically. In the meantime names for kinds of poem proliferated in Greek practice; some were named by metre, as in the iambic, and others by occasion or content, as in the marriage poem or *epithalamion*. Horace's *Ars poetica* had the greatest influence on subsequent literary criticism, and followed from the work of the Alexandrian scholars whose classifications of literature by kind and merit determined which works of which ancient authors were allowed to survive through manuscript copying. Horace offers an array of kinds of literature, including epic, tragedy, comedy, lyric, pastoral, satire, elegy, and epigram and in each case gives the rules or guidelines of good practice as he saw them. By choosing a kind of literature an author embraced expectations as to the sort of matter it would contain, and certain fundamental conventions for its arrangement and style. The style of poetry fit for tragedy, for example, was not to be used in comedy; plays should have five acts and any bloodiness should be kept offstage; an epic should begin *in medias res*.

Until the eighteenth century the theory of genre is always delivered prescriptively rather than descriptively, but this does not mean that it only concerns authors and cannot be applied by readers to texts. Aristotle's prescriptions, after all, had been based squarely on the practices of past tragedians, and took Sophocles' *Oedipus rex* as the ideal. Generic conventions offer readers the instruments with which to evaluate works of literature, but in the Renaissance such evaluation was not in the first instance inflexible or doctrinaire. Only with the rise of neoclassical criticism, the belated progeny of Aristotle's rediscovered *Poetics*, did rule-based criticism come to dominate. The best-known example is the doctrine of the dramatic unities of time, place, and action – the laws which stated that the events in a play should span no more than a day, should occur in one place, and should comprise a single action or chain of events. Outlined in Castelvetro's 1570 edition of the *Poetics*, the unities were recommended by Sidney and acknowledged by subsequent writers, but only came to dominate critical discourse in the later seventeenth century under the influence of the more rigorous French. For the committed neoclassical critic, Shakespeare simply wouldn't do, and only plays written strictly according to the unities were acceptable. When Shakespeare himself was writing, the attitude to rules was more relaxed, and this contributes to the distinctive and varied achievement of late sixteenth-century and early seventeenth-century English literature. Shakespeare knew what the unities were, and that Jonson liked to observe them. But he could enjoy flouting them in *The Winter's Tale* (*c*.1611) as much as he could enjoy observing them in *The Tempest* (*c*.1611). Literature is not in this period the slave of theory, but a critical reader of it: literature and criticism exist in a state of fruitful symbiosis.

It was only in the sixteenth century that the triad of the epic, dramatic and lyric genres was firmly established, but from the start it struggled to contain those kinds of poetry which derived not from classical models but from medieval ones, and especially those mixed kinds which combined elements from both sources. So at the same time as generic criticism sought to combine Horace and Aristotle to develop a viable theory of genre, it had to account for tragicomedy, for works which mixed prose and verse, and for the heroic poem, with its combination of elements from classical epic and medieval romance. Sidney's own *Arcadia* is a heroic poem in prose with verse elements, an epic romance in five books or acts with a dramatic tragicomic plot structure, and direct influences from Homer and Virgil as well as classical drama, the Greek prose romance, the medieval chivalric romance, the sixteenth-century heroic poem, the Renaissance prose romance, classical pastoral poetry and the Renaissance pastoral romance. Spenser's *The Faerie Queene* offers an even more bewildering blend. In *The Defence of Poesy*, Sidney's simple argument about such brilliant generic mixing is that 'if severed they be good, the conjunction cannot be hurtful' (p. 25). And yet such mixtures only hold together because of the internal tension of each separate genre. Sidney and Spenser did not wish to write without generic convention, but to be able to play with it. And the reader's job is to know what is going on.

The most common appeal in judgements of generic correctness is to the principle of decorum or, in Puttenham's term, decency – to what is suitable or fitting. Each genre had its decorum – so that a one-liner would be a breach of decorum in a tragedy, and a grave moral discourse not fitting in a comedy. And the principle could also judge whether the language of a poem or play was suitable to the conventions of the metre or style employed. But decorum is invoked most insistently in relation to people: what is fitting behaviour in a certain kind of writing for a certain kind of person – a king, a general, a shopkeeper, a shepherd – and how they should be represented as speaking. And it always related to contemporary social order. An author might be criticized for failing to elevate the language of regal figures above that of their servants, or for allowing those servants to speak the same language as their masters. Both classical and Renaissance cultures shared rigid class systems which gave an edge to the discourse of decorum. In the period of the English Renaissance the social hierarchy was bolstered by sumptuary laws which determined what each rank was entitled or obliged to wear. To make a shepherd speak as well as a knight – an accusation wrongly levelled by Jonson at Sidney – was therefore a sort of stylistic crime, an anarchistic blow struck against a necessary social order.[14]

Rhetoric

Book I of Puttenham's *Art of English Poesy* is a history of poetry at the same time as an effort to prescribe the conventions of the different genres; the result is that its prescriptions seem more than normally anachronistic. Sidney's theory is conceived primarily in terms of the heroic poem, and specific treatment of individual genres is only offered in passing, when Sidney defends poetry by its parts, and when he turns to assess the state of English literature. Daniel is even less concerned with generic questions. For many English Renaissance critics, Horace was too well-known to need repeating, and said all that was needed. They were far more concerned about the theory and practice of words than that of matter. As we have seen, rhetorical *elocutio*, the stage of composition which dressed ideas in words, was the focus of literary criticism in the rhetorical tradition. Puttenham's Book 3 is about the use in poetry not of rhetoric in general, but of *elocutio* in particular. Again, Abraham Fraunce's *The Arcadian Rhetoric* (1588), influenced by Ramus' restriction of rhetoric to only *elocutio* and *pronuntiatio*, offered a handbook of these two stages with illustrations from Homer, Virgil, Du Bartas (French), Tasso (Italian), Boscán (Spanish), and Sidney, as yet available only in manuscript. And he was followed by John Hoskyns, whose manuscript *Directions for Speech and Style* (c.1599) was based almost exclusively on examples from Sidney's *Arcadia*, and confirmed the strong association between the best new writing and a firm grasp of *elocutio*.

From the theory of *elocutio* come many of the critical standards which writers aimed at and readers could apply. Rhetoric distinguished types of style – most commonly the grand, middle, and low or plain, but also intermediate styles between each of these. Competing models might offer not three but four styles, as in the *On Style* of the Greek critic Demetrius, which dealt with the plain, the grand, the elegant, and the forceful styles. In developing their theories of style Renaissance critics absorbed suggestions that the three main styles were respectively best suited to moving, delighting, and teaching. A style, especially in prose, might be labelled for the author whose model the writer followed – Ciceronian, Senecan or Tacitean. Relatedly, rhetoric had amassed a set of labels for particular stylistic virtues, usually arranged into sets and subsets. These included such virtues as purity, clarity, correctness (in relation to decorum), grandeur, rapidity, sincerity, solemnity, vehemence, abundance, sweetness and simplicity. At its simplest a style was about the amplitude of syntactic units (from small to large), about the types of rhetorical figures deemed suitable (mostly schemes, mostly tropes, a middle course), and about the amount of variety in the deployment of different kinds of sentence shape or figure. The efforts of writers to form their own styles on the best models and to deploy them correctly were met by the ability of readers to appreciate writing in terms of the various styles and virtues.

Renaissance prose modelled itself in theory and practice on classical example, and notably in its adoption of the classical model of the rhetorical period. The period, or periodic sentence, is all about rhythm, and its theory is a theory of rhythm rather than of meaning. The theorists even treated the use of verse rhythms in prose, a practice which was highly recommended, especially at climactic moments. Punctuation in the periodic sentence is also about distinguishing units of rhythm rather than dependent or independent units of sense (as we now use it). It is because of these differences that Renaissance prose can be hard to follow, that in editions in the original spelling and punctu-ation that punctuation may be somewhat perplexing, and that in editions in modernized punctuation – like this one – that punctuation may not always seem quite to work. The period is a long sentence made up of various parts, all clearly related to each other syntactically; these parts will balance each other, highlighting antithesis as well as producing a satisfying rhythm and internal logic. 'Suspended syntax' is a name often given to this style, since it tends to build towards a conclusion which is held in suspense, and it is only at the conclusion that the relations of the many interdependent parts become clear. The word 'period' means a circuit, and therefore signifies a completed, measured circle of meaning. The period comprises two other units of rhythm: the smallest is called the comma, and the intermediate unit is called the colon. Marks of punctuation borrowed the terms for these units and sometimes coincide with them: what we call a full stop is still in American English called a 'period'.

The opening sentences in this edition provide a good example of the periodic style. In the following quotations, the original punctuation has been preserved; it is not perfect even in its own terms, but since it marks units of rhythm fairly well, it is instructive:

> When the right virtuous Edward Wotton and I, were at the Emperor's court together, we gave ourselves to learn horsemanship of John Pietro Pugliano, one that with great commendation had the place of an esquire in his stable: and he according to the fertileness of the Italian wit, did not only afford us the demonstration of his practice, but sought to enrich our minds with the contemplations therein, which he thought most precious.

So far we have one period ending at the full stop; it comprises two *cola* divided by the colon, and each colon is made up of four *commata*, marked by the commas, so that each half of the sentence is rhythmically balanced. Sidney continues:

> But with none I remember mine ears were at any time more loaden, than when (either angered with slow payment, or moved with our learner-like admiration) he exercised his speech in the praise of his faculty. He said soldiers were the noblest estate of mankind, and horsemen the noblest of soldiers. He said they were the masters of war, and ornaments of peace, speedy goers and strong abiders, triumphers both in camps and courts: nay to so unbelieved a point he proceeded, as that no earthly thing bred such wonder to a prince, as to be a good horseman.

Here Sidney's middle style employs various schemes, including the parallel syntax of *isocolon* ('He said ... He said ...') and the mirror structure of *chiasmus* ('soldiers ... noblest ... noblest ... soldiers'). And we notice a general tendency to balance and antithesis at the smallest and largest levels, proceeding by pairs contrasted or complemented.

Elocutio gives us the balanced periodic style, and the possibility of its antithesis. It gives us the patterning of words through rhetorical schemes. And it gives us the transformations or turns in words and their meanings through tropes. In each case literary effect is constructed according to a model, and that model is established in relation to accepted norms – how people speak in particular everyday situations, what word order is normal and expected, what meanings and usages raise no eyebrows. If anything is typical of the Renaissance literary mentality, it is this habit of conceiving of patterns and transformations in relation to models, norms, and conventions. The simplest way to see this is to think of the plots of Shakespeare's plays as sentences, and to observe how they too proceed through the embracing or rejecting of models and conventions, through balanced, antithetical construction, through stylized patternings of subplot and mirrored characters, through transformations and turns. The *elocutio* of Puttenham's Book 3 gives us much more than the tools with which to analyse particular lines and stanzas of verse.

Versification

The other aspect of words given special prominence by English Renaissance critics was their arrangement in verse. And it was because this was an area in which classical models could not be converted into English straightforwardly that a debate developed which focused, as no other area of literary criticism was able to, the issue of dependence on the ancients versus independence from them. Old English verse had been accentual in nature, its lines regulated by patterns of accents but with variable syllable counts; the accents were hammered home by alliteration. Since the Norman invasion English language and literature had developed in close proximity to French, and although some writers of the fourteenth and fifteenth centuries tried to revive the old alliterative and accentual verse, the poetry of Geoffrey Chaucer and his successors was not unlike French medieval verse, which counted syllables rather than accents. In the sixteenth century, as today, there were different opinions about the line Chaucer wrote. Did the line used in *Troilus and Criseyde* (written *c.*1385) and *The Canterbury Tales* (written in the 1380s and 1390s) have a fixed number of syllables, obscured by changes in pronunciation? Did it have four stresses in each line, as a vestige of the Old English alliterative verse, or did it have five, as a forerunner of the Elizabethan pentameter? The line written by Sir Thomas Wyatt in the early sixteenth century is not substantially different, and it is only with the Earl of Surrey and some of his late-Henrician contemporaries that the modern system emerges clearly. In Surrey, as in the verse of George Gascoigne, the line is fixed in respect both of syllable count and of accentual pattern, and we have true accentual–syllabic verse. That the rules had evolved was not registered by all, and Puttenham, for one, remains confused. But the future belonged to the accentual-syllabic system.

At the same time, in the middle of the sixteenth century, scholar poets were attempting to rethink English versification far more radically. The impulse was humanist and, in its English form, Protestant. Our verse, like other European poetry, was felt to be most characterized by its use of rhyme, and rhyme was seen as a monkish corruption of Latin verse belonging to the Dark Ages. Roger Ascham in *The Schoolmaster* (1570), was one of the first openly to criticize 'our rude beggarly rhyming, brought first into Italy by Goths and Huns, when all good verse and all good learning too were destroyed by them, and after carried into France and Germany, and at last received into England by men of excellent wit indeed, but of small learning and less judgement in that behalf'.[15] But he was only following similar movements in other European countries in suggesting that it might be better to write verses in the vernacular according to the quantitative system of the Greeks and Romans. Quantitative poetry, musical in origin, is regulated neither by syllable count nor by accent, but by patterning syllables according to their length. Either naturally or by the application of elaborate rules, syllables would be designated long or short; a long syllable took twice as long to say as a short one. Lines of quantitative verse were built of distinct feet, units of two or more syllables either long or short. From the iamb (short-long), for example, could be composed an iambic line of various lengths, and some metres also allowed for combinations of feet and substitutions of one foot for another. The heroic line of Homer and Virgil, seen as the pinnacle of the classical achievement, was the dactylic hexameter. Of its six feet, the penultimate had to be a dactyl (long-short-short), and the final foot a spondee (long-long), but the other four could be either, making it a metre of varied and flexible rhythm.

The most important experiments with the classical system were headed by Sidney in the late 1570s and early 1580s, and are famously discussed in a printed exchange of letters between the poet Edmund Spenser and his friend Gabriel Harvey, a Cambridge academic. Their discussions are fairly technical, concerning such vexed questions as whether ordinary pronunciation or artificial rules are the best guide to quantity – if the rules tell us that the second syllable of 'carpenter' is long, does it matter how we pronounce it? And Spenser's quantitative poetry does him little credit. In Sidney's hands, though, the quantitative system becomes a vehicle which at its best introduces a completely new sound into English verse. Literary history tends to put these experiments down as a misguided attempt to make a major road out of a dead end. But it is important to notice that they coincide exactly with the period in which the rules and conventions of the accentual-syllabic system were being settled, and it is equally important to recognize that this is no coincidence.

We can look at an example of the iambic pentameter of George Gascoigne, the author of *Certain Notes of Instruction*:

> I smile sometimes, although my grief be great,
> To hear and see these lovers paint their pain;
> And how they can in pleasant rhymes repeat
> The passing pangs, which they in fancies feign.
> But if I had such skill to frame a verse,
> I could more pain than all their pangs rehearse.
>   ('Gascoigne's Passion', ll. 1–6)

The problem with this kind of poetry, as Sidney realized, is that it has no movement apart from what can be described metrically – every unit of sense, like every line, is composed of five regular iambic feet. If we were to pretend that this was prose, it would not sound any different, and the iambic pattern is beaten out by an alliterative stamping of feet. What Gascoigne and his contemporaries had achieved was the establishing beyond any doubt of the accentual-syllabic system. Sidney's response was twofold. On the one hand to see what would happen if the English language were to have other metrical systems imposed on it. And on the other hand to grant the accentual-syllabic system the status of a set of abstract rules to which any line of verse must confirm absolutely, but could confirm as quietly as it wished. The significance of the second response is especially lasting. Sidney recognized that the metrical system could be conceptualized independently of the words and phrases which realize it in verse. It became abstract, a set of rules to which a line of verse must conform rather than a way each line must sound. It could then be stretched, put under pressure, realized very literally in some lines and only just in others; and always for effect. There are many signs of this new way of thinking about metre in Sidney's poetry. One is that a syllable does not have to be thumped to be stressed – it just needs to bear more stress than its neighbour. So as a line is pronounced there will be all kinds of fluent and shifting emphases, rather than a binary pattern of ons and offs, heavy and light syllables. But the most obvious sign of a new flexibility is the reversed foot, and the most common example of that is the reversed first foot, inverting the stress pattern of the first two syllables, so that the line begins with a stressed syllable. Once the rules become abstract it is possible to manipulate the imagined pattern, by reaching in and turning the first, or the third, or the fourth foot. The line still conforms to the rule within the dispensation of this new licence. Examples of all these effects can be seen in the sestet of *Astrophil and Stella*, 47:

> Virtue, awake: beauty but beauty is;
>   I may, I must, I can, I will, I do
> Leave following that, which it is gain to miss.
>   Let her go. Soft, but here she comes. Go to,
> Unkind, I love you not—: O me, that eye
> Doth make my heart give to my tongue the lie.

These developments were helped along by the experiments of Sidney and his contemporaries with the quantitative system. It

seems to have been the case that the Latin verses on which
schoolboys were brought up were recited according to an
accepted Anglicized pronunciation, and not in the musical way
which would demonstrate each syllable's quantity audibly. It is
likely that English verses in classical metres were treated similarly: once a word had been bound into the quantitative pattern
it was free to be pronounced as it would be in ordinary speech.
The poems which resulted were not, therefore, intended to be
chanted in a strict way, and, as in the new accentual-syllabic
poems, English phraseology could be put in tension with a
different metrical pattern. It is possible to argue, in fact, that
Sidney's quantitative experiments taught him to separate metre
and rhythm in the first place. The sound patterns and rhythms
which result are strikingly new. We may look at a brief example,
and observe how Sidney gives order by the use of rhetorical
schemes which pattern his phrases in parallel – the broad term
for such parallel constructions is *isocolon*; when we have phrases
beginning with the same word we call it *anaphora*; when phrases
end in the same way, we have *epistrophe*; when they do both,
we have *symploce*. All of these devices are used here as a way of
patterning the phrases in the absence of rhyme. The metrical
pattern in each line is dactyl (long-short-short), trochee (long-
short), spondee (long-long):

> For though my sense be from me,
> And I be dead who want sense,
> Yet do we both live in you.

> Turnèd anew by your means,
> Unto the flower that ay turns,
> As you, alas, my Sun, bends:

> Thus do I fall to rise thus,
> Thus do I die to live thus,
> Changed to a change, I change not.

> Thus may I not be from you,
> Thus be my senses on you,

Thus what I think is of you,
Thus what I seek is in you:
All what I am, it is you.
(*Certain Sonnets*, 25, ll. 21–34)

The classical experiments encouraged poets to think about other ways of patterning their lines, and the rhetorical figures treated by Puttenham became increasingly common in both kinds of verse. The experiments also taught poets to view the accentual-syllabic system in terms of feet, with stress or its lack substituted for length and shortness respectively. They taught them to separate rhythm and metre, enabling the intonations and rhythms of speech to find their way into verse. And they encouraged them to do without rhyme on occasion. Arguably, and in spite of the important earlier precedents of Surrey and Thomas Norton's and Thomas Sackville's tragedy *Gorboduc* (*c.*1561) in introducing blank verse to epic and drama, the blank verse of Shakespeare and Milton would not have been possible without this period of experimentation and rapid evolution.

At the same time, a third, parallel, area of activity saw Sidney and others learning from Continental poetry, experimenting with the old fixed forms like the sestina, imitating such complex forms as the Petrarchan *canzone*, translating Continental poems or the words of songs in such a way as to reproduce the original verse form, and imitating particular features of French and Italian versification. This activity brings new materials – images, conceits, arguments, personae – into English verse, and brings such features as the trochaic line and the feminine ending into English prosody. Lyric poetry especially was greatly enriched by this less contentious area of experiment.

SIDNEY, PUTTENHAM, DANIEL

Sidney

Sir Philip Sidney was born in 1554 and died in 1586. Knighted in 1583 only so that he could stand proxy for a foreign prince in a courtly ceremony, the man who for most of his career was

Mr Philip Sidney could nevertheless claim aristocratic descent. His mother was the daughter of the Duke of Northumberland, and for most of his life Sidney was the heir to her two brothers, the Earl of Warwick and Robert Dudley, Earl of Leicester, Queen Elizabeth's first and most lasting favourite. And his family was at the centre of Elizabethan politics: Sidney's father, at various points in time, ran both Ireland and Wales for the Queen. Sidney was therefore brought up for a significant career at court, and great things came to be expected of the talented and charismatic young man who in 1572, after studying at Shrewsbury School and Christ Church, Oxford, was packed off on a three-year grand tour of the Continent. This period gave him a network of Protestant correspondents in France, Germany, and the Low Countries, and helped to form his internationalist outlook on politics and culture. It also took him to Italy, the seat of the Renaissance. In the years that followed the Queen granted Sidney a few diplomatic duties, but although he figured prominently in court entertainments and tilts, preferment was slower to come Sidney's way than he felt he deserved. He may have ruined his chances of advancement in 1579 by writing a letter to Elizabeth I in which, speaking for a faction headed by his uncle Leicester, he set out the reasons why she should not marry the French Duke of Alençon. His literary writings, which are assumed to date from 1577 onwards, are usually presented, with his encouragement, as the fruits of enforced idleness. We should not be misled. *The Defence of Poesy* shows that Sidney had real ambitions for the future of English literature; his patronage of other writers, including Spenser, shows that he would back up his convictions with his limited financial resources; and his own works show him exploring every kind of writing and taking English literature forward by leaps and bounds. His successors saw him as their master in prose style and versification, and in the sonnet sequence *Astrophil and Stella* and the prose romance *Arcadia* they found two works which were to have an enormous impact on subsequent writing.

Sidney's works remained in manuscript during his lifetime, although whilst the *Arcadia* seems to have circulated fairly freely, *Astrophil and Stella* and *The Defence of Poesy* were probably read by fewer people. When he died in the Low Countries in 1586, as one of the leaders of the English force sent to help the Dutch Protestants resist Catholic Spain, he was known principally as a promising courtier and a generous patron. He was given, in early 1587, an elaborate funeral in St Paul's Cathedral, preceded by a massive procession through London. Though cynics point out that this might have helped to distract a querulous nation after the execution of Mary Queen of Scots eight days earlier, it also speaks for the value put on him by those friends and family he left behind. And it was friends and family who eventually took charge of printing his literary remains. Bounced into action by the plan of a London printer to put out an unauthorized edition, Sidney's close friend Fulke Greville was behind the printing in 1590 of *The Countess of Pembroke's Arcadia*, the prose romance named for Sidney's sister. Sidney had completed the work in around 1580 and had subsequently undertaken a large-scale revision of it, each of the first three books more than doubling in size. But he left the work unfinished, in the middle of an extended epic episode which had taken the work far away from its framework of a pastoral romance with chivalric inset tales and verse interludes. It was this unfinished revision which Greville decided to have printed, and this authorized text was followed straightaway, in 1591, by an unauthorized printing of Sidney's sonnet sequence *Astrophil and Stella*. At this point Sidney's sister took over, and in 1593, at her instigation, appeared an edition of the *Arcadia* with an ending tacked on from the original version. This was followed in 1595 by *The Defence of Poesy*, beaten to the shops by a pirated version entitled *An Apology for Poetry*, which was subsequently withdrawn. In 1598 all three works were gathered together, along with an early courtly entertainment and a selection of poems called *Certain Sonnets*, in an edition of the *Arcadia* which was in effect Sidney's collected works. This book was reprinted frequently in the subsequent century, proving a far bigger seller than the works of Shakespeare, Jonson, Spenser or Donne.

Other Englishmen had written works of criticism in Latin:

important precursors are an oration in praise of poetry ascribed to Henry Dethick and John Rainolds (*c.*1572), and Richard Wills' *De re poetica* ('On Poetry', 1573). But the *Defence* is the first attempt at sustained literary criticism in English, and remains one of the very best. The editor of *Literary Criticism: Plato to Dryden* judges that 'If we could have but one sixteenth-century book on poetry, it should be that of Sidney'.[16] Sidney can stand for all the rest – a score of significant works of French, Italian, and neo-Latin criticism – because he has absorbed and learned from them. Ideas resembling his theories can be found in such works, to the extent that there is very little in Sidney's *Defence* which is truly original. But it gives those ideas a force, clarity, and cohesion which they had lacked in the more pedantic and expansive treatises of the Continental critics. Why did Sidney write it? There are different ways of answering this question. A controversy was raging in England in the late 1570s and early 1580s, as Puritans attacked all manner of games and pastimes, and especially the theatre, which they saw as a danger to public morals, both for the subject matter represented, and because of the sorts of things which happen when large numbers of people are gathered together for purposes other than worship. Stephen Gosson had dedicated one such Puritan attack, *The School of Abuse*, to Sidney in 1579 and, Spenser tells his friend Harvey, 'was for his labour scorned, if at least it be in the goodness of that nature to scorn'.[17] Thomas Lodge replied to Gosson, and Gosson wrote several subsequent works; other, often anonymous, authors joined in on either side. The works have little to say about literature, and are not represented in this edition. The controversy may have encouraged Sidney to gather his thoughts about literature, but he says little about drama, nothing about the stage, and only engages generally with the argument that poetry is 'the nurse of abuse' in the section in which he refutes well-known charges. If the *Defence* sets out to answer anyone, it is Plato.

Perhaps a better answer is that Sidney was genuinely interested in the theory of literature and in the prospects for English literature. This certainly tallies with his efforts in his other writings, and even fifteen years after it had been written, the impact of the printed *Defence* was more positive than negative: it was valued less as a defence than as a manifesto. Sidney typically frustrates attempts to understand his motives, however. He himself calls the work 'this ink-wasting toy of mine' at its close, and undercuts it at the opening by comparing it to the self-interested praise of horsemanship of his riding instructor. The irony of the cleverest writers in this edition is a joy, but it muddies the waters no end. We might compare Sidney to Harington, who tells us in the preface to his English version of Ariosto, *Orlando Furioso* (1591), that when translating an episode in which the hero is rebuked by an enchantress in the form of his tutor:

> straight I began to think that my tutor, a grave and learned man, and one of a very austere life, might say to me in like sort, 'Was it for this that I read Aristotle and Plato to you, and instructed you so carefully both in Greek and Latin, to have you now become a translator of Italian toys?' But while I thought thus, I was aware that it was no toy that could put such an honest and serious consideration into my mind.[18]

The resort to irony and paradox involves criticism in the game with meaning which is literature. The treatises which should tell us how to interpret must themselves be interpreted. We are further confused if we remember that Sidney's *Defence* is a piece of rhetoric. Modelled closely on the form of the classical oration, it is both a speech for the defence in a court of philosophical law and an epideictic praise of poetry. Even when rhetorical theory attempts to insist that the good orator must be a good man and must believe what he says, it makes clear enough that the important thing is not to believe but to be believed: the job of persuasion does not require conviction, only the ability to be convincing. Sidney may therefore be more intent on winning the argument than on building a viable literary theory, and this aspect certainly accounts for a common experience: the *Defence* will carry you along with it, charm you into submission, and have you reaching for superlatives, but you will not be able to recount its arguments afterwards.

A wide range of classical and modern works got Sidney thinking about literary theory. He is familiar with Plato's dialogues, including the *Republic* and the *Phaedrus*; he has read Aristotle's *Poetics* and *Rhetoric*; like most of his contemporaries he knows Horace's *Ars poetica* backwards. He is unlikely to have read Longinus' *On the Sublime*, a work which made little impact before the later seventeenth century, but he has read the rhetoric books of Cicero and, probably, Quintilian, and Plutarch's influential essay on 'How the Young Man Ought to Study Poetry'. Claims are often made for particular affinities to various medieval and Renaissance critics, philosophers, and theologians, but it seems most likely that Sidney absorbed much current and recent thinking informally, in conversation or at second hand. It is possible that he read, or dipped into, recent works of criticism in Italian by Minturno, Castelvetro, Mazzoni, Tasso, and others, and it is certain that he had some familiarity with the general shape of literary practice and theory in France and Spain. But particular modern sources have proved hard to establish. The exception is the lengthy Latin treatise *Poetices libri septem* ('Seven Books on Poetics') of 1561, written by the Frenchman Julius Caesar Scaliger. Even here, though, Sidney's attention is highly selective, and he is not put off by Scaliger's ability to ignore all literature not written in Greek or Latin. Sidney is no philosopher, and, for all his impressive scholarship, no scholar. His interest is not so much in what others say as in what their writings can help him to think; he applies his poet's imagination to the task of assembling a single edifice from the assorted fragments of previous writers, and what he produces is entirely his own.

Sidney is notably ahead of his time in England in his careful use of Aristotle's *Poetics*; that his application of it was less rigid than was common in the later seventeenth century further complicates the picture. Here again, in a way, he is ahead of the game – he can see that much is to be learned from Aristotle, but he absorbs rather than reflects this learning in his development of the literary theory presented in the *Defence* and in his writing of, for instance, the *Arcadia*. Those familiar with the cultural montages and patchworks of postmodernism will enjoy this characteristically Elizabethan approach to the writings of the past. All sources and influences can be combined; no writer is so grand that they may not be twisted beyond recognition, taken out of context, or merged into a hybrid with another. Sidney's theory can reconcile Plato and Aristotle because it comes naturally to him to think round categories. And his fiction can merge Homer, Virgil, the *Poetics*, the *Ars poetica*, Heliodorus, Ariosto, the popular romance, Montemayor and many more because writing and reading is more interesting that way.

The Defence of Poesy is a defence of imaginative literature. Sidney follows Aristotle in insisting that the origin of 'poesy' and 'poetry' from the Greek word for 'making' means that poetry signifies the making of fictions, and not the use of verse. Histories in verse may not be poems; prose romances are. Sidney's own *Arcadia*, a prose romance with verse interludes, is therefore a poem throughout, and its author a poet. This extension of the key term is important, for it allows us to read Sidney's theory both sideways, as applying to all Renaissance literature, and forwards, as applying equally to eighteenth-century novels or twenty-first-century films. At the work's centre stands a simple definition, sharing elements with other such definitions from rhetorical and literary treatises, but adding a twist of Sidney's own: 'Poesy, therefore, is an art of imitation, for so Aristotle termeth it in the word *mimēsis*, that is to say, a representing, counterfeiting or figuring forth – to speak metaphorically, a speaking picture – with this end: to teach and delight' (p. 10). Three elements make up this definition. The first is the Aristotelian version of imitation as the representation of an action according to naturalistic principles of necessity and probability. The second element is the rhetorical and Horatian goal of teaching and delighting. The third element, introduced with Sidney's characteristic wordplay, is the metaphor of the speaking picture. The comparison of literature to painting goes back via Plutarch and Horace to the early Greek poet Simonides' observation that painting is silent poetry and poetry talking painting. Horace, relatedly, observes that things seen impress the imagination more than things spoken, and a parallel rhetorical tradition emphasizes appeals to the mind's eye through vivid description (the figure of *enargeia*). Sidney also draws on recent developments in the theory of painting as well as on the prevalence of visual metaphors in the philosophy of understanding. But that the 'speaking picture' of fiction appears to be the link between the author's act of representation and the teaching and delighting of the reader is an original touch. It is also far from straightforward. Aristotle had insisted that fiction imitates an action first of all, and characters only as a consequence – plot is the soul of the literary work. But in view of Sidney's emphasis later in the *Defence* on exemplary characters or 'images', we may be inclined to take the speaking picture not as an image of the plot but as a portrait of an exemplary character. This, however, is to simplify Sidney's point. The sum of what the poem represents is likened to a picture, and because language is its medium it has a voice. If we think of portraits this is only to engage the strand of metaphors which sees a whole work as an individual with a voice and a body – a surrogate for the work's author.

Sidney gives an ideal account of poetry. He speaks 'of the art and not of the artificer' (p. 20). If criticisms can be levelled at that art because of particular poems and poets, we should 'not say that poetry abuseth man's wit, but that man's wit abuseth poetry' (p. 35). And it is an ideal account of an idealizing poetry. In one of the most famous passages in the *Defence*, Sidney likens the work of the poet to that of nature (pp. 8–9). All other forms of learning are based on nature; only poetry can create its own world. He introduces this section by telling us that those other arts are 'actors and players, as it were, of what nature will have set forth' (p. 8). To 'set forth' is to write, express or publish: Sidney subtly invokes the common image of the book of nature (in this case as a dramatic text) to align creation with writing even before he compares the poet to nature. He goes on: 'Nature never set forth the earth in so rich tapestry as divers poets have done, neither with so pleasant rivers, fruitful trees, sweet-smelling flowers, nor whatsoever else may make the too-much-loved earth more lovely: her world is brazen, the poets only deliver a golden' (p. 9). Sidney's argument comes to depend on the ability of poetry not to differ from nature but to exceed it, and this is the clearest example of how his theory diverges, for

its own purposes, from most practice: Sidney's ideal poetry
does not only represent Aristotelian universals, but things and
characters 'better than nature bringeth forth' (p. 8), both 'what
may be and should be' (p. 11). Sidney goes on to borrow from
the Neoplatonic response to Plato's critique of imitation. The
poet works by forming an '*idea* or fore-conceit of the work',
and it is this Platonic ideal form which he imitates. The idea as
form rather than substance is also what is impressed on the
mind of the receptive reader. Sidney even says that the skill of
the poet lies in the making of the idea, not the work itself, and
the proof of that skill not in the work but in the work's ability
to transform its reader: 'not only to make a Cyrus, which had
been but a particular excellency as nature might have done, but
to bestow a Cyrus upon the world to make many Cyruses, if
they will learn aright why and how that maker made him' (p. 9).
Imitation as *mimesis* and imitation as readerly emulation are
bridged by the power of the authorial idea.

Since the authority of imaginative literature is made to depend
on its ability to teach, rather than only to give pleasure or
impress critics, Sidney must set it beside the other disciplines –
philosophy and history. Sidney read philosophy and was deeply
attached to the study of history, but for the purposes of his
argument he sacrifices poetry's two rivals. Philosophy gives only
precepts, whereas poetry can exemplify those precepts and give
the reader a lifelike instance of the beautiful and the good.
History is bound by what is supposed to have happened, so its
characters will be a mixture of good and bad, and its events
lacking in reason and coherence; if the historian is to teach he
must poetically impose order and pattern on his materials. What
is more, poetry is unique in having the power to move its readers
both 'with desire to be taught' and 'to do that which it doth
teach' (p. 22). Sidney remembers the third element of the rhetorical triad, submerged both in Horace and in his own central
definition, and makes moving the clinching argument. In its
ideal form poetry is thoroughly rhetorical, concerned with transforming individuals and the world around it, teaching not what
to think but what to do, and inspiring the reader with a desire
to act accordingly.

   Sidney did not have to take his arguments this far. Plutarch, in his essay on 'How the Young Man Ought to Study Poetry', which Sidney studied closely, insists that poetry 'is an imitation of the lives and manners of men, who are not perfect, pure, and irreproachable, but involved in passions, false opinions, and ignorance'.[19] Homer's heroes are mixtures of virtue and vice, like real people, and the reader must learn to discriminate bad from good. This argument, though, would let history back into the reckoning, and so Sidney, relying heavily on a few good characters (Cyrus and Aeneas foremost), sticks to his idealist guns. He also almost completely ignores allegory, a topic covered in depth in Harington's *Apology* and central to any reading of Spenser's *The Faerie Queene*. Sidney would have seen it as a dated medieval system which detracts from the rhetorical purpose and responsibility of the author by making it possible to read a wholesome moral into any story; his silence, though, has not stopped critics from making allegories of his own literary works. Any lingering feeling that Sidney's rhetorical fiction may not be justified and that the representation of realities may be preferable is extinguished brilliantly in the section in which Sidney disposes of the charge that poets are liars. All other forms of learning deal in affirmations, and those affirmations are often found to be untrue: 'Now, for the poet, he nothing affirms, and therefore never lieth, for, as I take it, to lie is to affirm that to be true which is false' (p. 34). Historians lie in trying to tell the truth; the poet only deals in ideals and so can concentrate on the higher truths which are the province of the philosopher. Fiction is not only justified and defended; it is transformed into the best form of knowledge and means of learning, the surest route to virtue.

   At times Sidney seems to present poetry as an irresistible force, just as the orators do rhetoric, as a perfect mechanism which delights, moves, and teaches a passive reader; the reader is then compared to a child, tricked into taking the sugar-coated pill. But ultimately Sidney follows Plutarch in requiring activity from the reader – he puts meaning in the reader's hands. The feigned Cyrus, the perfect image of virtue created by the poet, can only 'make many Cyruses, if they will learn aright why and how that maker made him' (p. 9). The reader must ask questions, must want to learn both the why and the how. This concession offers us a slender bridge between Sidney's theory and his practice. His *Arcadia* is stocked with characters whose evident vices we are meant to laugh at and shun; and its central characters, two princes and two princesses, are equipped with most of the virtues Sidney's theory would have us be moved to emulate. But the princes especially, like the Homeric heroes Plutarch refers to, have their bad sides too: they make mistakes, and are driven to unjustifiable actions by their passions. They are human. Sidney's model only holds if we accept that in practice it requires more effort from the reader. The same can be said of that other great Elizabethan monument, Spenser's *The Faerie Queene*. The theory of poetry is simple. But poetry itself will always break theoretical models into pieces, turn those pieces into metaphors, look at them this way and that, and find a way of transforming them into something new and unexpected. The *Arcadia* is not a sixteenth-century *Aeneid*, but Sidney still intends that it will not only delight (as it certainly does) but that it will also transform its readers – that it will make them wiser and better and inspire them to act accordingly.

Puttenham

George Puttenham was born in around 1529 and died in 1590 or 1591. His maternal uncle was Sir Thomas Elyot, author of *The Book Named The Governor* (1531). Puttenham studied at Christ's College, Cambridge from 1546, may also have studied at Oxford, entered the Middle Temple in 1556, and spent time on the Continent after this date and probably before. Connected by birth or marriage to various significant courtiers, most of his writings seem to have had a court focus or occasion, although he appears never to have achieved any notable court position. He names many now lost works, including a poem to Edward VI, a treatise on decorum, a work on the history of English, a comedy *Gynecocratia* ('The Rule of Women'), an Arthurian verse romance, and a probably allegorical cycle of love poems illustrating rhetorical figures. Two other works survive in manuscript: a treatise defending Elizabeth I's treatment of Mary,

Queen of Scots, and *Partheniads* (*c.*1579–82), a series of poems in praise of Elizabeth I. The Queen granted him £1,000 in 1588 for his 'good, true, faithful, and acceptable service', and it was to Elizabeth that he evidently dedicated the manuscript of *The Art of English Poesy*.

Puttenham probably started to work on the *Art* in the late 1560s, may have finished most of Books 1 and 2 in the 1570s, and substantially revised the whole in the mid-1580s. It was printed in 1589 and new passages were still being added while it was in press. Although Puttenham was still working on his *Art* after Sidney's death, therefore, it is the work of a man belonging to the same generation as Sidney's father, and Puttenham's literary tastes are decidedly mid-century. The plan of the work is elegant. Book 1 is on poets and poesy, defining the art in terms familiar from Sidney and then offering a fanciful historical account of the different genres; Book 2 turns from matter to words, treating the subject of versification in considerable detail; Book 3 is on rhetoric in poetry, includes a substantial discussion of decorum in both *res* and *verba*, and is dominated by a systematic account of the rhetorical figures. Puttenham leans heavily on Scaliger and other Continental critics, on the *Institutio oratoria* of Quintilian, and on the *Epitome troporum ac schematum* ('Outline of Schemes and Tropes') of Susenbrotus (*c.*1541), which is typical of Renaissance rhetorical treatises in attending to *elocutio* alone. He is less interested than Sidney in classical philosophy and literary criticism, and although he has a good line in tongue-in-cheek pedantry, in general he seems happier to borrow uncritically and leave questions begged. He himself admits towards the end of Book 1 that 'what we have written of the ancient forms of poems we have taken from the best clerks writing in the same art' (p. 103). Of Book 2, however, he goes on to claim that 'we may truly affirm to have been the first devisers thereof ourselves, as *autodidaktoi*, and not to have borrowed it of any other by learning or imitation' (p. 103).

Puttenham is no Aristotle, and the affection in which he is held by students of the English Renaissance can appear like a very English love of the quaint and unintentionally comical. But the *Art* provides an important repository of normative views

lxiv   INTRODUCTION

about poetry, always memorably expressed, is usefully characteristic of Elizabethan literary culture in its guileless jumbling
together of all manner of disparate influences, and for all its
eccentricities is in certain parts important and influential. One
such part is Book 3. Puttenham borrows many of the details
from the conventional sources, but his tripartite distinction
between schemes, tropes, and figures of thought, while not
unprecedented, is unusual and coherent. The decision to give
English names to the figures combines the Renaissance urge to
absorb and compete with classical learning with a literary and
linguistic nationalism. Puttenham recognizes that some will
laugh at such colourful names as 'the fleering frump' and 'the
mingle-mangle', and probably wants us at least to smile, but his
serious purpose is to show that the Greek and Latin names
are not mysterious and sacred hieroglyphs but words directly
expressive of the action of the figure. At some points, especially
in Book 1, he may be criticized for not acknowledging how far
apart modern and ancient literature and society are, but his
instinct to demystify classical learning and apply it practically
to modern poetry is that of a model humanist. Book 3 goes
further than previous treatises in connecting rhetoric to poetry.
It neither presents a general rhetoric which the readers and
writers of verse, among others, may use, as Peacham does in
The Garden of Eloquence, nor repackages the details of rhetoric
in the form of a poetics, as Horace, Scaliger and Sidney do.
Instead it offers a purely literary rhetoric, a simple manual of
elocutio for the poet; for Puttenham, poetry is not like rhetoric,
it is rhetoric. Even so, Puttenham does not take every opportunity: the treatments of *prosopographia*, *topographia* and *pragmatographia* are too dependent on the rhetoricians' discussions
of the use of literary devices in the oration to realize that these
figures describe the basics of literature – character, scene, and
plot – and would merit more detailed treatment.

Book 2, the work of the autodidact, has great strengths and
considerable weaknesses. A comparison with Gascoigne and
Webbe shows that Puttenham's understanding of metre was
both idiosyncratic and dated. But his treatment of verse form is
superb. Subsequent poets such as Donne and Herbert produced

metrical forms of the bewildering variety which Puttenham's analysis of rhyme scheme and its relation to line length encouraged. Herbert also joined more poets than we would now credit in writing the shape poems discussed by Puttenham. Poetic form had deep significance for a culture which thought through analogies and liked to find macrocosms reflected in microcosms. The structure and harmony of the universe was felt to be echoed in poetic and musical forms as it was in social structures. Because man, too, was a complex structure echoing the order of the cosmos, different musical modes and, Puttenham adds by analogy, kinds of poetic form operated in distinct ways on his mind and heart. The poetic form resembles Sidney's '*idea* or fore-conceit of the work', since it is the first thing which Puttenham's poet/maker creates, and it has an independent strength and significance. In this area Puttenham coincides with Sidney's own poetic practice and that of the subsequent generation of lyric poets, and in his emphasis on the visual aspect of poetic form helps us to see Renaissance lyric poetry in a more revealing light.

Puttenham's prose style merits some consideration. Like Sidney's, it demands affection for its wit and plain speaking. But where both Sidney and Daniel rise to the persuasive eloquence required by Cicero and Quintilian, Puttenham often falls short, the flood of eloquence restricted to a rustically babbling stream. This is deliberate. His rhetorical *ethos* or character is avuncular, self-deprecating, and generous, more adept at the shaggy dog story than the wisecrack. And yet he writes to a queen, and tells us that his intended audience is one of ladies and courtiers. His gentle sense of the comical and incongruous is delightful, as when he likens the classical period to a traveller on horseback and its three elements (comma, colon, and period) to a brief stop, a lunch break, and an overnight stay. His prose lacks the finely tuned cadence of Sidney's and Daniel's; but they are far better poets with far more sophisticated ears. One stylistic habit is seen everywhere: like many of his contemporaries he is fond of proceeding by twos. To take an example: 'implying thereby how, by his discreet and wholesome lessons uttered in harmony and with melodious instruments, he brought the rude and savage people to a more civil and orderly life, nothing, as it seemeth, more prevailing or fit to redress and edify the cruel and sturdy courage of man than it' (p. 61). Many of the words which face each other across Puttenham's conjunctions are synonyms. The technique belonged in the mixed language which Puttenham had written a history of. For most things English had an Anglo-Saxon term and an Anglo-Norman one; and the Latinate element represented by the influence of French was being fortified by the many borrowings from Latin which expanded the English lexicon in the sixteenth and seventeenth centuries. Puttenham is not frightened to employ neologisms when he wants to, but he sympathizes with those of the previous generation who had called for a purification of English and a return to its Anglo-Saxon origins; he employs many archaic, rustic or unusual Saxonisms. Often the use of doublets will allow a new word to be complemented and glossed by an old one, but here the habit is instinctive, a badge of mixed origins.

Harington comments rather gleefully that Puttenham's own poems prove, ironically, that poetry 'is a gift and not an art' (p. 263). Puttenham tends to overvalue his own art, telling us that Wyatt has translated this sonnet by Petrarch but giving us his own version, referring to a celebrated *blason* by Sidney but quoting instead his own rather embarrassing celebration of Elizabeth. In this last instance, at least, he has an excuse. Rhetorical figures are always personified by Puttenham, made into characters who represent a type of behaviour with regard to language. The Queen's body stands as a frontispiece to Puttenham's *Art*, and stands behind it throughout. And the Queen comes metaphorically to stand for the *Art* when he implicitly likens her to the rhetorical figure *exergasia*, a figure of beauty and final polish which he offers last and in a chapter of its own. This conclusive figure is illustrated by one of her own poems, and she in turn is described as 'the most beautiful, or rather beauty, of queens' (p. 189): Puttenham turns her into an abstraction, a sort of rhetorical figure writ large. In Book 1 she is the ultimate poet or maker not for her own verses but for her ability to make men, and she presides over the opening and closing chapters of the work. She is the *Art*'s master, or mistress, figure. Her presence guarantees that Puttenham's work becomes *the* art of Elizabethan poetry.

Daniel

Samuel Daniel was born in 1562 or 1563 and studied at Oxford in the early 1580s. His first publication, in 1585, was a translation of a book of *imprese*, and for five years or so he was employed in the household of Sir Edward Dymoke. In 1591, perhaps with Daniel's complicity, some of his sonnets were printed at the end of the pirated edition of Sidney's *Astrophil and Stella*. This enabled Daniel to dedicate an authorized edition of his *Delia* to Sidney's sister, the Countess of Pembroke, in the following year, and Daniel was subsequently taken into her household at Wilton where he probably taught her sons and worked with her on various literary projects. At her request he wrote a play *Cleopatra* (1594), on proper classical lines, which served as a companion piece to her *Antonius* (1592), a translation from the French of Robert Garnier. Daniel rapidly achieved a high reputation as a lyric poet, and was encouraged to attempt more ambitious projects. In 1595 the first four books of his *Civil Wars*, a poetic account of the Wars of the Roses, were printed, dedicated to a new patron, Lord Mountjoy. Other associations with important courtiers, including Fulke Greville, were developed at this time, and in 1599 appeared Daniel's *Poetical Essays*, which reprinted the *Civil Wars* (now grown to five books), *Cleopatra*, and *The Complaint of Rosamond* (originally a companion to *Delia*), and included also the *Letter from Octavia* and *Musophilus: Containing a General Defence of Learning*.

Musophilus, excerpts of which are included here, is a dialogue between two speakers, Musophilus and Philocosmus, who represent opposing positions on the value of the intellectual and contemplative life, and of learning, eloquence and literature. Philocosmus is worldly and cynical, Musophilus an idealistic and defensive alter ego of Daniel. Daniel dedicated the poem to Greville, and in a later printing wrote that the work represents his own self-examination in a period of crisis when he almost gave up writing. In 1601 and 1602 Daniel's *Works* appeared, adding a sixth book of the *Civil Wars* and a revised *Delia*. Daniel appears to have had a good standing with the Queen, and when she died in 1603 he acted quickly to secure his place at court. He wrote a *Panegyric Congratulatory*, either performed or given in manuscript to the new King, James VI of Scotland, as he made his trip south to London. When the work was printed a little later in 1603 it included a selection of verse epistles to prominent courtiers and, in its second issue, Daniel's *Defence of Rhyme*, a timely essay on the tension between tradition and innovation in English literary and, through a substantial strand of metaphors and analogies, political culture. Daniel came to enjoy the patronage of James VI and I's Queen, Anne of Denmark, and his career at the Jacobean court included commissions to write masques, entertainments, and pastoral dramas for court performance. In 1604 he was rather unsuccessfully employed by Queen Anne as Licensor of the Children of the Queen's Revels, and in 1605 he wrote a play for this children's company, *Philotas*, the resemblance of whose classical theme to the recent fall of the Earl of Essex landed Daniel in trouble with the authorities. By now he seems to have earned the dislike of Ben Jonson, Daniel's rival for the attentions of several key courtiers and for court masque commissions. Daniel steered clear of Jonson's theatrical turf, finished the *Civil Wars* (dedicating its last book to the Countess of Pembroke) and embarked on his largest project, a prose history of England, starting from the Conquest, and ending with the death of Edward III in 1377, which was published in instalments in 1612 and 1618. He died in 1619, and came to be most valued as a historian, both for the clarity and strength of his prose and for his unusually modern approach. Daniel was not the slave of accepted accounts and legends, but scrutinized sources and formed his own objective and sometimes revisionist views. Just as in the *Defence of Rhyme*, he shows an uncommon ability to look sympathetically at the issues and mentalities of England's medieval past, and a profound sense of the limits of historical knowledge and the dangers of wishful thinking.

Daniel's *Defence of Rhyme* is his most celebrated work, which is odd when we consider that it is an intervention in a debate about versification. Daniel had never picked up the classical strand of Sidney's prosodic legacy, and as the publication of English verses in classical metres dwindled through the 1590s he would not have expected ever to have to argue about this issue. But the publication in 1601 of Thomas Campion's *Observations in the Art of English Poesy* left Daniel in no doubt that something had to be said, and that he was the one to say it. Campion (1567–1620) was educated at Cambridge and Gray's Inn, and was to study medicine at Caen in France, receiving a medical degree in 1605. A handful of his poems had been included alongside Daniel's in the 1591 *Astrophil and Stella*, and his Latin *Poemata* ('Poems') were published in 1595. Campion's greatest talent is as a lyric poet, and in this area he continues to have a substantial reputation. His ear for verbal melody is matched only by Tennyson's, and is evidence of the musical gifts which saw him contribute to the music for several masques which he devised. He published a number of songbooks between 1601 and 1617 for which he wrote the words and in most cases the music; his songs are characterized by elegance, simplicity and wit, and achieve a match of words and music – in rhythm, intonation, syntax and mood – which is rarely found elsewhere. As a Latinist, composer and writer of lyric poetry, Campion's interest in the question of metrics is unsurprising. Music made verse quantitative, and in one song Campion wrote a strictly quantitative text which he set quantitatively, using only two note values for the long and short syllables. But for the most part the theory advanced in *Observations* is kept separate from his practice as poet and composer, a weakness which Daniel pounces on.

As an alternative to barbaric rhyme, Campion suggests various ways of introducing greater regulation into metre. His quantitative system is moderate, allowing many licences in the construction of lines, and leads in the examples he gives to a supple rhythm which avoids the monotony of some accentual-syllabic lines (Gascoigne's, for instance) and to which earlier quantitative experiments, especially with the hexameter, also tended. Daniel's response is to accuse Campion of reinventing the wheel, showing that Campion's theory makes little possible that was not already. The debate thus comes down to rhyme, and to the view of English cultural history which can argue that a revolution in versification is desirable. Daniel's arguments about the value of rhyme in tying stanzas together are eloquent and persuasive, but it is when he thinks more generally about English culture that his *Defence* really takes wing. The succession of James I had not been certain. Elizabeth I had always refused to name a successor, and there were fears of a fight for the crown and of foreign claims which might see a Catholic on the throne. Even if James did become King of England, it was feared that a monarch who saw himself as a significant political philosopher might wish to reform the English law and institutions along Scottish or other lines. Daniel's *Defence of Rhyme* becomes a defence of custom and the traditional, unwritten, English constitution and common law, gentle advice to a new monarch about the attachment of the freeborn English to their ancient rights. In this respect it predicts the relations between literature and politics which operate in the period of the Civil War and in the works of John Milton. Pretending that English rhyme is as old as the hills, rather than a recent innovation brought to England by French invaders, Daniel is able to base his argument on what is natural to English. There is no answer to his appeal to 'custom that is before all law, nature that is above all art' (p. 210) which does not sound like pettiness and innovation for its own sake. And Daniel is able to explode Campion's simplistic picture of English cultural history (in which the monkish Dark Ages only end with the advent of the North European humanists of the early sixteenth century) with a roll-call of scholars of the Italian Renaissance of the two previous centuries. Daniel also insists on the value and integrity of medieval scholarship and society. He likens England's ancient constitution to its solid Gothic buildings and initiates an important reappraisal of medieval culture. Human nature is always the same; what looks like progress is only change. Daniel makes his argument with Campion not an isolated argument over technicalities but a fight for the soul of English culture; the right of the English to do things their way is defended against the knee-jerk classicizing implicit in the humanist project. And yet

Daniel's copious Latin quotations demonstrate that he stands
not against classical learning, but against its misuse, that he is
not anti-humanist, but wishes rather to see a better and more
realistic marriage of the classical and the vernacular.

It is the metaphors Daniel uses which give coherence and
scope to the *Defence*. These are not only the political images of
the 'state of rhyme', of reformation, parliament and citizenry,
but a series of structural metaphors which liken the action of
poetic form to the divine construction of the cosmos or, in
common with Puttenham, to the construction of buildings.
Daniel is a poet of the firm monosyllables which form the
building blocks of English verse, and his language has a kinetic
strength which is most felt when it refuses to be moved. Only
Daniel can come out with the poetic prose of 'we must stand
bound to stay' (p. 227), six monosyllables, four of them verbs
of compulsion and stasis. Daniel expands his argument by metaphor, analogy and connection until it operates almost on a
cosmic scale, and it is this which makes his relativistic conclusion
such a glorious shock. Even if Campion had initially felt minded
to reply, there is really nothing which can be said in answer to
Daniel's closing words: 'But this is but a character of that
perpetual revolution which we see to be in all things that never
remain the same, and we must herein be content to submit
ourselves to the law of time, which in few years will make all
that for which we now contend *nothing*' (p. 233).

OTHER VOICES

The remaining texts gathered in this edition offer a selection of
analogues, alternative emphases, paradigmatic statements, and
examples of literary criticism in verse. It is impossible in an
edition of this size to offer a comprehensive account of the
development of literary criticism in the English Renaissance, but
it is hoped that these selections will help the reader to follow
various lines of development. The passages chosen are rich in
implication and connection to the three main texts, and also fill
a few representative gaps.

George Gascoigne was born in around 1534 and died in 1577.
Educated at Trinity College, Cambridge, he entered Gray's Inn
in 1555 and tried unsuccessfully to make his way at court. In
1561 he married Elizabeth Breton, a widow and the mother of
the poet Nicholas Breton. However, she was already married,
and Gascoigne was involved in protracted legal proceedings to
secure their marriage and her property. Gascoigne was frequently involved in legal wrangling, usually without success,
and also failed as a farmer and member of Parliament. He had
some success in attracting patronage, but his mounting debts
may have caused his ejection from Gray's Inn and did lead to a
spell in Bedford Gaol for debt. Between 1572 and 1574 he
joined the English expedition to aid the Dutch against Spain,
ending with four months as a Spanish prisoner. After his return
he concentrated on courting patronage and having his works
printed (he claimed that the 1573 edition of *A Hundred Sundry
Flowers* was unauthorized), and in 1575 appeared *The Posies
of George Gascoigne*, which ends with *Certain Notes of Instruction Concerning the Making of Verse or Rhyme in English*.
Among the innovative works included in these collections are
Supposes, a prose comedy based on Ariosto; *Jocasta*, a blank
verse tragedy derived from Euripides; and *The Adventures of
Master F.I.*, a raunchy novella; other works published separately
include the verse satire, *The Steel Glass* (1576). His many poems
play on occasions and personae, blurring fact and fiction (we
do not, for example, know if the addressee of *Certain Notes of
Instruction* actually existed), and Gascoigne uses his works
to advertise his courtly connections and soldiery. Although
Drayton, in the 1620s, saw him as obsolete ('To Henry
Reynolds', ll. 73–8), the later Elizabethans agreed that he was
of great importance; as Nashe put it in 1589: 'Master Gascoigne
is not to be abridged of his deserved esteem, who first beat the
path to that perfection which our best poets have aspired to
since his departure'.[20] Above all, Gascoigne was praised for his
metrical facility, and *Certain Notes of Instruction* marked a
significant step forward, providing a simple metrical theory
which accounted for current practices and encouraged the
refinements of the subsequent generation. It is often referred to

as the first piece of literary criticism in English, and therefore makes an appropriate point of departure.

Henry Peacham was a clergyman about whom little is known. His *Garden of Eloquence* was first printed in 1577 and an expanded edition followed in 1593. It is a treatment of the rhetorical figures based on the *Epitome troporum ac schematum* of Susenbrotus (c.1541) and sees rhetoric as having a broad scope. As Peacham's title pages make clear, rhetoric is for readers as well as writers, and applies not only to oratory but to poetry and scripture too. Peacham's treatise is well organized and contains a great deal of original thought. In 1593 he adds to his accounts of the figures notes on 'the use' and 'the caution', demonstrating a strong sense that each figure must contribute appropriately to a coherent whole. The current edition includes the 1577 dedicatory preface and a passage from the 1593 dedication. Each offers a highly eloquent account of the importance of eloquence, and of the figures in particular.

William Webbe's *A Discourse of English Poetry* (1586) tells us that its author was a 'graduate', and that he worked as a tutor in the family of Edward Suliard, an Essex gentleman. The work combines standard humanist learning and a university outlook with a relish for contemporary English verse. Webbe is up to date and has a good ear; while his comments on poetry in general are conventional enough, his observations on versification are of real value. Like many of his contemporaries in the 1580s, including Sidney and Puttenham, he knows that he ought to prefer quantitative versification, but he is no dogmatist. His treatise includes quantitative translations of Virgil's first and second eclogues, and of the hymn in praise of Cynthia from the 'April' eclogue of Spenser's *The Shepheardes Calender* (1579). The brief selection given here complements and adds to Gascoigne's *Certain Notes of Instruction*.

Sir John Harington (c.1561–1612) was the godson of Queen Elizabeth I and was educated at Eton, King's College, Cambridge, and Lincoln's Inn. Following the practices of his father, he was a great collector and compiler of literary manuscripts, and his family's manuscripts provide an important, and in some cases unique, source for the study of Tudor poetry. It was supposedly at Elizabeth I's command that he translated Ludovico Ariosto's great heroic poem *Orlando furioso*. His 1591 translation was followed in 1596 by *A New Discourse of a Stale Subject, Called the Metamorphosis of Ajax* [i.e. 'a jakes'], a wittily discursive account of Harington's invention of the water closet which attempts to gain court patronage and royal favour. The plan backfired, and Harington turned soldier, accompanying the Earl of Essex to Ireland in 1599; after the accession of James VI of Scotland as James I of England he repaired his reputation somewhat, acting as a tutor to the King's oldest son, Prince Henry. Numerous letters and short works survive, including a tract on the succession supporting King James VI's claim to the English throne and a translation of *Aeneid*, Book 6; his *Epigrams*, which circulated in different manuscript configurations in his lifetime, were printed posthumously in 1615. Harington's abiding reputation is of a well-educated wit, and a lively observer of his fellow humans and himself. As an introduction to his Ariosto he wrote 'A Preface, or rather a Brief Apology of Poetry, and of the Author and Translator of this Poem', the first part of which is included here. It borrows heavily from Sidney's *Defence of Poesy*, which Harington evidently possessed in manuscript, at times referring the reader to a work which was not to be printed for another four years, at other times lifting phrases without acknowledgement. Harington joined in the general veneration of Sidney in the literary and court culture of the 1590s, especially after the printing of *Arcadia* in 1590 and *Astrophil and Stella* in 1591. Whilst his debts in this case tread a fine line between imitation and plagiarism, he would have believed that direct borrowing could do Sidney little harm, and his use of the *Defence* shows how important it was recognized to be even before it was printed. His many original touches, including a useful account of allegory, and his brilliant writing justify his inclusion here.

Francis Bacon (1561–1626) is one of the most significant figures of the English Renaissance. Educated at Trinity College, Cambridge, he was admitted to Gray's Inn in 1582 and was a successful barrister and MP. He early aspired to a significant position at court, but made little progress under Elizabeth I,

INTRODUCTION

in spite, or perhaps because, of the fact that his cause was championed by the Earl of Essex. Under James I he rose rapidly, from Solicitor General in 1607 to Lord Chancellor in 1618, and was made Viscount St Albans in 1621. But he fell spectacularly, after admitting to taking bribes as a judge. His *Essays or Counsels, Civil and Moral* (1597) were expanded in editions of 1612 and 1625, and offer snapshots of new ideas and old wisdom on a great variety of subjects. The majority of his other writings form part of his 'Great Instauration' [restoration, renewal], an ambitious attempt to reform knowledge and learning. This gave to the later seventeenth century the preference for the study of the natural world and for the use of the inductive method which was to prove so fundamental to scientific and philosophical progress. Where most previous learning proceeded by deduction, from a conclusion to the evidence which would support it, and tended therefore to argue in support of old truths, the inductive method worked from the gathering of details to hypotheses about their significance which might be tested experimentally. *The Advancement of Learning* of 1605 represents the first part of the Great Instauration, a new classification of the branches of knowledge, including literature. Bacon seeks to replace theoretical writing about knowledge which is overly disputative, rhetorical or whimsical with a more scientific approach. The passage from the second book of the *Advancement* shows how that approach could nevertheless accord with Sidney's model of poetry as a sort of idealizing moral rhetoric.

Little is known of the early life of Michael Drayton (1563–1631), except that he lived as a boy in the service of the Gooderes of Nottinghamshire. In 1593 he published *Idea: The Shepherds' Garland*, a set of Spenserian eclogues, and followed this with a Petrarchan sonnet sequence, *Idea's Mirror* (1594). His poems on subjects from English history include *Mortimeriados* (1596), revised as *The Barons' Wars* (1603), and *England's Heroical Epistles* (1597), which imitates the *Heroides* of Ovid. In 1612 he published the first part of *Poly-Olbion* (published complete in 1622), a long topographical poem which embeds history and legend in the English landscape. He was not as successful as some of his friends and contemporaries in securing celebrity, patronage or advancement, and many of his later works are marked by a nostalgia for the Elizabethan period and its literary themes. His works, often revised, were printed in various collections, one of the last of which was *The Battle of Agincourt* (1627), which includes the epistle 'To Henry Reynolds, of Poets and Poesy'. The epistle versifies the brief synoptic history of English literature of which the last chapter of Puttenham's Book 1, itself an afterthought, is perhaps the first example. Drayton's remarks are typical of the period in avoiding any false appearance of objectivity. They are introduced by delightful accounts of evenings of literary chat with Reynolds, and of Drayton as a young would-be poet. Drayton's survey is characterized by the confidence seen in such accounts from the 1590s on that England had finally produced a body of literary work which could stand comparison to the canons of Greece, Rome, and modern Italy.

Sir William Alexander (?1567–1640) was a Scottish poet, courtier and statesman. He is thought to have been educated at Stirling, Glasgow, and Leiden, was a tutor to Prince Henry, and came to the English court with King James I in 1603. A member of the household of Prince Henry and, after his death in 1612, Prince Charles, he was made Master of Requests in 1614 and was granted jurisdiction over Nova Scotia and Canada in 1621. When Charles I became King in 1625, Alexander was sent back to Scotland as Secretary of State (in 1626); he was raised to the peerage in 1630 and made Earl of Stirling in 1633. He died insolvent in London in 1640, the beleagured Secretary of State of a nation which had resisted Charles I's imposition on it of episcopacy (Church government by bishops) and the English Prayer Book. Alexander's works include a collection of sonnets and other lyric poems, *Aurora* (1604), a long poem on *Doomsday* (1614) and four tragedies on classical themes and along classical lines. In around 1617 was published Alexander's bridging passage linking Book 3 of Sidney's incomplete revised *Arcadia* to the ending supplied in 1593 from Books 3–5 of the original version. It is an accomplished piece of Sidney imitation and offers an interesting perspective on the work. Bound into unsold copies of the 1613 edition of the *Arcadia*, it was printed with it in subsequent editions (including that in the Penguin Classics series). Alexander collaborated with King James I on a verse translation of the Psalms which was printed in 1631; Alexander had been granted a monopoly on its printing for thirty-one years. A friend of William Drummond of Hawthornden since around 1613, he addressed to him at some point in the 1630s a brief set of critical reflections, *Anacrisis* ('An Enquiry'), which was not printed until 1711. Alexander's literary tastes and critical views show that he is a devotee of Sidney, but the work also represents a staging post between the eloquent and digressive style of Renaissance literary criticism, where a critic's argument may be frequently hijacked by his metaphors, and a more concise, aphoristic style directly based on Horace, which was the vehicle of the more rule-laden neoclassical criticism of the later seventeenth century.

It is with Horace that this edition ends, as one signpost to the road ahead. His translator, Ben Jonson (1572/3–1637), might have received ampler representation in this anthology, but at no point does he deliver a sustained piece of criticism. His brief dramatic prefaces combine general critical reflection with engagement with particular issues and private quarrels. A great deal of material on literature and rhetoric is contained in *Timber, or Discoveries*, published posthumously in 1640, but the work is in essence a commonplace book of fragmentary thoughts and maxims, some developed more fully than others, which are often highly, and complicatedly, derivative. And his 'Conversations with Drummond of Hawthornden' offer much of interest to the student of Jonson or Jacobean literature more generally, including his unguarded, and not always flattering, reflections on Sidney, Daniel, Drayton and others. Jonson's scattered remarks and evidence of wide reading show that he could have been a critic of real significance. But his failure to write a treatise, even the 'Observations' on Horace he was promising his readers in 1605, is typical of the pause for thought in the Jacobean and Caroline periods which accounts for this edition's concentration on Elizabethan sources. Jonson is represented here by his 'A Fit of Rhyme against Rhyme', a witty

afterword on the Campion–Daniel controversy, and by selections from his translation of Horace's *Ars poetica*. The Roman
lyric poet lived from 65 BC to 8 BC and enjoyed the patronage
of the first Roman emperor, Augustus. Horace offered Jonson
a role model in his successful pursuit of the patronage of James I,
and was also his most important literary model. Jonson's verse
epistles are Horatian in style, with their emphasis on the values
of friendship, conviviality, self-knowledge and temperance, and
his plays are influenced by the dramatical rules to be gathered
from the *Ars poetica*. This brief assemblage of critical reflections,
at 476 lines Horace's longest poem, was written as a verse epistle
to the Pisos, a family of budding writers. Though given the title
Ars poetica by Quintilian, it is arranged as a letter rather than
as a treatise, and thus in its form provides a direct model for
Drayton (in verse) and Alexander (in prose). Its influence is
felt equally strongly in treatises of the early sixteenth century
(Marco Girolamo Vida's Latin verse *De arte poetica* ['On the
Art of Poetry'] of 1527) and the early eighteenth (Pope's verse
Essay on Criticism of 1711). The passages selected here are
some of those most cited and followed in the period up to 1640.

NOTES

Where possible reference is given to collections detailed in Further
Reading. Quotations from classical texts are in most cases from editions in the Loeb Classical Library series.

1.   *Classical Literary Criticism*, ed. Penelope Murray (Penguin
     Classics, 2000), 55. Hereafter *CLC*.
2.   *Elizabethan Critical Essays*, ed. G. G. Smith, 2 vols. (Oxford,
     1904), 1.226–7. Hereafter *ECE*.
3.   *Ben Jonson*, ed. C. H. Herford, and Percy and Evelyn Simpson,
     11 vols. (Oxford, 1925–52), 8.567; *English Renaissance Literary
     Criticism*, ed. Brian Vickers (Oxford, 1999), 559. Hereafter
     ERLC.
4.   Desiderius Erasmus, *Literary and Educational Writings 2: De
     copia, De ratione studii*, ed. Craig R. Thompson, Collected Works
     of Erasmus 24 (Toronto, 1978), 670, 687.

5.   *The Anatomy of Absurdity* (1589), *ECE*, 1.334.
6.   *A Defence of Poetry, Music, and Stage Plays* [1579], *ECE*, 1.75.
7.   *Ancient Literary Criticism: The Principal Texts in New Transla-tions*, ed. D. A. Russell and M. Winterbottom (Oxford, 1972), 302. Hereafter *ALC*.
8.   *Ben Jonson*, 8.595; *ERLC*, 568.
9.   'How the Young Man Ought To Study Poetry', *Moralia* ('Moral Essays'), 18b, in *ALC*, 513–14.
10. Webbe, *ECE*, 1.251.
11. *ERLC*, 82.
12. *On the Sublime*, 22, in *CLC*, 141–2.
13. 'Humanist Education', in *The Cambridge History of Literary Criticism*, vol. 3: *The Renaissance*, ed. Glyn Norton (Cambridge, 1999), 153.
14. 'Conversations with William Drummond of Hawthornden', in *Ben Jonson*, ed. Ian Donaldson, The Oxford Authors (Oxford, 1985), 595 and 609; *ERLC*, 529 and 535.
15. *ECE*, 1.29–30; *ERLC*, 157.
16. *Literary Criticism: Plato to Dryden*, ed. Allan H. Gilbert (Detroit, 1962), 404. Hereafter Gilbert.
17. Spenser and Harvey, *Two Letters* (1580), *ECE*, 1.89.
18. *ECE*, 2.220; *ERLC*, 323.
19. *Moralia*, 26a, in *ALC*, 527.
20. Preface to Greene's *Menaphon* (1589), *ECE*, 1.315.

Further Reading

Subsections of this bibliography are ordered chronologically and/or generically, with the most useful works in each section tending to come first.

General Works, Reference, Historical and Cultural Background

The Cambridge History of Literary Criticism, vol. 1: *Classical Criticism*, ed. George A. Kennedy (Cambridge, 1989). An excellent survey in eleven chapters.

The Cambridge History of Literary Criticism, vol. 3: *The Renaissance*, ed. Glyn Norton (Cambridge, 1999). Sixty-one chapters covering a broad range of topics, some general, some specific, and with a good deal of overlap; especially useful are the sections on 'Poetics' and 'Structures of Thought', and four essays by Ann Moss.

William K. Wimsatt, Jr and Cleanth Brooks, *Literary Criticism: A Short History* (New York, 1957). A whistle-stop tour by two masters of the subject.

The New Princeton Encyclopedia of Poetry and Poetics, ed. Alex Preminger and T.V.F. Brogan (Princeton, 1993). A superb work of reference; detailed articles are the best place to start on any question and include substantial bibliographies: see e.g. 'Classical Poetics', 'Imitation', 'Platonism and Poetry', 'Renaissance Poetics', 'Representation and Mimesis', 'Rhetoric and Poetry' and articles on all aspects of versification.

Isabel Rivers, *Classical and Christian Ideas in English Renaissance Poetry: A Students' Guide*, 2nd edn (London, 1994).

Richard A. Lanham, *A Handlist of Rhetorical Terms*, 2nd edn (Berkeley and Los Angeles, 1991). Explains figures and other rhetorical terms; excellent appendix gives systematic overview of rhetoric.

Heinrich F. Plett, *English Renaissance Rhetoric and Poetics: A Systematic Bibliography of Primary and Secondary Sources* (Leiden and New York, 1995).

Susan Brigden, *New Worlds, Lost Worlds: The Rule of the Tudors, 1485–1603*, Penguin History of Britain (London, 2001).

Mark A. Kishlansky, *A Monarchy Transformed: Britain, 1603–1714*, Penguin History of Britain (London, 1997).

The Cambridge Companion to Renaissance Humanism, ed. Jill Kraye (Cambridge, 1996).

The Cambridge Companion to English Literature, 1500–1600, ed. Arthur F. Kinney (Cambridge, 2000).

George A. Kennedy, *A New History of Classical Rhetoric* (Princeton, 1994).

Brian Vickers, *In Defence of Rhetoric*, corrected edn (Oxford, 1989).

Rosalie Colie, *The Resources of Kind: Genre-Theory in the Renaissance* (Berkeley, 1973).

Derek Attridge, *Well-Weighed Syllables: Elizabethan Verse in Classical Metres* (Cambridge, 1974).

John Hollander, *Vision and Resonance: Two Senses of Poetic Form*, 2nd edn (New Haven and London, 1985).

Classical Texts

Classical Literary Criticism, ed. Penelope Murray (London, 2000). Plato's *Ion* and relevant passages from the *Republic*; Aristotle, *Poetics*; Horace, *The Art of Poetry*; Longinus, *On the Sublime*. Includes an excellent introduction.

Ancient Literary Criticism: The Principal Texts in New Translations, eds. D.A. Russell and M. Winterbottom (Oxford, 1972); abridged version, *Classical Literary Criticism*, eds.

Russell and Winterbottom (Oxford, 1989). Superb translations and helpful apparatus.

Aristotle's *Rhetoric* and most of Plato's dialogues are available
in the Penguin Classics series. Also useful is Plato, *Complete
Works*, ed. John M. Cooper (Indianapolis, 1997).

All classical texts are available in The Loeb Classical Library
series in the original Greek or Latin with facing translation;
the Loeb series is the only source for English translations of
Cicero's treatises, Quintilian, Plutarch's essay on the study of
poetry, and other important texts cited in the notes.

Renaissance Texts

Literary Criticism: Plato to Dryden, ed. Allan H. Gilbert
(Detroit, 1962). An excellent anthology especially useful for
its coverage of sixteenth-century Italian critics.

Elizabethan Critical Essays, ed. G.G. Smith, 2 vols. (Oxford,
1904; frequently reprinted). Though this and Spingarn
(below) may seem dated, they remain comprehensive and
well thought-out anthologies. Especially worthy of study are
works by Ascham, Lodge, Spenser, Harvey, Nashe and Meres.
Includes fuller texts of Webbe, Harington and Campion.

Critical Essays of the Seventeenth Century, ed. J.E. Spingarn,
3 vols. (Oxford, 1908; frequently reprinted). In vol. 1
(1603–50), works by Jonson, Chapman and Milton are
especially important, and fuller selections from Bacon and
Alexander are included. Volumes 2 (1650–85) and 3 (1685–
1700) take the story forward to the age of the critic.

English Literary Criticism: The Renaissance, ed. O.B. Hardison
(London, 1967).

Literary Criticism of Seventeenth-Century England, ed. Edward
W. Tayler (New York, 1967).

English Renaissance Literary Criticism, ed. Brian Vickers
(Oxford, 1999). A comprehensive selection with a useful
introduction; strong on rhetoric.

Augustan Critical Writing, ed. David Womersley (London,
1997). Covers the period 1660–1750.

Sidney

Sidney's *Defence* was until fairly recently more often known as the *Apology*. See p. lxxxvii.

An Apology for Poetry or The Defence of Poesy, ed. Geoffrey Shepherd, 2nd edn (Manchester, 1973); 3rd edn rev. R.W. Maslen (Manchester, 2002). Extensive introduction and commentary make this a useful source for further study; Shepherd's original introduction, replaced in Maslen's revised edition, is still valuable.

Sir Philip Sidney: The Major Works, ed. Katherine Duncan-Jones (Oxford, 2002); reissue of *Sir Philip Sidney*, ed. Katherine Duncan-Jones, The Oxford Authors (Oxford, 1989). Includes *Astrophil and Stella*, a selection of other poems, the *Defence*, and letters to Robert Sidney and Edward Denny on reading.

The Old Arcadia, ed. Katherine Duncan-Jones (Oxford, 1985).

The Countess of Pembroke's Arcadia, ed. Maurice Evans (London, 1977). The composite 'new' *Arcadia*.

For further work on Sidney, the Clarendon editions should be used: the *Poems*, ed. Ringler (Oxford, 1962), 'old' *Arcadia*, ed. Robertson (Oxford, 1973), *Miscellaneous Prose*, eds. Duncan-Jones and van Dorsten (Oxford, 1973), and 'new' *Arcadia*, ed. Skretkowicz (Oxford, 1987).

Katherine Duncan-Jones, *Sir Philip Sidney, Courtier Poet* (London, 1991). The standard biography.

John Buxton, *Sir Philip Sidney and the English Renaissance*, 3rd edn (London, 1987).

Sir Philip Sidney: An Anthology of Modern Criticism, ed. Dennis Kay (Oxford, 1987).

Essential Articles for the Study of Sir Philip Sidney, ed. Arthur F. Kinney (Hamden, Conn., 1986).

S.K. Heninger, Jr, *Sidney and Spenser: The Poet as Maker* (University Park, Pa., 1989). Important and clearly written study of the context and implications of Sidney's theory in the *Defence*, and its relation to the works of Sidney and Spenser.

Puttenham

The Arte of English Poesie, eds. Gladys Doidge Willcock and Alice Walker (Cambridge, 1936). No notes or commentary, but appendices and index, together with introduction, supply useful information.

Daniel

A new Oxford edition of the complete works, ed. John Pitcher, is forthcoming. In the meantime, the *Works* are available in Alexander B. Grosart's edition (London, 1885).

Poems and A Defence of Ryme, ed. A.C. Sprague (Cambridge, Mass., 1930; repr. Chicago, 1965). The standard edition of the shorter works, but lacks notes.

Selected Poetry and A Defense of Rhyme, eds. Geoffrey G. Hiller and Peter L. Groves (Asheville, N.C., 1998). A useful edition with apparatus and further reading.

Selected Poems of Thomas Campion, Samuel Daniel and Sir Walter Ralegh, ed. Ronald Levao (London, 2001).

Joan Rees, *Samuel Daniel: A Critical and Biographical Study* (Liverpool, 1964).

Richard Helgerson, *Forms of Nationhood: The Elizabethan Writing of England* (Chicago, 1992). Influential opening chapter on the political resonances of the *Defence*.

Editions of Other Authors

This list omits editions which are difficult to obtain or lack notes.

George Gascoigne, *A Hundreth Sundrie Flowres*, ed. G. W. Pigman III (Oxford, 2000). Text of 1573 with addition from *Posies* (1575) including 'Certain Notes of Instruction'.

Thomas Campion, *The Works*, ed. Walter R. Davis (Garden City, N.Y. and London, 1969).

Francis Bacon: The Major Works, ed. Brian Vickers (Oxford, 2002); reissue of *Francis Bacon*, ed. Brian Vickers, The Oxford Authors (Oxford, 1996).

Francis Bacon, *The Essays*, ed. John Pitcher (London, 1985).

Michael Drayton, *The Works*, ed. J.W. Hebel *et al.*, 5 vols., corrected edn (Oxford, 1961).

Ben Jonson, ed. Ian Donaldson, The Oxford Authors (Oxford, 1985).
Ben Jonson, ed. C.H. Herford, and Percy and Evelyn Simpson, 11 vols (Oxford, 1925–52).

The discovery of an important manuscript treatise, *The Model of Poesy* (*c.* 1600), by William Scott is reported by Stanley Wells in *The Times Literary Supplement*, 26 September 2003.

A Note on the Texts

Each text in this anthology has been edited directly from the first printed edition. Spelling and punctuation have been modernized, and paragraphing is editorial. Contractions and abbreviations have been expanded (so '&' becomes 'and'). Capitalization and italicization have been regularized, in line with modern usage (so proper names are not italicized). Greek words have been transliterated. Greek and Latin names are kept in the forms in which they are given (e.g. 'Hesiodus' in Puttenham, 'Hesiod' in Sidney), with spelling regularized. Modern European names are kept in the original, Anglicized, or Latinized forms in which they are given, with spelling regularized; intentions in this regard are not always clear (is 'Bocace' in Sidney a misspelling of 'Boccaccio' or an attempt to Anglicize?). Obsolete or archaic forms are not modernized (so 'sithence' does not become 'since'), but their spelling is regularized to accord with *The Oxford English Dictionary*. Where the form is counted by OED as simply a variant spelling, it is modernized. Thus, in the opening paragraph of Sidney's *Defence*, 'loaden' and 'spake' are retained whilst 'maisters' becomes 'masters'.

Difficult words and foreign-language quotations are glossed at the foot of the page; the presence of a gloss is indicated by this sign: *. Words used several times in a text are glossed once, at their first occurrence, and more often when their meaning is especially difficult for a modern reader. This method is preferred to that of providing a single glossary. In many cases a familiar word carries an unexpected meaning; without the indication of a gloss, the reader will tend to assume that the modern meaning applies and will not fully grasp the sense of the passage concerned. Superscript numbers in the text refer the reader to the notes for each work at the end of the volume.

A head-note at the start of the notes for each work gives details of the copy-text used, and of any significant issues relating to the text or its dating. It will be seen from the head-notes (e.g. Campion, Bacon) or from the text itself (e.g. Harington, Drayton) that the titles conventionally used to refer to the works are often shortened from their original form. Particular information on the organization or context of works (e.g. Sidney, Puttenham, Jonson), is also included in the head-notes if it is needed.

The text of Puttenham's *The Art of English Poesy* has been abridged for this edition. Omitted passages within individual chapters are indicated thus: [. . .]. On occasion, to enable a fluent reading, a brief summary of the omitted passage is given in the square brackets. The titles of omitted chapters are given in square brackets, and every single omitted figure in Book III is reported in this way also. It is hoped that the result gives a fuller sense of Puttenham than would otherwise be possible. Passages omitted in the selections from, e.g., Webbe and Campion, and in the abridgement of Harington, are treated in the same way.

The editing of Sidney's *The Defence of Poesy* is the only problematic case, and a full explanation is provided in the head-note. I am grateful to Viscount De L'Isle for permission to use the Penshurst manuscript in arriving at my text. We do not know what title, if any, Sidney gave his work. It was first printed in 1595 in two different editions: *The Defence of Poesy* (published by William Ponsonby, the authoritative publisher of all of Sidney's works) and *An Apology for Poetry* (published by Henry Olney). The large number of editions in the past two centuries based on Olney's text have popularized his title, *An Apology for Poetry*, but most scholars now prefer to use the title under which Sidney's work was reprinted throughout the seventeenth century, and which we must presume to have had the sanction of Sidney's family, who worked closely with Ponsonby. Ponsonby's title, *The Defence of Poesy*, has therefore been used in this edition.

The volume concludes with 'A Note on Rhetoric' and 'A Note on English Versification'. It is hoped that these will help to prevent the reader from being daunted by the theoretical material discussed by, for example, Puttenham and Daniel, and will prove a useful resource in their own right.

The illustrations in Book 2 of Puttenham's *The Art of English Poesy* and in Gascoigne's *Certain Notes of Instruction* are taken from copies of the original texts in Cambridge University Library (Puttenham: SSS.24.24; Gascoigne: Syn.7.5.27). They are reproduced by permission of the Syndics of Cambridge University Library.

SIR PHILIP SIDNEY
THE DEFENCE OF POESY
(*c.* 1580; printed 1595)

When the right virtuous Edward Wotton and I were at the Emperor's court together, we gave ourselves to learn horsemanship of John Pietro Pugliano, one that with great commendation had the place of an esquire in his stable.[1] And he, according to the fertileness of the Italian wit, did not only afford us the demonstration of his practice, but sought to enrich our minds with the contemplations therein, which he thought most precious. But with none I remember mine ears were at any time more loaden, than when (either angered with slow payment or moved with our learner-like admiration) he exercised his speech in the praise of his faculty.* He said soldiers were the noblest estate of mankind, and horsemen the noblest of soldiers. He said they were the masters of war and ornaments of peace, speedy goers and strong abiders,* triumphers both in camps* and courts. Nay, to so unbelieved a point he proceeded, as that no earthly thing bred such wonder to a prince as to be a good horseman – skill of government was but a *pedanteria** in comparison. Then would he add certain praises by telling what a peerless beast the horse was, the only serviceable* courtier without flattery, the beast of most beauty, faithfulness, courage, and such more, that if I had not been a piece of a logician before I came to him, I think he would have persuaded me to have wished myself a horse.[2] But thus much at least with his no few words he drave into me, that self-love is better than any gilding

* *faculty*: profession, branch of knowledge
* *strong abiders*: i.e. strong in sustaining an attack or standing their ground
* *in camps*: i.e. at war   * *pedanteria*: 'pedantry'
* *serviceable*: ready to do service, useful

to make that seem gorgeous wherein ourselves be parties. Wherein, if Pugliano's strong affection* and weak arguments will not satisfy you, I will give you a nearer example of myself, who (I know not by what mischance) in these my not old years and idlest times having slipped into the title of a poet am provoked to say something unto you in the defence of that my unelected vocation, which if I handle with more good will than good reasons, bear with me, since the scholar is to be pardoned that followeth the steps of his master. And yet I must say that, as I have more just cause to make a pitiful defence of poor poetry, which from almost the highest estimation of learning is fallen to be the laughing stock of children, so have I need to bring some more available proofs, since the former is by no man barred of his deserved credit, the silly latter[3] hath had even the names of philosophers used to the defacing* of it, with great danger of civil war among the Muses.

And first, truly, to all them that, professing learning, inveigh against poetry may justly be objected that they go very near to ungratefulness to seek to deface that which, in the noblest nations and languages that are known, hath been the first light-giver to ignorance, and first nurse whose milk by little and little enabled them to feed afterwards of tougher knowledges.[4] And will they now play the hedgehog that, being received into the den, drave out his host? Or rather the vipers, that with their birth kill their parents?[5] Let learned Greece in any of his manifold sciences* be able to show me one book before Musaeus, Homer, and Hesiod,[6] all three nothing else but poets. Nay, let any history be brought that can say any writers were there before them, if they were not men of the same skill, as Orpheus, Linus,[7] and some other are named, who, having been the first of that country that made pens deliverers of their knowledge to the posterity, may justly challenge to be called their fathers in learning; for not only in time they had this priority (although in itself antiquity be venerable), but went before them, as causes to draw with their charming sweetness the wild, untamed wits to an admiration of

---

* *affection*: prejudice   * *defacing*: discrediting, defaming
* *sciences*: branches of knowledge

knowledge. So, as Amphion was said to move stones with his poetry to build Thebes, and Orpheus to be listened to by beasts,[8] indeed stony and beastly people, so among the Romans were Livius Andronicus and Ennius;[9] so in the Italian language the first that made it aspire to be a treasure-house of science* were the poets Dante, Boccaccio and Petrarch; so in our English were Gower and Chaucer,[10] after whom, encouraged and delighted with their excellent fore-going, others have followed to beautify our mother tongue, as well in the same kind as in other arts.

This did so notably show itself, that the philosophers of Greece durst not* a long time appear to the world but under the masks of poets. So Thales, Empedocles and Parmenides sang their natural philosophy* in verses; so did Pythagoras and Phocylides their moral counsels; so did Tyrtaeus in war matters and Solon in matters of policy;[11] or rather they, being poets, did exercise their delightful vein in those points of highest knowledge which before them lay hid to the world. For that wise Solon was directly a poet it is manifest, having written in verse the notable fable of the Atlantic island, which was continued by Plato. And, truly, even Plato whosoever well considereth shall find that in the body of his work, though the inside and strength were philosophy, the skin, as it were, and beauty depended most of poetry. For all standeth upon dialogues, wherein he feigneth many honest burgesses* of Athens to speak of such matters that, if they had been set on the rack, they would never have confessed them, besides his poetical describing the circumstances of their meetings, as the well ordering of a banquet, the delicacy* of a walk, with interlacing mere tales, as Gyges' ring and others,[12] which who knoweth not to be flowers of poetry did never walk into Apollo's garden.[13]

And even historiographers,* although their lips sound of things done and verity be written in their foreheads, have been glad to borrow both fashion* and perchance weight of the poets. So Herodotus entitled his History by the name of the nine

* *science*: knowledge, learning   * *durst not*: did not dare
* *natural philosophy*: natural science   * *burgesses*: citizens
* *delicacy*: delightfulness   * *historiographers*: writers of history
* *fashion*: form

muses,[14] and both he and all the rest that followed him either stale or usurped of poetry their passionate describing of passions, the many particularities of battles which no man could affirm, or, if that be denied me, long orations put in the mouths of great kings and captains, which it is certain they never pronounced. So that truly neither philosopher nor historiographer could at the first have entered into the gates of popular judgements if they had not taken a great passport of poetry, which in all nations at this day where learning flourisheth not is plain to be seen, in all which they have some feeling of poetry.[15]

In Turkey, besides their law-giving divines, they have no other writers but poets.[16] In our neighbour country Ireland, where truly learning goeth very bare, yet are their poets held in a devout reverence. Even among the most barbarous and simple Indians, where no writing is, yet have they their poets, who make and sing songs which they call *areytos*, both of their ancestors' deeds and praises of their gods[17] – a sufficient probability that if ever learning come among them it must be by having their hard, dull wits softened and sharpened with the sweet delights of poetry, for, until they find a pleasure in the exercises of the mind, great promises of much knowledge will little persuade them that know not the fruits of knowledge. In Wales, the true remnant of the ancient Britons, as there are good authorities to show the long time they had poets, which they called 'bards', so through all the conquests of Romans, Saxons, Danes and Normans, some of whom did seek to ruin all memory of learning from among them, yet do their poets even to this day last – so as it is not more notable in soon beginning than in long continuing.[18] But since the authors of most of our sciences were the Romans, and before them the Greeks, let us a little stand upon their authorities, but even so far as to see what names they have given unto this now scorned skill.

Among the Romans a poet was called *vates*, which is as much as a diviner, foreseer or prophet, as by his conjoined words *vaticinium* and *vaticinari* is manifest[19] – so heavenly a title did that excellent people bestow upon this heart-ravishing knowledge. And so far were they carried into the admiration thereof, that they thought in the chanceable hitting upon any such verses

great foretokens of their following fortunes were placed. Whereupon grew the word of *Sortes Virgilianae*, when by sudden
opening Virgil's book they lighted upon any verse of his making,
whereof the histories of the emperors' lives are full, as of Albinus
the governor of our island, who in his childhood met with this
verse, *arma amens capio; nec sat rationis in armis*,* and in his
age performed it.[20] Which, although it were a very vain and
godless superstition (as also it was to think spirits were commanded by such verses, whereupon this word 'charms', derived
of *carmina*,* cometh), so yet serveth it to show the great reverence those wits were held in, and altogether not without ground,
since both the oracles of Delphos and Sibylla's prophecies were
wholly delivered in verses;[21] for that same exquisite observing
of number and measure* in the words, and that high-flying
liberty of conceit* proper to the poet, did seem to have some
divine force in it.

And may not I presume a little farther, to show the reasonable-
ness of this word *vates*, and say that the holy David's Psalms
are a divine poem? If I do, I shall not do it without the testimony
of great learned men both ancient and modern. But even the
name of 'Psalms' will speak for me, which, being interpreted, is
nothing but 'songs'; then, that it is fully written in metre, as all
learned Hebricians agree, although the rules be not yet fully
found;[22] lastly and principally, his handling his prophecy, which
is merely* poetical. For what else is the awaking his musical
instruments, the often and free changing of persons, his notable
prosopopoeias[23] when he maketh you, as it were, see God
coming in His majesty, his telling of the beasts' joyfulness and
hills' leaping, but a heavenly poesy, wherein almost he showeth
himself a passionate lover of that unspeakable and everlasting
beauty, to be seen by the eyes of the mind, only cleared by faith?
But, truly, now having named him, I fear me I seem to profane
that holy name, applying it to poetry, which is among us thrown
down to so ridiculous an estimation. But they that with quiet
judgements will look a little deeper into it shall find the end and

* *arma . . . armis*: 'frantic I seize arms; yet little purpose is there in arms'
* *carmina*: 'songs, incantations'   * *number and measure*: metre
* *conceit*: imagination   * *merely*: entirely

working of it such as, being rightly applied, deserveth not to be scourged out of the Church of God.

But now let us see how the Greeks named it, and how they deemed of it. The Greeks called him a 'poet',[24] which name hath, as the most excellent, gone through other languages. It cometh of this word, *poiein*, which is 'to make', wherein, I know not whether by luck or wisdom, we Englishmen have met with the Greeks in calling him a 'maker',[25] which name, how high and incomparable a title it is, I had rather were known by marking the scope of other sciences than by any partial allegation.*

There is no art delivered to mankind that hath not the works of nature for his principal object, without which they could not consist,* and on which they so depend as they become actors and players, as it were, of what nature will have set forth.* So doth the astronomer look upon the stars, and, by that he seeth, set down what order nature hath taken therein. So doth the geometrician and arithmetician in their divers sorts of quantities. So doth the musician in times tell you which by nature agree, which not.[26] The natural philosopher thereon hath his name, and the moral philosopher standeth upon the natural virtues, vices or passions of man: 'and follow nature,' saith he, 'therein, and thou shalt not err.' The lawyer saith what men have determined, the historian, what men have done. The grammarian speaketh only of the rules of speech, and the rhetorician and logician, considering what in nature will soonest prove and persuade, thereon give artificial rules, which still are compassed within the circle of a question, according to the proposed matter. The physician weigheth the nature of man's body, and the nature of things helpful or hurtful unto it. And the metaphysic, though it be in the second and abstract notions, and therefore be counted supernatural,* yet doth he indeed build upon the depth of nature. Only the poet, disdaining to be tied to any such subjection, lifted up with the vigour of his own invention, doth grow in effect into another nature, in making things either better than nature bringeth forth or, quite anew, forms such as never were

* *partial allegation*: biased assertion   * *consist*: exist
* *set forth*: arranged, expressed, narrated, published
* *supernatural*: outside the physical world

in nature, as the heroes, demigods, cyclopes, chimeras, furies
and such like. So as he goeth hand in hand with nature, not
enclosed within the narrow warrant* of her gifts but freely
ranging only within the zodiac of his own wit.* Nature never
set forth the earth in so rich tapestry as divers poets have done,
neither with so pleasant rivers, fruitful trees, sweet-smelling
flowers, nor whatsoever else may make the too-much-loved
earth more lovely: her world is brazen,* the poets only deliver
a golden.[27]

But let those things alone and go to man, for whom as the
other things are, so it seemeth in him her uttermost cunning is
employed,[28] and know whether she have brought forth so true
a lover as Theagenes, so constant a friend as Pylades, so valiant
a man as Orlando, so right a prince as Xenophon's Cyrus, so
excellent a man every way as Virgil's Aeneas.[29] Neither let this
be jestingly conceived, because the works of the one be essential,
the other in imitation or fiction, for any understanding knoweth
the skill of each artificer* standeth in that *idea* or fore-conceit
of the work, and not in the work itself.[30] And that the poet hath
that *idea* is manifest by delivering them forth* in such excellency
as he had imagined them; which delivering forth also is not
wholly imaginative, as we are wont to say by them that build
castles in the air, but so far substantially it worketh, not only to
make a Cyrus, which had been but a particular excellency as
nature might have done, but to bestow a Cyrus upon the world
to make many Cyruses, if they will learn aright why and how
that maker made him.[31]

Neither let it be deemed too saucy* a comparison to balance
the highest point of man's wit with the efficacy* of nature, but
rather give right honour to the heavenly Maker of that maker,
who, having made man to His own likeness, set him beyond
and over all the works of that second nature;[32] which in nothing
he showeth so much as in poetry, when, with the force of a

* *warrant*: licence, permission   * *wit*: mind, understanding
* *brazen*: brass   * *artificer*: artist, poet
* *delivering them forth*: writing them up, imprinting them in the mind of the
reader   * *saucy*: disrespectful, presumptuous
* *efficacy*: mode of working, power

divine breath, he* bringeth things forth surpassing her* doings
– with no small arguments to the incredulous of that first
accursed fall of Adam, since our erected wit maketh us know
what perfection is, and yet our infected will keepeth us from
reaching unto it.[33] But these arguments[34] will by few be understood, and by fewer granted. Thus much I hope will be given
me, that the Greeks with some probability of reason gave him
the name above all names of learning.

Now let us go to a more ordinary opening* of him, that the
truth may be the more palpable; and so I hope, though we get
not so unmatched a praise as the etymology of his names will
grant, yet his very description, which no man will deny, shall
not justly be barred from a principal commendation. Poesy,
therefore, is an art of imitation, for so Aristotle termeth it in the
word *mimēsis*, that is to say, a representing, counterfeiting* or
figuring forth – to speak metaphorically, a speaking picture –
with this end: to teach and delight.[35] Of this have been three
general kinds. The chief, both in antiquity and excellency, were
they that did imitate* the unconceivable excellencies of God.
Such were David in his Psalms, Solomon in his Song of Songs,
in his Ecclesiastes and Proverbs, Moses and Deborah in their
Hymns, and the writer of Job, which, beside other, the learned
Emanuel Tremellius and Franciscus Junius do entitle the poetical
part of the Scripture.[36] Against these none will speak that hath
the Holy Ghost in due holy reverence. In this kind, though in a
full wrong divinity, were Orpheus, Amphion, Homer in his
Hymns,[37] and many other both Greeks and Romans. And this
poesy must be used by whosoever will follow St James' counsel[38]
in singing psalms when they are merry, and I know is used with
the fruit of comfort by some, when in sorrowful pangs of their
death-bringing sins they find the consolation of the never-
leaving goodness.

The second kind is of them that deal with matters philosophical, either moral, as Tyrtaeus, Phocylides, Cato; or natural, as

---

* *he*: i.e. the poet   * *her*: i.e. nature   * *opening*: exposition, definition
* *counterfeiting*: imitating, making after a pattern
* *imitate*: represent, figure forth

Lucretius and Virgil's *Georgics*; or astronomical, as Manilius and Pontanus; or historical, as Lucan;[39] which who mislike, the fault is in their judgement quite out of taste, and not in the sweet food of sweetly uttered knowledge.

But because this second sort is wrapped within the fold of the proposed subject, and takes not the course of his own invention, whether they properly be poets or no let grammarians dispute, and go to the third, indeed right poets, of whom chiefly this question[40] ariseth, betwixt whom and these second is such a kind of difference as betwixt the meaner sort of painters, who counterfeit only such faces as are set before them, and the more excellent, who having no law but wit bestow that in colours upon you which is fittest for the eye to see – as the constant though lamenting look of Lucretia, when she punished in herself another's fault, wherein he painteth not Lucretia, whom he never saw, but painteth the outward beauty of such a virtue.[41] For these third be they which most properly do imitate to teach and delight, and to imitate borrow nothing of what is, hath been or shall be, but range, only reined with learned discretion, into the divine consideration of what may be and should be.[42] These be they that, as the first and most noble sort may justly be termed *vates*, so these are waited on* in the excellentest languages and best understandings with the fore-described name of poets. For these indeed do merely make to imitate, and imitate both to delight and teach, and delight to move men to take that goodness in hand, which without delight they would fly as from a stranger, and teach to make them know that goodness whereunto they are moved[43] – which being the noblest scope* to which ever any learning was directed, yet want there not idle tongues to bark at them.

These be subdivided into sundry more special denominations. The most notable be the heroic, lyric, tragic, comic, satiric, iambic, elegiac, pastoral[44] and certain others, some of these being termed according to the matter they deal with, some by the sorts of verses they liked best to write in. For indeed the

* *waited on*: accompanied   * *scope*: object, purpose

greatest part of poets have apparelled their poetical inventions
in that numbrous* kind of writing which is called verse – indeed
but apparelled, verse being but an ornament and no cause to
poetry, since there have been many most excellent poets that
never versified, and now swarm many versifiers that need never
answer to the name of poets.[45] For Xenophon, who did imitate
so excellently as to give us *effigiem iusti imperii* – the portraiture
of a just empire – under the name of Cyrus, as Cicero saith of
him, made therein an absolute heroical poem. So did Heliodorus
in his sugared invention of that picture of love in Theagenes and
Charikleia.[46] And yet both these wrote in prose, which I speak
to show that it is not rhyming and versing that maketh a poet
(no more than a long gown maketh an advocate, who though
he pleaded in armour should be an advocate and no soldier),
but it is that feigning* notable images of virtues, vices or what
else,[47] with that delightful teaching, which must be the right
describing note* to know a poet by; although indeed the senate
of poets hath chosen verse as their fittest raiment,* meaning, as
in matter they passed all in all, so in manner to go beyond them,
not speaking, table talk fashion, or like men in a dream, words
as they chanceably fall from the mouth, but peising* each syllable of each word by just proportion, according to the dignity
of the subject.[48]

Now, therefore, it shall not be amiss first to weigh this latter
sort of poetry by his works,* and then by his parts, and if in
neither of these anatomies he be condemnable, I hope we shall
obtain a more favourable sentence.* This purifying of wit, this
enriching of memory, enabling of judgement, and enlarging of
conceit,* which commonly we call learning, under what name
soever it come forth, or to what immediate end soever it be
directed, the final end is to lead and draw us to as high a
perfection as our degenerate souls, made worse by their clayey
lodgings,[49] can be capable of. This, according to the inclination
of the man, bred many-formed impressions. For some, that

---

* *numbrous*: metrical   * *feigning*: making, representing
* *note*: name, distinguishing mark   * *raiment*: dress   * *peising*: weighing
* *works*: effects, results   * *sentence*: judgement
* *conceit*: understanding, power of thought

thought this felicity principally to be gotten by knowledge, and
no knowledge to be so high or heavenly as acquaintance with
the stars, gave themselves to astronomy; others, persuading
themselves to be demigods if they knew the causes of things,
became natural and supernatural philosophers. Some an admirable delight drew to music; and some the certainty of demonstration to the mathematics. But all, one and other, having this
scope: to know, and by knowledge to lift up the mind from the
dungeon of the body to the enjoying his own divine essence.
But when by the balance of experience it was found that the
astronomer, looking to the stars, might fall in a ditch,[50] that
the inquiring philosopher might be blind in himself, and the
mathematician might draw forth a straight line with a crooked
heart,[51] then, lo, did proof, the overruler of opinions, make
manifest that all these are but serving sciences, which, as they
have each a private end in themselves, so yet are they all directed
to the highest end of the mistress-knowledge, by the Greeks
called *architektonikē*, which stands as I think in the knowledge
of a man's self, in the ethic and politic consideration, with the
end of well-doing and not of well-knowing only[52] – even as the
saddler's next* end is to make a good saddle, but his further
end to serve a nobler faculty, which is horsemanship, so the
horseman's to soldiery, and the soldier not only to have the skill
but to perform the practice of a soldier. So that the ending end
of all earthly learning being virtuous action, those skills that
most serve to bring forth that have a most just title to be princes
over all the rest.

   Wherein, if we can, show we the poet's nobleness, by setting
him before his other competitors. Among whom as principal
challengers step forth the moral philosophers,[53] whom me
thinketh I see coming towards me with a sullen gravity, as
though they could not abide vice by daylight, rudely clothed,
for to witness outwardly their contempt of outward things,
with books in their hands against glory, whereto they set their
names,[54] sophistically speaking against subtlety,* and angry
with any man in whom they see the foul fault of anger. These

* *next*: nearest   * *subtlety*: sophistry

men, casting largess as they go of definitions, divisions and distinctions,[55] with a scornful interrogative* do soberly ask whether it be possible to find any path so ready to lead a man to virtue as that which teacheth what virtue is, and teacheth it not only by delivering forth his very being, his causes and effects, but also by making known his enemy vice, which must be destroyed, and his cumbersome servant passion, which must be mastered, by showing the generalities that containeth it and the specialities that are derived from it;[56] lastly, by plain setting down how it extendeth itself out of the limits of a man's own little world* to the government of families and maintaining of public societies.

The historian scarcely giveth leisure to the moralist to say so much, but that he – loaden with old mouse-eaten records, authorizing himself for the most part upon other histories whose greatest authorities are built upon the notable foundation of hearsay, having much ado to accord* differing writers and to pick truth out of partiality, better acquainted with a thousand years ago than with the present age, and yet better knowing how this world goeth than how his own wit runneth, curious for antiquities and inquisitive* of novelties, a wonder to young folks and a tyrant in table talk – denieth in a great chafe* that any man for teaching of virtue and virtuous actions is comparable to him. 'I am *testis temporum, lux veritatis, vita memoriae, magistra vitae, nuntia vetustatis.**[57] The philosopher,' saith he, 'teacheth a disputative* virtue, but I do an active. His virtue is excellent in the dangerless Academy of Plato, but mine showeth forth her honourable face in the battles of Marathon, Pharsalia, Poitiers and Agincourt.[58] He teacheth virtue by certain abstract considerations, but I only bid you follow the footing of them that have gone before you. Old-aged experience goeth beyond the fine-witted philosopher, but I give the experience of many ages. Lastly, if he make the songbook, I put

---

* *interrogative*: question   * *little world*: microcosm   * *accord*: reconcile
* *inquisitive*: suspicious   * *chafe*: heat, rage
* *testis ... vetustatis*: 'the witness of passing ages, the light of truth, the life of memory, the mistress of life, she who brings tidings of antiquity'
* *disputative*: theoretical

the learner's hand to the lute, and if he be the guide, I am the light.' Then would he allege* you innumerable examples, confirming story by stories, how much the wisest senators and princes have been directed by the credit of history, as Brutus, Alphonsus of Aragon, and who not, if need be?[59] At length, the long line of their disputation maketh a point* in this, that the one giveth the precept, and the other the example.

Now whom shall we find, since the question standeth for the highest form in the school of learning,[60] to be moderator?* Truly, as me seemeth, the poet; and if not a moderator, even the man that ought to carry the title from them both, and much more from all other serving sciences. Therefore compare we the poet with the historian and with the moral philosopher, and if he go beyond them both, no other human skill can match him. For as for the divine, with all reverence it is ever to be excepted, not only for having his scope as far beyond any of these as eternity exceedeth a moment, but even for passing each of these in themselves. And for the lawyer, though *ius** be the daughter of justice, and justice the chief of virtues, yet because he seeketh to make men good rather *formidine poenae* than *virtutis amore*,*[61] or, to say righter, doth not endeavour to make men good, but that their evil hurt not others, having no care, so he be a good citizen, how bad a man he be, therefore as our wickedness maketh him necessary, and necessity maketh him honourable, so is he not, in the deepest truth, to stand in rank with these who all endeavour to take naughtiness* away and plant goodness even in the secretest cabinet* of our souls. And these four are all that any way deal in the consideration of men's manners,* which being the supreme knowledge, they that best breed it deserve the best commendation.

The philosopher, therefore, and the historian are they which would win the goal, the one by precept, the other by example; but both, not having both, do both halt.* For the philosopher,

---

* *allege*: cite   * *point*: (punning on) full stop, period
* *moderator*: judge, chair   * *ius*: 'right, law'
* *formidine poenae . . . virtutis amore*: 'through fear of punishment . . . through the love of virtue'   * *naughtiness*: wickedness
* *cabinet*: private chamber   * *manners*: morals   * *halt*: walk with a limp

setting down with thorny arguments the bare rule, is so hard of utterance, and so misty to be conceived, that one that hath no other guide but him shall wade in him till he be old before he shall find sufficient cause to be honest. For his knowledge standeth so upon the abstract and general, that happy is that man who may understand him, and more happy that can apply what he doth understand.[62] On the other side, the historian, wanting the precept, is so tied not to what should be but to what is, to the particular truth of things and not to the general reason of things, that his example draweth no necessary consequence, and therefore a less fruitful doctrine.*

Now doth the peerless poet perform both, for whatsoever the philosopher saith should be done, he giveth a perfect picture of it in someone by whom he presupposeth it was done, so as he coupleth the general notion with the particular example. A perfect picture I say, for he yieldeth to the powers of the mind an image of that whereof the philosopher bestoweth but a wordish description, which doth neither strike, pierce nor possess the sight of the soul so much as that other doth.[63] For as in outward things, to a man that had never seen an elephant or a rhinoceros, who should tell him most exquisitely* all their shapes, colour, bigness and particular marks, or of a gorgeous palace an architector,* with declaring the full beauties, might well make the hearer able to repeat, as it were by rote, all he had heard, yet should never satisfy his inward conceit with being witness to itself of a true lively* knowledge; but the same man, as soon as he might see those beasts well painted, or the house well in model, should straightways grow, without need of any description, to a judicial* comprehending of them: so no doubt the philosopher, with his learned definitions, be it of virtues or vices, matters of public policy or private government, replenisheth the memory with many infallible grounds of wisdom, which notwithstanding lie dark before the imaginative and judging power,[64] if they be not illuminated or figured forth by the speaking picture of poesy.

* *doctrine*: lesson   * *exquisitely*: accurately   * *architector*: architect
* *lively*: living, lifelike   * *judicial*: judicious, just

Tully taketh much pains, and many times not without poetical helps, to make us know the force love of our country hath in us.[65] Let us but hear old Anchises speaking in the midst of Troy's flames, or see Ulysses, in the fullness of all Calypso's delights, bewail his absence from barren and beggarly Ithaca.[66] Anger, the Stoics said, was a short madness: let but Sophocles bring you Ajax on a stage, killing or whipping sheep and oxen thinking them the army of Greeks with their chieftains Agamemnon and Menelaus,[67] and tell me if you have not a more familiar insight into anger than finding in the schoolmen* his *genus* and difference.* See whether wisdom and temperance in Ulysses and Diomedes, valour in Achilles, friendship in Nisus and Euryalus[68] even to an ignorant man carry not an apparent shining;* and contrarily, the remorse of conscience in Oedipus, the soon repenting pride in Agamemnon, the self-devouring cruelty in his father Atreus, the violence of ambition in the two Theban brothers, the sour sweetness of revenge in Medea,[69] and, to fall lower, the Terentian Gnatho and our Chaucer's Pandar so expressed that we now use their names to signify their trades;[70] and finally, all virtues, vices and passions so in their own natural seats laid to the view, that we seem not to hear of them, but clearly to see through them.

But even in the most excellent determination of goodness, what philosopher's counsel can so readily direct a prince as the feigned Cyrus in Xenophon, or a virtuous man in all fortunes as Aeneas in Virgil, or a whole commonwealth as the way of Sir Thomas More's *Utopia*?[71] I say the way, because where Sir Thomas More erred it was the fault of the man and not of the poet, for that way[72] of patterning a commonwealth was most absolute,* though he perchance hath not so absolutely performed it. For the question is, whether the feigned image of poetry or the regular instruction of philosophy hath the more force in teaching. Wherein if the philosophers have more rightly showed themselves philosophers than the poets have attained

* *schoolmen*: medieval scholastic philosophers
* *difference*: distinguishing characteristic
* *apparent shining*: visible splendour   * *absolute*: perfect

to the high top of their profession (as in truth *mediocribus esse poetis / non di, non homines, non concessere columnae*)*[73] it is, I say again, not the fault of the art, but that by few men that art can be accomplished.

Certainly, even our Saviour Christ could as well have given the moral commonplaces of uncharitableness and humbleness as the divine narration of Dives and Lazarus, or of disobedience and mercy as that heavenly discourse of the lost child and the gracious father,[74] but that His through-searching wisdom knew the estate of Dives burning in hell and of Lazarus in Abraham's bosom would more constantly, as it were, inhabit both the memory and judgement; truly, for myself, me seems I see before mine eyes the lost child's disdainful prodigality turned to envy a swine's dinner: which by the learned divines are thought not historical acts but instructing parables.

For conclusion, I say the philosopher teacheth, but he teacheth obscurely, so as the learned only can understand him: that is to say, he teacheth them that are already taught. But the poet is the food for the tenderest stomachs; the poet is indeed the right popular philosopher. Whereof Aesop's tales[75] give good proof, whose pretty allegories, stealing under the formal tales* of beasts, make many, more beastly than beasts, begin to hear the sound of virtue from these dumb speakers.

But now may it be alleged, that if this imagining of matters be so fit for the imagination, then must the historian needs surpass, who bringeth you images of true matters, such as indeed were done, and not such as fantastically or falsely may be suggested to have been done. Truly, Aristotle himself, in his discourse of poesy, plainly determineth this question, saying that poetry is *philosophōteron* and *spoudaioteron* – that is to say, it is more philosophical and more studiously serious than history. His reason is, because poesy dealeth with *katholou*, that is to say with the universal consideration, and the history with *kath' hekaston*, the particular. Now, saith he, the universal weighs what is fit to be said or done, either in likelihood or

---

* *mediocribus . . . columnae*: 'neither gods, nor men, nor booksellers can put up with mediocrity in poets'
* *the formal tales*: i.e. the outward form of tales

necessity, which the poesy considereth in his imposed names; and the particular only marketh whether Alcibiades did or suffered this or that.[76] Thus far Aristotle: which reason of his, as all his, is most full of reason. For indeed if the question were whether it were better to have a particular act truly or falsely set down, there is no doubt which is to be chosen, no more than whether you had rather have Vespasian's picture right as he was or at the painter's pleasure, nothing resembling.[77] But if the question be for your own use and learning, whether it be better to have it set down as it should be or as it was, then certainly is more doctrinable* the feigned Cyrus in Xenophon than the true Cyrus in Justin, and the feigned Aeneas in Virgil than the right Aeneas in Dares Phrygius; as, to a lady that desired to fashion her countenance to the best grace, a painter should more benefit her to portrait a most sweet face, writing 'Canidia' upon it, than to paint Canidia as she was, who Horace sweareth was full ill-favoured.[78]

If the poet do his part aright, he will show you in Tantalus, Atreus,[79] and such like, nothing that is not to be shunned, in Cyrus, Aeneas, Ulysses each thing to be followed, where the historian, bound to tell things as things were, cannot be liberal – without he will be poetical – of a perfect pattern,* but, as in Alexander or Scipio himself, show doings, some to be liked, some to be misliked – and then how will you discern what to follow but by your own discretion, which you had without reading Quintus Curtius?[80] And whereas a man may say, though in universal consideration[81] of doctrine* the poet prevaileth, yet that the history, in his saying such a thing was done, doth warrant* a man more in that he shall follow, the answer is manifest: that if he stand upon that 'was' – as if he should argue, because it rained yesterday, therefore it should rain today – then indeed hath it some advantage to a gross* conceit; but if he know an example only informs a conjectured likelihood, and so go by reason, the poet doth so far exceed him, as he is to frame

* *doctrinable*: instructive
* *cannot be liberal ... pattern*: is not free, without being poetical, to give a perfect pattern   * *doctrine*: what is to be taught   * *warrant*: assure
* *gross*: ignorant, dull

his example to that which is most reasonable, be it in warlike, politic or private matters, where the historian in his bare 'was' hath many times that which we call fortune to overrule the best wisdom – many times he must tell events whereof he can yield no cause, or if he do, it must be poetically.

For, that a feigned example hath as much force to teach as a true example (for as for to move it is clear, since the feigned may be tuned to the highest key of passion), let us take one example wherein an historian and a poet did concur. Herodotus and Justin do both testify that Zopyrus, King Darius' faithful servant, seeing his master long resisted by the rebellious Babylonians, feigned himself in extreme disgrace of his king, for verifying of which he caused his own nose and ears to be cut off, and so, flying to the Babylonians, was received and for his known valour so far credited that he did find means to deliver them over to Darius;[82] much like matter doth Livy record of Tarquinius and his son.[83] Xenophon excellently feigneth such another stratagem performed by Abradatas in Cyrus' behalf.[84] Now would I fain know, if occasion be presented unto you to serve your prince by such an honest dissimulation, why you do not as well learn it of Xenophon's fiction as of the others' verity; and truly so much the better, as you shall save your nose by the bargain, for Abradatas did not counterfeit so far. So then the best of the historian is subject to the poet: for whatsoever action or faction,* whatsoever counsel, policy or war stratagem the historian is bound to recite,* that may the poet, if he list,* with his imitation make his own, beautifying it both for further teaching and more delighting as it please him, having all from Dante's heaven to his hell[85] under the authority of his pen. Which if I be asked what poets have done so, as I might well name some, so yet say I, and say again, I speak of the art and not of the artificer.

Now, to* that which commonly is attributed to the praise of history, in respect of the notable learning is got by marking the success,* as though therein a man should see virtue exalted and

---

* *faction*: course of conduct   * *recite*: relate   * *list*: wish   * *to*: as to
* *success*: outcome, upshot

vice punished, truly that commendation is peculiar to poetry, and far off from history; for indeed poetry ever sets virtue so out in her best colours, making fortune her well-waiting handmaid, that one must needs be enamoured of her. Well may you see Ulysses in a storm and in other hard plights,[86] but they are but exercises of patience and magnanimity,* to make them shine the more in the near-following prosperity. And of the contrary part, if evil men come to the stage, they ever go out (as the tragedy writer answered to one that misliked the show of such persons) so manacled as they little animate folks to follow them.[87] But the history, being captived to the truth of a foolish world, is many times a terror from well-doing, and an encouragement to unbridled wickedness. For see we not valiant Miltiades rot in his fetters; the just Phocion and the accomplished Socrates put to death like traitors; the cruel Severus live prosperously; the excellent Severus miserably murdered; Sulla and Marius dying in their beds; Pompey and Cicero slain then when they would have thought exile a happiness?[88] See we not virtuous Cato driven to kill himself, and rebel Caesar so advanced that his name yet after sixteen hundred years lasteth in the highest honour?[89] And mark but even Caesar's own words of the forenamed Sulla (who in that only did honestly, to put down his dishonest tyranny), *literas nescivit*,* as if want of learning caused him to do well.[90] He meant it not by poetry, which, not content with earthly plagues, deviseth new punishments in hell for tyrants, nor yet by philosophy, which teacheth *occidendos esse*,*[91] but no doubt by skill in history, for that indeed can afford you Cypselus, Periander, Phalaris, Dionysius,[92] and I know not how many more of the same kennel, that speed* well enough in their abominable injustice of usurpation.[93]

I conclude therefore that he excelleth history, not only in furnishing the mind with knowledge, but in setting it forward to that which deserveth to be called and accounted good, which setting forward and moving[94] to well-doing indeed setteth the laurel crown upon the poets as victorious,[95] not only of the

---

* *magnanimity*: fortitude, great-spiritedness
* *literas nescivit*: 'he was ignorant of letters'
* *occidendos esse*: 'that they must fall'   * *speed*: prosper

historian, but over the philosopher, howsoever in teaching it may be questionable.* For suppose it be granted, that which I suppose with great reason may be denied, that the philosopher, in respect of his methodical proceeding, doth teach more perfectly than the poet; yet do I think that no man is so much *philophilosophos** as to compare the philosopher in moving with the poet. And, that moving is of a higher degree than teaching, it may by this appear, that it is well nigh both the cause and effect of teaching. For who will be taught, if he be not moved with desire to be taught? And what so much good doth that teaching bring forth (I speak still of moral doctrine) as that it moveth one to do that which it doth teach? For, as Aristotle saith, it is not *gnōsis* but *praxis** must be the fruit;[96] and how *praxis* can be, without being moved to practise, it is no hard matter to consider.

The philosopher showeth you the way, he informeth you of the particularities, as well of the tediousness of the way, as of the pleasant lodging you shall have when your journey is ended, as of the many by-turnings that may divert you from your way. But this is to no man but to him that will read him, and read him with attentive, studious painfulness; which constant desire whosoever hath in him hath already passed half the hardness of the way, and therefore is beholding to the philosopher but for the other half. Nay truly, learned men have learnedly thought that where once reason hath so much overmastered passion as that the mind hath a free desire to do well, the inward light each mind hath in itself is as good as a philosopher's book, since in nature we know it is well to do well, and what is well and what is evil, although not in the words of art which philosophers bestow upon us; for out of natural conceit the philosophers drew it.[97] But to be moved to do that which we know, or to be moved with desire to know – *hoc opus, hic labor est.**[98]

Now therein of all sciences (I speak still of human, and according to the human conceit)[99] is our poet the monarch. For

----

* *it may be questionable*: i.e. who gets the crown for teaching alone may be debatable   * *philophilosophos*: 'a philosopher lover'
* *gnōsis . . . praxis*: 'knowing . . . doing'
* *hoc . . . est*: 'this is the labour, this is the toil'

he doth not only show the way, but giveth so sweet a prospect into the way as will entice any man to enter into it; nay, he doth as if your journey should lie through a fair vineyard – at the very first give you a cluster of grapes that, full of that taste, you may long to pass further. He beginneth not with obscure definitions, which must blur the margent* with interpretations* and load the memory with doubtfulness,* but he cometh to you with words set in delightful proportion, either accompanied with or prepared for the well-enchanting skill of music,[100] and with a tale, forsooth, he cometh unto you, with a tale which holdeth children from play and old men from the chimney corner;[101] and pretending* no more, doth intend the winning of the mind from wickedness to virtue. Even as the child is often brought to take most wholesome things by hiding them in such other as have a pleasant taste, which if one should begin to tell them the nature of the aloes or rhabarbarum they should receive, would sooner take their physic at their ears than at their mouth,[102] so is it in men (most of which are childish in the best things till they be cradled in their graves): glad they will be to hear the tales of Hercules, Achilles, Cyrus, Aeneas, and hearing them must needs hear the right description of wisdom, valour and justice, which if they had been barely (that is to say, philo-sophically) set out, they would swear they be brought to school again.

That imitation whereof poetry is hath the most conveniency* to nature of all other,[103] insomuch that, as Aristotle saith, those things which in themselves are horrible, as cruel battles, unnatu-ral monsters, are made in poetical imitation delightful.[104] Truly, I have known men that even with reading *Amadis de Gaule*,[105] which God knoweth wanteth much of a perfect poesy, have found their hearts moved to the exercise of courtesy, liberality and especially courage. Who readeth Aeneas carrying old Anchises on his back that wisheth not it were his fortune to perform so excellent an act? Whom doth not those words of Turnus move (the tale of Turnus having planted his image in

* *margent*: margin of a book   * *interpretations*: i.e. commentary
* *doubtfulness*: ambiguity   * *pretending*: claiming
* *conveniency*: congruity, propriety

the imagination): *fugientem haec terra videbit? / usque adeone mori miserum est?**[106] Where the philosophers, as they scorn to delight, so must they be content little to move (saving wrangling whether *virtus** be the chief or the only good, whether the contemplative or the active life do excel),[107] which Plato and Boethius well knew, and therefore made mistress Philosophy very often borrow the masquing raiment of Poesy.[108] For even those hard-hearted, evil men who think virtue a school name,* and know no other good but *indulgere genio*,*[109] and therefore despise the austere admonitions of the philosopher and feel not the inward reason they stand upon, yet will be content to be delighted, which is all the good-fellow* poet seemeth to promise, and so steal to see the form of goodness (which seen, they cannot but love) ere themselves be aware, as if they took a medicine of cherries.

Infinite proofs of the strange effects of this poetical invention might be alleged; only two shall serve, which are so often remembered as I think all men know them. The one of Menenius Agrippa who, when the whole people of Rome had resolutely divided themselves from the senate, with apparent show of utter ruin, though he were for that time an excellent orator, came not among them upon trust of figurative speeches or cunning insinuations,[110] and much less with far-fet* maxims of philosophy, which, especially if they were Platonic, they must have learned geometry before they could well have conceived,[111] but, forsooth, he behaves himself like a homely and familiar poet. He telleth them a tale, that there was a time when all the parts of the body made a mutinous conspiracy against the belly, which they thought devoured the fruits of each other's labour; they concluded, they would let so unprofitable a spender starve. In the end, to be short, for the tale is notorious, and as notorious that it was a tale, with punishing the belly they plagued themselves. This, applied by him, wrought such effect in the people,

---

* *fugientem ... est*: 'shall this land see [Turnus] in flight? Is death so very sad?'   * *virtus*: 'virtue'
* *a school name*: i.e. a purely academic, theoretical issue
* *indulgere genio*: 'to follow their own devices'
* *good-fellow*: good companion, or thief   * *far-fet*: far-fetched

as I never read that only words brought forth but then so sudden and so good an alteration, for upon reasonable conditions a perfect reconcilement ensued.[112] The other is of Nathan the prophet, who, when the holy David had so far forsaken God as to confirm* adultery with murder, when he was to do the tenderest office of a friend in laying his own shame before his eyes, sent by God to call again so chosen a servant – how doth he it, but by telling of a man whose beloved lamb was ungratefully* taken from his bosom, the application most divinely true, but the discourse itself feigned, which made David (I speak of the second and instrumental cause) as in a glass see his own filthiness, as that heavenly psalm of mercy well testifieth?[113]

By these, therefore, examples and reasons I think it may be manifest that the poet with that same hand of delight doth draw the mind more effectually than any other art doth, and so a conclusion not unfitly ensue: that as virtue is the most excellent resting place for all worldly learning to make his end of, so poetry, being the most familiar* to teach it, and most princely to move towards it, in the most excellent work is the most excellent workman. But I am content not only to decipher him by his works (although works in commendation or dispraise must ever hold a high authority),[114] but more narrowly will examine his parts, so that (as in a man), though all together may carry a presence full of majesty and beauty, perchance in some one defectuous* piece we may find blemish.

Now in his parts, kinds or species,[115] as you list to term them, it is to be noted that some poesies have coupled together two or three kinds: as the tragical and comical, whereupon is risen the tragi-comical. Some, in the manner, have mingled prose and verse, as Sannazaro and Boethius.[116] Some have mingled matters heroical and pastoral.[117] But that cometh all to one in this question, for if severed they be good, the conjunction cannot be hurtful.[118] Therefore, perchance forgetting some, and leaving some as needless to be remembered, it shall not be amiss in a

---

* *confirm*: add to   * *ungratefully*: harshly
* *familiar*: courteous, friendly   * *defectuous*: defective

word to cite the special kinds, to see what faults may be found in the right use of them.[119]

Is it then the pastoral poem which is misliked?[120] (For perchance where the hedge is lowest they will soonest leap over.) Is the poor pipe disdained, which sometimes, out of Meliboeus' mouth, can show the misery of people under hard lords or ravening soldiers, and again, by Tityrus, what blessedness is derived to them that lie lowest from the goodness of them that sit highest;[121] sometimes, under the pretty tales of wolves and sheep, can include the whole considerations of wrongdoing and patience;[122] sometimes show that contentions for trifles can get but a trifling victory, where perchance a man may see that even Alexander and Darius, when they strave who should be cock of this world's dunghill, the benefit they got was that the after-livers may say:

> Haec memini, et victum frustra contendere Thyrsim.
>   ex illo Corydon, Corydon est tempore nobis?*[123]

Or is it the lamenting elegiac, which in a kind heart would move rather pity than blame;[124] who bewails with the great philosopher Heraclitus[125] the weakness of mankind and the wretchedness of the world; who surely is to be praised, either for compassionate accompanying just causes of lamentations, or for rightly painting out how weak be the passions of woefulness? Is it the bitter but wholesome iambic, who rubs the galled mind in making shame the trumpet of villainy, with bold and open crying out against naughtiness?[126] Or the satiric, who *omne vafer vitium ridenti tangit amico*;*[127] who sportingly never leaveth till he make a man laugh at folly, and, at length ashamed, to laugh at himself, which he cannot avoid without avoiding the folly; who, while *circum praecordia ludit*,* giveth us to feel how many headaches a passionate life bringeth us to,

---

* *Haec ... nobis*: 'This I remember, and how Thyrsis, vanquished, strove in vain. From that day it is Corydon, Corydon with us'
* *omne ... amico*: 'the rascal, probes every fault of his friend while making him laugh'   * *circum ... ludit*: 'he plays with the secrets of his heart'

how, when all is done, *est Ulubris, animus si nos non deficit aequus*?*[128]

No? Perchance it is the comic, whom naughty* play-makers and stage-keepers have justly made odious.[129] To the arguments of abuse I will answer after;[130] only thus much now is to be said – that the comedy is an imitation of the common errors of our life, which he representeth in the most ridiculous and scornful sort that may be, so as it is impossible that any beholder can be content to be such a one. Now, as in geometry the oblique must be known as well as the right,[131] and in arithmetic the odd as well as the even, so in the actions of our life who seeth not the filthiness of evil wanteth a great foil to perceive the beauty of virtue. This doth the comedy handle so in our private and domestical matters as, with hearing it, we get, as it were, an experience what is to be looked for of a niggardly Demea, of a crafty Davus, of a flattering Gnatho, of a vainglorious Thraso;[132] and not only to know what effects are to be expected, but to know who be such, by the signifying badge given them by the comedian.[133] And little reason hath any man to say that men learn the evil by seeing it so set out, since, as I said before, there is no man living, but, by the force truth hath in nature, no sooner seeth these men play their parts but wisheth them *in pistrinum*,* although perchance the sack of his own faults lie so behind his back[134] that he seeth not himself dance the same measure;* whereto yet nothing can more open his eyes than to find his own actions contemptibly set forth.

So that the right use of comedy will, I think, by nobody be blamed. And much less of the high and excellent tragedy, that openeth the greatest wounds, and showeth forth the ulcers that are covered with tissue; that maketh kings fear to be tyrants, and tyrants manifest their tyrannical humours; that with stirring the affects* of admiration* and commiseration teacheth the

---

* *est ... aequus*: '[what we are looking for] is at Ulubrae, if our equanimity doesn't fail us'   * *naughty*: wicked
* *in pistrinum*: 'in the mill', i.e. sentenced to hard labour
* *measure*: type of dance: i.e. 'dance to the same tune'   * *affects*: emotions
* *admiration*: surprise, wonderment

uncertainty of this world, and upon how weak foundations
gilden roofs are builded;[135] that maketh us know:

> qui sceptra saevus duro imperio regit
> timet timentes; metus in auctorem redit.*[136]

But how much it can move, Plutarch yieldeth a notable testimony of the abominable tyrant Alexander Pheraeus, from
whose eyes a tragedy well made and represented drew abundance of tears, who without all pity had murdered infinite
numbers, and some of his own blood;[137] so as he that was not
ashamed to make matters for tragedies yet could not resist the
sweet violence of a tragedy. And if it wrought no further good
in him, it was that he, in despite of himself, withdrew himself
from hearkening to that which might mollify* his hardened
heart. But it is not the tragedy they do mislike, for it were too
absurd to cast out so excellent a representation of whatsoever
is most worthy to be learned.

Is it the lyric that most displeaseth, who with his tuned lyre
and well-accorded voice giveth praise, the reward of virtue, to
virtuous acts; who gives moral precepts and natural problems;
who sometime raiseth up his voice to the height of the heavens
in singing the lauds* of the immortal God?[138] Certainly I must
confess my own barbarousness: I never heard the old song of
Percy and Douglas that I found not my heart moved more than
with a trumpet, and yet is it sung but by some blind crowder,*[139]
with no rougher voice than rude* style – which being so evil
apparelled in the dust and cobwebs of that uncivil age, what
would it work trimmed in the gorgeous eloquence of Pindar?[140]
In Hungary I have seen it the manner at all feasts and other such
meetings to have songs of their ancestors' valour, which that
right soldierlike nation think one of the chiefest kindlers of
brave courage.[141] The incomparable Lacedemonians* did not
only carry that kind of music ever with them to the field, but

* *qui . . . redit*: 'the tyrant who rules harshly fears those who fear him; terror
rebounds on its agent'   * *mollify*: soften   * *lauds*: praises
* *crowder*: fiddler, minstrel   * *rude*: uncultivated
* *Lacedemonians*: Spartans

even at home, as such songs were made, so were they all content
to be singers of them, when the lusty men were to tell what they
did, the old men what they had done, and the young what they
would do.[142] And where a man may say that Pindar many times
praiseth highly victories of small moment, matters rather of
sport than virtue, as it may be answered, it was the fault of the
poet and not of the poetry, so indeed the chief fault was in the
time and custom of the Greeks, who set those toys* at so high
a price that Philip of Macedon reckoned a horserace won at
Olympus among his three fearful* felicities.[143] But as the unimit-
able Pindar often did, so is that kind most capable and most fit
to awake the thoughts from the sleep of idleness to embrace
honourable enterprises.

   There rests the heroical,[144] whose very name I think should
daunt all backbiters. For by what conceit can a tongue be
directed to speak evil of that which draweth with him no less
champions than Achilles, Cyrus, Aeneas, Turnus, Tydeus and
Rinaldo;[145] who doth not only teach and move to a truth, but
teacheth and moveth to the most high and excellent truth;
who maketh magnanimity* and justice shine through all misty
fearfulness and foggy desires; who, if the saying of Plato and
Tully be true, that who could see virtue would be wonderfully
ravished with the love of her beauty[146] – this man sets her out
to make her more lovely in her holiday apparel[147] to the eye of
any that will deign not to disdain until they understand? But if
anything be already said in the defence of sweet poetry, all
concurreth to the maintaining the heroical, which is not only a
kind, but the best and most accomplished kind of poetry. For
as the image of each action stirreth and instructeth the mind, so
the lofty image of such worthies most inflameth the mind with
desire to be worthy, and informs with counsel how to be worthy.
Only let Aeneas be worn in the tablet of your memory – how he
governeth himself in the ruin of his country, in the preserving
his old father, and carrying away his religious ceremonies; in
obeying God's commandment to leave Dido, though not only

* *toys*: trifles   * *fearful*: inspiring awe, reverence; ominous
* *magnanimity*: greatness of soul, nobility

all passionate kindness but even the human consideration of virtuous gratefulness would have craved other of him; how in storms, how in sports, how in war, how in peace, how a fugitive, how victorious, how besieged, how besieging, how to strangers, how to allies, how to enemies, how to his own; lastly, how in his inward self, and how in his outward government[148] – and I think in a mind not prejudiced with a prejudicating humour he will be found in excellency fruitful, yea even as Horace saith, *melius Chrysippo et Crantore.**[149]

But truly I imagine it falleth out with these poet-whippers as with some good women, who often are sick but in faith they cannot tell where – so the name of poetry is odious to them, but neither his cause nor effects, neither the sum that contains him nor the particularities descending from him, give any fast handle to their carping dispraise.

Since then poetry is of all human learnings the most ancient, and of most fatherly antiquity, as from whence other learnings have taken their beginnings; since it is so universal that no learned nation doth despise it, nor barbarous nation is without it; since both Roman and Greek gave such divine names unto it, the one of prophesying, the other of making, and that indeed that name of making is fit for him, considering that where all other arts retain themselves within their subject, and receive, as it were, their being from it, the poet, only, only bringeth his own stuff, and doth not learn a conceit out of a matter but maketh matter for a conceit;* since, neither his description nor end containing any evil, the thing described cannot be evil; since his effects be so good as to teach goodness and to delight the learners; since therein (namely in moral doctrine, the chief of all knowledges) he doth not only far pass the historian, but for instructing is well nigh comparable to the philosopher, for moving leaves him behind him; since the Holy Scripture (wherein there is no uncleanness) hath whole parts in it poetical, and that even our Saviour Christ vouchsafed to use the flowers of it; since all his kinds are not only in their united forms but in

* *melius . . . Crantore*: 'better than Chrysippus and Crantor'
* *doth not . . . conceit*: does not take his fore-conceit from events but creates events which will form a satisfying fore-conceit

their severed dissections fully commendable – I think (and think I think rightly) the laurel crown appointed for triumphant captains doth worthily of all other learnings honour the poet's triumph.[150] But because we have ears as well as tongues, and that the lightest reasons that may be will seem to weigh greatly if nothing be put in the counterbalance, let us hear, and as well as we can ponder, what objections be made against this art which may be worthy either of yielding or answering.

First, truly, I note not only in these *misomousoi** – poet-haters – but in all that kind of people who seek a praise by dispraising others, that they do prodigally spend a great many wandering words in quips and scoffs, carping and taunting at each thing, which, by stirring the spleen, may stay the brain from a through-beholding* the worthiness of the subject. Those kind of objections, as they are full of a very idle easiness, since there is nothing of so sacred a majesty but that an itching tongue may rub itself upon it, so deserve they no other answer, but instead of laughing at the jest to laugh at the jester. We know a playing wit can praise the discretion of an ass, the comfortableness of being in debt, and the jolly commodities of being sick of the plague;[151] so of the contrary side, if we will turn Ovid's verse, *ut lateat virtus proximitate mali*, that good lie hid in nearness of the evil,[152] Agrippa will be as merry in showing the vanity of science as Erasmus was in the commending of folly;[153] neither shall any man or matter escape some touch of these smiling railers. But for Erasmus and Agrippa, they had another foundation* than the superficial part would promise. Marry, these other pleasant fault-finders, who will correct the verb before they understand the noun, and confute others' knowledge before they confirm* their own[154] – I would have them only remember that scoffing cometh not of wisdom, so as the best title in true English they get with their merriments is to be called good fools, for so have our grave forefathers ever termed that humorous kind of jesters.

But that which giveth greatest scope to their scorning humour

* *misomousoi*: 'haters of the Muses'
* *through-beholding*: thorough consideration
* *another foundation*: i.e. a profounder point   * *confirm*: prove

is rhyming and versing. It is already said (and, as I think, truly said), it is not rhyming and versing that maketh poesy: one may be a poet without versing, and a versifier without poetry. But yet presuppose it were inseparable, as indeed it seemeth Scaliger judgeth:[155] truly it were an inseparable commendation. For if *oratio* next to *ratio*, speech next to reason, be the greatest gift bestowed upon mortality,[156] that cannot be praiseless which doth most polish that blessing of speech, which considers each word not only, as a man may say, by his forcible quality,* but by his best measured quantity, carrying even in themselves a harmony – without* perchance number, measure, order, proportion be in our time grown odious. But lay aside the just praise it hath, by being the only fit speech for music (music, I say, the most divine striker of the senses),[157] thus much is undoubtedly true, that if reading be foolish without remembering, memory being the only treasure* of knowledge, those words which are fittest for memory are likewise most convenient for knowledge. Now, that verse far exceedeth prose in the knitting up of the memory, the reason is manifest: the words (besides their delight, which hath a great affinity to memory) being so set, as one cannot be lost but the whole work fails, which accusing itself calleth the remembrance back to itself and so most strongly confirmeth it. Besides, one word so, as it were, begetting another, as, be it in rhyme or measured* verse, by the former a man shall have a near guess to the follower. Lastly, even they that have taught the art of memory have showed nothing so apt for it as a certain room divided into many places well and thoroughly known.[158] Now, that hath the verse in effect perfectly, every word having his natural seat, which seat must needs make the word remembered. But what needeth more in a thing so known to all men? Who is it that ever was a scholar that doth not carry away some verses of Virgil, Horace or Cato, which in his youth he learned, and even to his old age serve him for hourly lessons, as *percontatorem fugito, nam*

* *forcible quality*: accent or pitch   * *without*: unless
* *treasure*: treasury
* *rhyme or measured verse*: accentual-syllabic rhymed verse or quantitative verse

*garrulus idem est;** *dum sibi quisque placet, credula turba sumus?**[159] But the fitness it hath for memory is notably proved by all delivery of arts, wherein for the most part, from grammar to logic, mathematics, physic and the rest, the rules chiefly necessary to be borne away are compiled in verses.[160] So that verse being in itself sweet and orderly, and being best for memory, the only handle of knowledge, it must be in jest that any man can speak against it.

Now then go we to the most important imputations laid to the poor poets. For ought I can yet learn, they are these. First, that there being many other more fruitful knowledges, a man might better spend his time in them than in this. Secondly, that it is the mother of lies. Thirdly, that it is the nurse of abuse, infecting us with many pestilent desires, with a siren's sweetness drawing the mind to the serpent's tail of sinful fancies*[161] (and herein especially comedies give the largest field to ear,* as Chaucer saith);[162] how both in other nations and in ours, before poets did soften us, we were full of courage, given to martial exercises, the pillars of manlike liberty, and not lulled asleep in shady idleness with poets' pastimes. And lastly and chiefly, they cry out with open mouth as if they had overshot Robin Hood, that Plato banished them out of his commonwealth.[163] Truly this is much, if there be much truth in it.[164]

First, to the first. That a man might better spend his time is a reason indeed, but it doth, as they say, but *petere principium*.* For if it be, as I affirm, that no learning is so good as that which teacheth and moveth to virtue, and that none can both teach and move thereto so much as poetry, then is the conclusion manifest, that ink and paper cannot be to a more profitable purpose employed. And certainly, though a man should grant their first assumption, it should follow (methinks) very unwillingly that good is not good because better is better. But I still and utterly deny that there is sprung out of earth a more fruitful knowledge.

---

* *percontatorem . . . est*: 'avoid a questioner, for he is also a prattler'
* *dum . . . sumus*: 'while each pleases himself, we are a credulous crowd'
* *fancies*: fantasies   * *ear*: plough
* *petere principium*: 'beg the question'

To the second, therefore, that they should be the principal liars,[165] I answer paradoxically but truly, I think truly, that of all writers under the sun the poet is the least liar – and though* he would, as a poet can scarcely be a liar. The astronomer with his cousin the geometrician can hardly escape when they take upon them to measure the height of the stars. How often, think you, do the physicians lie, when they aver things good for sicknesses which afterwards send Charon a great number of souls drowned in a potion before they come to his ferry?[166] And no less of the rest which take upon them to affirm. Now, for the poet, he nothing affirms, and therefore never lieth, for, as I take it, to lie is to affirm that to be true which is false. So as the other artists, and especially the historian, affirming many things, can in the cloudy knowledge of mankind hardly escape from many lies. But the poet, as I said before, never affirmeth; the poet never maketh any circles about your imagination,[167] to conjure you to believe for true what he writes; he citeth not authorities of other histories, but even for his entry* calleth the sweet Muses to inspire into him a good invention[168] – in troth, not labouring to tell you what is or is not, but what should or should not be. And therefore, though he recount things not true, yet because he telleth them not for true, he lieth not, without we will say that Nathan lied in his speech before-alleged to David, which as a wicked man durst scarce say, so think I none so simple would say that Aesop lied in the tales of his beasts – for who thinks that Aesop wrote it for actually true were well worthy to have his name chronicled among the beasts he writeth of. What child is there, that coming to a play and seeing 'Thebes' written in great letters upon an old door doth believe that it is Thebes? If then a man can arrive to that child's age to know that the poet's persons and doings are but pictures what should be and not stories what have been, they will never give the lie* to things not affirmatively but allegorically and figuratively written; and therefore, as in history, looking for truth, they may go away full fraught with falsehood, so in poesy, looking but for fiction, they

* *and though*: even if   * *entry*: opening words
* *give the lie*: make an accusation of lying

shall use the narration but as an imaginative ground-plot of a profitable invention.[169] But hereto is replied, that the poets give names to men they write of, which argueth a conceit of an actual truth, and so, not being true, proves a falsehood. And doth the lawyer lie then, when under the names of 'John of the Stile' and 'John of the Nokes'[170] he puts his case? But that is easily answered: their naming of men is but to make their picture the more lively* and not to build any history.[171] Painting men, they cannot leave men nameless. We see we cannot play at chess but that we must give names to our chessmen, and yet methinks he were a very partial champion of truth that would say we lied for giving a piece of wood the reverend title of a 'bishop'. The poet nameth Cyrus or Aeneas no other way than to show what men of their fames, fortunes, and estates should* do.

Their third is, how much it abuseth men's wit, training it to wanton sinfulness and lustful love: for indeed that is the principal, if not only, abuse I can hear alleged. They say the comedies rather teach than reprehend amorous conceits.* They say the lyric is larded with passionate sonnets, the elegiac weeps the want of his mistress, and that even to the heroical Cupid hath ambitiously climbed. Alas, Love, I would thou couldst as well defend thyself as thou canst offend others; I would those on whom thou dost attend could either put thee away or yield good reason why they keep thee. But grant love of beauty to be a beastly fault (although it be very hard, since only man and no beast hath that gift to discern beauty); grant that lovely name of love to deserve all hateful reproaches (although even some of my masters the philosophers spent a good deal of their lamp oil in setting forth the excellency of it);[172] grant, I say, whatsoever they will have granted, that not only love but lust, but vanity, but – if they list – scurrility possesseth many leaves of the poets' books: yet think I, when this is granted, they will find their sentence may with good manners put the last words foremost, and not say that poetry abuseth man's wit, but that man's wit abuseth poetry.

For I will not deny but that man's wit may make poesy, which

---

* *lively*: lifelike   * *should*: ought to, or would   * *conceits*: minds, ideas

should be *eikastikē*, which some learned have defined figuring forth good things, to be *phantastikē*, which doth contrariwise infect the fancy with unworthy objects,[173] as the painter that should give to the eye either some excellent perspective, or some fine picture, fit for building or fortification,[174] or containing in it some notable example, as Abraham sacrificing his son Isaac, Judith killing Holofernes, David fighting with Goliath,[175] may leave those and please an ill-pleased* eye with wanton shows of better-hidden matters. But what, shall the abuse of a thing make the right use odious? Nay, truly, though I yield that poesy may not only be abused, but that being abused, by the reason of his sweet charming force, it can do more hurt than any other army of words, yet shall it be so far from concluding* that the abuse should give reproach to the abused, that contrariwise it is a good reason, that whatsoever, being abused, doth most harm, being rightly used (and upon the right use each thing conceiveth his title)* doth most good.[176] Do we not see skill of physic, the best rampire* to our often assaulted bodies, being abused, teach poison, the most violent destroyer? Doth not knowledge of law, whose end is to even and right all things, being abused, grow the crooked fosterer of horrible injuries? Doth not (to go to the highest) God's word abused breed heresy, and His name abused become blasphemy? Truly, a needle cannot do much hurt, and as truly (with leave of ladies be it spoken) it cannot do much good. With a sword thou mayst kill thy father, and with a sword thou mayst defend thy prince and country. So that, as in their calling poets fathers of lies they said nothing, so in this their argument of abuse they prove the commendation.

They allege herewith, that before poets began to be in price,* our nation had set their heart's delight upon action and not imagination, rather doing things worthy to be written than writing things fit to be done. What that before-time was, I think scarcely Sphinx can tell,[177] since no memory is so ancient that hath the precedence of poetry. And certain it is, that in our plainest homeliness yet never was the Albion nation[178] without

* *ill-pleased*: pleased by ill things   * *concluding*: proving
* *title*: right, entitlement   * *rampire*: rampart, defensive mound of earth
* *price*: esteem

poetry. Marry, this argument, though it be levelled against poetry, yet is it indeed a chain shot* against all learning, or bookishness as they commonly term it. Of such mind were certain Goths, of whom it is written, that having in the spoil of a famous city taken a fair library, one hangman, belike fit to execute the fruits of their wits, who had murdered a great number of bodies, would have set fire in it. 'No,' said another, very gravely, 'take heed what you do, for while they are busy about these toys, we shall with more leisure conquer their countries.'[179] This indeed is the ordinary doctrine of ignorance, and many words sometimes I have heard spent in it. But because this reason is generally against all learning as well as poetry, or rather all learning but poetry; because it were too large a digression to handle it, or at least too superfluous, since it is manifest that all government of action is to be gotten by knowledge, and knowledge best by gathering many knowledges, which is reading – I only with Horace, to him that is of that opinion, *iubeo stultum esse libenter*.*[180]

For as for poetry itself, it is the freest from this objection, for poetry is the companion of camps. I dare undertake *Orlando furioso*, or honest King Arthur,[181] will never displease a soldier, but the quiddity of *ens* and *prima materia*[182] will hardly agree with a corslet.* And therefore, as I said in the beginning, even Turks and Tartars are delighted with poets. Homer, a Greek, flourished before Greece flourished, and, if to a slight conjecture a conjecture may be opposed, truly it may seem, that as by him their learned men took almost their first light of knowledge, so their active men received their first motions* of courage. Only Alexander's example may serve, who by Plutarch is accounted of such virtue that fortune was not his guide but his footstool,[183] whose acts speak for him though Plutarch did not* – indeed the phoenix of warlike princes.[184] This Alexander left his schoolmaster, living Aristotle, behind him, but took dead Homer with him. He put the philosopher Callisthenes to death, for his seeming-philosophical, indeed mutinous, stubbornness, but the

---

* *chain shot*: cannon shot of two balls joined by a chain
* *iubeo . . . libenter*: 'cheerfully bid him be a fool'   * *corslet*: body armour
* *motions*: stirrings   * *though Plutarch did not*: even if Plutarch had not

chief thing he was ever heard to wish for was that Homer had been alive. He well found he received more bravery of mind by the pattern of Achilles than by hearing the definition of fortitude.[185] And therefore, if Cato misliked Fulvius for carrying Ennius with him to the field, it may be answered that, if Cato misliked it, the noble Fulvius liked it, or else he had not done it. For it was not the excellent Cato Uticensis, whose authority I would much more have reverenced, but it was the former, in truth a bitter punisher of faults, but else a man that had never well sacrificed to the Graces. He misliked and cried out against all Greek learning, and yet, being eighty years old, began to learn it, belike* fearing that Pluto understood not Latin. Indeed, the Roman laws allowed no person to be carried to the wars but he that was in the soldiers' roll. And therefore, though Cato misliked his unmustered* person, he misliked not his work. And if he had, Scipio Nasica (judged by common consent the best Roman) loved him; both the other Scipio brothers, who had by their virtues no less surnames than of Asia and Afric, so loved him that they caused his body to be buried in their sepulture.* So as Cato's authority, being but against his person, and that answered with so far greater than himself, is herein of no validity.[186]

But now indeed my burden is great, now Plato's name is laid upon me,[187] whom, I must confess, of all philosophers I have ever esteemed most worthy of reverence; and with good reason, since of all philosophers he is the most poetical.[188] Yet if he will defile the fountain[189] out of which his flowing streams have proceeded, let us boldly examine with what reasons he did it. First, truly, a man might maliciously object that Plato, being a philosopher, was a natural enemy of poets.[190] For indeed, after the philosophers had picked out of the sweet mysteries of poetry the right discerning true points of knowledge, they forthwith putting it in method, and making a school art of that which the poets did only teach by a divine delightfulness, beginning to spurn at their guides, like ungrateful prentices were not content

* *belike*: perhaps   * *unmustered*: not enlisted, not enrolled
* *sepulture*: sepulchre

to set up shops for themselves, but sought by all means to discredit their masters; which, by the force of delight, being barred them, the less they could overthrow them, the more they hated them. For indeed, they found for Homer seven cities strave who should have him for their citizen, where many cities banished philosophers as not fit members to live among them.[191] For only repeating certain of Euripides' verses many Athenians had their lives saved of the Syracusans, where the Athenians themselves thought many philosophers unworthy to live.[192] Certain poets, as Simonides and Pindarus, had so prevailed with Hiero the First, that of a tyrant they made him a just king; where Plato could do so little with Dionysius, that he himself of a philosopher was made a slave.[193] But who should do thus, I confess, should requite the objections made against poets with like cavillations* against philosophers, as likewise one should do that should bid one read *Phaedrus* or *Symposium* in Plato, or the discourse of love in Plutarch, and see whether any poet do authorize abominable filthiness as they do.[194] Again, a man might ask out of what commonwealth Plato did banish them: in sooth, thence where he himself alloweth community of women.[195] So as belike this banishment grew not for* effeminate wantonness, since little should poetical sonnets be hurtful when a man might have what woman he listed. But I honour philosophical instructions, and bless the wits which bred them, so as they be not abused, which is likewise stretched to poetry.*

St Paul himself (who yet, for the credit of poets, allegeth twice two* poets, and one of them by the name of a prophet)[196] setteth a watchword* upon philosophy – indeed upon the abuse.[197] So doth Plato upon the abuse, not upon poetry. Plato found fault that the poets of his time filled the world with wrong opinions of the gods, making light* tales of that unspotted essence, and therefore would not have the youth depraved with such opinions.[198] Herein may much be said; let this suffice. The poets did not induce such opinions, but did imitate those opinions

---

* *cavillations*: cavils, petty objections   * *for*: i.e. because of, for fear of
* *so as . . . poetry*: as long as they are not misused, and the same goes for poetry
* *twice two*: four   * *watchword*: word of warning
* *light*: wanton, lascivious

already induced. For all the Greek stories can well testify that the very religion of that time stood upon many, and many-fashioned,* gods, not taught so by the poets, but followed according to their nature of imitation.[199] Who list may read in Plutarch the discourses of Isis and Osiris, of the cause why oracles ceased, of the divine providence,[200] and see whether the theology of that nation stood not upon such dreams, which the poets indeed superstitiously observed; and truly, since they had not the light of Christ, did much better in it than the philosophers who, shaking off superstition, brought in atheism. Plato therefore, whose authority I had much rather justly construe than unjustly resist, meant not in general of poets, in those words of which Julius Scaliger saith *qua authoritate barbari quidam atque hispidi abuti velint ad poetas e republica exigendos,*[201] but only meant to drive out those wrong opinions of the Deity (whereof now, without further law,* Christianity hath taken away all the hurtful belief), perchance, as he thought, nourished by the then esteemed poets. And a man need go no further than to Plato himself to know his meaning, who in his dialogue called *Ion*[202] giveth high and rightly divine commendation unto poetry. So as Plato, banishing the abuse, not the thing – not banishing it, but giving due honour unto it – shall be our patron and not our adversary. For indeed I had much rather, since truly I may do it, show their mistaking* of Plato, under whose lion's skin they would make an ass-like braying against poesy,[203] than go about* to overthrow his authority, whom the wiser a man is, the more just cause he shall find to have in admiration, especially since he attributeth unto poesy more than myself do, namely to be a very inspiring of a divine force far above man's wit,[204] as in the forenamed dialogue is apparent.

Of the other side, who would show the honours have been by the best sort of judgements granted them, a whole sea of examples would present themselves: Alexanders, Caesars,[205]

---

* *many-fashioned*: in many forms, able to change their shape
* *qua . . . exigendos*: 'whose authority certain barbarous and uncouth men seek to use in order to expel poets from the republic'
* *law*: ado, or philosophical legislation   * *mistaking*: misreading
* *go about*: aim, endeavour

Scipios, all favourers of poets; Laelius, called the Roman
Socrates, himself a poet, so as part of *Heautontimoroumenos* in
Terence was supposed to be made by him;[206] and even the Greek
Socrates, whom Apollo confirmed to be the only wise man, is
said to have spent part of his old time in putting Aesop's fables
into verses.[207] And, therefore, full evil should it become his
scholar Plato to put such words in his master's mouth against
poets. But what need more? Aristotle writes the Art of Poesy –
and why, if it should not be written? Plutarch teacheth the use
to be gathered of them – and how, if they should not be read?[208]
And who reads Plutarch's either history or philosophy shall find
he trimmeth both their garments with guards* of poesy. But I
list not to defend poesy with the help of his underling historiography. Let it suffice to have showed it is a fit soil for praise to
dwell upon, and what dispraise may set upon it is either easily
overcome, or transformed into just commendation.

So that since the excellencies of it may be so easily and so
justly confirmed, and the low creeping objections so soon trod-
den down – it not being an art of lies, but of true doctrine; not
of effeminateness, but of notable stirring of courage; not of
abusing man's wit, but of strengthening man's wit; not banished,
but honoured by Plato – let us rather plant more laurels for to
engarland the poets' heads (which honour of being laureate, as
besides them only triumphant captains were, is a sufficient
authority to show the price they ought to be held in)[209] than
suffer the ill-savoured breath of such wrong-speakers once to
blow upon the clear springs of poesy.

But since I have run so long a career[210] in this matter, methinks,
before I give my pen a full stop, it shall be but a little more lost
time to inquire why England, the mother of excellent minds,
should be grown so hard a stepmother to poets, who certainly
in wit ought to pass all other, since all only proceedeth from
their wit, being indeed makers of themselves, not takers of
others.[211] How can I but exclaim, *Musa, mihi causas memora,
quo numine laeso?*∗[212] Sweet poesy, that hath anciently had

* *guards*: ornamental trimmings
* *Musa . . . laeso*: 'Tell me, O Muse, the cause; by which offended deity . . .'

kings, emperors, senators, great captains such as, besides a thousand others, David, Hadrian, Sophocles, Germanicus,[213] not only to favour poets, but to be poets; and of our nearer times can present for her patrons a Robert, King of Sicily, the great King Francis of France, King James of Scotland, such cardinals as Bembus and Bibbiena, such famous preachers and teachers as Beza and Melanchthon, so learned philosophers as Fracastorius and Scaliger, so great orators as Pontanus and Muretus, so piercing wits as George Buchanan, so grave counsellors as – besides many, but before all – that Hospital of France,[214] than whom I think that realm never brought forth a more accomplished judgement more firmly builded upon virtue – I say these, with numbers of others, not only to read others' poesies, but to poetize for others' reading: that poesy, thus embraced in all other places, should only find in our time a hard welcome in England, I think the very earth lamenteth it, and therefore decketh our soil with fewer laurels than it was accustomed. For heretofore poets have in England also flourished, and, which is to be noted, even in those times when the trumpet of Mars did sound loudest.[215] And now that an over-faint quietness[216] should seem to strew the house* for poets, they are almost in as good reputation as the mountebanks at Venice.[217] Truly, even that,* as of the one side it giveth great praise to poesy, which like Venus (but to better purpose) had rather be troubled in the net with Mars than enjoy the homely quiet of Vulcan,[218] so serves it for a piece of a reason why they are less grateful* to idle England, which now can scarce endure the pain of a pen. Upon this necessarily followeth, that base men with servile wits undertake it, who think it enough if they can be rewarded of the printer; and so, as Epaminondas is said with the honour of his virtue to have made an office, by his exercising it, which before was contemptible, to become highly respected,[219] so these men, no more but setting their names to it, by their own disgracefulness disgrace the most graceful poesy. For now, as if all the Muses were got with child to bring forth

* *strew the house*: with rushes and flowers, i.e. prepare a welcome
* *that*: i.e. the relationship between poetry and war   * *grateful*: acceptable

bastard poets, without any commission* they do post* over the banks of Helicon,[220] till they make the readers more weary than post horses; while in the meantime they, *queis meliore luto finxit praecordia Titan*,*[221] are better content to suppress the outflowings of their wit than, by publishing them, to be accounted knights of the same order.

But I, that before ever I durst aspire unto the dignity am admitted into the company of the paper-blurrers,* do find the very true cause of our wanting estimation is want of desert, taking upon us to be poets in despite of Pallas.[222] Now, wherein we want desert were a thankworthy labour to express; but if I knew, I should have mended myself. But I, as I never desired the title, so have I neglected the means to come by it; only, overmastered by some thoughts, I yielded an inky tribute unto them.[223] Marry, they that delight in poesy itself should seek to know what they do and how they do, and especially look themselves in an unflattering glass of reason, if they be inclinable unto it. For poesy must not be drawn by the ears: it must be gently led, or rather it must lead, which was partly the cause that made the ancient learned affirm it was a divine gift and no human skill, since all other knowledges lie ready for any that hath strength of wit. A poet no industry can make, if his own genius* be not carried into it, and therefore is it an old proverb – *orator fit, poeta nascitur*.* Yet confess I always, that as the fertilest ground must be manured,* so must the highest-flying wit have a Daedalus to guide him.[224] That Daedalus, they say, both in this and in other, hath three wings to bear itself up into the air of due commendation: that is, art, imitation and exercise.[225] But these, neither artificial rules nor imitative patterns,* we much cumber ourselves withal. Exercise indeed we do, but that very fore-backwardly, for where we should exercise to know, we exercise as having known, and so is our

---

* *without any commission*: without authority, without being asked
* *post*: hasten, travel with relays of horses ridden to exhaustion
* *queis . . . Titan*: 'whose hearts Prometheus formed from better clay'
* *blurrers*: smudgers, smearers, blotters   * *genius*: disposition, natural bent
* *orator . . . nascitur*: 'the orator is made, but the poet is born'
* *manured*: tilled, worked with the hands   * *patterns*: models

brain delivered of much matter which never was begotten by knowledge. For, there being two principal parts, matter to be expressed by words and words to express the matter, in neither we use art or imitation rightly. Our matter is *quodlibet*:* indeed, though wrongly, performing Ovid's verse, *quicquid conabor dicere, versus erit*;*[226] never marshalling it into any assured rank,* that almost the readers cannot tell where to find themselves.

Chaucer, undoubtedly, did excellently in his *Troilus and Criseyde*,[227] of whom truly I know not whether to marvel more, either that he in that misty time could see so clearly, or that we in this clear age go so stumblingly after him. Yet had he great wants, fit to be forgiven in so reverent an antiquity. I account the *Mirror of Magistrates* meetly* furnished of beautiful parts; and in the Earl of Surrey's lyrics many things tasting of a noble birth, and worthy of a noble mind.[228] The *Shepheardes Calender* hath much poetry in his eclogues, indeed worthy the reading, if I be not deceived. That same framing of his style to an old rustic language I dare not allow,* since neither Theocritus in Greek, Virgil in Latin, nor Sannazaro in Italian did affect it.[229] Besides these, I do not remember to have seen but few (to speak boldly) printed that have poetical sinews in them. For proof whereof, let but most of the verses be put in prose, and then ask the meaning; and it will be found that one verse did but beget another, without ordering at the first what should be at the last, which becomes a confused mass of words, with a tingling* sound of rhyme, barely accompanied with reason.[230]

Our tragedies and comedies not without cause cried out against, observing rules neither of honest civility nor skilful poetry – excepting *Gorboduc* (again, I say, of those that I have seen)* which, notwithstanding as it is full of stately speeches and well-sounding phrases, climbing to the height of Seneca's style, and as full of notable morality, which it doth most delightfully teach, and so obtain the very end of poesy, yet in truth it

* *quodlibet*: 'whatever we want'
* *quicquid . . . erit*: 'anything I try to say will come out as poetry'
* *rank*: order   * *meetly*: moderately, or suitably
* *allow*: approve of, praise   * *tingling*: ringing, tinkling   * *seen*: i.e. read

is very defectuous in the circumstances, which grieveth me, because it might not remain as an exact model of all tragedies.[231] For it is faulty both in place and time, the two necessary companions of all corporal* actions.[232] For where the stage should always represent but one place, and the uttermost time presupposed in it should be, both by Aristotle's precept and common reason, but one day, there is both many days and many places inartificially* imagined. But if it be so in *Gorboduc*, how much more in all the rest, where you shall have Asia of the one side and Afric of the other, and so many other under-kingdoms, that the player, when he cometh in, must ever begin with telling where he is, or else the tale will not be conceived? Now you shall have three ladies walk to gather flowers, and then we must believe the stage to be a garden. By and by we hear news of shipwreck in the same place, and then we are to blame if we accept it not for a rock. Upon the back of that comes out a hideous monster with fire and smoke, and then the miserable beholders are bound to take it for a cave. While in the meantime two armies fly in, represented with four swords and bucklers,* and then what hard heart will not receive it for a pitched field?*

Now, of time they are much more liberal. For ordinary it is that two young princes fall in love, after many traverses* she is got with child, delivered of a fair boy, he is lost, groweth a man, falls in love, and is ready to get another child – and all this in two hours' space, which how absurd it is in sense, even sense may imagine, and art hath taught, and all ancient examples justified, and at this day the ordinary players in Italy will not err in.[233] Yet will some bring in an example of *Eunuchus* in Terence, that containeth matter of two days,[234] yet far short of twenty years. True it is, and so was it to be played in two days, and so fitted to the time it set forth. And though Plautus have in one place done amiss, let us hit with him, and not miss with him.[235]

But they will say, 'How then shall we set forth a story which

* *corporal*: physical, material   * *inartificially*: inartistically
* *bucklers*: shields   * *pitched field*: battlefield   * *traverses*: misfortunes

containeth both many places and many times?' And do they not
know that a tragedy is tied to the laws of poesy and not of
history, not bound to follow the story, but having liberty either
to feign a quite new matter or to frame the history to the most
tragical conveniency?* Again, many things may be told which
cannot be showed, if they know the difference betwixt reporting
and representing: as, for example, I may speak, though I am
here, of Peru, and in speech digress from that to the description
of Calicut;[236] but in action I cannot represent it without Pacolet's
horse.[237] And so was the manner the ancients took, by some
*nuntius** to recount things done in former time or other place.
Lastly, if they will represent an history, they must not (as Horace
saith) begin *ab ovo*,* but they must come to the principal point
of that one action which they will represent.[238]

By example this will be best expressed. I have a story of
young Polydorus, delivered for safety's sake, with great riches,
by his father Priamus to Polymnestor, King of Thrace, in the
Trojan war time; he, after some years, hearing the overthrow
of Priamus, for to make the treasure his own, murdereth the
child; the body of the child is taken up by Hecuba; she, the
same day, findeth a sleight* to be revenged most cruelly of
the tyrant. Where now would one of our tragedy writers begin,
but with the delivery of the child? Then should he sail over into
Thrace, and so spend I know not how many years, and travel
numbers of places. But where doth Euripides? Even with the
finding of the body, the rest leaving to be told by the spirit of
Polydorus.[239] This need no further to be enlarged; the dullest
wit may conceive it.

But besides these gross absurdities, how all their plays be
neither right tragedies nor right comedies, mingling kings and
clowns, not because the matter so carrieth it, but thrust in
the clown by head and shoulders to play a part in majestical
matters, with neither decency* nor discretion, so as neither the
admiration and commiseration nor the right sportfulness is by
their mongrel tragicomedy obtained.[240] I know Apuleius did

* *conveniency*: propriety, decorum   * *nuntius*: 'messenger'
* *ab ovo*: 'from the egg'   * *sleight*: trick, stratagem   * *decency*: decorum

somewhat so, but that is a thing recounted with space of time, not represented in one moment.[241] And I know the ancients have one or two examples of tragicomedies, as Plautus hath *Amphitryo*;[242] but if we mark them well, we shall find that they never, or very daintily,* match hornpipes and funerals. So falleth it out that, having indeed no right comedy in that comical part of our tragedy, we have nothing but scurrility unworthy of any chaste ears, or some extreme show of doltishness,* indeed fit to lift up a loud laughter, and nothing else, where the whole tract* of a comedy should be full of delight, as the tragedy should be still maintained in a well-raised admiration.

But our comedians think there is no delight without laughter, which is very wrong, for though laughter may come with delight, yet cometh it not of delight, as though delight should be the cause of laughter; but well may one thing breed both together.[243] Nay, rather in themselves they have, as it were, a kind of contrariety. For delight we scarcely do, but in things that have a conveniency* to ourselves or to the general nature; laughter almost ever cometh of things most disproportioned to ourselves and nature. Delight hath a joy in it, either permanent or present; laughter hath only a scornful tickling. For example, we are ravished with delight to see a fair woman, and yet are far from being moved to laughter. We laugh at deformed creatures, wherein certainly we cannot delight. We delight in good chances; we laugh at mischances. We delight to hear the happiness of our friends or country, at which he were worthy to be laughed at that would laugh. We shall, contrarily, laugh sometimes to find a matter quite mistaken and go down the hill against the bias* in the mouth of some such men as, for the respect of them, one shall be heartily sorry he cannot choose but laugh, and so is rather pained than delighted with laughter.[244] Yet deny I not, but that they may go well together. For as in Alexander's picture well set out we delight without laughter, and in twenty mad

---

* *daintily*: sparingly, deftly   * *doltishness*: dullness, stupidity
* *tract*: course, duration   * *conveniency*: suitability, congruity
* *go down the hill against the bias*: metaphor from bowls, the slope of the ground counteracting the swerve of the ball

antics* we laugh without delight, so in Hercules painted with
his great beard and furious* countenance, in a woman's attire,
spinning at Omphale's commandment,[245] it breedeth both
delight and laughter: for the representing of so strange a power
in love procureth delight, and the scornfulness of the action
stirreth laughter. But I speak to this purpose, that all the end of
the comical part be not upon such scornful matters as stir
laughter only, but, mixed with it, that delightful teaching which
is the end of poesy. And the great fault even in that point of
laughter, and forbidden plainly by Aristotle,[246] is that they stir
laughter in sinful things, which are rather execrable than ridiculous; or in miserable, which are rather to be pitied than scorned.
For what is it to make folks gape at a wretched beggar, and a
beggarly clown;* or, against law of hospitality, to jest at
strangers, because they speak not English so well as we do?
What do we learn, since it is certain *nil habet infelix paupertas
durius in se, / quam quod ridiculos homines facit?*[247] But rather
a busy loving courtier, and a heartless threatening Thraso,
a self-wise-seeming schoolmaster, a wry-transformed* traveller:[248] these if we saw walk in stage names, which we play
naturally* – therein were delightful laughter and teaching
delightfulness, as, in the other, the tragedies of Buchanan[249] do
justly bring forth a divine admiration. But I have lavished out
too many words of this play matter. I do it because, as they are
excelling parts of poesy, so is there none so much used in
England, and none can be more pitifully abused; which, like an
unmannerly daughter showing a bad education, causeth her
mother Poesy's honesty* to be called in question.

Other sort of poetry almost have we none, but that lyrical
kind of songs and sonnets,[250] which, Lord, if He gave us so good
minds, how well it might be employed, and with how heavenly
fruits, both private and public, in singing the praises of the

---

* *antics*: grotesque plays or characters
* *furious*: mad   * *clown*: peasant
* *nil . . . facit*: 'of all the woes of luckless poverty none is harder to endure than
this, that it exposes men to ridicule'
* *wry-transformed*: diverted, twisted from a natural course
* *naturally*: in real life   * *honesty*: honour, chastity

immortal beauty, the immortal goodness of that God who giveth
us hands to write and wits to conceive; of which we might well
want words, but never matter, of which we could turn our eyes
to nothing, but we should ever have new-budding occasions.[251]
But truly, many of such writings as come under the banner of
unresistible love, if I were a mistress, would never persuade me
they were in love, so coldly they apply fiery speeches,[252] as men
that had rather read lovers' writings, and so caught up certain
swelling phrases (which hang together like a man that once told
my father that the wind was at northwest and by south, because
he would be sure to name winds enough), than that in truth
they feel those passions;[253] which easily, as I think, may be
bewrayed* by that same forcibleness or *energeia*[254] (as the
Greeks call it) of the writer. But let this be a sufficient, though
short, note that we miss the right use of the material point of
poesy.

Now, for the outside of it, which is words or (as I may term it)
diction,[255] it is even well worse, so is that honey-flowing matron
Eloquence apparelled, or rather disguised, in a courtesan-like
painted affectation: one time with so far-fet words that may
seem monsters but must seem strangers to any poor Englishman; another time with coursing* of a letter, as if they were
bound to follow the method of a dictionary;[256] another time with
figures and flowers extremely winter-starved.[257] But I would this
fault were only peculiar to versifiers, and had not as large
possession among prose-printers, and, which is to be marvelled,
among many scholars, and, which is to be pitied, among some
preachers. Truly, I could wish, if at least I might be so bold to
wish in a thing beyond the reach of my capacity, the diligent
imitators of Tully and Demosthenes, most worthy to be imitated, did not so much keep Nizolian paper-books of their
figures and phrases as, by attentive translation,* as it were,
devour them whole, and make them wholly theirs.[258] For now
they cast sugar and spice upon every dish that is served to the
table, like those Indians, not content to wear earrings at the fit

---

* *bewrayed*: betrayed   * *coursing*: hunting
* *translation*: transformation, adaptation

and natural place of the ears, but they will thrust jewels through their nose and lips, because they will be sure to be fine.[259] Tully, when he was to drive out Catiline, as it were with a thunderbolt of eloquence, often useth the figure of repetition, as *vivit. Vivit? Imo in senatum venit*,* [260] etc. Indeed inflamed with a well-grounded rage, he would have his words (as it were) double out of his mouth, and so do that artificially which we see men in choler do naturally.[261] And we, having noted the grace of those words, hale* them in sometimes to a familiar epistle, when it were too too much choler to be choleric.[262] How well store of *similiter cadenses*[263] doth sound with the gravity of the pulpit I would but invoke Demosthenes' soul to tell, who with a rare daintiness* useth them. Truly, they have made me think of the sophister* that with too much subtlety would prove two eggs three, and, though he might be counted a sophister, had none for his labour.[264] So these men, bringing in such a kind of eloquence, well may they obtain an opinion of a seeming fineness,* but persuade few, which should be the end of their fineness. Now for similitudes,* in certain printed discourses I think all herbarists,* all stories* of beasts, fowls and fishes, are rifled up, that they come in multitudes to wait upon any of our conceits, which certainly is as absurd a surfeit to the ears as is possible.[265] For the force of a similitude not being to prove anything to a contrary disputer, but only to explain to a willing hearer, when that is done, the rest is a most tedious prattling, rather over-swaying the memory from the purpose whereto they were applied than any whit informing the judgement, already either satisfied, or by similitudes not to be satisfied. For my part, I do not doubt, when Antonius and Crassus, the great forefathers of Cicero in eloquence, the one (as Cicero testifieth of them) pretended not to know art, the other not to set by it[266] (because with a plain sensibleness they might win credit of popular ears,

---

* *vivit... venit*: '[and yet this man] is alive. Alive did I say? Not only is he alive, but he attends the senate'   * *hale*: haul
* *daintiness*: discrimination, fastidiousness
* *sophister*: sophist, or senior Cambridge undergraduate
* *fineness*: splendour, subtlety   * *similitudes*: similes
* *herbarists*: [authors of] herbals   * *stories*: [natural] histories

which credit is the nearest step to persuasion, which persuasion is the chief mark* of oratory)[267] – I do not doubt, I say, but that they used these knacks* very sparingly, which who doth generally* use, any man may see doth dance to his own music, and so be noted by the audience more careful to speak curiously* than to speak truly. Undoubtedly (at least to my opinion undoubtedly), I have found in divers smally learned courtiers a more sound style than in some professors of learning, of which I can guess no other cause but that the courtier, following that which by practice he findeth fittest to nature, therein (though he know it not) doth according to art, though not by art; where the other, using art to show art and not to hide art[268] (as in these cases he should do), flieth from nature and indeed abuseth art.

But what? Methinks I deserve to be pounded* for straying from poetry to oratory. But both have such an affinity in the wordish consideration,[269] that I think this digression will make my meaning receive the fuller understanding, which is not to take upon me to teach poets how they should do, but only, finding myself sick among the rest, to show some one or two spots of the common infection grown among the most part of writers, that, acknowledging ourselves somewhat awry, we may bend* to the right use both of matter and manner; whereto our language giveth us great occasion, being indeed capable of any excellent exercising of it. I know some will say it is a mingled language.[270] And why not so much the better, taking the best of both the other?* Another will say it wanteth grammar. Nay, truly, it hath that praise that it wants not grammar: for grammar it might have, but it needs it not, being so easy in itself, and so void of those cumbersome differences of cases, genders, moods, and tenses, which I think was a piece of the Tower of Babylon's[271] curse, that a man should be put to school to learn his mother tongue. But for the uttering sweetly and properly the conceits of the mind, which is the end of speech, that hath it equally with

---

* *mark*: aim, target   * *knacks*: trinkets
* *generally*: everywhere   * *curiously*: artfully
* *pounded*: impounded (shut up in a pound like a stray animal)
* *bend*: direct our course, apply ourselves
* *both the other*: i.e. Anglo-Saxon and French

any other tongue in the world, and is particularly happy in compositions* of two or three words together,[272] near the Greek, far beyond the Latin, which is one of the greatest beauties can be in a language.

Now, of versifying there are two sorts, the one ancient, the other modern. The ancient marked the quantity of each syllable, and according to that framed his verse. The modern observing only number,* with some regard of the accent, the chief life of it standeth in that like sounding of the words which we call rhyme. Whether of these be the more excellent would bear many speeches: the ancient no doubt more fit for music, both words and time* observing quantity, and more fit lively to express divers passions by the low or lofty sound of the well-weighed syllable; the latter likewise with his rhyme striketh a certain music to the ear, and in fine, since it doth delight, though by another way, it obtains the same purpose, there being in either sweetness and wanting in neither majesty.[273] Truly, the English, before any vulgar* language I know, is fit for both sorts. For, for the ancient, the Italian is so full of vowels that it must ever be cumbered with elisions; the Dutch* so, of the other side, with consonants that they cannot yield the sweet sliding fit for a verse; the French in his whole language hath not one word that hath his accent in the last syllable saving two, called *antepenultima*; and little more hath the Spanish, and therefore very gracelessly may they use dactyls.[274] The English is subject to none of these defects. Now, for the rhyme,* though we do not observe quantity, yet we observe the accent very precisely, which other languages either cannot do, or will not do so absolutely. That *caesura*, or breathing place, in the midst of the verse neither Italian nor Spanish have; the French and we never almost fail of. Lastly, even the very rhyme itself, the Italian cannot put it in the last syllable, by the French named the masculine rhyme, but still* in the next to the last, which the French call the female, or the next before that, which the Italian term *sdrucciola*: the

* *compositions*: compounds   * *number*: i.e. syllable count
* *time*: i.e. musical measure   * *vulgar*: vernacular
* *Dutch*: German (*Deutsch*)
* *the rhyme*: i.e. the modern (accentual-)syllabic system   * *still*: always

example of the former is 'buono' / 'suono', of the *sdrucciola* is
'femina' / 'semina'. The French, of the other side, hath both the
male, as 'bon' / 'son', and the female, as 'plaise' / 'taise', but the
sdrucciola he hath not; where the English hath all three, as
'due' / 'true', 'father' / 'rather', 'motion' / 'potion'.[275] With much
more which might be said, but that already I find the triflingness
of this discourse is much too much enlarged.

So that since the ever-praiseworthy poesy is full of virtue-
breeding delightfulness, and void of no gift that ought to be in
the noble name of learning; since the blames* laid against it are
either false or feeble; since the cause why it is not esteemed in
England is the fault of poet-apes,* not poets; since, lastly, our
tongue is most fit to honour poesy, and to be honoured by
poesy, I conjure you all that have had the evil luck to read this
ink-wasting toy of mine, even in the name of the nine Muses,
no more to scorn the sacred mysteries of poesy, no more to
laugh at the name of poets, as though they were next inheritors
to fools, no more to jest at the reverent title of a rhymer, but to
believe with Aristotle that they were the ancient treasurers of
the Grecians' divinity; to believe with Bembus that they were
first bringers-in of all civility; to believe with Scaliger that no
philosopher's precepts can sooner make you an honest man than
the reading of Virgil; to believe with Clauserus, the translator of
Cornutus, that it pleased the heavenly Deity, by* Hesiod and
Homer, under the veil of fables to give us all knowledge, logic,
rhetoric, philosophy natural and moral and *quid non?*;*[276] to
believe with me that there are many mysteries contained in
poetry which of purpose were written darkly,* lest by profane
wits it should be abused; to believe with Landin that they are so
beloved of the gods, that whatsoever they write proceeds of a
divine fury;[277] lastly, to believe themselves when they tell you
they will make you immortal by their verses. Thus doing, your
name shall flourish in the printers' shops; thus doing, you shall
be of kin to many a poetical preface; thus doing, you shall be
most fair, most rich, most wise, most all – you shall dwell

---

* *blames*: charges   * *poet-apes*: poetasters, rhymesters
* *by*: through   * *quid non?*: 'what not?'
* *darkly*: obscurely, allegorically

upon superlatives;[278] thus doing, though you be *libertino patre natus*,*[279] you shall suddenly grow *Herculea proles* – *si quid mea carmina possunt*;*[280] thus doing, your soul shall be placed with Dante's Beatrix or Virgil's Anchises.[281] But if (fie of such a but) you be born so near the dull-making cataract* of Nilus that you cannot hear the planet-like music of poetry;[282] if you have so earth-creeping a mind that it cannot lift itself up to look to the sky of poetry, or rather by a certain rustical disdain will become such a mome* as to be a Momus of poetry;[283] then, though I will not wish unto you the ass's ears of Midas, nor to be driven by a poet's verses, as Bubonax was, to hang himself, nor to be rhymed to death, as is said to be done in Ireland;[284] yet thus much curse I must send you in the behalf of all poets: that while you live, you live in love, and never get favour for lacking skill of a sonnet, and when you die, your memory die from the earth for want of an epitaph.

* *libertino . . . natus*: 'son of a freedman'
* *Herculea proles*: 'a descendant of Hercules'
* *si . . . possunt*: 'if my songs can achieve anything'
* *cataract*: waterfall   * *mome*: blockhead, fool

GEORGE PUTTENHAM
THE ART OF
ENGLISH POESY
(1589)

THE FIRST BOOK
OF POETS AND POESY

CHAPTER I

*What a poet and poesy is, and who may be worthily said the
most excellent poet of our time*

A poet is as much to say as a maker. And our English name well
conforms with the Greek word, for of *poiein*, to make, they call
a maker *poeta*.[1] Such as (by way of resemblance, and reverently)
we may say of God, who, without any travail* to His divine
imagination, made all the world of nought, nor also by any
pattern or mould, as the Platonics with their *ideas* do fantastically suppose[2] – even so the very poet makes and contrives out
of his own brain both the verse and matter of his poem, and not
by any foreign copy* or example, as doth the translator, who
therefore may well be said a versifier, but not a poet.[3] The
premises considered, it giveth to the name and profession no
small dignity and pre-eminence, above all artificers scientific or
mechanical. And nevertheless, without any repugnancy* at all,
a poet may in some sort be said a follower or imitator, because
he can express the true and lively* of everything is set before
him[4] and which he taketh in hand to describe, and so in that
respect is both a maker and a counterfeiter,* and poesy an art
not only of making but also of imitation.[5] And this science
in his perfection cannot grow but by some divine instinct* –
the Platonics call it *furor*[6] – or by excellency of nature and

* *travail*: toil, exertion   * *copy*: pattern, original
* *repugnancy*: contradiction, inconsistency   * *lively*: living, lifelike (quality)
* *counterfeiter*: imitator   * *instinct*: prompting

complexion,* or by great subtlety* of the spirits and wit, or by much experience and observation of the world and course of kind,* or peradventure by all or most part of them. Otherwise, how was it possible that Homer, being but a poor private man and, as some say, in his later age blind, should so exactly set forth and describe, as if he had been a most excellent captain or general, the order and array of battles, the conduct of whole armies, the sieges and assaults of cities and towns; or, as some great prince's major-domo* and perfect surveyor* in court, the order, sumptuousness and magnificence of royal banquets, feasts, weddings and interviews; or, as a politician very prudent, and much inured* with the private and public affairs, so gravely examine the laws and ordinances civil, or so profoundly discourse in matters of estate* and forms of all politic regiment?*[7] Finally, how could he so naturally paint out the speeches, countenance and manners of princely persons and private: to wit, the wrath of Achilles, the magnanimity* of Agamemnon, the prudence of Menelaus, the prowess of Hector, the majesty of King Priamus, the gravity of Nestor, the policies and eloquence of Ulysses, the calamities of the distressed queens, and valiance of all the captains and adventurous knights in those lamentable wars of Troy?[8] It is therefore of poets thus to be conceived, that if they be able to devise and make all these things of themselves, without any subject of verity, that they be (by manner of speech) as creating gods; if they do it by instinct divine or natural, then surely much favoured from above; if by their experience, then no doubt very wise men; if by any precedent or pattern laid before them, then truly the most excellent imitators and counterfeiters of all others. But you (Madam), my most honoured and gracious, if I should seem to offer you this my device* for a discipline* and not a delight, I might well be reputed of all

---

* *complexion*: disposition, temperament   * *subtlety*: acuteness, cleverness
* *kind*: nature   * *major-domo*: steward, head servant
* *surveyor*: royal officer in charge of food   * *inured*: accustomed, familiar
* *estate*: state   * *regiment*: rule, government
* *magnanimity*: great-spiritedness   * *device*: project, work
* *discipline*: lesson, (course of) instruction

others the most arrogant and injurious, yourself being already, of any that I know in our time, the most excellent poet: forsooth, by your princely purse, favours and countenance making in manner what ye list – the poor man rich, the lewd* well-learned, the coward courageous, and vile both noble and valiant. Then for imitation no less, your person as a most cunning* counterfeiter lively representing Venus in countenance, in life Diana, Pallas for government, and Juno in all honour and regal magnificence.[9]

CHAPTER 2

That there may be an art of our English poesy, as well as there is of the Latin and Greek

Then, as there was no art in the world till by experience found out, so if poesy be now an art, and of all antiquity hath been among the Greeks and Latins, and yet were none until by studious persons fashioned and reduced* into a method of rules and precepts, then no doubt may there be the like with us. And if the art of poesy be but a skill appertaining to utterance,* why may not the same be with us as well as with them, our language being no less copious, pithy and significative than theirs, our conceits* the same, and our wits no less apt to devise and imitate than theirs were? If, again, art be but a certain order of rules prescribed by reason and gathered by experience, why should not poesy be a vulgar* art with us as well as with the Greeks and Latins, our language admitting no fewer rules and nice* diversities than theirs (but peradventure more, by a peculiar* which our speech hath, in many things differing from theirs,

---

* *lewd*: unlearned   * *cunning*: skilful   * *reduced*: ordered
* *utterance*: speech   * *conceits*: imaginations, understandings
* *vulgar*: vernacular; common, in general use
* *nice*: refined, cultured; particular
* *peculiar*: privilege, special dispensation or jurisdiction

and yet in the general points of that art allowed to go in common with them)? So as if one point,* perchance, which is their feet whereupon their measures* stand, and indeed is all the beauty of their poesy, and which feet we have not, nor as yet never went about to frame (the nature of our language and words not permitting it), we have instead thereof twenty other curious* points in that skill more than ever they had, by reason of our rhyme and tuneable* concords or symphony,* which they never observed.[10] Poesy therefore may be an art in our vulgar, and that very methodical and commendable.

CHAPTER 3

How poets were the first priests, the first prophets, the first legislators and politicians in the world

The profession and use of poesy is most ancient from the beginning – and not, as many erroneously suppose, after but before any civil society was among men. For it is written that poesy was the original cause and occasion of their first assemblies, when* before the people remained in the woods and mountains, vagrant and dispersed like the wild beasts, lawless and naked, or very ill clad, and of all good and necessary provision for harbour* or sustenance utterly unfurnished, so as they little differed for their manner of life from the very brute beasts of the field. Whereupon it is feigned* that Amphion and Orpheus, two poets of the first ages, one of them, to wit Amphion, builded up cities and reared walls with the stones that came in heaps to the sound of his harp, figuring* thereby the mollifying of hard and stony hearts by his sweet and eloquent persuasion; and Orpheus assembled the wild beasts to come in herds to hearken

---

* *So as if one point*: if they have one feature ['we have instead thereof twenty other'] *   * measures*: verse metres   * curious*: artful
* *tuneable*: musical, harmonious   * symphony*: harmony
* *when*: whereas   * harbour*: shelter   * feigned*: related, fabled
* *figuring*: representing allegorically

to his music, and by that means made them tame, implying thereby how, by his discreet and wholesome lessons uttered in harmony and with melodious instruments, he brought the rude* and savage people to a more civil and orderly life, nothing, as it seemeth, more prevailing or fit to redress and edify* the cruel and sturdy* courage* of man than it. And as these two poets, and Linus before them, and Musaeus also and Hesiodus, in Greece and Arcadia, so by all likelihood had more poets done in other places, and in other ages before them, though there be no remembrance left of them, by reason of the records by some accident of time perished and failing.[11]

Poets therefore are of great antiquity. Then, forasmuch as they were the first that intended* to the observation of nature and her works, and specially of the celestial courses, by reason of the continual motion of the heavens, searching after the first mover, and from thence by degrees coming to know and consider of the substances separate and abstract, which we call the divine intelligences* or good angels (*daemones*), they were the first that instituted sacrifices of placation, with invocations and worship to them, as to gods, and invented and established all the rest of the observances and ceremonies of religion, and so were the first priests and ministers of the holy mysteries. And because, for the better execution of that high charge and function, it behoved them to live chaste and in all holiness of life, and in continual study and contemplation, they came by instinct divine and by deep meditation and much abstinence (the same assubtiling* and refining their spirits) to be made apt to receive visions, both waking and sleeping, which made them utter prophesies and foretell things to come. So also were they the first prophets or seers, *videntes* (for so the Scripture termeth them in Latin after the Hebrew word),[12] and all the oracles and answers of the gods were given in metre or verse and published to the people by their direction. And for that they were aged and grave men, and of much wisdom and experience in the

* *rude*: uncivilized, barbarous   * *edify*: instruct, improve
* *sturdy*: fierce, ruthless   * *courage*: nature, disposition
* *intended*: directed their attention   * *intelligences*: spirits
* *assubtiling*: refining, sharpening

affairs of the world, they were the first lawmakers to the people
and the first politicians, devising all expedient means for the
establishment of commonwealth, to hold and contain the people
in order and duty by force and virtue of good and wholesome
laws, made for the preservation of the public peace and tranquillity; the same, peradventure, not purposely intended but
greatly furthered by the awe of their gods, and such scruple of
conscience as the terrors of their late-invented religion had led
them into.

CHAPTER 4

*How the poets were the first philosophers, the first astron-
omers and historiographers and orators and musicians of the
world*

Utterance also and language is given by nature to man for
persuasion of others and aid of themselves – I mean the first
ability to speak. For speech itself is artificial* and made by man,
and the more pleasing it is the more it prevaileth to such purpose
as it is intended for; but speech by metre is a kind of utterance
more cleanly couched* and more delicate* to the ear than prose
is, because it is more current* and slipper* upon the tongue,
and withal tuneable and melodious, as a kind of music, and
therefore may be termed a musical speech or utterance, which
cannot but please the hearer very well. Another cause is for that
it is briefer and more compendious, and easier to bear away and
be retained in memory, than that which is contained in multitude
of words, and full of tedious ambage* and long periods. It is,
beside, a manner of utterance more eloquent and rhetorical than
the ordinary prose which we use in our daily talk, because it is
decked and set out with all manner of fresh colours* and figures,

* *artificial*: made by art and according to rules
* *cleanly couched*: artfully arranged   * *delicate*: delightful
* *current*: smoothly flowing   * *slipper*: easily uttered
* *ambage*: circumlocution   * *colours*: rhetorical devices, ornaments

which maketh that it sooner inveigleth the judgement of man, and carrieth his opinion this way and that, whither soever the heart, by impression of the ear, shall be most affectionately bent and directed. The utterance in prose is not of so great efficacy, because not only it is daily used, and by that occasion the ear is overglutted with it, but is also not so voluble* and slipper upon the tongue, being wide and loose and nothing numerous,* nor contrived into measures and sounded with so gallant and harmonical accents, nor in fine* allowed that figurative conveyance,* nor so great licence in choice of words and phrases, as metre is.

So as the poets were also from the beginning the best persuaders, and their eloquence the first rhetoric of the world. Even so, it became that the high mysteries of the gods should be revealed and taught by a manner of utterance and language of extraordinary phrase* and brief and compendious, and above all others sweet and civil, as the metrical is. The same also was meetest* to register* the lives and noble gests* of princes and of the great monarchs of the world, and all other the memorable accidents* of time, so as the poet was also the first historiographer. Then, forasmuch as they were the first observers of all natural causes and effects in the things generable and corruptible, and from thence mounted up to search after the celestial courses and influences, and yet penetrated further to know the divine essences and substances separate, as is said before, they were the first astronomers and philosophers and metaphysics.* Finally, because they did altogether endeavour themselves to reduce the life of man to a certain method of good manners, and made the first differences between virtue and vice, and then tempered* all these knowledges and skills with the exercise of a delectable music by melodious instruments, which withal

* *voluble*: moving rapidly, fluent
* *numerous*: rhythmic, harmonious, measured   * *in fine*: at last, in short
* *conveyance*: manner of expression, style   * *phrase*: style
* *meetest*: best, most fitting   * *register*: record   * *gests*: deeds
* *accidents*: events
* *metaphysics*: metaphysicians, philosophers concerned with first principles
* *tempered*: balanced, strengthened

served them to delight their hearers and to call the people together by admiration* to a plausible* and virtuous conversation,* therefore were they the first philosophers ethic and the first artificial musicians of the world. Such was Linus, Orpheus, Amphion and Musaeus, the most ancient poets and philosophers of whom there is left any memory by the profane writers. King David also, and Solomon his son, and many other of the holy prophets wrate in metres and used to sing them to the harp, although to many of us ignorant of the Hebrew language and phrase, and not observing it, the same seem but a prose.[13] It cannot be, therefore, that any scorn or indignity should justly be offered to so noble, profitable, ancient and divine a science* as poesy is.

CHAPTER 5

How the wild and savage people used a natural poesy in versicle* and rhyme as our vulgar is

And the Greek and Latin poesy was by verse numerous and metrical, running upon pleasant feet, sometimes swift, sometime slow (their words very aptly serving that purpose), but without any rhyme or tuneable concord in the end of their verses, as we and all other nations now use. But the Hebrews and Chaldees, who were more ancient than the Greeks, did not only use a metrical poesy, but also with the same a manner of rhyme, as hath been of late observed by learned men.[14] Whereby it appeareth that our vulgar rhyming poesy[15] was common to all the nations of the world besides, whom the Latins and Greeks in special* called barbarous. So as it was, notwithstanding, the first and most ancient poesy, and the most universal, which two points do otherwise give to all human inventions and affairs no small credit. This is proved by

* *admiration*: wonder, reverence   * *plausible*: praiseworthy, acceptable
* *conversation*: mode of society   * *science*: branch of learning
* *versicle*: verse   * *in special*: in particular

certificate* of merchants and travellers, who by late navigations have surveyed the whole world, and discovered large countries and strange peoples wild and savage, affirming that the American,* the Perusian,* and the very* cannibal do sing and also say their highest and holiest matters in certain rhyming versicles and not in prose; which proves also that our manner of vulgar poesy is more ancient than the artificial of the Greeks and Latins, ours coming by instinct of nature, which was before art or observation, and used with the savage and uncivil, who were before all science or civility, even as the naked by priority of time is before the clothed, and the ignorant before the learned. The natural poesy therefore, being aided and amended by art and not utterly altered or obscured, but some sign left of it (as the Greeks and Latins have left none), is no less to be allowed* and commended than theirs.

CHAPTER 6

How the rhyming poesy came first to the Grecians and Latins, and had altered and almost spilt* their manner of poesy

But it came to pass, when fortune fled far from the Greeks and Latins and that their towns flourished no more in traffic,* nor their universities in learning, as they had done continuing* those monarchies, the barbarous conquerors invading them with innumerable swarms of strange* nations, the poesy metrical of the Grecians and Latins came to be much corrupted and altered, insomuch as there were times that the very Greeks and Latins themselves took pleasure in rhyming verses, and used it as a rare* and gallant* thing. Yea, their orators' proses nor the doctors' sermons* were acceptable to princes, nor yet to the

* *certificate*: witness, assurance   * *American*: Native American
* *Perusian*: Peruvian   * *the very*: even the
* *allowed*: approved of, praised   * *spilt*: destroyed   * *traffic*: trade
* *continuing*: during   * *strange*: foreign   * *rare*: fine, splendid
* *gallant*: excellent   * *doctors' sermons*: teachers' discourses

common people, unless it went in manner of tuneable rhyme or metrical sentences, as appears by many of the ancient writers about that time and since. And the great princes and popes and sultans would one salute and greet another – sometime in friendship and sport, sometime in earnest and enmity – by rhyming verses, and nothing seemed clerkly* done but must be* done in rhyme. Whereof we find divers examples from the time of the Emperors Gratian and Valentian downwards.[16] For thenabouts began the declination* of the Roman Empire by the notable inundations of the Huns and Vandals in Europe, under the conduct of Totila and Attila and other their generals. This brought the rhyming poesy in grace* and made it prevail in Italy and Greece (their own long time cast aside and almost neglected), till, after many years, that the peace of Italy and of the Empire occidental* revived new clerks,* who, recovering and perusing the books and studies of the civiler ages, restored all manner of arts, and that of the Greek and Latin poesy withal, into their former purity and neatness.[17] Which, nevertheless, did not so prevail but that the rhyming poesy of the barbarians remained still in his reputation: that one in the school,* this other in courts of princes, more ordinary and allowable.

CHAPTER 7

How in the time of Charlemagne and many years after him the Latin poets wrote in rhyme

And this appeareth evidently by the works of many learned men who wrote about the time of Charlemagne's reign in the Empire occidental, where the Christian religion became, through the excessive authority of popes and deep devotion of princes,

---

* *clerkly*: learnedly   * *but must be*: unless it was   * *declination*: decline
* *grace*: favour   * *Empire occidental*: Western Roman Empire
* *clerks*: scholars   * *in the school*: amongst scholars and teachers

strongly fortified and established by erection of orders monastical, in which many simple clerks for devotion sake and
sanctity were received more than for any learning, by which
occasion and the solitariness of their life waxing studious, without discipline or instruction by any good method, some of them
grew to be historiographers, some poets, and, following either
the barbarous rudeness* of the time or else their own idle
inventions, all that they wrote to the favour or praise of princes
they did it in such manner of minstrelsy, and thought themselves no small fools when they could make their verses go all
in rhyme. [*examples of political and religious uses of rhymed
Latin verse*]

And as this was used in the greatest and gayest matters of
princes and popes, by the idle invention of monastical men then
reigning all in their superlative,* so did every scholar and secular
clerk or versifier when he wrote any short poem or matter of
good lesson put it in rhyme, whereby it came to pass that all
your old proverbs and common sayings, which they would have
plausible* to the reader and easy to remember and bear away,
were of that sort. [. . .] Thus, what in writing of rhymes and
registering of lies was the clergy of that fabulous* age wholly
occupied.

[*examples of formal conceits*]

Thus you may see the humours and appetites of men how
diverse and changeable they be in liking new fashions, though
many times worse than the old, and not only in the manner of
their life and use of their garments, but also in their learnings
and arts, and specially of their languages.

---

* *rudeness*: lack of civilization or education   * *superlative*: pre-eminence
* *plausible*: gratifying   * *fabulous*: legendary, fabled

CHAPTER 8

In what reputation poesy and poets were in old time with princes and otherwise generally, and how they be now become contemptible and for what causes

For the respects aforesaid, in all former ages and in the most civil countries and commonwealths, good poets and poesy were highly esteemed and much favoured of the greatest princes. For proof whereof we read how much Amyntas, King of Macedonia made of the tragical poet Euripides, and the Athenians of Sophocles; in what price the noble poems of Homer were holden with Alexander the Great,[18] insomuch as every night they were laid under his pillow, and by day were carried in the rich jewel coffer of Darius, lately before vanquished by him in battle; and not only Homer, the father and prince of the poets, was so honoured by him, but for his sake all other meaner poets, insomuch as Choerilus, one no very great good poet, had for every verse well made a Philip's noble* of gold,[19] amounting in value to an angel* English, and so for every hundred verses (which a cleanly* pen could speedily despatch) he had a hundred angels. And since Alexander the Great, how Theocritus, the Greek poet, was favoured by Ptolemy, King of Egypt, and Queen Berenice his wife, Ennius, likewise, by Scipio, prince of the Romans, Virgil also by the Emperor Augustus.[20] And in later times how much were Jean de Meung and Guillaume de Lorris made of by the French kings, and Geoffrey Chaucer, father of our English poets, by Richard the Second, who, as it was supposed, gave him the manor of Ewelme in Oxfordshire; and Gower to Henry the Fourth, and Hardyng to Edward the Fourth.[21] Also how Francis the French king made Saint-Gelais, Salmonius Macrinus and Clement Marot of his privy chamber for their excellent skill in vulgar and Latin poesy.[22] And King Henry the Eighth, her Majesty's father, for a few Psalms of David turned into English metre by Sternhold made him groom

* *noble*: gold coin   * *angel*: gold coin   * *cleanly*: deft

of his privy chamber and gave him many other good gifts.[23] And one Gray, what good estimation did he grow unto with the same King Henry, and afterward with the Duke of Somerset, Protector, for making certain merry ballads, whereof one chiefly was 'The hunt is up, the hunt is up'?[24] And Queen Mary, his daughter, for one epithalamy or nuptial song made by Vargas, a Spanish poet, at her marriage with King Philip in Winchester, gave him during his life two hundred crowns' pension.[25]

Nor this reputation was given them in ancient times altogether in respect that poesy was a delicate* art, and the poets themselves cunning* prince-pleasers, but for that also they were thought for their universal knowledge to be very sufficient men for the greatest charges in their commonwealths, were it for counsel or for conduct, whereby no man need to doubt but that both skills may very well concur and be most excellent in one person. For we find that Julius Caesar, the first Emperor and a most noble captain, was not only the most eloquent orator of his time, but also a very good poet, though none of his doings therein be now extant.[26] And Quintus Catulus a good poet, and Cornelius Gallus, treasurer of Egypt;[27] and Horace, the most delicate* of all the Roman lyrics,* was thought meet* and by many letters of great instance provoked to be Secretary of Estate to Augustus the Emperor, which nevertheless he refused, for his unhealthfulness' sake, and being a quiet-minded man and nothing ambitious of glory, *non voluit accedere ad Rempublicam,* * as it is reported.[28] And Ennius, the Latin poet, was not, as some perchance think, only favoured by Scipio the African for his good making of verses, but used as his familiar* and counsellor in the wars for his great knowledge and amiable conversation.[29] And long before that, Antimenides and other Greek poets, as Aristotle reports in his *Politics*, had charge in the wars.[30] And Tyrtaeus the poet, being also a lame man and halting upon one leg, was chosen by the oracle of the gods from the Athenians to be general of the Lacedemonians' army, not

* *delicate*: delightful, elegant   * *cunning*: learned, skilful
* *delicate*: skilful   * *lyrics*: lyric poets   * *meet*: suitable
* *non ... Rempublicam*: 'he did not want to take part in politics'
* *familiar*: close friend

for his poetry, but for his wisdom and grave persuasions, and subtle stratagems whereby he had the victory over his enemies.[31] So as the poets seemed to have skill not only in the subtleties of their art, but also to be meet for all manner of functions civil and martial, even as they found favour of the times they lived in, insomuch as their credit and estimation generally was not small.

But in these days, although some learned princes may take delight in them, yet universally it is not so. For as well poets as poesy are despised, and the name become, of honourable, infamous, subject to scorn and derision, and rather a reproach than a praise to any that useth it. For commonly who so is studious in the art or shows himself excellent in it, they call him in disdain a 'fantastical'; and a light-headed or fantastical man (by conversion) they call a poet. And this proceeds through the barbarous ignorance of the time, and pride of many gentlemen and others, whose gross heads not being brought up or acquainted with any excellent art, nor able to contrive or in manner conceive any matter of subtlety in any business or science, they do deride and scorn it in all others as superfluous knowledges and vain sciences, and whatsoever device* be of rare invention they term it 'fantastical', construing it to the worst side; and among men such as be modest and grave and of little conversation, nor delighted in the busy life and vain ridiculous actions of the popular, they call him in scorn a 'philosopher' or 'poet', as much to say as a fantastical man, very injuriously (God wot),* and to the manifestation of their own ignorance, not making difference betwixt terms. For as the evil and vicious disposition of the brain hinders the sound judgement and discourse of man with busy and disordered fantasies, for which cause the Greeks call him *phantastikos*, so is that part,[32] being well affected,* not only nothing disorderly or confused with any monstrous imaginations or conceits,* but very formal,* and in his much multiformity uniform, that is, well proportioned, and so passing clear, that by it as by a glass or

---

* *device*: plan, contrivance, conceit, piece of writing   * *wot*: knows
* *affected*: disposed   * *conceits*: ideas, imaginings
* *formal*: methodical, sane

mirror are represented unto the soul all manner of beautiful visions, whereby the inventive part of the mind is so much holpen as without it no man could devise any new or rare thing. And where it is not excellent in his kind, there could be no politic captain,* nor any witty* engineer or cunning artificer, nor yet any law-maker or counsellor of deep discourse; yea, the prince of philosophers sticks* not to say *animam non intellegere absque phantasmate*,* which text to another purpose Alexander Aphrodisias well noteth, as learned men know.[33]

And this fantasy may be resembled to a glass, as hath been said, whereof there be many tempers* and manner of makings, as the perspectives* do acknowledge, for some be false glasses and show things otherwise than they be indeed, and others right as they be indeed, neither fairer nor fouler, nor greater nor smaller. There be again of these glasses that show things exceeding fair and comely; others that show figures very monstrous and ill-favoured. Even so is the fantastical part of man (if it be not disordered) a representer of the best, most comely and beautiful images or appearances of things to the soul and according to their very truth. If otherwise, then doth it breed chimeras and monsters in man's imaginations, and not only in his imaginations but also in all his ordinary actions and life which ensues. Wherefore, such persons as be illuminated with the brightest irradiations of knowledge and of the verity and due proportion of things, they are called by the learned men not *phantastikoi* but *euphantasiōtoi*,*[34] and of this sort of fantasy are all good poets, notable captains stratagematic, all cunning artificers and engineers, all legislators, politicians and counsellors of estate, in whose exercises the inventive part is most employed and is to the sound and true judgement of man most needful.

This diversity in the terms perchance every man hath not

---

* *politic captain*: political, or shrewd, leader   * *witty*: wise, clever
* *sticks*: scruples, hesitates
* *animam ... phantasmate*: 'the mind does not think without an image'
* *tempers*: mixtures, types   * *perspectives*: optical instruments
* *phantastikoi ... euphantasiōtoi*: 'fantastics' ... 'those having good imaginations'

noted, and thus much be said in defence of the poet's honour, to the end no noble and generous mind be discomforted in the study thereof; the rather for that worthy and honourable memorial* of that noble woman, twice French queen, Lady Anne of Britanny, wife first to King Charles VIII and after to Louis XII, who, passing one day from her lodging toward the King's side, saw in a gallery Master Alain Chartier[35] the King's secretary, an excellent maker or poet, leaning on a table's end asleep, and stooped down to kiss him, saying thus in all their hearings: 'We may not of princely courtesy pass by and not honour with our kiss the mouth from whence so many sweet ditties* and golden poems have issued.' But methinks at these words I hear some smilingly say, 'I would be loath to lack living of my own till the prince gave me a manor of Ewelme for my rhyming.'[36] And another to say, 'I have read that the lady Cynthia came once down out of her sky to kiss the fair young lad Endymion as he lay asleep,[37] and many noble queens that have bestowed kisses upon their princes paramours, but never upon any poets.' The third, methinks, shruggingly saith, 'I kept not to sit sleeping with my poesy till a queen came and kissed me.' But what of all this? Princes may give a good poet such convenient* countenance* and also benefit as are due to an excellent artificer, though they neither kiss nor coax* them and the discreet poet looks for no such extraordinary favours, and as well doth he honour by his pen the just, liberal or magnanimous prince as the valiant, amiable or beautiful, though they be every one of them the good gifts of God. So it seems not altogether the scorn and ordinary disgrace offered unto poets at these days is cause why few gentlemen do delight in the art, but for that liberality is come to fail in princes, who for their largesse were wont to be accounted the only patrons of learning and first founders* of all excellent artificers.

Besides, it is not perceived that princes themselves do take any pleasure in this science, by whose example the subject is commonly led and allured to all delights and exercises, be they

* *memorial*: story   * *ditties*: songs, lyric poems   * *convenient*: suitable
* *countenance*: favour, support, patronage   * *coax*: make a pet of
* *founders*: supporters, patrons

good or bad, according to the grave saying of the historian: *rex multitudinem religione implevit, quae semper regenti similis est.**[38] And peradventure, in this iron and malicious age of ours, princes are less delighted in it, being over-earnestly bent and affected to the affairs of empire and ambition, whereby they are, as it were, enforced to endeavour themselves to arms and practices of hostility, or to intend to the right policing* of their states, and have not one hour to bestow upon any other civil or delectable art of natural or moral doctrine, nor scarce any leisure to think one good thought in perfect and godly contemplation, whereby their troubled minds might be moderated and brought to tranquillity. So as it is hard to find in these days of noblemen or gentlemen any good mathematician, or excellent musician, or notable philosopher, or else a cunning poet, because we find few great princes much delighted in the same studies. Now, also, of such among the nobility or gentry as be very well seen* in many laudable sciences, and especially in making or poesy, it is so come to pass that they have no courage to write, and if they have, yet are they loath to be known of their skill. So as I know very many notable gentlemen in the court that have written commendably and suppressed it again, or else suffered it to be published without their own names to it, as if it were a discredit for a gentleman to seem learned, and to show himself amorous of any good art.[39] In other ages it was not so, for we read that kings and princes have written great volumes and published them under their own regal titles. As to begin with Solomon, the wisest of kings; Julius Caesar, the greatest of emperors; Hermes Trismegistus, the holiest of priests and prophets; Evax, King of Arabia, wrote a book of precious stones in verse; Prince Avicenna of physic and philosophy; Alphonsus, King of Spain, his astronomical tables; Almanzor, a king of Morocco, diverse philosophical works;[40] and, by their regal example, our late sovereign lord King Henry the Eighth wrate a book in defence of his faith, then persuaded that it was the true and apostolical doctrine, though it hath appeared otherwise since, yet his

---

* *rex . . . est*: 'the king filled the people with reverence, which is always similar to ruling'   * *policing*: regulation, governing   * *seen*: versed

honour and learned zeal was nothing less to be allowed.[41]
Queens, also, have been known studious and to write large
volumes, as Lady Margaret of France, Queen of Navarre,[42] in
our time. But of all others the Emperor Nero was so well learned
in music and poesy as, when he was taken by order of the senate
and appointed to die, he offered violence to himself and said, O
quantus artifex pereo!,* as much to say as how is it possible a
man of such science and learning as myself should come to this
shameful death?[43] The Emperor Octavian, being made executor
to Virgil, who had left by his last will and testament that his
books of the Aeneidos should be committed to the fire as things
not perfected by him, made his excuse for infringing the dead's
will by a number of verses most excellently written, whereof
these are part:

> frangatur potius legum veneranda potestas,
> quam tot congestos noctesque diesque labores
> hauserit una dies;*

and put his name to them.[44] And before him his uncle and father
adoptive Julius Caesar was not ashamed to publish under his
own name his commentaries of the French and Britain wars.

Since, therefore, so many noble emperors, kings and princes
have been studious of poesy and other civil arts, and not
ashamed to bewray* their skills in the same, let none other
meaner person despise learning, nor (whether it be in prose or
in poesy) if they themselves be able to write, or have written
anything well or of rare invention, be any whit squeamish to let
it be published under their names, for reason serves it, and
modesty doth not repugn.*

* O . . . pereo!: 'O, how great an artist is undone!'
* frangatur . . . dies: 'rather let the sacred force of laws be broken, than that the
great labours of days and nights one day should consume'
* bewray: betray, show   * repugn: object, oppose

CHAPTER 9

How poesy should not be employed upon vain conceits, or
vicious, or infamous

Wherefore, the nobility and dignity of the art considered, as
well by universality as antiquity and the natural excellence of
itself, poesy ought not to be abased and employed upon any
unworthy matter and subject, nor used to vain purposes, which
nevertheless is daily seen, and that is to utter conceits* infamous
and vicious, or ridiculous and foolish, or of no good example
and doctrine;* albeit in merry matters (not unhonest) being used
for man's solace* and recreation, it may be well allowed, for,
as I said before, poesy is a pleasant manner of utterance, varying
from the ordinary, of purpose to refresh the mind by the ear's
delight. Poesy also is not only laudable because I said it was a
metrical speech used by the first men, but because it is a metrical
speech corrected and reformed by discreet judgements, and with
no less cunning and curiosity* than the Greek and Latin poesy,
and by art beautified and adorned, and brought far from the
primitive rudeness of the first inventors: otherwise it might be
said to me that Adam and Eve's aprons* were the gayest*
garments because they were the first, and the shepherds' tent or
pavilion* the best housing because it was the most ancient and
most universal – which I would not have so taken, for it is not
my meaning but that art and cunning* concurring with nature,
antiquity and universality, in things indifferent* and not evil,
do make them more laudable. And right so our vulgar rhyming
poesy, being by good wits brought to that perfection we see, is
worthily to be preferred before any other manner of utterance
in prose, for such use and to such purpose as it is ordained, and
shall hereafter be set down more particularly.

---

* *conceits*: witty notions   * *doctrine*: lesson   * *solace*: entertainment
* *curiosity*: artfulness   * *aprons*: i.e. fig leaves   * *gayest*: finest
* *pavilion*: large tent   * *cunning*: skill, knowledge
* *indifferent*: unimportant, neutral

CHAPTER 10

The subject or matter of poesy

Having sufficiently said of the dignity of poets and poesy, now
it is time to speak of the matter or subject of poesy, which to
mine intent* is whatsoever witty and delicate conceit of man
meet or worthy to be put in written verse, for any necessary use
of the present time, or good instruction of the posterity. But the
chief and principal is the laud,* honour and glory of the immortal gods (I speak now in phrase of the gentiles);* secondly, the
worthy gests of noble princes; the memorial and registry of all
great fortunes; the praise of virtue and reproof of vice; the
instruction of moral doctrines; the revealing of sciences natural
and other profitable arts; the redress* of boisterous and sturdy
courages* by persuasion; the consolation and repose of temperate minds; finally, the common solace of mankind in all his
travails and cares of this transitory life. And in this last sort,
being used for recreation only, may allowably bear matter not
always of the gravest or of any great commodity* or profit, but
rather in some sort vain, dissolute or wanton, so it be not very
scandalous and of evil example. But as our intent is to make this
art vulgar for all Englishmen's use, and therefore are of necessity
to set down the principal rules therein to be observed, so in mine
opinion it is no less expedient to touch briefly all the chief points
of this ancient poesy of the Greeks and Latins, so far forth as it
conformeth with ours, so as it may be known what we hold of
them as borrowed and what as of our own peculiar.* Wherefore,
now that we have said what is the matter of poesy, we will
declare the manner and forms of poems used by the ancients.

---

* *intent*: meaning, understanding   * *laud*: praise
* *gentiles*: heathens, pagans   * *redress*: correction
* *boisterous and sturdy courages*: violent and fierce dispositions
* *commodity*: benefit   * *peculiar*: property

CHAPTER II

*Of poems and their sundry forms, and how thereby the
ancient poets received surnames**

As the matter of poesy is diverse, so was the form of their poems
and manner of writing, for all of them wrote not in one sort,
even as all of them wrote not upon one matter. Neither was
every poet alike cunning in all as in some one kind of poesy, nor
uttered with like felicity. But wherein any one most excelled,
thereof he took a surname, as to be called a poet heroic, lyric,
elegiac, epigrammatist or otherwise. Such therefore as gave
themselves to write long histories of the noble gests of kings and
great princes, intermeddling the dealings of the gods, half-gods*
or heroes of the gentiles, and the great and weighty consequences
of peace and war, they called poets heroic, whereof Homer was
chief and most ancient among the Greeks, Virgil among the
Latins. Others, who more delighted to write songs or ballads of
pleasure to be sung with the voice and to the harp, lute or
cithern* and such other musical instruments, they were called
melodious poets (*melici*) or, by a more common name, lyric
poets, of which sort was Pindarus,* Anacreon and Callimachus,
with others, among the Greeks, Horace and Catullus among the
Latins. There were another sort, who sought the favour of fair
ladies, and coveted to bemoan their estates* at large and the
perplexities of love in a certain piteous verse called elegy, and
thence were called elegiac: such among the Latins were Ovid,
Tibullus and Propertius. There were also poets that wrote only
for the stage, I mean plays and interludes, to recreate the people
with matters of disport, and to that intent did set forth in shows
– pageants, accompanied with speech – the common behaviours
and manner of life of private persons, and such as were the
meaner sort of men, and they were called comical poets, of
whom among the Greeks Menander and Aristophanes were

* *surnames*: titles   * *half-gods*: demigods
* *cithern*: medieval stringed instrument   * *Pindarus*: i.e. Pindar
* *estates*: conditions

most excellent, with the Latins Terence and Plautus. Besides
those poets comic there were other who served also the stage
but meddled not with so base matters, for they set forth
the doleful falls of unfortunate and afflicted princes, and were
called poets tragical. Such were Euripides and Sophocles with
the Greeks, Seneca among the Latins. There were yet others
who mounted nothing so high as any of them both, but in base
and humble style, by manner of dialogue, uttered the private
and familiar talk of the meanest sort of men, as shepherds, haywards* and such like. Such was among the Greeks
Theocritus, and Virgil among the Latins; their poems were
named eclogues, or shepherdly talk. There was yet another kind
of poet, who intended to tax the common abuses and vice of the
people in rough and bitter speeches, and their invectives were
called satires and themselves satirics. Such were Lucilius,
Juvenal and Persius among the Latins, and with us he that wrote
the book called *Piers Plowman*. Others, of a more fine and
pleasant head, were given wholly to taunting and scoffing at
undecent* things, and in short poems uttered pretty, merry
conceits, and these men were called epigrammatists. There
were others that, for the people's good instruction and trial of
their own wits, used in places of great assembly to say by rote
numbers of short and sententious metres, very pithy and of good
edification, and thereupon were called poets mimists,[45] as who
would say imitable and meet to be followed for their wise and
grave lessons. There was another kind of poem, invented only
to make sport, and to refresh the company with a manner of
buffoonery or counterfeiting of merry speeches, converting all
that which they had heard spoken before to a certain derision
by a quite contrary sense; and this was done when comedies or
tragedies were a-playing, and that between the acts, when the
players went to make ready for another, there was great silence
and the people waxed weary – then came in these manner of
counterfeit vices (they were called *pantomimi*),[46] and all that
had before been said, or great part of it, they gave a cross*
construction to it very ridiculously. Thus have you how the

---

* *haywards*: herdsmen   * *undecent*: improper   * *cross*: contrary

names of the poets were given them by the forms of their poems
and manner of writing.

CHAPTER 12

*In what form of poesy the gods of the gentiles were praised
and honoured*

The gods of the gentiles were honoured by their poets in hymns,
which is an extraordinary and divine praise, extolling and mag-
nifying them for their great powers and excellency of nature in
the highest degree of laud, and yet therein their poets were after
a sort restrained, so as they could not with their credit untruly
praise their own gods, or use in their lauds any manner of gross
adulation or unveritable report: for in any writer untruth and
flattery are counted most great reproaches. Wherefore, to praise
the gods of the gentiles, for that by authority of their own
fabulous records they had fathers and mothers, and kindred and
allies, and wives and concubines, the poets first commended
them by their genealogies or pedigrees, their marriages and
alliances, their notable exploits in the world for the behoof* of
mankind, and yet, as I said before, none otherwise than the
truth of their own memorials might bear, and in such sort as it
might be well avouched* by their old written reports; though in
very deed they were not from the beginning all historically true,
and many of them very fictions, and such of them as were true
were grounded upon some part of an history or matter of verity,
the rest altogether figurative and mystical, covertly applied to
some moral or natural sense, as Cicero setteth it forth in his
books *De natura deorum.*[47] For to say that Jupiter was son to
Saturn, and that he married his own sister Juno, might be true,
for such was the guise* of all great princes in the oriental part
of the world both at those days, and now is. Again, that he loved
Danae, Europa, Leda, Callisto and other fair ladies, daughters

---

* *behoof*: benefit   * *avouched*: certified   * *guise*: manner

to kings, besides many meaner women, it is likely enough, because he was reported to be a very incontinent person, and given over to his lusts, as are for the most part all the greatest princes. But that he should be the highest god in heaven, or that he should thunder and lighten, and do many other things very unnaturally and absurdly; also that Saturnus should geld his father Caelus, to the intent to make him unable to get any more children, and other such matters as are reported by them – it seemeth to be some witty device and fiction made for a purpose, or a very notable and impudent lie, which could not be reasonably suspected by the poets, who were otherwise discreet and grave men, and teachers of wisdom to others.[48] Therefore, either to transgress the rules of their primitive records, or to seek to give their gods honour by belying them (otherwise than in that sense which I have alleged), had been a sign not only of an unskilful poet but also of a very impudent and lewd man: for untrue praise never giveth any true reputation.

But with us Christians, who be better disciplined,* and do acknowledge but one God Almighty, everlasting and in every respect self-suffisant* (autarkēs),[49] reposed in all perfect rest and sovereign bliss, not needing or exacting any foreign help or good – to Him we cannot exhibit overmuch praise, nor belie Him any ways, unless it be in abasing His excellency by scarcity of praise, or by misconceiving His divine nature, weening* to praise Him, if we impute to Him such vain delights and peevish affections as commonly the frailest men are reproved for: namely, to make Him ambitious of honour; jealous and difficult in His worships; terrible, angry, vindictive; a lover, a hater, a pitier; and indigent* of man's worship; finally, so passionate as in effect He should be altogether anthrōpopathēs.* To the gods of the gentiles they might well attribute these infirmities, for they were but the children of men, great princes and famous in the world, and not for any other respect divine than by some resemblance of virtue they had to do good and to benefit many.

* disciplined: instructed   * self-suffisant: self-sufficient
* weening: thinking   * indigent: needy
* anthrōpopathēs: 'having human feelings'

So as to the God of the Christians such divine praise might be verified, to the other gods none, but figuratively or in mystical sense, as hath been said. In which sort the ancient poets did indeed give them great honours and praises, and made to them sacrifices and offered them oblations of sundry sorts, even as the people were taught and persuaded by such placations and worships to receive any help, comfort or benefit to themselves, their wives, children, possessions or goods. For if that opinion were not, who would acknowledge any god, the very etymology of the name with us of the north parts of the world declaring plainly the nature of the attribute, which is all one as if we say good (*bonus*) or a giver of good things?[50] Therefore, the gentiles prayed for peace to the goddess Pallas; for war (such as thrived by it) to the god Mars; for honour and empire to the god Jupiter; for riches and wealth to Pluto; for eloquence and gain to Mercury; for safe navigation to Neptune; for fair weather and prosperous winds to Aeolus; for skill in music and leechcraft* to Apollo; for free life and chastity to Diana; for beauty and good grace, as also for issue and prosperity in love, to Venus; for plenty of crop and corn to Ceres; for seasonable* vintage to Bacchus; and for other things to others, so many things as they could imagine good and desirable, and to so many gods as they supposed to be authors thereof, insomuch as fortune was made a goddess and the fever quartan* had her altars, such blindness and ignorance reigned in the hearts of men at that time – and whereof it first proceeded and grew, besides the opinion hath been given, appeareth more at large in our books of *Hierotechnē*,[51] the matter being of another consideration than to be treated of in this work. And these hymns to the gods was the first form of poesy, and the highest and the stateliest, and they were sung by the poets as priests, and by the people or whole congregation as we sing in our churches the Psalms of David. But they did it commonly in some shady groves of tall timber trees, in which places they reared altars of green turf and bestrewed them all over with flowers, and upon them offered

* *leechcraft*: skill in healing   * *seasonable*: occurring at the right time
* *fever quartan*: quartan fever, characterized by paroxysms every fourth day

their oblations and made their bloody sacrifices (for no kind of
gift can be dearer than life), of such quick cattle* as every god
was in their conceit most delighted in, or in some other respect
most fit for the mystery:* temples or churches or other chapels
than these they had none at those days.

CHAPTER 13

*In what form of poesy vice and the common abuses of man's
life was reprehended*

Some perchance would think that next after the praise and
honouring of their gods should commence the worshippings
and praise of good men, and specially of great princes and
governors of the earth, in sovereignty and function next unto
the gods. But it is not so, for before that came to pass the poets
or holy priests chiefly studied the rebuke of vice, and to carp at
the common abuses, such as were most offensive to the public
and private, for as yet, for lack of good civility and wholesome
doctrines, there was greater store of lewd lurdans* than of
wise and learned lords or of noble and virtuous princes and
governors. So as next after the honours exhibited to their
gods, the poets, finding in man generally much to reprove and
little to praise, made certain poems in plain metres, more like to
sermons or preachings than otherwise, and when the people
were assembled together in those hallowed places dedicate to
their gods – because they had yet no large halls or places of
conventicle,* nor had any other correction of their faults but
such as rested only in rebukes of wise and grave men, such as at
these days make the people ashamed rather than afeard – the
said ancient poets used for that purpose three kinds of poems
reprehensive,* to wit the satire, the comedy and the tragedy.
And the first and most bitter invective against vice and vicious

* *quick cattle*: livestock   * *mystery*: rite   * *lurdans*: layabouts, loafers
* *conventicle*: assembly   * *reprehensive*: containing reproof

men was the satire, which, to the intent their bitterness should breed none ill will, either to the poets or to the reciters (which could not have been chosen if they had been openly known), and, besides, to make their admonitions and reproofs seem graver and of more efficacy, they made wise* as if the gods of the woods, whom they called satyrs or sylvans, should appear and recite those verses of rebuke, whereas indeed they were but disguised persons under the shape of satyrs, as who would say these terrene* and base gods, being conversant with man's affairs and spyers-out of all their secret faults, had some great care over man, and desired by good admonitions to reform the evil of their life, and to bring the bad to amendment, by those kind of preachings; whereupon the poets, inventors of the device, were called satirists.[52]

CHAPTER 14

How vice was afterward reproved by two other manner of poems better reformed than the satire, whereof the first was comedy, the second tragedy

But when these manner of solitary speeches and recitals of rebuke uttered by the rural gods out of bushes and briars seemed not to the finer heads sufficiently persuasive, nor so popular as if it were reduced into action of many persons or by many voices lively* represented to the ear and eye, so as a man might think it were even now a-doing, the poets devised to have many parts played at once by two or three or four persons that debated the matters of the world, sometimes of their own private affairs, sometimes of their neighbours', but never meddling with any princes' matters nor such high personages, but commonly of merchants, soldiers, artificers, good honest householders and also of unthrifty youths, young damsels, old nurses, bawds,

---

* *wise*: in such a manner   * *terrene*: earthly   * *lively*: realistically

brokers, ruffians and parasites,* with such like, in whose
behaviours lieth in effect the whole course and trade of man's
life, and therefore tended altogether to the good amendment of
man by discipline and example. It was also much for the solace
and recreation of the common people by reason of the pageants
and shows. And this kind of poem was called comedy, and
followed next after the satire, and by that occasion was somewhat sharp and bitter, after the nature of the satire, openly and
by express names taxing men more maliciously and impudently
than became,* so as they were enforced for fear of quarrel and
blame to disguise their players with strange apparel, and, by
colouring their faces and carrying hats and caps of diverse
fashions, to make themselves less known. But as time and experience do reform everything that is amiss, so this bitter poem
called the Old Comedy, being disused and taken away, the New
Comedy came in place,[53] more civil and pleasant a great deal,
and not touching any man by name but in a certain generality
glancing at every abuse, so as from thenceforth, fearing none ill
will or enmity at anybody's hands, they left aside their disguisings and played bareface; till one Roscius Gallus, the most
excellent player among the Romans, brought up these vizards,*
which we see at this day used, partly to supply the want of
players, when there were more parts than there were persons,
or that it was not thought meet to trouble and pester princes'
chambers with too many folks: now, by the change of a vizard
one man might play the king and the carter,* the old nurse and
the young damsel, the merchant and the soldier, or any other
part he listed, very conveniently. There be that say Roscius did
it for another purpose, for being himself the best histrion* or
buffoon* that was in his days to be found, insomuch as Cicero
said Roscius contended with him, by variety of lively gestures,
to surmount the copy* of his speech, yet because he was squint-
eyed and had a very unpleasant countenance, and looks which
made him ridiculous or rather odious to the presence, he devised

---

* *parasites*: flatterers   * *became*: was becoming   * *vizards*: masks
* *carter*: a type – any lowly, uncultured person   * *histrion*: actor
* *buffoon*: comic actor   * *copy*: copiousness

these vizards to hide his own ill-favoured face.[54] And thus much touching the comedy.

CHAPTER 15

In what form of poesy the evil and outrageous behaviours of princes were reprehended

But because, in those days when the poets first taxed by satire and comedy, there was no great store of kings or emperors or such high estates (all men being yet for the most part rude and in a manner popularly egall),* they could not say of them or of their behaviours anything to the purpose, which cases of princes are sithence* taken for the highest and greatest matters of all. But after that some men among the more became mighty and famous in the world, sovereignty and dominion having learned them all manner of lusts and licentiousness of life, by which occasions also their high estates and felicities fell many times into most low and lamentable fortunes, whereas before in their great prosperities they were both feared and reverenced in the highest degree, after their deaths, when the posterity stood no more in dread of them, their infamous life and tyrannies were laid open to all the world, their wickedness reproached, their follies and extreme insolencies derided, and their miserable ends painted out in plays and pageants, to show the mutability of fortune and the just punishment of God in revenge of a vicious and evil life. These matters were also handled by the poets and represented by action, as that of the comedies, but because the matter was higher than that of the comedies the poets' style was also higher and more lofty, the provision* greater, the place more magnificent; for which purpose also the players' garments were made more rich and costly and solemn, and every other thing appertaining, according to that rate. So as, where the satire was pronounced by rustical and naked sylvans speaking

* *egall*: equal   * *sithence*: since   * *provision*: preparation

out of a bush, and the common players of interludes called *planipedes*[55] played barefoot upon the floor, the later comedies upon scaffolds* and by men well and cleanly hosed and shod, these matters of great princes were played upon lofty stages, and the actors thereof ware upon their legs buskins* of leather called *cothurni* and other solemn habits,* and for a special pre-eminence did walk upon those high corked shoes or pantofles which now they call in Spain and Italy *cioppini*.[56] And because those buskins and high shoes were commonly made of goats' skins very finely tanned and died into colours, or for that, as some say, the best player's reward was a goat to be given him, or for that, as other think, a goat was the peculiar sacrifice to the god Pan, king of all the gods of the woods, forasmuch as a goat in Greek is called *tragos*, therefore these stately plays were called tragedies.[57] And thus have ye four sundry forms of poesy dramatic reprehensive, and put in execution by the feat and dexterity of man's body, to wit, the satire, Old Comedy, New Comedy and tragedy, whereas all other kind of poems except eclogue – whereof shall be entreated* hereafter – were only recited by mouth or sung with the voice to some melodious instrument.

CHAPTER 16

In what form of poesy the great princes and dominators* of the world were honoured

But as the bad and illaudable parts of all estates* and degrees were taxed by the poets in one sort or another, and those of great princes by tragedy in especial (and not till after their deaths), as hath been before remembered, to the intent that such exemplifying (as it were) of their blames and adversities, being

---

* *scaffolds*: (temporary) platforms   * *buskins*: boots   * *habits*: garments
* *entreated*: handled, treated   * *dominators*: rulers, lords
* *estates*: ranks

now dead, might work for a secret reprehension to others that were alive, living in the same or like abuses, so was it great reason that all good and virtuous persons should for their well-doings be rewarded with commendation, and the great princes above all others with honours and praises, being for many respects of greater moment to have them good and virtuous than any inferior sort of men. Wherefore the poets, being indeed the trumpeters of all praise and also of slander (not slander, but well-deserved reproach), were in conscience and credit bound next after the divine praises of the immortal gods to yield a like rateable* honour to all such amongst men as most resembled the gods by excellency of function, and had a certain affinity with them by more than human and ordinary virtues showed in their actions here upon earth. They were therefore praised by a second degree of laud, showing their high estates, their princely genealogies and pedigrees, marriages alliances and such noble exploits as they had done in the affairs of peace and of war to the benefit of their people and countries, by invention of any noble science or profitable art, or by making wholesome laws or enlarging of their dominions by honourable and just con-quests, and many other ways. Such personages among the gen-tiles were Bacchus, Ceres, Perseus, Hercules, Theseus and many other, who thereby came to be accounted gods and half-gods or goddesses – heroes – and had their commendations given by hymn accordingly, or by such other poems as their memory was thereby made famous to the posterity for ever after, as shall be more at large said in place convenient. [. . .]

[*Chapter 17 – Of the places where their interludes or poems dramatic were represented to the people*]

---

* *rateable*: proportional

CHAPTER 18

Of the shepherds' or pastoral poesy called eclogue, and to
what purpose it was first invented and used

Some be of opinion, and the chief of those who have written in
this art among the Latins, that the pastoral poesy, which we
commonly call by the name of eclogue and bucolic, a term
brought in by the Sicilian poets, should be the first of any other,
and before the satire, comedy or tragedy, because, say they, the
shepherds' and haywards' assemblies and meetings when they
kept their cattle and herds in the common fields and forests was
the first familiar conversation,* and their babble and talk under
bushes and shady trees the first disputation and contentious
reasoning, and their fleshly heats growing of ease the first idle
wooings, and their songs made to their mates or paramours
either upon sorrow or jollity of courage* the first amorous
musics; sometime, also, they sang and played on their pipes for
wagers, striving who should get the best game* and be counted
cunningest. All this I do agree unto, for no doubt the shepherd's
life was the first example of honest fellowship, their trade the
first art of lawful acquisition or purchase, for at those days
robbery was a manner of purchase; so saith Aristotle in his
books of the *Politics*, and that pasturage* was before tillage,*
or fishing, or fowling, or any other predatory art or chevisance.*[58] And all this may be true, for before there was a
shepherd, keeper of his own or of some other body's flock, there
was none owner in the world, quick cattle being the first property
of any foreign* possession (I say foreign because alway men
claimed property in their apparel and armour, and other like
things made by their own travail and industry), nor thereby was
there yet any good town or city or king's palace where pageants
and pomps might be showed by comedies or tragedies. But, for

* *conversation*: mode of society   * *courage*: heart, spirit
* *best game*: victory   * *pasturage*: grazing
* *tillage*: cultivation, agriculture
* *chevisance*: provision of the means of life   * *foreign*: other than personal

all this, I do deny that the eclogue should be the first and most ancient form of artificial* poesy, being persuaded that the poet devised the eclogue long after the other dramatic poems, not of purpose to counterfeit or represent the rustical manner of loves and communications, but under the veil of homely persons and in rude* speeches to insinuate and glance at greater matters, and such as perchance had not been safe to have been disclosed in any other sort, which may be perceived by the eclogues of Virgil, in which are treated by figure* matters of greater importance than the loves of Tityrus and Corydon.[59] These eclogues came after* to contain and inform moral discipline for the amendment of man's behaviour, as be those of Mantuan[60] and other modern poets.

CHAPTER 19

Of historical poesy, by which the famous acts of princes and the virtuous and worthy lives of our forefathers were reported

There is nothing in man, of all the potential* parts of his mind (reason and will except), more noble or more necessary to the active life than memory, because it maketh most to a sound judgement and perfect worldly wisdom, examining and comparing the times past with the present, and, by them both considering the time to come, concludeth with a steadfast resolution what is the best course to be taken in all his actions and advices* in this world. It came upon this reason, experience to be so highly commended* in all consultations of importance, and preferred before any learning or science, and yet experience is no more than a mass of memories assembled – that is, such trials as man hath made in time before. Right so, no kind of argument

---

* *artificial*: governed by rules of art   * *rude*: unrefined
* *by figure*: allegorically   * *after*: later   * *potential*: powerful
* *advices*: plans
* *It came . . . commended*: i.e. For this reason experience came to be so highly commended

in all the oratory craft doth better persuade and more universally satisfy than example, which is but the representation of old memories and like successes* happened in times past. For these regards the poesy historical is, of all other, next the divine most honourable and worthy, as well for the common benefit as for the special comfort every man receiveth by it, no one thing in the world with more delectation* reviving our spirits than to behold, as it were in a glass, the lively image of our dear fore-fathers, their noble and virtuous manner of life, with other things authentic, which because we are not able otherwise to attain to the knowledge of by any of our senses, we apprehend them by memory, whereas the present time and things so swiftly pass away as they give us no leisure almost to look into them, and much less to know and consider of them thoroughly. The things future, being also events very uncertain and such as cannot possibly be known because they be not yet, cannot be used for example nor for delight otherwise than by hope, though many promise the contrary, by vain and deceitful arts taking upon them to reveal the truth of accidents* to come, which, if it were so as they surmise, are yet but sciences merely conjec-tural, and not of any benefit to man or to the commonwealth where they be used or professed. Therefore the good and exemp-lary things and actions of the former ages were reserved only to the historical reports of wise and grave men; those of the present time left to the fruition and judgement of our senses; the future as hazards and uncertain events utterly neglected and laid aside for magicians and mockers* to get their livings by – such manner of men as, by negligence of magistrates and remissness*[61] of laws, every country breedeth great store of.

These historical men nevertheless used not the matter so precisely to wish that all they wrote should be accounted true, for that was not needful nor expedient to the purpose, namely to be used either for example or for pleasure, considering that many times it is seen a feigned matter or altogether fabulous, besides that it maketh more mirth than any other, works no less

---

* *successes*: fortunes, events   * *delectation*: delight   * *accidents*: events
* *mockers*: deceivers, phonies   * *remissness*: negligence, relaxation

good conclusions for example than the most true and veritable, but often times more, because the poet hath the handling of them to fashion at his pleasure, but not so of the other, which must go according to their verity and none otherwise, without the writer's great blame.[62] Again, as ye know, more, and more excellent, examples may be feigned in one day by a good wit than many ages through man's frailty are able to put in ure,* which made the learned and witty men of those times to devise many historical matters of no verity at all, but with purpose to do good and no hurt, as using them for a manner of discipline and precedent of commendable life. Such was the commonwealth of Plato and Sir Thomas More's *Utopia*,[63] resting all in device* but never put in execution, and easier to be wished than to be performed. And you shall perceive that histories were of three sorts – wholly true and wholly false, and a third holding part of either, but for honest recreation – and good example they were all of them. And this may be apparent to us not only by the poetical histories but also by those that be written in prose. For as Homer wrate a fabulous or mixed report of the siege of Troy, and another of Ulysses' errors* or wanderings, so did Musaeus compile a true treatise of the life and loves of Leander and Hero – both of them heroic, and to none ill edification. Also, as Thucydides wrate a worthy and veritable history of the wars betwixt the Athenians and the Peloponneses, so did Xenophon, a most grave philosopher and well-trained courtier and counsellor, make another (but feigned and untrue) of the childhood of Cyrus, King of Persia – nevertheless both to one effect, that is for example and good information* of the posterity.[64]

Now because the actions of mean and base personages tend in very few cases to any great good example (for who passeth* to follow the steps and manner of life of a craftsman, shepherd or sailor, though he were his father or dearest friend – yea, how almost is it possible that such manner of men should be of any virtue* other than their profession requireth?), therefore was

---

* *ure*: practice   * *device*: plan, scheme   * *errors*: wanderings
* *information*: instruction   * *passeth*: attempts   * *virtue*: particular skill

nothing committed to history but matters of great and excellent
persons and things, that the same by irritation* of good courages
(such as emulation causeth) might work more effectually; which
occasioned the story-writer to choose an higher style fit for his
subject, the prosaic* in prose, the poet in metre. And the poet's
was by verse hexameter for his* gravity and stateliness most
allowable; neither would they intermingle him with any other
shorter measure, unless it were in matters of such quality as
became best to be sung with the voice and to some musical
instrument, as were with the Greeks all your hymns and *encomia*
of Pindarus and Callimachus,[65] not very* histories but a manner
of historical reports, in which cases they made those poems in
variable measures and coupled a short verse with a long to serve
that purpose the better. And we ourselves who compiled this
treatise have written for pleasure a little brief romance or historical ditty in the English tongue of the isle of Great Britain, in
short and long metres, and by breaches* or divisions, to be more
commodiously sung to the harp in places of assembly, where
the company shall be desirous to hear of old adventures and
valiances* of noble knights in times past, as are those of King
Arthur and his knights of the Round Table, Sir Bevis of Southampton, Guy of Warwick, and others like.[66] Such as have not
premonition* hereof, and consideration of the causes alleged,*
would peradventure reprove and disgrace* every romance or
short historical ditty for that they be not written in long metres
or verses Alexandrines,* according to the nature and style of
large histories – wherein they should do wrong, for they be
sundry forms of poems and not all one.

* *irritation*: arousing   * *prosaic*: prosaist, prose writer   * *his*: its
* *very*: true   * *by breaches*: in sections   * *valiances*: feats of valour
* *premonition*: prior notification   * *alleged*: cited
* *disgrace*: disparage, discredit   * *verses Alexandrines*: twelve-syllable lines

CHAPTER 20

In what form of poesy virtue in the inferior sort was commended

In every degree and sort of men virtue is commendable, but not egally* – not only because men's estates are unegall, but for that also virtue itself is not in every respect of egall value and estimation. For continence in a king is of greater merit than in a carter, the one having all opportunities to allure him to lusts, and ability to serve his appetites, the other, partly for the baseness of his estate wanting such means and occasions, partly by dread of laws more inhibited and not so vehemently carried away with unbridled affections, and therefore deserve not, in the one and the other, like praise nor equal reward, by the very ordinary course of distributive justice. Even so, parsimony and illiberality are greater vices in a prince than in a private person, and pusillanimity and injustice likewise. For, to the one, fortune hath supplied enough to maintain them in the contrary virtues (I mean fortitude, justice, liberality, and magnanimity), the prince having all plenty to use largesse by, and no want or need to drive him to do wrong; also all the aids that may be to lift up his courage and to make him stout and fearless – *augent animos fortunae*,* saith the mimist,[67] and very truly, for nothing pulleth down a man's heart so much as adversity and lack. Again, in a mean* man prodigality and pride are faults more reprehensible than in princes, whose high estates do require in their countenance, speech and expense a certain extraordinary,* and their functions enforce them sometime to exceed the limits of mediocrity,* not excusable in a private person, whose manner of life and calling hath no such exigence.* Besides, the good and bad of princes is more exemplary, and thereby of greater moment, than the private persons'. Therefore it is that the inferior* persons with their inferior virtues have a certain inferior praise,

* *egally*: equally   * *augent . . . fortunae*: 'riches increase spirits'
* *mean*: lowly, or middling   * *extraordinary*: something extraordinary
* *mediocrity*: moderation   * *exigence*: need   * *inferior*: lower in status

to guerdon* their good with and to comfort them to continue a laudable course in the modest and honest life and behaviour. But this lieth not in written lauds so much as in ordinary reward and commendation to be given them by the mouth of the superior magistrate. For histories were not intended to so general and base a purpose, albeit many a mean soldier and other obscure persons were spoken of and made famous in stories, as we find of Irus the beggar and Thersites the glorious noddy,* whom Homer maketh mention of.[68] But that happened (and so did many like memories of mean men) by reason of some greater personage or matter that it was long of,* which therefore could not be an universal case nor chance to every other good and virtuous person of the meaner sort. Wherefore the poet, in praising the manner of life or death of any mean person, did it by some little ditty or epigram or epitaph, in few verses and mean* style conformable to his subject. So have you how the immortal gods were praised by hymns; the great princes and heroic personages by ballads* of praise called *encomia*; both of them* by historical reports of great gravity and majesty; the inferior persons by other slight poems.

[*Chapter 21 – The form wherein honest and profitable arts and sciences were treated*]

CHAPTER 22

In what form of poesy the amorous affections and allurements were uttered

The first founder of all good affections is honest love, as the mother of all the vicious is hatred. It was not therefore without reason that so commendable, yea honourable a thing as love well meant, were it in princely estate or private, might in all civil

* *guerdon*: reward   * *glorious noddy*: boastful fool
* *long of*: on account of   * *mean*: middling   * *ballads*: songs
* *both of them*: i.e. both 'great princes' and 'heroic personages'

commonwealths be uttered in good form and order, as other
laudable things are. And because love is of all other human
affections the most puissant* and passionate, and most general
to all sorts and ages of men and women, so as, whether it be of
the young or old, or wise or holy, or high estate or low, none
ever could truly brag of any exemption in that case, it requireth
a form of poesy variable, inconstant, affected,* curious and
most witty of any others, whereof the joys were to be uttered in
one sort, the sorrows in another, and by the many forms of
poesy the many moods and pangs of lovers thoroughly to be
discovered* – the poor souls sometimes praying, beseeching, sometime honouring, advancing, praising, another while
railing, reviling and cursing, then sorrowing, weeping,
lamenting, in the end laughing, rejoicing and solacing the
beloved again, with a thousand delicate devices, odes, songs,
elegies, ballads, sonnets and other ditties, moving one way and
another to great compassion.

[*Chapter 23 – The form of poetical rejoicings*]

CHAPTER 24

The form of poetical lamentations

Lamenting is altogether contrary to rejoicing – every man saith
so – and yet is it a piece of joy to be able to lament with ease
and freely to pour forth a man's inward sorrows and the griefs
wherewith his mind is surcharged. This was a very necessary
device of the poet and a fine, besides his poetry to play also the
physician, and not only by applying a medicine to the ordinary
sickness of mankind but by making the very grief itself (in part)
cure of the disease. Now are the causes of man's sorrows many:
the death of his parents, friends, allies and children (though
many of the barbarous nations do rejoice at their burials and

* *puissant*: powerful   * *affected*: artificial   * *discovered*: revealed

sorrow at their births); the overthrows and discomfits* in battle, the subversions of towns and cities, the desolations of countries; the loss of goods and worldly promotions, honour and good renown; finally, the travails and torments of love forlorn or ill bestowed, either by disgrace, denial, delay, and twenty other ways that well-experienced lovers could recite. Such of these griefs as might be refrained or holpen by wisdom and the party's own good endeavour, the poet gave none order to sorrow* them. [. . .] But death, the irrecoverable loss, death, the doleful departure of friends that can never be recontinued by any other meeting or new acquaintance, besides our uncertainty and suspicion of their estates and welfare in the places of their new abode, seemeth to carry a reasonable pretext of just sorrow. Likewise the great overthrows in battle and desolations of countries by wars, as well for the loss of many lives and much liberty as for that it toucheth the whole state, and every private man hath his portion in the damage. Finally, for love, there is no frailty in flesh and blood so excusable as it, no comfort or discomfort greater than the good and bad success thereof, nothing more natural to man, nothing of more force to vanquish his will and to inveigle his judgement. Therefore, of death and burials, of the adversities by wars, and of true love lost or ill bestowed are the only sorrows that the noble poets sought by their art to remove or appease, not with any medicament of a contrary temper, as the Galenists use to cure *contraria contrariis,** but, as the Paracelsians, who cure *similia similibus,** making one dolour to expel another and, in this case, one short sorrowing the remedy of a long and grievous sorrow.[69] [. . .] The third sorrowing was of loves, by long lamentation in elegy (so was their song called), and it was in a piteous manner of metre, placing a limping pentameter after a lusty hexameter,[70] which made it go dolorously more than any other metre.

[*Chapter 25 – Of the solemn rejoicings at the nativity of princes' children*]

* *discomfits*: defeats   * *sorrow*: lament
* *contraria contrariis*: 'opposites by opposites'
* *similia similibus*: 'like by like'

CHAPTER 26

The manner of rejoicings at marriages and weddings

As the consolation of children well begotten is great, no less but
rather greater ought to be that which is occasion of children,
that is honourable matrimony, a love by all laws allowed, not
mutable nor encumbered with such vain cares and passions as
that other love, whereof there is no assurance but loose and
fickle affection occasioned for the most part by sudden sights
and acquaintance of no long trial or experience, nor upon
any other good ground wherein any surety may be conceived.
Wherefore the civil poet could do no less in conscience and
credit than as he had before done to the ballad of birth, now
with much better devotion to celebrate by his poem the cheerful
day of marriages, as well princely as others, for that hath always
been accounted with every country and nation, of never so
barbarous people, the highest and holiest of any ceremony
appertaining to man – a match, forsooth, made for ever and not
for a day, a solace provided for youth, a comfort for age, a knot
of alliance and amity indissoluble. Great rejoicing was therefore
due to such a matter and to so gladsome a time.

This was done in ballad wise,* as the natal* song, and was
sung very sweetly by musicians at the chamber door of the
bridegroom and bride, at such times as shall be hereafter
declared, and they were called epithalamies, as much to say as
ballads at the bedding of the bride[71] – for such as were sung at
the board* at dinner or supper were other musics and not
properly epithalamies. Here, if I shall say that which appertaineth to the art and disclose the mystery of the whole matter, I
must and do with all humble reverence bespeak* pardon of the
chaste and honourable ears, lest I should either offend them
with licentious speech or leave them ignorant of the ancient
guise* in old times used at weddings, in my simple opinion

* *ballad wise*: ballad fashion   * *natal*: of birth
* *board*: table, when laden with food   * *bespeak*: ask for
* *guise*: manner

nothing reprovable. This epithalamy was divided by breaches
into three parts to serve for three several fits,* [72] or times to be
sung. The first breach was sung at the first part of the night,
when the spouse and her husband were brought to their bed,
and at the very chamber door, where in a large utter-room*
used to be (besides the musicians) good store of ladies or gentlewomen of their kinsfolks and others who came to honour the
marriage. And the tunes of the songs were very loud and shrill,
to the intent there might no noise be heard out of the bedchamber
by the screaking* and outcry of the young damsel feeling the
first forces of her stiff and rigorous* young man, she being, as
all virgins, tender and weak, and unexpert in those manner
of affairs. For which purpose also, they used by old nurses
(appointed to that service) to suppress the noise by casting of
pots full of nuts round about the chamber upon the hard floor
or pavement, for they used no mats nor rushes as we do now.
So as the ladies and gentlewomen should have their ears so
occupied, what with music and what with their hands wantonly
scambling* and catching after the nuts, that they could not
intend* to hearken after any other thing. This was, as I said, to
diminish the noise of the laughing, lamenting spouse. The tenor
of that part of the song was to congratulate the first acquaintance
and meeting of the young couple, allowing of their parents'
good discretions in making the match, then afterward to sound
cheerfully to the onset and first encounters of that amorous
battle, to declare the comfort of children and increase of love
by that mean chiefly caused, the bride showing herself every
ways well disposed, and still supplying occasions of new lusts
and love to her husband by her obedience and amorous embrac-
ings and all other allurements.

About midnight or one of the clock the musicians came again
to the chamber door (all the ladies and other women, as they
were of degree,* having taken their leave and being gone to
rest). This part of the ballad was to refresh the faint and wearied

---

* *fits*: songs or sections of a song   * *utter-room*: outer room, antechamber
* *screaking*: screaming   * *rigorous*: rigid
* *scambling*: scrambling, scrabbling   * *intend*: turn their attention
* *as they were of degree*: in order of precedence by rank or family connection

bodies and spirits, and to animate new appetites with cheerful words, encouraging them to the recontinuance of the same entertainments, praising and commending (by supposal)* the good conformities of them both and their desire one to vanquish the other by such friendly conflicts: alleging that the first embracements never bred bairns* by reason of their overmuch affection and heat, but only made passage for children and enforced greater liking to the late-made match; that the second assaults were less rigorous, but more vigorous and apt to advance the purpose of procreation; that, therefore, they should persist in all good appetite with an invincible courage to the end. This was the second part of the epithalamy.

In the morning, when it was fair, broad day and that by likelihood all turns were sufficiently served,* the last acts of the interlude being ended, and that the bride must within few hours arise and apparel herself, no more as a virgin, but as a wife, and about dinnertime must by order come forth *sicut sponsa de thalamo**[73] very demurely and stately, to be seen and acknowledged of her parents and kinsfolks whether she were the same woman or a changeling, or dead or alive, or maimed* by any accident nocturnal, the same musicians came again with this last part, and greeted them both with a psalm* of new applausions,* for that they had either of them so well behaved themselves that night, the husband to rob his spouse of her maidenhead and save her life, the bride so lustily to satisfy her husband's love and scape with so little danger of her person; for which good chance that they should make a lovely truce and abstinence of that war till next night, sealing the placard* of that lovely league with twenty manner of sweet kisses; then by good admonitions informed them to the frugal and thrifty life all the rest of their days, the good man getting and bringing home, the wife saving that which her husband should get, therewith to be the better able to keep good hospitality, according to

---

* *by supposal*: as they supposed, or as is supposed   * *bairns*: children
* *turns . . . served*: purposes . . . accomplished
* *sicut . . . thalamo*: 'like a bride from the marriage-bed'   * *maimed*: injured
* *psalm*: song   * *applausions*: approval, commendation
* *placard*: official document

their estates, and to bring up their children (if God sent any) virtuously, and the better by their own example; finally to persevere all the rest of their life in true and inviolable wedlock. This ceremony was omitted when men married widows or such as had tasted the fruits of love before (we call them well-experienced young women), in whom there was no fear of danger to their persons, or of any outcry at all, at the time of those terrible* approaches.

Thus much touching the usage of epithalamy or bedding ballad of the ancient times, in which if there were any wanton or lascivious matter more than ordinary, which they called *Fescennina licentia,**[74] it was borne withal for that time because of the matter no less requiring. Catullus hath made of them one or two very artificial and civil, but none more excellent than, of late years, a young nobleman, of Germany as I take it, Johannes Secundus, who in that and in his poem *De basiis* passeth any of the ancient or modern poets in my judgement.[75]

CHAPTER 27

The manner of poesy by which they uttered their bitter taunts and privy nips, or witty scoffs, and other merry conceits*

But all the world could not keep, nor any civil ordinance to the contrary so prevail, but that men would and must needs utter their spleens in all ordinary matters also, or else it seemed their bowels would burst. Therefore the poet devised a pretty-fashioned poem short and sweet (as we are wont to say), and called it *epigramma*, in which every merry conceited man might, without any long study or tedious ambage,* make his friend sport and anger his foe, and give a pretty nip or show a sharp conceit in few verses. For this epigram is but an inscription or writing made as it were upon a table, or in a window, or upon

---

* *terrible*: terrifying   * *Fescennina licentia*: 'Fescennine licence'
* *privy*: intimate, private   * *ambage*: circumlocution

the wall or mantle of a chimney,[76] in some place of common resort where it was allowed every man might come or be sitting to chat and prate, as now in our taverns and common tabling houses, where many merry heads meet and scribble with ink, with chalk, or with a coal such matters as they would every man should know and descant* upon. Afterward the same came to be put in paper and in books, and used as ordinary missives, some of friendship, some of defiance, or as other messages of mirth. [further background, including an anecdote about Virgil]

CHAPTER 28

Of the poem called epitaph used for memorial of the dead

An epitaph is but a kind of epigram, only applied to the report of the dead person's estate and degree, or of his other good or bad parts, to his commendation or reproach, and is an inscription such as a man may commodiously write or engrave upon a tomb in few verses,[77] pithy, quick and sententious, for the passer-by to peruse and judge upon without any long tarriance;* so as if it exceed the measure of an epigram, it is then (if the verse be correspondent) rather an elegy than an epitaph, which error many of these bastard rhymers commit, because they be not learned nor (as we are wont to say) their craft's masters, for they make long and tedious discourses and write them in large tables* to be hanged up in churches and chancels over the tombs of great men and others, which be so exceeding long as one must have half a day's leisure to read one of them, and must be called away before he come half to the end – or else be locked into the church by the sexton, as I myself was once served reading an epitaph in a certain cathedral church of England. They be ignorant of poesy that call such long tales by the name of epitaphs; they might better call them elegies, as I said before, and then ought neither to be engraven nor hanged up in tables.

* *descant*: discourse, make remarks   * *tarriance*: delay   * *tables*: boards

I have seen them nevertheless upon many honourable tombs of these late times erected, which do rather disgrace than honour either the matter or maker.

[*Chapter 29 – A certain ancient form of poesy by which men did use to reproach their enemies*]

CHAPTER 30

Of short epigrams, called posies

There be also other like* epigrams that were sent usually for New Year's gifts, or to be printed or put upon their banqueting dishes of sugar-plate* or of marchpanes* and such other dainty meats* as by the courtesy and custom every guest might carry from a common feast home with him to his own house, and were made for the nonce. They were called *nenia* or *apophoreta*,[78] and never contained above one verse, or two at the most, but the shorter the better; we call them posies,[79] and do paint them nowadays upon the backsides of our fruit trenchers* of wood, or use them as devices in rings, and arms, and about such courtly pursuits.

So have we remembered and set forth to your Majesty very briefly all the commended forms of the ancient poesy, which we in our vulgar makings* do imitate and use under these common names: interlude, song, ballad, carol and ditty – borrowing them also from the French, all saving this word 'song', which is our natural Saxon English word; the rest, such as time and usurpation by custom have allowed us, out of the primitive Greek and Latin, as comedy, tragedy, ode, epitaph, elegy, epigram and other more. And we have purposely omitted all such nice or scholastical curiosities* not meet for your Majesty's

---

* *other like*: other kinds of, other similar   * *sugar-plate*: flat cake of sugar
* *marchpanes*: marzipan   * *meats*: foodstuffs   * *trenchers*: platters
* *vulgar makings*: vernacular poems
* *nice . . . curiosities*: fussy or pedantic conceits

contemplation in this our vulgar art, and what we have written of the ancient forms of poems we have taken from the best clerks writing in the same art. The part that next followeth, to wit of proportion, because the Greeks nor Latins never had it in use, nor made any observation, no more than we do of their feet, we may truly affirm to have been the first devisers thereof ourselves, as *autodidaktoi*,* and not to have borrowed it of any other by learning or imitation, and thereby trusting to be holden the more excusable if anything in this our labours happen either to mislike* or to come short of the author's purpose, because commonly the first attempt in any art or engine* artificial is amendable, and in time by often experiences reformed. And so, no doubt, may this device of ours be, by others that shall take the pen in hand after us.

CHAPTER 31

Who in any age have been the most commended writers in our English poesy, and the author's censure given upon them*[80]

It appeareth by sundry records of books both printed and written that many of our countrymen have painfully travailed* in this part; of whose works some appear to be but bare translations, other some matters of their own invention and very commendable, whereof some recital shall be made in this place, to the intent chiefly that their names should not be defrauded of such honour as seemeth due to them for having by their thankful studies so much beautified our English tongue, as at this day it will be found our nation is in nothing inferior to the French or Italian for copy* of language, subtlety of device, good method and proportion in any form of poem, but that they may compare with the most, and perchance pass a great many of them. And I will not reach above the time of King Edward the Third and

* *autodidaktoi*: self-taught persons, autodidacts   * *mislike*: be displeasing
* *engine*: contrivance, product of ingenuity   * *censure*: judgement, criticism
* *travailed*: laboured   * *copy*: copiousness

Richard the Second for any that wrote in English metre,[81] because before their times, by reason of the late Norman conquest, which had brought into this realm much alteration both of our language and laws, and therewithal a certain martial barbarousness, whereby the study of all good learning was so much decayed as long time after no man, or very few, intended* to write in any laudable science – so as beyond that time there is little or nothing worth commendation to be found written in this art.

And those of the first age were Chaucer and Gower, both of them, as I suppose, knights.[82] After whom followed John Lydgate, the monk of Bury, and that nameless who wrote the satire called *Piers Plowman*.[83] Next him followed Hardyng the chronicler, then in King Henry the Eighth's time Skelton, (I wot not for what great worthiness) surnamed the poet laureate.[84] In the latter end of the same king's reign sprong up a new company of courtly makers, of whom Sir Thomas Wyatt the elder and Henry, Earl of Surrey were the two chieftains, who having travelled into Italy, and there tasted the sweet and stately measures and style of the Italian poesy, as novices newly crept out of the schools of Dante, Ariosto and Petrarch, they greatly polished our rude and homely manner of vulgar poesy from that it had been before, and for that cause may justly be said the first reformers of our English metre and style.[85] In the same time, or not long after, was the Lord Nicholas Vaux, a man of much facility in vulgar makings.[86] Afterward, in King Edward the Sixth's time, came to be in reputation for the same faculty Thomas Sternhold, who first translated into English certain Psalms of David, and John Heywood the epigrammatist, who for the mirth and quickness of his conceits, more than for any good learning was in him, came to be well benefited by the King.[87] But the principal man in this profession at the same time was Master Edward Ferrers, a man of no less mirth and felicity that way, but of much more skill and magnificence in his metre, and therefore wrate for the most part to the stage, in tragedy and sometimes in comedy or interlude, wherein he gave the

* *intended*: endeavoured

King so much good recreation as he had thereby many good rewards.[88] In Queen Mary's time flourished above any other Dr Phaer, one that was well learned and excellently well translated into English verse heroical certain books of Virgil's *Aeneidos*.[89] Since him followed Master Arthur Golding, who with no less commendation turned into English metre the *Metamorphoses* of Ovid, and that other doctor who made the supplement to those books of Virgil's *Aeneidos* which Master Phaer left undone.[90]

And in her Majesty's time that now is are sprong up another crew of courtly makers – noblemen and gentlemen of her Majesty's own servants – who have written excellently well, as it would appear if their doings could be found out and made public with the rest. Of which number is first that noble gentleman Edward, Earl of Oxford, Thomas, Lord of Buckhurst, when he was young, Henry, Lord Paget, Sir Philip Sidney, Sir Walter Ralegh, Master Edward Dyer, Master Fulke Greville, Gascoigne, Breton, Turberville and a great many other learned gentlemen, whose names I do not omit for envy but to avoid tediousness, and who have deserved no little commendation.[91]

But of them all particularly this is mine opinion: that Chaucer, with Gower, Lydgate and Harding, for their antiquity ought to have the first place, and Chaucer as the most renowned of them all for the much learning appeareth to be in him above any of the rest. And though many of his books be but bare translations out of the Latin and French, yet are they well handled, as his books of *Troilus and Criseyde* and *The Romaunt of the Rose*, whereof he translated but one half (the device was Jean de Meung's, a French poet).[92] *The Canterbury Tales* were Chaucer's own invention, as I suppose, and where he showeth more the natural* of his pleasant wit than in any other of his works; his similitudes,* comparisons and all other descriptions are such as cannot be amended. His metre heroical of *Troilus and Criseyde* is very grave and stately, keeping the staff* of seven and the verse of ten;[93] his other verses of *The Canterbury*

* *natural*: natural inclination, character   * *similitudes*: similes
* *staff*: stanza

Tales be but riding rhyme,* nevertheless very well becoming the
matter of that pleasant pilgrimage, in which every man's part is
played with much decency.* Gower, saving for his good and
grave moralities,* had nothing in him highly to be commended,
for his verse was homely and without good measure, his words
strained much deal* out of the French writers, his rhyme
wrested, and in his inventions small subtlety. The applications
of his moralities are the best in him, and yet those many times
very grossly bestowed;* neither doth the substance of his works
sufficiently answer the subtlety of his titles. Lydgate, a translator
only and no deviser of that which he wrate, but one that wrate
in good verse. Harding, a poet epic or historical, handled himself
well according to the time and manner of his subject. He that
wrote the satire of *Piers Plowman* seemed to have been a mal-
content of that time, and therefore bent himself wholly to tax
the disorders of that age, and specially the pride of the Roman
clergy, of whose fall he seemeth to be a very true prophet; his
verse is but loose metre and his terms hard and obscure, so as
in them is little pleasure to be taken. Skelton, a sharp satirist,
but with more railing and scoffery than became a poet laureate:
such, among the Greeks, were called *pantomimi*,[94] with us,
buffoons, altogether applying their wits to scurrilities and other
ridiculous matters. Henry, Earl of Surrey and Sir Thomas Wyatt,
between whom I find very little difference, I repute them (as
before) for the two chief lanterns of light to all others that have
since employed their pens upon English poesy: their conceits
were lofty, their styles stately, their conveyance* cleanly,* their
terms proper, their metre sweet and well proportioned, in all
imitating very naturally and studiously their master Francis
Petrarca. The Lord Vaux's commendation lieth chiefly in the
facility of his metre and the aptness of his descriptions, such as he
taketh upon him to make, namely in sundry of his songs, wherein
he showeth the counterfeit action very lively* and pleasantly.

* *riding rhyme*: rhyming couplets   * *decency*: decorum
* *moralities*: moral lessons   * *much deal*: to a great extent
* *grossly bestowed*: clumsily expressed
* *conveyance*: manner of expression, style   * *cleanly*: according to art
* *lively*: realistically, in a lifelike manner

Of the latter sort I think thus: that for tragedy the Lord of Buckhurst and Master Edward Ferrers, for such doings as I have seen of theirs, do deserve the highest price;* the Earl of Oxford and Master Edwards of her Majesty's Chapel for comedy and interlude;[95] for eclogue and pastoral poesy Sir Philip Sidney and Master Chaloner, and that other gentleman who wrate the late *Shepheardes Calender*;[96] for ditty and amorous ode I find Sir Walter Ralegh's vein most lofty, insolent* and passionate; Master Edward Dyer for elegy most sweet, solemn and of high conceit; Gascoigne for a good metre and for a plentiful vein; Phaer and Golding for a learned and well-corrected verse, specially in translation clear and very faithfully answering their author's intent. Others have also written with much facility, but more commendably perchance if they had not written so much nor so popularly. But last in recital and first in degree is the Queen our sovereign lady, whose learned, delicate, noble muse easily surmounteth all the rest that have written before her time or since for sense, sweetness and subtlety, be it in ode, elegy, epigram or any other kind of poem heroic or lyric wherein it shall please her Majesty to employ her pen, even by as much odds as her own excellent estate and degree exceedeth all the rest of her most humble vassals.

* *price*: estimation, honour   * *insolent*: extravagant, unusual

THE SECOND BOOK
OF PROPORTION POETICAL

CHAPTER I

Of proportion poetical

It is said by such as profess the mathematical sciences that all things stand by* proportion, and that without it nothing could stand* to be good or beautiful. The doctors of our theology, to the same effect but in other terms, say that God made the world by number, measure and weight;¹ some for 'weight', say 'tune', and peradventure better, for weight is a kind of measure, or of much conveniency* with it, and therefore in their descriptions be always coupled together *statica* and *metrica*, weight and measures. Hereupon it seemeth the philosopher gathers a triple proportion, to wit, the arithmetical, the geometrical and the musical. And by one of these three is every other proportion guided of the things that have conveniency by relation, as the visible by light, colour and shadow; the audible by stirs,* times* and accents; the odorable by smells of sundry temperaments;* the tastible by savours to the rate;* the tangible by his objects in this or that regard. Of all which we leave to speak, returning to our poetical proportion, which holdeth of* the musical, because, as we said before, poesy is a skill to speak and write harmonically, and verses or rhyme be a kind of musical

---

* *stand by*: depend upon   * *stand*: manage, remain, be judged
* *conveniency*: congruity, similarity   * *stirs*: motions, rhythms
* *times*: units of measurement   * *temperaments*: mixtures, qualities
* *to the rate*: in proportion   * *holdeth of*: belongs to, has affinity with

utterance,* by reason of a certain congruity in sounds pleasing the ear, though not perchance so exquisitely as the harmonical concents* of the artificial* music, consisting in strained* tunes, as is the vocal music, or that of melodious instruments, as lutes, harps, regals,* records* and such like. And this our proportion poetical resteth in five points: staff,* measure, concord,* situation and figure,* all which shall be spoken of in their places.

CHAPTER 2

Of proportion in staff

'Staff', in our vulgar* poesy, I know not why it should be so called, unless it be for that we understand it for a bearer or supporter of a song or ballad, not unlike the old, weak body that is stayed up by his staff and were not otherwise able to walk or stand upright. The Italian called it *stanza*, as if we should say a resting place.[2] And if we consider well the form of this poetical staff, we shall find it to be a certain number of verses* allowed to go altogether and join without any intermission, and do, or should, finish up all the sentences of the same with a full period,* unless it be in some special cases, and there to stay till another staff follow of like sort. And the shortest staff containeth not under four verses, nor the longest above ten: if it pass that number it is rather a whole ditty* than properly a staff. Also, for the more part the staves stand rather upon* the even number of verses than the odd, though there be of both sorts.

The first proportion, then, of a staff is by *quatrain*, or four

---

* *utterance*: speech   * *concents*: concords, harmonies
* *artificial*: made by art   * *strained*: having a strain or melody
* *regals*: small, portable organs   * *records*: recorders   * *staff*: stanza
* *concord*: rhyme   * *figure*: shape   * *vulgar*: vernacular
* *verses*: lines of verse   * *full period*: complete sentence, full stop, period
* *ditty*: poem   * *stand . . . upon*: consist . . . of, depend . . . on

verses; the second of five verses, and is seldom used; the third by *sixain* or six verses, and is not only most usual but also very pleasant to the ear. The fourth is in seven verses, and is the chief of our ancient proportions used by any rhymer writing anything of historical or grave poem, as ye may see in Chaucer and Lydgate, the one writing the loves of Troilus and Cressida, the other of the fall of princes, both by them translated, not devised.[3] The fifth proportion is of eight verses, very stately and heroic, and which I like better than that of seven because it receiveth better band.* The sixth is of nine verses, rare* but very grave. The seventh proportion is of ten verses, very stately, but in many men's opinion too long; nevertheless of very good grace and much gravity. Of eleven and twelve I find none ordinary staves used in any vulgar language, neither doth it serve well to continue any historical report, or ballad, or other song, but is a ditty of itself and no staff; yet some modern writers have used it, but very seldom. Then last of all have ye a proportion to be used in the number of your staves, as to a carol and a ballad, to a song and a round or virelay.[4] For to an historical poem no certain number is limited, but as the matter falls out. Also, a distich or couple* of verses is not to be accounted a staff, but serves for a continuance, as we see in elegy, epitaph, epigram or such metres, of plain concord,* not harmonically intertangled as some other songs of more delicate* music be.

A staff of four verses containeth in itself matter sufficient to make a full period or complement* of sense,[5] though it do not always so, and therefore may go by divisions.* A staff of five verses is not much used, because he that cannot comprehend* his period in four verses will rather drive it into six than leave it in five, for that the even number is more agreeable to the ear than the odd is. A staff of six verses is very pleasant to the ear, and also serveth for a greater complement than the inferior* staves, which maketh him more commonly to be used. A staff

---

* *band*: cohesion, bond, binding quality   * *rare*: fine, splendid
* *couple*: couplet   * *concord*: rhyme, rhyme scheme
* *delicate*: skilful, elegant   * *complement*: completion, full allowance
* *by divisions*: i.e. the period may extend across quatrains
* *comprehend*: conclude, contain   * *inferior*: having fewer lines

of seven verses, most usual with our ancient makers,* also the staff of eight, nine and ten, of larger complement than the rest, are only used by the later makers, and unless they go with very good band do not so well as the inferior staves. Therefore, if ye make your staff of eight by two fours not intertangled, it is not a *huitain* or a staff of eight but two quatrains;[6] so is it in ten verses – not being intertangled they be but two staves of five.

CHAPTER 3

Of proportion in measure

Metre and measure is all one, for what the Greeks call *metron* the Latins call *mensura*,[7] and is but the quantity of a verse, either long or short. The quantity with them consisteth in the number of their feet, and with us in the number of syllables which are comprehended in every verse, not regarding his* feet otherwise than that we allow, in scanning our verse, two syllables to make one short portion (suppose it a foot) in every verse. And after that sort ye may say we have feet in our vulgar rhymes, but that is improperly. For a foot, by his sense natural, is a member* of office and function, and serveth to three purposes, that is to say, to go,* to run and to stand still, so as he must be sometimes swift, sometimes slow, sometime unegally* marching or peradventure steady. And if our feet poetical want these qualities, it cannot be said a foot in sense translative* as here. And this cometh to pass by reason of the evident motion and stir* which is perceived in the sounding of our words not always egall.* For some ask longer, some shorter time to be uttered in, and so, by the philosopher's definition, stir is the true measure of time.

The Greeks and Latins, because their words happened to be of many syllables and very few of one syllable, it fell out right with them to conceive, and also to perceive, a notable diversity

---

* *makers*: poets   * *his*: its   * *member*: limb, component part
* *go*: walk   * *unegally*: unequally   * *translative*: metaphorical
* *stir*: motion, rhythm   * *egall*: equal

of motion and times in the pronunciation of their words. And therefore to every bissyllable* they allowed two times, and to a trisyllable three times, and to every polysyllable more according to his quantity, and their times were some long, some short, according as their motions were slow or swift. For the sound of some syllables stayed the ear a great while, and others slid away so quickly as if they had not been pronounced. Then every syllable being allowed one time, either short or long, it fell out that every tetrasyllable had four times, every trisyllable three, and the bissyllable two, by which observation every word, not under that size, as he ran or stood in a verse was called by them a foot of such and so many times: namely, the bissyllable was either of two long times, as the *spondeus*, or two short, as the *pyrrhichius*, or of a long and a short, as the *trochaeus*, or of a short and a long, as the *iambus*. The like rule did they set upon the word trisyllable,* calling him a foot of three times, as the *dactylus* of a long and two short, the *molossus* of three long, the *tribrachys* of three short, the *amphibrachys* of two long and a short, the *amphimacer* of two short and a long.[8] The word of four syllables they called a foot of four times, some or all of them either long or short; and yet, not so content,* they mounted higher, and because their words served well thereto they made feet of six times. But this proceeded more of curiosity* than otherwise; for whatsoever foot pass the trisyllable is compounded of his inferior, as every number arithmetical above three is compounded of the inferior numbers, as twice two make four, but the three is made of one number, *videlicet* * of two and an unity.[9]

Now because our natural and primitive language of the Saxon English bears not any words (at least very few) of more syllables than one (for whatsoever we see exceed cometh to us by the alterations of our language grown upon many conquests and otherwise), there could be no such observation of times in the sound of our words, and for that cause we could not have the feet which the Greeks and Latins have in their metres. [. . .]

* *bissyllable*: disyllable   * *trisyllable*: trisyllabic
* *not so content*: not content with this   * *curiosity*: artfulness
* *videlicet*: namely (viz.)

This was a pretty fantastical observation of them, and yet
brought their metres to have a marvellous good grace, which
was in Greek called *rhythmos*, whence we have derived this
word 'rhyme',[10] but improperly and not well, because we have
no such feet or times or stirs in our metres by whose sympathy
or pleasant conveniency with the ear we could take any delight.
This *rhythmos* of theirs is not therefore our rhyme, but a certain
musical numerosity* in utterance, and not a bare number as
that of the arithmetical computation is, which therefore is not
called *rhythmos* but *arithmos*.* Take this away from them, I
mean the running of their feet, there is nothing of curiosity
among them more than with us, nor yet so much.

CHAPTER 4

How many sorts of measures we use in our vulgar*

To return from rhyme to our measure again, it hath been said
that according to the number of the syllables contained in every
verse the same is said a long or short metre, and his shortest
proportion is of four syllables and his longest of twelve; they
that use it above pass the bounds of good proportion.[11] And
every metre may be as well in the odd as in the even syllable,
but better in the even, and one verse may begin in the even,
and another follow in the odd, and so keep a commendable
proportion.

The verse that containeth but two syllables, which may be in
one word, is not usual; therefore many do deny him to be a
verse, saying that it is but a foot, and that a metre can have no
less than two feet at the least. But I find it otherwise, as well
among the best Italian poets as also with our vulgar makers,
and that two syllables serve well for a short measure in the first
place,* and middle, and end of a staff, and also in diverse

* *numerosity*: rhythmic quality   * *arithmos*: number
* *measures*: metres   * *place*: position

GEORGE PUTTENHAM

situations and by sundry distances,* and is very passionate and of good grace, as shall be declared more at large in the chapter of proportion by situation. The next measure is of two feet or of four syllables, and then one word tetrasyllable* divided in the midst makes up the whole metre, as thus: 'Rêvé rêntlý'; or a trisyllable and one monosyllable, thus: 'Sovereign God'; or two bissyllables, and that is pleasant, thus: 'Restore again'; or with four monosyllables, and that is best of all, thus: 'When I do think'. I find no savour in a metre of three syllables, nor in effect in any odd, but they may be used for variety's sake, and specially being interlaced* with others. The metre of six syllables is very sweet and delicate,* as thus:

> O God, when I behold
> This bright heaven so high,
> By thine own hands of old
> Contrived so cunningly.

The metre of seven syllables is not usual; no more is that of nine and eleven. Yet, if they be well composed, that is, their cesure*[12] well appointed, and their last accent which makes the concord, they are commendable enough, as in this ditty, where one verse is of eight, another is of seven, and in the one the accent upon the last, in the other upon the last save one:

> The smoky sighs, the bitter tears
> That I in vain have wasted,
> The broken sleeps, the woe and fears
> That long in me have lasted,
> Will be my death, all by thy guilt
> And not by my deserving,
> Since so inconstantly thou wilt
> Not love but still be swerving.*[13]

---

* *in diverse ... distances*: i.e. in different positions within the stanza and separated from each other by different numbers of lines
* *tetrasyllable*: tetrasyllabic   * *interlaced*: alternated, interwoven
* *delicate*: delightful, elegant   * *cesure*: caesura
* *swerving*: wavering, forsaking

And all the reason why these metres in odd[14] syllable are allowable is for that the sharp accent* falls upon the *penultima* or last save one syllable of the verse, which doth so drown the last as he seemeth to pass away in manner unpronounced, and so make the verse seem even. But if the accent fall upon the last, and leave two flat* to finish* the verse, it will not seem so, for the oddness will more notoriously appear. As, for example, in the last verse before recited, 'Not love but still be swerving', say thus: 'Love it is a marvellous thing'. Both verses be of egall quantity, viz. seven syllables apiece, and yet the first seems shorter than the latter, who shows a more* oddness than the former by reason of his sharp accent which is upon the last syllable, and makes him more audible than if he had slid away with a flat accent, as the word 'swérving'.[15]

Your ordinary rhymers use very much their measures in the odd, as nine and eleven, and the sharp accent upon the last syllable, which therefore makes him go ill-favouredly and like a minstrel's music. Thus said one in a metre of eleven, very harshly in mine ear, whether it be for lack of good rhyme or of good reason, or of both, I wot* not:

> Now suck child and sleep child, thy mother's own joy,
> Her only sweet comfort to drown all annoy;
> For beauty surpassing the azurèd sky
> I love thee my darling, as ball of mine eye.*[16]

This sort of composition in the odd I like not, unless it be holpen* by the cesure or by the accent, as I said before.

The metre of eight is no less pleasant than that of six, and the cesure falls just* in the middle, as this of the Earl of Surrey's: 'When raging love, with extreme pain'.[17] The metre of ten syllables is very stately and heroical, and must have his cesure fall upon the fourth syllable and leave six behind him, thus: 'I serve at ease, and govern all with woe'. This metre of twelve syllables the Frenchman calleth a verse *Alexandrine*, and is with

* *sharp accent*: accent, stress   * *flat*: unstressed   * *finish*: make up
* *more*: greater   * *wot*: know   * *as . . . eye*: i.e. as much as my eyeballs
* *holpen*: helped   * *just*: right

our modern rhymers most usual; with the ancient makers it was
not so, for before Sir Thomas Wyatt's time they were not used
in our vulgar; they be for grave and stately matters fitter than
for any other ditty of pleasure. Some makers write in verses of
fourteen syllables, giving the cesure at the first eight, which
proportion is tedious, for the length of the verse keepeth the ear
too long from his delight, which is to hear the cadence or the
tuneable* accent in the end of the verse. Nevertheless, that of
twelve, if his cesure be just in the middle, and that ye suffer him
to run at full length and do not, as the common rhymers do, or
their printer for sparing of paper, cut them off in the midst,
wherein they make in two verses but half rhyme – they do very
well, as wrote the Earl of Surrey, translating the book of the
preacher: 'Solomon, David's son, King of Jerusalem'.[18] This
verse is a very good Alexandrine, but perchance would have
sounded more musically if the first word had been a dissyllable
or two monosyllables, and not a trisyllable, having his sharp
accent upon the *antepenultima* as it hath, by which occasion it
runs like a dactyl and carries the two later syllables away so
speedily as it seems but one foot in our vulgar measure, and by
that means makes the verse seem but of eleven syllables, which
oddness is nothing pleasant to the ear.[19] Judge somebody
whether it would have done better if it might have been said
thus, 'Robóham David's son, King of Jerusalem', letting the
sharp accent fall upon 'bo', or thus, 'Restóre King Dávid's són
untó Jerúsalém', for now the sharp accent falls upon 'bo', and
so doth it upon the last in 'restóre', which was not in the other
verse.[20]

But because we have seemed to make mention of cesure, and
to appoint his place in every measure, it shall not be amiss to
say somewhat more of it, and also of such pauses as are used in
utterance, and what commodity* or delectation* they bring
either to the speakers or to the hearers.

---

* *tuneable*: musical   * *commodity*: comfort, convenience
* *delectation*: delight

CHAPTER 5

Of cesure

There is no greater difference betwixt a civil and brutish utterance than clear distinction of voices; and the most laudable languages are always most plain and distinct, and the barbarous most confuse* and indistinct. It is therefore requisite that leisure be taken in pronunciation, such as may make our words plain and most audible and agreeable to the ear; also, the breath asketh to be now and then relieved with some pause or stay more or less, besides that the very nature of speech (because it goeth by clauses of several* construction and sense) requireth some space betwixt them with intermission of sound, to the end they may not huddle one upon another so rudely and so fast that the ear may not perceive their difference.

For these respects the ancient reformers of language invented three manner of pauses, one of less leisure than another, and such several intermissions of sound to serve (besides easement to the breath) for a treble distinction of sentences or parts of speech as they happened to be more or less perfect* in sense. The shortest pause or intermission they called *comma*, as who would say a piece of a speech cut off. The second they called *colon*, not a piece but, as it were, a member for his larger length, because it occupied twice as much time as the *comma*.[21] The third they called *periodus*, for a complement* or full pause, and as a resting place and perfection of so much former speech as had been uttered, and from whence they needed not to pass any further, unless it were to renew more matter to enlarge the tale.*[22]

This cannot be better represented than by example of these common travellers by the highways, where they seem to allow themselves three manner of stays or easements:* one a-horseback, calling perchance for a cup of beer or wine, and having

---

* *confuse*: confused   * *several*: distinct   * *perfect*: complete
* *complement*: completion   * *tale*: discourse, narration
* *easements*: stops for rest and refreshment

drunken it up, rides away and never lights;* about noon he cometh to his inn, and there baits* himself and his horse an hour or more; at night, when he can conveniently travel no further, he taketh up his lodging and rests himself till the morrow, from whence he followeth the course of a further voyage, if his business be such. Even so, our poet, when he hath made one verse, hath, as it were, finished one day's journey, and the while* easeth himself with one bait at the least, which is a comma or cesure, in the mid-way if the verse be even and not odd, otherwise in some other place, and not just* in the middle. If there be no cesure at all, and the verse long, the less is the maker's skill and hearer's delight. [rules for caesural placement in different lengths of line]

So may you see that the use of these pauses or distinctions is not generally with the vulgar poet as it is with the prose writer, because, the poet's chief music lying in his rhyme or concord, to hear the symphony* he maketh all the haste he can to be at an end of his verse, and delights not in many stays by the way, and therefore giveth but one cesure to any verse; and thus much for the sounding of a metre. Nevertheless, he may use in any verse both his comma, colon and interrogative point* as well as in prose. But our ancient rhymers, as Chaucer, Lydgate and others, used these cesures either very seldom or not at all, or else very licentiously,* and many times made their metres (they called them riding rhyme)[23] of such unshapely words as would allow no convenient cesure, and therefore did let their rhymes run out at length and never stayed till they came to the end. Which manner though it were not to be misliked in some sort of metre, yet in every long verse the cesure ought to be kept precisely, if it were but to serve as a law to correct the licentiousness of rhymers, besides that it pleaseth the ear better and showeth more cunning* in the maker by following the rule of his restraint. For a rhymer that will be tied to no rules at all, but

* *lights*: alights   * *baits*: stops to rest and refresh
* *the while*: along the way   * *just*: exactly   * *symphony*: concord, rhyme
* *interrogative point*: question mark
* *licentiously*: freely, bending or breaking the rules
* *cunning*: knowledge, skill

range as he list,* may easily utter what he will, but such manner
of poesy is called, in our vulgar, rhyme doggerel, with which
rebuke we will in no case our maker should be touched.* Therefore before all things let his rhyme and concords be true, clear
and audible, with no less delight than almost the strained* note
of a musician's mouth, and not dark* or wrenched* by wrong
writing, as many do to patch up their metres, and so follow in
their art neither rule, reason nor rhyme.

  Much more might be said for the use of your three pauses,
comma, colon and period, for perchance it be not all a matter
to use many commas and few, nor colons likewise, or long
and short periods, for it is diversely used by divers good writers.
But because it appertaineth more to the orator or writer in
prose than in verse I will say no more in it than thus, that they
be used for a commodious* and sensible* distinction of clauses
in prose, since every verse is, as it were, a clause of itself and
limited with a cesure howsoever the sense bear, perfect or imperfect, which difference is observable betwixt the prose and
the metre.

CHAPTER 6

Of proportion in concord, called symphony or rhyme

Because we use the word rhyme, though by manner of abusion,*24 yet to help that fault again we apply it in our vulgar
poesy another way very commendably and curiously.* For,
wanting the currentness* of the Greek and Latin feet, instead
thereof we make in the ends of our verses a certain tuneable
sound, which anon after* with another verse reasonably distant
we accord together in the last fall* or cadence, the ear taking

* list: please   * touched: implicated   * strained: melodic
* dark: obscure   * wrenched: twisted   * commodious: convenient
* sensible: perceptible   * abusion: misapplication, abuse
* curiously: excellently, artfully   * currentness: fluency
* anon after: immediately after   * fall: resolution, cadence

pleasure to hear the like tune reported* and to feel his return.
And for this purpose serve the monosyllables of our English
Saxons* excellently well, because they do naturally and indifferently receive any accent, and in them, if they finish the verse,
resteth the shrill accent* of necessity, and so doth it not in the
last of every bissyllable, nor of every polysyllable word.[25]

But, to the purpose: 'rhyme', is a borrowed word from the
Greeks by the Latins and French, from them by us Saxon
Angles,* and by abusion as hath been said; and therefore it shall
not do amiss to tell what this *rhythmos* was with the Greeks,
for what is it with us hath been already said. There is an
accountable* number which we call arithmetical (*arithmos*), as
one, two, three. There is also a musical or audible number,
fashioned by stirring of tunes* and their sundry times* in the
utterance of our words, as when the voice goeth high or low, or
sharp or flat, or swift or slow, and this is called *rhythmos* or
numerosity,[26] that is to say, a certain flowing utterance by
slipper* words and syllables, such as the tongue easily utters
and the ear with pleasure receiveth, and which flowing of words
with much volubility* smoothly proceeding from the mouth
is in some sort harmonical, and breedeth to the ear a great
compassion.* This point grew by the smooth and delicate running of their feet, which we have not in our vulgar, though we
use as much as may be the most flowing words and slippery
syllables that we can pick out; yet do not we call that by the
name of rhyme, as the Greeks did, but do give the name of
rhyme only to our concords or tuneable concents* in the latter
end of our verses, and which concords the Greeks nor Latins
never used in their poesy till, by the barbarous soldiers, out of
the camp* it was brought into the court, and thence to the
school,* as hath been before remembered.[27] And yet the Greeks

* *reported*: echoed   * *English Saxons*: Anglo-Saxon
* *shrill accent*: sharp accent, stress   * *Saxon Angles*: Anglo-Saxons
* *accountable*: able to be added up   * *stirring of tunes*: uttering of sounds
* *times*: units of time   * *slipper*: easily uttered
* *volubility*: rapid, fluent motion   * *compassion*: sympathy
* *concents*: concords, harmonies   * *camp*: military sphere
* *school*: academic sphere

and Latins both used a manner of speech by clauses of like termination, which they called *homoioteleuton*,[28] and was the nearest that they approached to our rhyme, but is not our right concord. So as we in abusing this term 'rhyme' be nevertheless excusable, applying it to another point in poesy no less curious than their rhythm or numerosity, which indeed passed the whole verse throughout, whereas our concords keep but the latter end of every verse, or perchance the middle and the end in metres that be long.[29]

[*Chapter 7 – Of accent, time and stir perceived evidently in the distinction of man's voice, and which makes the flowing of a metre*]

CHAPTER 8

Of your cadences by which your metre is made symphonical:* when they be sweetest and most solemn in a verse

As the smoothness of your words and syllables, running upon feet of sundry quantities, make with the Greeks and Latins the body of their verses numerous or rhythmical, so in our vulgar poesy, and of all other nations at this day, your verses answering each other by couples,* or at larger distances, in good *cadence* is it that maketh your metre symphonical. This cadence is the fall of a verse in every last word with a certain tuneable sound, which being matched with another of like sound do make a *concord*. And the whole cadence is contained sometime in one syllable, sometime in two, or in three at the most. For above the *antepenultima* there reacheth no accent (which is chief cause of the cadence), unless it be by usurpation in some English words to which we give a sharp accent upon the fourth, as 'hónourable', 'mátrimony', 'pátrimony', 'míserable', and such other as would neither make a sweet cadence nor easily find any word of like

* *symphonical*: harmonious   * *couples*: couplets

quantity to match them.[30] And the accented syllable, with all
the rest under* him, make the cadence, and no syllable above,*
as in these words, 'agílity' / 'facílity', 'subjéction' / 'diréction',
and these bissyllables, 'ténder' / 'slénder', 'trústy' / 'lústy'. But
always the cadence which falleth upon the last syllable of a verse
is sweetest and most commendable; that upon the *penultima*
more light and not so pleasant; but falling upon the *antepenultima* is most unpleasant of all, because they make your metre
too light and trivial, and are fitter for the epigrammatist or
comical poet than for the lyric and elegiac, which are accounted
the sweeter musics.[31]

But though we have said that, to make good concord, your
several verses should have their cadences like, yet must there be
some difference in their orthography, though not in their sound.
As, if one cadence be 'constraín', the next 'restraín', or one
'aspíre', another 'respíre', this maketh no good concord because
they are all one, but if ye will exchange both these consonants
of the accented syllable, or void but one of them away, then will
your cadences be good and your concord too, as to say 'restrain' /
'refrain' / 'remain', 'aspire' / 'desire' / 'retire'; which rule, nevertheless, is not well observed by many makers, for lack of good
judgement and a delicate ear.[32] And this may suffice to show the
use and nature of your cadences, which are in effect all the
sweetness and cunning in our vulgar poesy.

CHAPTER 9

*How the good maker will not wrench his word to help his
rhyme, either by falsifying his accent or by untrue orthography*

Now there cannot be in a maker a fouler fault than to falsify his
accent to serve his cadence, or by untrue orthography to wrench
his words to help his rhyme, for it is a sign that such a maker is
not copious* in his own language, or (as they are wont to say)

* *under*: after   * *above*: before   * *copious*: of abundant resource

not half his craft's master. [. . .] For since the chief grace of our vulgar poesy consisteth in the symphony, as hath been already said, our maker must not be too licentious* in his concords, but see that they go even, just and melodious in the ear, and right so in the numerosity or currentness* of the whole body of his verse, and in every other of his proportions. For a licentious maker is in truth but a bungler and not a poet. Such men were in effect the most part of all your old rhymers, and specially Gower, who to make up his rhyme would for the most part write his terminant* syllable with false orthography, and many times not stick to put in a plain French word for an English; and so, by your leave, do many of our common rhymers at this day. [. . .] Such extreme licentiousness is utterly to be banished from our school, and better it might have been borne with in old rhyming writers, because they lived in a barbarous age, and were grave, moral men but very homely poets, such also as made most of their works by translation out of the Latin and French tongue, and few or none of their own engine,* as may easily be known to them that list* to look upon the poems of both languages.

Finally, as ye may rhyme with words of all sorts, be they of many syllables or few, so nevertheless is there a choice by which to make your cadence (before remembered) most commendable. For some words of exceeding great length, which have been fetched from the Latin inkhorn[33] or borrowed of strangers,* the use of them in rhyme is nothing pleasant, saving perchance to the common people, who rejoice much to be at plays and interludes and, besides their natural ignorance, have at all such times their ears so attentive to the matter, and their eyes upon the shows of the stage, that they take little heed to the cunning of the rhyme, and therefore be as well satisfied with that which is gross as with any other finer and more delicate.

* *licentious*: disregarding accepted rules   * *currentness*: fluency, rhythm
* *terminant*: final   * *engine*: ingenuity, invention   * *list*: choose, care
* *strangers*: foreigners

CHAPTER 10

Of concord in long and short measures, and by near or far distances, and which of them is most commendable

But this ye must observe withal, that, because your concords contain the chief part of music in your metre, their distances may not be too wide or far asunder, lest the ear should lose the tune* and be defrauded of his delight; and whensoever ye see any maker use large and extraordinary distances ye must think he doth intend to show himself more artificial than popular, and yet therein is not to be discommended, for respects that shall be remembered in some other place of this book.[34]

Note also that rhyme or concord is not commendably used both in the end and middle of a verse, unless it be in toys* and trifling poesies, for it showeth a certain lightness either of the matter or of the maker's head, albeit these common rhymers use it much.[35] For, as I said before, like as the symphony in a verse of great length is, as it were, lost by looking after him,* and yet may the metre be very grave and stately, so on the other side doth the overbusy and too speedy return of one manner of tune too much annoy and, as it were, glut the ear; unless it be in small and popular musics sung by these *cantabanqui** upon benches and barrels' heads, where they have none other audience than boys or country fellows that pass by them in the street, or else by blind harpers or such like tavern minstrels that give a fit* of mirth for a groat,* and their matters being for the most part stories of old time, as the tale of Sir Thopas, the reports of Bevis of Southampton, Guy of Warwick, Adam Bell and Clym of the Clough,[36] and such other old romances or historical rhymes, made purposely for recreation of the common people at Christmas dinners and bride-ales,* and in taverns and alehouses

* *tune*: sound   * *toys*: light compositions, trifles
* *looking after him*: having to look for it
* *cantabanqui*: 'singers on platforms, common ballad-singers' (*cantambanci*)
* *fit*: song   * *groat*: silver coin worth four pennies
* *bride-ales*: wedding-feasts

and such other places of base resort. Also, they be used in carols and rounds and such light or lascivious poems, which are commonly more commodiously uttered by these buffoons* or vices* in plays than by any other person. Such were the rhymes of Skelton (usurping the name of a poet laureate),[37] being indeed but a rude,* railing rhymer, and all his doings ridiculous; he used both short distances and short measures, pleasing only the popular ear: in our courtly maker we banish them utterly. Now also have ye in every song or ditty concord by compass, and concord intertangled, and a mixt* of both: what that is and how they be used shall be declared in the chapter of proportion by situation.

CHAPTER 11

Of proportion by situation

This proportion consisteth in placing of every verse in a staff or ditty by such reasonable distances as may best serve the ear for delight, and also to show the poet's art and variety of music. And the proportion is double: one, by marshalling the metres and limiting their distances, having regard to the rhyme or concord, how they go and return; another, by placing every verse, having a regard to his measure and quantity only and not to his concord, as to set one short metre to three long, or four short and two long, or a short measure and a long, or of divers lengths with relation one to another.[38] Which manner of situation, even without respect of the rhyme, doth alter the nature of the poesy and make it either lighter or graver, or more merry or mournful, and many ways passionate* to the ear and heart of the hearer, seeming for this point that our maker by his measures and concords of sundry proportions doth counterfeit the harmonical tunes of the vocal and instrumental musics: as

* *buffoons*: comic actors   * *vices*: characters in morality plays
* *rude*: unlearned, ignorant   * *mixt*: mixture
* *passionate*: emotive, vehement

the Dorian, because his falls,* sallies* and compass* be divers* from those of the Phrygian, the Phrygian likewise from the Lydian, and all three from the Aeolian, Mixolydian and Ionian, mounting and falling from note to note such as be to them peculiar,* and with more or less leisure or precipitation.[39] Even so, by diversity of placing and situation of your measures and concords, a short with a long and by narrow or wide distances, or thicker or thinner bestowing of them, your proportions differ, and breedeth a variable and strange* harmony not only in the ear but also in the conceit* of them that hear it, whereof this may be an ocular* example:

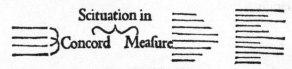

Where ye see the concord or rhyme in the third distance, and the measure in the fourth, sixth or second distances,[40] whereof ye may devise as many other as ye list, so the staff be able to bear it. And I set you down an ocular example because ye may the better conceive it. Likewise, it so falleth out most times your ocular proportion doth declare the nature of the audible, for if it please the ear well, the same represented by delineation* to the view pleaseth the eye well, and è converso;* and this is by a natural sympathy between the ear and the eye, and between tunes* and colours, even as there is the like between the other senses and their objects, of which it appertaineth not here to speak.

Now, for the distances usually observed in our vulgar poesy, they be in the first, second, third and fourth verse, or if the verse be very short in the fifth and sixth, and in some manner of musics far above. And the first distance for the most part goeth

* falls: cadences   * sallies: movement, rhythms
* compass: range of notes, sequence of intervals   * divers: different, other
* peculiar: proper   * strange: singular, causing wonder
* conceit: mind, imagination   * ocular: visual
* by delineation: diagrammatically   * è converso: vice versa
* tunes: tones, sounds

all by distich or couples of verses agreeing in one cadence, and do pass so speedily away and so often return again as their tunes are never lost nor out of the ear, one couple supplying another so nigh and so suddenly. And this is the most vulgar proportion of distance or situation, such as used Chaucer in his *Canterbury Tales*, and Gower in all his works.

Second distance is when ye pass over one verse and join the first and the third, and so continue on till another like distance fall in, and this is also usual and common, as:[41]

Third distance is when your rhyme falleth upon the first and fourth verse, overleaping two; this manner is not so common, but pleasant and allowable enough. In which case the two verses

ye leave out are ready to receive their concords by the same distance or any other ye like better.[42]

[...]

There be larger distances also, as when the first concord falleth upon the sixth verse, and is very pleasant if they be joined with other distances not so large, as:[43]

There be also of the seventh, eighth, tenth and twelfth distance, but then they may not go thick but two or three such distances serve to proportion a whole song, and all between must be of other less distances and these wide distances serve for coupling of staves[44] or for to declare high and passionate or grave matter, and also for art. Petrarch hath given us examples hereof in his *canzoni*.[45] [. . .] And all that can be objected against this wide distance is to say that the ear, by losing his concord, is not satisfied. So is indeed the rude and popular ear, but not the learned,[46] and therefore the poet must know to whose ear he maketh his rhyme and accommodate himself thereto, and not give such music to the rude and barbarous as he would to the learned and delicate ear.

[*further Petrarchan example*]

Besides all this there is in situation of the concords two other points: one, that it go by plain and clear compass not entangled; another, by interweaving one with another by knots* or, as it were, by band* – which is more or less busy* and curious, all as the maker will double or redouble his rhyme or concords and set his distances far or nigh, of all which I will give you ocular examples, as thus:[47]

And first, in a quatrain there are but two proportions:[48]

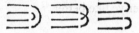

For four verses in this last sort coupled are but two distichs and not a staff quatrain or of four.

[*proportions of larger stanzas, from five lines to twelve*]

Now, ye may perceive by these proportions before described that there is a band to be given every verse in a staff, so as none fall out alone or uncoupled, and this band maketh that the staff is said fast and not loose, even as ye see in buildings of stone or brick the mason giveth a band, that is a length to two breadths, and upon necessity divers other sorts of bands, to hold in the

* *knots*: decorative designs formed of crossing lines
* *band*: cohesion, binding   * *busy*: elaborate, intricate

work fast and maintain the perpendicularity of the wall.[49] So, in any staff of seven or eight or more verses, the coupling of the more metres by rhyme or concord is the faster* band, the fewer the looser band. And, therefore, in a huitain, he that putteth four verses in one concord and four in another concord, and in a *dizain* five, showeth himself more cunning and also more copious in his own language. For he that can find two words of concord cannot find four or five or six unless he have his own language at will. Sometime, also, ye are driven of necessity to close and make band more than ye would, lest otherwise the staff should fall asunder and seem two staves: and this is in a staff of eight and ten verses, whereas without a band in the middle it would seem two quatrains or two *quintains*, which is an error that many makers slide away with.* Yet Chaucer and others, in the staff of seven and six, do almost as much amiss, for they shut up the staff with a distich, concording* with none other verse that went before, and maketh but a loose rhyme, and yet, because of the double cadence in the last two verses, serve the ear well enough.[50] And as there is in every staff band, given to the verses by concord more or less busy, so is there in some cases a band given to every staff, and that is by one whole verse running alone throughout the ditty or ballad, either in the middle or end of every staff. The Greeks called such uncoupled verse* *epimonē*, the Latins *versus intercalaris*.[51]

Now, touching the situation of measures, there are as many or more proportions of them, which I refer to the maker's fantasy* and choice, contented with two or three ocular examples and no more:[52]

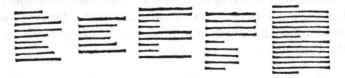

---

* *faster*: stronger, more secure   * *slide away with*: sneakily get away with
* *concording*: rhyming   * *uncoupled verse*: an unrhymed line
* *fantasy*: imagination

Which manner of proportion by situation of measures giveth more efficacy to the matter oftentimes than the concords themselves, and, both proportions concurring together as they needs must, it is of much more beauty and force to the hearer's mind.[53]

To finish the learning* of this division,* I will set you down one example of a ditty written extempore with this device,* showing not only the promptness of wit in the maker but also great art and a notable memory. Make me, saith this writer to one of the company, so many strokes or lines with your pen as ye would have your song contain verses, and let every line bear his several* length, even as ye would have your verse of measure, suppose of four, five, six or eight or more syllables, and set a figure of every number at the end of the line, whereby ye may know his measure. Then, where you will have your rhyme or concord to fall, mark it with a compassed* stroke or semicircle passing over those lines, be they far or near in distance, as ye have seen before described.[54] And because ye shall not think the maker hath premeditated beforehand any such-fashioned ditty, do ye yourself make one verse,* whether it be of perfect or imperfect* sense, and give it him for a theme to make all the rest upon. If ye shall perceive the maker do keep the measures and rhyme as ye have appointed him, and besides do make his ditty sensible* and ensuant* to the first verse in good reason, then may ye say he is his craft's master. For if he were not of a plentiful discourse, he could not upon the sudden shape an entire ditty upon your imperfect theme or proposition in one verse. And if he were not copious in his language, he could not have such store of words at commandment as should supply your concords. And if he were not of a marvellous good memory, he could not observe the rhyme and measures after the distances of your limitation, keeping with all gravity and good sense in the whole ditty.

---

* *learning*: lesson   * *division*: chapter   * *device*: stratagem, trick
* *several*: distinct   * *compassed*: curved   * *verse*: line of verse
* *perfect or imperfect*: complete or incomplete   * *sensible*: comprehensible
* *ensuant*: following appropriately

CHAPTER 12

Of proportion in figure[55]

Your last proportion is that of figure, so called for that it yields an ocular representation,[56] your metres being by good symmetry reduced into certain geometrical figures, whereby the maker is restrained to keep him within his bounds and showeth not only more art but serveth also much better for briefness and subtlety of device,* and for the same respect are also fittest for the pretty amorets* in court to entertain their servants and the time withal, their delicate wits requiring some commendable exercise to keep them from idleness. [. . .]

[*various shapes itemized and then exemplified: lozenge, triangle, spire or pyramid, pillar*]

The roundel or sphere. The most excellent of all the figures geometrical is the round,* for his many perfections. First, because he is even and smooth, without any angle or interruption, most voluble* and apt to turn and to continue motion, which is the author of life; he containeth in him the commodious description of every other figure,[57] and for his ample capacity doth resemble the world or universe, and for his indefiniteness, having no special place of beginning nor end, beareth a similitude* with God and eternity. [. . .]

*Of the square or quadrangle equilater.** The square is of all other accounted the figure of most solidity and steadfastness, and for his own stay and firmity requireth none other base than himself. And therefore, as the roundel or sphere is appropriate to the heavens, the spire to the element of the fire, the triangle to the air, and the lozenge to the water, so is the square for his inconcussible* steadiness likened to the earth; which perchance might be the reason that the prince of philosophers in his first book of the *Ethics* termeth a constant-minded man, even egall

---

* *device*: design, conceit   * *amorets*: sweethearts, amorous girls
* *round*: circle, sphere   * *voluble*: capable of rotation, apt to revolve
* *similitude*: resemblance   * *equilater*: having equal sides, equilateral
* *inconcussible*: firmly fixed, unshakeable

132   GEORGE PUTTENHAM

and direct on all sides and not easily overthrown by every little adversity, *hominem quadratum*, a square man.[58] Into this figure may ye reduce your ditties by using no more verses than your verse is of syllables, which will make him fall out square. [...] I need not give you any example, because in good art all your ditties, odes, and epigrams should keep and not exceed the number of twelve verses, and the longest verse to be of twelve syllables and not above, but under that number as much as ye will.

[*oval; then an added section on devices, emblems, and imprese, and on anagrams*]

[*Chapter 13 – How, if all manner of sudden innovations were not very scandalous, specially in the laws of any language or art, the use of the Greek and Latin feet might be brought into our vulgar poesy, and with good grace enough; Chapter 14 – A more particular declaration of the metrical feet of the ancient poets Greek and Latin, and chiefly of the feet of two times; Chapter 15 – Of your feet of three times, and first of the dactyl; Chapter 16 – Of all your other feet of three times, and how well they would fashion a metre in our vulgar; Chapter 17 – Of your verses perfect and defective, and that which the Grecians called the half foot; Chapter 18 – Of the breaking your bissyllables and polysyllables, and when it is to be used*]

THE THIRD BOOK
OF ORNAMENT

CHAPTER I

Of ornament poetical[1]

As, no doubt, the good proportion of anything doth greatly adorn and commend* it, and right so our late-remembered proportions do to our vulgar* poesy, so is there yet requisite to the perfection of this art another manner of exornation,* which resteth in the fashioning of our maker's* language and style to such purpose as it may delight and allure as well the mind as the ear of the hearers with a certain novelty and strange manner of conveyance,* disguising it no little from the ordinary and accustomed, nevertheless making it nothing the more unseemly or misbecoming but rather decenter* and more agreeable to any civil ear and understanding. And as we see in these great madams* of honour, be they for personage or otherwise never so comely and beautiful, yet if they want their courtly habiliments,* or at leastwise such other apparel as custom and civility have ordained to cover their naked bodies, would be half ashamed or greatly out of countenance to be seen in that sort, and perchance do then think themselves more amiable in every man's eye when they be in their richest attire – suppose of silks or tissues* and costly embroideries – than when they go in cloth

* *commend*: grace, set off to advantage   * *vulgar*: vernacular
* *exornation*: adornment, decoration   * *maker's*: poet's
* *conveyance*: expression, style   * *decenter*: more decorous
* *madams*: ladies of rank   * *habiliments*: clothes
* *tissues*: rich cloths interwoven with gold or silver

or in any other plain and simple apparel, even so cannot our vulgar poesy show itself either gallant* or gorgeous* if any limb be left naked and bare and not clad in his kindly* clothes and colours,* such as may convey them somewhat out of sight, that is, from the common course of ordinary speech and capacity of the vulgar judgement, and yet, being artificially* handled, must needs yield it much more beauty and commendation.

This ornament we speak of is given to it by figures and figurative speeches, which be the flowers, as it were, and colours[2] that a poet setteth upon his language by art, as the embroiderer doth his stone* and pearl or passements* of gold upon the stuff* of a princely garment, or as the excellent painter bestoweth the rich orient colours upon his table of portrait;* so, nevertheless, as if the same colours in our art of poesy (as well as in those other mechanical arts) be not well tempered,* or not well laid, or be used in excess, or never so little disordered or misplaced, they not only give it no manner of grace at all but rather do disfigure the stuff and spill* the whole workmanship, taking away all beauty and good liking from it, no less than, if the crimson taint* which should be laid upon a lady's lips or right in the centre of her cheeks should by some oversight or mishap be applied to her forehead or chin, it would make (ye would say) but a very ridiculous beauty. Wherefore the chief praise and cunning* of our poet is in the discreet* using of his figures, as the skilful painter's is in the good conveyance* of his colours and shadowing traits* of his pencil,* with a delectable* variety, by all measure and just proportion and in places most aptly to be bestowed.

* *gallant*: fine, ornate   * *gorgeous*: magnificently dressed
* *kindly*: proper, natural   * *colours*: [also:] rhetorical figures
* *artificially*: by art, skilfully   * *stone*: precious stone
* *passements*: lace, gimp, braid   * *stuff*: material
* *table of portrait*: portrait, board on which portrait is painted
* *tempered*: mixed, balanced   * *spill*: destroy   * *taint*: tincture
* *cunning*: learning, skill   * *discreet*: judicious
* *conveyance*: imparting, management   * *traits*: touches, strokes
* *pencil*: fine brush   * *delectable*: delightful

[*Chapter 2 – How our writing and speeches public ought to be figurative, and if they be not, do greatly disgrace the cause and purpose of the speaker and writer*]

CHAPTER 3

How ornament poetical is of two sorts, according to the double virtue and efficacy of figures

This ornament, then, is of two sorts: one to satisfy and delight the ear only, by a goodly outward show set upon the matter with words and speeches smoothly and tuneably* running; another by certain intendments* or sense of such words and speeches inwardly working a stir to the mind. That first quality the Greeks called *enargeia*, of this word, *argos*, because it giveth a glorious lustre and light; this latter they called *energeia*, of *ergon*, because it wrought with a strong and virtuous operation.[3] And figure breedeth them both: some serving to give gloss only to a language, some to give it efficacy by sense, and so, by that means, some of them serve the ear only, some serve the conceit* only and not the ear; there be of them also that serve both turns as common servitors* appointed for the one and the other purpose, which shall be hereafter spoken of in place. But because we have alleged before that ornament is but the good or rather beautiful habit* of language and style, and figurative speeches the instrument wherewith we burnish our language, fashioning it to this or that measure and proportion, whence finally resulteth a long and continual phrase* or manner of writing or speech which we call by the name of style, we will first speak of language, then of style, lastly of figure, and declare their virtue and differences, and also their use and best

---

* *tuneably*: musically, harmoniously   * *intendments*: meanings
* *conceit*: mind, imagination   * *common servitors*: general servants
* *habit*: dress   * *phrase*: diction, style

application, and what portion in exornation every one of them bringeth to the beautifying of this art.

CHAPTER 4

Of language

Speech* is not natural to man, saving for his only ability to speak, and that he is by kind* apt to utter all his conceits* with sounds and voices diversified many manner of ways, by means of the many and fit instruments he hath by nature to that purpose, as a broad and voluble* tongue, thin and moveable lips, teeth even and not shagged,* thick ranged, a round vaulted palate and a long throat, besides an excellent capacity of wit that maketh him more disciplinable* and imitative than any other creature.[4] Then, as to the form and action of his speech, it cometh to him by art and teaching, and by use or exercise. But after a speech is fully fashioned to the common* understanding, and accepted by consent of a whole country and nation, it is called a language, and receiveth none allowed alteration but by extraordinary occasions, by little and little, as it were insensibly, bringing in of many corruptions that creep along with the time. Of all which matters we have more largely spoken in our books of the originals and pedigree of the English tongue.[5] Then, when I say language, I mean the speech wherein the poet or maker writeth, be it Greek or Latin or, as our case is, the vulgar* English. And when it is peculiar unto a country it is called the mother speech of that people (the Greeks term it *idiōma*): so is ours at this day the Norman English. Before the Conquest of the Normans it was the Anglo-Saxon, and before that the British, which, as some will, is at this day the Welsh or, as others affirm,

* *speech*: i.e. language   * *kind*: nature   * *conceits*: ideas
* *voluble*: easily moved   * *shagged*: jagged
* *disciplinable*: able to be taught   * *common*: general
* *vulgar*: commonly used, vernacular

the Cornish; I, for my part, think neither of both as they be now spoken and pronounced.

This part in our maker or poet must be heedily* looked unto, that it be natural, pure and the most usual of all his country; and for the same purpose rather that which is spoken in the king's court, or in the good towns and cities within the land, than in the marches* and frontiers, or in port towns, where strangers* haunt for traffic's* sake, or yet in universities, where scholars use much peevish* affectation of words out of the primitive languages,* or, finally, in any uplandish* village or corner of a realm, where is no resort but of poor, rustical or uncivil people. Neither shall he follow the speech of a craftsman or carter or other of the inferior sort, though he be inhabitant or bred in the best town and city in this realm, for such persons do abuse good speeches by strange accents or ill-shapen sounds and false orthography.* But he shall follow generally the better brought-up sort, such as the Greeks call *charientes*,[6] men civil and graciously behavioured and bred. Our maker, therefore, at these days shall not follow *Piers Plowman*, nor Gower, nor Lydgate, nor yet Chaucer,[7] for their language is now out of use with us. Neither shall he take the terms of Northern-men, such as they use in daily talk (whether they be noblemen or gentlemen or of their best clerks,* all is a matter), nor, in effect, any speech used beyond the river of Trent,* though no man can deny but that theirs is the purer English Saxon at this day, yet it is not so courtly nor so current as our Southern English is; no more is the far Westernman's speech. Ye shall therefore take the usual speech of the court and that of London and the shires lying about London within 60 miles and not much above. I say not this but that in every shire of England there be gentlemen and others that speak, but specially write, as good Southern as we of Middlesex or Surrey do, but not the common people of every

* *heedily*: heedfully, with attention   * *marches*: borders
* *strangers*: foreigners   * *traffic's*: trade's   * *peevish*: foolish
* *primitive languages*: i.e. Greek and Latin   * *uplandish*: remote
* *orthography*: spelling   * *clerks*: scholars
* *beyond . . . Trent*: i.e. beyond the Midlands

shire, to whom the gentlemen and also their learned clerks do
for the most part condescend.* But herein we are already ruled
by the English dictionaries and other books written by learned
men,[8] and therefore it needeth none other direction in that
behalf, albeit, peradventure, some small admonition be not
impertinent: for we find in our English writers many words and
speeches amendable, and ye shall see in some many inkhorn*
terms so ill-affected,[9] brought in by men of learning, as preachers
and schoolmasters, and many strange terms of other languages,
by secretaries and merchants and travellers, and many dark*
words and not usual nor well sounding, though they be daily
spoken in court. Wherefore great heed must be taken by our
maker in this point that his choice be good. And peradventure
the writer hereof be in that behalf * no less faulty than any other,
using many strange and unaccustomed words and borrowed
from other languages, and in that respect himself no meet*
magistrate to reform the same errors in any other person. But
since he is not unwilling to acknowledge his own fault, and can
the better tell how to amend it, he may seem a more excusable
corrector of other men's; he intendeth, therefore, for an indifferent way* and universal benefit to tax himself first and before
any others.

[*Puttenham discusses his own lexicon, neologisms and
borrowings*]
But herein the noble poet Horace hath said enough to satisfy us
all in these few verses:

>   multa renascentur quae iam cecidere, cadentque
>   quae nunc sunt in honore vocabula, si volet usus,
>   quem penes arbitrium est et vis et norma loquendi.[10]

Which I have thus Englished, but nothing with so good grace,
nor so briefly as the poet wrote:

---

* *condescend*: i.e. accord with in speech   * *inkhorn*: pedantic, scholarly
* *dark*: obscure   * *behalf*: respect   * *meet*: appropriate
* *indifferent way*: impartial approach

> Many a word yfall'n shall eft* arise,
> And such as now been* held in highest prize
> Will fall as fast, when use and custom will,*
> Only umpires of speech, for force and skill.

CHAPTER 5

Of style

Style is a constant and continual phrase* or tenor* of speaking and writing, extending to the whole tale or process* of the poem or history and not properly to any piece or member of a tale, but is of words, speeches and sentences[11] together a certain contrived form and quality, many times natural to the writer, many times his peculiar* by election* and art, and such as either he keepeth by skill or holdeth on by ignorance, and will not, or peradventure cannot, easily alter into any other. So we say that Cicero's style and Sallust's were not one, nor Caesar's and Livy's, nor Homer's and Hesiodus', nor Herodotus' and Thucydides', nor Euripides' and Aristophanes', nor Erasmus' and Budaeus' styles.[12] And because this continual course and manner of writing or speech showeth the matter and disposition of the writer's mind more than one or few words or sentences can show, therefore there be that have called style the image of man, *mentis character*,* for man is but his mind, and as his mind is tempered* and qualified,* so are his speeches and language at large; and his inward conceits be the mettle of his mind and his manner of utterance the very warp and woof of his conceits, more plain or busy, and intricate or otherwise affected after the

* *eft*: again   * *been*: are   * *will*: wish   * *phrase*: style, diction
* *tenor*: course   * *process*: course of the narrative
* *peculiar*: own property   * *election*: choice
* *mentis character*: 'the mark of the mind'
* *tempered*: made up, constituted
* *qualified*: endowed with certain qualities

rate.* Most men say that not any one point in all physiognomy is so certain as to judge a man's manners* by his eye; but more assuredly, in mine opinion, by his daily manner of speech and ordinary writing. For if the man be grave, his speech and style is grave; if light-headed, his style and language also light; if the mind be haughty and hot, the speech and style is also vehement and stirring; if it be cold and temperate, the style is also very modest; if it be humble, or base and meek, so is also the language and style. And yet, peradventure not altogether so, but that every man's style is for the most part according to the matter and subject of the writer, or so ought to be, and conformable thereunto. Then again may it be said as well, that men do choose their subjects according to the mettle of their minds, and therefore a high-minded man chooseth him high and lofty matter to write of, the base courage,* matter base and low, the mean* and modest mind, mean and moderate matters after the rate. Howsoever it be, we find that under these three principal complexions* (if I may with leave so term them), high, mean and base style, there be contained many other humours or qualities of style, as the plain and obscure, the rough and smooth, the facile and hard, the plentiful and barren, the rude and eloquent, the strong and feeble, the vehement and cold styles,[13] all which in their evil are to be reformed, and the good to be kept and used.

But generally, to have the style decent* and comely it behoveth the maker or poet to follow the nature of his subject: that is, if his matter be high and lofty, that the style be so too, if mean, the style also to be mean, if base, the style humble and base accordingly. And they that do otherwise use it, applying to mean matter high and lofty style, and to high matters style either mean or base, and to the base matters the mean or high style, do utterly disgrace their poesy and show themselves nothing skilful in their art, nor having regard to the decency* which is the chief praise of any writer. Therefore, to rid all lovers of learning from

* *after the rate*: accordingly   * *manners*: moral character
* *courage*: spirit, mind   * *mean*: middling, intermediate
* *complexions*: qualities   * *decent*: decorous, according to decorum
* *decency*: decorum

that error, I will, as near as I can, set down which matters be high and lofty, which be but mean, and which be low and base, to the intent the styles may be fashioned to the matters, and keep their *decorum* and good proportion in every respect. [*digression on decorum in Homer and Virgil*] But still methinks that in all decency the style ought to conform with the nature of the subject. Otherwise, if a writer will seem to observe no decorum at all, nor pass* how he fashion his tale* to his matter, who doubteth but he may in the lightest cause speak like a pope and in the gravest matters prate like a parrot, and find words and phrases enough to serve both turns, and neither of them commendably. For neither is all that may be written of kings and princes such as ought to keep a high style, nor all that may be written upon a shepherd to keep the low, but according to the matter reported, if that be of high or base nature. For every petty pleasure and vain delight of a king are not to be accounted high matter for the height of his estate,* but mean and perchance very base and vile. Nor so a poet or historiographer could decently with a high style report the vanities of Nero, the ribaldries of Caligula, the idleness of Domitian and the riots of Heliogabalus; but well the magnanimity and honourable ambition of Caesar, the prosperities of Augustus, the gravity of Tiberius, the bounty of Trajan, the wisdom of Aurelius[14] and generally all that which concerned the highest honours of emperors, their birth, alliances, government, exploits in war and peace and other public affairs. For they be matter stately and high, and require a style to be lift up and advanced by choice of words, phrases, sentences and figures high, lofty, eloquent and magnific* in proportion. So be the mean matters to be carried with all words and speeches of smoothness and pleasant moderation, and finally the base things to be holden within their tether, by a low, mild and simple manner of utterance, creeping rather than climbing, and marching rather than mounting upwards with the wings of the stately subjects and style.

* *pass*: care, regard   * *tale*: narration
* *estate*: status, condition, position   * *magnific*: magnificent

CHAPTER 6

Of the high, low and mean subject*

The matters therefore that concern the gods and divine things
are highest of all other to be couched in writing; next to them
the noble gests* and great fortunes of princes, and the notable
accidents* of time, as the greatest affairs of war and peace –
these be all high subjects, and therefore are delivered over to the
poets hymnic and historical, who be occupied either in divine
lauds* or in heroical reports.[15] The mean matters be those that
concern mean men, their life and business, as lawyers, gentlemen and merchants, good householders and honest citizens,
and which sound neither to* matters of state nor of war, nor
leagues, nor great alliances, but smatch* all the common conversation, as of the civiler and better sort of men. The base and low
matters be the doings of the common artificer,* servingman,
yeoman, groom, husbandman,* day-labourer, sailor, shepherd,
swineherd and such like of homely calling, degree and bringing-
up. So that, in every of the said three degrees, not the selfsame
virtues be egally* to be praised, nor the same vices egally to be
dispraised, nor their loves, marriages, quarrels, contracts and
other behaviours be like high, nor do require to be set forth with
the like style, but every one in his degree and decency. Which
made that all hymns and histories and tragedies were written in
the high style, all comedies and interludes and other common
poesies of loves and such like in the mean style, all eclogues and
pastoral poems in the low and base style; otherwise they had
been utterly disproportioned. Likewise, for the same cause,
some phrases and figures* be only peculiar to the high style,
some to the base or mean, some common to all three, as shall
be declared more at large hereafter when we come to speak of
figure and phrase. Also, some words and speeches and sentences

* *mean*: middle   * *gests*: deeds   * *accidents*: events   * *lauds*: praises
* *sound . . . to*: touch, have a connection to   * *smatch*: smack of, taste of
* *artificer*: craftsman   * *husbandman*: farmer   * *egally*: equally
* *figures*: rhetorical figures

do become the high style that do not become the other two, and contrariwise, as shall be said when we talk of words and sentences. Finally, some kind of measure* and concord* do not beseem* the high style that well become the mean and low, as we have said speaking of concord and measure. But generally the high style is disgraced and made foolish and ridiculous by all words affected, counterfeit and puffed up, as it were a wind-ball,* carrying more countenance* than matter; and cannot be better resembled* than to these midsummer pageants in London, where to make the people wonder are set forth great and ugly giants, marching as if they were alive and armed at all points,* but within they are stuffed full of brown paper and tow,* which the shrewd* boys, underpeering, do guilefully discover* and turn to a great derision. Also, all dark and unaccustomed words, or rustical and homely, and sentences* that hold too much of the merry and light, or infamous and unshamefast,* are to be accounted of the same sort, for such speeches become not princes, nor great estates, nor them that write of their doings, to utter or report and intermingle with the grave and weighty matters.

CHAPTER 7

Of figures and figurative speeches

As figures be the instruments of ornament in every language, so be they also in a sort abuses,* or rather trespasses,* in speech,[16] because they pass the ordinary limits of common utterance,* and be occupied of purpose to deceive the ear and also the mind,

* measure: metre   * concord: rhyme   * beseem: suit
* wind-ball: inflated ball used in an early modern precursor of volleyball
* countenance: show   * resembled: compared
* at all points: in every part   * tow: coarse fibres   * shrewd: mischievous
* discover: reveal   * sentences: sayings
* infamous and unshamefast: vile and immodest   * abuses: misuses, deceits
* trespasses: transgressions   * utterance: speech

drawing it from plainness and simplicity to a certain doubleness, whereby our talk is the more guileful and abusing.* For what else is your metaphor but an inversion of sense by transport;* your allegory but[17] a duplicity of meaning or dissimulation under covert and dark intendments; one while speaking obscurely and in riddle called *aenigma*; another while by common proverb or adage called *paroemia*; then by merry scoff called *ironia*; then by bitter taunt called *sarcasmus*; then by periphrase or circumlocution when all might be said in a word or two; then by incredible comparison giving credit, as by your *hyperbole*; and many other ways seeking to inveigle and appassionate* the mind?[18] Which thing made the grave judges Areopagites* (as I find written) to forbid all manner of figurative speeches to be used before them in their consistory of justice, as mere illusions to the mind and wresters* of upright judgement,[19] saying that to allow such manner of foreign and coloured* talk to make the judges affectioned* were all one as if the carpenter before he began to square his timber would make his squire* crooked, insomuch as the straight and upright mind of a judge is the very rule of justice till it be perverted by affection.* This, no doubt, is true, and was by them gravely considered. But in this case, because our maker or poet is appointed not for a judge but rather for a pleader, and that of pleasant and lovely causes and nothing perilous, such as be those for the trial of life, limb or livelihood, and before judges neither sour nor severe, but in the ear of princely dames, young ladies, gentlewomen and courtiers, being all for the most part either meek of nature or of pleasant humour, and that all his abuses tend but to dispose the hearers to mirth and solace* by pleasant conveyance* and efficacy of speech, they are not in truth to be accounted vices, but for virtues in the poetical science very commendable. On the other side, such trespasses in speech (whereof there be many)

* *abusing*: deceiving   * *transport*: transfer   * *appassionate*: impassion
* *Areopagites*: members of the court of the Areopagus at Athens
* *wresters*: distorters, twisters   * *coloured*: figurative, feigned
* *affectioned*: swayed by the affections, biased   * *squire*: carpenter's square
* *affection*: emotion, feeling   * *solace*: enjoyment
* *conveyance*: expression

as give dolour and disliking to the ear and mind by any foul indecency* or disproportion of sound, situation* or sense, they be called, and not without cause, the vicious parts or rather heresies of language, whereof the matter resteth much in the definition and acceptance of this word 'decorum', for whatsoever is so cannot justly be misliked. In which respect it may come to pass that what the grammarian setteth down for a vitiosity* in speech may become a virtue and no vice;[20] contrariwise, his commended figure may fall into a reproachful* fault – the best and most assured remedy whereof is generally to follow the saying of Bias:[21] *ne quid nimis.* So as in keeping measure,* and not exceeding nor showing any defect in the use of his figures, he cannot lightly do amiss, if he have besides (as that must needs be) a special regard to all circumstances of the person, place, time, cause and purpose he hath in hand, which being well observed it easily avoideth all the recited inconveniences,* and maketh now and then very vice go for a formal* virtue in the exercise of this art.

[*Chapter 8 – Six points set down by our learned forefathers for a general regiment* of all good utterance, be it by mouth or by writing*]

CHAPTER 9

How the Greeks first, and afterward the Latins, invented new names for every figure, which this author is also enforced to do in his vulgar

The Greeks were a happy people for the freedom and liberty of their language, because it was allowed them to invent any new

* *indecency*: indecorum   * *situation*: stanza form
* *vitiosity*: vice, defect, fault   * *reproachful*: blameworthy
* *ne quid nimis*: 'nothing to excess'   * *measure*: metre
* *inconveniences*: incongruities, absurdities   * *formal*: methodical
* *regiment*: method, rule

name that they listed,* and to piece many words together to make of them one entire, much more significative* than the single word.[22] So, among other things, did they to their figurative speeches devise certain names. The Latins came somewhat behind them in that point, and, for want of convenient single words to express that which the Greeks could do by cobbling many words together, they were fain to use the Greeks' still, till after many years that the learned orators and good grammarians among the Romans, as Cicero, Varro, Quintilian[23] and others, strained themselves to give the Greek words Latin names, and yet nothing so apt and fitty.* The same course are we driven to follow in this description, since we are enforced to cull* out for the use of our poet or maker all the most commendable figures. Now, to make them known (as behoveth), either we must do it by the original Greek name, or by the Latin, or by our own. But when I consider to what sort of readers I write, and how ill-faring* the Greek term would sound in the English ear, then also how short the Latins come to express many of the Greek originals, finally, how well our language serveth to supply the full signification of them both, I have thought it no less lawful, yea peradventure, under licence of the learned, more laudable, to use our own natural,* if they be well chosen and of proper signification, than to borrow theirs. So shall not our English poets, though they be to seek* of the Greek and Latin languages, lament for lack of knowledge sufficient to the purpose of this art.

And in case any of these new English names given by me to any figure shall happen to offend, I pray that the learned will bear with me, and to think the strangeness thereof proceeds but of novelty and disacquaintance with our ears, which in process of time and by custom will frame* very well. And such others as are not learned in the primitive languages, if they happen to hit upon any new name of mine so ridiculous in their opinion as may move them to laughter, let such persons yet assure themselves that such names go as near as may be to their

* *listed*: pleased   * *significative*: having meaning   * *fitty*: fitting
* *cull*: select   * *ill-faring*: ill-conditioned, sickly   * *natural*: native terms
* *to seek*: ignorant   * *frame*: supply the need

originals, or else serve better to the purpose of the figure than
the very original, reserving always that such new name should
not be unpleasant in our vulgar nor harsh upon the tongue, and,
where it shall happen otherwise, that it may please the reader
to think that hardly any other name in our English could be
found to serve the turn better. Again, if, to avoid the hazard of
this blame, I should have kept the Greek or Latin still, it would
have appeared a little too scholastical* for our makers, and a
piece of work more fit for clerks than for courtiers, for whose
instruction this travail* is taken. And if I should have left out
both the Greek and Latin name, and put in none of our own
neither, well perchance might the rule of the figure have been
set down, but no convenient name to hold him in memory. It was
therefore expedient we devised for every figure of importance his
vulgar name, and to join the Greek or Latin original with them,
after that sort much better satisfying as well the vulgar* as the
learned learner, and also the author's own purpose, which is to
make of a rude* rhymer a learned and a courtly poet.

CHAPTER 10

*A division of figures, and how they serve in exornation of
language*

And because our chief purpose herein is for the learning of ladies
and young gentlewomen or idle courtiers, desirous to become
skilful in their own mother tongue and for their private recreation to make now and then ditties* of pleasure, thinking for
our part none other science* so fit for them and the place as
that which teacheth *beau semblant*,* the chief profession as well
of courting* as of poesy: since to such manner of minds nothing
is more cumbersome than tedious doctrines and scholarly

---

* *scholastical*: academic, pedantic   * *travail*: labour
* *vulgar*: uneducated   * *rude*: unlearned   * *ditties*: lyric poems
* *science*: form of learning   * *beau semblant*: fine-seeming
* *courting*: courtiership

methods of discipline,* we have in our own conceit devised a new and strange* model of this art, fitter to please the court than the school, and yet not unnecessary for all such as be willing themselves to become good makers in the vulgar, or to be able to judge of other men's makings.[24] Wherefore, intending to follow the course which we have begun, thus we say: that though the language of our poet or maker, being pure and cleanly, and not disgraced by such vicious parts as have been before remembered in the chapter of language, be sufficiently pleasing and commendable for the ordinary use of speech, yet is not the same so well appointed for all purposes of the excellent poet as when it is gallantly arrayed in all his colours which figure can set upon it; therefore we are now further to determine of figures and figurative speeches.

Figurative speech is a novelty of language evidently (and yet not absurdly) estranged* from the ordinary habit and manner of our daily talk and writing; and figure itself is a certain lively or good grace set upon words, speeches and sentences[25] to some purpose and not in vain, giving them ornament or efficacy by many manner of alterations in shape, in sound and also in sense: sometime by way of surplusage,* sometime by defect,* sometime by disorder or mutation, and also by putting into our speeches more pith and substance, subtlety, quickness, efficacy or moderation, in this or that sort tuning and tempering* them by amplification, abridgement, opening, closing, enforcing, meekening* or otherwise disposing them to the best purpose. Whereupon the learned clerks who have written methodically of this art in the two master languages, Greek and Latin, have sorted all their figures into three ranks; and the first they bestowed upon the poet only, the second upon the poet and orator indifferently,* the third upon the orator alone.[26] And that first sort of figures doth serve the ear only, and may be therefore called 'auricular'; your second serves the conceit* only

* *discipline*: instruction   * *strange*: singular, causing wonder
* *estranged*: altered, removed   * *surplusage*: excess, addition
* *defect*: deficiency, lack   * *tempering*: mixing, balancing
* *meekening*: softening   * *indifferently*: alike, without distinction
* *conceit*: mind, imagination

and not the ear, and may be called 'sensable',* not sensible*
nor yet sententious; your third sort serves as well the ear as the
conceit, and may be called 'sententious' figures, because not
only they properly appertain to full sentences,*[27] for beautifying
them with a current* and pleasant numerosity,* but also giving
them efficacy, and enlarging the whole matter besides with
copious amplifications.[28] I doubt not but some busy* carpers
will scorn at my new-devised terms, 'auricular' and 'sensable',
saying that I might with better warrant have used in their
steads these words, 'orthographical' or 'syntactical',[29] which the
learned grammarians left ready-made to our hands and do
import* as much as the other that I have brought; which thing,
peradventure, I deny not in part, and nevertheless for some
causes thought them not so necessary. But with these manner of
men I do willingly bear, in respect of their laudable endeavour
to allow* antiquity and fly innovation; with like benevolence I
trust they will bear with me writing in the vulgar speech and
seeking by my novelties to satisfy not the school but the court,
where, as[30] they know very well, all old things soon wax stale
and loathsome, and the new devices* are ever dainty and delicate,* the vulgar instruction requiring also vulgar and com-
municable terms, not clerkly* or uncouth,* as are all these of
the Greek and Latin languages primitively received, unless they
be qualified,* or by much use and custom allowed and our ears
made acquainted with them.

Thus, then, I say that auricular figures be those which work
alteration in the ear by sound, accent, time and slipper volubility* in utterance, such as for that respect was called by the
ancients numerosity[31] of speech. And not only the whole body
of a tale in poem or history may be made in such sort pleasant
and agreeable to the ear, but also every clause by itself, and

---

* *sensable*: of sense, of meaning   * *sensible*: perceptible, of the senses
* *sentences*: [also:] complete thoughts   * *current*: fluent
* *numerosity*: fluency, harmony   * *busy*: fussy   * *import*: signify
* *allow*: approve of   * *devices*: contrivances, ideas, conceits
* *dainty and delicate*: pleasant and delightful   * *clerkly*: scholarly
* *uncouth*: unknown, unfamiliar   * *qualified*: described, explained
* *slipper volubility*: easy fluency

every single word carried in a clause, may have their pleasant sweetness apart. And so long as this quality extendeth but to the outward tuning of the speech, reaching no higher than the ear and forcing the mind little or nothing, it is that virtue which the Greeks call *enargeia*,[32] and is the office of the auricular figures to perform. Therefore, as the members of language at large are whole sentences, and sentences are compact* of clauses, and clauses of words, and every word of letters and syllables, so is the alteration (be it but of a syllable or letter) much material* to the sound and sweetness of utterance. Wherefore beginning first at the smallest alterations, which rest in letters and syllables, the first sort of our figures auricular we do appoint to single words as they lie in language, the second to clauses of speech, the third to perfect* sentences and to the whole mass or body of the tale, be it poem or history, written or reported.

[*Chapter 11 – Of auricular figures appertaining to single words, and working by their divers sounds and audible tunes alteration to the ear only and not to the mind*]

CHAPTER 12

Of auricular figures pertaining to clauses of speech, and by them working no little alteration to the ear

As your single words may be many ways transfigured to make the metre or verse more tuneable* and melodious, so also may your whole and entire clauses be in such sort contrived by the order of their construction as the ear may receive a certain recreation,* although the mind for any novelty of sense be little or nothing affected. And therefore all your figures of grammatical construction, I account them but merely auricular in that they reach no further than the ear, to which there will appear

---

* *compact*: made up   * *material*: important   * *perfect*: complete
* *tuneable*: musical   * *recreation*: pleasurable exercise

some sweet or unsavoury point to offer you dolour or delight, either by some evident defect, or surplusage, or disorder, or immutation* in the same speeches, notably altering either the congruity grammatical, or the sense, or both.

[ellipsis, *or the figure of default*; zeugma, *or the single supply*; prozeugma, *or the ringleader*; mesozeugma, *or the middle-marcher*; hypozeugma, *or the rearwarder*; syllepsis, *or the double supply*; hypozeuxis, *or the substitute*]

Aposiopesis,* *or the figure of silence.* Ye have another auricular figure of defect, and is when we begin to speak a thing and break off in the middle way, as if either it needed no further to be spoken of, or that we were ashamed or afraid to speak it out. It is also sometimes done by way of threatening, and to show a moderation of anger. The Greeks call him *aposiopesis*; I, the figure of silence or of interruption indifferently.

If we do interrupt our speech for fear, this may be an example, where as one durst* not make the true report as it was, but staid halfway for fear of offence, thus:

> He said you were – I dare not tell you plain,
> For words, once out, never return again.

If it be for shame, or that the speaker suppose it would be indecent to tell all, then thus, as he that said to his sweetheart, whom he checked for secretly whispering with a suspected person:

> And did ye not come by his chamber door,
> And tell him that – ? Go to, I say no more.

If it be for anger, or by way of menace, or to show a moderation of wrath as the grave and discreeter sort of men do, then thus:

> If I take* you with such another cast,*
> I swear by God – but let this be the last;

---

* *immutation*: mutation   * *aposiopesis*: 'becoming silent'
* *durst*: dared   * *take*: catch   * *cast*: trick

thinking to have said further, viz., 'I will punish you'. If it be for none of all these causes, but upon some sudden occasion that moves a man to break off his tale, then thus:

> He told me all at large – lo, yonder is the man:
> Let himself tell the tale that best tell can.

This figure is fit for fantastical heads and such as be sudden* or lack memory. I know one of good learning that greatly blemisheth his discretion* with this manner of speech, for if he be in the gravest matter of the world talking, he will upon the sudden, for the flying of a bird overthwart the way,* or some other such slight cause, interrupt his tale and never return to it again.

   [prolepsis, *or the propounder*]

CHAPTER 13

Of your figures auricular working by disorder

Hyperbaton,* *or the trespasser*. To all their speeches which wrought by disorder the Greeks gave a general name, *hyperbaton*, as much to say as the 'trespasser'; and because such disorder may be committed many ways it receiveth sundry particulars* under him, whereof some are only proper to the Greeks and Latins and not to us,[33] other some ordinary in our manner of speeches, but so foul and intolerable as I will not seem to place them among the figures, but do range them as they deserve among the vicious or faulty speeches.[34]

   Parenthesis,* *or the inserter*. Your first figure of tolerable disorder is *parenthesis* or, by an English name, the 'inserter', and is when ye will seem, for larger information or some other purpose, to piece or graff* in the midst of your tale an unnecess-

---

* *sudden*: hasty, lacking in forethought, apt to improvise
* *discretion*: judgement, discernment   * *overthwart the way*: across the path
* *hyperbaton*: 'transposed'   * *particulars*: parts, sub-categories
* *parenthesis*: 'insertion'   * *graff*: graft

ary parcel of speech, which nevertheless may be thence* without
any detriment to the rest. The figure is so common that it needeth
none example; nevertheless, because we are to teach ladies and
gentlewomen to know their school points and terms appertaining to the art, we may not refuse to yield examples even in
the plainest cases, as that of Master Dyer's, very aptly:

> But now, my dear (for so my love makes me to call you still –
> That love, I say, that luckless love, that works me all this ill).[35]

[...]

Hysteron proteron,* or the preposterous.* Ye have another
manner of disordered speech, when ye misplace your words or
clauses and set that before which should be behind, and è
converso.* We call it in English proverb the cart before the
horse, the Greeks call it *hysteron proteron*, we name it the
preposterous, and if it be not too much used is tolerable enough,
and many times scarce perceivable, unless the sense be thereby
made very absurd; as he that described his manner of departure
from his mistress said thus, not much to be misliked, 'I kissed
her cherry lip and took my leave', for 'I took my leave and kissed
her'. And yet I cannot well say whether a man use to kiss before
he take his leave, or take his leave before he kiss, or that it be
all one business: it seems the taking leave is by using some speech
entreating licence of departure, the kiss a knitting-up of the
farewell and, as it were, a testimonial of the licence, without
which here in England one may not presume of courtesy to
depart – let young courtiers decide this controversy. One,
describing his landing upon a strange* coast, said thus, pre-
posterously: 'When we had climbed the cliffs, and were ashore'.
Whereas he should have said, by good order: 'When we were
come ashore, and climbèd had the cliffs.' For one must be on
land ere he can climb. And as another said: 'My dame that bred
me up, and bare me in her womb'. Whereas the bearing is before

---

* *may be thence*: i.e. may be taken away
* *hysteron proteron*: 'the latter first'
* *preposterous*: reversed (Latin *praeposterus*)   * *è converso*: vice versa
* *strange*: foreign

the bringing up. All your other figures of disorder, because they rather seem deformities than beauties of language, for so many of them as be notoriously undecent* and make no good harmony, I place them in the chapter of vices hereafter following.

[Chapter 14 – Of your figures auricular that work by surplusage; Chapter 15 – Of auricular figures working by exchange: enallage, or the figure of exchange; hypallage, or the changeling; Chapter 16 – Of some other figures which, because they serve chiefly to make the metres tuneable and melodious, and affect not the mind but very little, be placed among the auricular: homoeoteleuton, or the like-loose; paroemion, or the figure of like letter; asyndeton, or the loose language; polysyndeton, or the couple-clause; hirmus, or the long-loose; epitheton, or the qualifier; hendiadys, or the figure of twins]

CHAPTER 17

Of the figures which we call sensable, because they alter and affect the mind by alteration of sense; and first in single words

The ear having received his due satisfaction by the auricular figures, now must the mind also be served with his natural delight by figures sensable,[36] such as by alteration of intendments* affect the courage* and give a good liking to the conceit.* And first, single words have their sense and understanding altered and figured many ways, to wit, by transport,* abuse,* cross-naming,* new-naming, change of name. This will seem very dark to you unless it be otherwise explained more particularly; and first, of transport.

Metaphora,* or the figure of transport. There is a kind of wresting* of a single word from his own right signification to

* undecent: unbecoming, against decorum   * intendments: meanings
* courage: heart   * conceit: mind   * transport: transfer
* abuse: misuse, deceit   * cross-naming: misnaming
* metaphora: 'transference'   * wresting: turning, twisting

another not so natural, but yet of some affinity or conveniency*
with it, as to say 'I cannot digest your unkind words' for 'I
cannot take them in good part'; or, as the man of law said, 'I
feel you not' for 'I understand not your case', because he had
not his fee in his hand; or, as another said to a mouthy advocate,
'Why barkest thou at me so sore?'; or to call the top of a tree,
or of a hill, the crown of a tree or of a hill: for, indeed, 'crown'
is the highest ornament of a prince's head, made like a close*
garland, or else the top of a man's head where the hair winds
about, and because such term is not applied naturally to a tree
or to a hill, but is transported from a man's head to a hill or
tree, therefore it is called by metaphor or the figure of transport.
And three causes moves us to use this figure. One for necessity
or want of a better word, thus:

> As the dry ground that thirsts after a shower
> Seems to rejoice when it is well ywet,*
> And speedily brings forth both grass and flower
> If lack of sun or season do not let.*

Here, for want of an apter and more natural word to declare
the dry temper* of the earth, it is said to thirst and to rejoice,
which is only proper to living creatures, and yet, being so
inserted, doth not so much swerve from the true sense but that
every man can easily conceive the meaning thereof. [*second
cause: pleasure and ornament*] Then also do we it sometimes to
enforce a sense and make the word more significative, as thus:

> I burn in love, I freeze in deadly hate,
> I swim in hope, and sink in deep despair.[37]

These examples I have the willinger given you to set forth the
nature and use of your figure metaphor, which of any other,
being choicely made, is the most commendable and most
common.

* *conveniency*: congruity, similarity   * *close*: closed   * *ywet*: wetted
* *let*: hinder   * *temper*: condition

[catachresis, *or the figure of abuse*]

Metonymia,* *or the misnamer.* Now doth this understanding or secret conceit reach many times to the only nomination* of persons or things in their names, as of men, or mountains, seas, countries and such like, in which respect the wrong naming, or otherwise naming of them than is due, carrieth not only an alteration of sense but a necessity of intendment figuratively.* As when we call love by the name of Venus, fleshly lust by the name of Cupid, because they were supposed by the ancient poets to be authors and kindlers of love and lust; Vulcan for fire, Ceres for bread, Bacchus for wine by the same reason. Also, if one should say to a skilful craftsman known for a glutton or common drunkard, that had spent all his goods on riot and delicate fare, 'Thy hands they made thee rich, thy palate made thee poor', it is meant his travail and art made him wealthy, his riotous life had made him a beggar. And as one that boasted of his housekeeping said that never a year passed over his head that he drank not in his house every month four tuns* of beer and one hogshead of wine, meaning not the casks or vessels but that quantity which they contained. These and such other speeches, where ye take the name of the author for the thing itself, or the thing containing for that which is contained, and in many other cases do, as it were, wrong name the person or the thing, so, nevertheless, as it may be understood, it is by the figure *metonymia*, or misnamer.

[antonomasia, *or the surnamer*]

Onomatopoeia,* *or the new-namer.* Then also is the sense figurative when we devise a new name to anything, consonant, as near as we can, to the nature thereof, as to say 'flashing of lightning', 'clashing of blades', 'clinking of fetters', 'chinking of money', and, as the poet Virgil said of the sounding a trumpet, 'ta-ra-tant', *taratantara;*[38] or as we give special names to the voices of dumb beasts, as to say a horse neigheth, a lion brays, a swine grunts, a hen cackleth, a dog howls, and a hundred

---

* *metonymia*: 'change of name'   * *only nomination*: naming only
* *necessity . . . figuratively*: unavoidable figurative meaning
* *tuns*: large beer casks   * *onomatopoeia*: 'the making of words'

more such new names as any man hath liberty to devise, so it be
fitty for the thing which he covets to express.

[epitheton, *or the qualifier; otherwise the figure of attribution*]

Metalepsis, * *or the far-fet.** But the sense is much altered, and
the hearer's conceit strangely entangled, by the figure *metalepsis*,
which I call the far-fet, as when we had rather fetch a word a
great way off than to use one nearer hand to express the matter
as well and plainer. And it seemeth the deviser of this figure had
a desire to please women rather than men, for we use to say, by
manner of proverb, things far-fet and dear bought are good for
ladies. So in this manner of speech we use it: leaping over the
heads of a great many words, we take one that is furthest off to
utter our matter by, as Medea, cursing her first acquaintance
with Prince Jason, who had very unkindly forsaken her, said,

> Woe worth* the mountain that the mast bare,
> Which was the first causer of all my care,[39]

where she might as well have said 'Woe worth our first meeting',
or 'Woe worth the time that Jason arrived with his ship at my
father's city in Colchis, when he took me away with him', and
not so far off as to curse the mountain, that bare the pine tree,
that made the mast, that bare the sails, that the ship sailed with,
which carried her away. A pleasant gentleman came into a lady's
nursery and saw her, for her own pleasure, rocking of her young
child in the cradle, and said to her:

> I speak it madam without any mock:
> Many a such cradle may I see you rock.

'God's Passion, whoreson,' said she. 'Would thou have me bear
more children yet?' 'No, madam,' quoth the gentleman, 'but I
would have you live long, that ye might the better pleasure your
friends.' For his meaning was that as every cradle signified a
new-born child, and every child the leisure of one year's birth,
and many years a long life, so by wishing her to rock many

---

* *metalepsis*: 'substitution'   * *far-fet*: farfetched   * *worth*: betide

cradles of her own he wished her long life. Virgil said: *post multas mea regna videns mirabor aristas?*[40] Thus in English:

> After many a stubble shall I come
> And wonder at the sight of my kingdom?

By stubble the poet understood years, for harvests come but once every year, at leastways* with us in Europe. This is spoken by the figure of far-fet, *metalepsis*.

[emphasis, *or the reinforcer*; litotes, *or the moderator*]

Paradiastole,* *or the curry-favel*.* But if such moderation of words tend to flattery, or soothing, or excusing, it is by the figure *paradiastole*, which therefore nothing improperly we call the curry-favel, as when we make the best of a bad thing, or turn a signification to the more plausible sense, as to call an unthrift* a liberal gentleman, the foolish-hardy* valiant or courageous, the niggard thrifty, a great riot or outrage an youthful prank, and suchlike terms, moderating and abating the force of the matter by craft,* and for a pleasing purpose, as appeareth by these verses of ours,[41] teaching in what cases it may commendably be used by courtiers.

[meiosis, *or the disabler*; tapinosis, *or the abaser*]

Synecdoche,* *or the figure of quick conceit*. Then, again, if we use such a word (as many times we do) by which we drive the hearer to conceive more, or less, or beyond, or otherwise than the letter expresseth, and it be not by virtue of the former figures metaphor and abase and the rest, the Greeks then call it *synecdoche*, the Latins *subintellectio*8 or understanding, for by part we are enforced to understand the whole, by the whole part, by many things one thing, by one many, by a thing precedent a thing consequent, and generally one thing out of another by manner of contrariety to the word which is spoken, *aliud*

---

* *at leastways*: at least   * *paradiastole*: 'putting together of dissimilar things'
* *curry-favel*: one who solicits favour by flattery   * *unthrift*: spendthrift
* *foolish-hardy*: foolhardy   * *craft*: skill, ingenuity
* *synecdoche*: 'understanding one thing with another'
* *subintellectio*: 'understanding a little'

ex alio.* Which, because it seemeth to ask a good, quick and pregnant capacity, and is not for an ordinary or dull wit so to do, I chose to call him the figure not only of conceit, after the Greek original, but also of quick conceit. As for example, we will give none because we will speak of him again in another place, where he is ranged among the figures sensable appertaining to clauses.

CHAPTER 18

Of sensable figures altering and affecting the mind by alteration of sense or intendments in whole clauses or speeches

As by the last-remembered figures the sense of single words is altered, so by these that follow is that of whole and entire speech, and first by the courtly figure *allegoria*, which is when we speak one thing and think another, and that our words and our meanings meet not. The use of this figure is so large, and his virtue of so great efficacy, as it is supposed no man can pleasantly utter and persuade without it, but in effect is sure never or very seldom to thrive and prosper in the world that cannot skilfully put in ure,* insomuch as not only every common courtier but also the gravest counsellor, yea, and the most noble and wisest prince of them all are many times enforced to use it, by example (say they) of the great emperor who had it usually in his mouth to say *qui nescit dissimulare nescit regnare.**[42] Of this figure, therefore, which for his duplicity we call the figure of 'false semblant* or dissimulation', we will speak first, as of the chief ringleader and captain of all other figures either in the poetical or oratory science.

Allegoria, * *or the figure of false semblant.* And ye shall know that we may dissemble, I mean speak otherwise than we think,

* *aliud ex alio*: 'one thing from another'   * *ure*: use
* *qui . . . regnare*: 'who knows not how to dissimulate knows not how to reign'
* *semblant*: seeming, appearance   * *allegoria*: 'other speaking'

in earnest as well as in sport, under covert and dark terms and in learned and apparent* speeches, in short sentences and by long ambage* and circumstance* of words, and finally as well when we lie as when we tell truth. To be short, every speech wrested from his own natural signification to another not altogether so natural is a kind of dissimulation, because the words bear contrary countenance to the intent. But properly and in his principal virtue *allegoria* is when we do speak in sense translative* and wrested from the own* signification, nevertheless applied to another not altogether contrary but having much conveniency* with it, as before we said of the metaphor: as, for example, if we should call the commonwealth a ship, the prince a pilot, the counsellors mariners, the storms wars, the calm and haven peace,[43] this is spoken all in allegory. And because such inversion of sense in one single word is by the figure metaphor, of whom we spake before, and this manner of inversion extending to whole and large speeches, it maketh the figure allegory to be called a long and perpetual metaphor. [. . .] Virgil, in his shepherdly poems called *Eclogues*, used as rustical but fit allegory for the purpose, thus: *claudite iam rivos, pueri; sat prata biberunt.*[44] Which I English thus: 'Stop up your streams, my lads, the meads have drunk their fill.' As much to say, 'Leave off now, ye have talked of the matter enough', for the shepherds' guise in many places is by opening certain sluices to water their pastures, so as when they are wet enough they shut them again. This application is full allegoric.

Ye have another manner of allegory, not full but mixed, as he that wrate thus:

> The clouds of care have covered all my coast,
> The storms of strife do threaten to appear;
> The waves of woe, wherein my ship is tossed,

* *apparent*: seemingly plausible   * *ambage*: circumlocution
* *circumstance*: beating about the bush, indirectness
* *translative*: metaphorical, involving transference of meaning
* *the own*: its own   * *conveniency*: affinity, congruency

THE ART OF ENGLISH POESY

> Have broke the banks, where lay my life so dear;
> Chips of ill chance are fall'n amidst my choice,
> To mar the mind that meant for to rejoice.[45]

I call him not a full allegory, but mixed, because he discovers*
withal what the 'cloud', 'storm', 'wave' and the rest are, which
in a full allegory should not be discovered, but left at large* to
the reader's judgement and conjecture.

Aenigma,* *or the riddle.* We dissemble again under covert
and dark speeches when we speak by way of riddle (*aenigma*),
of which the sense can hardly be picked out but by the party's
own assoil.* [. . .] My mother had an old woman in her nursery
who in the winter nights would put us forth many pretty riddles,
whereof this is one:

> I have a thing, and rough it is,
> And in the midst a hole iwis;*
> There came a young man with his gin,*
> And he put it a handful in.

The good old gentlewoman would tell us that were children
how it was meant by a furred glove. Some other naughty body
would peradventure have construed it not half so mannerly.*
The riddle is pretty, but that it holds too much of the *cacemphaton* or foul speech,[46] and may be drawn to a reprobate*
sense.

[*paroemia, or proverb*]

Ironia,* *or the dry mock.* Ye do likewise dissemble when ye
speak in derision or mockery, and that may be many ways,
as sometime in sport, sometime in earnest, and privily,* and
apertly,* and pleasantly, and bitterly. But first by the figure
ironia, which we call the dry mock, as he that said to a bragging

* *discovers*: reveals   * *at large*: at liberty
* *aenigma*: 'speaking in riddles'   * *assoil*: solution
* *iwis*: assuredly, indeed   * *gin*: tool   * *mannerly*: decently
* *reprobate*: depraved   * *ironia*: 'dissembling'
* *privily*: secretly, privately   * *apertly*: openly

ruffian, that threatened he would kill and slay, 'No doubt you
are a good man of your hands'.* Or as it was said by a French
king to one that prayed* his reward, showing how he had been
cut in the face at a certain battle fought in his service: 'Ye
may see,' quoth the King, 'what it is to run away and look
backwards.' And as Alfonso, King of Naples[47] said to one that
proffered to take his ring when he washed before dinner, 'This
will serve another well', meaning that the gentleman had another
time taken them and, because the King forgot to ask for them,
never restored his ring again.

[sarcasmus, *or the bitter taunt*; asteismus, *or the merry scoff,
otherwise the civil jest*; mycterismus, *or the fleering frump;**
antiphrasis, *or the broad flout*; charientismus, *or the privy nip*]
All these be soldiers to the figure *allegoria*, and fight under the
banner of dissimulation.

Hyperbole,* *or the overreacher; otherwise called the loud
liar*. Nevertheless, ye have yet two or three other figures that
smatch* a spice of* the same false semblant, but in another sort
and manner of phrase, whereof one is when we speak in the
superlative and beyond the limits of credit, that is by the figure
which the Greeks call *hyperbole*, the Latins *dementiens*[48] or the
lying figure; I, for his immoderate excess, call him the overreacher, right with his original, or 'loud liar', and methinks not
amiss. Now, when I speak that which neither I myself think to
be true, nor would have any other body believe, it must needs
be a great dissimulation, because I mean nothing less than that
I speak; and this manner of speech is used when either we would
greatly advance or greatly abase the reputation of any thing or
person, and must be used very discreetly, or else it will seem
odious. For although a praise or other report may be allowed
beyond credit, it may not be beyond all measure, specially in
the proseman,* as he that was Speaker in a parliament of King
Henry the Eighth's reign, in his oration, which ye know is of

* *good man of your hands*: man of skill and valour
* *prayed*: asked for, begged   * *fleering frump*: sneering gibe
* *hyperbole*: 'excessive throw'   * *smatch*: smack of, taste of
* *a spice of*: a kind of   * *proseman*: author of prose

ordinary* to be made before the Prince at the first assembly of both Houses, would seem to praise his Majesty thus: 'What should I go about* to recite your Majesty's innumerable virtues, even as much as if I took upon me to number the stars of the sky, or to tell the sands of the sea?' This *hyperbole* was both *ultra fidem* and also *ultra modum*,* and therefore of a grave and wise counsellor made the Speaker to be accounted a gross flattering fool. Peradventure if he had used it thus it had been better, and nevertheless a lie too, but a more moderate lie and no less to the purpose of the King's commendation, thus: 'I am not able with any words sufficiently to express your Majesty's regal virtues; your kingly merits, also, towards us your people and realm are so exceeding many as your praises therefore are infinite, your honour and renown everlasting.' And yet all this, if we shall measure it by the rule of exact verity, is but an untruth, yet a more cleanly commendation than was Master Speaker's. [. . .]

Periphrasis,* *or the figure of ambage.* Then have ye the figure *periphrasis*, holding somewhat of the dissembler, by reason of a secret intent not appearing by the words, as when we go about the bush and will not in one or a few words express that thing which we desire to have known, but do choose rather to do it by many words, as we ourselves wrote of our sovereign lady thus:

> Whom princes serve, and realms obey,
> And greatest of Briton kings begot,
> She came abroad even yesterday,
> When such as saw her knew her not.[49]

And the rest that followeth, meaning her Majesty's person, which we would seem to hide, leaving her name unspoken, to the intent the reader should guess at it, nevertheless, upon the matter, did so manifestly disclose it as any simple judgement

* *of ordinary*: according to custom   * *go about*: beat about the bush
* *ultra fidem . . . ultra modum*: 'beyond belief' . . . 'beyond due measure'
* *periphrasis*: 'talking around'

might easily perceive by whom it was meant, that is by Lady
Elizabeth, Queen of England and daughter to King Henry the
Eighth; and therein resteth the dissimulation. It is one of the
gallantest figures among the poets, so* it be used discreetly and
in his right kind,* but many of these makers that be not half
their craft's masters do very often abuse it, and also many
ways. For if the thing or person they go about to describe
by circumstance be by the writer's improvidence* otherwise
bewrayed,* it looseth the grace of a figure. As he that said,

> The tenth of March, when Aries received
> Dan Phoebus'* rays into his hornèd head,[50]

intending to describe the spring of the year, which every man
knoweth of himself, hearing the day of March named. The
verses be very good, the figure nought worth if it were meant in
periphrase for the matter: that is, the season of the year, which
should have been covertly disclosed by ambage, was by and by
blabbed out by naming the day of the month, and so the purpose
of the figure disappointed. Peradventure it had been better to
have said thus:

> The month and day when Aries received
> Dan Phoebus' rays into his hornèd head.

For now there remaineth for the reader somewhat to study and
guess upon, and yet the springtime to the learned judgement
sufficiently expressed. [. . .]

Synecdoche, *or the figure of quick conceit*. Now, for the
shutting up of this chapter, will I remember you farther of that
manner of speech which the Greeks call *synecdoche* and we the
figure of 'quick conceit', who, for the reasons before alleged,
may be put under the speeches *allegorical*, because of the darkness and duplicity of his sense. As, when one would tell me how
the French King was overthrown at St-Quentin,[51] I am enforced

* *so*: as long as   * *in his right kind*: according to its natural character
* *improvidence*: carelessness, lack of foresight   * *bewrayed*: betrayed
* *Dan Phoebus'*: Apollo's (i.e. the sun's)

to think that it was not the King himself in person, but the Constable of France with the French King's power. Or if one would say the town of Antwerp were famished, it is not so to be taken, but of the people of the town of Antwerp.[52] And this conceit being drawn aside, and (as it were) from one thing to another, it encumbers the mind with a certain imagination what it may be that is meant and not expressed; as he that said to a young gentlewoman, who was in her chamber making herself unready,* 'Mistress, will ye give me leave to unlace your petticoat?', meaning (perchance) the other thing that might follow such unlacing. In the old time, whosoever was allowed to undo his lady's girdle, he might lie with her all night, wherefore the taking of a woman's maidenhead away was said to undo her girdle: *virgineam dissoluit zonam*,* saith the poet,[53] conceiving out of a thing precedent a thing subsequent. This may suffice for the knowledge of this figure 'quick conceit'.

CHAPTER 19

Of figures sententious, otherwise called rhetorical

Now if our presupposal be true, that the poet is of all other the most ancient orator, as he that by good and pleasant persuasions first reduced* the wild and beastly people into public societies and civility of life, insinuating unto them under fictions with sweet and coloured speeches many wholesome lessons and doctrines, then no doubt there is nothing so fit for him as to be furnished with all the figures that be rhetorical, and such as do most beautify language with eloquence and sententiousness.* Therefore, since we have already allowed to our maker his auricular figures, and also his sensable, by which all the words and clauses of his metres are made as well tuneable to the ear as

---

* *making . . . unready*: getting undressed
* *virgineam . . . zonam*: 'loosed the virginal belt'   * *reduced*: ordered
* *sententiousness*: fullness of meaning

stirring to the mind, we are now by order* to bestow upon him those other figures which may execute both offices, and all at once to beautify and give sense and sententiousness to the whole language at large. So as if we should entreat our maker to play also the orator, and whether it be to plead, or to praise, or to advise,[54] that in all three cases he may utter and also persuade both copiously and vehemently.

And your figures rhetorical, besides their remembered ordinary virtues, that is, sententiousness and copious amplification, or enlargement, of language,[55] do also contain a certain sweet and melodious manner of speech, in which respect they may, after a sort, be said auricular, because the ear is no less ravished with their current* tune than the mind is with their sententiousness. For the ear is properly but an instrument of conveyance for the mind, to apprehend the sense by the sound. And our speech is made melodious or harmonical not only by strained* tunes, as those of music, but also by choice of smooth words; and, thus or thus marshalling them in their comeliest construction and order, and as well by sometimes sparing, sometimes spending them more or less liberally, and carrying or transporting of them farther off or nearer, setting them with sundry relations and variable forms in the ministry and use of words, do breed no little alteration in man. For, to say truly, what else is man but his mind? Which whosoever have skill to compass* and make yielding and flexible, what may not he command the body to perform? He, therefore, that hath vanquished the mind of man hath made the greatest and most glorious conquest. But the mind is not assailable unless it be by sensible* approaches, whereof the audible is of greatest force for instruction or discipline, the visible for apprehension of exterior knowledges, as the philosopher saith.[56] Therefore, the well-tuning of your words and clauses to the delight of the ear maketh your information no less plausible to the mind than to the ear – no, though* you filled them with never so much sense and sententiousness. Then, also, must the whole tale (if it tend to persuasion) bear his just

* *by order*: in order   * *current*: fluent   * *strained*: melodic
* *compass*: win round   * *sensible*: perceptible   * *though*: even if

and reasonable measure, being rather with the largest than with the scarcest.* For like as one or two drops of water pierce not the flint stone, but many and often droppings do, so cannot a few words (be they never so pithy or sententious) in all cases and to all manner of minds make so deep an impression as a more multitude of words to the purpose, discreetly and without superfluity uttered, the mind being no less vanquished with large load of speech than the limbs are with heavy burden. Sweetness of speech, sentence and amplification are therefore necessary to an excellent orator and poet, ne* may in no wise be spared from any of them.

And first of all others your figure that worketh by iteration or repetition of one word or clause doth much alter and affect the ear and also the mind of the hearer, and therefore is counted a very brave* figure both with the poets and rhetoricians, and this repetition may be in seven sorts.

Anaphora,* *or the figure of report.** Repetition in the first degree we call the figure of report, according to the Greek original, and is when we make one word begin and, as they are wont to say, lead the dance to many verses in suit, as [. . .] this, written by Sir Walter Ralegh of his greatest mistress in most excellent verses:

> In vain mine eyes, in vain you waste your tears,
> In vain my sighs the smokes of my despairs,
> In vain you search the earth and heav'ns above,
> In vain ye seek, for fortune keeps my love.[57]

[. . .]

[antistrophe, *or the counter-turn;* symploce, *or the figure of reply*]

Anadiplosis,* *or the redouble.* Ye have another sort of repetition, when with the word by which you finish your verse ye begin the next verse with the same, as thus:

---

* *being rather . . . scarcest:* i.e. being grouped rather with the most copious narrations than with the most meagre   * *ne:* nor
* *brave:* splendid, handsome   * *anaphora:* 'carrying back'
* *report:* echo, repeated sound   * *anadiplosis:* 'repetition'

> Comfort it is for man to have a wife,
> Wife chaste, and wise, and lowly all her life.

Or thus:

> Your beauty was the cause of my first love –
> Love, while I live, that I may sore repent.

The Greeks call this figure *anadiplosis*; I call him the redouble, as the original bears.

Epanalepsis, * *or the echo sound; otherwise, the slow return.* Ye have another sort of repetition, when ye make one word both begin and end your verse, which therefore I call the slow return, otherwise the echo sound, as thus:

> Much must he be belov'd that loveth much;
> Fear many must he needs, whom many fear.[58]

Unless I called him the echo sound I could not tell what name to give him, unless it were the slow return.

Epizeuxis, * *the underlay, or cuckoo-spell.* Ye have another sort of repetition, when in one verse or clause of a verse ye iterate one word without any intermission, as thus: 'It was Maryne, Maryne that wrought mine woe.' And this, bemoaning the departure of a dear friend:

> The chiefest staff of mine assurèd stay, *
> With no small grief, is gone, is gone away.

And that of Sir Walter Ralegh's, very sweet:

> With wisdom's eyes had but blind fortune seen,
> Then had my love my love forever been.[59]

The Greeks call him *epizeuxis,* the Latins *subiunctio;* * we may

---

* *epanalepsis*: 'resumption'   * *epizeuxis*: 'fastening together'
* *stay*: support   * *subiunctio*: 'joining'

call him the underlay.[60] Methinks if we regard his manner of iteration, and would depart from the original, we might very properly in our vulgar, and for pleasure, call him the cuckoo-spell, for right as the cuckoo repeats his lay, which is but one manner of note, and doth not insert any other tune betwixt, and sometimes for haste stammers out two or three of them, one immediately after another, as 'cuck, cuck, cuckoo', so doth the figure *epizeuxis* in the former verses, 'Maryne, Maryne', without any intermission at all.

Ploce,* *or the doubler.* Yet have ye one sort of repetition, which we call the doubler, and is as the next before, a speedy iteration of one word, but with some little intermission by inserting one or two words between, as, in a most excellent ditty written by Sir Walter Ralegh, these two closing verses:

> Yet when I saw myself to you was true,
> I loved myself, because myself loved you.[61]

[...]

Now also be there many other sorts of repetition, if a man would use them, but are nothing commendable and therefore are not observed in good poesy, as a vulgar rhymer who doubled one word in the end of every verse, thus: '... adieu, adieu', '... my face, my face'. And another that did the like in the beginning of his verse, thus: 'To love him and love him, as sinners should do.' These repetitions be not figurative but fantastical, for a figure is ever used to a purpose, either of beauty or of efficacy, and these last recited be to no purpose, for neither can ye say that it urges affection, nor that it beautifieth or enforceth the sense, nor hath any other subtlety in it, and therefore is a foolish impertinency* of speech and not a figure.

Prosonomasia,* *or the nicknamer.* Ye have a figure by which ye play with a couple of words or names much resembling, and because the one seems to answer the other by manner of allusion, and doth, as it were, nick* him, I call him the nicknamer. If any

---

* *ploce*: 'plaiting'   * *impertinency*: absurdity
* *prosonomasia*: 'naming'   * *nick*: suit, resemble

other man can give him a fitter English name, I will not be angry, but I am sure mine is very near the original sense of *prosonomasia*, and rather a byname* given in sport than a surname given of any earnest purpose. As Tiberius the Emperor, because he was a great drinker of wine, they called him by way of derision to his own name 'Caldius Biberius Mero', instead of Claudius Tiberius Nero,[62] and so a jesting friar that wrate against Erasmus called him by resemblance to his own name 'Errans mus',* and are maintained by the figure *prosonomasia*, or the nicknamer. [. . .] Now, when such resemblance happens between words of another nature and not upon men's names, yet doth the poet or maker find pretty sport to play with them in his verse, specially the comical poet and the epigrammatist. Sir Philip Sidney in a ditty played very prettily with these two words 'love' and 'live', thus:

> And all my life I will confess,
> The less I love, I live the less.[63]

[. . .] Or as one replied to his mistress, charging him with some disloyalty towards her:

> Prove me, madam, ere ye fall to reprove:
> Meek minds should rather excuse than accuse.

Here the words 'prove' and 'reprove', 'excuse' and 'accuse', do pleasantly encounter and (as it were) mock one another by their much resemblance, and this is by the figure *prosonomasia*, as well as if they were men's proper names alluding to each other.

Traductio,* *or the tranlacer*. Then have ye a figure which the Latins call *traductio*, and I the tranlacer, which is when ye turn and tranlace* a word into many sundry shapes, as the tailor doth his garment, and after that sort do play with him in your ditty, as thus:

* *byname*: nickname   * *Errans mus*: 'wandering/erring mouse'
* *traductio*: 'leading along, transferring'
* *tranlace*: transpose, convey from one form to another

> Who lives in love, his life is full of fears
> To lose his love, livel'hood, or liberty.
> But lively sprites that young and reckless be
> Think that there is no living like to theirs.

[...] Here ye see how [...] this word 'life' is tranlaced into 'live', 'living', 'lively', 'livel'hood'. [...]

Anthypophora, * or the figure of response. Ye have a figurative speech which the Greeks call *anthypophora*, I name him the response, and is when we will seem to ask a question to the intent we will answer it ourselves, and is a figure of argument and also of amplification. Of argument because, proponing* such matter as our adversary might object and then to answer it ourselves, we do unfurnish and prevent him of such help as he would otherwise have used for himself; then, because such objection and answer spend much language, it serves as well to amplify and enlarge our tale. [...] Edward, Earl of Oxford, a most noble and learned gentleman, made in this figure of response an emblem of desire, otherwise called Cupid, which, for his excellency and wit, I set down some part of the verses for example:

> When wert thou born, Desire?
> *In pomp and prime of May.*
> By whom, sweet boy, wert thou begot?
> *By good conceit,* men say.*
> Tell me, who was thy nurse?
> *Fresh youth, in sugared joy.*
> What was thy meat and daily food?
> *Sad sighs with great annoy.*
> What hadst thou then to drink?
> *Unfeignèd lovers' tears.*
> What cradle wert thou rockèd in?
> *In hope devoid of fears.*[64]

---

* *anthypophora*: 'reply'   * *proponing*: propounding, proposing
* *conceit*: opinion

[synoeciosis, *or the cross-coupling;* antanaclasis, *or the rebound*]

Climax, * *or the marching figure.* Ye have a figure which, as well by his Greek and Latin originals[65] and also by allusion to the manner of a man's gait or going, may be called the marching figure, for after the first step all the rest proceed by double the space, and so in our speech one word proceeds double to the first that was spoken, and goeth, as it were, by strides or paces. It may as well be called the climbing figure, for *climax* is as much to say as a ladder, as in one of our epitaphs showing how a very mean* man by his wisdom and good fortune came to great estate and dignity:

> His virtue made him wise, his wisdom brought him wealth,
> His wealth won many friends, his friends made much supply
> Of aids in weal* and woe, in sickness and in health:
> Thus came he from alow* to sit in seat so high.

Or as Jean de Meung, the French poet:

> Peace makes plenty, plenty makes pride,
> Pride breeds quarrel, and quarrel brings war,
> War brings spoil, and spoil poverty,
> Poverty patience, and patience peace:
> So peace brings war, and war brings peace.[66]

Antimetabole, * *or the counter-change.* Ye have a figure which takes a couple of words to play with in a verse, and by making them to change and shift one into other's place they do very prettily exchange and shift the sense, as [. . .] thus:

> We wish not peace to maintain cruel war,
> But we make war to maintain us in peace.

---

* *climax*: 'ladder'   * *mean*: lowly   * *weal*: prosperity
* *alow*: in a low condition or estate   * *antimetabole*: 'turning about'

Or thus:

> If poesy be, as some have said,
> A speaking picture to the eye,
> Then is a picture not denied
> To be a mute poesy.[67]

[...]

[insultatio, *or the disdainful;* antitheton, *or the rencounter;* erotema, *or the questioner;* ecphonesis, *or the outcry;* brachylogia, *or the cutted comma;* parison, *or the figure of even;* synonymia, *or the figure of store;* metanoia, *or the penitent;* antanagoge, *or the recompencer*]

Epiphonema,* *or the surclose.* Our poet in his short ditties, but specially playing the epigrammatist, will use to conclude and shut up his epigram with a verse or two, spoken in such sort as it may seem a manner of allowance* to all the premises, and that with a joyful approbation, which the Latins call *acclamatio;** we therefore call this figure the surclose or consenting close. As Virgil, when he had largely spoken of Prince Aeneas' success and fortunes, concluded with this close: *tantae molis erat Romanam condere gentem.*[68] In English, thus:

> So huge a piece of work it was and so high,
> To rear the house of Roman progeny.

Sir Philip Sidney very prettily closed up a ditty in this sort:

> What med'cine, then, can such disease remove,
> Where love breeds hate, and hate engenders love?[69]

And we, in a 'Partheniad' written of her Majesty, declaring to what perils virtue is generally subject and applying that fortune to herself, closed it up with this *epiphonema:*

* *epiphonema:* 'finishing touch, exclamation'
* *allowance:* praise, approbation   * *acclamatio:* 'acclamation'

> Then if there be
> Any so cankered heart to grutch*
> At your glories, my Queen, in vain
> Repining at your fatal* reign,
> It is for that they feel too much
> Of your bounty.[70]

As who would say her own overmuch lenity and goodness made her ill-willers the more bold and presumptuous. [...]

Auxesis,* *or the advancer*. It happens many times that, to urge and enforce the matter we speak of, we go still mounting by degrees and increasing our speech with words or with sentences of more weight one than another, and is a figure of great both efficacy and ornament. As he that, declaring the great calamity of an infortunate* prince, said thus:

> He lost besides his children and his wife,
> His realm, renown, liege,* liberty, and life.

By which it appeareth that to any noble prince the loss of his estate ought not to be so grievous as of his honour, nor any of them both like to the lack of his liberty, but that life is the dearest detriment* of any other. We call this figure, by the Greek original, the advancer or figure of increase, because every word that is spoken is one of more weight than another.
[...]

[meiosis, *or the disabler;* epanodos, *or the figure of retire;* dialysis, *or the dismemberer*]

Merismus,* *or the distributer*. Then have ye a figure very meet* for orators or eloquent persuaders, such as our maker or poet must in some cases show himself to be, and is when we may conveniently utter a matter in one entire speech or proposition, and will rather do it piecemeal and by distribution of every part for amplification sake. As, for example, he that might

* *grutch*: complain, grouch   * *fatal*: destined   * *auxesis*: 'increase'
* *infortunate*: subject to ill fortune   * *liege*: those faithful to him
* *detriment*: loss   * *merismus*: 'division'   * *meet*: appropriate

say a house was outrageously plucked down will not be satisfied so to say, but rather will speak it in this sort: they first undermined the ground-sills,* they beat down the walls, they unfloored the lofts, they untiled it, and pulled down the roof. For so indeed is a house pulled down by circumstances,* which this figure of distribution doth set forth every one apart, and therefore I name him the distributor according to his original. As wrate the Tuscan poet* in a sonnet which Sir Thomas Wyatt translated with very good grace, thus:

> Set me whereas* the sun doth parch the green,
> Or where his beams do not dissolve the ice,
> In temperate heat where he is felt and seen,
> In presence pressed of people mad or wise;
> Set me in high or yet in low degree,
> In longest night or in the shortest day,
> In clearest sky or where clouds thickest be,
> In lusty youth or when my hairs are grey;
> Set me in heav'n, in earth, or else in hell,
> In hill or dale, or in the foaming flood,
> Thrall or at large,* alive whereso* I dwell,
> Sick or in health, in evil fame or good:
> Hers will I be, and only with this thought
> Content myself, although my chance be naught.[71]

All which might have been said in these two verses:

> Set me wheresoever ye will,
> I am and will be yours still.

[. . .] This figure serves for amplification, and also for ornament, and to enforce persuasion mightily. Sir Geoffrey Chaucer, father of our English poets, hath these verses following in the distributor:

---

* *ground-sills*: foundations   * *circumstances*: details, particulars
* *the Tuscan poet*: i.e. Petrarch   * *whereas*: where
* *Thrall . . . large*: enslaved or free   * *whereso*: wherever

When faith fails in priests' saws,*
And lords' hests* are holden for laws,
And robbery is ta'en for purchase,
And lechery for solace,*
Then shall the realm of Albion
Be brought to great confusion.[72]

Where he might have said as much in these words: 'When vice abounds and virtue decayeth in Albion, then' etc. [. . .]

Epimone,* *or the love-burden.** The Greek poets who made musical ditties to be sung to the lute or harp did use to link their staves* together with one verse running throughout the whole song by equal distance, and was, for the most part, the first verse of the staff, which kept so good sense and conformity with the whole as his often repetition did give it greater grace. They called such linking verse *epimone*, the Latins *versus intercalaris*,* and we may term him the love-burden,[73] following the original, or, if it please you, the long repeat: in one respect because that one verse alone beareth the whole burden of the song, according to the original, in another respect for that it comes by large distances to be often repeated. As in this ditty made by the noble knight Sir Philip Sidney:

My true love hath my heart and I have his,
By just exchange one for another given;
I hold his dear, and mine he cannot miss* –
There never was a better bargain driven.
    My true love hath my heart and I have his.

His heart in me keeps him and me in one,
My heart in him his thoughts and senses guides;
He loves my heart, for once it was his own,
I cherish his because in me it bides:
    My true love hath my heart and I have his.[74]

* *saws*: sayings, commands   * *hests*: commands, behests
* *solace*: pleasure   * *epimone*: 'delay'   * *burden*: refrain
* *staves*: stanzas   * *versus intercalaris*: 'verse for insertion'
* *miss*: be without

[paradoxon, *or the wonderer;* aporia, *or the doubtful;* epitrope, *or the figure of reference*]

Parrhesia, * *or the licentious.* The fine* and subtle persuader, when his intent is to sting his adversary, or else to declare his mind in broad and liberal speeches which might breed offence or scandal, he will seem to bespeak pardon beforehand, whereby his licentiousness may be the better borne withal, as he that said:

> If my speech hap t'offend you any way,
> Think it their fault that force me so to say.[75]

[anacoenosis, *or the impartener;* paromologia, *or the figure of admittance*]

Aetiologia, * *or the reason-renderer, or the tell-cause.* In many cases we are driven for better persuasion to tell the cause that moves us to say thus or thus, or else when we would fortify our allegations by rendering reasons to every one: this assignation of cause the Greeks called *aetiologia,* which if we might without scorn of a new-invented term call 'tell-cause' it were right according to the Greek original. And, I pray you, why should we not, and with as good authority as the Greeks? Sir Thomas Smith, her Majesty's principal Secretary and a man of great learning and gravity, seeking to give an English word to this Greek word *agamos,** called it 'spite-wed' or 'wed-spite'.[76] Master Secretary Wilson, giving an English name to his *Art of Logic,* called it 'Witcraft'.[77] Methink I may be bold with like liberty to call the figure *aetiologia* 'tell-cause'. And this manner of speech is always confirmed[78] with these words: 'for', 'because', and such other confirmatives. The Latins, having no fit name to give it in one single word, gave it no name at all, but by circumlocution. We also call him the reason-renderer, and leave the right English word 'tell-cause'[79] much better answering the Greek original. Aristotle was most excellent in use of this figure, for he never propones* any allegation or makes any

* *parrhesia:* 'free-spokenness' * *fine:* skilful
* *aetiologia:* 'giving a cause' * *agamos:* unmarried
* *propones:* puts forward

surmise but he yields a reason or cause to fortify and prove it, which gives it great credit. For example ye may take these verses, first pointing, then confirming by similitudes:*

> When fortune shall have spit out all her gall,
> I trust good luck shall be to me allowed:
> For I have seen a ship in haven fall,
> After the storm had broke both mast and shroud.*[80]

[. . .] And in this other ditty of ours, where the lover complains of his lady's cruelty, rendering for every surmise a reason, and by telling the cause seeketh (as it were) to get credit, thus:

> Cruel you be who can say nay,
> Since ye delight in others' woe;
> Unwise am I, ye may well say,
> For that I have honoured you so.
> But blameless I, who could not choose,
> To be enchanted by your eye;
> But ye to blame, thus to refuse
> My service, and to let me die.

[dicaeologia, *or the figure of excuse*]

Noema,* *or the figure of close conceit*. Speaking before of the figure *synecdoche*, we called him 'quick conceit', because he inured* in a single word only by way of intendment or large meaning, but such as was speedily discovered by every quick wit, as by the half to understand the whole, and many other ways appearing by the examples. But by this figure *noema* the obscurity of the sense lieth not in a single word but in an entire speech, whereof we do not so easily conceive the meaning but, as it were, by conjecture, because it is witty and subtle or dark, which makes me therefore call him in our vulgar the 'close conceit'. As he that said by* himself and his wife: 'I thank God in forty winters that we have lived together never any of our

---

* *similitudes*: similes, resemblances   * *shroud*: sail   * *noema*: 'thought'
* *inured*: operated   * *by*: of

neighbours set us at one' – meaning that they never fell out in all that space, which had been the directer speech and more apert,* and yet by intendment amounts all to one, being nevertheless dissemblable and in effect contrary. Paulet, Lord Treasurer of England and first Marquess of Winchester, with the like subtle speech gave a quip to Sir William Gifford, who had married the Marquess's sister, and all her lifetime could never love her nor like of her company, but when she was dead made the greatest moan for her in the world, and with tears and much lamentation uttered his grief to the Lord Treasurer: 'O, good brother,' quoth the Marquess, 'I am right sorry to see you now love my sister so well' – meaning that he showed his love too late and should have done it while she was alive. A great counsellor, somewhat forgetting his modesty, used these words: 'God's Lady, I reckon myself as good a man as he you talk of, and yet I am not able to do so.' 'Yea, sir,' quoth the party, 'your Lordship is too good to be a man; I would ye were a saint' – meaning he would he were dead, for none are shrined for saints* before they be dead.

[horismus, *or the definer of difference*]

Procatalepsis,* *or the presumptous; otherwise the figure of presupposal.* It serveth many times to great purpose to prevent* our adversary's arguments and take upon us to know before what our judge or adversary or hearer thinketh, and that we will seem to utter it before it be spoken or alleged by them, in respect of which boldness to enter so deeply into another man's conceit or conscience, and to be so privy of another man's mind, gave cause that this figure was called the 'presumptuous'.[81] I will also call him the figure of presupposal or the preventer, for by reason we suppose before what may be said, or perchance would be said, by our adversary or any other, we do prevent them of their advantage, and do catch the ball (as they are wont to say) before it come to the ground.

Paralepsis,* *or the passager.* It is also very many times used

---

* *apert*: open   * *shrined for saints*: proclaimed or venerated as saints
* *procatalepsis*: 'seizing in advance'   * *prevent*: anticipate
* *paralepsis*: 'leaving aside'

for a good policy in pleading or persuasion to make wise* as if
we set but light of the matter, and that therefore we do pass it
over slightly, when indeed we do then intend most effectually,*
and despitefully* if it be invective, to remember it. It is also
when we will not seem to know a thing, and yet we know it well
enough, and may be likened to the manner of women, who, as
the common saying is, will say nay and take it:

> I hold my peace, and will not say, for shame,
> The much untruth of that uncivil dame:
> For if I should her colours kindly blaze,*
> It would so make the chaste ears amaze. etc.

[commoratio, *or the figure of abode*; metastasis, *or the flitting
figure, or the remove*; parecbasis, *or the straggler*; expeditio, *or
the speedy dispatcher*; comparatio, *or the paragon, or the figure
of comparison*][82]

Dialogismus,* *or the right reasoner.* We are sometimes
occasioned in our tale to report some fine speech from another
man's mouth, as what a king said to his privy council or subject,
a captain to his soldier, a soldier to his captain, a man to a
woman, and contrariwise; in which report we must always
give to every person his fit and natural,* and that which best
becometh him. For that speech becometh a king which doth not
a carter, and a young man that doth not an old, and so in every
sort and degree. Virgil speaking in the person of Aeneas, Turnus
and many other great princes, and sometimes of meaner men,
ye shall see what decency* every of their speeches holdeth with
the quality, degree and years of the speaker. To which examples
I will for this time refer you. So if, by way of fiction, we will
seem to speak in another man's person, as if King Henry the
Eighth were alive and should say, of the town of Boulogne,
'What we by war to the hazard of our person hardly* obtained,
our young son without any peril at all for little money delivered

* *wise*: in such a manner   * *effectually*: explicitly   * *despitefully*: cruelly
* *her colours kindly blaze*: describe her qualities according to their nature
* *dialogismus*: 'debate'   * *fit and natural*: appropriate and natural character
* *decency*: decorum   * *hardly*: boldly, with difficulty

up again'; or if we should feign King Edward the Third, understanding how his successor Queen Mary had lost the town of
Calais by negligence, should say 'That which the sword won,
the distaff hath lost' – this manner of speech is by the figure
dialogismus, or the right reasoner.[83]

Gnome,* *or the director;* Sententia,* *or the sage sayer.* In
weighty causes and for great purposes wise persuaders use grave
and weighty speeches, specially in matter of advice or counsel,
for which purpose there is a manner of speech to allege* texts
or authorities of witty sentence, such as smatch* moral doctrine
and teach wisdom and good behaviour. By the Greek original
we call him the director; by the Latin he is called *sententia*; we
may call him the sage sayer, thus:

> Nature bids us, as a loving mother,
> To love ourselves first and next to love another.[84]

> The prince that covets all to know and see
> Had need full mild and patient to be.[85]

> Nothing sticks faster by us, as appears,
> Than that which we learn in our tender years.[86]

And that which our sovereign lady wrate in defiance of fortune:

> Never think you fortune can bear the sway,
> Where virtue's force can cause her to obey.[87]

Heed must be taken that such rules or sentences* be choicely
made and not often used, lest excess breed loathsomeness.

[synathroesmus, *or the heaping figure*]

Apostrophe,* *or the turn-tale.* Many times, when we have
run a long race in our tale spoken to the hearers, we do suddenly
fly out and either speak or exclaim at some other person or

* *gnome*: 'thought, opinion'
* *sententia*: 'opinion, thought, sentence, maxim'
* *allege*: cite   * *smatch*: smack of   * *sentences*: sententiae, maxims
* *apostrophe*: 'turning away'

thing, and therefore the Greeks call such figure (as we do) the turn-way or turn-tale, and breedeth by such exchange a certain recreation to the hearers' minds, as this used by a lover to his unkind mistress:

> And as for you (fair one), say now by proof ye find
> That rigour and ingratitude soon kill a gentle mind.[88]

And as we in our 'Triumphals', speaking long to the Queen's Majesty, upon the sudden we burst out in an exclamation to Phoebus,* seeming to draw in a new matter, thus:

> But, O Phoebus,
> All glistering in thy gorgeous gown,
> Wouldst thou vouchsafe to slide adown
> And dwell with us,
>
> But for a day,
> I could tell thee close in thine ear
> A tale that thou hadst liefer* hear,
> I dare well say,
>
> Than e'er thou wert
> To kiss that unkind runaway,
> Who was transformed to boughs of bay
> For her cursed heart, etc.[89]

Hypotyposis,* *or the counterfeit representation.* The matter and occasion leadeth us many times to describe and set forth many things in such sort as it should appear they were truly before our eyes, though they were not present, which to do it requireth cunning, for nothing can be kindly* counterfeit or represented in his absence but by great discretion in the doer. And if the things we covet to describe be not natural or not veritable, then yet the same asketh more cunning to do it,

---

* *Phoebus*: Apollo, i.e. the sun   * *liefer*: rather
* *hypotyposis*: 'sketch, outline'   * *kindly*: naturally, characteristically

THE ART OF ENGLISH POESY

because to feign* a thing that never was, nor is like to be, proceedeth of a greater wit and sharper invention than to describe things that be true.

Prosopographia, * or the counterfeit countenance.[90] And these be things that a poet or maker is wont to describe, sometimes as true or natural, and sometimes to feign as artificial and not true, viz. the visage, speech and countenance of any person absent or dead. And this kind of representation is called the counterfeit countenance, as Homer doth in his *Iliades* diverse personages, namely Achilles and Thersites, according to the truth and not by fiction;[91] and as our poet Chaucer doth in his *Canterbury Tales* set forth the Summoner, Pardoner, Manciple and the rest of the pilgrims, most naturally and pleasantly.

Prosopopoeia, * or the counterfeit impersonation. But if ye will feign any person with such features, qualities and conditions, or if ye will attribute any human quality, as reason or speech, to dumb creatures or other insensible things, and do study (as one may say) to give them a human person, it is not *prosopographia* but *prosopopoeia*, because it is by way of fiction. And no prettier examples can be given to you thereof than in *The Romaunt of the Rose*, translated out of French by Chaucer,[92] describing the persons of avarice, envy, old age and many others, whereby much morality is taught.

Chronographia, * or the counterfeit time. So if we describe the time or season of the year, as winter, summer, harvest, day, midnight, noon, evening or such like, we call such description the counterfeit time, *chronographia*; examples are everywhere to be found.

Topographia, * or the counterfeit place. And if this description be of any true place, city, castle, hill, valley or sea, and such like, we call it the counterfeit place, *topographia*; or if ye feign places untrue, as heaven, hell, paradise, the house of fame, the palace of the sun, the den of sleep and such like, which ye shall see in poets: so did Chaucer very well describe the country of

---

* *feign*: represent, create in fiction   * *prosopographia*: 'writing a face/mask'
* *prosopopoeia*: 'making a face/mask'   * *chronographia*: 'time-writing'
* *topographia*: 'place-writing'

Saluces* in Italy, which ye may see in his report of the Lady Grisild.[93]

Pragmatographia,* *or the counterfeit action.* But if such description be made to represent the handling of any business, with the circumstances belonging thereunto, as the manner of a battle, a feast, a marriage, a burial, or any other matter that lieth in feat and activity, we call it then the counterfeit action, *pragmatographia.* In this figure the Lord Nicholas Vaux,[94] a noble gentleman and much delighted in vulgar making, and a man otherwise of no great learning but having herein a marvellous facility, made a ditty representing the battle and assault of Cupid so excellently well as, for the gallant and proper application of his fiction in every part, I cannot choose but set down the greatest part of his ditty, for in truth it cannot be amended:

> When Cupid scalèd first the fort,
> Wherein my heart lay wounded sore,
> The batt'ry was of such a sort,
> That I must yield or die therefore.*
> There saw I Love upon the wall,
> How he his banner did display;
> 'Alarm, alarm' he gan to call,
> And bade his soldiers keep array.*
> The arms the which that Cupid bare
> Were piercèd hearts with tears besprent,*
> In silver and sable,* to declare
> The steadfast love he always meant.
> There might you see his band all dressed
> In colours like to white and black,
> With powder and with pellets pressed,
> To bring them forth to spoil and sack.
> Good will, the master of the shot,
> Stood in the rampire* brave and proud;

* *Saluces*: Saluzzo   * *pragmatographia*: 'writing an action'
* *therefore*: on account of it   * *array*: rank, order
* *besprent*: besprinkled   * *sable*: (heraldic) black   * *rampire*: rampart

> For expense of powder he spared not
> 'Assault, assault' to cry aloud.
> There might you hear the cannons roar,
> Each piece discharging a lover's look, etc.[95]

Homoeosis,* *or resemblance.* As well to a good maker and poet as to an excellent persuader in prose the figure of similitude* is very necessary, by which we not only beautify our tale but also very much enforce and enlarge it. I say enforce, because no one thing more prevaileth with all ordinary judgements than persuasion by similitude. Now because there are sundry sorts of them which also do work after diverse fashions in the hearers' conceits, I will set them all forth by a triple division, exempting the general similitude as their common ancestor, and I will call him by the name of resemblance, without any addition, from which I derive three other sorts, and give every one his particular name: as resemblance by portrait or imagery, which the Greeks call *icon*; resemblance moral or mystical, which they call *parabola*; and resemblance by example, which they call *paradigma*. And first we will speak of the general resemblance or bare similitude, which may be thus spoken:

> But as the wat'ry showers delay the raging wind,
> So doth good hope clean put away despair out of my mind.[96]

And in this other, likening the forlorn lover to a stricken deer:

> Then as the stricken deer withdraws himself alone,
> So do I seek some secret place where I may make my moan.[97]

[. . .]

Icon,* *or resemblance by imagery.* But when we liken an human person to another, in countenance, stature, speech or other quality, it is not called bare resemblance, but resemblance

---

* *homoeosis*: 'likeness, resemblance'   * *similitude*: simile, resemblance
* *icon*: 'image'

by imagery or portrait, alluding to the painter's term, who yieldeth to the eye a visible representation of the thing he describes and painteth in his table.* [. . .] And this manner of resemblance is not only performed by likening of lively* creatures one to another, but also of any other natural thing bearing a proportion of similitude, as to liken yellow to gold, white to silver, red to the rose, soft to silk, hard to the stone, and such like. Sir Philip Sidney, in the description of his mistress, excellently well handled this figure of resemblance by imagery, as ye may see in his book of *Arcadia*.[98] And ye may see the like, of our doings, in a 'Partheniad' written of our sovereign lady, wherein we resemble every part of her body to some natural thing of excellent perfection in his kind, as of her forehead, brows and hair, thus:

> Of silver was her forehead high,
> Her brows two bows of ebony,
> Her tresses trussed were, to behold,
> Frizzled and fine as fringe of gold.

And of her lips:

> Two lips wrought out of ruby rock,
> Like leaves to shut and to unlock;
> As portal door in prince's chamber,
> A golden tongue in mouth of amber.

And of her eyes:

> Her eyes, God wot* what stuff they are –
> I durst* be sworn each is a star,
> As clear and bright as wont to guide
> The pilot in his winter tide.

---

* *table*: board on which picture is painted   * *lively*: living
* *wot*: knows   * *durst*: dare

And of her breasts:

> Her bosom, sleek as Paris plaster,
> Held up two balls of alabaster;
> Each bias* was a little cherry,
> Or else I think a strawberry.[99]

And all the rest that followeth, which may suffice to exemplify your figure of *icon*, or resemblance by imagery and portrait.

Parabola,* *or resemblance mystical*. But whensoever, by your similitude, ye will seem to teach any morality or good lesson by speeches mystical and dark or far-fet, under a sense metaphorical applying one natural thing to another, or one case to another, inferring by them a like consequence in other cases, the Greeks call it *parabola*, which term is also by custom accepted of us; nevertheless, we may call him in English the resemblance mystical, as when we liken a young child to a green twig which ye may easily bend every way ye list; or an old man who laboureth with continual infirmities to a dry and drixy* oak. Such parables were all the preachings of Christ in the Gospel, as those of the wise and foolish virgins, of the evil steward, of the labourers in the vineyard, and a number more.[100] And they may be feigned* as well as true, as those fables of Aesop, and other apologues* invented for doctrine sake by wise and grave men.

Paradigma,* *or resemblance*[101] *by example*. Finally, if in matter of counsel or persuasion we will seem to liken one case to another, such as pass ordinarily in man's affairs, and do compare the past with the present, gathering probability of like success to come in the things we have presently in hand, or if ye will draw the judgements precedent and authorized by antiquity as veritable, and peradventure feigned and imagined for some purpose, into similitude or dissimilitude with our present actions

---

* *bias*: the weight on one side of a bowling ball; i.e. nipple
* *parabola*: 'setting alongside'   * *drixy*: decayed   * *feigned*: fictitious
* *apologues*: moral fables
* *paradigma*: 'model, comparison, showing alongside'

GEORGE PUTTENHAM

and affairs, it is called resemblance by example. As if one should say thus: Alexander the Great, in his expedition to Asia, did thus; so did Hannibal coming into Spain; so did Caesar in Egypt; therefore all great captains and generals ought to do it. And thus again: it hath been always usual among great and magnanimous princes in all ages not only to repulse any injury and invasion from their own realms and dominions, but also with a charitable and princely compassion to defend their good neighbours princes and potentates from all oppression of tyrants and usurpers; so did the Romans by their arms restore many kings of Asia and Afric expulsed out of their kingdoms; so did King Edward I re-establish Balliol rightful owner of the crown of Scotland against Robert le Bruce, no lawful king;[102] so did King Edward the Third aid Dam* Peter, King of Spain against Henry, bastard and usurper;[103] so have many English princes holpen with their forces the poor dukes of Brittany, their ancient friends and allies, against the outrages of the French kings; and why may not the Queen our sovereign lady, with like honour and godly zeal, yield protection to the people of the Low Countries, her nearest neighbours, to rescue them, a free people, from the Spanish servitude?[104] [. . .]

CHAPTER 20

The last and principal figure of our poetical ornament

Exergasia,* *or the gorgeous.* For the glorious lustre it setteth upon our speech and language the Greeks call it *exergasia*, the Latin *expolitio*,* a term transferred from these polishers of marble or porphyrite, who, after it is rough-hewn and reduced to that fashion they will, do set upon it a goodly glass,* so smooth and clear as ye may see your face in it, or otherwise as

---

* *Dam*: Lord   * *exergasia*: 'working out'   * *expolitio*: 'polishing'
* *glass*: glaze, gloss

it fareth by the bare and naked body, which, being attired in rich and gorgeous apparel, seemeth to the common usage of the eye much more comely and beautiful than the natural. So doth this figure (which therefore I call the gorgeous) polish our speech and, as it were, attire it with copious and pleasant amplifications and much variety of sentences, all running upon one point and to one intent; so as I doubt whether I may term it a figure or rather a mass of many figurative speeches applied to the beautifying of our tale or argument.[105] In a work of ours entitled *Philocalia* we have strained to show the use and application of this figure and all others mentioned in this book, to which we refer you.[106] I find none example in English metre so well maintaining this figure as that ditty of her Majesty's own making, passing sweet and harmonical, which figure being, as his very original name purporteth, the most beautiful and gorgeous of all others, it asketh in reason to be reserved for a last complement,* and deciphered* by the art of a lady's pen, herself being the most beautiful, or rather beauty, of queens. And this was the occasion. Our sovereign Lady perceiving how by the Scottish Queen's residence within this realm at so great liberty and ease (as were scarce meet for so great and dangerous a prisoner) bred secret factions among her people and made many of the nobility incline to favour her party, some of them desirous of innovation in the state, others aspiring to greater fortunes by her liberty and life, the Queen, our sovereign Lady, to declare that she was nothing ignorant of those secret practices, though she had long with great wisdom and patience dissembled it, writeth this ditty most sweet and sententious, not hiding from all such aspiring minds the danger of their ambition and disloyalty. Which afterward fell out most truly by the exemplary chastisement of sundry persons who, in favour of the said Scottish Queen declining from her Majesty, sought to interrupt the quiet of the realm by many evil and undutiful practices.[107] The ditty is as followeth:

* *complement*: completion, finishing touch
* *deciphered*: represented, expressed

The doubt of future foes exiles my present joy,
And wit me warns to shun such snares as threaten mine annoy.
For falsehood now doth flow, and subject faith doth ebb,
Which would not be if reason ruled, or wisdom weaved the web.
But clouds of toys* untried do cloak aspiring minds,
Which turn to rain of late repent by course of changèd winds.
The top of hope supposed the root of ruth will be,
And fruitless all their graffèd* guiles, as shortly ye shall see.
Then dazzled eyes with pride, which great ambition blinds,
Shall be unsealed by worthy wights, whose foresight falsehood
    finds.
The daughter of debate, that eke* discord doth sow
Shall reap no gain where former rule hath taught still peace to
    grow.
No foreign banished wight shall anchor in this port:
Our realm it brooks no stranger's force – let them elsewhere
    resort.
Our rusty sword with rest shall first his edge employ
To poll* their tops that seek such change and gape for future
    joy.[108]

In a work of ours entitled *Philocalia*, where we entreat of the
loves between prince Philo and Lady Calia in their mutual
letters, messages and speeches, we have strained our muse to
show the use and application of this figure, and of all others.

CHAPTER 21

*Of the vices or deformities in speech and writing principally
noted by ancient poets*

It hath been said before how, by ignorance of the maker, a good
figure may become a vice, and, by his good discretion, a vicious

---

* *toys*: notions, flimsy schemes   * *graffèd*: grafted   * *eke*: also, moreover
* *poll*: cut off the top of a tree, or behead

speech go for a virtue in the poetical science.[109] This saying is to
be explained and qualified, for some manner of speeches are
always intolerable and such as cannot be used with any decency,
but are ever undecent:* namely, barbarousness, incongruity, ill
disposition,* fond affectation, rusticity and all extreme darkness, such as it is not possible for a man to understand the
matter without an interpreter. All which parts are generally to
be banished out of every language, unless it may appear that the
maker or poet do it for the nonce, as it was reported by* the
philosopher Heraclitus[110] that he wrote in obscure and dark
terms of purpose not to be understood, whence he merited the
nickname 'Scotinus'.* Otherwise, I see not but the rest of the
common faults may be borne with sometimes, or pass without
any great reproof, not being used overmuch or out of season, as
I said before. So as every surplusage,* or preposterous* placing,
or undue iteration, or dark word, or doubtful* speech are not
so narrowly to be looked upon in a large poem, nor specially in
the pretty poesies and devices of ladies and gentlewomen
makers, whom we would not have too precise poets, lest, with
their shrewd wits, when they were married they might become
a little too fantastical wives. Nevertheless, because we seem to
promise an art, which doth not justly admit any wilful error in
the teacher, and to the end we may not be carped at by these
methodical men that we have omitted any necessary point in
this business to be regarded, I will speak somewhat touching
these vitiosities* of language particularly and briefly, leaving no
little to the grammarians for maintenance of the scholastical
war and altercations[111] – we, for our part, condescending in this
device* of ours to the appetite of princely personages and other
so tender and queasy complexions* in court as are annoyed
with nothing more than long lessons and overmuch good order.

* *undecent*: lacking in decorum, improper
* *ill disposition*: bad setting-out, misplacing   * *by*: of
* *Scotinus*: 'the Obscure'   * *surplusage*: excess
* *preposterous*: inverted, topsy-turvy   * *doubtful*: ambiguous
* *vitiosities*: vices   * *device*: work, project   * *complexions*: dispositions

GEORGE PUTTENHAM

CHAPTER 22

Some vices in speeches and writing are always intolerable,
some others now and then borne withal by licence of approved
authors and custom.

[barbarismus, *or foreign speech;* solecismus, *or incongruity*]

Cacozelia, * *or fond* * affectation. Ye have another intolerable
ill manner of speech, which by the Greek's original we may call
fond affectation, and is when we affect new words and phrases
other than the good speakers and writers in any language, or
than custom hath allowed; and is the common fault of young
scholars not half well studied, before they come from the university or schools, and when they come to their friends, or
happen to get some benefice* or other promotion in their
countries,* will seem to coin fine words out of the Latin and to
use newfangled speeches, thereby to show themselves, among
the ignorant, the better learned.

[soraismus, *or the mingle-mangle;* cacosyntheton, *or the mis-*
placer; cacemphaton, *or the figure of foul speech;* tautologia, *or*
the figure of self-saying; hysteron proteron, *or the preposterous;*
acyron, *or the uncouth*]

The vice of surplusage; pleonasmus, * *or too full speech.* Also,
the poet or maker's speech becomes vicious* and unpleasant by
nothing more than by using too much surplusage, and this lieth
not only in a word or two more than ordinary, but in whole
clauses, and peradventure large sentences, impertinently*
spoken, or with more labour and curiosity* than is requisite.
The first surplusage the Greeks call *pleonasmus,* I call him 'too
full speech', and is no great fault, as if one should say 'I heard it
with mine ears and saw it with mine eyes', as if a man could
hear with his heels, or see with his nose. We ourselves used this

* *cacozelia*: 'bad zeal, misplaced affectation'   * *fond*: foolish
* *benefice*: church living
* *countries*: counties, i.e. their own part of the country
* *pleonasmus*: 'excess, redundancy'   * *vicious*: corrupt, faulty
* *impertinently*: absurdly   * *curiosity*: artfulness

superfluous speech in a verse written of our mistress, nevertheless not much to be misliked, for even a vice sometime, being seasonably used, hath a pretty grace:

> For ever may my true love live and never die,
> And that mine eyes may see her crowned a queen.[112]

As, if she lived ever, she could ever die, or that one might see her crowned without his eyes.

Macrologia, * or long language. Another part of surplusage is called *macrologia*, or long language, when we use large clauses or sentences more than is requisite to the matter; it is also named by the Greeks *perissologia*.* As he that said: 'The ambassadors, after they had received this answer at the King's hands, they took their leave and returned home into their country from whence they came.' [...]

Periergia, * or over-labour; otherwise called the curious. Another point of surplusage lieth not so much in superfluity of your words as of your travail* to describe the matter which ye take in hand, and that ye over-labour yourself in your business. And therefore the Greeks call it *periergia*; we call it over-labour, jump* with the original, or rather 'the curious', for his overmuch curiosity and study to show himself fine in a light matter. As one of our late makers, who in most of his things wrote very well, in this (to mine opinion) more curiously than needed, the matter being ripely considered; yet is his verse very good, and his metre cleanly. His intent was to declare how upon the tenth day of March he crossed the river of Thames to walk in St George's Field; the matter was not great, as ye may suppose:

> The tenth of March, when Aries received
> Dan Phoebus' rays into his hornèd head,
> And I myself by learnèd lore perceived
> That Ver* approached and frosty winter fled,

* *macrologia*: 'speaking at length'
* *perissologia*: 'speaking too much, wordiness'
* *periergia*: 'over-elaboration'   * *travail*: labour, effort
* *jump*: exactly agreeing   * *Ver*: spring

> I crossed the Thames to take the cheerful air
> In open fields, the weather was so fair.[113]

First, the whole matter is not worth all this solemn circumstance to describe the tenth day of March, but if he had left it at the two first verses it had been enough. But when he comes with two other verses to enlarge his description, it is not only more than needs but also very ridiculous, for he makes wise as, if he had not been a man learned in some of the mathematics ('by learnèd lore'), that he could not have told that the 10th of March had fallen in the spring of the year, which every carter, and also every child, knoweth without any learning. Then, also, when he saith 'Ver approached and frosty winter fled', though it were a surplusage (because one season must needs give place to the other), yet doth it well enough pass without blame in the maker. These, and a hundred more of such faulty and impertinent speeches, may ye find amongst us vulgar poets, when we be careless of our doings.

Tapinosis,* *or the abaser.* It is no small fault in a maker to use such words and terms as do diminish and abase the matter he would seem to set forth, by impairing the dignity, height, vigour, or majesty of the cause he takes in hand. [. . .]

Bomphiologia,* *or pompous speech.* Others there be that fall into the contrary vice, by using such bombasted* words as seem altogether farced* full of wind, being a great deal too high and lofty for the matter, whereof ye may find too many in all popular rhymers.

Amphibologia,* *or the ambiguous.* Then have ye one other vicious speech with which we will finish this chapter, and is when we speak or write doubtfully,* and that the sense may be taken two ways. Such ambiguous terms they call *amphibologia;* we call it the ambiguous, or figure of sense uncertain. As, if one should say 'Thomas Taylor saw William Tyler drunk', it is indifferent* to think either the one or the other drunk. Thus said

* *tapinosis:* 'reduction, humiliation'
* *bomphiologia:* 'booming, buzzing words'   * *bombasted:* stuffed, padded
* *farced:* stuffed   * *amphibologia:* 'double-meaning, ambiguity'
* *doubtfully:* ambiguously   * *indifferent:* equally apt

a gentleman in our vulgar, prettily notwithstanding, because he did it not ignorantly but for the nonce:

> I sat by my lady, soundly sleeping,
> My mistress lay by me, bitterly weeping.

No man can tell by this whether the mistress or the man slept or wept. These doubtful speeches were used much in the old times by their false prophets, as appeareth by the oracles of Delphos and of the Sibyl's prophecies,[114] devised by the religious persons of those days to abuse the superstitious people, and to encumber their busy brains with vain hope or vain fear. [...] Our maker shall therefore avoid all such ambiguous speeches, unless it be when he doth it for the nonce and for some purpose.

CHAPTER 23

What it is that generally makes our speech well pleasing and commendable, and of that which the Latins call decorum

In all things, to use decency* is it only that giveth everything his good grace, and without which nothing in man's speech could seem good or gracious, insomuch as many times it makes a beautiful figure fall into a deformity, and on the other side a vicious speech seem pleasant and beautiful. This decency is therefore the line and level* for all good makers to do their business by. But herein resteth the difficulty, to know what this good grace is and wherein it consisteth, for peradventure it be easier to conceive than to express. We will therefore examine it to the bottom, and say that everything which pleaseth the mind or senses, and the mind by the senses as by means instrumental, doth it for some amiable point or quality that is in it, which draweth them to a good liking and contentment with their

* *decency*: seemliness, decorum
* *line and level*: (builder's/carpenter's) plumb-line and level

proper* objects. But that cannot be if they discover* any ill-favouredness or disproportion to the parts apprehensive:* as, for example, when a sound is either too loud or too low, or otherwise confuse, the ear is ill affected; so is the eye if the colour be sad* or not luminous* and recreative,* or the shape of a membered* body without his due measures and symmetry; and the like of every other sense in his proper function. These excesses or defects, or confusions and disorders, in the sensible objects are deformities, and unseemly to the sense. In like sort the mind: for the things that be his mental objects hath his good graces and his bad, whereof the one contents him wondrous well, the other displeaseth him continually, no more nor no less than ye see the discords of music do to a well-tuned ear. The Greeks call this good grace of everything in his kind *to prepon*,* the Latins *decorum*; we in our vulgar call it by a scholastical term, 'decency'; our own Saxon English term is 'seemliness',[115] that is to say for his good shape and utter* appearance well pleasing the eye; we call it also 'comeliness', for the delight it bringeth coming towards us, and to that purpose may be called 'pleasant approach';[116] so as, every way seeking to express this *prepon* of the Greeks and *decorum* of the Latins, we are fain in our vulgar tongue to borrow the term which our eye only, for his noble prerogative over all the rest of the senses, doth usurp, and to apply the same to all good, comely, pleasant and honest things, even to the spiritual* objects of the mind, which stand no less in the due proportion of reason and discourse than any other material thing doth in his sensible beauty, proportion and comeliness.

Now because this comeliness resteth in the good conformity of many things and their sundry circumstances* with respect one to another, so as there be found a just correspondency between them by this or that relation, the Greeks call it

---

* *proper*: own particular   * *discover*: reveal
* *parts apprehensive*: mind and senses   * *sad*: dark, dull
* *luminous*: bright   * *recreative*: pleasurable
* *membered*: having limbs or parts   * *to prepon*: 'the fitting'
* *utter*: outer   * *spiritual*: intellectual   * *circumstances*: particulars

analogy,* or a convenient* proportion. This lovely conformity,
or proportion, or conveniency* between the sense and the sensible hath nature herself first most carefully observed in all her
own works, then also by kind* graffed it in the appetites of
every creature working by intelligence to covet and desire, and
in their actions to imitate and perform, and of man chiefly before
any other creature, as well in his speeches as in every other part
of his behaviour. And this in generality and by an usual term is
that which the Latins call *decorum*. So, albeit we before alleged
that all our figures be but transgressions of our daily speech, yet
if they fall out decently, to the good liking of the mind or ear
and to the beautifying of the matter or language, all is well; if
indecently, and to the ear's and mind's misliking (be the figure
of itself never so commendable), all is amiss: the election* is the
writer's, the judgement is the world's, as theirs to whom the
reading appertaineth. But since the actions of man, with their
circumstances, be infinite, and the world likewise replenished
with many judgements, it may be a question who shall have the
determination of such controversy as may arise, whether this or
that action or speech be decent or indecent. And verily it seems
to go all by discretion,* not perchance of everyone, but by a
learned and experienced discretion. For otherwise seems the
decorum to a weak and ignorant judgement than it doth to one
of better knowledge and experience, which showeth that it
resteth in the discerning part of the mind, so as he who can
make the best and most differences of things by reasonable
and witty* distinction is to be the fittest judge or sentencer of
'decency'.[117]

[...]

It were too busy a piece of work for me to tell you of all the
parts of decency and indecency which have been observed in the
speeches of man and in his writings, and this that I tell you is

* *analogy*: i.e. *analogia*: 'ratio, correspondence, proportion'
* *convenient*: suitable, commensurate
* *conveniency*: congruency, correspondence   * *by kind*: naturally
* *election*: choice   * *discretion*: judgement, discernment
* *witty*: judicious

rather to solace your ears with pretty conceits after a sort of long scholastical precepts, which may happen have doubled them, rather than for any other purpose of institution or doctrine,* which to any courtier of experience is not necessary in this behalf.* And as they appear by the former examples to rest in our speech and writing, so do the same by like proportion consist in the whole behaviour of man, and that which he doth well and commendably is ever decent, and the contrary undecent, not in every man's judgement always one, but after* their several discretion and by circumstance diversly, as by the next chapter shall be showed.

CHAPTER 24

Of decency in behaviour, which also belongs to the consideration of the poet or maker

And there is a decency to be observed in every man's action and behaviour, as well as in his speech and writing, which some, peradventure, would think impertinent* to be treated of in this book, where we do but inform the commendable fashions of language and style. But that is otherwise, for the good maker or poet, who is in decent speech and good terms to describe all things, and with praise or dispraise to report every man's behaviour, ought to know the comeliness of an action as well as of a word, and thereby to direct himself, both in praise and persuasion or any other point that pertains to the orator's art. Wherefore, some examples we will set down of this manner of decency in behaviour, leaving you for the rest to our book which we have written *De Decoro*,[118] where ye shall see both parts* handled more exactly. And this decency of man's behaviour, as well as of his speech, must also be deemed* by discretion, in which regard the thing that may well become one man to do

* *institution or doctrine*: education or instruction   * *behalf*: respect
* *after*: according to   * *impertinent*: irrelevant
* *both parts*: i.e. of speech and behaviour   * *deemed*: judged

may not become another, and that which is seemly to be done in this place is not so seemly in that, and at such a time decent but at another time undecent, and in such a case, and for such a purpose, and to this and that end, and by this and that event, perusing all the circumstances with like consideration.[119]

[...]

And with these examples I think sufficient to leave, giving you information of this one point, that all your figures poetical or rhetorical are but observations of strange* speeches, and such as without any art at all we should use and commonly do, even by very nature, without discipline;*[120] but more or less aptly and decently, or scarcely or abundantly, or of this or that kind of figure, and one of us more than another, according to the disposition of our nature, constitution of the heart, and facility of each man's utterance. So as we may conclude that nature herself suggesteth the figure in this or that form, but art aideth the judgement of his use and application, which gives me occasion finally, and for a full conclusion to this whole treatise, to inform you in the next chapter how art should be used in all respects, and specially in this behalf of language, and when the natural is more commendable than the artificial, and contrariwise.

CHAPTER 25

That the good poet or maker ought to dissemble his art, and in what cases the artificial is more commended than the natural, and contrariwise

And now (most excellent Queen), having largely* said of poets and poesy and about what matters they be employed, then of all the commended forms of poems, thirdly of metrical proportions, such as do appertain to our vulgar art, and last of all set forth

* *strange*: unusual, singular   * *discipline*: instruction
* *largely*: at great length, fully

the poetical ornament, consisting chiefly in the beauty and gallantness* of his language and style, and so have apparelled him,
to our seeming, in all his gorgeous habiliments;* and pulling
him first from the cart to the school, and from thence to the
court, and preferred him to your Majesty's service, in that
place of great honour and magnificence to give entertainment
to princes, ladies of honour, gentlewomen and gentlemen and,
by his many moods* of skill, to serve the many humours of men
thither haunting and resorting, some by way of solace,* some
of serious advice, and in matters as well profitable as pleasant
and honest: we have, in our humble conceit, sufficiently performed our promise, or rather duty, to your Majesty in the
description of this art, so, always, as we leave him not unfurnished of one piece that best beseems that place of any other,
and may serve as a principal good lesson for all good makers to
bear continually in mind in the usage of this science, which is
that, being now lately become a courtier, he show not himself a
craftsman, and merit to be disgraded* and with scorn sent back
again to the shop,* or other place of his first faculty* and calling,
but that so wisely and discreetly he behave himself as he may
worthily retain the credit of his place and profession of a very
courtier, which is, in plain terms, cunningly* to be able to
dissemble.

[...]

These, and many such like, disguisings do we find in man's
behaviour, and specially in the courtiers of foreign countries,
where in my youth I was brought up, and very well observed
their manner of life and conversation, for of mine own country
I have not made so great experience. Which parts, nevertheless,
we allow not now in our English maker, because we have given
him the name of an honest man and not of an hypocrite. And,
therefore, leaving these manner of dissimulations to all base-
minded men, and of vile nature or mystery,* we do allow our

* *gallantness*: splendour, excellence   * *habiliments*: clothes
* *moods*: forms, modes   * *solace*: entertainment
* *disgraded*: deposed, deprived of status   * *shop*: workshop
* *faculty*: trade, profession   * *cunningly*: skilfully
* *mystery*: trade, profession

courtly poet to be a dissembler only in the subtleties of his art –
that is, when he is most artificial* so to disguise and cloak it as
it may not appear, nor seem to proceed from him by any study
or trade* of rules, but to be his natural,* nor so evidently to be
descried as every lad that reads him shall say he is a good
scholar, but will rather have him to know his art well, and little
to use it.[121]

[. . .]

But, now, because our maker or poet is to play many parts
and not one alone – as first to devise his plot or subject, then to
fashion his poem, thirdly to use his metrical proportions, and
last of all to utter with pleasure and delight, which rests in his
manner of language and style as hath been said, whereof the
many moods* and strange phrases are called figures – it is
not altogether with him as with the craftsman, nor altogether
otherwise than with the craftsman. For, in that he useth his
metrical proportions by appointed and harmonical measures
and distances, he is like the carpenter or joiner, for, borrowing
their timber and stuff of nature, they appoint and order it by art
otherwise than nature would do, and work effects in appearance
contrary to hers. Also, in that which the poet speaks or reports
of another man's tale or doings, as Homer of Priamus or
Ulysses,[122] he is as the painter or carver that work by imitation
and representation in a foreign* subject. In that he speaks
figuratively, or argues subtly, or persuades copiously and vehemently, he doth as the cunning gardener, that, using nature as a
coadjutor,* furthers her conclusions, and many times makes
her effects more absolute and strange. But for that, in our maker
or poet, which rests only in device,* and issues from an excellent
sharp and quick invention, holpen by a clear and bright fantasy
and imagination, he is not as the painter, to counterfeit the
natural by the like* effects and not the same, nor as the gardener,
aiding nature to work both the same and the like, nor as the
carpenter, to work effects utterly unlike, but, even as nature

* *artificial*: artful, skilful   * *trade*: course, method
* *natural*: natural disposition, gift   * *moods*: forms
* *foreign*: not his own   * *coadjutor*: assistant
* *device*: invention, devising   * *like*: similar

herself, working by her own peculiar virtue* and proper*
instinct, and not by example, or meditation, or exercise, as all
other artificers do, is then most admired when he is most natural
and least artificial. And in the feats of his language and utterance,
because they hold as well of nature to be suggested and uttered
as by art to be polished and reformed, therefore shall our poet
receive praise for both, but more by knowing of his art than by
unseasonable* using it, and be more commended for his natural
eloquence than for his artificial, and more for his artificial well
dissembled than for the same overmuch affected and grossly or
undiscreetly bewrayed,* as many makers and orators do.

The Conclusion

And with this (my most gracious sovereign Lady) I make
an end, humbly beseeching your pardon in that I have pre-
sumed to hold your ears so long annoyed with a tedious trifle.
So as, unless it proceed more of your own princely and natural
mansuetude* than of my merit, I fear greatly lest you may think
of me as the philosopher Plato did of Anniceris, an inhabitant
of the city Cyrene, who, being in troth a very active and artificial
man in driving of a prince's chariot, or coach (as your Majesty's
might be),[123] and knowing it himself well enough, coming one
day into Plato's school and having heard him largely dispute in
matters philosophical, 'I pray you,' quoth he, 'give me leave also
to say somewhat of mine art'; and indeed showed so many tricks
of his cunning, how to launch forth and stay, and change pace,
and turn and wind his coach this way and that way, uphill,
downhill and also in even or rough ground, that he made the
whole assembly wonder at him. Quoth Plato, being a grave
personage, 'Verily, in mine opinion, this man should be utterly
unfit for any service of greater importance than to drive a coach
– it is great pity that so pretty* a fellow had not occupied his

* *virtue*: power   * *proper*: own, inherent
* *unseasonable*: at the wrong times   * *bewrayed*: revealed, exposed
* *mansuetude*: gentleness, mildness   * *pretty*: clever

brains in studies of more consequence.'[124] Now, I pray God it be not thought so of me in describing the toys* of this our vulgar art. But when I consider how everything hath his estimation by opportunity, and that it was but the study of my younger years, in which vanity reigned; also, that I write to the pleasure of a lady and a most gracious queen, and neither to priests nor to prophets or philosophers; besides, finding by experience that many times idleness is less harmful than unprofitable occupation, daily seeing how these great aspiring minds and ambitious heads of the world,* seriously searching to deal in matters of state, be often times so busy and earnest that they were better be unoccupied and peradventure altogether idle – I presume so much upon your Majesty's most mild and gracious judgement, howsoever you conceive of mine ability to any better or greater service, that yet in this attempt ye will allow of my loyal and good intent, always endeavouring to do your Majesty the best and greatest of those services I can.

* *toys*: trifling notions   * *heads of the world*: worldly characters

SAMUEL DANIEL
A DEFENCE OF RHYME
(1603)

To all the worthy lovers and learned professors of rhyme within His Majesty's dominions, S.D.*

Worthy gentlemen, about a year since, upon the great reproach given to the professors* of rhyme and the use thereof, I wrote a private letter as a defence of mine own undertakings in that kind to a learned gentleman, a great friend of mine,[1] then in court, which I did rather to confirm myself in mine own courses, and to hold him from being won from us, than with any desire to publish the same to the world. But now, seeing the times to promise a more regard to the present condition of our writings, in respect of our sovereign's happy inclination this way[2] (whereby we are rather to expect an encouragement to go on with what we do than that any innovation should check us with a show of what it would do in another kind, and yet do nothing but deprave),* I have now given a greater body to the same argument, and here present it to your view under the patronage of a noble earl,[3] who in blood and nature is interessed* to take our part in this cause, with others who cannot, I know, but hold dear the monuments that have been left unto the world in this manner of composition, and who I trust will take in good part this my defence, if not as it is my particular,*

---

* *S.D.*: *salutem dicit* ('greetings'); possibly also *suis dedit* ('[the author] has presented [the work] to them' and 'S[amuel] D[aniel]'
* *professors*: those who practice, or claim allegiance to
* *deprave*: disparage   * *is interessed*: has a legal concern
* *particular*: personal concern

yet in respect of the cause I undertake, which I here invoke you all to protect.

Sa: D.

To William Herbert, Earl of Pembroke.

The general custom and use of rhyme in this kingdom, noble Lord, having been so long (as if from a grant of nature) held unquestionable made me to imagine that it lay altogether out of the way of contradiction, and was become so natural as we should never have had a thought to cast it off into reproach or be made to think that it ill became our language. But now I see, when there is opposition made to all things in the world by words, we must now at length likewise fall to contend for words themselves, and make a question whether they be right or not. For we are told how that our measures* go wrong, all rhyming is gross, vulgar, barbarous, which if it be so, we have lost much labour to no purpose; and, for mine own particular,* I cannot but blame the fortune of the times and mine own genius* that cast me upon so wrong a course, drawn with the current of custom and an unexamined example. Having been first encouraged or framed thereunto by your most worthy and honourable mother, receiving the first notion for the formal ordering of those compositions at Wilton,[4] which I must ever acknowledge to have been my best school, and thereof always am to hold a feeling and grateful memory, afterward, drawn farther on by the well-liking and approbation of my worthy Lord,[5] the fosterer of me and my muse, I adventured to bestow all my whole powers therein, perceiving it agreed so well both with the complexion of the times and mine own constitution, as I found not wherein I might better employ me. But yet now, upon the great discovery of these new measures[6] threatening to overthrow the whole state of rhyme in this kingdom, I must either stand out to defend or else be forced to forsake myself and give over all. And though irresolution and a self-distrust be the most apparent faults of

---

* *measures*: metres, lines of verse   * *particular*: part, case
* *genius*: disposition

my nature, and that the least check of reprehension, if it savour of reason, will as easily shake my resolution as any man's living, yet in this case I know not how I am grown more resolved and, before I sink, willing to examine what those powers of judgement are that must bear me down and beat me off from the station of my profession, which by the law of nature I am set to defend.

And the rather for that this detractor (whose commendable rhymes, albeit now himself an enemy to rhyme, have given heretofore to the world the best notice of his worth)[7] is a man of fair parts and good reputation, and therefore the reproach forcibly cast from such a hand may throw down more at once than the labours of many shall in long time build up again, specially upon the slippery foundation of opinion and the world's inconstancy, which knows not well what it would have, and

> discit enim citius meminitque libentius illud
> quod quis deridet, quam quod probat et veneratur.*[8]

And he who is thus become our unkind adversary must pardon us if we be as jealous of our fame and reputation as he is desirous of credit by his new-old art, and must consider that we cannot, in a thing that concerns us so near, but have a feeling of the wrong done, wherein every rhymer in this universal island as well as myself stands interested.* So that, if his charity had equally drawn with his learning, he would have forborne to procure the envy of so powerful a number upon him, from whom he cannot but expect the return of a like measure of blame, and only have made way to his own grace by the proof of his ability without the disparaging of us, who would have been glad to have stood quietly by him, and perhaps commended his adventure, seeing that evermore of one science another may be born, and that these sallies made out of the quarter of our

* discit . . . veneratur: 'more quickly learns and more gladly recalls what one derides than what one approves and esteems'
* interessed: concerned, touched in reputation

set knowledges are the gallant proffers only of attemptive*
spirits, and commendable though they work no other effect than
make a bravado;* and I know it were *indecens, et morosum
nimis, alienae industriae modum ponere.** We could well have
allowed of his numbers* had he not disgraced our rhyme, which
both custom and nature doth most powerfully defend – custom
that is before all law, nature that is above all art. Every language
hath her proper number or measure fitted to use and delight,
which custom, entertaining by the allowance of the ear, doth
indenize* and make natural. All verse is but a frame of words
confined within certain measure, differing from the ordinary
speech and introduced the better to express men's conceits,*
both for delight and memory. Which frame of words consisting
of *rhythmus* or *metrum*, number or measure,[9] are disposed into
divers fashions, according to the humour of the composer and
the set of the time. And these *rhythmi*, as Aristotle saith, are
familiar amongst all nations, and *è naturale et sponte fusa
composizione,**[10] and they fall as naturally already in our language as ever art can make them, being such as the ear of itself
doth marshal in their proper rooms,* and they of themselves
will not willingly be put out of their rank; and that in such a
verse as best comports with the nature of our language.

And for our rhyme (which is an excellency added to this work
of measure, and a harmony far happier than any proportion
antiquity could ever show us) doth add more grace and hath
more of delight than ever bare numbers,* howsoever they can
be forced to run in our slow language, can possibly yield. Which,
whether it be derived of *rhythmus* or of *romance* (which were
songs the bards and druids about Reims used, and thereof were
called *remensi*, as some Italians hold),[11] or howsoever, it is
likewise number and harmony of words, consisting of an

* *attemptive*: given to bold attempts, venturous
* *make a bravado*: challenge to fight, put on a daring display
* *indecens . . . ponere*: 'inappropriate and too pedantic to appoint the method
for another's efforts'   * *numbers*: verse metres
* *indenize*: naturalize, give rights of citizenship to an alien
* *conceits*: ideas
* *è . . . composizione*: 'are of a natural and spontaneous composition'
* *proper rooms*: own positions   * *bare numbers*: unrhymed verses

agreeing sound in the last syllables of several* verses, giving both to the ear an echo of a delightful report,* and to the memory a deeper impression of what is delivered therein. For as Greek and Latin verse consists of the number and quantity of syllables, so doth the English verse of measure and accent.[12] And though it doth not strictly observe long and short syllables, yet it most religiously respects the accent, and as the short and the long make number, so the acute and grave accent[13] yield harmony; and harmony is likewise number, so that the English verse then hath number, measure and harmony in the best proportion of music, which, being more certain and more resounding, works that effect of motion* with as happy success as either the Greek or Latin. And so natural a melody is it, and so universal, as it seems to be generally born with all the nations of the world, as an hereditary eloquence proper* to all mankind. The universality argues the general power of it: for if the barbarian use it, then it shows that it sways the affection of the barbarian; if civil nations practise it, it proves that it works upon the hearts of civil nations; if all, then that it hath a power in nature on all. Georgevicz' *De Turcarum moribus*[14] hath an example of the Turkish rhymes just* of the measure of our verse of eleven syllables in feminine rhyme,[15] never begotten, I am persuaded, by any example in Europe, but born no doubt in Scythia, and brought over Caucasus and Mount Taurus. The Slavonian* and Arabian tongues acquaint a great part of Asia and Afric with it; the Muscovite, Polack, Hungarian, German, Italian, French and Spaniard use no other harmony of words. The Irish, Briton, Scot, Dane, Saxon, English and all the inhabitors of this island either have hither brought, or here found, the same in use. And such a force hath it in nature, or so made by nature, as the Latin numbers, notwithstanding their excellency, seemed not sufficient to satisfy the ear of the world, thereunto accustomed, without this harmonical cadence, which made the most learned of all nations labour with exceeding travail to bring those numbers likewise unto it, which many did

* *several*: separate   * *report*: answering sound (in music)
* *motion*: moving, persuading   * *proper*: belonging   * *just*: exactly
* *Slavonian*: Slavonic

with that happiness as neither their purity of tongue nor their material contemplations are thereby any way disgraced, but rather deserve to be reverenced of all grateful posterity with the due regard of their worth. And for *Schola Salerna* and those *Carmina proverbialia*,[16] who finds not therein more precepts for use, concerning diet, health and conversation, than Cato, Theognis[17] or all the Greeks and Latins can show us in that kind of teaching? – and that in so few words, both for delight to the ear and the hold of memory, as they are to be embraced of all modest readers that study to know and not to deprave.*

Methinks it is a strange imperfection that men should thus overrun the estimation of good things with so violent a censure, as though it must please none else because it likes not them. Whereas *oportet arbitratores esse non contradictores eos qui verum iudicaturi sunt*,* saith Aristotle,[18] though he could not observe it himself. And mild charity tells us:

> non ego paucis
> offendar maculis, quas aut incuria fudit
> aut humana parum cavit natura.*[19]

For all men have their errors, and we must take the best of their powers and leave the rest as not appertaining to us.

'Ill customs are to be left',[20] I grant it. But I see not how that can be taken for an ill custom which nature hath thus ratified, all nations received, time so long confirmed; the effects such as it performs those offices of motion for which it is employed, delighting the ear, stirring the heart, and satisfying the judgement in such sort as I doubt whether ever single numbers* will do in our climate if they show no more work of wonder than yet we see. And if ever they prove to become anything, it must

---

* *deprave*: vilify, slander
* *oportet . . . sunt*: 'it behoves those who would judge truly to be arbiters and not prosecutors'
* *non . . . natura*: 'I shall not take offence at a few blots which a careless hand has let drop, or human frailty has failed to avert'
* *single numbers*: unrhymed quantitative verses

be by the approbation of many ages that must give them their strength for any operation, or before the world will feel where the pulse, life and energy lies, which now we are sure where to have in our rhymes, whose known frame hath those due stays* for the mind, those encounters of touch* as makes the motion certain, though the variety be infinite. Nor will the general sort for whom we write (the wise being above books) taste these laboured measures[21] but as an orderly prose when we have all done, for this kind acquaintance and continual familiarity ever had betwixt our ear and this cadence is grown to so intimate a friendship, as it will now hardly ever be brought to miss* it. For be the verse never so good, never so full, it seems not to satisfy nor breed that delight as when it is met and combined with a like sounding accent, which seems as the jointure* without which it hangs loose and cannot subsist but runs wildly on, like a tedious fancy without a close.[22] Suffer* then the world to enjoy that which it knows, and what it likes, seeing that whatsoever form[23] of words doth move, delight and sway the affections of men, in what Scythian[24] sort soever it be disposed* or uttered, that is true number, measure, eloquence and the perfection of speech, which I said hath as many shapes as there be tongues or nations in the world, nor can with all the tyrannical rules of idle rhetoric be governed otherwise than custom and present observation will allow. And being now the trim* and fashion of the times, to suit a man otherwise cannot but give a touch of singularity,* for when he hath all done he hath but found other clothes to the same body, and peradventure not so fitting as the former. But could our adversary hereby set up the music of our times to a higher note of judgement and discretion, or could these new laws of words better our imperfections, it were a happy attempt; but when hereby we shall but, as it were, change prison, and put off these fetters to receive others, what have we gained? As good still to use rhyme and a little reason as neither rhyme nor reason, for no doubt as idle wits will write in that kind as do now in this: imitation will after, though it break her

* *stays*: supports or pauses   * *encounters of touch*: joins, meetings of lines
* *miss*: do without   * *jointure*: joint   * *suffer*: allow
* *disposed*: arranged   * *trim*: modish dress   * *singularity*: eccentricity

neck – *scribimus indocti doctique poemata passim.**[25] And this
multitude of idle writers can be no disgrace to the good, for the
same fortune in one proportion or other is proper in a like
season to all states in their turn, and the same unmeasurable
confluence of scribblers happened when measures were most in
use among the Romans, as we find by this reprehension:

> mutavit mentem populus levis et calet uno
> scribendi studio; pueri patresque severi
> fronde comas vincti cenant et carmina dictant.*[26]

So that their plenty seems to have bred the same waste and
contempt as ours doth now, though it had not power to disvalue
what was worthy of posterity, nor keep back the reputation of
excellencies destined to continue for many ages. For seeing it is
matter that satisfies the judicial,* appear it in what habit* it will,
all these pretended proportions of words, howsoever placed,
can be but words, and peradventure serve but to embroil our
understanding: whilst seeking to please our ear we enthral* our
judgement, to delight an exterior sense we smooth up a weak
confused sense, affecting sound to be unsound, and all to seem
servum pecus,*[27] only to imitate the Greeks and Latins, whose
felicity in this kind might be something to themselves, to whom
their own *idioma** was natural, but to us it can yield no other
commodity than a sound. We admire them not for their smooth-
gliding words, nor their measures, but for their inventions[28]
(which treasure, if it were to be found in Welsh and Irish, we
should hold those languages in the same estimation); and they
may thank their sword that made their tongues so famous and
universal as they are. For to say truth, their verse is many
times but a confused deliverer of their excellent conceits, whose
scattered limbs we are fain to look out and join together to
discern the image of what they represent unto us.[29] And even

* *scribimus . . . passim*: 'skilled or unskilled, we scribble poetry, all alike'
* *mutavit . . . dictant*: 'The fickle public has changed its taste and is fired
throughout with a scribbling craze; sons and grave fathers dine crowned with
leaves and dictate their poems'   * *judicial*: judicious   * *habit*: dress
* *enthral*: enslave   * *servum pecus*: 'slavish herd'   * *idioma*: 'idiom'

the Latins, who profess not to be so licentious* as the Greeks,
show us many times examples but of strange cruelty, in torturing
and dismembering of words in the midst, or disjoining such as
naturally should be married and march together by setting them
as far asunder as they can possibly stand – that sometimes,
unless the kind reader, out of his own good nature, will stay*
them up by their measure, they will fall down into flat prose,
and sometimes are no other indeed in their natural sound.[30] And
then, again, when you find them disobedient to their own laws
you must hold it to be *licentia poetica*[31] and so dispensable.*
The striving to show their changeable measures in the variety of
their odes[32] have been very painful, no doubt, unto them, and
forced them thus to disturb the quiet stream of their words,
which by a natural succession otherwise desire to follow in their
due course. But such affliction doth laboursome curiosity* still
lay upon our best delights (which ever must be made strange
and variable), as if art were ordained to afflict nature, and that
we could not go but in fetters. Every science, every profession,
must be so wrapped up in unnecessary intrications,* as if it were
not to fashion but to confound the understanding, which makes
me much to distrust man, and fear that our presumption goes
beyond our ability and our curiosity is more than our judgement,
labouring ever to seem to be more than we are, or laying greater
burdens upon our minds than they are well able to bear, because
we would not appear like other men.

And indeed I have wished there were not that multiplicity of
rhymes as is used by many in sonnets,[33] which yet we see in
some so happily to succeed, and hath been so far from hindering
their inventions as it hath begot conceit* beyond expectation,
and comparable to the best inventions of the world; for sure in
an eminent spirit whom nature hath fitted for that mystery*
rhyme is no impediment to his conceit,* but rather gives him

* *licentious*: able to disregard conventional rules   * *stay*: hold
* *licentia poetica*: 'poetic licence'
* *dispensable*: allowable, subject to dispensation
* *curiosity*: (excessive) ingenuity   * *intrications*: complications, intricacies
* *conceit*: ingenious expression   * *mystery*: occupation
* *conceit*: imagination

wings to mount and carries him, not out of his course but as it were beyond his power to a far happier flight. All excellencies being sold us at the hard price of labour, it follows, where we bestow most thereof we buy the best success; and rhyme, being far more laborious than loose measures (whatsoever is objected), must needs, meeting with wit and industry, breed greater and worthier effects in our language. So that if our labours have wrought out a manumission from bondage and that we go at liberty, notwithstanding these ties, we are no longer the slaves of rhyme, but we make it a most excellent instrument to serve us. Nor is this certain limit observed in sonnets any tyrannical bounding of the conceit,[34] but rather a reducing it *in gyrum*,* and a just form, neither too long for the shortest project nor too short for the longest, being but only employed for a present passion. For the body of our imagination being as an unformed chaos without fashion, without day, if by the divine power of the spirit it be wrought into an orb of order and form,[35] is it not more pleasing to nature, that desires a certainty and comports not with that which is infinite, to have these closes,* rather than not to know where to end or how far to go, especially seeing our passions are often without measure? And we find the best of the Latins many times either not concluding, or else otherwise in the end than they began. Besides, is it not most delightful to see much excellently ordered in a small room, or little gallantly disposed and made to fill up a space of like capacity, in such sort that the one would not appear so beautiful in a larger circuit nor the other do well in a less, which often we find to be so, according to the powers of nature, in the workman? And these limited proportions and rests of stanzas consisting of six, seven or eight lines[36] are of that happiness, both for the disposition* of the matter, the apt planting the sentence where it may best stand to hit, the certain close of delight with the full body of a just period well carried, is such as neither the Greeks or Latins ever attained unto.[37] For their boundless running on often so confounds the reader that, having

* *in gyrum*: 'into a circle or circuit'   * *closes*: stops, cadences
* *disposition*: arrangement

once lost himself, must either give off unsatisfied, or uncertainly cast back to retrieve the escaped sense, and to find way again into his matter.

Methinks we should not so soon yield our consents captive to the authority of antiquity, unless we saw more reason; all our understandings are not to be built by the square* of Greece and Italy. We are the children of nature as well as they; we are not so placed out of the way of judgement but that the same sun of discretion shineth upon us; we have our portion of the same virtues as well as of the same vices: *et Catilinam / quocumque in populo videas, quocumque sub axe.**38 Time and the turn of things bring about these faculties according to the present estimation, and *res temporibus, non tempora rebus, servire oportet.** So that we must never rebel against use: *quem penes arbitrium est et vis et norma loquendi.**39 It is not the observing of trochaics nor their iambics that will make our writings ought the wiser; all their poesy, all their philosophy, is nothing unless we bring the discerning light of conceit with us to apply it to use. It is not books, but only that great book of the world and the all-overspreading grace of heaven that makes men truly judicial. Nor can it be but a touch of arrogant ignorance to hold this or that nation barbarous, these or those times gross, considering how this manifold creature man, wheresoever he stand in the world, hath always some disposition of worth, entertains* the order of society, affects* that which is most in use, and is eminent in some one thing or other that fits his humour and the times. The Grecians held all other nations barbarous but themselves, yet Pyrrhus, when he saw the well-ordered marching of the Romans, which made them see their presumptuous error, could say it was no barbarous manner of proceeding.40 The Goths, Vandals and Longobards,* whose

---

* *square*: builder's square; also standard, pattern
* *et ... axe*: 'and you may see a Catiline [traitor] among any people, under any sky'
* *res ... oportet*: 'things should serve the times, and not the times things'
* *quem ... loquendi*: '[if usage so will it,] in whose hands lies the judgement, the power and the rule of speech'   * *entertains*: maintains
* *affects*: prefers, tends towards, strives after   * *Longobards*: Lombards

coming down like an inundation overwhelmed, as they say, all the glory of learning in Europe, have yet left us still their laws and customs as the originals of most of the provincial constitutions of Christendom, which well considered with their other courses of government may serve to clear them from this imputation of ignorance. And though the vanquished never yet spake well of the conqueror, yet even through the unsound coverings of malediction* appear those monuments of truth as argue well their worth and proves them not without judgement, though without Greek and Latin.

Will not experience confute us if we should say the state of China, which never heard of anapaestics, trochees and tribrachs,[41] were gross, barbarous and uncivil? And is it not a most apparent ignorance, both of the succession of learning in Europe and the general course of things, to say that 'all lay pitifully deformed in those lack-learning times from the declining of the Roman empire till the light of the Latin tongue was revived by Reuchlin, Erasmus and More',[42] when for three hundred years before them, about the coming down of Tamburlaine into Europe,[43] Franciscus Petrarca (who then no doubt likewise found whom to imitate) showed all the best notions of learning in that degree of excellency, both in Latin prose and verse and in the vulgar* Italian, as all the wits of posterity have not yet much overmatched him in all kinds to this day?[44] His great volumes written in moral philosophy show his infinite reading and most happy power of disposition; his twelve Eclogues, his *Africa* containing nine books of* the last Punic war, with his three books of Epistles in Latin verse, show all the transformations of wit and invention that a spirit naturally born to the inheritance of poetry and judicial knowledge could express. All which notwithstanding wrought him not that glory and fame with his own nation as did his poems in Italian, which they esteem above all whatsoever wit could have invented in any other form than wherein it is, which questionless they will not change with the best measures Greeks or Latins can show them, howsoever our adversary imagines.[45] Nor could this very same

---

* *malediction*: slander   * *vulgar*: everyday, vernacular   * *of*: on

innovation in verse, begun amongst them by C. Tolomei,[46] but die in the attempt, and was buried as soon as it came born, neglected as a prodigious and unnatural issue amongst them; nor could it never induce Tasso,[47] the wonder of Italy, to write that admirable poem of Jerusalem, comparable to the best of the ancients, in any other form than the accustomed verse. And with Petrarch lived his scholar Boccaccius,[48] and near about the same time Johannes Ravenensis,[49] and from these, *tanquam ex equo Troiano*,*[50] seems to have issued all those famous Italian writers: Leonardus Aretinus, Laurentius Valla, Poggius, Blondus and many others.[51] Then Emmanuel Chrysolaras, a Constantin-opolitan gentleman renowned for his learning and virtue, being employed by John Paleologus, Emperor of the East, to implore the aid of Christian princes for the succouring of perishing Greece, and understanding in the meantime how Bajazeth was taken prisoner by Tamburlaine and his country freed from danger, stayed still at Venice and there taught the Greek tongue, discontinued before in these parts the space of seven hundred years.[52] Him followed Bessarion, George Trapezuntius, Theodore Gaza[53] and others, transporting philosophy beaten by the Turk out of Greece into Christendom. Hereupon came that mighty confluence of learning in these parts, which, returning as it were *per postliminium** and here meeting then with the new invented stamp of printing,[54] spread itself indeed in a more universal sort than the world ever heretofore had it, when Pomponius Laetus, Aeneas Sylvius, Angelus Politianus, Hermo-laus Barbarus, Johannes Pico de Mirandola,[55] the miracle and phoenix of the world, adorned Italy and wakened up other nations likewise with this desire of glory, long before it brought forth Reuchlin, Erasmus and More – worthy men, I confess, and the last a great ornament to this land, and a rhymer.[56] And yet long before all these, and likewise with these, was not our nation behind in her portion of spirit and worthiness, but concurrent with the best of all this lettered world. Witness venerable Bede,[57] that flourished above a thousand years since;

* *tanquam . . . Troiano*: 'as from the Trojan horse'
* *per postliminium*: 'through a return to former privileges'

Aldelmus Durotelmus[58] that lived in the year 739, of whom
we find this commendation registered: *omnium poetarum
sui temporis facile primus, tantae eloquantiae, maiestatis et
eruditionis homo fuit, ut nunquam satis admirari possim unde
illi in tam barbara ac rudi aetate facundia accreverit, usque
adeo omnibus numeris tersa, elegans et rotunda, versus edidit
cum antiquitate de palma contendentes.* Witness Josephus
Devonius, who wrote *De bello Troiano** in so excellent a
manner, and so near resembling antiquity, as, printing his work
beyond the seas, they have ascribed it to Cornelius Nepos, one
of the ancients.[59]

What, should I name Walterus Map, Gulielmus Nigellus,
Gervasius Tilburiensis, Bracton, Bacon, Ockham[60] and an infinite catalogue of excellent men, most of them living about four
hundred years since and have left behind them monuments of
most profound judgement and learning in all sciences? So that
it is but the clouds gathered about our own judgement that
makes us think all other ages wrapped up in mists, and the great
distance betwixt us that causes us to imagine men so far off to
be so little in respect of ourselves. We must not look upon the
immense course of times past as men overlook* spacious and
wide countries from off high mountains, and are never the near
to judge of the true nature of the soil or the particular site and
face of those territories they see; nor must we think, viewing the
superficial figure of a region in a map, that we know straight
the fashion and place as it is; or, reading an history (which is
but a map of men, and doth no otherwise acquaint us with the
true substance of circumstances than a superficial card* doth
the seaman with a coast never seen, which always proves other
to the eye than the imagination forecast it), that presently we
know all the world and can distinctly judge of times, men and
manners just as they were, when the best measure of man is to

* *omnium . . . contendentes*: 'easily the foremost of all the poets of his time, he
was a man of such eloquence, majesty and erudition that I can never enough
admire how in such a barbarous and uncultivated age he achieved in all metres
a pure, elegant and full eloquence; he published verses which contend with
antiquity for the palm'   * *De . . . Troiano*: 'Of the Trojan War'
* *overlook*: look out over   * *card*: navigational chart

be taken by his own foot, bearing ever the nearest proportion to himself, and is never so far different and unequal in his powers that he hath all in perfection at one time and nothing at another. The distribution of gifts are universal, and all seasons hath them in some sort. We must not think but that there were Scipios, Caesars, Catos and Pompeys[61] born elsewhere than at Rome; the rest of the world hath ever had them in the same degree of nature, though not of state.* And it is our weakness that makes us mistake or misconceive in these delineations of men the true figure of their worth; and our passion and belief is so apt to lead us beyond truth, that unless we try them by the just compass of humanity, and as they were men, we shall cast their figures in the air when we should make their models upon earth. It is not the contexture* of words but the effects of action that gives glory to the times. We find they had *mercurium in pectore* though not *in lingua*,*[62] and in all ages, though they were not Ciceronians,[63] they knew the art of men, which only is *ars artium*,* the great gift of heaven, and the chief grace and glory on earth; they had the learning of government and ordering their state, eloquence enough to show their judgements. And it seems the best times followed Lycurgus' counsel: *literas ad usum saltem discebant, reliqua omnis disciplina erat, ut pulchre parerent ut labores perferrent*,*[64] etc. Had not unlearned Rome laid the better foundation, and built the stronger frame of an admirable state, eloquent Rome had confounded it utterly, which, we saw, ran the way of all confusion, the plain course of dissolution in her greatest skill.[65] And though she had not power to undo herself, yet wrought she so that she cast herself quite away from the glory of a commonwealth and fell upon that form of state she ever most feared and abhorred of all other. And then scarce was there seen any shadow of policy under her first emperors, but the most horrible and gross confusion that could be conceived, notwithstanding it still endured, preserving

---

* *state*: circumstance, status   * *contexture*: weaving together
* *mercurium . . . lingua*: 'eloquence in the heart' . . . 'in speech'
* *ars artium*: 'the art of arts'
* *literas . . . perferrent*: 'at least they learned letters for use; all their remaining skill was that they might obey graciously, and endure their labours'

not only a monarchy locked up in her own limits, but there-withal held under her obedience so many nations so far distant, so ill affected, so disorderly commanded and unjustly con-quered, as it is not to be attributed to any other fate but to the first frame of that commonwealth, which was so strongly jointed and with such infinite combinations interlinked, as one nail or other ever held up the majesty thereof. There is but one learning, which *omnes gentes habent scriptum in cordibus suis*,*[66] one and the self-same spirit that worketh in all. We have but one body of justice, one body of wisdom throughout the whole world, which is but apparelled according to the fashion of every nation.

Eloquence and gay words are not of the substance of wit; it is but the garnish of a nice* time, the ornaments that do but deck the house of a state, and *imitatur publicos mores*:* hunger is as well satisfied with meat served in pewter as silver. Discretion is the best measure, the rightest foot,[67] in what habit soever it run. Erasmus, Reuchlin and More brought no more wisdom into the world with all their new-revived words than we find was before; it bred not a profounder divine than St Thomas, a greater lawyer than Bartolus, a more acute logician than Scotus.[68] Nor are the effects of all this great amass* of eloquence so admirable or of that consequence but that *impexa illa antiqui-tatis** can yet* compare with them.[69] Let us go no further but look upon the wonderful architecture of this state of England, and see whether they were deformed times that could give it such a form, where there is no one the least pillar of majesty but was set with most profound judgement and borne up with the just conveniency* of prince and people, no court of justice but laid by the rule and square of nature, and the best of the best commonwealths that ever were in the world – so strong and substantial as it hath stood against all the storms of factions, both of belief and ambition, which so powerfully beat upon

* *omnes . . . suis*: 'all peoples have written in their hearts'
* *nice*: refined, cultured   * *imitatur . . . mores*: 'it follows popular custom'
* *amass*: accumulation
* *impexa . . . antiquitatis*: 'that unpolished antiquity'   * *yet*: still
* *conveniency*: agreement

it, and all the tempestuous alterations of humorous* times whatsoever, being continually in all ages furnished with spirits fit to maintain the majesty of her own greatness, and to match in an equal concurrency* all other kingdoms round about her with whom it had to encounter. But this innovation, like a viper, must ever make way into the world's opinion through the bowels of her own breeding, and is always born with reproach in her mouth. The disgracing others is the best grace it can put on to win reputation of wit, and yet is it never so wise as it would seem, nor doth the world ever get so much by it as it imagineth, which being so often deceived, and seeing it never performs so much as it promises, methinks men should never give more credit unto it. For, let us change never so often, we cannot change man: our imperfections must still run on with us. And therefore the wiser nations have taught men always to use *moribus legibusque presentibus etiamsi deteriores sint.** The Lacedemonians,* when a musician – thinking to win himself credit by his new invention, and be before his fellows – had added one string more to his crowd,* brake his fiddle and banished him the city, holding the innovator, though in the least things, dangerous to public society. It is but a fantastic giddiness to forsake the way of other men, especially where it lies tolerable: *ubi nunc est res publica, ibi simus potius quam, dum illam veterem sequimur, simus in nulla.**[70] But shall we not tend to perfection?[71] Yes, and that ever best by going on in the course we are in, where we have advantage, being so far onward, of him that is but now setting forth. For we shall never proceed if we be ever beginning, nor arrive at any certain port sailing with all winds that blow: *non convalescit planta quae saepius transfertur,**[72] and therefore let us hold on in the course we have undertaken, and not still be wandering. Perfection is not the portion of man, and, if it were, why may we not as well get to

---

* *humorous*: capricious   * *concurrency*: rivalry
* *moribus . . . sint*: 'present customs and laws even if they are inferior'
* *Lacedemonians*: Spartans   * *crowd*: ancient Celtic fiddle
* *ubi . . . nulla*: 'let us abide with the state as it now is rather than, by pursuing its old form, find ourselves with no state at all'
* *non . . . transfertur*: 'a plant which is too often moved can never flourish'

it this way as another, and suspect these great undertakers,* lest
they have conspired with envy to betray our proceedings, and
put us by* the honour of our attempts, with casting us back
upon another course, of purpose to overthrow the whole action
of glory when we lay the fairest for it, and were so near our
hopes? I thank God that I am none of these great scholars, if
thus their high knowledges do but give them more eyes to look
out into uncertainty and confusion, accounting myself, rather,
beholding to my ignorance, that hath set me in so low an
under-room of conceit* with other men and hath given me as
much distrust as it hath done hope, daring not adventure to go
alone, but plodding on the plain tract* I find beaten by custom
and the time, contenting me with what I see in use. And, surely,
methinks these great wits should rather seek to adorn than to
disgrace the present – bring something to it without taking from
it what it hath. But it is ever the misfortune of learning to be
wounded with her own hand. *Stimulos dat emula virtus,**[73] and
when there is not ability to match what is, malice will find out
engines* either to disgrace or ruin it with a perverse encounter
of some new impression;* and, which is the greatest misery, it
must ever proceed from the powers of the best reputation, as if
the greatest spirits were ordained to endanger the world, as the
gross are to dishonour it, and that we were to expect *ab optimis
periculum, a pessimis dedecus publicum.**[74] Emulation, the
strongest pulse that beats in high minds, is oftentimes a wind,
but of the worst effect; for whilst the soul comes disappointed
of the object it wrought on, it presently forges another, and even
cozens itself and crosses all the world rather than it will stay to
be under her desires, falling out with all it hath to flatter and
make fair that which it would have. So that it is the ill success
of our longings that with Xerxes makes us to whip the sea and
send a cartel of defiance* to Mount Athos,[75] and the fault laid

---

* *undertakers*: entrepreneurs   * *put us by*: divert us from
* *conceit*: understanding   * *tract*: track
* *Stimulos . . . virtus*: 'rivalry in excellence serves to spur on'
* *engines*: contrivances   * *impression*: onslaught
* *ab . . . publicum*: 'from the best, public peril, from the worst, public shame'
* *cartel of defiance*: challenge

upon others' weakness is but a presumptuous opinion of our own strength, who must not seem to be mastered.

But, had our adversary taught us by his own proceedings this way of perfection, and therein framed us a poem of that excellency as should have put down* all and been the master-piece of these times, we should all have admired him. But to deprave the present form of writing and to bring us nothing but a few loose and uncharitable epigrams,[76] and yet would make us believe those numbers were come to raise the glory of our language, giveth us cause to suspect the performance, and to examine whether this new art *constat sibi** or *aliquid sit dictum quod non sit dictum prius.**[77]

First, we must here imitate the Greeks and Latins, and yet we are here showed to disobey them, even in their own numbers and quantities: taught to produce* what they make short, and make short what they produce; made believe to be showed measures in that form we have not seen, and no such matter; told that here is the perfect art of versifying, which in conclusion is yet confessed to be unperfect[78] – as if our adversary, to be opposite to us, were become unfaithful to himself, and, seeking to lead us out of the way of reputation, hath adventured to intricate* and confound him* in his own courses, running upon most uneven grounds, with imperfect rules, weak proofs and unlawful laws, whereunto the world, I am persuaded, is not so unreasonable as to subscribe, considering the unjust authority of the law-giver. For who hath constituted* him to be the Rhadamanthus[79] thus to torture syllables and adjudge them their perpetual doom, setting his *theta*[80] or mark of condem-nation upon them to endure the appointed sentence of his cruelty as he shall dispose? As though there were that disobedience in our words as they would not be ruled or stand in order without so many intricate laws, which would argue a great perverseness amongst them, according to that *in pessima republica plurimae leges;**[81] or that they were so far gone from the quiet freedom

---

* *put down*: conquered   * *constat sibi*: 'is self-consistent'
* *aliquid . . . prius*: 'something would be said which has not been said before'
* *produce*: make long   * *intricate*: entangle   * *him*: i.e. himself
* *constituted*: appointed   * *in . . . leges*: 'the most laws in the worst state'

of nature that they must thus be brought back again by force. And now in what case were this poor state of words if in like sort another tyrant the next year should arise and abrogate these laws and ordain others clean contrary according to his humour, and say that they were only right, the others unjust: what disturbance were there here, to whom should we obey? Were it not far better to hold us fast to our old custom than to stand thus distracted with uncertain laws, wherein right shall have as many faces as it pleases passion to make it, that wheresoever men's affections stand it shall still look that way? What trifles doth our unconstant curiosity call up to contend for! What colours are there laid upon indifferent* things to make them seem other than they are! As if it were but only to entertain contestation amongst men, who, standing according to the prospective* of their own humour, seem to see the selfsame things to appear otherwise to them than either they do to other or are indeed in themselves, being but all one in nature.

For what ado have we here! What strange precepts of art about the framing of an iambic verse in our language, which, when all is done, reaches not* by a foot but falleth out to be the plain ancient verse consisting of ten syllables or five feet, which hath ever been used amongst us, time out of mind,[82] and for all this cunning and counterfeit name can or will be* any other in nature than it hath been ever heretofore! And this new 'dimeter' is but the half of this verse divided in two, and no other than the caesura or breathing place in the midst thereof, and therefore it had been as good to have put two lines in one, but only to make them seem diverse; nay, it had been much better for the true English reading and pronouncing thereof, without violating the accent, which now our adversary hath herein most unkindly done. For, being as we are to sound it according to 'our English march',[83] we must make a rest, and raise* the last syllable, which falls out very unnatural in 'desolate', 'funeral', 'Elizabeth', 'prodigal', and in all the rest saving the monosyllables.[84] Then

* *indifferent*: of no importance either way   * *prospective*: glass, mirror
* *reaches not*: falls short   * *can or will be*: i.e. cannot or will not be
* *raise*: lengthen or stress

follows the 'English trochaic', which is said to be a simple verse, and so indeed it is, being without rhyme; having here no other grace than that in sound it runs like the known measure of our former ancient verse, ending (as we term it according to the French) in a feminine foot, saving that it is shorter by one syllable at the beginning, which is not much missed by reason it falls full at the last.[85] Next comes the 'Elegiac', being the fourth kind, and that likewise is no other than our old accustomed measure of five feet; if there be any difference it must be made in the reading, and therein we must stand bound to stay where often we would not, and sometimes either break the accent or the due course of the word.[86] And now, for the other four kinds of numbers, which are to be employed for odes, they are either of the same measure, or such as have ever been familiarly used amongst us. So that of all these eight several kinds of new promised numbers you see what we have: only what was our own before, and the same but apparelled in foreign titles, which had they come in their kind and natural attire of rhyme, we should never have suspected that they had affected to be other or sought to degenerate into strange manners, which now we see was the cause why they were turned out of their proper habit and brought in as aliens, only to induce men to admire them as far-comers. But see the power of nature: it is not all the artificial coverings of wit that can hide their native and original condition, which breaks out through the strongest bands* of affectation and will be it self – do singularity* what it can. And as for those imagined quantities of syllables which have been ever held free and indifferent in our language[87] – who can enforce us to take knowledge of them, being *in nullius verba iurati*[*88] and owing fealty to no foreign invention, especially in such a case where there is no necessity in nature, or that it imports either the matter or form* whether it be so or otherwise? But every versifier that well observes his work finds in our language, without all these unnecessary precepts, what numbers best fit the nature of her

* *bands*: bindings   * *singularity*: dissent, eccentricity
* *in . . . iurati*: 'sworn in allegiance to nobody'
* *or . . . form*: i.e. it makes no difference to either content or form

idiom, and the proper places destined to such accents as she will not let in to any other rooms* than into those for which they were born. As, for example, you cannot make this fall into the right sound of a verse, 'None thinks reward rendered worthy his worth', unless you thus misplace the accent upon 'ren*dered*' and 'wor*thy*', contrary to the nature of these words, which showeth that two feminine numbers (or trochees, if so you will call them) will not succeed in the third and fourth place of the verse. And so likewise in this case, 'Though death doth consume, yet virtue preserves', it will not be a verse, though it hath the just* syllables, without the same number* in the second and the altering of the fourth place, in this sort: 'Though death doth ruin, virtue yet preserves.' Again, who knows not that we cannot kindly* answer a feminine number with a masculine rhyme, or (if you will so term it) a trochee with a spondee, as 'weakness' with 'confess', 'nature' and 'endure', only for that thereby we shall wrong the accent, the chief lord and grave governor of numbers. Also, you cannot in a verse of four feet place a trochee in the first without the like offence – as 'Yearly out of his wat'ry cell', for so you shall sound it 'Year*ly*', which is unnatural. And other such like observations usually occur, which nature and a judicial ear of themselves teach us readily to avoid.

But, now, for whom hath our adversary taken all this pains – for the learned, or for the ignorant, or for himself, to show his own skill? If for the learned it was to no purpose, for every grammarian in this land hath learned his *prosodia*[89] and already knows all this art of numbers. If for the ignorant it was vain, for if they become versifiers we are like to have lean numbers instead of fat rhyme;[90] and if Tully would have his orator skilled in all the knowledges appertaining to God and man,[91] what should they have who would be a degree above orators? Why then it was to show his own skill and what himself had observed; so he might well have done, without doing wrong to the honour of the dead, wrong to the fame of the living, and wrong to England in seeking to lay reproach upon her native ornaments and to

* *rooms*: places, positions   * *just*: right number of   * *number*: foot
* *kindly*: naturally

turn the fair stream and full course of her accents into the
shallow current of a loose[92] uncertainty, clean out of the way of
her known delight. And I had thought it could never have
proceeded from the pen of a scholar (who sees no profession
free from the impure mouth of the scorner) to say the reproach
of others' idle tongues is the curse of nature upon us,[93] when it
is rather her curse upon him that knows not how to use his
tongue. What, doth he think himself is now gotten so far out of
the way of contempt that his numbers are gone beyond the reach
of obloquy, and that – how frivolous or idle soever they shall
run – they shall be protected from disgrace, as though that light
rhymes and light numbers did not weigh all alike in the grave
opinion of the wise, and that it is not rhyme but our idle
arguments[94] that hath brought down to so base a reckoning the
price and estimation of writing in this kind, when the few good
things of this age, by coming together in one throng and press
with the many bad, are not discerned from them but overlooked
with them, and all taken to be alike? But when after-times shall
make a quest of inquiry[95] to examine the best of this age,
peradventure there will be found in the now contemned records
of rhyme matter not unfitting the gravest divine and severest
lawyer in this kingdom. But these things must have the date of
antiquity to make them reverend and authentical, for ever in the
collation* of writers men rather weigh their age than their
merit, and *legunt priscos cum reverentia, quando coetaneos non
possunt sine invidia.*[96] And let no writer in rhyme be any way
discouraged in his endeavour by this brave alarum* but rather
animated to bring up all the best of their powers, and charge
with all the strength of nature and industry upon contempt, that
the show of their real forces may turn back insolency into
her own hold.* For be sure that innovation never works any
overthrow but upon the advantage of a careless idleness. And
let this make us look the better to our feet, the better to our
matter, better to our manners.[97] Let the adversary that thought

* *collation*: bringing together, comparison
* *legunt . . . invidia*: 'they read the ancients with reverence, while they cannot
read their contemporaries without envy'   * *alarum*: call to arms
* *hold*: shelter, stronghold

to hurt us bring more profit and honour by being against us than if he had stood still on our side, for that* (next to the awe of heaven) the best rein, the strongest hand to make men keep their way is that which their enemy bears upon them; and let this be the benefit we make by being oppugned, and the means to redeem back the good opinion vanity and idleness have suffered to be won from us, which nothing but substance and matter can effect, for *scribendi recte sapere est et principium et fons.**[98]

When we hear music we must be in our ear, in the utter-room* of sense, but when we entertain judgement we retire into the cabinet and innermost withdrawing chamber of the soul; and it is but as music for the ear, *verba sequi fidibus modulanda Latinis*,* but it is a work of power for the soul, *numerosque modosque ediscere vitae.**[99] The most judicial and worthy spirits of this land are not so delicate,* or will owe so much to their ear, as to rest upon the outside of words and be entertained with sound, seeing that both number, measure and rhyme is but as the ground or seat whereupon is raised the work that commends it, and which may be easily at the first found out by any shallow conceit; as we see some fantastic* to begin a fashion which afterward gravity itself is fain to put on because it will not be out of the wear of other men, and *recti apud nos locum tenet error, ubi publicus factus est.**[100] And power and strength, that can plant itself anywhere, having built within this compass and reared it of so high a respect, we now embrace it as the fittest dwelling for our invention, and have thereon bestowed all the substance of our understanding to furnish it as it is. And therefore here I stand forth, only to make good the place we have thus taken up and to defend the sacred monuments erected

---

* *for that*: because
* *scribendi . . . fons*: 'of good writing the source and fount is wisdom'
* *utter-room*: outer room, antechamber
* *verba . . . Latinis*: 'words that will fit the music of the Latin lyre'
* *numerosque . . . vitae*: 'to master the rhythms and measures of life'
* *delicate*: given to sensuous pleasure or fastidious
* *fantastic*: person who dresses or behaves eccentrically
* *recti . . . est*: 'wrong views, when they have become prevalent, take the place, in our eyes, of what is right'

therein, which contain the honour of the dead, the fame of the living, the glory of peace, and the best power of our speech, and wherein so many honourable spirits have sacrificed to memory their dearest passions, showing by what divine influence they have been moved and under what stars they lived.

But yet now, notwithstanding all this which I have here delivered in the defence of rhyme, I am not so far in love with mine own mystery* or will seem so froward* as to be against the reformation and the better settling these measures of ours, wherein there be many things I could wish were more certain and better ordered, though myself dare not take upon me to be a teacher therein, having so much need to learn of others. And I must confess that, to mine own ear, those continual cadences of couplets used in long and continued poems are very tiresome and unpleasing, by reason that still, methinks, they run on with a sound of one nature and a kind of certainty which stuffs the delight rather than entertains it.[101] But yet, notwithstanding, I must not out of mine own daintiness* condemn this kind of writing, which peradventure to another may seem most delightful; and many worthy compositions we see to have passed with commendation in that kind. Besides, methinks sometimes to beguile the ear with a running out and passing over the rhyme, as no bound to stay us in the line where the violence of the matter will break through, is rather graceful than otherwise, wherein I find my Homer, Lucan, as if he gloried to seem to have no bounds albeit he were confined within his measures, to be in my conceit most happy.[102] For so thereby they who care not for verse or rhyme may pass it over without taking notice thereof, and please themselves with a well-measured prose. And I must confess my adversary hath wrought this much upon me – that I think a tragedy would indeed best comport with a blank verse and dispense with rhyme, saving in the chorus or where a sentence shall require a couplet.[103] And, to avoid this over-glutting the ear with that always certain and full encounter of rhyme, I have essayed in some of my epistles to alter the usual

* *mystery*: occupation   * *froward*: perverse, reluctant
* *daintiness*: fastidiousness

place of meeting and to set it further off by one verse, to try how I could disuse my own ear and to ease it of this continual burden, which indeed seems to surcharge it a little too much; but as yet I cannot come to please myself therein, this alternate or cross rhyme holding still the best place in my affection.[104]

Besides, to me this change of number in a poem of one nature sits not so well, as to mix uncertainly feminine rhymes with masculine, which, ever since I was warned of that deformity by my kind friend and countryman Master Hugh Sanford,[105] I have always so avoided it as there are not above two couplets in that kind in all my poem of the civil wars; and I would willingly, if I could, have altered it in all the rest, holding feminine rhymes to be fittest for ditties, and either to be set certain or else by themselves.[106] But in these things, I say, I dare not take upon me to teach that they ought to be so in respect myself holds them to be so or that I think it right, for indeed there is no right in these things that are continually in a wandering motion, carried with the violence of our uncertain likings, being but only the time that gives them their power. For if this right, or truth, should be no other thing than that we make it, we shall shape it into a thousand figures, seeing this excellent painter man can so well lay* the colours which himself grinds in his own affections*[107] as that he will make them serve for any shadow and any counterfeit. But the greatest hinderer to our proceedings, and the reformation of our errors, is this self-love whereunto we versifiers are ever noted to be especially subject, a disease of all other the most dangerous, and incurable being once seated in the spirits, for which there is no cure but only by a spiritual remedy. *Multos puto ad sapientiam potuisse pervenire, nisi putassent se pervenisse.*[108] And this opinion of our sufficiency makes so great a crack in our judgement as it will hardly ever hold anything of worth: *caecus amor sui*,*[109] and though it would seem to see all without* it, yet certainly it discerns but little within. For there is not the simplest writer that will ever

---

* *lay*: apply   * *affections*: dispositions, inclinations, partialities
* *Multos . . . pervenisse*: 'I think many might have been able to arrive at wisdom, if they hadn't thought they had already arrived'
* *caecus . . . sui*: 'self-love is blind'   * *without*: outside

tell himself he doth ill, but, as if he were the parasite* only to soothe his own doings, persuades him that his lines cannot but please others which so much delight himself: *Suffenus est quisque sibi,**

> neque idem umquam
> aeque est beatus ac poema cum scribit:
> tam gaudet in se tamque se ipse miratur.*[110]

And, the more to show that he is so, we shall see him evermore in all places and to all persons repeating his own compositions, and *quem vero arripuit, tenet occiditque legendo.*[111]

Next to this deformity stands our affectation, wherein we always bewray* ourselves to be both unkind and unnatural to our own native language in disguising or forging strange or unusual words, as if it were to make our verse seem another kind of speech out of the course of our usual practice, displacing our words or investing new only upon a singularity, when our own accustomed phrase, set in the due place, would express us more familiarly and to better delight than all this idle affectation of antiquity or novelty can ever do.[112] And I cannot but wonder at the strange presumption of some men that dare so audaciously adventure to introduce any whatsoever foreign words, be they never so strange, and of themselves, as it were, without a parliament, without any consent or allowance, establish them as free-denizens* in our language. But this is but a character of that perpetual revolution which we see to be in all things that never remain the same, and we must herein be content to submit ourselves to the law of time, which in few years will make all that for which we now contend *nothing*.

---

* *parasite*: flatterer   * *Suffenus . . . sibi*: 'each is a Suffenus to himself'
* *neque . . . miratur*: 'at the same time he is never so happy as when he is writing a poem, he delights in himself and admires himself so much'
* *quem . . . legendo*: 'if he catches a man, he holds him fast and reads him to death'   * *bewray*: betray
* *free-denizens*: aliens naturalized and given rights of citizenship

SELECTED PASSAGES

GEORGE GASCOIGNE

Certain Notes of Instruction (1575)

Certain notes of instruction concerning the making of verse or rhyme in English, written at the request of Master Eduardo Donati[1]

Signor Eduardo, since promise is debt, and you (by the law of friendship) do burden me with a promise that I should lend you instructions towards the making of English verse or rhyme, I will assay to discharge the same, though not so perfectly as I would, yet as readily as I may. And therewithal I pray you consider that *quot homines, tot sententiae*,* especially in poetry, wherein (nevertheless) I dare not challenge any degree,* and yet will I at your request adventure to set down my simple skill in such simple manner as I have used, referring the same hereafter to the correction of the laureate.* And you shall have it in these few points following.

The first and most necessary point that ever I found meet* to be considered in making of a delectable* poem is this: to ground it upon some fine invention.[2] For it is not enough to roll in pleasant words, nor yet to thunder in 'rim, ram, ruff, by letter' (quoth my master Chaucer),[3] nor yet to abound in apt vocables* or epithets, unless the invention have in it also *aliquid salis*.* By this *aliquid salis* I mean some good and fine device* showing

---

* *quot . . . sententiae*: 'there are as many opinions as there are men' (proverbial)
* *challenge any degree*: claim any rank/merit
* *the laureate*: i.e. those true poets who claim entitlement to wear the laurel wreath   * *meet*: appropriate   * *delectable*: delightful
* *vocables*: words, terms, names   * *aliquid salis*: 'some salt, wit, sense'
* *device*: plan, design, conceit

the quick capacity of a writer, and where I say 'some good and
fine invention' I mean that I would have it both fine and good;
for many inventions are so superfine* that they are *vix** good,
and, again, many inventions are good and yet not finely handled.
And for a general forewarning: what theme soever you do take
in hand, if you do handle it but *tanquam in oratione perpetua**
and never study for some depth of device in the invention, and
some figures* also in the handling thereof, it will appear to the
skilful reader but a tale of a tub.* To deliver unto you general
examples it were almost unpossible, sithence* the occasions of
inventions are (as it were) infinite; nevertheless, take in worth*
mine opinion, and perceive my further meaning in these few
points. If I should undertake to write in praise of a gentlewoman,
I would neither praise her crystal eye, nor her cherry lip, etc.,
for these things are *trita et obvia*.* But I would either find
some supernatural cause* whereby my pen might walk in the
superlative degree, or else I would undertake to answer for any
imperfection that she hath, and thereupon raise the praise of
her commendation. Likewise, if I should disclose my pretence
in love, I would either make a strange* discourse of some
intolerable passion, or find occasion to plead by the example
of some history, or discover* my disquiet in shadows* *per
allegoriam*,* or use the covertest mean that I could to avoid the
uncomely customs of common writers. Thus much I adventure
to deliver unto you (my friend) upon the rule of invention,
which of all other rules is most to be marked and hardest to
be prescribed in certain and infallible rules. Nevertheless, to
conclude therein, I would have you stand most upon the excellency of your invention, and stick* not to study deeply for some

* *superfine*: over-refined   * *vix*: 'hardly'
* *tanquam ... perpetua*: 'as if in plain prose'
* *figures*: rhetorical ornaments
* *a tale of a tub*: a cock and bull story, rubbish (proverbial)
* *sithence*: since   * *take in worth*: take in good part, be content with
* *trita et obvia*: 'trite and obvious'
* *supernatural cause*: e.g. by writing of Venus and Cupid
* *strange*: unusual, singular   * *discover*: reveal
* *shadows*: allegorical representations   * *per allegoriam*: 'through allegory'
* *stick*: scruple, hesitate, be reluctant

fine device. For that being found, pleasant words will follow well enough and fast enough.[4]

2. Your invention being once devised, take heed that neither pleasure of rhyme nor variety of device do carry you from it: for as to use obscure and dark phrases in a pleasant sonnet* is nothing delectable, so to intermingle merry jests in a serious matter is an *indecorum*.[5]

3. I will next advise you that you hold the just measure* wherewith you begin your verse. I will not deny but this may seem a preposterous* order, but because I covet rather to satisfy you particularly than to undertake a general tradition,* I will not so much stand upon the manner as the matter of my precepts. I say, then, remember to hold the same measure wherewith you begin, whether it be in a verse of six syllables, eight, ten, twelve, etc. And though this precept might seem ridiculous unto you, since every young scholar can conceive that he ought to continue in the same measure wherewith he beginneth, yet do I see and read many men's poems nowadays which, beginning with the measure of twelve in the first line and fourteen in the second (which is the common kind of verse)[6] they will yet (by that time they have passed over a few verses) fall into fourteen and fourteen, *et sic de similibus*,* the which is either forgetfulness or carelessness.

4. And in your verses remember to place every word in his natural emphasis* or sound: that is to say, in such wise,* and with such length or shortness, elevation or depression of syllables, as it is commonly pronounced or used.[7] To express the same we have three manner of accents, *gravis, levis et circumflexa*,* the which I would English thus: the long accent, the short accent, and that which is indifferent. The grave accent is marked by this charact:* /. The light accent is noted thus: \. And the circumflex or indifferent is thus signified: ~. The grave accent is drawn out or elevate, and maketh that syllable long

* *sonnet*: lyric poem   * *hold the just measure*: keep to the same metre
* *preposterous*: inverted, topsy-turvy   * *tradition*: method
* *et . . . similibus*: 'etc'.   * *emphasis*: pattern of stress, pronunciation
* *wise*: a manner   * *gravis . . . circumflexa*: 'heavy, light and circumflex'
* *charact*: sign

whereupon it is placed. The light accent is depressed or snatched up, and maketh that syllable short upon the which it lighteth. The circumflex accent is indifferent, sometimes short, sometimes long, sometimes depressed and sometimes elevate.[8] For example of the emphasis or natural sound of words, this word 'treasure' hath the grave accent upon the first syllable, whereas if it should be written in this sort, 'treasúre', now were the second syllable long, and that were clean contrary to the common use wherewith it is pronounced. For further explanation hereof, note you that commonly nowadays in English rhymes (for I dare not call them English verses)[9] we use none other order but a foot of two syllables, whereof the first is depressed or made short and the second is elevate or made long,[10] and that sound or scanning continueth throughout the verse. We have used in times past other kinds of metres, as for example this following:[11]

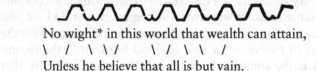

No wight* in this world that wealth can attain,
\ / \ / \ / \ / \ /
Unless he believe that all is but vain.

Also, our father Chaucer hath used the same liberty in feet and measures that the Latinists do use, and whosoever do peruse and well consider his works, he shall find that although his lines are not always of one selfsame number of syllables, yet, being read by one that hath understanding, the longest verse and that which hath most syllables in it will fall (to the ear) correspondent unto that which hath fewest syllables in it, and, likewise, that which hath in it fewest syllables shall be found yet to consist of words that have such natural sound as may seem equal in length to a verse which hath many more syllables of lighter accents.[12] And, surely, I can lament that we are fallen into such a plain and simple manner of writing, that there is none other foot used but one, whereby our poems may justly be called rhythms and cannot by any right challenge* the name of a verse.[13] But since it is so, let us take the ford as we find it and let me set down

---

* *wight*: person   * *challenge*: lay claim to

unto you such rules or precepts that even in this plain foot of
two syllables you wrest* no word from his natural and usual
sound. I do not mean hereby that you may use none other
words but of two syllables, for therein you may use discretion
according to occasion of matter. But my meaning is that all the
words in your verse be so placed as the first syllable may sound
short or be depressed, the second long or elevate, the third short,
the fourth long, the fifth short, etc. For example of my meaning
in this point mark these two verses:

I understand your meaning by your eye.

\   / \ /\   / \   / \   /

Your meaning I understand by your eye.

In these two verses there seemeth no difference at all, since the
one hath the very selfsame words that the other hath, and yet
the latter verse is neither true* nor pleasant, and the first verse
may pass the musters. The fault of the latter verse is that this
word 'understand' is therein so placed as the grave accent falleth
upon '-der-' and thereby maketh '-der-' in this word 'understand'
to be elevated, which is contrary to the natural or usual pronunciation, for we say 'ùndèrstánd', and not 'ùndérstànd'.[14]

5. Here by the way, I think it not amiss to forewarn you that
you thrust as few words of many syllables into your verse as
may be, and hereunto I might allege many reasons. First, the
most ancient English words are of one syllable, so that the more
monosyllables that you use, the truer Englishman you shall
seem, and the less you shall smell of the inkhorn.[15] Also, words
of many syllables do cloy a verse and make it unpleasant,
whereas words of one syllable will more easily fall to be short
or long as occasion requireth, or will be adapted to become
circumflex or of an indifferent sound.[16]

6. I would exhort you also to beware of rhyme without
reason.[17] My meaning is hereby that your rhyme lead you not
from your first invention, for many writers, when they have laid

* *wrest*: twist, distort   * *true*: (metrically) correct

the platform* of their invention, are yet drawn sometimes by rhyme to forget it, or at least to alter it, as, when they cannot readily find out a word which may rhyme to the first* (and yet continue their determinate* invention), they do then either botch it up with a word that will rhyme (how small reason soever it carry with it), or else they alter their first word and so percase* decline* or trouble their former invention. But do you always hold your first determined invention, and do rather search the bottom of your brains for apt words than change good reason for rumbling* rhyme.

7. To help you a little with rhyme (which is also a plain young scholar's lesson), work thus. When you have set down your first verse, take the last word thereof and count over all the words of the selfsame sound by order of the alphabet. As, for example, the last word of your first line is 'care'; to rhyme therewith you have 'bare', 'clare',* 'dare', 'fare', 'gare',* 'hare', and 'share', 'mare', 'snare', 'rare', 'stare' and 'ware', etc. Of all these take that which best may serve your purpose, carrying reason with rhyme, and if none of them will serve so, then alter the last word of your former verse, but yet do not willingly alter the meaning of your invention.

8. You may use the same figures or tropes in verse which are used in prose, and in my judgement they serve more aptly, and have greater grace in verse than they have in prose. But yet therein remember this old adage, *ne quid nimis*,*[18] as many writers which do not know the use of any other figure than that which is expressed in repetition of sundry words beginning all with one letter, the which (being modestly used) lendeth good grace to a verse, but they do so hunt a letter to death that they make it *crambe*,* and *crambe bis positum mors est*;*[19] therefore, *ne quid nimis*.[20]

---

* *platform*: ground-plan   * *to the first*: i.e. with the first line
* *determinate*: determined   * *percase*: perhaps
* *decline*: turn aside, cause to deviate   * *rumbling*: murmuring and rambling
* *clare*: clear   * *gare*: eager, or a spear
* *ne quid nimis*: 'nothing to excess'   * *crambe*: 'cabbage, old hat'
* *crambe . . . est*: 'cabbage served up twice is death'

9. Also, as much as may be, eschew strange* words, or *obsoleta et inusitata*,* unless the theme do give just occasion. Marry, in some places a strange word doth draw attentive reading, but yet I would have you therein to use discretion.[21]

10. And, as much as you may, frame your style to perspicuity and to be sensible,* for the haughty obscure verse doth not much delight, and the verse that is too easy is like a tale of a roasted horse;* but let your poem be such as may both delight and draw attentive reading, and therewithal may deliver such matter as be worth the marking.

11. You shall do very well to use your verse after the English phrase,* and not after the manner of other languages. The Latinists do commonly set the adjective after the substantive, as, for example, *femina pulchra, aedes altae*,* etc., but if we should say in English 'a woman fair', 'a house high', etc., it would have but small grace, for we say 'a good man', and not 'a man good', etc. And yet I will not altogether forbid it you, for in some places it may be borne, but not so hardly* as some use it which write thus: 'Now let us go to temple ours', 'I will go visit mother mine', etc. Surely, I smile at the simplicity* of such devisers, which might as well have said it in plain English phrase, and yet have better pleased all ears, than they satisfy their own fancies by such superfineness. Therefore, even as I have advised you to place all words in their natural or most common and usual pronunciation, so would I wish you to frame all sentences in their mother phrase and proper *idioma*,* and yet sometimes (as I have said before) the contrary may be borne, but that is rather where rhyme enforceth, or *per licentiam poeticam*,* than it is otherwise lawful or commendable.

* *strange*: unusual, foreign   * *obsoleta et inusitata*: obsolete and rare
* *sensible*: intelligible
* *a tale of a roasted horse*: a pointless or nonsensical story (proverbial)
* *phrase*: mode of expression, idiom
* *femina ... altae*: *femina* = 'a woman', *pulchra* = 'fair', *aedes* = 'houses', *altae* = 'high'   * *hardly*: strenuously, harshly
* *simplicity*: stupidity, ignorance   * *idioma*: 'idiom'
* *per licentiam poeticam*: 'by poetic licence'

12. This poetical licence is a shrewd fellow, and covereth many faults in a verse. It maketh words longer, shorter, of more syllables, of fewer, newer, older, truer, falser and, to conclude, it turkeneth* all things at pleasure: for example, 'ydone' for 'done', 'adown' for 'down', 'o'ercome' for 'overcome', 'ta'en' for 'taken', 'power' for 'pow'r', 'heaven' for 'heav'n',[22] 'thews' for good parts or good qualities, and a number of other which were but tedious and needless to rehearse, since your own judgement and reading will soon make you espy such advantages.

13. There are also certain pauses or rests in a verse, which may be called 'cesures',[23] whereof I would be loath to stand* long, since it is at discretion of the writer, and they have been first devised (as should seem) by the musicians. But yet thus much I will adventure to write: that, in mine opinion, in a verse of eight syllables the pause will stand best in the midst; in a verse of ten it will best be placed at the end of the first four syllables; in a verse of twelve, in the midst; in verses of twelve in the first and fourteen in the second we place the pause commonly in the midst of the first and at the end of the first eight syllables in the second; in rhyme royal it is at the writer's discretion, and forceth not* where the pause be until the end of the line.[24]

14. And here, because I have named rhyme royal, I will tell you also mine opinion as well of that as of the names which other rhymes* have commonly borne heretofore. Rhyme royal is a verse of ten syllables, and seven such verses make a staff,* whereof the first and third lines do answer (across) in like terminations and rhyme, the second, fourth, and fifth do likewise answer each other in terminations, and the two last do combine and shut up the sentence. This hath been called rhyme royal, and surely it is a royal kind of verse, serving best for grave discourses.[25] There is also another kind called ballad, and thereof are sundry sorts. For a man may write ballad in a staff of six lines, every line containing eight or six syllables, whereof

---

* *turkeneth*: twists, transforms   * *stand*: delay, insist
* *forceth not*: does not matter   * *rhymes*: verse forms   * *staff*: stanza

the first and third, second and fourth do rhyme across, and the
fifth and sixth do rhyme together in conclusion. You may write
also your ballad of ten syllables, rhyming as before is declared,
but these two* were wont to be most commonly used in ballad,
which proper name was (I think) derived of this word in Italian,
'ballare', which signifieth 'to dance'; and, indeed, those kinds of
rhymes serve best for dances or light matters.[26] Then have you
also a rondelet, the which doth always end with one selfsame
foot or repetition, and was thereof (in my judgement) called a
rondelet.[27] This may consist of such measure* as best liketh the
writer. Then have you sonnets. Some think that all poems (being
short) may be called sonnets, as indeed it is a diminutive word
derived of 'suonare',* but yet I can best allow to call those
sonnets which are of fourteen lines, every line containing ten
syllables. The first twelve do rhyme in staves of four lines by
cross metre, and the last two, rhyming together, do conclude
the whole.[28] There are dizains and sixains, which are of ten lines
and of six lines, commonly used by the French, which some
English writers do also term by the name of sonnets. Then is
there an old kind of rhyme called virelays, derived (as I have
read) of this word 'vert', which betokeneth green, and 'lay',
which betokeneth a song, as if you would say 'green songs'. But
I must tell you by the way that I never read any verse which I
saw by authority called 'virelay' but one, and that was a long
discourse in verses* of ten syllables, whereof the four first did
rhyme across, and the fifth did answer to the first and third,
breaking off there and so going on to another termination. Of
this I could show example of imitation in mine own verses
written to the Right Honourable the Lord Grey of Wilton upon
my journey into Holland, etc.[29] There are also certain poems
devised of ten syllables, whereof the first* answereth in termination with the fourth, and the second and third answer each
other. These are more used by other nations than by us; neither
can I tell readily what name to give them.[30] And the commonest
sort of verse which we use nowadays (viz. the long verse of

* *these two*: i.e. lines of eight or six syllables   * *measure*: metre
* *suonare*: 'to sound' (Italian)   * *verses*: lines   * *the first*: i.e. the first line

twelve and fourteen syllables) I know not certainly how to name it, unless I should say that it doth consist of poulter's* measure, which giveth twelve for one dozen and fourteen for another.[31] But let this suffice (if it be not too much) for the sundry sorts of verses which we use nowadays.

15. In all these sorts of verses whensoever you undertake to write, avoid prolixity and tediousness, and ever, as near as you can, do finish the sentence* and meaning at the end of every staff, where you write staves, and at the end of every two lines where you write by couples* or poulter's measure. For I see many writers which draw* their sentences in length and make an end at latter Lammas,* for, commonly, before they end the reader hath forgotten where he began. But do you (if you will follow my advice) eschew prolixity and knit up your sentences as compendiously as you may, since brevity (so that* it be not drowned in obscurity) is most commendable.

16. I had forgotten a notable kind of rhyme called riding rhyme, and that is such as our master and father Chaucer used in his *Canterbury Tales*, and in divers other delectable and light enterprises.[32] But though it come to my remembrance somewhat out of order, it shall not yet come altogether out of time, for I will now tell you a conceit* which I had before forgotten to write. You may see (by the way) that I hold a preposterous* order in my traditions,* but, as I said before, I write moved by good will and not to show my skill. Then, to return to my matter, as this riding rhyme serveth most aptly to write a merry tale, so rhyme royal is fittest for a grave discourse,* ballads are best of matters of love, and rondelets most apt for the beating or handling of an adage or common proverb; sonnets serve as well in matters of love as of discourse, dizains and sixains for short fantasies,* virelays for an effectual* proposition, although by the name you might otherwise judge of virelays, and the long

* *poulter's*: poulterer's, poultryman's, chicken dealer's
* *sentence*: [also] thought   * *by couples*: in couplets   * *draw*: draw out
* *at latter Lammas*: i.e. never (proverbial)   * *so that*: as long as
* *conceit*: notion, idea, device   * *preposterous*: topsy-turvy
* *traditions*: methods   * *discourse*: discussion, narrative
* *fantasies*: fancies, conceits, fictions   * *effectual*: pertinent

verse of twelve and fourteen syllables, although it be nowadays used in all themes, yet in my judgement it would serve best for psalms and hymns.[33]

I would stand longer in these traditions, were it not that I doubt* mine own ignorance, but, as I said before, I know that I write to my friend, and, affying* myself thereupon, I make an end.

---

* *doubt*: suspect, fear   * *affying*: trusting

HENRY PEACHAM

from *The Garden of Eloquence* (1577; 1593)

From the 1577 edition

To the Right Reverend Father in God, John Aylmer, by God's permission Lord Bishop of London,[1] *Henry Peacham wisheth a long and happy life with prosperous success in all godly affairs.*

When we consider and call to mind (Right Reverend) the great might and worthiness of wisdom, then do we perfectly perceive and evidently see that God of His goodness hath poured forth His divine virtue* into the mind of man far more largely, and much more abundantly, than in any other creature upon the face of the whole earth. Whereby He hath made man able not only to govern himself, and to live after* a most goodly order, but also to subdue the monstrous beasts to his will. By this divine virtue and intellective* power man doth seek, find out and comprehend the causes of things, he doth meditate and muse upon the wonderful works of God, he searcheth out the secrets of nature, and climbeth up to the knowledge of sapience supernatural;* he learneth the cunning reasons* of numbers, the mathematical demonstrations, the motions of stars, the course and alteration of times, the musical concent* of harmonies and diversity of tunes;* he conceiveth trim devices,* and is full of many profitable and pleasant inventions; he seeth what is comely for his dignity, and to what end he is created, which

---

* *virtue*: power   * *after*: in   * *intellective*: of the understanding
* *sapience supernatural*: wisdom of things outside the physical world
* *cunning reasons*: learned ratios   * *concent*: concord
* *tunes*: tones, sounds   * *trim devices*: fine ideas

no other is able to do. And to the end that this sovereign rule of reason might spread abroad her beautiful branches, and that wisdom might bring forth most plentifully her sweet and pleasant fruits for the common use and utility of mankind, the Lord God hath joined to the mind of man speech, which He hath made the instrument of our understanding and key of conceptions, whereby we open the secrets of our hearts and declare our thoughts to other.[2] And herein it is that we do so far pass and excel all other creatures, in that we have the gift of speech and reason, and not they, for we see what difference there is between those men in whom these two virtues do smally* appear and brute beasts that have no understanding. Therefore, how worthy of high commendations are those men that, perceiving this, do bestow their studies, their travail* and their time to obtain wisdom and eloquence, the only ornaments whereby man's life is beautified and a praise most precious purchased!

For by these manner of studies we see that many have attained to a great excellency in their kind, who have got to themselves and their country many commodities,* clothed themselves with ample honours, and deserved by their worthy works to be praised for ever of posterity. Of this sort among the Grecians we see was Demosthenes, Plato, Aristotle, among the Latins Marcus Tullius Cicero, Lucius Crassus, Marcus Antonius, Fabius Quintilianus,[3] most famous and renowned orators, and many other more who, by their earnest travails, obtained these two most notable treasures, whose excellent wisdom is now wondered at, and their singular eloquence had in great admiration, whose worthy praises the injury of time shall never be able to oppress, nor the devouring course of years strong enough to abolish or darken the brightness of their glory. For their honours posterity shall uphold, and their noble renown everlasting memory shall maintain, whose worthy works may be sufficient examples how we should apply our studies, which are both fraughted* with great wisdom and garnished with goodly eloquence.

* *smally*: very little   * *travail*: labour   * *commodities*: benefits
* *fraughted*: laden

Many, not perceiving the nigh and necessary conjunction of these two precious jewels, do either affect* fineness of speech and neglect the knowledge of things, or, contrariwise, covet understanding and contemn the art of eloquence. And therefore it cometh to pass that such take great pains and reap small profits; they ever seek and never find the thing they would fainest* have – the one sort of these speak much to small purpose, and the other (though they be wise) are not able aptly to express their meaning. From which calamity they are free, that do use a right judgement in applying their studies so that their knowledge may be joined with apt utterance,* and their copy* of speech with matter of importance: that is to say, that their eloquence may be wise, and their wisdom eloquent.

And therefore (Right Reverend), when of late I had considered the needful assistance that the one of these do require of the other, that wisdom do require the light of eloquence and eloquence the fertility of wisdom, and saw many good books of philosophy and precepts of wisdom set forth in English, and very few of eloquence, I was of a sudden moved to take this little garden in hand, and to set therein such figurative flowers, both of grammar and rhetoric,[4] as do yield the sweet savour of eloquence, and present to the eyes the goodly and beautiful colours of elocution,[5] such as shine in our speech like the glorious stars in firmament; such as beautify it, as flowers of sundry colours a gallant* garland; such as garnish it, as precious pearls a gorgeous garment; such as delight the ears, as pleasant reports,* repetitions and running points* in music; whose utility is so great that I cannot sufficiently praise them, and the knowledge of them so necessary that no man can read profitably or understand perfectly either poets, orators or the holy scriptures without them,[6] nor any orator able by the weight of his words to persuade his hearers, having no help of them – but being well stored with such plausible furniture,* how wonderfully shall his persuasions

---

* *affect*: aim at, prefer   * *fainest*: most gladly   * *utterance*: speech
* *copy*: copiousness, abundance of resource   * *gallant*: splendid
* *reports*: echoes, answering phrases   * *points*: passages, phrases
* *plausible furniture*: praiseworthy equipment

take place in the minds of men, and his words pierce into their inward parts!

For by figures, as it were by sundry streams, that great and forcible flood of eloquence is most plentifully and pleasantly poured forth.[7] By the great might of figures, which is no other thing than wisdom speaking eloquently,[8] the orator may lead his hearers which way he list, and draw them to what affection* he will: he may make them to be angry, to be pleased, to laugh, to weep and lament; to love, to abhor and loathe; to hope, to fear, to covet,* to be satisfied, to envy, to have pity and compassion; to marvel, to believe, to repent; and, briefly, to be moved with any affection that shall serve best for his purpose. By figures he may make his speech as clear as the noon day, or, contrariwise, as it were with clouds and foggy mists, he may cover it with darkness;* he may stir up storms and troublesome tempests, or, contrariwise, cause and procure a quiet and silent calmness; he may set forth any matter with a goodly perspicuity, and paint out any person, deed, or thing so cunningly* with these colours that it shall seem rather a lively image* painted in tables* than a report expressed with the tongue. Finally, the force of figures is so great that the strength of apt and eloquent pleading and speaking consisteth (saith Fabius)* in these kind of exornations.*[9]

And now (Right Reverend), this little work, although with no little labour having finished as well as I could, but not as I would, the fame of your wisdom, learning and knowledge, mixed with humility and godly courtesy, and the love you bear to the lovers of learning and travailers* in the same, have moved me to attempt your Lordship with the dedication hereof, in hope that your Lordship will accept my well-meaning, which is (as far as my small ability is able to extend) to profit this my country, and especially the studious youth of this realm, and such as have

---

* *affection*: emotion, feeling   * *covet*: wish for, wish to do something
* *darkness*: obscurity   * *cunningly*: skilfully
* *lively image*: lifelike picture   * *in tables*: on boards
* *Fabius*: Quintilian (Marcus Fabius Quintilianus)
* *exornations*: adornments, decorations   * *travailers*: labourers

not the understanding of the Latin tongue;[10] sure I am it may profit many, and I dare be bold to say it can hurt none. Concerning confutations of cavils* and answers to the envious* I will now spend no time, for* troubling of your Lordship, but make an end, beseeching your Lordship to take to your protection this little treatise, the fruit of my travails, as a token of my good will, which, at the next edition, I trust, shall come forth more perfect and trimly published, which now lack of leisure hath left undone. Almighty God preserve your Lordship, and give you in this life an happy time, and after time that blessed eternity that is prepared for the faithful.

From North Mimms, the 24th of April, your Lordship's in Christ to command,

Henry Peacham

From the 1593 edition

From the Dedication *To the Right Honourable Sir John Puckering, knight, Lord Keeper of the Great Seal of England*[11]

So mighty is the power of this happy union (I mean of wisdom and eloquence), that by the one the orator forceth and by the other he allureth, and by both so worketh that what he commendeth is beloved, what he dispraiseth is abhorred, what he persuadeth is obeyed, and what he dissuadeth is avoided; so that he is, in a manner, the Emperor of men's minds and affections,* and next to the omnipotent God in the power of persuasion, by grace and divine assistance. The principal instruments of man's help in this wonderful effect are those figures and forms of speech contained in this book, which are the fruitful branches of elocution* and the mighty streams of eloquence, whose utility, power and virtue I cannot sufficiently commend, but, speaking by similitude,* I say they are as stars to give light, as cordials* to comfort, as harmony to delight, as pitiful spectacles to move sorrowful passions, and as

* *cavils*: quibbling objections   * *the envious*: ill-willers   * *for*: to avoid
* *affections*: emotions   * *elocution*: style, eloquence   * *similitude*: simile
* *cordials*: medicines, tonics

orient* colours to beautify reason. Finally, they are as martial instruments both of defence and invasion,[12] and, being so, what may be either more necessary or more profitable for us than to hold those weapons always ready in our hands, wherewith we may defend ourselves, invade our enemies, revenge our wrongs, aid the weak, deliver the simple* from dangers, conserve true religion, and confute idolatry? For look what the sword may do in war, this virtue may perform in peace, yet with great difference, for that with violence, this with persuasion, that with shedding of blood, this with piercing the affections, that with desire of death, this with special regard of life.

* *orient*: precious, resplendent   * *simple*: poor, humble

WILLIAM WEBBE

from *A Discourse of English Poetry* (1586)

The most usual and frequented kind of our English poetry hath
always run upon, and to this day is observed in, such equal
number of syllables and likeness of words that in all places one
verse either immediately, or by mutual interposition,* may be
answerable* to another, both in proportion of length and ending
of lines in the same letters. Which rude* kind of verse, though
(as I touched before) it rather discrediteth our speech, as
borrowed from the barbarians, than furnisheth the same with
any comely ornament, yet, being so engraffed* by custom and
frequented by the most part,* I may not utterly disallow* it, lest
I should seem to call in question the judgement of all our famous
writers, which have won eternal praise by their memorable
works compiled in that verse.[1]

For my part, therefore, I can be content to esteem it as a thing
the perfection whereof is very commendable, yet so as,* with
others, I could wish it were by men of learning and ability
bettered and made more artificial,* according to the worthiness
of our speech.*

[...]

There be three special notes necessary to be observed in the
framing of our accustomed English rhyme.[2] The first is that one
metre or verse be answerable to another in equal number of feet
or syllables, or proportionable to the tune whereby it is to be

---

* *by mutual interposition*: with other lines of different lengths and/or rhymes
interposed   * *answerable*: correspondent   * *rude*: unlearned, unrefined
* *engraffed*: engrafted   * *the most part*: the majority
* *disallow*: refuse to praise/sanction   * *so as*: as long as, at the same time as
* *artificial*: artful, according to rules of art   * *speech*: language

read or measured.*³ The second, to place the words in such sort as none of them be wrested* contrary to the natural inclination or affectation* of the same, or more truly the true quantity* thereof. The third, to make them fall together mutually in rhyme, that is, in words of like sound, but so as the words be not disordered for the rhyme's sake, nor the sense hindered. [. . .]

Of the kinds of English verses which differ in number of syllables, there are almost infinite, which every way alter according to his fancy or to the measure of that metre wherein it pleaseth him to frame his ditty.* Of the best and most frequented I will rehearse* some. The longest verse in length which I have seen used in English consisteth of sixteen syllables, each two verses rhyming together, thus:

> Where virtue wants and vice abounds, there wealth is but a
>   baited hook,
> To make men swallow down their bane,* before on danger
>   deep they look.

This kind is not very much used at length thus, but is commonly divided, each verse into two, whereof each shall contain eight syllables and rhyme crosswise, the first to the third and the second to the fourth, in this manner:

> Great wealth is but a baited hook,
> Where virtue wants and vice abounds,
> Which men devour before they look,
> So them in dangers deep it drowns.⁴

Another kind next in length to this is where each verse hath fourteen syllables, which is the most accustomed of all other, and especially used of all the translators of the Latin poets for the most part, thus:

* *measured*: i.e. matched in rhythm or metre   * *wrested*: twisted, turned
* *affectation*: inclination
* *quantity*: (in classical metrics) length or shortness   * *ditty*: (lyric) poem
* *rehearse*: mention, give an account of   * *bane*: poison, ruin

> My mind with fury fierce inflamed of late, I know not how,
> Doth burn Parnassus hill to see, adorned with laurel bough.[5]

Which may be likewise, and so it often is, divided,[6] each verse
into two, the first having eight syllables, the second six, whereof
the two sixes shall always rhyme, and sometimes the eights,
sometimes not, according to the will of the maker:

> > My mind with fury fierce inflamed
> > Of late, I know not how,
> > Doth burn Parnassus hill to see,
> > Adorned with laurel bough.[7]

There are now, within this compass,* as many sorts of verses
as may be devised differences of numbers, whereof some consist
of equal proportions,* some of long and short together, some
of many rhymes in one staff* (as they call it), some of cross
rhyme, some of counter rhyme,[8] some rhyming with one word
far distant from another, some rhyming every third or fourth
word; and so, likewise, all manner of ditties appliable to every
tune that may be sung or said, distinct from prose or continued
speech.

[*examples of verse forms from* The Shepheardes Calender]

These sorts of verses for brevity's sake have I chosen forth of
him, whereby I shall avoid the tedious rehearsal of all the kinds
which are used, which I think would have been unpossible,
seeing they may be altered to as many forms as the poets please.
Neither is there any tune or stroke* which may be sung or
played on instruments which hath not some poetical ditties
framed according to the numbers* thereof: some to 'Rogero',
some to 'Trenchmore', some to 'Downright Squire', to galliards,
to pavans, to jigs, to brawls, to all manner of tunes, which every
fiddler knows better than myself, and therefore I will let them
pass.[9]

---

* *this compass*: this range, these limits   * *proportions*: line lengths
* *staff*: stanza   * *stroke*: metrical/rhythmic pattern
* *numbers*: metre, rhythm

[. . .]

Now for the second point. The natural course of most English verses seemeth to run upon the old iambic stroke, and I may well think by all likelihood it had the beginning thereof.* For if you mark the right quantity of our usual verses, ye shall perceive them to contain in sound the very property of iambic feet, as thus:

       ˘ _ ˘ _ ˘ _ ˘ _ ˘ _ ˘ _ ˘ _

   I that my slender oaten pipe in verse was wont to sound[10]

For transpose any of those feet in pronouncing, and make short either the two, four, six, eight, ten, twelve syllable, and it will (do what you can) fall out very absurdly.

Again, though our words cannot well be forced to abide the touch* of position and other rules of *prosodia*,*[11] yet is there such a natural force or quantity in each word that it will not abide any place but one without some foul disgrace; as for example, try any verse, as this:

       ˘ _ ˘ _ ˘ _ ˘ _ ˘ _ ˘ _ ˘ _

   Of shapes transformed to bodies strange I purpose to entreat[12]

Make the first syllable long, or the third, or the fifth, and so forth, or, contrariwise, make the other syllables to admit the shortness of one of them places, and see what a wonderful defacing* it will be to the words,[13] as thus:

       _ ˘ _ ˘ _ ˘ _ ˘ _ ˘ _ ˘ _ ˘

   Of strange bodies transformed to shapes purpose I to entreat

So that this is one especial thing to be taken heed of in making a good English verse, that, by displacing,* no word be wrested against his natural propriety, whereunto you shall perceive each

* *thereof*: i.e. from the nature of English (verse)   * *touch*: test, trial
* *prosodia*: 'prosody'   * *defacing*: spoiling, disfiguring
* *displacing*: transposition, putting out of place

word to be affected,* and may easily discern it in words of two syllables or above, though some there be of indifferency* that will stand in any place.[14]

Again, in couching the whole sentence the like regard is to be had that we exceed not too boldly in placing the verb out of his order and too far behind the noun, which the necessity of rhyme may oftentimes urge. For though it be tolerable in a verse to set words so extraordinarily as other speech will not admit, yet heed is to be taken, lest by too much affecting that manner we make both the verse unpleasant and the sense obscure.[15] And sure it is a wonder to see the folly of many in this respect, that use not only too much of this overthwart* placing, or rather displacing, of words in their poems and verses, but also in their prose or continued writings, where they think to roll most smoothly and flow most eloquently: there, by this means, come forth their sentences, dragging at one another's tail as they were tied together with points,* where often you shall tarry (scratching your head) a good space before you shall hear his principal verb or special word, lest his singing grace, which in his sentence is contained, should be less, and his speech seem nothing poetical.[16]

The third observation is the rhyme or like ending of verses, which, though it is of least importance, yet hath won such credit among us that of all other it is most regarded of the greatest part of readers. And surely, as I am persuaded, the regard of writers to this hath been the greatest decay of that good order of versifying, which might ere this have been established in our speech. In my judgement, if there be any ornament in the same it is rather to be attributed to the plentiful fullness of our speech, which can afford rhyming words sufficient for the handling of any matter, than to the thing itself for any beautifying it bringeth to a work, which might be adorned with far more excellent colours than rhyming is. Notwithstanding, I cannot but yield unto it (as custom requireth) the deserved praises, especially where it is with good judgement ordered. And I think them

* *affected*: inclined   * *indifferency*: i.e. able to be stressed or unstressed
* *overthwart*: crosswise, perverse   * *points*: cord fastenings

right worthy of admiration for their readiness and plenty of wit
and capacity who can with facility entreat* at large, and, as
we call it, extempore, in good and sensible rhyme upon some
unacquainted matter.

---

entreat: treat

SIR JOHN HARINGTON

A Brief Apology of Poetry (1591)

A Preface, or rather a Brief Apology* of Poetry, and of the Author and Translator of this Poem

The learned Plutarch, in his Laconical Apothegms, tells of a sophister* that made a long and tedious oration in praise of Hercules, and, expecting at the end thereof for some great thanks and applause* of the hearers, a certain Lacedaemonian* demanded him who had dispraised Hercules.[1] Methinks the like may be now said to me, taking upon me the defence of poesy, for surely if learning in general were of that account* among us as it ought to be among all men, and is among wise men, then should this my apology of poesy (the very first nurse and ancient grandmother of all learning)[2] be as vain and superfluous as was that sophister's, because it might then be answered, and truly answered, that no man disgraced it. But sith* we live in such a time in which nothing can escape the envious tooth and back-biting tongue of an impure mouth, and wherein every blind corner hath a squint-eyed Zoilus[3] that can look aright upon no man's doings (yea, sure there be some that will not stick* to call Hercules himself a dastard,* because, forsooth, he fought with a club and not at the rapier and dagger),[4] therefore I think no man of judgement will judge this my labour needless, in seeking to remove away those slanders that either the malice of those that love it not or the folly of those that understand it not hath

---

* *Apology*: speech in defence   * *sophister*: sophist
* *applause*: commendation   * *Lacedaemonian*: Spartan
* *account*: estimation, importance   * *sith*: since
* *stick*: scruple, hesitate   * *dastard*: malicious coward

devised against it. For indeed, as the old saying is, *scientia non habet inimicum praeter ignorantem* – knowledge hath no foe but the ignorant.[5]

But now[6] because I make account* I have to deal with three sundry kinds of reprovers – one of those that condemn all poetry, which (how strong head soever they have) I count but a very weak faction; another of those that allow poetry, but not this particular poem, of which kind sure there cannot be many; a third of those that can bear with the art, and like of the work, but will find fault with my not well handling of it, which they may not only probably but I doubt* too truly do, being a thing as commonly done as said that where the hedge is lowest, there doth every man go over[7] – therefore against these three I must arm me with the best defensive weapons I can, and if I happen to give a blow now and then in mine own defence, and, as good fencers use, to ward and strike at once, I must crave pardon of course,* seeing our law allows that is done *se defendendo*,* and the law of nature teacheth *vim vi repellere.*

First, therefore, of poetry itself,[8] for those few that generally disallow* it might be sufficient to allege* those many that generally approve it, of which I could bring in such an army, not of soldiers but of famous kings and captains,* as not only the sight but the very sound of them were able to vanquish and dismay the small forces of our adversaries. For who would once dare to oppose himself against so many Alexanders, Caesars, Scipios[9] (to omit infinite other princes, both of former and later ages, and of foreign and nearer countries), that with favour, with study, with practice, with example, with honours, with gifts, with preferments, with great and magnificent cost have encouraged and advanced poets and poetry? As witness the huge theatres and amphitheatres, monuments of stupendous charge,* made only for tragedies and comedies, the works of poets, to be represented on. But all those aids and defences I

---

* *make account*: expect, reckon   * *doubt*: fear
* *of course*: as a matter of course   * *se defendendo*: 'in self-defence'
* *vim vi repellere*: 'to repel force with force'
* *disallow*: refuse to praise/sanction   * *allege*: cite   * *captains*: leaders
* *charge*: cost

leave as superfluous: my cause I count so good, and the evidence so open,* that I neither need to use the countenance* of any great state to bolster it, nor the cunning of any subtle* lawyer to enforce it – my meaning is, plainly and *bona fide*,* confessing all the abuses* that can truly be objected against some kind of poets, to show you what good use there is of poetry.

Neither do I suppose it to be greatly behoveful* for this purpose to trouble you with the curious* definitions of a poet and poesy, and with the subtle distinctions of their sundry kinds;[10] nor to dispute how high and supernatural the name of a maker is, so christened in English by that unknown godfather that this last year save one, viz. 1589, set forth a book called the *Art of English Poetry*;[11] and least of all do I purpose to bestow any long time to argue whether Plato, Xenophon and Erasmus, writing fictions and dialogues in prose, may justly be called poets, or whether Lucan, writing a story* in verse, be an historiographer,* or whether Master Phaer translating Virgil, Master Golding translating Ovid's *Metamorphoses*, and myself in this work that you see be any more than versifiers, as the same *Ignoto*ted* termeth all translators.[12] For as for all, or the most part, of such questions, I will refer you to Sir Philip Sidney's Apology,[13] who doth handle them right learnedly, or to the forenamed treatise, where they are discoursed more largely,* and where, as it were, a whole receipt* of poetry is prescribed, with so many new-named figures* as would put me in great hope, in this age to come, would breed many excellent poets – save for one observation that I gather out of the very same book. For though the poor gentleman laboureth greatly to prove, or rather to make, poetry an art, and reciteth, as you may see in the plural number, some pluralities of patterns,* and parcels* of his own poetry, with diverse pieces of Partheniads and hymns

* *open*: evident, plain, easy to understand
* *countenance*: support, patronage   * *subtle*: cunning, sly
* *bona fide*: 'in good faith'   * *abuses*: misuses
* *behoveful*: useful, beneficial, necessary   * *curious*: artful
* *story*: history   * *historiographer*: historian
* *Ignoto*: Unknown, Anonymous   * *more largely*: at greater length
* *receipt*: recipe   * *figures*: rhetorical ornaments
* *patterns*: examples, models   * *parcels*: parts, portions, passages

in praise of the most praiseworthy,*[14] yet, whatsoever he would prove by all these, sure in my poor opinion he doth prove nothing more plainly than that which Master Sidney and all the learneder sort that have written of it do pronounce, namely that it is a gift and not an art.[15] I say he proveth it because, making himself and many others so cunning* in the art, yet he showeth himself so slender a gift in it, deserving to be commended as Martial praiseth one that he compares to Tully:

> carmina quod scribis Musis et Apolline nullo,
> audari debes: hoc Ciceronis habes.*[16]

But to come to the purpose, and to speak after the phrase* of the common sort, that term all that is written in verse poetry, and, rather in scorn than in praise, bestow the name of a poet on every base rhymer and ballad-maker, this I say of it, and I think I say truly, that there are many good lessons to be learned out of it, many good examples to be found in it, many good uses to be had of it, and that therefore it is not, nor ought not to be, despised by the wiser sort, but so to be studied and employed as was intended by the first writers and devisers thereof, which is to soften and polish the hard and rough dispositions of men, and make them capable of* virtue and good discipline.*

I cannot deny but to us that are Christians, in respect of the high end of all, which is the health of our souls, not only poetry but all other studies of philosophy are in a manner vain and superfluous – yea, (as the wise man saith) whatsoever is under the sun is vanity of vanities, and nothing but vanity.[17] But sith we live with men and not with saints, and because few men can embrace this strict and stoical divinity;* or rather, indeed, for that the holy scriptures in which those high mysteries of our salvation are contained are a deep and profound study, and not subject to every weak capacity, no, nor to the highest wits and

---

* *the most praiseworthy*: i.e. Queen Elizabeth   * *cunning*: learned, skilful
* *carmina . . . habes*: 'you write verses without Apollo and the Muses. You deserve praise; this habit you have of Cicero's'   * *phrase*: style, idiom
* *capable of*: open to, able to comprehend   * *discipline*: moral instruction
* *divinity*: theology

judgements except they be first illuminate by God's spirit or instructed by his teachers and preachers – therefore we do first read some other authors, making them, as it were, a looking glass to the eyes of our mind, and then, after we have gathered more strength, we enter into profounder studies of higher mysteries, having first, as it were, enabled our eyes by long beholding the sun in a basin of water at last to look upon the sun itself. So we read how that great Moses, whose learning and sanctity is so renowned over all nations, was first instructed in the learning of the Egyptians before he came to that high contemplation of God, and familiarity (as I may so term it) with God.[18] So the notable prophet Daniel was brought up in the learning of the Chaldeans, and made that the first step of his higher vocation to be a prophet.[19] If, then, we may by the example of two such special servants of God spend some of our young years in studies of humanity,* what better and more meet* study is there for a young man than poetry, specially heroical poetry, that with her sweet stateliness doth erect the mind and lift it up to the consideration of the highest matters, and allureth them, that of themselves would otherwise loathe them, to take and swallow and digest the wholesome precepts of philosophy, and many times even of the true divinity? Wherefore Plutarch,[20] having written a whole treatise of the praise of Homer's works, and another of reading poets, doth begin this latter with this comparison: that as men that are sickly and have weak stomachs or dainty* tastes do many times think that flesh most delicate to eat that is not flesh, and those fishes that be not fish, so young men (saith he) do like best that philosophy that is not philosophy, or that is not delivered as philosophy – and such are the pleasant writings of learned poets, that are the popular philosophers and the popular divines.[21] Likewise Tasso,[22] in his excellent work of *Gerusalemme liberata*, likeneth poetry to the physic that men give unto little children when they are sick; his verse is this [. . .], speaking to God with a pretty *prosopopoeia*:[23]

---

* *humanity*: language and literature, secular culture   * *meet*: fitting
* *dainty*: fastidious

> Thou know'st the wanton worldlings* ever run
> To sweet Parnassus' fruits; how, otherwhile,
> The truth well sauced with pleasant verse hath won
> Most squeamish stomachs with the sugared style;
> So the sick child, that potions all doth shun,
> With comfits* and with sugar we beguile,
> And cause him take a wholesome sour receipt:*
> He drinks, and saves his life with such deceit.

This is then that honest fraud, in which (as Plutarch saith) he that is deceived is wiser than he that is not deceived, and he that doth deceive is honester than he that doth not deceive.[24]

[*arguments against poetry*: that it is a nurse of lies, a pleaser of fools, a breeder of dangerous errors, and an enticer to wantonness][25]

And first for lying,[26] I might if I list* excuse it by the rule of *poetica licentia*,* and claim a privilege given to poetry, whose art is but an imitation (as Aristotle calleth it), and therefore are allowed to feign* what they list,[27] according to that old verse:

> iuridicis, Erebo, fisco, fas vivere rapto;
> militibus, medicis, tortori, occidere ludo est;
> mentiri, astronomis, pictoribus atque poetis.[28]

Which because I count it without reason, I will English without rhyme:

> Lawyers, Hell and the Exchequer are allowed to live on spoil;
> Soldiers, physicians and hangmen make a sport of murder;
> Astronomers, painters and poets may lie by authority.

Thus you see that poets may lie if they list *cum privilegio*.* But what if they lie least of all other men? What if they lie not at all?

* *worldlings*: worldly-minded persons
* *comfits*: sugar-coated nuts or seeds   * *receipt*: medicine
* *list*: please   * *poetica licentia*: 'poetic licence'
* *feign*: create fictionally, represent
* *cum privilegio*: 'with (official) privilege, with special permission'

Then I think that great slander is very unjustly raised upon them. For in my opinion they are said properly to lie that affirm that to be true that is false; and how other arts can free themselves from this blame,* let them look that profess them, but poets, never affirming any for true, but presenting them to us as fables and imitations, cannot lie though* they would.[29] And because this objection of lies is the chief, and that upon which the rest be grounded, I will stand* the longer upon the clearing thereof.

The ancient poets have indeed wrapped, as it were, in their writings divers and sundry meanings, which they call the senses or mysteries thereof. First of all for the literal sense (as it were the utmost* bark or rind), they set down in manner of an history the acts and notable exploits of some persons worthy memory. Then, in the same fiction, as a second rind and somewhat more fine, as it were nearer to the pith and marrow, they place the moral sense, profitable for the active life of man,[30] approving virtuous actions and condemning the contrary. Many times also, under the selfsame words, they comprehend* some true understanding of natural philosophy, or sometimes of politic* government, and now and then of divinity; and these same senses that comprehend so excellent knowledge we call the allegory, which Plutarch defineth to be when one thing is told and by that another is understood.[31] Now, let any man judge if it be a matter of mean* art or wit to contain in one historical narration, either true or feigned, so many, so diverse, and so deep conceits.* But for making the matter more plain I will allege an example thereof.

Perseus, son of Jupiter, is feigned by the poets to have slain Gorgon, and after that conquest achieved to have flown up to heaven.[32] The historical sense is this: Perseus, the son of Jupiter by the participation* of Jupiter's virtues that were in him, or rather coming of the stock of one of the kings of Crete or Athens so called,[33] slew Gorgon, a tyrant in that country ('Gorgon' in

* *blame*: charge   * *though*: even if   * *stand*: delay, insist
* *utmost*: outermost   * *comprehend*: include   * *politic*: political, civil
* *mean*: ordinary   * *conceits*: ideas   * *participation*: sharing

Greek signifieth earth), and was for his virtuous parts* exalted
by men up unto heaven. Morally it signifieth this much: Perseus,
a wise man, son of Jupiter, endued with virtue from above,
slayeth sin and vice, a thing base and earthly signified by Gorgon,
and so mounteth up to the sky of virtue. It signifies in one kind
of allegory thus much: the mind of man, being gotten* by God,
and so the child of God, killing and vanquishing the earthliness
of this gorgonical nature, ascendeth up to the understanding of
heavenly things, of high things, of eternal things, in which
contemplation consisteth the perfection of man. This is the
natural allegory, because man one of the chief works of nature.[34]
It hath also a more high and heavenly allegory: that the heavenly
nature, daughter of Jupiter, procuring with her continual
motion corruption and mortality in the inferior bodies, severed
itself at last from these earthly bodies and flew up on high,
and there remaineth for ever. It hath also another theological
allegory: that the angelical nature, daughter of the most high
God the creator of all things, killing and overcoming all bodily
substance, signified by Gorgon, ascended into heaven.

The like infinite allegories I could pick out of other poetical
fictions, save that I would avoid tediousness. It sufficeth me
therefore to note this: that the men of greatest learning and
highest wit* in the ancient times did of purpose conceal these
deep mysteries of learning and, as it were, cover them with the
veil of fables and verse, for sundry causes.[35] One cause was that
they might not be rashly abused by profane wits, in whom
science* is corrupted like good wine in a bad vessel. Another
cause why they wrote in verse was conservation of the memory
of their precepts, as we see yet the general rules almost of every
art, not so much* as husbandry, but they are oftener recited and
better remembered in verse than in prose.[36] Another, and a
principal cause of all, is to be able with one kind of meat and
one dish (as I may so call it) to feed divers tastes: for the weaker
capacities will feed themselves with the pleasantness of the
history and sweetness of the verse; some that have stronger

---

* *parts*: qualities, character   * *gotten*: begotten   * *wit*: understanding
* *science*: knowledge   * *not so much*: none so much

stomachs will, as it were, take a further taste of the moral sense; a third sort, more high-conceited* than they, will digest the allegory. So as indeed it hath been thought, by men of very good judgement, such manner of poetical writing was an excellent way to preserve all kind of learning from that corruption which now it is come to since they left that mystical writing of verse.

Now, though, I know the example and authority of Aristotle and Plato be still urged against this, who took to themselves another manner of writing. First, I may say indeed that laws were made for poor men and not for princes, for these two great princes of philosophy brake that former allowed* manner of writing; yet Plato still preserved the fable, but refused the verse. Aristotle, though rejecting both, yet retained still a kind of obscurity, insomuch he answered Alexander, who reproved him in a sort for publishing the sacred secrets of philosophy, that he had set forth* his books in a sort, and yet not set them forth, meaning that they were so obscure that they would be understood by few, except they came to him for instructions, or else without* they were of very good capacity and studious of philosophy.[37] But (as I say) Plato, howsoever men would make him an enemy of poetry (because he found indeed just fault with the abuses of some comical poets of his time, or some that sought to set up new and strange religions), yet you see he kept still that principal part of poetry, which is fiction and imitation;[38] and as for the other part of poetry, which is verse, though he used it not, yet his master Socrates even in his old age wrote certain verses, as Plutarch testifieth.[39]

But because I have named the two parts of poetry, namely invention or fiction and verse, let us see how well we can authorize the use of both these. First for fiction, against which, as I told before, many inveigh, calling it by the foul name of lying, though notwithstanding, as I then said, it is farthest from it. Demosthenes, the famous and renowned orator, when he would persuade the Athenians to war against Philip, told them a solemn tale how the wolves on a time sent ambassadors to the

* *more high-conceited*: more high-minded, of greater intellectual power
* *allowed*: approved   * *set forth*: published   * *without*: unless

sheep, offering them peace if they would deliver up the dogs that kept their folds, with all that long circumstance* (needless to be repeated), by which he persuaded them far more strongly than if he should have told them in plain terms that Philip sought to bereave them of their chief bulwarks and defences, to have the better ability to overthrow them.[40] [. . .] But, to go higher, did not our Saviour Himself speak in parables? As that divine parable of the sower, that comfortable* parable of the prodigal son, that dreadful* parable of Dives and Lazarus,[41] though I know of this last many of the Fathers* hold that it is a story* indeed and no parable. But in the rest it is manifest that He that was all holiness, all wisdom, all truth used parables, and even such as discreet* poets use, where a good and honest and wholesome allegory is hidden in a pleasant and pretty fiction. And therefore for that part of poetry, of imitation, I think nobody will make any question but it is not only allowable but godly and commendable, if the poet's ill handling of it do not mar and pervert the good use of it.

The other part of poetry, which is verse,[42] as it were the clothing or ornament of it, hath many good uses. Of the help of memory I spake somewhat before, for the words being couched together in due order, measure and number, one doth, as it were, bring on another, as myself have often proved, and so, I think, do many beside; though for my own part I can rather boast of the marring a good memory than of having one, yet I have ever found that verse is easier to learn and far better to preserve in memory than is prose. Another special grace in verse is the forcible manner of phrase,* in which, if it be well made, it far excelleth loose speech or prose. A third is the pleasure and sweetness to the ear, which makes the discourse pleasant unto us oftentime when the matter itself is harsh and unacceptable.* For mine own part I was never yet so good a husband* to take any delight to hear one of my ploughmen tell how an acre of

---

* *circumstance*: detail   * *comfortable*: affording spiritual comfort
* *dreadful*: causing dread   * *Fathers*: Church Fathers   * *story*: history
* *discreet*: judicious   * *phrase*: expression   * *unacceptable*: unpleasing
* *husband*: farmer

wheat must be fallowed and twifallowed,* and how cold land
should be burned, and how fruitful land must be well harrowed.
But when I hear one read Virgil, where he saith:

> saepe etiam steriles incendere profuit agros
> atque levem stipulam crepitantibus urere flammis;
> sive inde occultas vires et pabula terrae
> pinguia concipiunt, sive illis omne per ignem
> excoquitur vitium atque exsudat inutilis umor,*[43] etc.

and after:

> Multum adeo, rastris glaebas qui frangit inertis
> vimineasque trahit crates, iuvat arva . . .*[44]

with many other lessons of homely husbandry, but delivered in
so good verse that methinks all that while I could find in my
heart to drive the plough.

But now for the authority of verse, if it be not sufficient to say
for them that the greatest philosophers and gravest senators that
ever were have used them both in their speeches and in their
writings,[45] that precepts of all arts have been delivered in them,
that verse is as ancient a writing as prose, and indeed more
ancient in respect that the oldest works extant be verse, as
Orpheus, Linus, Hesiodus and others beyond memory of man
or mention almost of history[46] – if none of these will serve for
the credit of it, yet let this serve, that some part of the Scripture
was written in verse, as the Psalms of David, and certain other
songs of Deborah, of Solomon and others, which the learnedest
divines do affirm to be verse, and find that they are in metre,
though the rule of the Hebrew verse they agree not on.[47] Sufficeth

---

* *twifallowed*: (of fallow land) ploughed a second time
* *saepe . . . umor*: 'often, too, it has been useful to fire barren fields, and burn
the light stubble in crackling flames; whether it be that the earth derives thence
hidden strength and rich nutriment, or that in the flame every taint is baked out
and the useless moisture sweats from it . . .'
* *Multum . . . arva*: 'Yea, and much service does he do the land who with the
mattock breaks up the sluggish clods, and drags over it wicker hurdles . . .'

it me only to prove that by the authority of sacred scriptures both parts of poesy – invention, or imitation, and verse – are allowable, and consequently that great objection of lying is quite taken away and refuted.

Now, the second objection is pleasing of fools.[48] I have already showed how it displeaseth not wise men. Now if it have this virtue too, to please the fools and ignorant, I would think this an article of praise not of rebuke; wherefore I confess that it pleaseth fools, and so pleaseth them that, if they mark it and observe it well, it will in time make them wise. For in verse is both goodness and sweetness, rhubarb and sugar candy, the pleasant and the profitable, wherefore, as Horace saith, *omne tulit punctum qui miscuit utile dulci.**[49] He that can mingle the sweet and the wholesome, the pleasant and the profitable, he is indeed an absolute good writer, and such be poets if any be such: they present unto us a pretty tale, able to keep a child from play and an old man from the chimney corner.[50] [. . .]

Now, for the breeding of errors, which is the third objection,[51] I see not why it should breed any when none is bound to believe that they write, nor they look not to have their fictions believed in the literal sense. And therefore he that well examines whence errors spring shall find the writers of prose, and not of verse, the authors and maintainers of them. And this point I count so manifest as it needs no proof.

The last reproof is lightness* and wantonness. This is indeed an objection of some importance, sith, as Sir Philip Sidney confesseth, Cupido* is crept even into the heroical poems and consequently makes that, also, subject to this reproof.[52] I promised in the beginning not partially to praise poesy, but plainly and honestly to confess that that might truly be objected against it, and if anything may be, sure it is this lasciviousness. Yet this I will say: that of all kind of poesy the heroical is least infected therewith. The other kinds I will rather excuse than

* *omne . . . dulci*: 'He has won every vote who has blended profit and pleasure'
* *lightness*: wantonness, lewdness, incontinence
* *Cupido*: Cupid, Desire

defend, though of all the kinds of poesy it may be said: where any scurrility and lewdness is found, there poetry doth not abuse us, but writers have abused poetry.[53] And briefly to examine all the kinds. First, the tragical is merely* free from it, as representing only the cruel and lawless proceedings of princes, moving nothing but pity or detestation.[54] The comical, whatsoever foolish playmakers make it offend in this kind, yet being rightly used it represents them so as to make the vice scorned and not embraced. The satiric is merely free from it, as being wholly occupied in mannerly* and covertly reproving of all vices. The elegy is still mourning; as for the pastoral, with the sonnet or epigram, though many times they savour of wantonness and love and toying, and now and then, breaking the rules of poetry, go into plain scurrility, yet even the worst of them may be not ill applied, and are, I must confess, too delightful, insomuch as Martial saith: *laudant illa, sed ista legunt.**[55] And, in another place:

> erubuit posuitque meum Lucretia librum,
> sed coram Bruto; Brute, recede: leget.*[56]

Lucretia (by which he signifies any chaste matron) will blush and be ashamed to read a lascivious book. But how? Not except Brutus be by, that is, if any grave man should see her read it. But if Brutus turn his back, she will to it again and read it all.[57]

But to end this part of my apology: as I count and conclude heroical poesy allowable, and to be read and studied without all exception, so I may as boldly say that tragedies well handled be a most worthy kind of poesy, that comedies may make men see and shame at their own faults, that the rest may be so written and so read as much pleasure and some profit may be gathered out of them, and, for mine own part, as Scaliger writeth of

---

* *merely*: wholly, actually   * *mannerly*: decently, properly, morally
* *laudant . . . legunt*: 'that they praise but this they read'
* *erubuit . . . leget*: 'Lucretia blushed and put my book aside, but that was in front of Brutus. Brutus, withdraw: she will read.'

Virgil, so I believe that the reading of a good heroical poem may make a man both wiser and honester.[58] [. . .] Finally, if comedies may be so made as the beholders may be bettered by them, without all doubt all other sorts of poetry may bring their profit as they do bring delight, and if all, then much more the chief of all, which by all men's consent is the heroical. And thus much be said for poesy.[59]

SAMUEL DANIEL

from *Musophilus: Containing a General
Defence of Learning* (1599)

[*Philocosmus engages Musophilus in debate*]

> *Philocosmus*
> [. . .]
55   Besides, so many so confusedly sing,
>   Whose divers discords have the music marred,
>   And in contempt that mystery* doth bring,
>   That he must sing aloud* that will be heard.
>   And the received opinion of the thing,
60   For* some unhallowed strings that vildly* jarred,*
>   Hath so unseasoned* now the ears of men
>   That who doth touch the tenor of that vein
>   Is held but vain, and his unreck'ned* pen
>   The title but of levity doth gain:
65   A poor light gain to recompense their toil
>   That thought to get eternity the while.[1]
>   And therefore leave the left and outworn course
>   Of unregarded ways, and labour how
>   To fit the times with what is most in force:
70   Be new with men's affections* that are now;
>   Strive not to run an idle counter-course,
>   Out from the scent* of humours men allow.*
>   [. . .]

* *mystery*: trade, profession (of poetry)   * *aloud*: loudly
* *For*: because of   * *vildly*: vilely   * *jarred*: clashed discordantly
* *unseasoned*: made unappreciative   * *unreck'ned*: ignored, not esteemed
* *affections*: predilections   * *Out from the scent*: off the scent (like a hound)
* *allow*: approve, praise

Musophilus
[. . .]
But yet, in all this interchange of all,
  Virtue, we see, with her fair grace, stands fast: 140
  For what high races hath there come to fall,
  With low disgrace, quite vanishèd and past,
  Since Chaucer lived, who yet lives and yet shall,
  Though (which I grieve to say) but in his last!²
Yet what a time hath he wrested from time,   145
  And won upon the mighty waste of days,
  Unto th'immortal honour of our clime,*
  That by his means came first adorned with bays,*
  Unto the sacred relics of whose rhyme
  We yet are bound in zeal to offer praise!   150
And could our lines begotten in this age
  Obtain but such a blessed hand* of years,
  And scape* the fury of that threat'ning rage*
  Which in confusèd clouds ghastly appears,
  Who would not strain his travails to engage,*   155
  When such true glory should succeed his cares?*
But whereas he came planted in the spring,
  And had the sun before him of respect,
  We, set in th'autumn, in the withering
  And sullen season of a cold defect,*   160
  Must taste those sour distastes* the times do bring
  Upon the fullness of a cloyed neglect;
Although the stronger constitutions shall
  Wear out* th'infection of distemp'rèd days,
  And come with glory to outlive this fall,*   165
  Recov'ring of another spring of praise,
  Cleared from th'oppressing humours,* wherewithal

* *clime*: region, country   * *bays*: the poet's laurels
* *hand*: hand dealt in cards   * *scape*: escape
* *that threat'ning rage*: i.e. oblivion
* *his travails to engage*: to pledge his toil   * *cares*: efforts, pains
* *defect*: deficiency, failure of the sun to shine   * *distastes*: aversions, nausea
* *Wear out*: last, survive   * *fall*: autumn   * *humours*: whimsies, fancies

The idle multitude surcharge* their lays.*
Whenas perhaps the words thou scornest now
170   May live, the speaking picture[3] of the mind,
The extract of the soul that laboured how
To leave the image of herself behind,
Wherein posterity, that love to know,
The just proportion of our spirits may find.
175   For these lines are the veins, the arteries,
And undecaying life-strings of those hearts
That still shall pant, and still shall exercise
The motion spirit and nature both imparts,*
And shall with those alive so sympathize,
180   As, nourished with their powers, enjoy their parts.*
O blessèd letters, that combine in one
All ages past, and make one live with all!
By you we do confer with who are gone,
And the dead living unto counsel call;
185   By you th'unborn shall have communion
Of what we feel, and what doth us befall.
Soul of the world,[4] knowledge, without thee
What hath the earth that truly glorious is?
Why should our pride make such a stir to be,
190   To be forgot? What good is like to this,
To do worthy the writing, and to write
Worthy the reading and the world's delight?
[. . .]

Philocosmus
[. . .]
Alas, poor fame, in what a narrow room,*
As an encagèd parrot, art thou pent
Here amongst us, where ev'n as good* be dumb
As speak and to be heard with no attent?*
415   How can you promise of the time to come

---

* *surcharge*: attack, burden   * *lays*: poems, songs
* *The . . . imparts*: the motion (activity) which both spirit and nature impart
* *parts*: qualities, abilities   * *room*: space
* *ev'n as good*: it is as good to   * *attent*: attention

Whenas the present are so negligent?
Is this the walk* of all your wide renown,
    This little point, this scarce discernèd isle,
    Thrust from the world, with whom our speech
        unknown
    Made never any traffic of our style?⁵   420
    And is this all, where all this care is shown,
    T'enchant your fame to last so long a while?
    And, for that happier tongues* have won so much,
    Think you to make your barbarous language such?
Poor narrow limits for so mighty pains,   425
    That cannot promise any foreign vent;*
    And yet, if here too all your wondrous veins*
    Were generally known, it might content,
    But lo, how many reads not, or disdains
    The labours of the chief and excellent!   430
How many thousands never heard the name
    Of Sidney, or of Spencer, or their books?
    And yet brave* fellows, and presume of* fame,
    And seem to bear down all the world with looks.
    What then shall they expect of meaner frame,   435
    On whose endeavours few or none scarce looks?
Do you not see these pamphlets, libels,* rhymes,
    These strange confusèd tumults of the mind,
    Are grown to be the sickness of these times,
    The great disease inflicted on mankind?   440
    Your virtues, by your follies, made your crimes
    Have issue with your indiscretion joined.*
[. . .]
Men find that action is another thing
    Than what they in discoursing papers read.
    The world's affairs require in managing

---

* *walk*: region, extent
* *for that happier tongues*: because more fortunate languages (i.e. Greek and
Latin)   * *vent*: outlet   * *veins*: qualities, styles   * *brave*: splendid
* *presume of*: they expect   * *libels*: little books
* *issue with your indiscretion joined*: taken issue with your lack of judgement

480   More arts than those wherein you clerks* proceed.
        Whilst timorous knowledge stands considering,
        Audacious ignorance hath done the deed.
        For who knows most, the more he knows to doubt:
        The least discourse* is commonly most stout.*
485   This sweet enchanting knowledge turns you clean
            Out from the fields of natural delight,
        And makes you hide, unwilling to be seen
            In th'open concourse of a public sight:
        This skill wherewith you have so cunning* been
490   Unsinews all your powers, unmans you quite.
        Public society and commerce of men
            Require another grace, another port;*
        This eloquence, these rhymes, these phrases then,
            Begot in shades, do serve us in no sort:
495   Th'unmaterial* swellings of your pen
            Touch not the spirit that action doth import.*
        [. . .]
505   Yet do I not dislike, that in some wise
            Be sung the great heroical deserts
        Of brave renownèd spirits, whose exercise*
            Of worthy deeds may call up* others' hearts,
        And serve a model for posterities,
510   To fashion them fit for like glorious parts;[6]
        But so that all our spirits may tend hereto:
        To make it not our grace to say, but do.

Musophilus
[. . .]
And for my part, if only one allow*
    The care my labouring spirits take in this,
    He is to me a theatre large enow,*
560   And his applause* only sufficient is:

* *clerks*: scholars   * *discourse*: reasoning   * *stout*: vigorous, resolute
* *cunning*: learned, clever   * *port*: behaviour, manner, style
* *unmaterial*: immaterial   * *import*: bring about, involve
* *exercise*: practice   * *call up*: provoke, incite   * *allow*: approve
* *enow*: enough   * *applause*: praise, commendation

All my respect* is bent but to his brow;
That is my all, and all I am is his.[7]
And if some worthy spirits be pleasèd too,
It shall more comfort breed, but not more will.
But what if none? It cannot yet undo   565
The love I bear unto this holy skill:
This is the thing that I was born to do;
This is my scene, this part must I fulfil.
[. . .]
Power above powers, O heavenly Eloquence,
That with the strong rein of commanding words   930
Dost manage, guide, and master th'eminence*
Of men's affections more than all their swords![8]
Shall we not offer to thy excellence
The richest treasure that our wit affords?
Thou that canst do much more with one poor pen   935
Than all the powers of princes can effect,
And draw, divert, dispose and fashion men
Better than force or rigour can direct:
Should we this ornament of glory, then,
As th'unmaterial fruits of shades,[9] neglect?   940
Or should we careless come behind the rest
In power of words, that go before in worth,
Whenas our accents,* equal to the best,
Is able greater wonders to bring forth,
When all that ever hotter* spirits expressed   945
Comes* bettered by the patience of the north?*
And who, in time, knows whither we may vent
The treasure of our tongue, to what strange* shores
This gain of our best glory shall be sent
T'enrich unknowing nations with our stores;   950
What worlds in th'yet unformèd Occident*

* *respect*: regard, consideration, attention
* *master th'eminence*: achieve the mastery; or control the most superior
* *accents*: language
* *hotter*: less temperate, and from warmer, more southerly climes
* *Comes*: becomes, comes to be   * *the north*: i.e. northern Europe, England
* *strange*: foreign   * *Occident*: West (i.e. America)

　　　　　May come* refined with th'accents that are ours?
　　　　Or who can tell for what great work in hand
　　　　　The greatness of our style is now ordained;[10]
955　　　What powers it shall bring in, what spirits command,
　　　　　What thoughts let out, what humours keep restrained,
　　　　　What mischief it may powerfully withstand,
　　　　　And what fair ends may thereby be attained?
　　　　And as for poesy (mother of this force),[11]
960　　　That breeds, brings forth and nourishes this might,
　　　　　Teaching it in a loose, yet measured, course[12]
　　　　　With comely motions how to go upright,*
　　　　　And, fost'ring it with bountiful discourse,
　　　　　Adorns it thus in fashions of delight:
965　　What should I say? since it is well approved*
　　　　　The speech of heav'n, with whom they have
　　　　　　　commerce
　　　　　That only seem out of themselves removed,[13]
　　　　　And do with more than human skills converse –
　　　　　Those numbers,* wherewith heav'n and earth are
　　　　　　moved,
970　　　Show weakness speaks in prose, but power in verse.
　　　　[. . .]

---

* *come*: come to be　　　* *go upright*: walk, stand on its own feet
* *approved*: attested, known　　　* *Those numbers*: that metre

THOMAS CAMPION

from *Observations in the Art of English Poesy* (1602)

The first chapter, entreating of numbers* in general*

There is no writing too brief, that without obscurity compre-
hends* the intent of the writer. These my late observations in
English poesy I have thus briefly gathered that they might prove
the less troublesome in perusing, and the more apt to be retained
in memory. And I will first generally handle the nature of
numbers. Number is *discreta quantitas,**[1] so that when we speak
simply of number we intend* only the dissevered* quantity, but
when we speak of a poem written in number we consider not
only the distinct number of the syllables but also their value,
which is contained in the length or shortness of their sound.[2] As
in music we do not say a strain* of so many notes, but so many
semibreves (though sometimes there are no more notes than
semibreves),[3] so in a verse the numeration of the syllables is not
so much to be observed as their weight and due proportion. In
joining of words to harmony* there is nothing more offensive
to the ear than to place a long syllable with a short note, or a
short syllable with a long note, though in the last the vowel
often bears it out. The world is made by symmetry and proportion, and is in that respect compared to music, and music to
poetry:[4] for Terence saith, speaking of poets, *artem qui tractant*

---

* *entreating*: treating   * *numbers*: (quantitative) metre
* *comprehends*: encompasses
* *discreta quantitas*: 'quantity composed of distinct units'   * *intend*: mean
* *dissevered*: discrete, distinct   * *strain*: tune, musical phrase, section
* *joining . . . harmony*: i.e. setting words to music

musicam,* confounding music and poetry together.[5] What music can there be where there is no proportion observed? Learning first flourished in Greece; from thence it was derived unto the Romans – both diligent observers of the number and quantity of syllables, not in their verses only but likewise in their prose.[6] Learning, after the declining of the Roman Empire and the pollution of their language through the conquest of the barbarians, lay most pitifully deformed till the time of Erasmus, Reuchlin, Sir Thomas More and other learned men of that age,[7] who brought the Latin tongue again to light, redeeming it with much labour out of the hands of the illiterate monks and friars, as a scoffing book entitled *Epistolae obscurorum virorum** may sufficiently testify.[8] In those lack-learning times, and in barbarized Italy, began that vulgar and easy kind of poesy which is now in use throughout most parts of Christendom, which we abusively* call 'rhyme' and 'metre', of *rhythmus* and *metrum*,[9] of which I will now discourse.

The second chapter, declaring the unaptness* of rhyme in poesy

I am not ignorant that whosoever shall by way of reprehension examine the imperfections of rhyme must encounter with many glorious* enemies, and those very expert and ready at their weapon, that can, if need be, extempore (as they say) rhyme a man to death;[10] besides, there is grown a kind of prescription* in the use of rhyme, to forestall the right of true numbers; as also the consent of many nations – against all which it may seem a thing almost impossible and vain to contend. All this and more cannot deter me from a lawful defence of perfection, or make me any whit the sooner adhere to that which is lame and

---

* *artem . . . musicam*: 'who labour in the art of music'
* *Epistolae . . . virorum*: 'Letters of Obscure Men'   * *abusively*: incorrectly
* *unaptness*: unsuitability, inappropriateness
* *glorious*: proud, haughty; or illustrious
* *prescription*: authority of custom, claim founded upon long use

unbeseeming. For custom, I allege* that ill uses are to be abolished, and that things naturally imperfect cannot be perfected
by use. Old customs, if they be better, why should they not be
recalled,* as the yet flourishing custom of numerous* poesy
used among the Romans and Grecians? But the unaptness of
our tongues and the difficulty of imitation disheartens us; again,
the facility* and popularity of rhyme creates as many poets as
a hot summer flies.

But let me now examine the nature of that which we call
rhyme. By rhyme is understood that which ends in the like
sound, so that verses in such manner composed yield but a
continual repetition of that rhetorical figure which we term
similiter desinentia,*[11] and that, being but *figura verbi*,* ought
(as Tully* and all other rhetoricians have judicially* observed)
sparingly to be used, lest it should offend the ear with tedious
affectation.[12] Such was that absurd following of the letter*
amongst our English so much of late affected,* but now hissed
out of Paul's Churchyard.[13] [...] The ear is a rational sense,
and a chief judge of proportion, but in our kind of rhyming
what proportion is there kept, where there remains such a
confused inequality of syllables? Iambic and trochaic feet, which
are opposed by nature, are by all rhymers confounded; nay,
oftentimes they place instead of an iambic the foot *pyrrhichius*,
consisting of two short syllables, curtailing their verse, which
they supply* in reading with a ridiculous and unapt* drawing*
of their speech.[14] As for example: 'Was it my destiny or dismal
chance?' In this verse the two last syllables of the word 'destiny',
being both short, and standing for a whole foot in the verse,
cause the line to fall out shorter than it ought by nature.[15] [...]
But the noble Grecians and Romans, whose skilful monuments
outlive barbarism, tied themselves to the strict observation of

* *allege*: declare, assert   * *recalled*: revived, restored
* *numerous*: quantitative   * *facility*: easiness
* *similiter desinentia*: 'like endings'
* *figura verbi*: 'a figure of words, a scheme'   * *Tully*: Cicero
* *judicially*: judiciously   * *following of the letter*: alliteration
* *affected*: aimed at, preferred   * *supply*: make up for
* *unapt*: inappropriate   * *drawing*: drawing out, elongation

poetical numbers, so abandoning the childish titillation of rhyming that it was imputed a great error to Ovid for setting forth*
this one rhyming verse: *quot caelum stellas, tot habet tua Roma puellas.* *[16]

[...]

But there is yet another fault in rhyme altogether intolerable, which is that it enforceth a man oftentimes to abjure his matter, and extend a short conceit beyond all bounds of art. For in quatorzains* methinks the poet handles his subject as tyrannically as Procrustes the thief his prisoners, whom, when he had taken, he used to cast upon a bed, which if they were too short to fill he would stretch them longer, if too long he would cut them shorter.[17] Bring before me now any the most self-loved rhymer, and let me see if without blushing he be able to read his lame halting rhymes. Is there not a curse of nature laid upon such rude* poesy, when the writer is himself ashamed of it, and the hearers in contempt call it rhyming and ballading? What divine in his sermon, or grave counsellor in his oration, will allege the testimony* of a rhyme?[18] But the divinity* of the Romans and Grecians was all written in verse, and Aristotle, Galen[19] and the books of all the excellent philosophers are full of the testimonies of the old poets. By them was laid the foundation of all human wisdom, and from them the knowledge of all antiquity is derived. I will propound* but one question, and so conclude this point. If the Italians, Frenchmen and Spaniards that with commendation have written in rhyme were demanded* whether they had rather the books they have published (if their tongue would bear it) should remain as they are in rhyme or be translated into the ancient numbers of the Greeks and Romans, would they not answer 'into numbers'?[20] What honour were it then for our English language to be the first that after so many years of barbarism could second* the perfection

---

* *setting forth*: publishing
* *quot . . . puellas*: 'as many stars as has the sky, so many girls has your Rome'
* *quatorzains*: fourteen-line poems, i.e. sonnets   * *rude*: rough, unlearned
* *allege the testimony*: cite as a proof   * *divinity*: theology, religion
* *propound*: propose   * *demanded*: asked   * *second*: match

of the industrious Greeks and Romans? Which how it may be effected, I will now proceed to demonstrate.

The third chapter, of our English numbers in general

There are but three feet which generally distinguish the Greek and Latin verses: the dactyl, consisting of one long syllable and two short, as vīvĕrĕ;* the trochee, of one long and one short, as vītă;* and the iambic, of one short and one long, as ămōr.* The spondee, of two long, the tribrach, of three short, the anapaestic, of two short and a long, are but as servants to the first. Divers other feet, I know, are by the grammarians cited, but to little purpose.[21] The heroical verse that is distinguished by the dactyl hath been oftentimes attempted in our English tongue, but with passing* pitiful success; and no wonder, seeing it is an attempt altogether against the nature of our language. For both the concourse* of our monosyllables make our verses unapt to slide,*[22] and, also, if we examine our polysyllables we shall find few of them, by reason of their heaviness, willing to serve in place of a dactyl. Thence it is that the writers of English heroics do so often repeat 'Amyntas', 'Olympus', 'Avernus', 'Erinys' and such like borrowed words to supply the defect of our hardly entreated* dactyl.[23] I could in this place set down many ridiculous kinds of dactyls which they use, but that it is not my purpose here to incite men to laughter.

If we therefore reject the dactyl as unfit for our use (which of necessity we are enforced to do), there remain only the iambic foot, of which the iambic verse is framed, and the trochee, from which the trochaic numbers have their original.* Let us now then examine the property of these two feet, and try if they consent* with the nature of our English syllables. And first for

---

* *vivere*: 'to live'   * *vita*: 'life'   * *amor*: 'love'
* *passing*: exceedingly   * *concourse*: running together, flocking together
* *slide*: flow smoothly   * *hardly entreated*: harshly treated
* *original*: origin   * *consent*: agree, harmonize

the iambics, they fall out so naturally in our tongue, that if we examine our own writers, we shall find they unawares hit oftentimes upon the true iambic numbers, but always aim at them as far as their ear, without the guidance of art, can attain unto, as it shall hereafter more evidently appear.[24] The trochaic foot, which is but an iambic turned over and over, must of force* in like manner accord in proportion with our British syllables, and so produce an English trochaical verse. Then, having these two principal kinds of verses, we may easily out of them derive other forms, as the Latins and Greeks before us have done, whereof I will make plain demonstration, beginning at the iambic verse.

[*The fourth chapter, of the iambic verse; The fifth chapter, of the iambic dimeter, or English march; The sixth chapter, of the English trochaic verse; The seventh chapter, of the English elegiac verse*]

The eighth chapter, of ditties and odes

To descend orderly from the more simple numbers to them that are more compounded,* it is now time to handle such verses as are fit for ditties* or odes,[25] which we may call lyrical, because they are apt to be sung to an instrument, if they were adorned with convenient* notes.
[. . .]
   The second kind consists of: dimeter, whose first foot may either be a spondee or a trochee; the two verses* following are both of them trochaical, and consist of four feet, the first of either of them being a spondee or trochee, the other three only trochees; the fourth and last verse is made of two trochees.[26] The number is voluble* and fit to express any amorous conceit.*

* *of force*: of necessity   * *compounded*: complex, composite
* *ditties*: songs, lyric poems   * *convenient*: suitable, commensurate
* *verses*: lines   * *voluble*: fluent, easily moved   * *conceit*: thought, idea

The example

> Rose-cheeked Laura, come,
> Sing thou smoothly with thy beauty's
> Silent music, either other*
> > Sweetly gracing.

> Lovely forms do flow
> From concent* divinely framèd:
> Heav'n is music, and thy beauty's
> > Birth is heavenly.

> These dull notes we sing
> Discords need for helps to grace them.
> Only beauty, purely loving,
> > Knows no discord,

> But still moves delight,
> Like clear springs renewed by flowing,
> Ever perfect, ever in them-
> > Selves eternal.

[...]

The ninth chapter, of the Anacreontic verse

[*summary of the eight verse forms presented*] These numbers, which by long observation I have found agreeable with the nature of our syllables, I have set forth for the benefit of our language, which I presume the learned will not only imitate, but also polish and amplify* with their own inventions. Some ears, accustomed altogether to the fatness of rhyme,[27] may perhaps except* against the cadences* of these numbers. But let any man judicially* examine them, and he shall find they close of themselves so perfectly that the help of rhyme were not only in them superfluous, but also absurd. [...]

* *either other*: each the other   * *concent*: concord, harmony
* *amplify*: augment   * *except*: take exception, object
* *cadences*: line endings, closes   * *judicially*: judiciously

The tenth chapter, of the quantity of English syllables

[extensive rules]

These rules concerning the quantity of our English syllables I have disposed* as they came next into my memory; others more methodical time and practice may produce. In the mean season,* as the grammarians leave many syllables to the authority of poets,[28] so do I likewise leave many to their judgements; and withal thus conclude, that there is no art begun and perfected at one enterprise.[29]

---

* *disposed*: ordered, arranged   * *mean season*: meantime

FRANCIS BACON

from *The Advancement of Learning* (1605)

Poesy is a part of learning, in measure of words* for the most
part restrained, but in all other points extremely licensed,* and
doth truly refer to the imagination,[1] which, being not tied to the
laws of matter, may at pleasure join that which nature hath
severed, and sever that which nature hath joined, and so make
unlawful* matches and divorces of things: *pictoribus atque
poetis*,* etc.[2] It is taken in two senses, in respect of words or
matter.[3] In the first sense it is but a character of style and
belongeth to arts of speech, and is not pertinent for the present.
In the latter it is (as hath been said) one of the principal portions
of learning, and is nothing else but feigned* history, which may
be styled* as well in prose as in verse.[4]

The use of this feigned history hath been to give some shadow
of satisfaction to the mind of man in those points wherein the
nature of things doth deny it, the world being in proportion*
inferior to the soul, by reason whereof there is agreeable to the
spirit of man a more ample greatness, a more exact goodness
and a more absolute variety than can be found in the nature of
things. Therefore, because the acts or events of true history have
not that magnitude which satisfieth the mind of man, poesy
feigneth acts and events greater and more heroical; because true

---

* *measure of words*: poetic metre   * *licensed*: free from regulation
* *unlawful*: i.e. against the laws of nature
* *pictoribus atque poetis*: 'to painters and poets [has always been granted an
equal right in venturing to do anything they wished]'   * *feigned*: fictitious
* *styled*: written, expressed
* *in proportion*: in matters of form and symmetry

history propoundeth the successes* and issues of actions not so agreeable to the merits of virtue and vice, therefore poesy feigns them more just in retribution* and more according to revealed providence; because true history representeth actions and events more ordinary and less interchanged,* therefore poesy endueth them with more rareness, and more unexpected and alternative* variations.[5] So as it appeareth that poesy serveth and conferreth to magnanimity,* morality and to delectation.*[6] And therefore it was ever thought to have some participation of divineness, because it doth raise and erect* the mind by submitting the shows* of things to the desires of the mind, whereas reason doth buckle* and bow the mind unto the nature of things. And we see that by these insinuations* and congruities with man's nature and pleasure, joined also with the agreement and consort* it hath with music, it hath had access* and estimation in rude* times and barbarous regions where other learning stood excluded.[7]

* *successes*: outcomes, results   * *retribution*: reward and punishment
* *interchanged*: varied   * *alternative*: alternating
* *magnanimity*: greatness of soul, nobility   * *delectation*: delight
* *erect*: rouse, stir up   * *shows*: appearances
* *buckle*: bind, submit, bend   * *insinuations*: persuasive suggestions
* *consort*: accord, partnership   * *access*: admittance, approval
* *rude*: uncivilized

MICHAEL DRAYTON

'To Henry Reynolds, of Poets and Poesy' (1627)

To my most dearly loved friend Henry Reynolds, Esquire,[1] *of poets and poesy*

My dearly lovèd friend, how oft have we
In winter evenings (meaning to be free)*
To some well-chosen place used to retire,
And there with moderate meat,* and wine, and fire
Have passed the hours contentedly with chat,   5
Now talked of this, and then discoursed of that,
Spoke our own verses 'twixt ourselves, if not
Other men's lines which we by chance had got,
Or some stage pieces famous long before,
Of which your happy* memory had store!   10
And I remember you much pleasèd were
Of those who livèd long ago to hear,
As well as of those, of these latter times,
Who have enriched our language with their rhymes,
And, in succession, how still up they grew,*   15
Which is the subject that I now pursue.
For from my cradle (you must know that) I
Was still* inclined to noble poesy,
And when that once *Pueriles* I had read,
And newly had my Cato construèd,[2]   20
In my small self I greatly marvelled then,
Amongst all other, what strange kind of men

---

* *meaning to be free*: intending to talk frankly   * *meat*: food
* *happy*: ready   * *up . . . grew*: developed   * *still*: always

These poets were. And, pleasèd with the name,
To my mild tutor merrily I came
25   (For I was then a proper goodly page,*
Much like a pygmy, scarce ten years of age),
Clasping my slender arms about his thigh.
'O my dear master! Cannot you,' quoth I,
'Make me a poet? Do it, if you can,
30   And you shall see I'll quickly be a man.'
Who me thus answered, smiling: 'Boy,' quoth he,
'If you'll not play the wag,* but I may see
You ply* your learning, I will shortly read
Some poets to you.' Phoebus* be my speed,
35   To't hard went I, when shortly he began,
And first read to me honest Mantuan,
Then Virgil's *Eclogues*;[3] being entered* thus,
Methought I straight had mounted Pegasus,
And in his full career* could make him stop,
40   And bound* upon Parnassus' bicleft* top.[4]
I scorned your ballet* then, though* it were done
And had for Finis, William Elderton.[5]
But soft, in sporting with this childish jest,
I from my subject have too long digressed.
45   Then to the matter that we took in hand:
Jove and Apollo for the Muses stand.*

      That noble Chaucer, in those former times,
The first enriched our English with his rhymes,
And was the first of ours that ever brake
50   Into the Muses' treasure, and first spake
In weighty numbers,* delving in the mine
Of perfect knowledge, which he could refine
And coin for current, and as much as then
The English language could express to men

* *page*: boy, boy-servant   * *play the wag*: play truant
* *ply*: apply yourself to   * *Phoebus*: Apollo, god of poetry
* *entered*: begun, introduced   * *full career*: gallop (here, flight) at full stretch
* *bound*: leap, spring up   * *bicleft*: split in two, having two peaks
* *ballet*: ballad   * *though*: even if
* *for . . . stand*: take the part of, defend   * *numbers*: verse

He made it do, and by his wondrous skill 55
Gave us much light from his abundant quill.

And honest Gower,[6] who in respect of* him
Had only sipped at Aganippe's brim;[7]
And though in years this last was him before,*
Yet fell he far short of the other's store. 60

When after those, four ages very near,
They with the Muses which conversèd were
That princely Surrey, early in the time
Of the Eighth Henry, who was then the prime
Of England's noble youth; with him there came 65
Wyatt,[8] with reverence whom we still do name.
Amongst our poets, Bryan had a share
With the two former, which accounted are
That time's best makers,* and the authors were
Of those small poems, which the title bear 70
Of *Songs and Sonnets*,[9] wherein oft they hit
On many dainty passages of wit.

Gascoigne and Churchyard after them again,
In the beginning of Eliza's* reign,
Accounted were great meterers many a day, 75
But not inspirèd with brave fire;* had they
Lived but a little longer, they had seen
Their works before them to have buried been.[10]

Grave moral Spenser after these came on,
Than whom I am persuaded there was none 80
Since the blind bard* his *Iliads* up did make[11]
Fitter a task like that to undertake,
To set down boldly, bravely* to invent,
In all high knowledge surely excellent.

The noble Sidney with this last arose, 85
That heroë* for numbers and for prose,

---

* *in respect of*: in comparison with   * *him before*: ahead of him, i.e. older
* *makers*: poets   * *Eliza*: Queen Elizabeth I
* *brave fire*: splendid passion, imagination, genius   * *the blind bard*: Homer
* *bravely*: splendidly   * *heroë*: hero [common trisyllabic form]

That throughly* paced* our language, as to show
The plenteous English hand in hand might go
With Greek and Latin, and did first reduce
90   Our tongue from Lyly's writing, then in use:
Talking of stones, stars, plants, of fishes, flies,
Playing with words, and idle similes,[12]
As th'English apes* and very zanies* be
Of everything that they do hear and see,
95   So, imitating his ridiculous tricks,
They spake and writ all like mere lunatics.

Then Warner, though his lines were not so trimmed,
Nor yet his poem so exactly limbed*[13]
And neatly jointed, but the critic may
100   Easily reprove him, yet thus let me say
For my old friend: some passages there be
In him, which I protest have taken me
With almost wonder, so fine, clear and new
As yet they have been equallèd by few.

105   Neat Marlowe, bathèd in the Thespian* springs,
Had in him those brave translunary* things
That the first poets had; his raptures were
All air and fire, which made his verses clear:
For that fine madness still he did retain,
110   Which rightly should possess a poet's brain.[14]

And surely Nashe, though he a proser were,
A branch of laurel yet deserves to bear.
Sharply satiric was he,[15] and that way
He went, since that his being, to this day
115   Few have attempted, and I surely think
Those words shall hardly be set down with ink
Shall scorch and blast so as his could, where he
Would inflict vengeance; and be it said of thee,

---

* *throughly*: thoroughly, perfectly   * *paced*: measured (the poetic feet of)
* *apes*: imitators, copycats   * *zanies*: poor mimics
* *limbed*: given limbs, articulated
* *Thespian*: of the Muses, of Mount Helicon
* *translunary*: beyond the moon, visionary

Shakespeare, thou hadst as smooth a comic vein,
Fitting the sock, and in thy natural brain   120
As strong conception, and as clear a rage,
As anyone that trafficked* with the stage.[16]
   Amongst these Samuel Daniel, whom if I
May speak of, but to censure do deny,
Only have heard some wise men him rehearse*   125
To be too much historian in verse:
His rhymes were smooth, his metres well did close,
But yet his manner better fitted prose.[17]
   Next these,* learn'd Jonson in this list I bring,
Who had drunk deep of the Pierian* spring,   130
Whose knowledge did him worthily prefer,*
And long was lord here of the theatre;
Who in opinion made our learn'd'st to stick,*
Whether in poems rightly dramatic
Strong Seneca or Plautus, he or they   135
Should bear the buskin or the sock away.[18]
   Others again here livèd in my days,
That have of us deservèd no less praise
For their translations than the daintiest wit
That on Parnassus thinks he high'st doth sit,   140
And for a chair may 'mongst the Muses call,
As the most curious* maker of them all:
As reverent Chapman, who hath brought to us
Musaeus, Homer and Hesiodus
Out of the Greek,[19] and by his skill hath reared   145
Them to that height, and to our tongue endeared,*
That were those poets at this day alive,
To see their books thus with us to survive,
They would think, having neglected them so long,
They had been written in the English tongue.   150

---

* *trafficked*: had dealings   * *rehearse*: declare
* *Next these*: next to these   * *Pierian*: sacred to the Muses, poetic
* *prefer*: advance   * *stick*: be unable to decide   * *curious*: artful, skilful
* *endeared*: enhanced the value of, tied in obligations, made dear

And Sylvester, who from the French more weak
Made Bartas of his six days' labour speak
In natural English, who, had he there stayed,*
He had done well, and never had bewrayed*
His own invention to have been so poor,
Who still wrote less, in striving to write more.[20]
    Then dainty* Sandys, that hath to English done
Smooth sliding Ovid, and hath made him run
With so much sweetness and unusual* grace,
As though the neatness of the English pace
Should tell the jetting* Latin that it came
But slowly after, as though stiff and lame.[21]
    So Scotland sent us hither, for our own,
That man whose name I ever would have known
To stand by mine, that most ingenious knight,
My Alexander, to whom in his right
I want extremely, yet in speaking thus
I do but show the love that was 'twixt us,
And not his numbers,* which were brave and high,
So like his mind was his clear poesy;
And my dear Drummond, to whom much I owe
For his much love, and proud I was to know
His poesy; for which two worthy men
I Menstry still shall love, and Hawthornden.[22]
    Then the two Beaumonts and my Browne arose,[23]
My dear companions, whom I freely chose
My bosom friends; and in their several ways
Rightly born poets, and in these last days
Men of much note, and no less nobler parts,
Such as have freely told to me their hearts,
As I have mine to them. But if you shall
Say, in your knowledge, that these be not all
Have writ in numbers, be informed that I
Only myself to these few men do tie

155

160

165

170

175

180

---

* *stayed*: stopped   * *bewrayed*: revealed   * *dainty*: pleasant
* *unusual*: unaccustomed   * *jetting*: swaggering   * *numbers*: verses

Whose works oft printed, set on every post,*   185
To public censure subject have been most.
For such whose poems, be they ne'er so rare,*
In private chambers that encloistered* are,
And by transcription* daintily* must go,
As though the world unworthy were to know   190
Their rich composures,* let those men that keep
These wondrous relics in their judgement deep
And cry them up* so, let such pieces be
Spoke of by those that shall come after me:
I pass* not for them.[24] Nor do mean to run   195
In quest of these that them applause have won
Upon our stages in these latter days,
That are so many: let them have their bays*
That do deserve it; let those wits that haunt
Those public circuits,* let them freely chant   200
Their fine composures, and their praise pursue.
And so, my dear friend, for this time adieu.

* *set . . . post*: i.e. well publicised   * *rare*: fine, splendid
* *encloistered*: imprisoned, confined
* *by transcription*: through manuscript copying
* *daintily*: fastidiously, sparingly   * *composures*: compositions
* *cry . . . up*: praise, talk up   * *pass*: care, concern myself
* *bays*: poet's laurels   * *circuits*: spheres

SIR WILLIAM ALEXANDER

from *Anacrisis. Or a Censure of some Poets
Ancient and Modern* (c.1635)

Language is but the apparel of poesy, which may give beauty,
but not strength. And when I censure* any poet, I first dissolve
the general contexture* of his work in several* pieces, to see
what sinews it hath, and to mark what will remain behind when
that external gorgeousness, consisting in the choice or placing
of words, as if it would bribe the ear to corrupt the judgement,
is first removed, or at least only marshalled in its own degree.*¹
I value language as a conduit, the variety thereof to several
shapes, and adorned truth or witty* inventions that which it
should deliver.² I compare a poem to a garden,³ the disposing*
of the parts of the one to the several walks of the other, the
decorum kept in descriptions, and representing of persons,⁴ to
the proportions and distances to be observed in such things as
are planted therein, and the variety of invention to the diversity
of flowers thereof, whereof three sorts do chiefly please me: a
grave sentence,* by which the judgement may be bettered; a
witty conceit,* which doth harmoniously delight the spirits; and
a generous rapture expressing magnanimity,* whereby the mind
may be inflamed for great things.⁵ All the rest, for the most part,
is but a naked narration or gross staff to uphold the general
frame, yet the more apt, if well contrived and eloquently

---

* *censure*: criticize, form a judgement on
* *contexture*: fabric, body, connected structure   * *several*: separate
* *marshalled . . . degree*: arranged according to rank, put in its place
* *witty*: of the mind, clever   * *disposing*: arrangement
* *grave sentence*: serious moral dictum   * *witty conceit*: clever idea, plot
* *magnanimity*: greatness of soul, nobility

delivered, to angle* vulgar readers, who perchance can scarce conceive the other.*

[. . .]

Many would bound the boundless liberty of a poet, binding him only to the birth of his own brains, affirming that there can be no perfection but in a fiction,[6] not considering that the ancients, upon whose example they ground their opinion, did give faith unto those fables – whereby they would abuse our credulity – not only as to true history but as to true divinity, since containing the greatness of their gods and grounds of their religion, which they in their own kind did strive superstitiously to extol; so that hereby they would either make our religion or our affection thereunto inferior unto theirs,[7] and imaginary matters to be more celebrated than true deeds, whose envied price,* affectionately* looked upon, must beget a generous emulation in any virtuous reader's mind.

The treasures of poesy cannot be better bestowed than upon the apparelling of truth, and truth cannot be better apparelled to please young lovers than with the excellencies of poesy. I would allow that an epic poem should consist altogether of a fiction, that the poet, soaring above the course of nature, making the beauty of virtue to invite and the horror of vice to affright the beholders, may liberally furnish his imaginary man with all the qualities requisite for the accomplishing of a perfect creature, having power to dispose of all things at his own pleasure.[8] But it is more agreeable* with the gravity of a tragedy that it be grounded upon a true history, where the greatness of a known person, urging regard,* doth work the more powerfully upon the affections. As for the satirist and epigrammatist, they may mix both the two, who, shadowing truth with fables and discovering true persons with feigned names, may, by alluding to antiquity, tax the modern times. I have heard some, with a pretended theological austerity, condemn the reading of fictions

* *angle*: entice, catch   * *the other*: i.e. sentence, conceit and rapture
* *envied price*: value causing wish to emulate
* *affectionately*: earnestly, zealously   * *agreeable*: concordant, congruent
* *regard*: attention, sympathy

as only breathing a contagious dissoluteness to empoison the spirits, where such works must be acknowledged as the chief springs of learning, both for profit and pleasure, showing things as they should be, where histories represent them as they are, many times making vice to prosper and virtue to prove miserable.[9]

[. . .] But I confess that the *Arcadia* of Sir Philip Sidney (either being considered in the whole or in several lineaments)* is the most excellent work that, in my judgement, hath been written in any language that I understand, affording many exquisite types of perfection for both the sexes, leaving the gifts of nature, whose value doth depend upon the beholders, wanting no virtue whereof a human mind could be capable,[10] as, for men, magnanimity, carriage,* courtesy, valour, judgement, discretion, and, in women, modesty, shamefastness,* constancy, continency, still accompanied with a tender sense of honour; and his chief persons being eminent for some singular virtue, and yet all virtues being united in every one of them, men equally excelling both for martial exercise and for courtly recreations, showing the author, as he was indeed, alike well versed both in learning and arms. It was a great loss to posterity that his untimely death did prevent the accomplishing* of that excellent work.[11]

---

* *several lineaments*: separate outlines, plots   * *carriage*: conduct
* *shamefastness*: modesty, propriety   * *accomplishing*: completion

BEN JONSON

'A Fit of Rhyme against Rhyme' (before 1637)

Rhyme, the rack of finest wits,*
That expresseth but by fits,*
      True conceit,*
Spoiling senses of their treasure,
Cozening judgement with a measure,   5
      But false weight;
Wresting* words from their true calling,
Propping verse, for fear of falling
      To the ground;[1]
Jointing* syllabs, drowning letters,   10
Fast'ning vowels, as* with fetters
      They were bound![2]
Soon as lazy thou wert known,[3]
All good poetry hence was flown,
      And art banished.   15
For a thousand years together
All Parnassus' green did wither,
      And wit vanished;
Pegasus did fly away,
At the wells no Muse did stay,   20
      But bewailèd
So to see the fountain dry,
And Apollo's music die,
      All light failèd.[4]

* *wits*: minds, understandings
* *fits*: paroxysms, and sections of a poem or song (here, stanzas)
* *conceit*: thought, fancy, imagining   * *Wresting*: twisting, wrenching
* *Jointing*: dismembering, disjointing; connecting at the joints   * *as*: as if

25   Starveling* rhymes did fill the stage,
                  Not a poet in an age
                        Worth a-crowning.[5]
                  Not a work deserving bays,*
                  Nor a line deserving praise,
30   Pallas* frowning.
                  Greek was free from rhyme's infection,
                  Happy* Greek, by this protection,
                      Was not spoilèd.
                  Whilst the Latin, Queen of tongues,
35   Is not yet free from rhyme's wrongs,
                      But rests foilèd.*[6]
                  Scarce the hill* again doth flourish,
                  Scarce the world a wit doth nourish,
                      To restore
40   Phoebus* to his crown again,
                  And the Muses to their brain,
                      As before.
                  Vulgar* languages that want
                  Words and sweetness, and be scant
45   Of true measure,
                  Tyran* rhyme hath so abusèd
                  That they long since have refusèd
                      Other cesure.*[7]
                  He that first invented thee,
50   May his joints tormented be,
                      Cramp'd for ever;
                  Still may syllabs jar* with time,*
                  Still may reason war with rhyme,
                      Resting never;

---

* *Starveling*: lean, poverty-stricken   * *bays*: the poet's laurels
* *Pallas*: Athena, goddess of wisdom, and arts and crafts
* *Happy*: blessed, fortunate
* *rests foilèd*: remains defeated, polluted, trampled down
* *the hill*: i.e. Parnassus   * *Phoebus*: Apollo   * *Vulgar*: vernacular
* *Tyran*: tyrant   * *cesure*: close, ending, caesura
* *jar*: clash discordantly   * *time*: metre, poetic or musical

May his sense, when it would meet   55
The cold tumour* in his feet,
            Grow unsounder;[8]
And his title be long fool,
That in rearing such a school
            Was the founder!   60

* *tumour*: swelling

BEN JONSON

from Horace, his Art of Poetry (before 1637)

si vis me flere . . .[1]
    The comic matter will not be expressed
In tragic verse; no less Thyestes' feast[2]
Abhors low numbers* and the private strain,*
Fit for the sock.[3] Each subject should retain
125   The place allotted it, with decent thews.*
If now the turns,* the colours,* and right hues
Of poems here described I can nor* use
Nor know t'observe, why (i'the Muses' name)
Am I called poet? Wherefore, with wrong shame
130   Perversely modest, had I rather owe*
To ignorance still than either learn or know?
Yet sometime doth the comedy excite
Her voice, and angry Chremes[4] chafes outright
With swelling throat. And oft the tragic wight*
135   Complains in humble phrase: both Telephus
And Peleus,[5] if they seek to heart-strike us
That are spectators with their misery
When they are poor and banished, must throw by
Their bombard* phrase and foot-and-half-foot words.*
140   'Tis not enough th'elaborate* Muse affords

---

* *numbers*: verse   * *private strain*: everyday idiom
* *decent thews*: fitting attributes or customs, manners according to decorum
* *turns*: tropes   * *colours*: rhetorical figures   * *nor*: neither
* *owe*: admit, own   * *wight*: person, character
* *bombard*: large, swollen jug, i.e. inflated (Horace: *ampulla*)
* *foot-and-half-foot words*: words a foot and a half in length (Horace: *sesqui-pedalia verba*)   * *elaborate*: careful, labouring

Her poems beauty, but a sweet delight
To work the hearers' minds still to their plight.
Men's faces still with such as laugh are prone
To laughter; so they grieve with those that moan.
If thou wouldst have me weep, be thou first drowned   145
Thyself in tears, then me thy loss will wound,
Peleus or Telephus.[6] If you speak vile
And ill-penned things, I shall or sleep, or smile.
Sad language fits sad looks; stuffed* menacings,
The angry brow; the sportive, wanton things;   150
And the severe, speech ever serious.

in medias res[7]
He* thinks not how to give you smoke from light,
But light from smoke,[8] that he may draw his bright
Wonders forth after, as Antiphates,   205
Scylla, Charybdis, Polypheme,[9] with these.
Nor from the brand with which the life did burn
Of Meleager brings he the return
Of Diomede;[10] nor Troy's sad war begins
From the two eggs that did disclose the twins.[11]   210
He ever hastens to the end, and so
(As if he knew it) raps* his hearer to
The middle of his matter, letting go
What he dispairs, being handled, might not show;*
And so well feigns,* so mixeth cunningly*   215
Falsehood with truth, as no man can espy
Where the midst differs from the first, or where
The last doth from the midst disjoined* appear.

Scribendi recte, sapere . . .[12]
     The very root of writing well, and spring,   440
Is to be wise; thy matter first to know,
Which the Socratic writings best can show,

* *stuffed*: full   * *He*: i.e. Homer, or one like him
* *raps*: hurries (Horace: *rapit*)   * *show*: shine, come off
* *feigns*: represents, imitates, makes in fiction   * *cunningly*: skilfully
* *disjoined*: disunited, disjointed, discrepant

And, where the matter is provided still,
There words will follow, not against their will.[13]

445   He that hath studied well the debt,* and knows
What to his country, what his friends he owes,
What height of love a parent will fit* best,
What brethren, what a stranger,* and his guest,
Can tell a statesman's duty, what the arts

450   And office of a judge are, what the parts*
Of a brave chief sent to the wars – he can,
Indeed, give fitting dues to every man.[14]
And I still bid the learned maker* look
On life, and manners, and make those his book,

455   Thence draw forth true expressions. For sometimes
A poem of no grace, weight, art in rhymes,
With specious places,* and being humoured* right,
More strongly takes the people with delight,
And better stays* them there, than all fine noise

460   Of verse mere matter-less, and tinkling toys.

Aut prodesse volunt aut delectare poetae . . .
    omne tulit punctum qui miscuit utile dulci[15]

477   Poets would either profit, or delight,
Or, mixing sweet and fit, teach life the right.*
[. . .]
    Be brief in what thou wouldst command, that so
The docile* mind may soon thy precepts know,

505   And hold them faithfully; for nothing rests,
But flows out, that o'erswelleth in full breasts.*
    Let what thou feign'st for pleasure's sake be near

---

* *the debt*: duty   * *fit*: suit, befit   * *stranger*: foreigner, visitor
* *parts*: qualities, function, office (Horace: *partes*)   * *maker*: poet
* *specious places*: plausible, splendid passages or commonplaces (Horace: *speciosa locis*)
* *humoured*: with appropriate morals and manners, with accurately drawn characters (Horace: *morata*)   * *stays*: keeps
* *teach life the right*: instruct life as to that which is right   * *docile*: teachable
* *breasts*: minds, hearts (Horace: *pectore*)

The truth;[16] nor let thy fable think what e'er
It would must be, lest it alive would draw
The child, when Lamia's dined,[17] out of her maw.*   510
The poems void of profit our grave men
Cast out by voices;* want they pleasure, then
Our gallants give them none,[18] but pass them by.
But he hath every suffrage* can apply
Sweet mixed with sour to his reader, so   515
As doctrine* and delight together go:
This book will get the Sosii[19] money, this
Will pass the seas, and, long as nature is,
Will honour make the far-known author live.

dormitat Homerus . . . Ut pictura poesis[20]
          Sometimes I hear good Homer snore,
But I confess that in a long work sleep
May with some right upon an author creep.
   As painting, so is poesy. Some man's hand*
Will take you more, the nearer that you stand,   540
As some the farther off; this loves the dark,
This, fearing not the subtlest* judge's mark,*
Will in the light be viewed; this once the sight
Doth please, this ten times over will delight.

* *maw*: stomach   * *voices*: opinion, common judgement
* *suffrage*: vote, approbation   * *doctrine*: teaching
* *hand*: style, skill
* *subtlest*: most discriminating, having most critical acumen
* *mark*: attention, scrutiny

A Note on Rhetoric

The following outline is indebted to Richard A. Lanham, *A Handlist of Rhetorical Terms*, 2nd edn (Berkeley and Los Angeles, 1991), 163–80.

THE AIM

to teach, to delight, to move (*docere, delectare, movere*)

THE THREE KINDS

deliberative	persuasion and dissuasion, political debate
judicial/forensic	legal argument, prosecution or defence
epideictic/demonstrative	praise and dispraise, often ceremonial

THE BASIC SKILLS

(and the sections under which most textbooks treat rhetoric; sometimes called the *five parts*)

invention	choice of contents (*inventio*)
disposition	arrangement of contents (*dispositio*)
elocution	choice of figures and style of expression (*elocutio*)
memory	committing the above to memory (*memoria*)
delivery	performing the oration (*actio* and/or *pronuntiatio*)

INVENTIO

Finding out matter (*res*), including strategies of self-presentation (*ethos*) and moving the audience (*pathos*), means of proof (from evidence to a good argument), types of argument (*topoi*, topics) and commonplaces (*loci communes*).

DISPOSITIO

In literary terms, plot or form. In rhetoric, the arrangement of matter into the accepted form of the oration: (i) *exordium* (opening); (ii) *narratio* (narration, setting out the facts and the issue); (iii) *divisio* or *propositio* or *partitio* (division, breaking the issue into different points of agreement and disagreement); (iv) *confirmatio* (proof, delivering one's arguments); (v) *confutatio* (refuting one's opponent's arguments); (vi) *conclusio* or *peroratio* (peroration, summing up and moving the audience with a final appeal). The Greek terms for exordium (*prooimion*) and peroration (*epilogos*) are familiar as the literary terms proem and epilogue.

ELOCUTIO

The primary focus for literary rhetoric, concerned with words (*verba*). There were typically three kinds of style (grand, middle or mixed, and low or plain), though other systems were outlined, and a common distinction is also made between the Attic or unornamented style and the Asiatic or ornamented style. Particular stylistic virtues, including clarity and decorum (the doctrine that language and action should be verisimilar and appropriate to the genre and style), were treated. The rhetorical figures were categorized by distinguishing between schemes (devices which are about the patterning and arrangement of words; sometimes called figures of speech) and tropes (meaning 'turns': devices which involve changes of meaning, like metaphor; sometimes called figures of thought). On occasion, as in Puttenham, figures of speech are divided into schemes and tropes and a third category, figures of thought, contains complex figures which combine scheme and trope.

MEMORIA

The classical art of memory taught the student to visualize a complex memory building or theatre of memory into which the elements of the oration would be inserted in particular places. The oration would be performed by recalling each of these 'places' in order. Performance could include a degree of interplay between the oration as prepared and the possibility of improvisation. What was remembered and performed might be not a set sequence of words but rather a careful outline indicating, for instance, that at one point a particular commonplace was to be ornamented with a particular figure of speech.

ACTIO/PRONUNTIATIO

The two terms correspond to gesture and voice, both of which required training and planning. The complex system of gestural language by the particular position and movement of body and hands fed into early modern acting techniques.

A Note on English Versification

Rhythm and Metre

Versification depends on the interplay between the imposed metres of verse and the natural rhythms of speech.

English verse is for the most part accentual-syllabic. Whereas French verse has a fixed number of syllables per line and variable stresses, and Old English verse has a fixed pattern of accents and a variable number of syllables, English verse tends to be fixed in both respects. The accentual-syllabic system was accepted in practice by the middle of the sixteenth century and in theory by the final quarter of the sixteenth century. Popular verse, instanced in ballads and songs, tended to greater accentual regularity and aided the observation that English metre depends on accent for its organization.

Each line of English verse is composed of a number of units of accented (or 'stressed') and unaccented (or 'unstressed') syllables (feet). The common system of notation, borrowed from classical metrics, marks a stressed syllable ' ¯ ' and an unstressed syllable ' ˘ '; an alternative system is also given below. The first two kinds of feet only are common; in each case the name of the foot (e.g. iamb) gives its name to the metre (e.g. iambic):

Duple Metres

iamb	iambic	˘ –	x /
trochee	trochaic	– ˘	/ x
spondee	spondaic	– –	/ /
pyrrhic	pyrrhic	˘ ˘	x x

Triple Metres

anapaest	anapaestic	˘ ˘ –	x x /
dactyl	dactylic	– ˘ ˘	/ x x
amphibrach	amphibrachic	˘ – ˘	x / x

NB (i) these terms cannot be used to describe any cluster of syllables within a line, but only those clusters which are feet; (ii) it is debatable whether there can actually be a spondee or a pyrrhic in a line of English verse, since the best definition of a foot in accentual-syllabic verse is one stressed syllable plus nought to two unstressed syllables; (iii) poems in triple metres tend to use a mixture of anapaestic, dactylic and amphibrachic lines, and to employ substitution, where a two-syllable foot replaces a three-syllable one.

The name given to the metre tells us how many feet are in each line (not how many syllables):

one foot:	monometer
two feet:	dimeter
three feet:	trimeter
four feet:	tetrameter
five feet:	pentameter
six feet:	hexameter
seven feet:	heptameter
eight feet:	octameter

Examples: iambic pentameter; trochaic tetrameter; iambic hexameter (also called alexandrine).

Lines tend to contain a pause, often after the second or third accented syllable – a caesura. Since the caesura is most often and most obviously simply a manifestation of a syntactical, not a metrical, rule (i.e. the end of a clause), it is a term of rather limited usefulness. The syntax of a sentence tends to follow the division of verse into lines. Where this is regularly the case you will see punctuation at the ends of lines (the verse would then be described as end-stopped). Where not, you will see enjambment – i.e. the running-on of sense beyond the ends of the lines. As a general rule, poetic effect tends to reside in deviations from regularity, or in extreme regularity. A common example is a trochee as the first foot of an iambic line ('reversed first foot', 'foot inversion' or 'trochaic substitution').

The accentual-syllabic system does not require that each accented syllable in a line bear the same amount of speech stress as every other, but rather that it be relatively more stressed than the unaccented syllables around it. Thus Marvell's 'To a green thought in a green shade' is scanned not as pyrrhic, spondee, pyrrhic, spondee, which would be impossible, but as iambic tetrameter with the first and third feet reversed: – ‿ | ‿ – | – ‿ | ‿ –

Certain syllables may be omitted through elision (e.g. 'Th'expense

of spirit in a waste of shame', Shakespeare, sonnet 129). In other cases
a single syllable may be split in two for the sake of the metre: (e.g. 'Let
me be loved, or else not lovèd be', Sidney, 'old' Arcadia, OA 20, l. 14).
The original printers usually omitted the silent 'e', sometimes replacing
it with an apostrophe, meaning that an 'e' not omitted was to be
pronounced: 'Let me be lov'd, or else not loved be'.

The Quantitative Alternative

English prosodic terminology derives from classical metrics; this is why
it retains some awkwardness and is frequently challenged (e.g. are
there really feet or caesurae? What is accent?). It began to be applied
to English verse in the second half of the sixteenth century, at a time
when the accentual-syllabic system was becoming firmly established in
theory and practice. This development coincided with, and was affected
by, a movement aimed at using the classical system to organize English
verse. Classical Greek and Latin verse is quantitative and unrhymed.
Syllables are of either long or short quantity and the feet detailed
above, along with many others, are composed of long and short syllables instead of stressed and unstressed syllables. A long syllable
demands twice the time in pronunciation as a short. Some poets (like
Sidney) concentrated on imitating the varied forms of Greek and Latin
lyric poetry. Others copied the dactylic hexameter of epic. A line of
hexameter (also forming the first line in an elegiac couplet, as in the
example below – Ovid, *Heroides* ['Heroines'], 1.1) has six feet; the last
must be a spondee (- -), the penultimate a dactyl (- ‿ ‿); the others
may be spondee or dactyl; caesura (‖) occurs in the third or fourth foot:

_ ‿‿ | _ ‿‿ |_‖_ |_ ‿ ‿|_ ‿ ‿|_ _
Haec tua Penelope lento tibi mittit, Ulixe

In an Elizabethan imitation:

_ _ | _ ‿ ‿|_‖_ | _ _|_ ‿ ‿|_ _
Constant Penelope sends to thee, careless Ulysses

In the more successful experiments, speech stress coincides with
quantity, so that the long syllables will also be stressed, and the first
syllable of a spondee is more stressed than the second; the result is
that the verse moves rhythmically and accords with natural speech
patterns, as in this example (Sidney, 'Old' *Arcadia*, OA 12, l. 1), which

is written in Sapphics, the verse form named after the Greek lyric poet Sappho:

$$\_\ \cup\ |\ \_\ \_\ |\ \_\ \cup\ \cup\ |\ \_\ \cup|\ \_\ \_$$

If mine eyes can speak to do hearty errand

Rhyme

A masculine ending is a single stressed syllable at the end of a line. If the line rhymes, it is called a masculine rhyme ('rye' / 'die'). A feminine ending is an unstressed syllable at the end of a line. This is to be expected in trochaic verse, but is an effective variation in iambic verse, where the syllable will be extra-metrical. A feminine rhyme is where both the sounds after the stressed rhyme syllable are identical ('riot' / 'diet'). A triple rhyme (sometimes called a double feminine rhyme) is where two unstressed syllables follow the final stressed syllable, and all three syllables are a part of the rhyme ('rioting' / 'dieting').

Where the rhyme doesn't quite work, it is a half rhyme. If the rhyming syllables have similar spelling but differ in pronunciation, it is an eye rhyme (e.g. 'plough' / 'rough'). It is important to realize that with older texts half rhymes may have worked in the pronunciation of the time.

The form of the opening stanza is repeated in successive stanzas. A rhyme scheme or 'stanza form' is described by allocating successive letters of the alphabet to successive rhymes: e.g. the simple quatrain *abab* (a pattern known as cross rhyme) or *abba* (known as counter rhyme or envelope rhyme).

Examples of Forms

1. Sidney, *Astrophil and Stella*, sonnet 47: iambic pentameter, *abbaabba cdcdee* (Italian octave plus English sestet).

> What, have I thus betrayed my liberty?
>   Can those black beams such burning marks engrave
>   In my free side? or am I born a slave,
> Whose neck becomes such yoke of tyranny?
> Or want I sense to feel my misery?
>   Or spirit, disdain of such disdain to have,
>   Who for long faith, though daily help I crave,
> May get no alms, but scorn of beggary?

> Virtue, awake: beauty but beauty is;
> I may, I must, I can, I will, I do
> Leave following that, which it is gain to miss.
> Let her go. Soft, but here she comes. Go to,
> Unkind, I love you not—: O me, that eye
> Doth make my heart give to my tongue the lie.

2. Sidney, *Astrophil and Stella*, song 8: trochaic tetrameter *aabb*, alternating masculine and feminine rhymes.

> In a grove most rich of shade,
> Where birds wanton music made,
> May, then young, his pied weeds showing,
> New perfumed with flowers fresh growing . . .

3. Sidney's translation of Psalm 23: iambic *abbacc*, lines 1 and 4 tetrameter, 2 and 5 trimeter, 3 and 6 dimeter.

> The Lord, the Lord my shepherd is,
> And so can never I
>   Taste misery.
> He rests me in green pasture his;
> By waters still and sweet
>   He guides my feet.

4. Shakespeare, *The Rape of Lucrece*. Rhyme royal: iambic pentameter, *ababbcc*.

> At last she calls to mind where hangs a piece
> Of skilful painting made for Priam's Troy,
> Before the which is drawn the power of Greece,
> For Helen's rape the city to destroy,
> Threat'ning cloud-kissing Ilion with annoy;
> Which the conceited painter drew so proud
> As heav'n, it seemed, to kiss the turrets bowed.

Notes

SIR PHILIP SIDNEY: THE DEFENCE OF POESY

Text: *The defence of poesie. By Sir Phillip Sidney, knight.* (1595)

On Sidney (1554–1586), see the Introduction, pp. lii–lxii. Written between 1579 and 1585, and most probably in 1580–1, the *Defence* was not printed until after Sidney's death, and after both the *Arcadia* and *Astrophil and Stella* had already been printed. It was entered in the Stationers' Register to William Ponsonby, the authorized printer of his works, in November 1594, but not printed immediately. In April 1595 it was entered under the title *An Apology for Poetry* to the bookseller Henry Olney, and this edition was first into print. When it was realized that Olney had infringed Ponsonby's right, Olney's edition was withdrawn, remaining copies being reissued with the title page of Ponsonby's edition, which had appeared at some subsequent point in 1595. Two manuscript copies also exist, so a total of four different texts survive, each deriving, indirectly, from a putative lost original. These are: a contemporary manuscript copy at the Sidneys' home, Penshurst Place; a markedly inferior manuscript at the Norfolk County Record Office in Norwich; and the two printed editions, *The Defence of Poesy* (published by Ponsonby) and *An Apology for Poetry* (published by Olney), both printed in 1595. The modernized Clarendon edition of the *Defence* in *Miscellaneous Prose of Sir Philip Sidney*, ed. Katherine Duncan-Jones and Jan van Dorsten (Oxford, 1973) is based on two texts: the Penshurst manuscript, which was owned by Sidney's brother Robert, and Ponsonby's *The Defence of Poesy*. Some other editors (e.g. Shepherd) have preferred to base their texts on Olney's *Apology*, since it is well punctuated and carefully produced. Van Dorsten, however, shows that the Penshurst manuscript and Ponsonby's printed edition are textually superior, even though the latter takes less care than Olney's edition over layout and 'accidentals' (spelling and punctuation). Nevertheless, the differences between the Penshurst manuscript and the two printed texts are relatively minor: all three represent Sidney's text admirably. I have therefore based my edition on Ponsonby's text, with frequent comparison to Olney's, and have made full use of the textual apparatus in the Clarendon edition in incorporating what seem authoritative readings and forms from the other texts, especially the Penshurst manuscript; these have then been checked against the originals, and the whole text has been checked against the Penshurst manuscript. The result is not therefore a simple reproduction of any one text, as all the other texts in this anthology are, but it is an appropriate compromise. I have been far less free than van Dorsten in introducing readings from the Penshurst manuscript which are not supported by the other texts. One notable exception is the entertaining crux where three texts report 'a man that once told *me* the wind was at northwest and by south' but Penshurst reads 'a man that once told *my father*', which I have preferred. If a reading in Ponsonby is not inferior and has the support of at least one other text, I have tended to prefer it over Penshurst; and I have in a few places preferred Ponsonby against all the other texts where its reading makes better sense. In general, I find Ponsonby to be a better text than van Dorsten describes; what is more, from it derive all reprintings of the *Defence* before the era of modern editions, so it has a historical claim to priority. The reader is referred to the apparatus of the Clarendon edition for the evidence used in arriving at this text.

The careful structure of the *Defence* follows the guidelines of the rhetoric books. A plan follows, with the names given to each section supplied from Thomas Wilson, *The Art of Rhetoric* (1553):

The entrance or beginning [exordium]
  Sidney, Pugliano, and the praise of horsemanship
The narration
  poetry is ancient and universal; argument from etymology (*vates*, poet/maker); second nature, *idea*
The proposition
  definition: 'Poesy ... is an art of imitation ... with this end: to teach and delight.'
The division or several parting of things
  genera ('general kinds'): divine poetry, philosophical poetry, 'right' poetry
  species ('sundry more special denominations'): heroic, lyric, tragic, comic, satiric, iambic, elegiac, pastoral
  poesy = feigning images, not versifying

The confirmation
  'works', in relation to *architektonikē*: philosophy and history;
  more exemplary than philosophy; more universal than history;
  superior to philosophy in 'moving'; sweet medicine
  'parts' (species), in reverse order
  summary of arguments
The confutation
  'poet-haters' and the scorn of verse
  four charges: a waste of time; 'the mother of lies'; 'the nurse of
  abuse'; 'Plato banished them'
[Digression]
  state of poetry in England; art, imitation and exercise; matter
  and manner
  matter: notable achievements; tragedy, comedy, the unities,
  decorum, laughter or delight; lyric
  manner: *elocutio*; versification
The conclusion [peroration]

1. *When the right virtuous ... esquire in his stable*: The young
    Sidney undertook a European tour between 1572 and 1575. In
    Vienna between autumn 1574 and spring 1575, at the court of
    the Holy Roman Emperor Maximilian II, he befriended Edward
    Wotton (1548–1626), secretary to the English embassy there.
    Sidney would already have been an accomplished horseman but
    Vienna, then as now, was a centre of more advanced eques-
    trianism than was yet common in England: the celebrated Spanish
    Riding School, initially an adjunct of the imperial court and the
    probable scene of Sidney's encounter with Pugliano, was founded
    in 1572, and Pugliano, as Sidney indicates, would have been held
    in high esteem there (his office was one of considerable status).

2. *if I had not been a piece of a logician ... wished myself a horse*:
    Sidney was interested in contemporary developments in the theory
    of logic (including the work of the influential French logician
    Ramus) and had a reputation as a skilled disputant. Rather as
    Pugliano's oration in praise of the horseman and the horse is
    pricked by Sidney's logic, Sidney's own treatise in defence of the
    poet and poetry was subjected, at Sidney's request, to a punishing
    logical analysis by William Temple, Sidney's secretary in his last
    years; Temple points to a number of flaws in Sidney's arguments.
    The irony of this passage is enhanced by a habitual, though
    here submerged, play on words: Philip (*phil-hippos*) means
    'horselover'.

3. *since the former . . . the silly latter*: The 'former' is horsemanship, the 'silly [meaning 'poor'] latter' poetry. To make sense of the syntax here the reader must imagine '*but* the latter'.

4. *the first light-giver to ignorance, and first nurse . . . tougher knowledges*: Sidney's argument absorbs various classical commonplaces, including passages from Cicero and Horace. An especially important source is the extensive discussion in Strabo, *Geography*, 1.2.3–9 (*c* .17 AD), beginning: 'Every poet, according to Eratosthenes, aims at entertainment, not instruction. The ancients held a different view. They regarded poetry as a sort of primary philosophy, which was supposed to introduce us to life from our childhood, and teach us about character, emotion, and action in a pleasurable way.' Sidney is probably familiar with a passage in Sir Thomas Elyot, *The Book Named The Governor* (1530): 'For the name of a poet, whereat now, specially in this realm, men have such indignation that they use only poets and poetry in the contempt of eloquence, was in ancient time in high estimation, insomuch that all wisdom was supposed to be therein included and poetry was the first philosophy that ever was known, whereby men from their childhood were brought to the reason how to live well, learning thereby not only manners and natural affections but also the wonderful works of nature, mixing serious things with things that were pleasant . . .' *Literary Criticism: Plato to Dryden*, ed. Allan H. Gilbert (Detroit, 1962), 237. Hereafter, Gilbert. See also *English Renaissance Literary Criticism*, ed. Brian Vickers (Oxford, 1999), 64. Hereafter, *ERLC*.

5. *And will they now . . . kill their parents*: A fable of the snake and the hedgehog appears in various Renaissance collections of Aesopian fables, such as Johannes Camerarius, *Fabellae Aesopicae* (1564); for the vipers, see Pliny, *Natural History*, 10.82.2.

6. *Musaeus . . . Hesiod*: Musaeus: the author of *Hero and Leander*, *c.* 500 BC, the basis of Marlowe's poem and later translated by George Chapman, was merged with a mythical poet said to have been the pupil of Orpheus. Homer: the name associated with the greatest Greek epics, the *Iliad* and the *Odyssey*; perhaps a poet of the eighth century BC. Hesiod (eighth century BC): attributed to him were the *Theogony* and the *Works and Days*.

7. *Orpheus, Linus*: Mythical poet-musicians believed in the Renaissance to have been historical figures. Orpheus was a poet, priest and prophet said to be the son of Apollo and the Muse Calliope. Various writings were attributed to him in antiquity; those Orphic

hymns which survive are now thought to belong to the fifth century BC. Linus was the son of Apollo and the Muse Terpsichore, and the instructor of Orpheus and Hercules.

8.   *So, as Amphion was said to move stones . . . listened to by beasts*: Given the interpretation Sidney gives, his immediate source for these frequently cited examples of the power of music and poetry may be Horace, *Ars poetica*, 391–407: 'While men still roamed the woods, Orpheus, the holy prophet of the gods, made them shrink from bloodshed and brutal living; hence the fable that he tamed tigers and ravening lions; hence too the fable that Amphion, builder of Thebes' citadel, moved stones by the sound of his lyre . . .'

9.   *Livius Andronicus and Ennius*: A Greek captured in war, Livius Andronicus (c. 284–204 BC) became the first Latin poet and playwright. Ennius (239–169 BC) was the most important early Latin poet, author of the *Annales* ('Annals'), an epic on Roman history.

10.   *Dante, Boccaccio and Petrarch . . . Gower and Chaucer*: Dante Alighieri (1265–1321), Giovanni Boccaccio (1313–75), Francesco Petrarca (1304–74), John Gower (?1330–1408), Geoffrey Chaucer (c. 1343–1400): in each case the reader is expected to register that these are founding fathers of their respective national literatures and literary languages, and writers of broad philosophical and philological scope.

11.   *Thales, Empedocles and Parmenides . . . and Solon in matters of policy*: Early Greek thinkers. In all cases only fragments, if anything, survive, but a substantial body of writings was associated with them in the Renaissance, gathered by Sidney's friend the French scholar-printer Henri Estienne as *Poesis philosophus* ('Philosophical Poetry', 1573). The range of their writings, or reputations, is wide: Thales (fl. 585 BC), as an astronomer, geographer, mathematician and political scientist; Empedocles (fl. 450 BC) as a natural scientist and philosopher; Parmenides (fl. 475 BC) as a philosopher; Pythagoras (fl. 530 BC) as a philosopher and mathematician; Phocylides (fl. 560 BC) as a moralist; Tyrtaeus (fl. 670 BC), as a poet and general (or, according to tradition, a lame schoolmaster) whose poems were used as marching songs by the Spartans; Solon, as an Athenian legislator and democratic reformer (fl. 600 BC) who wrote poetry and to whom the story of Atlantis is attributed by Plato (*Timaeus*, 20d ff.).

12.   *even Plato . . . as Gyges' ring and others*: It was a common

observation that Plato, who banished poetry from his ideal republic, was the most poetic of prose philosophers. Cf. Quintilian,
Institutio oratoria, 10.1.81 and 5.11.39. Almost all of his works
are dialogues featuring his teacher Socrates; the *Symposium* is set
at a banquet, the *Phaedrus* during a walk in the country, and the
Republic (2.359–60) tells the story of Gyges, who found a ring
which made him invisible and used it to gain power.

13. *flowers of poetry . . . Apollo's garden*: Apollo is the god of poetry;
    the metaphor of poetical or rhetorical ornaments as flowers was
    common, giving us, for example, 'anthology', from the Greek for
    'gathering of flowers'.

14. *So Herodotus entitled his History . . . nine muses*: The *History* of
    Herodotus (*c*. 484–*c*. 420 BC) was divided into nine books, each
    named after one of the Muses, by later Alexandrian scholars.

15. *where learning flourisheth not . . . some feeling of poetry*: This
    topos may be traced back to Cicero's speech on behalf of Archias
    the poet, *Pro Archia poeta*, 8.19: 'even barbarians do not dis-
    honour the name of poet'; cf. Puttenham, pp. 64–5 and Daniel,
    p. 211.

16. *their law-giving divines . . . but poets*: The 'law-giving divines'
    are the mufti. Turkey fascinated Sidney's contemporaries, both
    as a military threat (the Ottoman Empire extended to Cyprus and
    into Hungary), and as a comparison point for Christian culture
    and history (as in the plays *Mustapha* and *Alaham*, both pub-
    lished posthumously in 1633, of Sidney's best friend Fulke
    Greville).

17. *the most barbarous and simple Indians . . . praises of their gods*:
    This anecdote is drawn from Peter Martyr's *Decades* (1516),
    translated by Richard Eden in *History of the West Indies* (1555).
    Sidney's version brings the American Indians into line with Plato's
    ideal republic, where 'the only poetry which will be admitted
    into our city are hymns to the gods and encomia to good men'
    (*Republic*, 607a).

18. *In Turkey . . . long continuing*: Sidney's interest in the countries
    discussed in this paragraph was genuine. His father had governed
    both Ireland and Wales; he invested in new world exploration
    and attempted to join Drake's expedition in 1585. Among works
    dedicated to him were John Derrick's *The Image of Ireland*
    (1581), Richard Hakluyt's *Diverse Voyages Touching the Dis-
    covery of America* (1582), Humphrey Lloyd's *The History of
    Cambria, Now Called Wales* (1584), Geoffrey of Monmouth's
    Britannicae Historiae (1585), and Nicolas de Nicolay's *The*

NOTES TO PP. 6–8

Navigations, Peregrinations and Voyages Made into Turkey (trans. Washington, 1585).

19. *a poet was called vates . . . is manifest*: Vates was the oldest Latin name for a poet but fell into disuse (*poeta*, derived from the Greek *poiëtës*, being preferred) until revived by Virgil (*Eclogues*, 7.27; 9.34) and Horace (*Odes*, e.g. 1.1.35; 2.20.3). *Vaticinium* means 'a prophesy', *vaticinari* 'to foretell' or 'to sing'. Cf. Puttenham, p. 61 and Harington, p. 262.

20. *Whereupon grew the word . . . and in his age performed it*: Sortes Virgilianae means 'Virgilian lots'; the practice is referred to in Lampridius' *Life of Alexander Severus*, 14.5 and Spartianus' *Life of Hadrian*, 2.8. Julius Capitolinus (*Life of Clodius Albinus*, 5.2), reports that as a child Clodius was obsessed with the quoted line from Virgil, *Aeneid*, 2.314. Advancing himself through his military prowess, Clodius was made Governor of Britain, and was proclaimed Emperor by his troops in 193 AD; he committed suicide after defeat by his rival Severus in 197 AD.

21. *oracles of Delphos and Sibylla . . . in verses*: The oracles of the Pythian priestess at Delphos, sacred to Apollo, were set down in hexameters. Oracles of the sibyl (or sibyls) were given in verse form. A collection was reputedly acquired by an early Roman king and continued to be consulted by the Roman senate at times of doubt. After their destruction in 83 BC subsequent collections were made or forged; fourteen books survive.

22. *even the name of 'Psalms' . . . the rules be not yet fully found*: 'Psalm' comes from the Greek *psalmos*, 'song accompanied on the harp'. The prosody of the apparently poetic sections of the Old Testament has been vigorously debated since early Christian times. St Jerome and the first-century AD Jewish historian Josephus both claimed to find classical metrics and verse forms in the Psalms, and similar claims were made until the twentieth century. The consensus now is that there is a system of patterning by clause length and word stress, but 'the rules be not yet fully found'.

23. *For what else . . . notable prosopopoeias*: The rhetorical figure *prosopopoeia* involves the personification of inanimate things and the giving of a voice to the absent or dead.

24. *the Greeks . . . a 'poet'*: See note 19 and cf. Puttenham, p. 57.

25. *in calling him a 'maker'*: The first recorded usage in the OED is from 1387–8.

26. *So doth the musician in times . . . which not*: A 'time' was in Renaissance prosody and music a unit of metrical measurement.

Renaissance music still lacked regular bar lines and time signatures, and mensural questions were pressing and complex. But
what Sidney is saying here is not clear, unless that certain rhythmic
patterns, especially in polyphonic music, are naturally right, and
others not.

27. *There is no art delivered to mankind ... her world is brazen, the
poets only deliver a golden*: Throughout this paragraph Sidney
follows Julius Caesar Scaliger, *Poetices libri septem* (1561), an
exhaustive and at times brilliant examination of literary theory.
Opening with the key Aristotelian idea that all arts and sciences
are bound by nature, Sidney introduces a Neoplatonic twist current in other areas of Renaissance theory of art and stated clearly
by Scaliger: that the artist is an imitator not of nature but of the
creative workings of nature, creating a 'second nature' (Sidney's
'another nature'). Cf. Puttenham, pp. 57–8, who makes the parallel between the divine and artistic maker more explicit than
Sidney wishes to ('poets ... be ... as creating gods'). See Ovid,
Metamorphoses, 1.89–150, for the four ages, of gold, silver,
brass, and (the current age) iron. The golden age is a once and
future perfect world, the brass world of nature far from perfect
and able to be exceeded by the imaginings of the poet.

28. *for whom ... employed*: With emphasis on '*for* whom' and '*in*
him' the point is that, as nature creates rivers, trees, and flowers
for man, so it is *in* his creation that 'her uttermost cunning is
employed'.

29. *as Theagenes ... as Virgil's Aeneas*: Theagenes, the lover of
Charikleia, is the hero of the fourth-century AD Greek prose
romance, Heliodorus' *Aethiopica*. Pylades was the faithful friend
of Orestes in Greek myth: see, e.g., Aeschylus' *Oresteia*. Orlando
was Roland in the medieval chivalric romances and became
Orlando in a series of fifteenth- and sixteenth-century Italian
verse romances, culminating in Ariosto's *Orlando furioso* (1532)
as translated by Harington. Xenophon wrote a fictional account
of the education of the sixth-century BC Persian King Cyrus,
admired founder of the Persian Empire, in the *Cyropaedia*. Aeneas
is the hero of Virgil's epic the *Aeneid*. The influence of Heliodorus,
Ariosto, Xenophon and Virgil is equally strong in Sidney's
romance the *Arcadia*.

30. *the works of the one ... not in the work itself*: Nature ('the one')
and the poet ('the other') are aligned, both skilful artificers able
to generate *ideas*, even though nature's ideas actually come into
existence ('essential') whereas the poet's can only be represented

on the page ('in imitation or fiction'). The *idea* (from the Greek *idein*, 'to see') is a Platonic concept, the immutable form of a thing which exists in a realm beyond the world of appearances, accessible only to the gods, glimpsed by the soul between incarnations on earth, and able to be remembered in visions by lovers and philosophers. According to this theory, every chair in the world is an imitation of the one eternal *idea* of the chair, and, Plato argued, any artist, copying what he finds in nature, is involved in making imitations of such imitations, at two removes from the *idea*. Sidney absorbs and reformulates a scattered Neoplatonic response to this doctrine. Cicero (*Orator*, 2.9–10) is expanded by Plotinus (*Enneads*, 5.8.1), ending: 'Pheidias wrought [his famous sculpture] the Zeus upon no model among things of sense but by apprehending what form Zeus must take if he chose to become manifest to sight.' This response is developed by Seneca (*Epistulae morales*, 65.7): 'it is [the idea] that the artist gazed upon when he created the work which he had decided to carry out. Now it makes no difference whether he has his pattern outside himself, that he may direct his glance to it, or within himself, conceived and placed there by himself.' Geoffrey Shepherd quotes an illuminating analogue from the Mannerist art theorist Federico Zuccaro, who probably met Sidney in England in 1575, in his edition of *An Apology for Poetry* (Manchester, 1973, 65–6), but concludes that 'Sidney's thinking about poetry could coincide with rather than derive directly from Mannerist theories about painting' (158). Sidney's 'idea or fore-conceit' comes close to Aristotle's *muthos*, or plot, 'the first principle and, as it were, soul of tragedy' (*Poetics*, 1450a; cf. 1461b for the relation of ideal to reality in the painted image).

31. *if they will learn . . . that maker made him*: Sidney's emphasis on the active responsibility of the reader, as opposed to any passive receptivity, is an important qualification. Cf. Plutarch, 'How the Young Man Ought to Study Poetry', for the responsibilities of teacher and pupil in interpretation: '[poetry] contains much that is pleasant and profitable to the young mind, but just as much that is confusing and misleading, if study is not properly directed' (*Moralia*, 15c; cf. 27e, 28c–d).

32. *made man to His own likeness . . . second nature*: Man is made in God's image; as God presides over nature, man presides over an image of nature, the second nature which he has power to shape at will.

33. *with no small arguments . . . reaching unto it*: Those incredulous

of Sidney's claim that the artist can create a second, golden nature are offered, but not supplied with, arguments about the postlapsarian relation between the soul or intellect, and its heavenly aspirations, and the will and its inherent sinfulness. Cf. his earlier description of the Psalmist as 'a passionate lover of that unspeakable and everlasting beauty, to be seen by the eyes of the mind, only cleared by faith' (p. 7).

34. *these arguments*: All the points relating to the poet as 'maker', the argument from etymology concluded here.

35. *Poesy, therefore ... to teach and delight*: Sidney's central definition follows Scaliger, *Poetices*, 1.1: 'What is called poesy describes not only what exists, but also non-existent things as if they existed, showing how they could or should exist. For the whole matter is comprehended in imitation. But imitation is only the means to the ultimate end, which is to teach with delight ... Poetry and the other arts represent things as they are, as a picture to the ear.' And parts of the definition are shared with sixteenth-century Italian critics such as Trissino, Castelvetro, Mazzoni and Tasso. But Sidney manages a much more elegant and condensed formulation. For Aristotle's *mimēsis*, well defined by Sidney, see *Poetics*, 1447a–1448b. For teaching and delighting see Horace, *Ars poetica*, 333–44 (see Jonson's translation, p. 307). The dictum that 'poetry is speaking painting and painting silent poetry' is attributed to the poet Simonides (*c.* 556–*c.* 468 BC) by Plutarch (*Moralia*, 346f; cf. 'How the Young Man Ought to Study Poetry', *Moralia*, 18a), and is frequently repeated; comparisons of poets to painters are ubiquitous in classical and Renaissance philosophy and literary criticism (see the famous passage of Horace, *Ars poetica*, 361–5, as translated by Jonson, p. 307), and inform the rhetorical figure of *enargeia* (see Quintilian, *Institutio oratoria*, 6.2.32). The words 'imitate' and 'imitation' refer not, with Plato, to a mere lifeless copying of something which is better in real life but rather, with Aristotle, to a realization ('figuring forth') of an idea.

36. *Emanuel Tremellius and Franciscus Junius ... the Scripture*: Tremellius (1510–80) and Junius (1545–1602) in their new Latin translation of the Bible from the Hebrew and Greek, *Biblia sacra* (1575), vol. 2, p. 4.

37. *Homer in his Hymns*: The mythic poems known as the Homeric hymns were ascribed to Homer but were actually composed by various poets from the late eighth century BC onwards.

38. *St James' counsel*: James 5:13. Psalm singing was something of a

Protestant craze in the sixteenth century, both in private devotions and, especially, in congregational worship.

39. *as Tyrtaeus ... as Lucan*: For Tyrtaeus and Phocylides see note 11. The *Distichs* of the third-century Dionysius Cato was a popular school text, from which schoolboys learnt Latin syntax as well as proverbial morality; see Drayton (p. 291, l. 20). Lucretius (95–52 BC) was the author of the philosophic poem in six books *De rerum natura* ('On the Nature of Things'). Virgil's *Georgics* are a fund of farming lore; see Harington, p. 270. Manilius is the first-century AD author of *Astronomica*, a poem in five books on astronomy and astrology. Pontanus (Giovanni Pontano) was the author of the late fifteenth-century neo-Latin astronomical poem *Urania*. The *Bellum civile* or *Pharsalia* of Lucan (39–65 AD) is an unfinished epic poem on the civil wars between Pompey and Caesar; for Daniel's admiration see p. 231.

40. *this question*: the subject of the *Defence*, and specifically the definition of poetry.

41. *lamenting look of Lucretia ... beauty of such a virtue*: The suicide of Lucretia after her rape by Tarquin was a popular theme with Renaissance artists and poets; see, most famously, Shakespeare's *The Rape of Lucrece* (1594). Sidney's formulation depends on the Platonic teaching that there is a fundamental connection between inward nature and outward appearance. He borrows from the responses to Plato's criticism of art cited in note 30.

42. *what may be and should be*: What 'should be' is primarily meant in the sense of 'according to rules "learned discretion"') of necessity and verisimilitude'. See Aristotle, *Poetics*, 1460a: 'One ought to prefer likely impossibilities to unconvincing possibilities'. The secondary sense, to our ears the primary sense, is 'what ought to be', in an ideal world.

43. *For these indeed do ... whereunto they are moved*: Sidney employs the rhetorical figure *gradatio* here. See Puttenham, p. 172 on 'Climax, *or the marching figure*'.

44. *heroic ... pastoral*: The list of kinds or genres is traditional, though that tradition, going back to Horace's *Ars poetica* and Quintilian's *Institutio oratoria* (10.1), is highly confused. Sidney retains the vestiges of Horace's taxonomy by verse form in his inclusion of 'iambic'. The only respect in which Sidney differs markedly from similar Renaissance lists is in his promotion of lyric above the two dramatic kinds; this is perhaps not surprising from a heroic and lyric poet.

45. *For indeed ... name of poets*: An important stage of Sidney's argument. Most previous critics distinguished between good poets and bad poets (or mere versers), but kept verse as a prerequisite of poetry. Cf. Elyot, *The Book Named the Governor*: 'They that make verses, expressing thereby none other learning but the craft of versifying, be not of ancient writers named poets, but only called versifiers' (Gilbert, 237; *ERLC*, 64). Sidney's most important precursor is Aristotle (*Poetics*, 1447b): 'people think, no doubt, that "makers" is applied to poets not because they make *mimēseis* but as a general term meaning "verse-makers", since they call "poets" or "makers" even those who publish a medical or scientific theory in verse. But as Homer and Empedocles have nothing in common except their metre, the latter had better be called a scientific writer, not a poet, if we are to use "poet" of the former.' See also *Poetics*, 1451b: 'the poet should be considered a maker of plots, not of verses, since he is a poet *qua* maker of *mimēsis* and the objects of his *mimēsis* are actions'.

46. *For Xenophon ... Theagenes and Charikleia*: For Xenophon and Heliodorus see note 29. Sidney refers to Cicero's *Epistola ad Quintum* ('Letter to Quintus'), 1.1.8. Cf. Spenser on Xenophon in his 'Letter to Ralegh' in the 1590 edition of *The Faerie Queene*: 'so much more profitable and gracious is doctrine by example than by rule' (*The Faerie Queene*, ed. Thoms P. Roche [London, 1978], 16).

47. *but it is that feigning ... virtues, vices or what else*: Sidney uses 'feigning' and its cognates in a precise sense related to its etymology, from the Latin *fingere*, 'to shape, form, make'; also derived from *fingere* is the word 'fiction', which most closely approaches what Sidney means by 'poesy'. In Aristotelian terms 'images of virtues' might be representations of particular virtuous actions, or might be representations of virtuous characters (Aristotle's *mimēsis* of *ēthos*, *Poetics*, 1450a), and 'images of ... vices' the contrary. It is tempting to equate 'images of virtue' with the 'speaking picture', and both with particular characters like Aeneas or Cyrus. But Sidney's terminology is not consistent.

48. *peising each syllable ... dignity of the subject*: Different subjects belong to different kinds, and each kind has a particular 'proportion' or verse form associated with it.

49. *clayey lodgings*: Genesis 2:7: 'And the Lord God formed man of the dust of the ground'; 'clay' was a frequent term for flesh and the human body.

NOTES TO PP. 13–14

50. *the astronomer . . . fall in a ditch*: Plato, *Theaetetus*, 174a, on the philosopher Thales.

51. *But when . . . crooked heart*: Cf. Seneca, *Epistulae morales*, 88, for this whole passage, and specifically 88.13: 'You know what a straight line is; but how does it benefit you if you do not know what is straight in this life of ours?' Sidney's omission of the musician from the list of shortcomings may be significant (he could have continued to follow Seneca, 88.9: 'rather bring my soul into harmony with itself, and let not my purposes be out of tune'), or may just be an oversight.

52. *by the Greeks called architektonikē . . . not of well-knowing only*: Sidney follows Aristotle, *Ethics*, 1.1–2 closely here. *Architektonikē* is the master-art or -science, equated by Aristotle with the political science, that is, the art of living in society. Cf. Greville's *A Dedication to Sir Philip Sidney*, known as the *Life of Sidney*, after a description of Sidney's *Arcadia* which follows the terms of the *Defence*: 'But the truth is, his end was not writing even while he wrote, nor his knowledge moulded for tables or schools, but both his wit and understanding bent upon his heart to make himself and others, not in words or opinion, but in life and action, good and great; in which architectonical art he was such a master . . .' (*The Prose Works of Fulke Greville, Lord Brooke*, ed. John Gouws [Oxford, 1986], 12).

53. *Among whom . . . moral philosophers*: Sidney's animation of opposing arguments employs the courtroom rhetorical figure of *prosopopoeia* to devastating effect (see note 23).

54. *with books . . . whereto they set their names*: From Cicero, *Pro Archia poeta*, 11.26: 'These same philosophers set their own names even upon the books in which they condemn the pursuit of glory.'

55. *definitions, divisions and distinctions*: Terms inherited from medieval scholasticism describing the stages of rhetorical and logical argument.

56. *by showing . . . derived from it*: i.e. an examination of genus and species.

57. *testis temporum . . . nuntia vetustatis*: Cicero, *De oratore*, 2.9.36.

58. *Marathon, Pharsalia, Poitiers and Agincourt*: The Athenians repulsed the Persians at Marathon (490 BC); Julius Caesar defeated Pompey at Pharsalia (48 BC); Edward the Black Prince led a small English army to victory at Poitiers and captured the French King (1356); Henry V defeated the French at Agincourt (1415).

59. *Brutus, Alphonsus of Aragon . . . if need be*: Both examples could be found in Thomas North's 1579 translation of Plutarch's *Lives*, itself a translation from the French edition of Jacques Amyot. According to Plutarch, Brutus (85–42 BC), the tyrannicide, studied and imitated his ancestors' deeds and was engaged in an epitome of the historian Polybius before the battle of Pharsalia; Alfonso V of Aragon and I of Naples and Sicily (1385–1458) cured himself of illness by reading about Alexander the Great, according to Amyot. Sidney's joke ('and who not, if need be?') is that historians make up stories about the exemplary power of history.

60. *Now whom . . . in the school of learning*: In logic and rhetoric the *quaestio* is the subject of debate, the central issue in an academic disputation; Sidney's metaphor here sets this *quaestio* for the top class 'in the school of learning', as a sort of finals exam.

61. *formidine poenae . . . virtutis amore*: From Horace, *Epistles*, 1.16.52–3.

62. *For the philosopher . . . what he doth understand*: Sidney borrows from Renaissance arguments for the pre-eminence of history (e.g. Amyot's preface to his Plutarch), which stress the superiority of example to precept.

63. *A perfect picture . . . as that other doth*: That things seen are perceived more acutely and readily than things heard was a commonplace of philosophy, rhetoric, and literary criticism: see e.g. Plato, *Phaedrus*, 250d; Horace, *Ars poetica*, 180–2; and Cicero, *De oratore*, 3.40.160–61, on creating verbal pictures.

64. *For as in outward things . . . imaginative and judging power*: Here and elsewhere Sidney adopts the standard Renaissance tripartite division of mind (or 'wit') into imagination (or 'conceit'), judgement, and memory. Not only were these categories associated respectively with three of the five separate parts of rhetoric – *inventio, dispositio, [elocutio], memoria* [and *actio*] – but they could also be aligned, as by Bacon in *The Advancement of Learning*, with the three liberal sciences Sidney investigates – judgement with philosophy, memory with history, and imagination with poetry. Cf. Bacon, p. 289 and note 1.

65. *Tully taketh much pains . . . hath in us*: As for example *De oratore*, 1.44.196, quoting Homer's Odysseus. Tully is Marcus Tullius Cicero (as Publius Vergilius Maro was Virgil).

66. *Let us but hear old Anchises . . . barren and beggarly Ithaca*: Virgil, *Aeneid*, 2.634–50; Homer, *Odyssey*, 5.149ff. and 215, perhaps influenced by Cicero's use (see note above).

67. *Anger, the Stoics said ... Agamemnon and Menelaus*: Horace, *Epistles*, 1.2.62: *ira furor brevis est*; cf. Seneca, *De ira* ('On Anger'), 1.1. What Sidney describes is not shown but reported in Sophocles' *Ajax*, but since Sidney's larger point is that poetry (rather than only drama, as in Horace, *Ars poetica*, 180–82) gives the mind the impression of seeing something, perhaps this hardly matters.

68. *Ulysses and Diomedes ... Nisus and Euryalus*: Characters in Homer's *Iliad* and (Nisus and Euryalus) in its Virgilian sequel the *Aeneid*.

69. *conscience in Oedipus ... revenge in Medea*: All characters in Greek tragedies, but Sidney may be thinking of their Roman counterparts – Seneca's *Oedipus*, *Agamemnon*, *Thyestes*, *Thebais*, and *Medea*.

70. *Terentian Gnatho and our Chaucer's Pandar ... signify their trades*: A 'Gnatho' (sycophant) and a 'pander' were both sixteenth-century coinages, after characters in the second-century BC dramatist Terence's *Eunuchus* and Chaucer's *Troilus and Criseyde* (written *c*. 1385).

71. *feigned Cyrus in Xenophon ... Sir Thomas More's Utopia*: For Cyrus and Aeneas see note 29. More's *Utopia* was printed in Latin in 1516 and in Ralph Robinson's English translation in 1551.

72. *that way*: i.e. the fictional mode (a traveller's account), as opposed to the philosophical discussion of Plato's *Republic*.

73. *mediocribus ... columnae*: Horace, *Ars poetica*, 372–3.

74. *Dives and Lazarus ... the lost child and the gracious father*: For Dives and Lazarus see Luke 16:19–31; for the Prodigal Son see Luke 15:11–32.

75. *Aesop's tales*: The earliest surviving collection of fables ascribed to the sixth-century BC Aesop is a metrical version by Babrius, *c*. 100 AD.

76. *Truly, Aristotle himself... Alcibiades did or suffered this or that*: Aristotle, *Poetics*, 1451b: 'The difference is that the one tells of what has happened, the other of the kinds of things that might happen. For this reason poetry is something more philosophical [*philosophōteron*] and more worthy of serious attention [*spoudaioteron*] than history; for poetry speaks more of universals [*katholou*], history of particulars [*kath' hekaston*]. By "universals" I mean the kinds of things a certain type of person will probably or necessarily say or do in a given situation; and this is the aim of poetry, although it gives individual names to characters.

"Particulars" are what, say, Alcibiades did, or what happened to him.' Sidney, for once perhaps, has the book open in front of him as he writes.

77. *For indeed if the question . . . nothing resembling*: This point goes further than Sidney takes it. The admirably straightforward and efficient first-century AD Emperor Vespasian was reputedly somewhat ugly; whilst a historian might seek a faithful portrait, a poet, following Sidney, might want to represent 'the outward beauty of such a virtue' (p. 11) or at least, following Aristotle (*Poetics*, 1454b), to 'emulate good portrait painters, who render personal appearance and produce likenesses, yet enhance people's beauty'.

78. *But if the question . . . was full ill-favoured*: Cyrus: Justinus (third century AD) abridged the now lost work of the Augustan historian Pompeius Trogus; an English translation by Arthur Golding was published in 1564; its account of Cyrus is no more historical than Xenophon's but lacks the fictive purpose of the *Cyropaedia*. Aeneas: Dares the Phrygian, mentioned in the *Iliad*, 5.9, was the reputed author of an eyewitness account of the Trojan war, transmitted in a Latin narrative ascribed to Cornelius Nepos (first century BC); its authenticity, accepted by medieval writers, was doubted by most sixteenth-century scholars. Canidia: see Horace, *Satires*, 1.8, for the witch Canidia's dishevelled appearance, further developed in *Epodes*, 5, where she tries to use spells to make Varus fall for her.

79. *Tantalus, Atreus*: Tantalus: more famous for his punishment in the underworld (tantalized by fruit above his head and water beneath, which he could never reach) than the various crimes attributed to him. Atreus: a descendant of Tantalus, Atreus quarrelled incessantly with his brother Thyestes, killing the latter's three sons and serving them up to him in a dish.

80. *Alexander or Scipio himself . . . without reading Quintus Curtius*: Scipio: Scipio Africanus (236–183 BC) was perhaps the greatest Roman general. Quintus Curtius was a first-century AD historian of Alexander the Great.

81. *universal consideration*: the phrase from the discussion of Aristotle in the preceding paragraph.

82. *Herodotus and Justin . . . deliver them over to Darius*: The story of the Persian King Darius is told in Herodotus (*History*, 3.153–60) and is lifted by Justinus (*Histories*, 1.10).

83. *much like matter . . . Tarquinius and his son*: See Livy, *Histories*, 1.53–4, on how Sextus, son of the last Roman king Tarquinius Superbus, pretended to be a deserter from Rome to Gabii.

84. *Xenophon excellently feigneth ... Abradatas in Cyrus' behalf*: See *Cyropaedia*, 5.3.8–19 and 6.1.39ff., for similar stories about Gadatas and Araspas; Abradatas (in Books 5–7) dies in Cyrus' service but is involved in no such stratagem: Sidney has misremembered.

85. *Dante's heaven to his hell*: Dante's *Divina commedia* ('Divine Comedy', *c.* 1310–21) had made little impact on English literature before this point, but, from his concluding references to Dante's editor Landino and to Beatrice, it does appear that Sidney read it.

86. *Well may you see Ulysses ... in other hard plights*: e.g. *Odyssey*, 5.

87. *And of the contrary part ... to follow them*: See Plutarch, 'How the Young Man Ought to Study Poetry', *Moralia*, 19e: 'Euripides is said to have answered critics who attacked his Ixion as impious and vile by saying: "But I didn't take him off the stage until he was nailed to the wheel."'

88. *For see we not valiant Miltiades ... exile a happiness*: Miltiades: Greek general who led the Greeks to victory over the Persians at Marathon in 490 BC; he died the following year after failing to capture Paros. Phocion: brilliant Athenian statesman and general condemned to death in 318 BC on dubious charges of high treason. Socrates: Greek philosopher, the hero of Plato's dialogues, condemned to death in 399 BC on trumped-up charges of corrupting the young. Severus: Lucius Septimius Severus, effective but ruthless Roman Emperor (193–211 AD), punished supporters of his rivals, including Clodius Albinus (see note 20). Severus: Alexander Severus, Emperor (222–35 AD), serious and religious but weak with the army; murdered by rebel soldiers. Sulla and Marius: Lucius Cornelius Sulla (138–78 BC), eventually elected dictator of Rome, and Gaius Marius (*c.* 157–86 BC), rivals during a period of bloody revolution in the Roman state. Pompey: Gnaeus Pompeius Magnus (106–48 BC), defeated by his rival Julius Caesar at Pharsalia, escaped to Egypt but was murdered on landing ashore. Cicero: Marcus Tullius Cicero (106–43 BC), Rome's greatest orator but politically naive (leading to temporary exile 58–57 BC); supporter of Pompey against Caesar and enemy of Antony, who had him murdered.

89. *See we not ... in the highest honour*: Marcus Porcius Cato Uticensis (95–46 BC), much praised by Cicero, supported Pompey against Julius Caesar (100–44 BC), and committed suicide after the defeat of Pompey's party, two years before Caesar was assas-

sinated. Sidney means both that Caesar's reputation is higher than it should be, and that his name was taken by subsequent emperors and adopted in other countries (Kaiser, Czar).

90. *And mark but even . . . caused him to do well*: The phrase 'put down his dishonest tyranny' refers to Sulla's own abdication of the dictatorship the year before his death (elliptically the mantle of tyranny is put down) rather than to Caesar's involvement with the later dismantling of Sulla's political system, long after Sulla's death; 'literas nescivit': Suetonius (*Julius Caesar*, 77) reports this pun, that 'Sulla did not know even the alphabet of politics, since he let others do all the dictating'.

91. *He meant it not . . . occidendos esse*: The deposition of tyrants was a current theme in political thought (e.g. the contemporary *Vindiciae contra tyrannos* ('Defence of Rights against Tyrants', 1579), probably the work of two of Sidney's closest Continental friends Hubert Languet and Philippe Duplessis-Mornay) and is acted out in episodes in Sidney's *Arcadia*.

92. *Cypselus, Periander, Phalaris, Dionysius*: Tyrants of Corinth (Cypselus and Periander, seventh century BC), Sicily (Phalaris, sixth century BC), and Syracuse (Dionysius, fifth century BC).

93. *Now, to that which commonly is attributed . . . abominable injustice of usurpation*: For the argument of this paragraph cf. Bacon, pp. 289–90.

94. *I conclude therefore . . . setting forward and moving*: Sidney uses a common formula – to teach (*docere*), to delight (*delectare*), and to move (*movere*). Traditionally the triple aim of rhetoric (see, e.g., Cicero, *De oratore*, 2.28.121 and *Orator*, 21.69; Quintilian, *Institutio oratoria*, 3.5.2), it had been claimed for poetry by Renaissance critics like Scaliger and Minturno.

95. *indeed setteth the laurel crown . . . poets as victorious*: See note 150.

96. *For, as Aristotle saith . . . praxis must be the fruit*: *Ethics*, 1.3: 'The end is not knowing, but doing'; cf. note 52.

97. *Nay truly, learned men . . . the philosophers drew it*: The philosophers deduced moral laws, so why can't we? On innate knowledge see Plato, *Meno*.

98. *hoc opus, hic labor est*: Virgil, *Aeneid*, 6.129, on Aeneas' path back up from the underworld.

99. *Now therein of all sciences . . . the human conceit*: Divinity is again removed from consideration.

100. *but he cometh to you . . . well-enchanting skill of music*: Sidney oddly shifts from his account of poetry as all fictional narrative,

in prose and in verse, to an account of the poet not only writing verse, but lyric verse at that: the accompaniment of music may describe some Homeric/bardic ideal for the performance of heroic poetry, but 'either accompanied with or prepared for' more specifically distinguishes between those lyric poems written to existing tunes and those whose verse form facilitates subsequent musical setting; Sidney wrote both kinds.

101. *with a tale ... from the chimney corner*: Cf. Cicero, *Pro Archia poeta*, 7.16. For Harington's use of this memorable phrase see p. 271.

102. *Even as the child ... than at their mouth*: *Aloēs*, aloes, or bitter aloes, is a bitter purgative made from the leaves of several species of aloe; rhabarbarum is rhubarb or rhubarb-root, also used as a purgative. For this image cf. the opening of Plutarch, 'How the Young Man Ought to Study Poetry', *Moralia*, 14d–f; Lucretius, *De rerum natura*, 4.11–25; and Harington, translating Tasso, p. 265.

103. *That imitation whereof poetry is ... to nature of all other*: 'That imitation whereof poetry is' distinguishes poetry from other kinds of imitation, such as painting and music, following Aristotle, *Poetics*, 1447a. It is not altogether clear what Sidney means by 'conveniency to nature'. He might, following *Poetics*, 1454a (characters must be morally good, suitable, lifelike, and consistent), be talking about verisimilitude. But he seems to be saying that poetry does not offend nature, since, as he goes on to say, it delights and tends to good even when it exhibits horror or evil.

104. *as Aristotle saith ... are made in poetical imitation delightful*: *Poetics*, 1448b: '*Mimēsis* is innate in human beings from childhood – indeed we differ from the other animals in being most given to *mimēsis* and in making our first steps in learning through it. And pleasure in instances of *mimēsis* is equally general ... we enjoy looking at the most exact portrayals of things we do not like to see in real life – the lowest animals, for instance, or corpses.'

105. *Amadis de Gaule*: A chivalric prose romance, Spanish originally, which gained great success in a French translation of 1540 and led to numerous spin-offs.

106. *Who readeth Aeneas ... usque adeone mori miserum est*: See Virgil, *Aeneid*, 2.705–804, for Aeneas carrying his father from the burning Troy. See *Aeneid*, 12.645–6, for Turnus' words: Turnus is the Rutulian king, betrothed to Lavinia, Aeneas' destined bride; these words come near the climax of the work, as he foresees death at Aeneas' hands.

107. *whether virtus be the chief . . . active life do excel*: Questions posed by philosophers and theologians, and addressed by schoolboys since antiquity.

108. *Plato and Boethius . . . raiment of Poesy*: Plato and Boethius, as philosophers, are not 'content little to move' and therefore do not 'scorn to delight': Sidney has already cited Plato's use of poetic fables and dramatic devices (see note 12); the Roman philosopher Boethius (*c.* 480–524 AD) wrote his *Consolation of Philosophy* as a dialogue, alternating prose and verse, with a personified female Philosophy.

109. *indulgere genio*: Persius (34–62 AD), *Satires*, 5.151.

110. *cunning insinuations*: An 'insinuation' is an indirect approach, but in English rhetoric books it is specifically a type of *exordium* or opening designed to win the favour of an audience strongly predisposed against the speaker or his case (Latin *insinuatio*: see Quintilian, *Institutio oratoria*, 4.1.42 and 48).

111. *much less with far-fet maxims . . . they could well have conceived*: According to a medieval commonplace, over the door of Plato's Academy was written 'Let no man enter who knows no geometry'.

112. *He telleth them a tale . . . perfect reconcilement ensued*: Best known to us from Shakespeare, *Coriolanus* (written *c.* 1608; printed 1623), Act 1, scene 1, this episode is recounted by both Livy (*Histories*, 2.32) and Plutarch (*Life of Coriolanus*); cf. Quintilian, *Institutio oratoria*, 5.11.17–21, on the oratorical use of examples *ex poeticis fabulis* ('from poetic stories'), citing Menenius' fable of the body and the belly at 5.11.19.

113. *The other is of Nathan . . . psalm of mercy well testifieth*: 2 Samuel 12:1–15; the first cause is God, the 'second and instrumental cause' the fable itself; 'that heavenly psalm of mercy' is Psalm 51, one of the seven penitential psalms.

114. *although works in commendation . . . a high authority*: If the *Defence* is engaged in 'commendation or dispraise' then it is not forensic oratory but epideictic or demonstrative oratory.

115. *parts, kinds or species*: what we would now call 'genres'.

116. *Some, in the manner . . . and Boethius*: Manner (*verba*) is as always opposed to matter (*res*), which follows. Influential examples of the *prosimetrum*, a work alternating verse and prose, include Boethius' *Consolation of Philosophy* (see note 108), and Dante's *La Vita Nuova* ('The New Life'). The *Arcadia* (1504) of Jacopo Sannazaro (1458–1530) is a rather limited pastoral narrative, its twelve prose sections alternating with twelve verse sections, but the work gave Sidney the title for his *Arcadia*.

117. *Some have mingled ... heroical and pastoral*: As in Sidney's *Arcadia* and Book VI of Spenser's *Faerie Queene*, and, on the Continent and to a lesser extent, in works by Montemayor and Tasso. The most balanced mixture of prose and verse, and pastoral and epic, is Sidney's *Arcadia* itself.

118. *But that cometh all to one ... the conjunction cannot be hurtful*: Sidney may believe this statement to be unexceptionable, since most of the great heroic poems of the sixteenth century mingle kinds in this way. But the stricter neoclassical position from which those poems would be criticized for breaching generic decorum was already nascent, and Sidney is on some questions (e.g. the dramatic unities and 'mongrel tragicomedy') in sympathy with it.

119. *Therefore ... in the right use of them*: Sidney follows the list of eight kinds given earlier (p. 11), in reverse order.

120. *Is it then ... which is misliked*: Pastoral, the lowest ranking of the genres in the traditional lists, had the status of both the first type of poetry for a writer to publish (as Spenser began his career with *The Shepheardes Calender*), and the first for a schoolboy to read, usually in the shape of Virgil's *Eclogues* and the neo-Latin eclogues of Mantuan (1448–1516): see Drayton, p. 292, ll. 36–7. See Puttenham, pp. 88–9 for an account which, like Sidney, draws attention to the use of pastoral to glance at other, political, matters.

121. *Is the poor pipe ... them that sit highest*: Virgil, *Eclogues*, 1, a dialogue between the dispossessed Meliboeus and the fortunate Tityrus (the latter probably representing Virgil, enjoying the patronage of Augustus).

122. *sometimes ... wrongdoing and patience*: For instance in Mantuan's ninth eclogue, a satire on the papal court, and Spenser's 'September' eclogue in *The Shepheardes Calender*, on the 'abuses ... and loose living of Popish prelates'.

123. *Haec memini ... Corydon est tempore nobis*: The closing lines of Virgil, *Eclogues*, 7.69–70, in which Meliboeus has narrated a contest between Corydon and Thyrsis. Similar poetic contests are found in Spenser and in the eclogues between each book of Sidney's *Arcadia*. Sidney compares such trivial struggles to the wars between Alexander the Great and the Persian King Darius III (defeated in 330 BC): Alexander may be famous but where is the Macedonian Empire now?

124. *Or is it ... rather pity than blame*: See Puttenham, pp. 95–6, for a fuller account of the genre. The Greek *elegeia* means 'lament' but in both Greek and Latin literature the mark of elegy was the use of

the elegiac couplet, which persisted in the Roman love elegies of
Ovid, Propertius and others, sidelined in Sidney's account.

125. *the great philosopher Heraclitus*: The Greek philosopher of the
sixth century, whose doctrine that everything is in a state of
constant flux Sidney glances at here; he wept, according to later
sources, at human folly.

126. *Is it the bitter . . . crying out against naughtiness*: Another genre
named for a verse form. Sidney follows Scaliger in calling the
direct and excoriating Juvenalian form of satire 'iambic' and
reserving the term 'satiric' for the gentler, comic approach of
Horace.

127. *omne vafer . . . tangit amico*: This and the following quotation
are from Persius, *Satires*, 1.116–17, on Horace: 'Horace, the
rascal, probes every fault of his friend while making him laugh;
and once inside he plays with the secrets of his heart'.

128. *est Ulubris . . . aequus*: Horace, *Epistles*, 1.11.30, substituting
nos ('we') for *te* ('you'): travelling does no good, the grass is
not greener elsewhere, you can be happy at Ulubrae [a rotten,
frog-infested town in the marshes] if you keep a well-balanced
mind.

129. *Perchance it is . . . justly made odious*: Cf. Puttenham on the
Old and New Comedy, pp. 83–5. Sidney applies the common
Renaissance criticism of early Greek comedy (represented by the
work of Aristophanes) to the contemporary Elizabethan stage.

130. *To the arguments . . . I will answer after*: Sidney is not, as has
been argued, promising to answer Gosson's *The School of Abuse*
(1579), the Puritan attack on the theatre dedicated rather inap-
propriately to Sidney; rather he is referring forward to the section
of the *Defence* in which he counters the four main arguments
against poetry, and specifically to the 'argument of abuse' dealt
with on pp. 35–8.

131. *Now, as in geometry . . . as the right*: 'Oblique' means 'crooked',
and 'right' can mean 'straight' (cf. the mathematician who can
'draw forth a straight line with a crooked heart', p. 13); at the
same time they are used in the technical senses of oblique and
right angles.

132. *a niggardly Demea . . . a vainglorious Thraso*: Stock characters in
the comedies of the Roman playwright Terence (*c.* 190–159 BC).

133. *but to know who be such . . . by the comedian*: The requirement
of *decorum*, that characters be self-consistent and appropriate;
cf. *Poetics*, 1454a and Horace, *Ars poetica*, 119–27.

134. *although perchance the sack . . . lie so behind his back*: In the

Aesopic fable retold in the first-century AD collections of both Babrius (66) and Phaedrus (4.10), man has two sacks, one filled with other men's faults, carried in front, one with his own, carried on his back where he cannot see it.

135. *And much less ... gilden roofs are builded*: For tragedy as concerned with great men, see Aristotle, *Poetics*, 1452b–1453a; for pity ('commiseration') and fear (Sidney habitually substitutes 'admiration', deliberately rather than through poor translation) see *Poetics*, 1452b–54a, following on from his central definition at 1449b: 'A tragedy is a *mimēsis* of a high, complete action, in verse, alternating dialogue and chorus, in dramatic, not narrative form, effecting through pity and fear the *catharsis* of such emotions.' Aristotle's method, offering a single, careful definition and then explaining and justifying its parts and terms, is the ultimate source of Sidney's method in the *Defence*, and that of other critics on the Continent.

136. *qui sceptra saevus ... in auctorem redit*: A popular tag from Seneca, *Oedipus*, 3.705–6 (which reads *qui sceptra duro saevus imperio regit*).

137. *Plutarch yieldeth ... some of his own blood*: See Plutarch, *Life of Pelopidas*, 29 (Alexander was a fourth century BC tyrant of Thessaly).

138. *Is it the lyric ... lauds of the immortal God*: Like Puttenham, Sidney to us seems unduly concerned with the epideictic rhetoric of praise and blame (there is no room for his own sonnets in this definition of lyric), but this is because the definition, for the purposes of theory rather than practice, sticks to tradition, and notably the example of Scaliger's *Poetices*, 1.44: lyric is sung to the lyre; chiefly hymns of praise, but also including songs about love and exhortations to good morals. See below p. 35, when Sidney answers the 'argument of abuse', for an admission that lyric, elegiac, and comedy are largely concerned with love.

139. *Certainly I must confess ... some blind crowder*: Some form of the ballad of Chevy Chase, dating from the fifteenth century, which tells of the enmity between Percy (of Northumberland) and the Scottish Douglas; both die in battle. Sidney may be talking from childhood experience: family accounts record that the eleven-year-old Sidney ordered a 'blind harper' to be paid for his performance. Cf. Puttenham on the repertoire of blind harpers, p. 124.

140. *what would it work ... eloquence of Pindar*: Pindar (518–438 BC) is known as the greatest Greek lyric poet; most of the

lyrics which survive celebrate victories at the four great Greek games.

141. *In Hungary . . . kindlers of brave courage*: Sidney spent several weeks in Hungary in 1573; the country was the eastern frontier of Christendom's struggle with the Ottoman Empire.

142. *The incomparable Lacedemonians . . . what they would do*: Sidney follows Plutarch's *Life of Lycurgus*, 21.

143. *so indeed the chief fault . . . three fearful felicities*: Mistaking, as was common, Mount Olympus for Olympia, site of the Games. The three 'felicities' were reported to Philip on the same day; the other two were a victory against the Illyrians and the birth of his son Alexander, later the Great (Plutarch's *Life of Alexander*, 3).

144. *There rests the heroical*: The heroical, or epic, was acknowledged to be the foremost literary kind by almost all authorities, only comparable to tragedy for the dignity of its subject matter, and preferable for its greater scope.

145. *no less champions than Achilles . . . Tydeus and Rinaldo*: Achilles is the hero of Homer's *Iliad* and the *Achilleis* of Statius (*c.* 45–96 AD); Tydeus is mentioned in Homer and is one of the seven against Thebes in Statius, *Thebais*; Rinaldo figures in Ariosto's *Orlando furioso*, and in Torquato Tasso's *Rinaldo* (1562) and *Gerusalemme liberata* ('Jerusalem Delivered', 1580–81). (For Cyrus, Aeneas and Turnus, see notes 29 and 106.)

146. *if the saying of Plato . . . love of her beauty*: Plato, *Phaedrus*, 250d, followed in Cicero, *De finibus* ('On Ends'), 2.16.52 and *De officiis* ('On Duties'), 1.5.14.

147. *this man sets her out . . . in her holiday apparel*: As opposed to the work clothes in which she is dressed by philosophers.

148. *Only let Aeneas be worn . . . in his outward government*: The image of the mind as a wax tablet (e.g. as a *tabula rasa*, a blank tablet) was common in Sidney's day. 'Tables' or 'tablets' were also boards on which portraits were painted; the image is thus closely related to the thread of visual metaphors centred on the 'speaking picture'. Sidney's list alludes to all the central matter of the *Aeneid*.

149. *yea even as Horace saith . . . Chrysippo et Crantore*: Horace, *Epistles*, 1.2.1–4: 'I have been reading afresh the author of the Trojan War [i.e. Homer] . . . He tells us what is noble, what is ignoble, what is profitable, what is not, more plainly and better than Chrysippus [a Stoic philosopher] and Crantor [a commentator on Plato].'

150. *the laurel crown . . . honour the poet's triumph*: A triumph was

'the entrance of a victorious commander with his army and spoils in solemn procession into Rome, permission for which was granted by the senate in honour of an important achievement in war' (*OED*). The victorious commander would then be crowned with laurel. The Roman tradition was adapted in 1341 when the poet Petrarch was given a triumph and crowned with laurel; thereafter dignified poets were crowned literally or figuratively with laurel (hence 'poet laureate').

151. *We know a playing wit . . . sick of the plague*: Cornelius Agrippa praised the ass (see note 153), and Francesco Berni both debt and the plague in *Il primo libro dell'opere burlesche* ('The First Book of Burlesque Works', 1558).

152. *if we will turn Ovid's verse . . . in nearness of the evil*: Inverting Ovid, *Ars amatoria* ('The Art of Love'), 2.661: *et lateat vitium proximitate boni* ('[call the short woman petite, and the fat ample,] and any fault may lie hid close to a good').

153. *so of the contrary side . . . commending of folly*: Bad things will be praised and, 'of the contrary side', good things will be ridiculed. Sidney refers to Agrippa, *De incertitudine et vanitate scientiarum at artium* (1530), translated as *Of the Vanity and Uncertainty of Arts and Sciences* (1569), a satire on learning which influenced, for instance, Sidney's portrayal of the paradoxes of scientists without self-knowledge on p. 13; and to Erasmus, *Moriae encomium* (1511), translated as *Praise of Folly* (1549).

154. *Marry, these other pleasant fault-finders . . . confirm their own*: Also inverting the proper order for an oration, as followed by Sidney: confirmation before confutation.

155. *But yet presuppose . . . it seemeth Scaliger judgeth*: Scaliger's *Poetices*, 1.2, *contra* Aristotle (see note 45).

156. *For if oratio . . . upon mortality*: Cf. Peacham, pp. 248-9 and note 2 for a version of this commonplace.

157. *But lay aside . . . striker of the senses*: Compare Sidney's account of lyric, p. 28, for the centrality of music to his theory of poetry. Music was believed by the ancients to be able to affect the mind in a very direct way. The music associated with each musical mode could represent and arouse a particular emotion; the theory stretches forward to Dryden's 'What passions cannot music raise and quell' ('A Song for St Cecilia's Day, 1687'), and was treated even in the political philosophy of Plato and Aristotle.

158. *Lastly, even they . . . thoroughly known*: This method originated in antiquity and is taught in the rhetoric books, *memoria* being the fourth part of oratory and the fourth stage of the oration. The

method gives us our word 'commonplaces' (*loci communes*), as well as 'topic' and 'topos' (from Greek *topos*, place). A medieval art of memory was developed from this tradition and taken up again in the sixteenth century.

159. *percontatorem fugito . . . credula turba sumus*: Horace, *Epistles*, 1.18.69; Ovid, *Remedium amoris* ('The Cure for Love'), 686.

160. *from grammar to logic . . . compiled in verses*: It was common to compose rhymed rules for all the disciplines Sidney mentions. On the famous medical verses of the 'Schola Salerna' see Daniel, p. 212.

161. *with a siren's sweetness . . . sinful fancies*: The sirens lured passing sailors to their deaths with their music; they were half woman, half bird, though Sidney has preferred the later tradition of depicting them as mermaids, perhaps because of the lure of the tale/tail pun. The possibility of equating poetry with the song of the sirens is recognized, e.g., by Plutarch ('How the Young Man Ought to Study Poetry', *Moralia*, 15d).

162. *herein especially . . . as Chaucer saith*: See Chaucer's *Knight's Tale*, 28 (only the phrase 'the largest field to ear', not any point about comedy).

163. *And lastly . . . of his commonwealth*: Cf. the proverb: 'Many speak of Robin Hood that never shot with his bow'. In this case Sidney means that people repeat Plato's arguments who know nothing of his philosophy. For Plato see note 187. Cf. Puttenham on *decorum*: 'And there is decency [*decorum*] in that every man should talk of the things they have best skill of, and not in that their knowledge and learning serveth them not to do, as we are wont to say "he speaketh of Robin Hood that never shot in his bow"' (*Art of English Poesy*, Book 3, chapter 23, not included in this edition).

164. *Now then go we . . . much truth in it*: The charges are traditional, and are dealt with by Boccaccio, Juan Luis Vives and others. Their emphasis depended on context. The first charge principally interested humanist educationalists, who defended the use of poetry in the curriculum. The second belongs to the sort of satiric attack on all forms of learning made by Agrippa. The third, social argument was bought by many secular and religious authorities, increasingly in Sidney's day, and was restated in Puritan attacks on the Elizabethan theatre. Plato's argument, the fourth charge, was a thorn in the side for the many poets who, like Sidney, loved Plato's dialogues.

165. *To the second . . . the principal liars*: 'Should' denotes a reported

statement. The question of whether poets lie or tell the truth is ancient. Plutarch reports 'the proverbial saying that "poets tell many lies"' ('How the Young Man Ought to Study Poetry', *Moralia*, 16a). When Hesiod is chosen as a poet by the Muses in his *Theogony* of *c.* 700 BC (21–34), they say 'we know how to tell many lies that resemble the truth'. Plutarch and others repeated the fine paradox about poetical deceit attributed to the rhetorician and sophist Gorgias (*c.* 485–376 BC): 'the deceiver is more just than the non-deceiver, and the deceived is wiser than the undeceived' (*Moralia*, 348d, and 'How the Young Man Ought to Study Poetry', *Moralia*, 15d). Sidney's response to an accusation which is at its sharpest in Plato (the poet is 'a maker of images and very far removed from the truth', *Republic*, 605b) is bound up with his theory of imitation and is essentially Aristotelian (*Poetics*, 1459b–1461b): 'In answer to the charge of not being true, one can say, "But perhaps it is as it should be"' (1460b).

166. *send Charon a great number . . . to his ferry*: In the Greek underworld, Charon was the ferryman who transported the souls of the dead across the river Styx.

167. *the poet never . . . your imagination*: The magic circles drawn on the ground by necromancers defined the area within which the magic worked.

168. *but even for his entry . . . a good invention*: The traditional epic invocation, as in Homer ('Sing, Muse, of the wrath of Achilles', *Iliad*, 1.1); 'invention' is the matter of the narrative or oration (the first part of rhetoric, *inventio*).

169. *use the narration but as an imaginative ground-plot of a profitable invention*: This is a confusing statement. 'Narration' meant 'story' and, in rhetoric, 'statement of facts of the case'; 'ground-plot' either meant 'foundation' or 'ground-plan'; 'invention', another rhetorical term, is the finding of matter for the poem or oration. Sidney is using the lexicon of rhetoric and poetics to describe not composition but interpretation and *praxis*. He means not 'treat the story as a mental outline of a useful plot', a mere circumlocution, but rather 'make use of the story in building in your own mind the foundations of some useful idea or course of action'. We become poets of our own lives in this dense metaphor.

170. *'John of the Stile' and 'John of the Nokes'*: Names used in fictitious legal cases (for instance in textbooks), meaning 'John who lives at the stile' and 'John who lives at the oak'.

171. *But that . . . build any history*: Cf. Aristotle, *Poetics*, 1451b: 'That poetry does aim at generality has long been obvious in the case

of comedy, where the poets make up the plot from a series of probable happenings and then give the persons any names they like.'

172. *But grant love of beauty . . . the excellency of it*: Sidney is principally aiming at Plato's *Symposium* and *Phaedrus*.

173. *For I will not deny . . . unworthy objects*: Plato makes this distinction in *Sophist*. Icastic or 'likeness-making' art occurs 'whenever someone produces an imitation by keeping to the proportions of length, breadth and depth of his model, and also by keeping to the appropriate colours of its parts' (235d–e). Fantastic art produces 'appearances that aren't likenesses' (236c), either by representing things which do not exist or by inaccurately representing those which do.

174. *as the painter that . . . building or fortification*: The early Renaissance painters were almost invariably skilled mathematicians and architects.

175. *as Abraham . . . with Goliath*: Biblical themes common in Renaissance art and poetry.

176. *Nay, truly . . . doth most good*: This argument and its examples are developed from discussions of the abuse of rhetoric in Aristotle, *Rhetoric*, 1.1.13 (1355b), and Quintilian, *Institutio oratoria*, 2.16.

177. *What that before-time . . . Sphinx can tell*: As being old enough and also adept with riddles.

178. *the Albion nation*: 'Albion' was an ancient name, supposedly predating 'Britain'.

179. *Of such mind were certain Goths . . . conquer their countries*: This story of the sack of Athens in 267 AD is told by Petrus Patricius in his continuation of Dio Cassius, *Roman Histories*, 54.17.

180. *iubeo stultum esse libenter*: Adapted from Horace, *Satires*, 1.1.63: 'Bid him be miserable'.

181. *Orlando furioso, or honest King Arthur*: Ariosto's epic *Orlando furioso*; the Arthurian stories (for instance of Sir Thomas Malory) seemed dated to the Elizabethans, hence 'honest' (= 'good old').

182. *the quiddity of ens and prima materia*: Scholastic terms: 'quiddity' means 'essential quality'; 'ens' is 'being'; 'prima materia' is 'first matter'. Poetry can inspire bravery, but philosophy is not going to win any battles.

183. *Only Alexander's example . . . but his footstool*: As Plutarch argued in *On the Fortune or Virtue of Alexander*.

344   NOTES TO PP. 37-8

184. *the phoenix of warlike princes*: People were often compared to
     the phoenix, for its uniqueness, not for its ability to be reborn.
185. *This Alexander . . . the definition of fortitude*: Anecdotes from
     Plutarch, *Life of Alexander*, and much repeated elsewhere. Alex-
     ander slept with a sword and a copy of Homer under his pillow;
     Callisthenes (died *c.* 327 BC) was in fact Alexander's official
     historian.
186. *And therefore, if Cato . . . is herein of no validity*: Ennius (239-
     169 BC) was brought to Rome by Cato and in 189 BC accom-
     panied the consul Fulvius Nobilior to the Aetolian War. Cato
     Censorius (234-149 BC) was a conservative, a stern moralist,
     and a frequent prosecutor of corruption, with an aversion to
     Greek culture. For his great-grandson Cato Uticensis see note
     89. Scipio Nasica opposed Cato's pursuit of the destruction of
     Carthage, arguing that Roman morals depended on having an
     enemy; Livy reports that Scipio Nasica was judged by the senate
     'to be the best of all the good men in the whole state'. The brothers
     Scipio Asiaticus and Scipio Africanus (236-183 BC) were sur-
     named for crucial victories in the wars against the Seleucids
     and Carthage respectively. The details about Ennius come from
     Cicero, *Pro Archia poeta*, 9.22 (a statue of Ennius is placed in the
     Scipios' tomb, not his body) and 11.27. Pluto, or Hades, was the
     Greek god of the Underworld.
187. *But now indeed . . . is laid upon me*: Sidney does not even need
     to state the charge. Plato deals with poetry in Books 2-3 and 10
     of the *Republic*. In Books 2-3, Socrates is concerned with the
     question of education, and the dangers of the moral values incul-
     cated by mythic poetry (because, for instance, children cannot
     distinguish between the allegorical and the literal); this develops
     into a discussion of the undesirability of *mimēsis*, since the same
     man cannot both copy another and do something worthwhile on
     his own account; also included is a preference for indirect over
     direct speech in narrative. In Book 10 Plato develops his theory
     of ideas and criticizes *mimēsis* from this angle; Socrates proves to
     his satisfaction that poets are incapable of educating or improving
     men or states; imitation is then shown to strengthen imagination
     at the expense of reason, and to encourage men to enjoy crying
     or laughing at things they would react to with more sense and
     restraint in real life. The argument concludes: 'So when you find
     admirers of Homer saying that he educated Greece and that for
     human management and education one ought to take him up and
     learn his lesson and direct one's whole life on his principles, you

must be kind and polite to them – they are as good as they are able to be – and concede that Homer is the foremost and most poetical of the tragic poets; but you must be clear in your mind that the only poetry admissible in our city is hymns to the gods and encomia to good men. If you accept the "sweetened Muse" in lyric or epic, pleasure and pain will be enthroned in your city instead of law and the principle which the community accepts as best in any given situation.' (606–7)

188. *of all philosophers he is the most poetical*: See note 12.

189. *Yet if he . . . the fountain*: If taken literally the 'fountain' is either Aganippe, on Mount Helicon, Castalia, on Mount Parnassus, or Hippocrene, on Mount Helicon, all sacred to Apollo and the Muses.

190. *First, truly . . . a natural enemy of poets*: Cf. *Republic*, 10, 607: 'there is an old quarrel between poetry and philosophy'. The remainder of the paragraph is a masterly instance of the rhetorical figure *paralepsis*: 'a man might maliciously object', but I shall refrain from doing so; see Puttenham, pp. 179–80.

191. *For indeed, they found . . . to live among them*: The Homeric anecdote is repeated by Cicero, *Pro Archia poeta*, 8.19, and became very popular. Among banished philosophers were Empedocles from his native town Acragas, and Anaxagoras and Protagoras the Sophist from Athens.

192. *For only repeating . . . many philosophers unworthy to live*: For 'Euripides' verses' see Plutarch, *Life of Nicias*. Socrates was the most celebrated philosopher condemned to death by the Athenians.

193. *Certain poets, as Simonides and Pindarus . . . was made a slave*: Both stories concern Greek rulers in Sicily. (i) Hieron (died 466 BC) was the tyrant of Gela and Syracuse, and a notable patron of the arts. Simonides (c. 556–c. 468 BC) was said to have effected his reconciliation with his brother Theron, tyrant of Acragas. Pindar was one of many prominent poets who stayed at Hieron's court, and celebrates him in several odes. (ii) Dionysius II ruled Syracuse from 367–344 BC; he wrote poetry and studied philosophy. In 366 BC his kinsman Dion persuaded him to invite Plato to Syracuse. For their efforts to turn Dionysius into the Platonic philosopher-king, Dion was suspected of conspiracy and exiled, and Plato forced to return to Athens; when in 360 BC Dionysius agreed to try again, Plato returned to Sicily, but this also failed. The story that Plato was sold into slavery by the Spartan ambassador to whom Dionysius I (c. 430–367 BC) had

given him is told by Cicero, *Pro Rabirio Postumo* ('On Behalf of Rabirius Postumus'), 9.23; the Spartans were famous scorners of philosophy.

194. *But who should do thus . . . as they do*: Sidney follows Scaliger, *Poetices*, 1.2. The sections on love in both *Phaedrus* and *Symposium* concern the love of older for younger men, a key part of educated Greek culture. Plutarch's 'On Love' includes the assertion that 'there is only one genuine love, the love of boys' (*Moralia*, 751).

195. *Again, a man might ask . . . community of women*: *Republic*, 5, arguing that women and children should not be considered the property of individual men.

196. *who yet, for the credit of poets . . . name of a prophet*: The whole parenthesis is missing in the 1595 *Defence* and is supplied here from the 1595 *Apology*; the more authoritative of the two manuscripts reads '(who yet, for the credit of poets, twice citeth poets, and one of them by the name of their prophet)', which may be preferable. St Paul twice cites poets, quotes them three times, and demonstrates knowledge of four. Acts 17:28: 'For in him we live, and move, and have our being; as certain also of your own poets have said', namely Aratus (early third century BC) and Cleanthes (?331–231 BC). Titus 1:12: 'One of themselves, even a prophet of their own, said, The Cretians are alway liars, evil beasts, slow bellies', quoting Epimenides of Crete. I Corinthians 15:33: 'Be not deceived: evil communications corrupt good manners', quoting the Greek comic dramatist Menander (342–292 BC).

197. *setteth a watchword upon philosophy . . . the abuse*: Colossians 2:8: 'Beware lest any man spoil you through philosophy and vain deceit, after the tradition of men, after the rudiments of the world, and not after Christ.'

198. *Plato found fault . . . with such opinions*: *Republic*, 2.377–3.392.

199. *imitation*: This is here used narrowly (icastic rather than fantastic imitation: see note 173).

200. *Who list may read . . . of the divine providence*: Essays in Plutarch's *Moralia*: 'On Isis and Osiris', 'On the Failure of the Oracles', 'On Divine Vengeance'.

201. *qua authoritate . . . e republica exigendos*: *Poetices*, 1.2.

202. *And a man need go . . . in his dialogue called Ion*: *Ion* is a short and beguilingly ironic dialogue between Socrates and the rhapsode (performer of poetry) Ion, in which Socrates develops a theory of poetic inspiration (picked up by Sidney and his con-

temporaries), but only in order to show that the poet and rhapsode know nothing about anything (which they ignored).

203. *under whose lion's skin . . . an ass-like braying against poesy*: In the Aesopian fable the ass puts on a lion's skin and passes for a fearsome lion until the wind blows it off (Babrius, 139), or, in another version, until a fox who had earlier heard him braying calls his bluff.

204. *he attributeth unto poesy . . . a divine force far above man's wit*: Sidney parts company with most of his predecessors in rejecting the doctrine of inspiration and the *furor poeticus* (on which see, e.g., Plato, *Phaedrus*, 245a); the only inspiration he allows is in the case of Scripture.

205. *Caesars*: Alluding primarily to Augustus Caesar's patronage of Horace and Virgil.

206. *Laelius, called the Roman Socrates . . . made by him*: Gaius Laelius (born *c.* 190 BC), nicknamed Sapiens ('wise'), appears as a speaker in several of Cicero's dialogues; Cicero also records (*Letters to Atticus*, 7.3.10) that Terence's plays were ascribed to him by many; Terence alludes to a debt in the prologues to *Heautontimoroumenos* ('The Self-Tormentor') and *The Brothers*.

207. *even the Greek Socrates . . . Aesop's fables into verses*: Socrates was confirmed to be the wisest man by the Delphic oracle, according to Plato (*Apology*, 21a). In Plato's *Phaedo* (60d–61b) he is represented as versifying Aesop in prison. Plutarch repeats this with a twist: 'Socrates, the lifelong striver for truth, found himself, when he set about composing poetry in obedience to a dream, no very convincing or gifted maker of lies; he therefore put Aesop's fables into verse, on the principle that where there is no fiction there is no poetry' ('How the Young Man Ought to Study Poetry', *Moralia*, 16c).

208. *Aristotle writes the Art of Poesy . . . if they should not be read*: I.e. Aristotle's *Poetics* and Plutarch's 'How the Young Man Ought to Study Poetry' (*Moralia*, 14d–37b), two of Sidney's most important sources.

209. *let us rather plant . . . the price they ought to be held in*: See note 150.

210. *I have run so long a career*: Most of the early meanings of 'career' concern horses – a gallop at full stretch, a racecourse, the jousting area of a tiltyard; Sidney is horse or rider in this image.

211. *since all only proceedeth . . . not takers of others*: A reiteration of Sidney's theory of poetic making and imitation.

212. *Musa . . . quo numine laeso*: The invocation at the start of Virgil, *Aeneid*, 1.8

213. *David, Hadrian, Sophocles, Germanicus*: King David, the psalm-ist; the Roman emperor Hadrian (76–138 AD), who wrote poetry; the politically active Greek tragedian Sophocles (496–406 BC); the 'great captain' Julius Caesar Germanicus (15 BC–19 AD), poet and dramatist.

214. *Robert, King of Sicily . . . that Hospital of France*: Robert II of Anjou (1309–43), patron of Petrarch; François I (1494–1547), patron and poet; either James I of Scotland (1394–1437), poet and patron, or James VI of Scotland and (later) I of England (1566–1625), tutored by Sidney's friend George Buchanan and a writer of poetry (see Daniel, *Defence*, note 2); Pietro Bembo (1470–1547), humanist scholar, poet and cardinal; Bernardo Dovizi, Cardinal Bibbiena (1470–1520), humanist and drama-tist; Théodore de Bèze (1519–1605), Calvinist editor of the New Testament, dramatist and (with Clement Marot) author of the French metrical version of the Psalms used by Sidney as a model for his psalm translations; Philip Melanchthon (1497–1560), German humanist educationalist, teacher and associate of Sidney's closest Continental friends, a selected translation of whose prayers and devotional poetry, *Godly Prayers* was dedi-cated to Sidney in 1579; Girolamo Fracastoro (1483–1553), polymath and poet; Julius Caesar Scaliger (1484–1558), scholar and poet, whose brilliant and learned *Poetices libri septem* ('Seven Books on Poetics') was a key source for Sidney; Giovanni Pontano (1426–1503), scholar, poet and diplomat, president of the Academy of Naples; Marc-Antoine Muret (1526–85), French humanist scholar; George Buchanan (1506–82), Scottish hu-manist poet, dramatist and pedagogue, author of an influential treatise of political theory and a Latin versification of the Psalms, tutor of James VI and greatly admired by Sidney; Michel de l'Hôpital (1503–73), jurist, Chancellor of France, patron and minor poet.

215. *For heretofore . . . the trumpet of Mars did sound loudest*: i.e. in times of continual wars (Mars is the god of war); a possible reference to the age of Chaucer and the Hundred Years' War.

216. *And now that an over-faint quietness*: A cowardly quietness in military affairs. Sidney was a so-called 'forward Protestant', one of a faction calling for military engagement on the Continent in defence of European Protestant interests, against the more pacific, isolationist policies of Elizabeth I.

217. *the mountebanks at Venice*: A later English traveller, Thomas Coryate, called the infamous Venetian street sellers 'natural orators'. Cf. the scene in which Jonson's Volpone pretends to be a mountebank selling quack medicine (*Volpone*, 2.2).

218. *which like Venus . . . homely quiet of Vulcan*: The lame blacksmith god Vulcan used a net to catch his wife Venus, goddess of love, and Mars, god of war, in adultery (Homer, *Odyssey*, 8.266–367).

219. *as Epaminondas is said . . . to become highly respected*: Plutarch in 'Principles of Statecraft' (*Moralia*, 811) recounts that the fourth-century BC Theban statesman and general was appointed *telearch* (giving him responsibility for gutters and sewers) and 'did not reject it, but said that the office does not make the man, but the man the office'.

220. *the banks of Helicon*: The mountain sacred to Apollo and the Muses; its 'banks' are those of its fountains, Aganippe and Hippocrene, which gave poetic inspiration.

221. *queis meliore . . . praecordia Titan*: Adapted from Juvenal, *Satires*, 14.34–5.

222. *in despite of Pallas*: Pallas Athena, goddess of wisdom, craft and war, whose Roman equivalent, Minerva, Horace mentions in a passage which Sidney had in mind as he wrote this and the previous paragraph: 'the man who knows not how dares to frame verses . . . But *you* will say nothing and do nothing against Minerva's will; such is your judgement, such your good sense' (*Ars poetica*, 366–90).

223. *But I, as I never desired the title . . . an inky tribute unto them*: A fashionable and characteristic gesture of *sprezzatura* ('careless disdain'), required of the courtier by the influential *Il Cortegiano* (1528) of Baldassare Castiglione, published in Thomas Hoby's English translation as *The Courtier* in 1561: the courtier is required 'to do his feats with a slight, as though they were rather naturally in him than learned with study, and use a recklessness [*sprezzatura*] to cover art, without minding greatly what he hath in hand, to a man's seeming' (*The Book of the Courtier*, ed. Virginia Cox [London, 1994], 367). The advice governs Sidney's rhetoric throughout the *Defence*.

224. *so must . . . have a Daedalus to guide him*: The mythical Greek inventor responsible for the Labyrinth and the wings which took Icarus, unheedful of his advice, too close to the sun; cf. Horace, *Odes*, 2.20.13 and 4.2.2.

225. *art, imitation and exercise*: The traditional triad. The meaning of

each is explained in the typical advice of the anonymous rhetoric manual *Ad Herennium* ('Rhetoric to Herennius'), 1.2.3: '[skill in speaking] we can acquire by three means: theory ['art'], imitation and practice ['exercise']. By theory is meant a set of rules that provide a definite method and system of speaking. Imitation stimulates us to attain, in accordance with a studied method, the effectiveness of certain models in speaking. Practice is assiduous exercise and experience in speaking.'

226. *performing Ovid's verse, quicquid . . . erit*: Adapting Ovid, *Tristia* ('Sad Things'), 9.10.26 (from past to future).

227. *Troilus and Criseyde*: The most popular of the poems of Geoffrey Chaucer (*c.* 1343–1400) with the Elizabethans, as Puttenham's references also testify. The brief survey of notable achievements is also one of notable defects. No author or work mentioned uses 'art or imitation rightly' in both 'words' and 'matter'.

228. *Mirror of Magistrates . . . worthy of a noble mind*: A collection of narratives on the misfortunes of kings and eminent people from English history, *A Mirror for Magistrates* was very much a work of parts and of multiple authorship; first appearing in 1559 it was enlarged in numerous subsequent additions. Forty of the lyrics of Henry Howard, Earl of Surrey (1517?–47) were printed in *Songs and Sonnets* ('Tottel's Miscellany', 1557), and Sidney would have known others in manuscript; Surrey's blank verse translation of Books 2 and 4 of the *Aeneid* was also printed in 1557.

229. *The Shepheardes Calender . . . did affect it*: Spenser's *The Shepheardes Calender* was published anonymously in 1579 and dedicated to Sidney. The language is both archaic and rustic; it was in fact thought that both the Greek poet Theocritus (*c.* 300–*c.* 250 BC) in his *Idylls* and Virgil in the *Eclogues* were aiming at a similar effect. Sannazaro, the author of *Arcadia*, was also admired for his *Piscatory Eclogues* (1526).

230. *For proof whereof . . . barely accompanied with reason*: Compare Gascoigne on 'rhyme without reason', p. 241.

231. *Our tragedies and comedies . . . model of all tragedies*: *Gorboduc* was a tragedy in blank verse by Thomas Sackville (1536–1608), who also contributed to *A Mirror for Magistrates*, and Thomas Norton (1532–84); first presented in 1561, it was printed in 1565. The plot concerns filial rivalry and civil war in ancient Britain, and moves between several courts; the mode is classical, in that action is reported rather than presented. The tragedies of Lucius Annaeus Seneca (*c.* 5 BC–65 AD) were used in schools, and their lofty and

moralizing language was taken up by the earlier Elizabethan dramatists. The influential Elizabethan translations were gathered in *Seneca his Ten Tragedies* (1581); the tragedies of the Greeks were almost completely ignored in this period.

232. *For it is faulty ... all corporal actions*: Sidney is ahead of his time in propounding the doctrine of the unities, which went on to dominate later seventeenth-century drama and dramatic theory. Clearly indicated in Scaliger's *Poetices*, it received its first full formulation in Lodovico Castelvetro's translation of Aristotle's *Poetics* with voluminous commentary, *Poetica d'Aristotele vulgarizzata et sposta* ('The Poetics of Aristotle Translated and Explained', 1570; 1576). It is often said that Castelvetro found what was not in Aristotle, but it is clear that something like a rule of the three unities governs classical drama, although not always very strictly, and was already, therefore, being adopted by those who translated or imitated the plays of Seneca, Plautus, Terence, and, to a lesser extent, the Greeks. Nevertheless, what Aristotle does say is clear enough. The unity of action, that a single, unified course of events should be represented, is indicated by Aristotle's definition of tragedy as 'a *mimēsis* of a complete, that is, of a whole action ... with a beginning, a middle and an end' (1450b; cf. 1449b–1450a), and his close discussion of what 'whole' means (1450b–1452a), including his criticism of episodic plots. The unity of time (usually interpreted as requiring that a passage of time of no more than twenty-four hours be represented) is indicated in Aristotle's remarks that tragedy differs from epic in length, 'tragedy attempting so far as possible to keep to the limit of one revolution of the sun or not much more or less, while epic is unfixed in time'. The unity of place (that the action should be confined to one place) follows from the unities of action and time. Clearly, Sidney could have found what he presents in Aristotle, perhaps aided by Scaliger. It is unlikely that he used Castelvetro. Sidney is to a degree anticipated by George Whetstone in the dedication to *Promos and Cassandra* (1578; a source for Shakespeare's *Measure for Measure*), though he is primarily concerned with Horatian decorum: 'The Englishman ... first grounds his work on impossibilities, then in three hours runs he through the world, marries, gets children, makes children men, men to conquer kingdoms, murder monsters, and bringeth gods from heaven and fetcheth devils from hell' (*Elizabethan Critical Essays*, ed G.G. Smith, 2 vols. (Oxford, 1925–52), 1.59; hereafter *ECE*; see also *ERLC*, 173). Although the unities are ignored by most

writing for the stage in the generation after Sidney, Jonson
frequently follows them, and Shakespeare enjoys both exploding
them in *The Winter's Tale* and observing them in *The Tempest*
(both plays written *c.* 1611).

233. *the ordinary players in Italy will not err in*: It is speculated that
Sidney may have witnessed the performance of popular comedies
when he was in Padua and Venice in 1574.

234. *Yet will some . . . matter of two days*: Sidney confuses *Eunuchus*
with another play, probably *Heautontimoroumenos*; the remarks
otherwise follow Scaliger, *Poetices*, 6.3.

235. *And though Plautus . . . not miss with him*: Scaliger criticizes
Plautus' *Captives* for spanning too much time (6.3).

236. *the description of Calicut*: Calicut (modern Kozhikode), on the
west coast of India, was a major trading port.

237. *Pacolet's horse*: The flying horse of the enchanter Pacolet in the
popular late-medieval romance *Valentine and Orson*. A version
of the story by Henry Watson was printed *c.* 1550 as *History of
Two Valiant Brethren, Valentine and Orson*.

238. *Lastly, if they will . . . which they will represent*: See p. 305
for Jonson's translation of Horace's famous advice: 'Nor does
[Homer] begin . . . the war of Troy from the egg [Helen of Troy
was born from an egg]. Ever he hastens to the issue, and hurries
his hearer into the story's midst [*in medias res*]' (*Ars poetica*,
147-9).

239. *I have a story . . . spirit of Polydorus*: Sidney follows Scaliger
(*Poetices*, 3.95) but includes more details from his knowledge of
the play, Euripides' *Hecuba*, drawing directly from the opening
speech of Polydorus' ghost in the phrases 'for safety's sake, with
great riches' and 'to make the treasure his own'. Priam ('Priamus')
and Hecuba are king and queen of Troy.

240. *But besides these gross absurdities . . . by their mongrel tragicomedy obtained*: For tragic 'admiration' and 'commiseration'
see note 135. Cf. Whetstone (continuing the quotation in note
232): 'And (that which is worst) their ground is not so unperfect
as their working indiscreet, not weighing, so the people laugh,
though they laugh them (for their follies) to scorn. Many times
(to make mirth) they make a clown companion with a king; in
their grave counsels they allow the advice of fools; yea, they use
one order of speech for all persons – a gross indecorum' (*ECE*
1.59–60; *ERLC*, 173–4).

241. *I know Apuleius . . . in one moment*: Apuleius was the
second-century AD author of the *Metamorphoses* (known as *The*

Golden Ass), a fantastical story with many inset narratives which influenced Sidney's *Arcadia*.

242. *And I know ... as Plautus hath Amphitryo*: In the prologue to *Amphitryo*, Plautus explicitly describes his play as a tragicomedy.

243. *But our comedians ... both together*: Sidney's theory of comedy follows Giangiorgio Trissino, *Poetica* ('Poetics'), part 6 (1563) in its distinction between laughter and delight. The distinction is present in Cicero, *Orator*, 26.87–90 and is developed on lines similar to Sidney's in Demetrius, *On Style*, 163–9. Aristotle discusses comedy briefly in the *Poetics* (1449a–b) and more fully in the *Ethics* (4.8); in the *Rhetoric* (1372a, 1419b) he refers to a full discussion of the ridiculous in the *Poetics*, which has been lost. Treatments of laughter by, e.g., Cicero (*De oratore*, 2.58.234–71.290) were concerned with oratory, but do not differ from Aristotle in treating it as concerned with ridicule.

244. *We shall, contrarily ... with laughter*: The gist of this rather perplexing sentence is that sometimes one will laugh rather painfully when people one respects drop clangers or speak with unintended irony.

245. *For as in Alexander's picture ... spinning at Omphale's commandment*: Following a prophecy, Hercules had to sell himself into slavery to cure his madness. He was bought by Omphale, Queen of Lydia and a love affair developed; while Omphale wore Hercules' lionskin, Hercules wore dresses and wove or span at her feet. Both Alexander and Hercules were popular subjects for classical and Renaissance painters.

246. *And the great fault ... forbidden plainly by Aristotle*: *Poetics*, 1449a–b: 'Comedy is, as I said, a *mimēsis* of people worse than are found in the world – "worse" in the particular sense of "uglier", as the ridiculous is a species of ugliness; for what we find funny is a blunder that does no serious damage or an ugliness that does not imply pain, the funny face, for instance, being one that is ugly and distorted, but not with pain.'

247. *nil habet infelix ... ridiculos homines facit*: Juvenal, *Satires*, 3.152–3.

248. *But rather a busy loving courtier ... a wry-transformed traveller*: Thraso is a braggart in Terence. Sidney created a 'self-wise-seeming schoolmaster' in Rombus, in his brief entertainment *The Lady of May* (1578 or 1579). The other character types came to be familiar in the plays of Shakespeare and his contemporaries.

249. *the tragedies of Buchanan*: See note 214.

250. *that lyrical kind of songs and sonnets*: 'Songs and sonnets' was a

catch-all term for lyric poems both intended for music and not; it was used as the title for Donne's lyrics, and for the collection edited by the publisher Richard Tottel, known as 'Tottel's Miscellany' (1557).

251. *of which we might well want words . . . new-budding occasions*: i.e. the first rhetorical stage of *inventio* poses no problems for the divine poet; that it does pose problems for the amorous poet is the foundation of the famous opening sonnet of Sidney's sequence *Astrophil and Stella*.

252. *so coldly they apply fiery speeches*: An allusion to the frequent use of oxymoron ('coldly . . . fiery') in the love poetry of Petrarch and his followers.

253. *But truly, many of such writings . . . in truth they feel those passions*: Again, the concern is rhetorical, with *ēthos*, the convincing character which the orator must portray in order to persuade. The similarities between the famous passage in Horace (*Ars poetica*, 102–3: 'If you would have me weep, you must first feel grief yourself'; see p. 305 for Jonson's translation) and Quintilian's treatment of *ēthos* and *pathos* are important indicators of the overlap between rhetoric and aesthetics at certain points: 'if we wish to give our words the appearance of sincerity, we must assimilate ourselves to the emotions of those who are genuinely so affected . . . Will he grieve who can find no trace of grief in the words with which I seek to move him to grief? Will he be angry, if the orator who seeks to kindle his anger shows no sign of labouring under the emotion which he demands from his audience? Will he shed tears if the pleader's eyes are dry? It is utterly impossible' (*Institutio oratoria*, 6.2.27). For the connection between the rhetorical arts and those of the lover cf. Ovid, *Ars amatoria*, esp. 1.459–62.

254. *that same forcibleness or energeia*: For *energeia*, a vigour of style 'inwardly working a stir to the mind', see Puttenham, p. 135.

255. *diction*: Sidney's word for rhetorical *elocutio*, its first use in this sense.

256. *another time with coursing . . . the method of a dictionary*: Sidney describes the passion for alliteration prevalent in early Elizabethan poetry; cf. his *Astrophil and Stella*, 15.5–6: 'You that do dictionary's method bring / Into your rhymes, running in rattling rows'.

257. *another time with . . . flowers extremely winter-starved*: On rhetorical 'flowers' see note 13.

258. *Truly, I could wish . . . make them wholly theirs*: In a typically

condensed sentence Sidney contrasts two ideologies of literary imitation: on the one hand, the careful copying of a single stylistic model; and on the other, the study of the styles of various authors and the transformation of the fruits of that study into one's own style. Cicero ('Tully') and the Greek orator Demosthenes were suggested by Quintilian and others as the best models for stylistic imitation (*Institutio oratoria*, 10.2). Many in the Renaissance took this further than Quintilian intended, aiming at a thorough Ciceronianism serviced by the *Thesaurus Ciceronianus* ('Ciceronian Thesaurus') of Marius Nizolius (1535) and their own commonplace-book collections of favourite sentences and phrases ('Nizolian paper-books'). Sidney was one of those who felt that such imitation was superficial – of words at the expense of matter. In a letter of 18 October 1580 he wrote to his brother Robert: 'So you can speak and write Latin not barbarously, I never require great study in Ciceronianism, the chief abuse of Oxford, *qui dum verba sectantur, res ipsas negligunt* [who, while they chase the words, neglect the matter itself]'. Jonson paraphrases the images associated with the two models of imitation in his *Discoveries*: 'To make use of one excellent man above the rest, and so to follow him till he grow very he, or so like him as the copy may be mistaken for the principal ... Not to imitate servilely, as Horace saith, and catch at vices for virtue, but to draw forth out of the best and choicest flowers with the bee, and turn all into honey'. This second, more pragmatic model, and its apian image, derives from Seneca, *Epistulae morales*, 84; its influential digestive metaphor informs Sidney's 'devour them whole, and make them wholly theirs'.

259. *like those Indians ... they will be sure to be fine*: This picture is based on early reports from travellers to South America.

260. *Tully, when he was ... Imo in senatum venit*: From the famous opening to Cicero's first oration against the conspirator Catiline (*In Catilinam*, 1), using the figure *epizeuxis* or *geminatio*; on 'this figure of repetition' which Puttenham calls 'the underlay, or cuckoo-spell', see p. 168.

261. *Indeed inflamed ... men in choler do naturally*: Cf. note 253, on *ēthos*.

262. *And we, having noted ... too too much choler to be choleric*: The meaning is both that the figure, belonging to the grand style, is so out of proportion in the middle or plain style of the familiar letter as to fail to communicate any anger, and, with a loud pun on 'colour' or figure of speech, that the use is simply too rhetorical

in that context to ring true. Sidney's own repetitions contribute to the joke.

263. *similiter cadenses*: *Similiter cadens* is the use of similar endings to successive words, phrases or sentences; Sidney affixes a deliberately bathetic English plural ending instead of giving the correct *similiter cadentia*.

264. *Truly, they have made ... had none for his labour*: A popular story about the pitfalls of specious arguing, told, for instance, by Thomas More in the *Confutation of Tyndale* (1532): 'as though a sophister would with a fond argument prove unto a simple soul that two eggs were three, because that there is one, and there be twain, and one and twain make three, the simple unlearned man, though he lack learning to foil his fond argument, hath yet wit enough to laugh thereat, and to eat two eggs himself and bid the sophister take and eat the third.'

265. *Now for similitudes ... as is possible*: Sidney is aiming particularly at the fashionable euphuistic style perfected by John Lyly in *Euphues, the Anatomy of Wit* (1578), a rather empty shell plastered with simile, antithesis, pun, and alliteration. On Sidney's liberation of English style from euphuism see Drayton, p. 294.

266. *For my part ... the other not to set by it*: De oratore, 2.1.4. Marcus Antonius (143–87 BC) wrote a lost treatise on rhetoric; Lucius Licinius Crassus (140–91 BC) was Cicero's teacher. Both are celebrated in Cicero's *Brutus* (46 BC) as the first Romans to be orators of the first rank (37.139–40.146), and are the main speakers in the dialogue sections of *De oratore*.

267. *because with a plain sensibleness ... the chief mark of oratory*: Sidney makes further ironic use of rhetorical figures, this time a parenthetic *gradatio* (see note 43).

268. *following that which by practice ... and not to hide art*: Two familiar formulations are used. (i) Art and nature; cf. Quintilian, *Institutio oratoria*, 3.2.3: 'It was, then, nature that created speech, and observation that originated the art of speaking'. (ii) The popular, post-classical Latin tag *ars est celare artem* ('the art is to hide art'). Cf. Puttenham, Book 3, chapters 24–5.

269. *But both have such ... in the wordish consideration*: For the connections between poetry and rhetoric see the Introduction, pp. xxxiv–xl and xliii–xlvii and, e.g., Cicero, *De oratore*, 1.16.70: 'The truth is that the poet is a very near kinsman of the orator, rather more heavily fettered as regards rhythm, but with ampler freedom in his choice of words, while in the use of many sorts of ornament he is his ally and almost his counterpart.'

270. *some will say it is a mingled language*: That is, mixed of Anglo-Saxon and Norman French, as well as absorbing many Latin loan words. Some sixteenth-century humanists thought, as Sir John Cheke put it, 'that our own tongue should be written clean and pure, unmixed and unmangled with borrowing of other tongues' (in a commendatory letter to Hoby's translation of Castiglione, *The Courtier*: see *The Book of the Courtier*, ed. Cox, 10). Spenser's poetry represents in part an attempt to write such a pure English. Cf. Daniel, p. 233.

271. *the Tower of Babylon's*: Babylon was believed to have been built on the site of the Tower of Babel.

272. *in compositions of two or three words together*: Sidney's use of compounds was recognized by writers in the subsequent generation as one of the most distinctive marks of his style. For a number of examples see the last paragraph of the *Defence*.

273. *Now, of versifying . . . wanting in neither majesty*: See 'A Note on English Versification'. Sidney contrasts the classical quantitative system with modern systems, either syllabic (e.g. French and Italian) or accentual-syllabic (English). The theory and experimental practice of writing quantitative English verses occupied Sidney and his associates in the late 1570s and 1580s, following on from earlier experiments in German, Italian, French and English. See Daniel and Campion in this volume. Among the 'many speeches' about which of the ancient and modern systems is the 'more excellent' is a passage at the end of two manuscript texts of the First Eclogues of Sidney's original *Arcadia*, in which two shepherds, Dicus and Lalus, speak for either system.

274. *therefore very gracelessly may they use dactyls*: The dactyl is a foot consisting of three syllables, the first long or stressed, the following two short or unstressed; it is the constituent unit of dactylic hexameter, the vehicle of epic verse.

275. *Lastly, even the very rhyme itself . . . 'motion' / 'potion'*: Sidney innovates as both poet and theorist in this area: he is the first to use the terms 'masculine' and 'female' (= feminine) of line endings, and in his poetry is the first habitually and schematically to use feminine and trisyllabic rhymes in English.

276. *but to believe with Aristotle . . . and quid non*: Aristotle: drawing on Boccaccio's misreading of *Metaphysics*, 3.4.12 in *De genealogia deorum* ('On the Genealogy of the Gods'), 14.8 and 15.8. Bembus: Pietro Bembo, possibly in his *Le prose* ('Prose Works', 1525), though the view was a popular one. Scaliger: throughout *Poetices*, and especially 3.19. Clauserus: Conrad Clauser,

German humanist editor of the *De natura deorum gentilium* ('On the Nature of the Greek Gods', 1543) of Lucius Annaeus Cornutus, first-century AD teacher of rhetoric and philosophy; Sidney draws on his preface here.

277. *to believe with Landin . . . proceeds of a divine fury*: Cristoforo Landino (1424–1504), influential Florentine humanist, editor of Dante's *Divina commedia*. Sidney draws on his prologue, where he outlines the theory of the *furor poeticus* which Sidney has already marginalized in his response to Plato: see note 204.

278. *Thus doing, your name shall flourish . . . superlatives*: Sidney is promising patrons that they will have many works dedicated to them, and in the fulsome terms of the typical verse or prose dedicatory epistle.

279. *libertino patre natus*: Horace, *Satires*, 1.6.6, on how the great aristocratic patron Maecenas does not 'curl up your nose at men of unknown birth, men like myself, a freedman's [former slave's] son'.

280. *si quid . . . possunt*: Virgil, *Aeneid*, 9.446, promising immortality to the dead friends Nisus and Euryalus: 'If aught my verse avail, no day shall ever blot you from the memory of time'.

281. *thus doing, your soul . . . with Dante's Beatrix or Virgil's Anchises*: In Dante, Beatrice inhabits Paradise; in Book 6 of the *Aeneid*, Aeneas travels to the underworld and meets his father Anchises in the Elysian fields.

282. *But if . . . the planet-like music of poetry*: Cicero, *Somnium Scipionis* ('Dream of Scipio'), 5.13 likens the inability to hear the music of the spheres (the machinery of cosmic harmony echoed in the hearts of ordered men and the forms of ordered poetry), even though it fills everyone's ears, to the deafness of those who live near the waterfalls of the Nile.

283. *a Momus of poetry*: From the Greek *mōmos*, ridicule, a personification of ridicule, sarcasm and carping criticism, the son or daughter of Night, and a popular character in poetical prefaces.

284. *then, though I will not . . . to be done in Ireland*: Midas adjudged the music of Pan (equivalent to mere versing) to be superior to the more sophisticated art of Apollo, and was rewarded with ass's ears (Ovid, *Metamorphoses*, 11.146ff.). Bubonax is a conflation of Bupalus, a sculptor, and the ugly satiric poet Hipponax (sixth century BC); Bupalus and a fellow-sculptor, Athenis, created a caricatured statue of Hipponax, and his violent verse response was said to have caused their suicides. The use of verse charms to kill vermin and people was widely attested in Elizabethan

accounts of Ireland; Sidney's own father was even threatened
with death by Irish bards.

GEORGE PUTTENHAM:
THE ART OF ENGLISH POESY

Text: *The arte of English poesie. Contrived into three bookes: the first
of poets and poesie, the second of proportion, the third of ornament.*
(1589)

On Puttenham (*c.* 1529–1590 or 1591), see the Introduction, pp. lxii–
lxvii. The *Art* was entered in the Stationers' Register to Thomas Orwin
on 9 November 1588, and the rights transferred to Richard Field on 7
April 1589. Neither here nor in the book itself is any author named,
but the authorship may have been an open secret at court. In a letter
to Field, who was also to print Harington's *Orlando Furioso* in 1591,
Harington requests the printer to print his prose passages 'in the same
print that Putnam's book is'. The attribution to Puttenham is now
accepted, and the case of George over his brother Richard generally
preferred. Perhaps begun in the mid-1560s, much of the work was
probably written in the 1570s, and then extended (especially in the
case of Book 3) and carefully revised in the 1580s. Emendations to the
1589 text which are not straightforward corrections of typesetters'
errors are indicated by a note giving the original reading, in the form
(1589: 'reading').

THE FIRST BOOK: OF POETS AND POESY

Puttenham's first book offers a historical overview of the origins of
poetry and a discussion of its separate kinds, and closes with a survey
of English poetry. The book was probably written for the most part in
the 1560s and 1570s, when the achievements of English vernacular
literature still seemed slight; by the mid-1580s, when the survey was
probably added, there was a little more to say, but still much more to
hope for. Book 1 is of course derivative. Like Sidney, Puttenham drew
a great deal from Julius Caesar Scaliger's *Poetices libri septem* (1561).
Scaliger's Book 1 gives a historical account of poetry, and consideration
of the kinds is divided between Books 1 and 3. Scaliger's Book 2 deals
with prosodic issues, as does Puttenham's, although here Puttenham must beat his own path through vernacular poetry and prosody.

Scaliger's Books 3 and 4 bring discussion of rhetorical figures into poetics, an important precedent for Puttenham's own project, although Book 3 of the *Art* is modelled on conventional rhetoric books. While, therefore, a suggestion of Puttenham's overall plan may be found in Scaliger, it is only in Book 1 that he follows him closely. Much of the conventional material of Puttenham's Book 1 is shared with Scaliger, and some of the accounts of individual kinds lean on him heavily, although Puttenham's jolly tone and candid head-scratching make his treatment far more entertaining (and, of course, far less scholarly) than Scaliger's. And the example of Scaliger, whose *Poetices* is about Greek and Latin literature and ignores modern vernacular literature completely, helps to explain why Puttenham's account of the origins, progress, and kinds of poetry in Book 1 seems to have so little to do with English practices. Perhaps the riotous chapter on the epithalamion (chapter 26) is the best instance of this, where Puttenham's tabloid anthropology gets a free rein. Had Puttenham read more in the vernacular treatises of French and Italian authors, he might have felt obliged to say more about modern English literature and culture. But he may also have felt restrained by the paucity of great English literature. The account in chapter 31 might have seemed sufficient, and the need to be prescriptive in relation to classical examples pressing as Elizabethan England waited for the great lyric, epic, and dramatic works which came flooding from the press in the 1590s.

1. *And our English name ... they call a maker poeta*: *Poeta* is in fact the Latin word, derived from the Greek *poiētēs*. Cf. Sidney, p. 8 for this argument from etymology.

2. *Such as ... with their ideas do fantastically suppose*: For Platonic ideas – the ideal forms of things rather than their actual appearances or instantiations – see Sidney, note 30. Puttenham may also be referring to the elaborate creation story presented in Plato's *Timaeus*, where the demiurge (craftsman god) creates the world by using the forms as patterns.

3. *even so ... a versifier, but not a poet*: Cf. Sidney, p. 12 and Harington, p. 262, taking up this point from a translator's point of view.

4. *the true and lively of everything is set before him*: All texts and editions read 'the true and lively of everything' at this point. Puttenham does use ellipsis of the noun elsewhere (e.g. in Book 3, p. 180, on representing speech: 'in which report we must always give to every person his fit and natural'), and this is probably more likely than that a word has been omitted accidentally. The sense of 'quality, essence' is possible, but that of 'image' might

make better sense in the context ('lively' is almost invariably coupled with the noun 'image' or verbs meaning 'to represent' in Renaissance literary theory).

5. *and so in that respect . . . but also of imitation*: For imitation cf. Sidney, p. 10 and note 35. Instead of eliding making and imitation, Puttenham distinguishes the two; cf. Sidney, p. 36 for Plato's distinction between fantastic and icastic (likeness-making) imitation.

6. *And this science . . . the Platonics call it furor*: The Latin *furor* is the equivalent of the Greek *mania*; on the *furor poeticus* see Plato, *Ion*, and *Phaedrus*, 245a.

7. *Otherwise, how was it possible . . . all politic regiment*: Puttenham's rather mundane examples recall Plato, who, both in *Ion* and the *Republic*, points out that you would not go to a poet to find out about generalship or politics, but to a general or politician, and that, therefore, the claim of poets to have knowledge and be teachers is flawed.

8. *Finally, how could he . . . lamentable wars of Troy*: Referring to Homer's *Iliad*.

9. *But you (Madam) . . . all honour and regal magnificence*: Queen Elizabeth, to whom the *Art* is apparently dedicated, is presented here as a poet or 'maker' of lives rather than verses – a maker not of poems but of other people and herself. The associations of Venus (love), Diana (chastity, hunting), Pallas Athena (war, wisdom and the arts) and Juno (queen of the gods) were variously and habitually claimed for Elizabeth I.

10. *So as if one point . . . which they never observed*: See A Note on English Versification for the differences between classical quantitative metrics and the English system.

11. *For it is written that . . . perished and failing*: For this account of the civilizing effect of poetry cf. Sidney, pp. 4–5 and Horace, *Ars poetica*, 391–407. For the mythical (Amphion, Orpheus, Linus, Musaeus) and ancient (Musaeus, Hesiod) poets see Sidney, notes 6, 7 and 8. Puttenham's account of the early history of poetry in the opening chapters has numerous points of contact with Sidney's, since both draw on conventional accounts and the same Continental critics.

12. *the first prophets or seers, videntes . . . after the Hebrew word*: Found in the Vulgate (the Latin translation of the Bible) in the singular form, *videns*, translated in the Authorized Version as 'seer' (e.g. 1 Chronicles, 9:22, 2 Chronicles, 29:25); it is surprising that Puttenham does not make the connection here to the Latin

word *vates*, meaning both prophet and poet (cf. Sidney, p. 6).

13. *although to many of us . . . the same seem but a prose*: For the Renaissance understanding of Hebrew scriptural verse see Sidney, p. 7.

14. *But the Hebrews and Chaldees . . . by learned men*: See the above note; Puttenham's remarks are based on various misunderstandings, both by Renaissance scholars, and of what they had said.

15. *vulgar rhyming poesy*: See *ERLC* (197), which suggests this emendation of the 1589 text's 'vulgar *running* poesy'. Manuscript 'riming' and 'ruñing' would be easily confused by the printer.

16. *from the time of . . . Valentian downwards*: That is, the later fourth century AD.

17. *till, after many years . . . former purity and neatness*: Puttenham's historiography is always vague. Compare Daniel for a more sophisticated account of the origins of the Renaissance. The Eastern Roman Empire collapsed with the fall of Constantinople to the Ottoman Turks in 1453, causing the influx of Greek learning into Italy traditionally seen as kick-starting the Renaissance. Puttenham, however, refers to the reinstitution of the Western Roman Empire (which had collapsed in the fifth century AD) in 800 AD when Charlemagne (*c.* 741–814 AD), who as King of the Franks and later Lombardy had conquered most of western Christendom, was crowned Emperor of the West by Pope Leo III.

18. *For proof whereof . . . Alexander the Great*: Euripides (*c.* 485–407 or 406 BC) spent his last years at the court of a previous King of Macedonia, Archelaus; Sophocles (496–406 BC) was a prominent and distinguished Athenian citizen as well as the foremost tragedian; Plutarch's account in the *Life of Alexander* of Alexander's admiration of Homer is also used by Sidney (p. 37).

19. *insomuch as Choerilus . . . a Philip's noble of gold*: See Horace, *Epistles*, 2.1.232–4; a *Philippus* was a gold coin struck by Philip II of Macedonia, Alexander's father.

20. *And since Alexander the Great . . . Virgil also by the Emperor Augustus*: Theocritus (*c.* 300–*c.* 250 BC), Greek pastoral poet, was supported by Ptolemy II, Greek ruler of Egypt; for Ennius and Scipio, see Sidney, p. 38 and note.

21. *And in later times . . . Hardyng to Edward the Fourth*: Guillaume de Lorris (d. 1237) started the *Roman de la rose*, which was finished by Jean de Meung (*c.* 1275); although John of Gaunt's patronage of Geoffrey Chaucer (*c.* 1343–1400) was more significant than that of his nephew and enemy Richard II, Puttenham's

point is to associate major figures from the first age of English poetry – Chaucer, John Gower (?1330–1408), and John Hardyng (1378–c. 1465) – with the patronage of monarchs. Ewelme (1589: 'new Holme', and, in a subsequent mention, 'new Elme') was probably given to Chaucer's son Thomas, who is buried in the church there along with his daughter Alice, Duchess of Suffolk.

22. *Also how Francis the French king . . . in vulgar and Latin poesy*: Melin de Saint-Gelais (1491–1559); Jean Salmon 'Macrinus' (1490–1557); Clement Marot (1496–1544).

23. *And King Henry the Eighth . . . many other good gifts*: Thomas Sternhold (d. 1549), versifier of the Psalms (completed by John Hopkins and others), and groom of the robes to Henry VIII.

24. *And one Gray . . . the hunt is up*: Possibly a William Gray (d. 1551) whose birthday verses to Edward Seymour (1506?– 1552), Duke of Somerset and Protector in the first years of the short reign of Edward VI, survive. 'The hunt is up' was a popular ballad to the tune of which other ballads were written.

25. *And Queen Mary . . . two hundred crowns' pension*: Not certainly identified.

26. *For we find that Julius Caesar . . . be now extant*: Caesar (100– 44 BC) was of course assassinated before he got close to being emperor. He was an able orator, though Puttenham seems to forget that Cicero (106–43 BC) has a somewhat stronger claim.

27. *And Quintus Catulus . . . and Cornelius Gallus, treasurer of Egypt*: Quintus Lutatius Catulus (d. 87 BC), one of the interlocutors in Cicero's *De oratore*, was a prominent Roman statesman and general who wrote poetry. Gaius Cornelius Gallus (*c.* 69– 26 BC), the subject of his friend Virgil's tenth eclogue, was a supporter of Augustus and was appointed the first *Praefectus* of Egypt after the fall of Cleopatra in 30 BC; very little of his love poetry survives.

28. *And Horace . . . as it is reported*: Horace (65–8 BC) became closely associated with the Emperor Augustus through his patron Maecenas; he turned down Augustus' invitation to become his secretary; Puttenham quotes Cicero, *De republica* ('On the Republic'), 1.5.9.1.

29. *And Ennius, the Latin poet . . . amiable conversation*: Ennius (239–169 BC) accompanied Fulvius Nobilior to the wars (Cicero, *Pro Archia poeta*, 11) and not Scipio Africanus, whom Ennius praises in his poem *Scipio*; cf. Sidney, p. 38.

30. *And long before that . . . had charge in the wars*: *Politics*, 3.1285a. Antimenides was the brother of the lyric poet Alcaeus.

31. *And Tyrtaeus the poet . . . victory over his enemies*: On Tyrtaeus (fl. 670 BC) cf. Sidney, p. 5 and note.

32. *that part*: The imagination; Puttenham uses the standard Renaissance tripartite division of mind (or 'wit') into imagination (or 'conceit'), judgement and memory.

33. *yea, the prince of philosophers . . . as learned men know*: Aristotle, *De memoria* ('On Memory'), 450a and *De anima* ('On the Soul'), 431a; Puttenham also refers to the Peripatetic philosopher Alexander of Aphrodisias (fl. 200 AD), celebrated as a commentator on Aristotle, and author of his own *De anima* ('On the Soul').

34. *not phantastikoi but euphantasiōtoi*: From Quintilian's important discussion of *ēthos* and *pathos*. We all dream and daydream: 'It is the man who is really sensitive to such impressions who will have the greatest power over the emotions. Some writers describe the possessor of this power of vivid imagination, whereby things, words and actions are presented in the most realistic manner, by the Greek word *euphantasiōtos* . . . From such impressions arises that *enargeia* . . . which makes us seem not so much to narrate as to exhibit the actual scene, while our emotions will be no less actively stirred than if we were present at the actual occurrence' (*Institutio oratoria*, 6.2.29–36).

35. *Master Alain Chartier*: Alain Chartier (*c.* 1385–*c.* 1433), author of *La belle dame sans mercy* (1424), secretary to Charles VI (1368–1422; reigned from 1380), whose wife was Isabella of Bavaria, and to Charles VII (1403–61; reigned from 1422), whose wife was Mary of Anjou. Chartier was long dead by the time of the reigns of Charles VIII (1470–98; reigned from 1483) and Louis XII (1462–1515; reigned from 1498).

36. *But methinks at these words . . . for my rhyming*: Referring to the story about Chaucer and Richard II, above, p. 68.

37. *the fair young lad Endymion as he lay asleep*: Endymion slept eternally and was visited nightly by Selene (the moon, also personified by the Greek goddess Artemis/Cynthia, and the Roman goddess Diana). Queen Elizabeth I was frequently represented as Cynthia, which is part of the fun here for Puttenham.

38. *rex multitudinem . . . regenti similis est*: Not identified.

39. *So as I know . . . amorous of any good art*: Puttenham engages with the gentlemanly preference for manuscript circulation and fear of the so-called 'stigma of print'. Sidney's works, for example, circulated in manuscript and were only printed in the decade after his death. Puttenham does not follow his own advice: his poems

remained in manuscript, apart from the fragments used as illustrations in the *Art*, and the *Art* itself was published anonymously.

40. *Julius Caesar, the greatest of emperors . . . diverse philosophical works*: Julius Caesar, assassinated in 44 BC, wrote the *Civil War* (after 48 BC) and the *Gallic War* (after 52 BC). Hermes Trismegistus ('thrice-great Hermes') was the name given by Neoplatonists to the Egyptian god Thoth; from the third century AD the name was attached to various Neoplatonic 'Hermetic' writings which acquired a new influence in the Renaissance. Evax is mentioned by some classical writers as an author and king of Arabia. Avicenna (980–1037 AD), Persian philosopher and physician, and commentator on Aristotle. Alfonso X 'the Wise' (*c.* 1221–84 AD), King of Castile and León, made his court at Toledo a centre for Christian, Arab, and Jewish scholars, and compiled a legal code. Almanzor: probably Ya'qūb al-Mansūr (*c.* 1160–99), third Mu'minid ruler.

41. *our late sovereign lord . . . was nothing less to be allowed*: Henry VIII's *Assertio septem sacramentorum* ('Defence of the Seven Sacraments', 1521), against Luther, which earned him the title *fidei defensor* ('Defender of the Faith') from Pope Leo X. His break from Rome was in the 1530s.

42. *as Lady Margaret of France, Queen of Navarre*: Margaret of Navarre (1492–1549), author of the collection of tales known after its printing in 1559 as the *Heptameron*.

43. *But of all others . . . this shameful death*: Suetonius, *Life of Nero*, 49.1, possibly via Erasmus, *Apophthegmata* ('Apophthegms').

44. *The Emperor Octavian . . . and put his name to them*: An interpolation in some texts of Donatus' *Life of Virgil*, 38–9; the full poem from which the lines are taken is no. 672 in the *Latin Anthology* (the lines quoted are ll. 20–22).

45. *There were others that . . . thereupon were called poets mimists*: Puttenham coins the term 'mimist'. A mime was an ancient farce, using stock characters; the word was also used of the actor who performed in mimes.

46. *There was another kind of poem . . . they were called pantomimi*: From the Greek *pantomīmos*, 'imitator of all'. Roman actors of dumb shows, representing various characters and scenes through mimicry.

47. *though in very deed . . . De natura deorum*: Cicero, *De natura deorum* ('On the Nature of the Gods'), throughout and, e.g., 1.14.36–16.43 and 2.23.60–28.70.

48. *But that he should be . . . teachers of wisdom to others*: This

argument indirectly addresses Plato, *Republic*, 2. Cf. Sidney, pp. 39–40.

49. *But with us Christians ... self-suffisant (autarkēs)*: The 1589 text reads '*autharcos*', confounding *autarkēs* ('self-sufficient') with *autarchos* ('sovereign', 'despot'), the spelling perhaps further influenced by 'author'.

50. *the very etymology of the name ... a giver of good things*: An etymological connection between 'good' and 'god' (or, for instance, in German 'gut' and 'Gott') seemed plausible, although it is not supported by modern philology.

51. *Hierotechnē*: 'sacred art/skill' (Puttenham's coinage, spelled '*Ierotekni*' in the original text). This seems to refer to one of the author's many lost works.

52. *And the first ... were called satirists*: This account of the origins of satire, typical for Puttenham in both following and colouring in conventional accounts (e.g. Scaliger's), depends on a faulty understanding of the etymology of 'satire' which arose in Roman times. The Latin *satira*, originally *satura*, came from *satura* (related to *satis*, 'enough'), a plate of various types of fruit or a dish composed of various ingredients, and hence a medley or hotchpotch. The word was later spelled *satyra*, on the erroneous assumption that the genre was actually connected with the Greek *saturos* (Latinized as *satyrus*), the mythical wood-deities, and the *saturoi*, the Satyr plays which concluded tragic trilogies.

53. *But as time and experience ... the New Comedy came in place*: Aristophanes (*c.* 448–380 BC) was the last major figure of the 'Old Comedy', and the only one whose plays survive; the 'New Comedy' of Menander (*c.* 342–292 BC) was taken up by the Romans Plautus (*c.* 254–184 BC) and Terence (*c.* 190–159 BC).

54. *till one Roscius Gallus ... to hide his own ill-favoured face*: Admired as both a comic and a tragic actor, Roscius Gallus did indeed play in a mask to hide his squint; he wrote a treatise on acting and oratory, ran a dramatic school, and was admired by Cicero, who on one occasion acted as his advocate in a civil suit. Cicero makes him a byword for perfection in any art (*De oratore*, 1.28.130), and throughout *De oratore* uses him as a touchstone in discussion of oratorical pronunciation and gesture.

55. *the common players of interludes called planipedes*: Latin *planipes* (sing.), 'flat-foot', 'barefoot'.

56. *they call in Spain and Italy cioppini*: A chopine (Spanish *chapin*) was indeed a high cork-soled shoe, worn in Spain and Italy, especially Venice, and used in England only on the stage. The

word exists in Spanish and French dictionaries only, but Putten-ham's contemporaries gave the word an Italian form (1589: 'Shoppini'). The word 'pantofle', more loosely any kind of slipper, was often used of this sort of shoe. For the tragic buskin and comic *soccus* see Drayton, note 18.

57. *forasmuch as a goat . . . stately plays were called tragedies*: The original meaning of 'tragedy' (Greek *tragōdia*, 'goat-song') remains disputed.

58. *All this I do agree unto . . . or chevisance*: *Politics*, 1.1256a–b.

59. *under the veil . . . Tityrus and Corydon*: Cf. Sidney, p. 26.

60. *Mantuan*: neo-Latin pastoral poet (1448–1516), much used in schools.

61. *remissness*: (1589: 'remisses').

62. *These historical men . . . the writer's great blame*: Cf. Sidney, pp. 18–21 and Bacon, p. 289. Puttenham's approach is different to Sidney's. All types of story are included in the category 'histori-cal poesy', including feigned histories like those of Virgil in the *Aeneid* or Sidney in the *Arcadia*, which for Sidney would occupy the very different category of 'heroical poesy'.

63. *Such was the commonwealth of Plato . . . Utopia*: i.e. Plato's *Republic*; More's *Utopia* was printed in Latin in 1516, and in Ralph Robinson's English translation in 1551; cf. Sidney, p. 17.

64. *For as Homer wrate . . . of the posterity*: Puttenham refers to Homer, *Iliad* and *Odyssey*; Musaeus' *Hero and Leander*; Thucyd-ides' *History* ('The Peloponnesian War'); and Xenophon's *Cyro-paedia* (cf. Sidney's constant reference to this).

65. *Hymns and encomia of Pindarus and Callimachus*: Pindar (518–438 BC): all his surviving work is panegyric. Callimachus (*c.* 310–*c.* 245 BC): hymns, epigrams and fragments of other works survive.

66. *old adventures and valiances . . . and others like*: Many verse and prose romances concerned the Arthurian legends; *Bevis of Hampton* and *Guy of Warwick* are popular medieval verse romances, both anonymous and written *c.* 1300. In each case contemporary ballad versions of these stories would have been known to Puttenham.

67. *augent animos fortunae, saith the mimist*: Not identified.

68. *Irus the beggar . . . Homer maketh mention of*: Irus in *Odyssey*, 18; Thersites in *Iliad*, 2.

69. *not with any medicament . . . a long and grievous sorrow*: Refer-ring to the followers of Galen (129–99 AD), the most influential

ancient medical theorist in the Middle Ages and Renaissance, and of Paracelsus (1493–1541), a controversial and influential physician who burned Galen's works. The differences between them are not as simple as Puttenham suggests, but Paracelsians 'did base much of their system on the doctrine of signatures, those apparent similarities between various levels of creation, so using a yellow plant to cure jaundice, for instance' (*ERLC*, 207 n. 31).

70. *placing a limping hexameter after a lusty hexameter*: The classical elegiac couplet.

71. *they were called epithalamies … at the bedding of the bride*: The Greek name *epithalamion* (pl. *epithalamia*) comes from *epi*, 'upon', and *thalamos*, 'bedchamber' or 'marriage-bed'.

72. *fits*: Cf. Jonson's 'A Fit of Rhyme against Rhyme'.

73. *sicut sponsa de thalamo*: Adapted from Psalm 19.5.

74. *Fescennina licentia*: 'Fescennine licence'. Fescennine verses, named after a town in Etruria, were a form of ribald or abusive Latin dialogue, surviving to later times in the form of lascivious wedding songs. Horace discusses them as part of the rustic origins of Latin drama in *Epistles*, 2.1.139–55 (*Fescennina … licentia*, l. 145).

75. *a young nobleman, of Germany … in my judgement*: The popular *Basia* ('Kisses' or 'Kissing Poems') of Johannes Secundus, an early sixteenth-century neo-Latin poet, depart from Catullus' famous poems on kissing, including 5 (*Vivamus, mea Lesbia*, 'Let us live and love, my Lesbia'), 7 and 99.

76. *For this epigram … or mantle of a chimney*: The Greek *epigramma* means 'inscription', from *epi*, 'upon', and *graphein*, 'to write'.

77. *An epitaph is … upon a tomb in few verses*: The Greek *epitaphion* comes from *epi*, 'upon', and *taphos*, 'stone'.

78. *They were called nenia or apophoreta*: While a *nenia* was a funeral song, or mournful song of any kind, the word was occasionally used (e.g. Horace, *Epistles*, 1.1.62) for a trifling or nursery song. *Apophoreta* were presents given to guests, especially at the Saturnalia (the Roman festival, in mid-December, in honour of Saturn); also the title of the fourteenth book of Martial's epigrams.

79. *never contained above one verse … we call them posies*: The term 'posy' is still used of bunches of flowers, although the flowers were originally metaphorical, since the word is simply a shortened form of 'poesy'. Renaissance poets exploited this double meaning: see, e.g., George Gascoigne's *A Hundreth Sundrie Flowres*

Bounde up in One Small Poesie (1573) and *The Posies of George Gascoigne* (1575).

80. *Who in any age . . . the author's censure given upon them*: This chapter is almost certainly a later interpolation, *c.* 1585, in a book for the most part anchored in the 1560s and 1570s; this impression seems confirmed by the end of the previous chapter, which points forward to Book 2 as if closing Book 1. Puttenham, following Continental examples, offers what is the first historical survey of English literature; this type of conspectus was attempted frequently in subsequent decades.

81. *And I will not reach . . . wrote in English metre*: i.e. the time of Chaucer (Edward III ruled 1327-77, Richard II 1377-99).

82. *those of the first age . . . as I suppose, knights*: Geoffrey Chaucer (*c.* 1343-1400), author of *The Canterbury Tales* and *Troilus and Criseyde*; John Gower (?1330-1408), author of the *Confessio Amantis* ('Confession of a Lover'). Neither was a knight.

83. *After whom followed . . . Piers Plowman*: John Lydgate (?1370-1449), who spent most of his life in the monastery of Bury St Edmunds, was the author of various Chaucerian works, and the *Troy Book* and *The Fall of Princes*, both translations. The great poem of the middle English alliterative revival, *Piers Plowman* (written and revised between *c.* 1367 and *c.* 1386), is now attributed on purely internal evidence to William Langland.

84. *Next him followed Hardyng . . . surnamed the poet laureate*: John Hardyng (1378-*c.* 1465), author of a verse history of Britain from the time of the mythical Brutus (supposed to be the great-grandson of Aeneas and founder of the British race) to 1437; John Skelton (?1460-1529), tutor to the future Henry VIII, satirical poet, and inventor of so-called skeltonic verse (on which see Book 2, p. 125), was created 'poet laureate' by both universities (see Sidney, note 150 for the significance of such laureations).

85. *In the latter end . . . our English metre and style*: Sir Thomas Wyatt (1503-42), as an imitator of Petrarch and classical authors, was an important forerunner of Elizabethan and Jacobean poets. Henry Howard, Earl of Surrey (?1517-47), like Wyatt an important imitator of Italian models, introduced the English sonnet form and was arguably the first knowingly to use the iambic pentameter in his innovative blank verse translation of *Aeneid* Books 2 and 4. Puttenham names three major Italian poets, although Petrarch is the most important model in both cases: Dante Alighieri (1265-1321), author of the *Divina Commedia*; Ludovico Ariosto (1474-1535), author of *Orlando furioso* and

satires imitated by Wyatt; and Francesco Petrarca (1304–74), author of the *Canzoniere* ('Poems').

86. *Lord Nicholas Vaux ... in vulgar makings*: Puttenham means Thomas, Lord Vaux (1509–56), whose poems were included in *Songs and Sonnets* ('Tottel's Miscellany', 1557) and *The Paradise of Dainty Devices* (1576), an important anthology of mid-century and early Elizabethan verse.

87. *Afterward, in King Edward the Sixth's time ... by the King*: Thomas Sternhold (d. 1549), whose common metre translations of the Psalms were augmented by John Hopkins and others; John Heywood (?1497–?1580), author of comic interludes, dialogue, satire and collections of proverbs and epigrams.

88. *But the principal man ... many good rewards*: Puttenham means George Ferrers (c. 1500–79), who planned and contributed to *A Mirror for Magistrates* (see Sidney, note 228) wrote plays and masques, and was Master of the King's Pastimes under Edward VI.

89. *In Queen Mary's time ... Virgil's Aeneidos*: Thomas Phaer (?1510–1560), lawyer, physician and translator of Books 1–9 and part of Book 10 of Virgil's *Aeneid*.

90. *Since him followed Master Arthur Golding ... Master Phaer left undone*: Arthur Golding (?1536–?1605) was a prolific translator, whose important version of Ovid's *Metamorphoses* was published in 1565–7; Thomas Twyne (1543–1613), physician, published a completed version of Phaer's *Aeneid* in 1584.

91. *Of which number is first ... no little commendation*: This list, dominated by manuscript authors, is given in order of rank rather than, necessarily, merit, beginning with nobles, continuing with gentry courtiers, and ending with Gascoigne, Breton and Turberville, neither courtiers nor given their first names by Puttenham, and, apart from Buckhurst, the only poets in print when Puttenham wrote: Edward de Vere, Earl of Oxford (1550–1604), author of various much-copied lyric poems; Thomas Sackville, Baron Buckhurst and later Earl of Dorset (1536–1608), contributor to *A Mirror for Magistrates*, author of *Gorboduc* with Thomas Norton (on which see Sidney, p. 44), and dedicatee of Campion's *Observations*; Henry, second Baron Paget, not now known as a poet; Sir Philip Sidney (1554–86), whose *Arcadia* Puttenham must have seen in manuscript; Sir Walter Ralegh (?1554–1618), favourite of Queen Elizabeth I, lyric poet and, later, author of *The History of the World* (1614); Edward Dyer (1543–1607), lyric poet and friend of Sidney; Fulke Greville, later Lord Brooke

(1554-1628), poet and dramatist, friend of Sidney and Dyer; George Gascoigne (c. 1534-77), on whom see the Introduction, p. lxxii; Nicholas Breton (?1555-1626), prolific verse and prose author; George Turberville (c. 1544-c. 1597), poet and translator.

92. *And though many of his books . . . Jean de Meung's, a French poet*: The story of *Troilus and Criseyde* is taken from Boccaccio's *Il filostrato*. Only the first 1,705 lines of *The Romaunt of the Rose* are now attributed to Chaucer; this translates the French of Guillaume de Lorris (d. 1237), the *Roman de la rose* being finished by Jean de Meung (c. 1275).

93. *the staff of seven and the verse of ten*: *Troilus and Criseyde* is written in 'rhyme royal', a seven-line stanza, with lines approximating Elizabethan pentameter in length. On these terms see Book 2.

94. *pantomimi*: The Latin form (in Greek *pantomīmos, -oi*).

95. *the Earl of Oxford . . . for comedy and interlude*: Richard Edwards (?1523-66), Master of the Children of the Chapel Royal (a company of child players), author of plays and entertainments, and compiler of *The Paradise of Dainty Devices*. No plays by Oxford are known.

96. *Master Chaloner, and that other gentleman . . . Shepheardes Calender*: Sir Thomas Chaloner (1521-65), who published Latin verses and translations from the Latin; by 'that other gentleman' Puttenham means Edmund Spenser (c. 1552-99), whose *Shepheardes Calender* was published under the name 'Immerito' in 1579.

THE SECOND BOOK:
OF PROPORTION POETICAL

As Puttenham claims at the end of chapter 30 of Book 1, the second Book of the *Art* is far more original than the first. There were numerous books of poetics and rhetoric for him to borrow from in Books 1 and 3 and in some of the general material in Book 2, but no one had previously treated the subject of English versification in any great detail. What is most original about Puttenham's observations is his discussion of rhyme and his emphasis on the patterning of rhyme schemes and the visual aspect of verse form (see especially chapter 11), since this opens a new avenue to our understanding of English Renaissance poetry. His treatment of metre is confused and confusing, caught between the loose lines of the earlier sixteenth century, the foot-based approach already outlined by Gascoigne, the classical experiments of Sidney and others which had both confirmed a foot-based prosody and liberated it from Gascoigne's over-regularity, and Puttenham's own sympathy for a syllabic prosody based on the example of Romance languages. It is important to remember that Puttenham probably wrote much of Book 2 in the 1560s and 1570s, before the theory and practice of first Gascoigne and then Sidney had become current. The notes may be supplemented by A Note on English Versification. Unless otherwise indicated, verse quotations are assumed to be of Puttenham's composition.

1. *The doctors of our theology . . . number, measure and weight*: Cf. Wisdom of Solomon (one of the Apocrypha), 11:21: 'Thou hast ordered all things by measure and number and weight'.

2. *The Italian called it stanza . . . a resting place*: The Italian *stanza* means 'room'.

3. *The fourth is in seven verses . . . translated, not devised*: *Troilus and Criseyde*, by Geoffrey Chaucer (*c.* 1343–1400), is based on *Il filostrato* by Boccaccio; *The Fall of Princes*, by John Lydgate (?1370–1449), is based on Boccaccio's *De casibus virorum illustrium* ('The Falls of Famous Men'). Both are written in 'rhyme royal' (*ababbcc*).

4. *Then last of all . . . a round or virelay*: With the exception of the generic 'song', all so-called fixed forms. Carol: medieval lyric of distinct verse + refrain structure. Ballad: in English any popular song, but the Old French *ballade* was a fixed form, typically three eight-line octosyllabic stanzas and a four-line *envoi*. Round: either the *rondel*, another French fixed form, of determined length with certain lines repeated, or the *rondeau*, a fixed form in three stanzas with only two rhymes, the opening words forming the refrain. Virelay: another French fixed form of three verses with refrains.

5. *A staff of four verses . . . full period or complement of sense*: The classical period (explained colourfully by Puttenham in chapter 5) was a unit of prose rhythm rather than of syntax, corresponding in size to a long sentence or short paragraph. It was divided ('by divisions') into *cola* and *commata*; our names for marks of punctuation – comma, colon, period – derive from the theory of the classical period.

6. *Therefore, if ye make your staff . . . but two quatrains*: That is to say, *abababcc* may be called a huitain, but *ababcdcd* may not.

7. *Metre and measure . . . the Latins call mensura*: 'Metre' derives

from the Greek *metron* (Latin *metrum*), 'measure' from the Latin *mensura*; both mean 'measure'.

8. *namely, the bissyllable ... two short and a long*: The English names for these feet: spondee (- -), pyrrhic (˘ ˘), trochee (- ˘), iamb (˘ -), dactyl (- ˘ ˘), molossus (- - -), tribrach (˘ ˘ ˘), amphibrach (˘ - ˘), amphimacer (- ˘ -); Puttenham reverses the definitions of amphibrach and amphimacer, and omits the anapaest (˘ ˘ -).

9. *But this proceeded ... of two and an unity*: As Puttenham uses 'number' here it cannot include the number one: a 'number' is an aggregate of things, whereas the number one is 'an unity', something complete in itself.

10. *which was in Greek ... this word 'rhyme'*: Both 'rhyme' and 'rhythm' derive from the Greek *rhythmos* (Latin *rhythmus*), denoting a flowing harmony or patterning in music or speech, as Puttenham explains in chapter 6. 'Rhythm' developed in the sixteenth century as an alternative, etymologically correct spelling of 'rime' (or 'ryme'), and later took on its separate meaning, at which point the spelling of 'rime' was also reformed; the two words are often synonymous in Puttenham's time.

11. *To return from rhyme ... bounds of good proportion*: Puttenham neglects the common 'fourteener' (used in works much admired by him, such as Golding's translation of Ovid's *Metamorphoses*) in suggesting that lines of more than twelve syllables 'pass the bounds of good proportion'.

12. *their cesure*: Puttenham intends to anglicize the Latin term *caesura*; this form derives from the French *césure*.

13. *The smoky sighs ... but still be swerving*: Anonymous, from the work Puttenham uses almost as a textbook, *Songs and Sonnets* (1557) (also known as 'Tottel's Miscellany'), no. 214, 1–4, 7–10.

14. *odd*: Emended (1589: 'all').

15. *And all the reason why ... as the word 'swérving'*: This passage demonstrates how Puttenham's ear and metrical theory lag behind the practice of most of the poets he quotes. By Sidney's time it would not be possible to alternate lines with odd and even numbers of syllables without this meaning a strict alternation of iambic and trochaic lines, or of masculine and feminine endings. The quoted example alternates masculine and feminine endings (the latter typically based on -ed and -ing endings) within an iambic scheme (alternating eight-syllable masculine tetrameter and seven-syllable feminine trimeter). The line 'Not love but still

be swerving' does indeed seem 'shorter' than the line 'Love it is a marvellous thing' because the latter is a four-stress (tetrameter) trochaic line and the former an iambic trimeter with a feminine ending. Both have seven syllables, but one has three stresses, the other four. Puttenham seems to hear the second line as something like iambic trimeter, with the stress on 'thing' somehow preventing that on either of the syllables of 'marvellous' (pronounced 'marv'lous'). Puttenham's musical terminology for syllable quality ('sharp', 'flat') recalls Gascoigne's, pp. 239–40.

16. *Now suck child . . . as ball of mine eye*: Found in manuscript, e.g. BL Harl. MS 7392, fol. 31ʳ. Puttenham's comments are again erroneous. The poem is metrically regular, but in a four-stress triple metre rather than the vaguely duple metre which Puttenham's ear is groping towards: 'Nŏw sūck chĭld ănd slēep chĭld, thў mōthĕr's ŏwn jŏy'.

17. *'When raging love, with extreme pain'*: The first line of a poem included in 'Tottel's Miscellany', no. 16.

18. *'Solomon, David's son, King of Jerusalem'*: Ecclesiastes, 1:1, in Surrey's paraphrase (which reads 'I Solomon') in poulter's measure (which alternates hexameter and fourteener lines). Cf. Webbe, p. 255, for the observation that long lines can be cut in half.

19. *This verse . . . oddness is nothing pleasant to the ear*: After Sidney, poets would deliberately aim at the effect in Surrey's line of reversing the first foot, so that the accent falls on the first syllable (the *'antepenultima'* in 'Sōlŏmŏn').

20. *Judge somebody . . . in the other verse*: There seems to be some corruption here, caused by the compositor's eye skipping between similar phrases in the manuscript copy. The intended sense may be: 'for now the sharp accent falls upon "restóre", and so doth it upon the last in "unto", which was not in the other verse.' Puttenham seems by this point in the chapter to have accepted the iambic pattern, as indicated by the marks of stress on every other syllable of 'Restóre King Dávid's són untó Jerúsalém'.

21. *The shortest pause . . . as the comma*: Puttenham's glosses allude to Greek etymology: *komma*, from *koptein*, 'to cut'; *kōlon*, 'limb'.

22. *The third they called periodus . . . to enlarge the tale*: See note 5, for the classical period. Puttenham's treatment of 'pauses' is symptomatic of the shift in the understanding of the comma-colon-period hierarchy from units of prose rhythm to the marks of punctuation which with increasing consistency were used to mark their respective ends.

23. *But our ancient rhymers . . . riding rhyme*: 'Riding rhyme' is the
      couplet form used by Chaucer and others, its line approximating
      in length to pentameter but probably regulated by a four-stress
      system. Many of Puttenham's contemporaries believed that
      Chaucer's line was close to that of sixteenth-century poets; it is
      true that Wyatt's line is closer to Chaucer's than is Gascoigne's,
      but the belief was supported either by discovering more metrical
      regularity in Chaucer than now seems feasible, or by perceiving
      less in the poets of the mid-century onwards than we now do.

24. *Because we use . . . though by manner of abusion*: See note 10.

25. *And for this purpose . . . every polysyllable word*: An accurate
      explanation of the preference in English versification for mascu-
      line rhyme: monosyllabic words can be stressed or unstressed
      'indifferently', and so, since the rhyme sound must be stressed 'of
      necessity', finding a masculine rhyme is far easier in English,
      with its many Anglo-Saxon monosyllables, than in the Romance
      languages; cf. Sidney, p. 52.

26. *There is an accountable number . . . rhythmos or numerosity*: On
      arithmos and *rhythmos* Puttenham follows Scaliger, *Poetices*,
      2.2.

27. *which concords the Greeks nor Latins . . . as hath been before
      remembered*: In Puttenham, Book 1, chapters 6–7.

28. *And yet the Greeks and Latins . . . homoioteleuton*: The figure of
      homoioteleuton ('same ending') is dealt with in Puttenham's Book
      3, chapter 16; in rhetorical theory it is of course a feature of
      the rhetorical patterning of prose (e.g. in the anonymous *Ad
      Herennium*, 4.20.28; Quintilian, *Institutio oratoria*, 9.3.77–80).

29. *or perchance the middle . . . in metres that be long*: An allusion
      either to internal rhyme schemes, or to verses in trimeter and
      tetrameter which might be grouped by twos into long lines of
      hexameter or fourteeners (on the obverse see note 18).

30. *unless it be by usurpation . . . to match them*: Puttenham is saying
      that a word like 'honourable' carries two stresses, and would in
      normal poetry be positioned so that its second stress, 'áble', was
      the last in the line and marked the beginning of a rhyme with
      such a word as 'miserable'. By counting, in each of the polysyllabic
      words given, only the greater of the two stresses, on the first
      syllable ('usurpation'), 'matrimony' can be rhymed with 'patri-
      mony' rather than only, say, 'milk and honey'.

31. *But always the cadence . . . the sweeter musics*: Puttenham's
      commonsense judgement seems borne out by subsequent practice,
      especially Byron's. However, Sidney did attempt to use polysyllabic

rhymes to amplify passion rather than comic effect, as in the elegiac lament for Basilius, 'Since that to death is gone that shepherd high' (*Poems of Sidney*, ed. Ringler, OA 75).

32. *As, if one cadence be . . . a delicate ear*: Rhyme cannot extend back to the initial consonant(s) of the last syllable cluster in the line, but is a matter only of the medial vowel and terminal consonant(s). The exception is 'rich rhyme', where words or syllables of identical sound differ either in meaning, or in meaning and spelling, e.g. 'may' / 'May', 'knight' / 'night'. Since spelling ('orthography') was flexible in early modern English, it could be manipulated to give the appearance of rhyme, or to play up or play down rich rhyme. The same, but to a lesser extent, went for pronunciation. Puttenham returns to these questions in the omitted portions of the following chapter.

33. *For some words . . . fetched from the Latin inkhorn*: Puttenham alludes lightly to the so-called 'inkhorn controversy'. The inkhorn was a portable vessel for carrying ink and came to symbolize pedantry. 'Inkhorn terms' or 'inkhornisms' were pedantic words usually derived from Latin and Greek. Some writers were excessive in their use of loan words and nonce words; whilst Puttenham coins many words of his own, and makes many inkhornisms current, he usually glosses them with a familiar term, and more generally utilizes a solid Anglo-Saxon lexicon. He returns in detail to this subject in Book 3, chapter 4.

34. *in some other place of this book*: In Book 3, chapter 25.

35. *Note also that . . . common rhymers use it much*: Various forms of internal rhyme patterning were popular in English and especially French medieval lyrics, derived from medieval Latin verse forms such as leonine rhyme and tail rhyme (the short rhyming lines *aabccb* developed by sectioning long internally rhymed lines). Sidney experimented with internal rhyme schemes.

36. *or else by blind harpers . . . Clym of the Clough*: Cf. Book I, p. 92 and Sidney, p. 28. Bevis of Hampton and Guy of Warwick are figures from medieval verse romances, and figured in contemporary ballad versions. Adam Bell and Clym of the Clough are northern equivalents of Robin Hood, figuring in numerous popular ballads. Chaucer parodies such tales in 'Chaucer's Tale of Sir Thopas' in *The Canterbury Tales*, both in its subject (Bevis and Guy are both mentioned) and in its use of tail rhyme.

37. *Such were the rhymes of Skelton . . . poet laureate*: See Book I, note 84.

38. *And the proportion is double . . . with relation one to another*:

Puttenham's simple observation that the lines of a stanza can be connected with each other by either rhyme or line length is of great importance to subsequent lyric practice. Classical stanzas were of course formed only by using a variety of line lengths, and the variety of verse forms used by such poets as Horace informs the assumption, both in this chapter and in the subsequent metrical experimentation it perhaps inspired, that variety is a virtue.

39. *Which manner of situation ... leisure or precipitation*: The ancient Greek modes were the equivalent of keys. The modes as used in medieval church music and heard by Puttenham derived from and were named after the classical modes but did not always correspond to them. A mode can be heard by playing an octave scale on the white notes of the piano keyboard and observing the different patterns of tones and semitones which make up the scale; these will vary depending on which note the scale begins on ('mounting and falling from note to note such as be to them peculiar'). Puttenham's observations derive from such discussions as Plato's (*Republic*, 397–403) and Aristotle's (*Politics*, 1341b– 1342b). Each mode had associated with it a certain type of music in respect of tempo ('more or less leisure or precipitation') and characteristic rhythms. Aristotle observes that melodies are divided into 'melodies of character, melodies of action, and passionate or inspiring melodies, each having a mode corresponding to it', and he notes the qualities of some of these modes: the Dorian 'is the gravest and manliest', the Phrygian mode suits Bacchic frenzy, the Lydian 'is suited to children of tender age, and possesses the elements both of order and of education'. The theory of modes is of great importance for an understanding of the direct equation assumed by Renaissance theorists between a type of poetic music and the emotions it could evoke. Cf. Sidney, note 157.

40. *Where ye see the concord ... fourth, sixth, or second distances*: 'In the third distance' means that two lines fall between the lines matched by either rhyme or line length. In fact the diagram represents, on the left, rhyme 'in the second distance' (rhyming *abab*), and, on the near right (working from the outside in), measure in the seventh, fifth, third and first distances, and, on the far right, in the first, second and third (but not in that order).

41. *Second distance is when ... as*: i.e. cross rhyme: *aba ...*

42. *In which case ... any other ye like better*: For example, *abcabc* or *abba*.

43. *There be larger distances . . . with other distances not so large, as*: E.g. *abccba*, which the diagram below represents.

44. *coupling of staves*: some longer stanzas would break down into shorter stanzaic units if rhymes were not shared between those shorter units.

45. *Petrarch hath given us . . . his canzoni*: The name *canzone* (from the Italian for 'song') is used of any Italian verse form, either sung or of musical origin. The Petrarchan *canzone*, however, was an elaborate lyric with lengthy, intricate stanzas.

46. *And all that can be objected . . . but not the learned*: Puttenham appears to be saying that it is 'not the learned' ear which is 'not satisfied' by the lengthy deferral of rhyme, but rather 'the rude and popular ear'.

47. *Besides all this . . . ocular examples, as thus*: 'Plain compass' (i.e. counter or envelope rhyme) requires mirror symmetry, so *abba* (as in the diagram) is of plain compass, as is *abccba*, but *abab* and *abcbca*, for example, are not. *Intertangle* is what we call cross rhyme, e.g. *ababab*, as in the diagram.

48. *And first, in a quatrain . . . but two proportions*: Illustrating envelope *abba*, and cross-rhymed *abab*, and two couplets *aabb*.

49. *Now, ye may perceive . . . perpendicularity of the wall*: Bricks or cut stones must be laid so that the joins in one course do not come vertically above or below the joins in neighbouring courses. This was usually achieved by laying bricks both with the long side showing (a 'stretcher') and with the short side showing (a 'header'), meaning the wall was at least as thick as the length (and two breadths) of a brick. The different patterns possible are still known as 'bonds'. Puttenham perhaps refers to that known as 'English bond', a course of stretchers alternating with a course of headers ('a length to two breadths'), ensuring that the joins of neighbouring courses did not coincide by setting headers alternatively over the centre of a stretcher and then over its join. Or he may refer to 'Flemish bond': while all that appears is a simple alternation of header and stretcher throughout each course, a cross-section from above shows the 'breadths' of two stretchers laid against the 'length' of one header. Architectural metaphors are of fundamental importance to Renaissance versification, but few theorists take them this literally.

50. *Yet Chaucer and others . . . serve the ear well enough*: An important observation about the lack of cohesion in many stanzas (including the English sonnet) which end with an independent couplet. Puttenham singles out the sextain *ababcc* and 'rhyme

royal' *ababbcc*, which combines the cohesion of 'intertangle' or cross rhyme in its first half and the independence of separate couplets in its second.

51. *And as there is ... versus intercalaris*: The *locus classicus* is Virgil, *Eclogues*, 8, a song from Damon followed by one from Alphesiboeus, each alternating three, four or five lines of hexameter with a repeated refrain line. Refrain poems and fixed forms based on repeating refrains were very common in medieval and early Renaissance lyric poetry. Cf. the treatment of *epimone* as a figure of speech in Book 3, p. 176.

52. The diagrams (from left to right) represent stanza forms according to line length, as follows (number of syllables): (i) 9 lines: 6, 8, 12, 12, 8, 6, 8, 10, 12; (ii) 6 lines: 10, 8, 6, 6, 8, 10; (iii) 9 lines: 10, 10, 4, 4, 10, 10, 4, 4, 10; (iv) 9 lines: 10, 10, 10, 10, 4, 6, 6, 6, 4; and (v) 14 lines: 4, 10, 10, 10, 10, 10, 4, 10, 10, 10, 10, 10, 10, 4.

53. *Which manner of proportion ... to the hearer's mind*: Rhyme did not always coincide with line length, but in the most common forms (e.g. ballad $a_8b_6a_8b_6$) it did; the second form here, for example, could match the 'plain compass' rhyme scheme *abccba*, to give $a_{10}b_8cc_6b_8a_{10}$.

54. *Then, where you will have ... as ye have seen before described*: Other poets, such as Drayton, used this system in print to explain their rhyme schemes, and it would seem that it was the only means available to poets for mapping out stanza forms, the alphabetical notation now used being a later development.

55. *Of proportion in figure*: Shape or pattern poetry (in Latin *carmina figurata*) takes its lead from six surviving Greek poems shaped as an axe, an egg, wings, two altars and a syrinx, and a third-century AD cycle of Latin poems shaped as squares. Popular in the early Middle Ages, it underwent a resurgence in the sixteenth century. Although most did not take Puttenham's cue, the shape poems of George Herbert (including 'The Altar' and 'Easter-wings') are well regarded, and the discipline was popular until scorned by the neoclassical poetics of the later seventeenth to eighteenth centuries.

56. *Your last proportion ... an ocular representation*: Puttenham goes on to exploit the various meanings of 'figure', as shape, diagram and image or emblem.

57. *he containeth in him ... of every other figure*: The sense is that all other shapes can be fitted within the circle, their 'description' being by the circumference described by the circle.

58.   *the prince of philosophers ... hominem quadratum, a square man*: Aristotle, *Ethics*, 1.10.11, possibly via Erasmus, *Adagia* ('Adages'), 4.8.35.

THE THIRD BOOK: OF ORNAMENT

Puttenham of course leans heavily on classical and contemporary neo-Latin rhetoric books, and notably on the great *Institutio oratoria* of the first-century AD Roman orator and teacher Quintilian and on the popular sixteenth-century compendium by Joannes Susenbrotus, *Epitome troporum ac schematum* ('Outline of Schemes and Tropes', *c.* 1541). He could also consult such recent English rhetorics as Wilson's *The Art of Rhetoric* (1553; 1560) and the first edition of Peacham's *The Garden of Eloquence* (1577). Many of his treatments of individual figures translate and/or versify the standard illustrations of figures from these and other rhetoric books, although Puttenham's characteristic plain speaking and eye for comedy adds a new dimension. What is unarguably original in his treatment, however, is that this is not simply a rhetoric which makes use of illustrations from the poets, but is a rhetoric *for* poets. Where every other rhetoric book is aimed at the production of speeches and prose composition, Puttenham transforms rhetorical theory into a theory of poetic style as part of a larger art of poetry. Because of the memorable English names given by Puttenham to the figures, and to give a sense of the overall shape of his taxonomy, figures omitted in this abridgement are nevertheless listed in the text. The Greek terms for rhetorical figures were transmitted to Puttenham via Latin and neo-Latin textbooks, and their spelling is given here in Latinized form. Unless otherwise indicated, poetic illustrations are assumed to be by Puttenham.

1.   *Of ornament poetical*: 'Ornament' is a key word in rhetorical theory. The Latin *ornamentum* and the related verb *exorno* initially referred to necessary equipment and accoutrements (such as military arms or the player's wardrobe) – to the equipment necessary to performing a particular function. Only later did the words come to be used of unnecessary decorations or embellishments. The related word *exornatio* (Puttenham's 'exornation'), frequently used by Cicero and the author of the *Rhetorica ad Herennium* for rhetorical embellishment and rhetorical figure, carries with it this ambiguity of (military) function versus mere decoration: on the one hand it is active, capable of damaging and protecting, of transforming a situation; on the other it is passive and unthreatening, simply to be appreciated by the eye. Putten-

ham exploits this 'double virtue' in chapter 3, on the efficacious *energeia* and the decorative *enargeia*. Cf. Peacham, pp. 250–53, for whom figures both 'garnish [speech], as precious pearls a gorgeous garment' and are 'martial instruments both of defence and invasion'.

2. *flowers ... and colours*: Both metaphors are deeply ingrained, cropping up frequently in rhetorical and poetic theory; colours were more usually used of types of argument or style, flowers of choice figures or phrases. For ornamental colours, flowers and precious stones see, e.g., Cicero, *De oratore*, 3.25.96, and Peacham, p. 250.

3. *That first quality ... strong and virtuous operation*: Enargeia means 'clearness, vividness', *argos* 'shining', *energeia* 'activity, operation, vigour' and *ergon* 'work'. Neither term had previously had the centrality which Puttenham gives them here, although in developing what is a useful distinction between kinds of ornament he misrepresents *enargeia* somewhat. For Quintilian, *enargeia* is a result of the convincing performance and evocation of emotion, 'which makes us seem not so much to narrate as to exhibit the actual scene, while our emotions will be no less actively stirred than if we were present at the actual occurrence'; *energeia*, in line with Puttenham, 'derives its name from action and finds its peculiar function in securing that nothing we say is tame' (*Institutio oratoria*, 6.2.32; 8.3.89). Demetrius, *On Style*, 209, discusses *enargeia* as a feature of the plain style, a simple matter of giving all the details of a description. *Enargeia*, then, is related to the visual, but it is a matter of compelling description which appeals to what Quintilian calls 'the eyes of the mind' (8.3.62), and not of mere 'lustre'.

4. *Speech is not natural to man ... than any other creature*: Language is not innate, but the potential to speak is. A squabble between the Anglo-Saxon term 'speech' and the French-derived 'language' is appropriately close to the surface in this paragraph. On imitation cf. Aristotle, *Poetics*, 1448b: '*Mimēsis* is innate in human beings from childhood – indeed we differ from the other animals in being most given to *mimēsis* and in making our first steps in learning through it'.

5. *in our books of the originals ... of the English tongue*: One of the many lost works referred to in the *Art*, it would, like the *Art*, have aimed to vindicate English in relation to both classical and Continental alternatives.

6. *such as the Greeks call charientes*: A term used by both Plato, in

the *Republic*, and Aristotle, in the *Politics*, contrasted to *hoi polloi*.

7. *Piers Plowman, nor Gower, nor Lydgate, nor yet Chaucer*: The major writers/texts of the fourteenth and early-fifteenth centuries.

8. *But herein we are already ruled . . . by learned men*: The sixteenth century saw the first English dictionaries, as a need was seen to gloss newer scholarly or inkhorn terms and loan words from other European languages. It also saw the first vernacular grammars and various works on the reform of the language and its orthography.

9. *many inkhorn terms so ill-affected*: On inkhorn terms see Book 2, note 33.

10. *multa renascentur . . . et vis et norma loquendi*: *Ars poetica*, 70–72; editions of Horace available to Puttenham read *vis*, 'force', in l. 72 where modern editions prefer *ius*, 'right'.

11. *words, speeches and sentences*: This combination occurs frequently and is ambiguous. It is more likely than not that an ascending hierarchy is implicit, so that 'speeches' might be glossed by 'phrases'; its use elsewhere in the book (often in the phrases 'words and speeches' and 'figurative speeches') must also intend this sense. The meaning of 'sentences' is less 'syntactical units' and more 'sayings' or 'whole thoughts verbalized' (Latin *sententiae*).

12. *So we say that . . . nor Erasmus' and Budaeus' styles*: Cicero, the orator, and Sallust, the historian, as noted models of Latin style, eloquent and terse respectively; Caesar and Livy as Roman historians; Homer and Hesiod as founding Greek poets; Herodotus and Thucydides as Greek historians; Euripides and Aristophanes as Greek dramatists, tragic and comic respectively; the Dutch Erasmus (*c.* 1467–1536) and the French Budaeus (Guillaume Budé, 1467–1540) as noted classical scholars.

13. *under these three principal complexions . . . the vehement and cold styles*: The tripartite classification of styles – the grand, the middle and the low or plain – was the most common in the rhetorical tradition. Discussions which directly or indirectly influence Puttenham's treatment include Cicero, *Orator*, 75–99 and Quintilian, *Institutio oratoria*, 12.10.58–72. Quintilian admits that there are 'intermediate styles compounded of the two which lie on either side' and that 'we may discover almost countless species of styles, each differing from the other by some fine shade of difference' (66–7). But alternatives to the tripartite scheme were also available, including the four styles – plain,

grand, elegant and forceful – of Demetrius' *On Style* (36), and
their various possible combinations.

14. *the vanities of Nero ... the wisdom of Aurelius*: Nero (37–
68 AD), Caligula (12–41 AD), Domitian (54–96 AD) and Heliogabalus (?204–22 AD): notorious, eccentric and for the most
part mad emperors. Julius Caesar (100–44 BC), Augustus
(63 BC–14 AD), Tiberius (42 BC–37 AD), Trajan (53–117 AD)
and Marcus Aurelius (121–180 AD): Caesar was a great leader
of Republican Rome but fears about the extent of his ambition
led to his assassination (which Puttenham clearly counts a mistake); as in Book 1, p. 69, Puttenham thinks of Caesar as an
emperor; the others were all militarily and politically successful
emperors who left good reputations, except for Tiberius, who
became deeply unpopular and whose character was assassinated
by the historian Tacitus; Puttenham may be confusing him with
Vespasian (9–79 AD).

15. *The matters therefore ... or in heroical reports*: See Puttenham's
Book 1, chapters 16 and 19.

16. *As figures be the instruments ... or rather trespasses, in speech*:
Cf. Quintilian: 'A *figure* ... is the term employed when we
give our language a conformation other than the obvious and
ordinary' (*Institutio oratoria*, 9.1.4; cf. 9.1.11).

17. *but*: (1589: 'by').

18. *one while speaking obscurely and in riddle called aenigma ...
appassionate the mind*: A sampling of some of the figures dealt
with in detail later on; 'periphrase' is *periphrasis*.

19. *Which thing made the grave judges Areopagites ... upright judgement*: A slight misrepresentation of Aristotle, *Rhetoric*,
1.1.1354a: 'For the arousing of prejudice, pity, anger and similar
emotions [which has previously been all that arts of rhetoric have
dealt with] has no connection with the matter in hand, but is
directed only to the judge, so that if it was the rule with all courts
as it actually is in some of the cities ... [rhetoricians] would have
nothing to say; for all men either believe that the laws should
proscribe such things or actually have such laws and ban speaking
off the point, as in the Areopagus, and this is a commendable
regulation.'

20. *In which respect ... a virtue and no vice*: Cf. Quintilian, *Institutio
oratoria*, 9.3.3.

21. *the saying of Bias*: Bias was a Greek philosopher, one of the
seven wise men of Greece. The saying is of uncertain origin; cf.
Gascoigne, p. 242 and Erasmus, *Adagia*, 1.6.96.

22. *to piece many words together ... more significative than the single word*: Cf. Sidney, p. 52, for the ability of English to match Greek in the forming of compounds.

23. *as Cicero, Varro, Quintilian*: Marcus Tullius Cicero (106–43 BC), the greatest Roman orator and author of a number of important works of rhetorical theory which were widely known and used in the Renaissance, including *De oratore* ('On the Orator'), *Brutus*, *Orator* ('The Orator'), and *De partitione oratoria* ('The Divisions of Rhetoric'); the influential *Ad C. Herennium de ratione dicendi* ('To Gaius Herennius on the Theory of Public Speaking'), known as *Ad Herennium*, was still thought to be his by some in Puttenham's day. Marcus Terentius Varro (116–27 BC), prolific Roman author, only part of whose *De lingua latina* ('On the Latin Tongue') survives. Marcus Fabius Quintilianus (*c.* 35–*c.* 100 AD), professor of rhetoric in Rome under Vespasian, whose *Institutio oratoria* ('The Education of an Orator') in twelve books was widely used in the Renaissance and is the best and most comprehensive of the classical treatises.

24. *or to be able to judge of other men's makings*: It is important to note that Puttenham here presents rhetoric as a skill necessary to readers and listeners as well as to writers.

25. *words, speeches and sentences*: See note 11.

26. *Whereupon the learned clerks ... the third upon the orator alone*: Classical rhetoric divides the rhetorical figures variously; confusions of system are compounded by confusions of translation, from Greek to Latin to English. The simplest division is between trope and scheme: a trope (Greek *tropos*, 'turn') is concerned with a change of meaning, such as through metaphor; a scheme (Greek *schēma*, 'form') is simply a particular patterning of words other than the ordinary. Quintilian treats first tropes and then schemes, which he calls figures (Latin *figurae*); these figures he divides into figures of speech ('that is of words, diction, expression, language, or style') and figures of thought ('that is of the mind, feeling, or conceptions'). For other authors the primary division is between figures of speech and figures of thought, and tropes may correspond to figures of thought or may be a sub-category of figures of speech (as in the *Rhetorica ad Herennium*). Richard Lanham's prescriptive scheme has much to recommend it, and corresponds to that of the *Rhetorica ad Herennium*: on the one hand we have figures of words, which may be either schemes or tropes, and on the other hand we have figures of thought (large-scale schemes or tropes, or combinations

of both). Puttenham is very much his own master in constructing his categories and in explaining his rationale, and is equally open to accusations of confusion. But his categories may be mapped on to Lanham's plan successfully: his first and second categories correspond to schemes ('auricular') and tropes ('sensable'), and his third category corresponds to figures of thought ('sententious'). See Lanham, *A Handlist of Rhetorical Terms* (Berkeley and Los Angeles, 1991), 178 and 154–7; Quintilian, *Institutio oratoria*, 8.6 and 9.1; *Ad Herennium*, 4.13–55. There is no warrant for Puttenham's claim that use of figures in the particular categories by poets or orators is restricted in any way; and it is a notion he is bound to ignore in the subsequent treatment. But cf. Peacham, *The Garden of Eloquence* (the 1577 edition) on grammatical schemes: these correspond to Puttenham's auricular figures and are subdivided into orthographical schemes ('lawful only to poets' because of poetic licence, on which see Gascoigne, p. 244) and syntactical schemes, some of which are in effect faults and may be used only by poets.

27. *your second serves the conceit ... they properly appertain to full sentences*: For the various related meanings of 'sensible', 'sensable' and 'sententious' cf. Quintilian, *Institutio oratoria*, 8.5.1–2: 'When the ancients used the word *sententia*, they meant a feeling, or opinion ... they regarded *sensus* as referring merely to the senses of the body. But modern usage applies *sensus* to concepts of the mind, while *sententia* is applied to striking reflections such as are more especially introduced at the close of our periods.'

28. *with copious amplifications*: 'Amplification' is a fundamental rhetorical device of expanding simple material (see, e.g., Quintilian, *Institutio oratoria*, 8.4). 'Copious' ('abundant') was a key term in Renaissance education and style, owing to Erasmus' hugely influential *De duplici copia rerum ac verborum* ('On the Twofold Copiousness of Subject Matter and Words'), its title drawn from a phrase in Quintilian. The phrase 'copious amplifications' has, therefore, a very positive sense indeed.

29. *'orthographical' or 'syntactical'*: Sub-categories of schemes in Peacham's *The Garden of Eloquence* (the 1577 edition).

30. *where, as*: (1589: 'whereas').

31. *numerosity*: Puttenham's word for *rhythmos* – see Book 2, note 10.

32. *it is that virtue which the Greeks call enargeia*: See note 3.

33. *some are only proper to the Greeks and Latins and not to us*:

Both Greek and Latin are inflected languages and therefore have far more flexibility in word order than English.

34. *but so foul and intolerable . . . among the vicious or faulty speeches*: In chapter 22.

35. *But now, my dear . . . that works me all this ill*: Edward Dyer (mentioned in Book 1, chapter 31), from a manuscript poem beginning 'Before I die, fair dame', ll. 9–10, in Steven W. May, *The Elizabethan Courtier Poets* (Columbia, Mo., 1991).

36. *sensable*: (1589: 'sensible').

37. *I burn in love . . . sink in deep despair*: A made-up pair of lines which, for its characteristic use of oxymoron, could belong to any Petrarchan sonnet; e.g. Wyatt's 'I find no peace', an imitation of a Petrarch sonnet, with its line 'I fear and hope, I burn and freeze like ice', poem no. 49 in 'Tottel's Miscellany' (see *Tottel's Miscellany*, ed. H. E. Rollins [Cambridge, Mass., 1965].)

38. *as the poet Virgil said . . . 'ta-ra-tant', taratantara*: In fact Ennius, *Annales* ('Annals'), fragment 143 (from Book 2): 'And the trumpet in terrible tones taratantara blared'; cf. Virgil, *Aeneid*, 9.503 for a similar line, but without the *onomatopoeia*.

39. *Woe worth the mountain . . . first causer of all my care*: From Euripides, *Medea*, 5.3, via Quintilian, *Institutio oratoria*, 5.10.83–84 (who uses Ennius' Latin translation).

40. *post multas mea regna videns mirabor aristas*: *Eclogues*, 1.69.

41. *as appeareth by these verses of ours*: This example, if it was ever written, was not printed.

42. *qui nescit dissimulare nescit regnare*: The maxim of Louis XI of France.

43. *if we should call . . . the calm and haven peace*: The allegory of the ship of state is the basis of Horace, *Odes*, 1.14, which Quintilian takes as the opening example in his account of allegory (*Institutio oratoria*, 8.6.44). On allegory cf. Harington, p. 266.

44. *claudite iam rivos, pueri; sat prata biberunt*: *Eclogues*, 3.111.

45. *The clouds of care . . . that meant for to rejoice*: George Gascoigne, 'A cloud of care', from 'The Adventures of Master F.I.' in *A Hundreth Sundry Flowres* (1573 [ed. G. W. Pigman III, Oxford, 2000]).

46. *cacemphaton or foul speech*: Puttenham deals with the figure *cacemphaton*, by which a foul meaning or double-entendre is imparted to a word or phrase, in chapter 22.

47. *Alfonso, King of Naples*: Alfonso V of Aragon and I of Naples and Sicily (1385–1458).

48. *that is by the figure . . . the Latins dementiens*: The Latin word

dementiens means 'mad'; Puttenham may intend *mentiens*, 'lying'.

49. *Whom princes serve ... knew her not*: From the *Partheniads*, which survive in manuscript (British Library MS Cotton Vesp. E.8); Puttenham quotes poem no. 4, lines 1–4.

50. *The tenth of March ... his hornèd head*: George Gascoigne, 'A loving lady, being wounded in the springtime', in *A Hundred Sundry Flowers*. Puttenham returns to the attack of these opening lines in his account of '*Periergia*', or over-labour'; Gascoigne, however, is using irony alongside *periphrasis*, making fun of the narrator who introduces the lady's lament.

51. *the French King was overthrown at St-Quentin*: By the Spanish in 1557.

52. *Or if one would say ... the people of the town of Antwerp*: Antwerp fell to the Spanish in August 1585 after a long siege. On the Dutch wars see the conclusion of chapter 19 and note 104.

53. *virgineam dissoluit zonam, saith the poet*: Taken from Susenbrotus, *Epitome troporum ac schematum*, on synecdoche (which reads *soluit* for *dissoluit*); possibly it is modelled on, or associated in Puttenham's mind with, Catullus' poem no. 2, l. 13: *quod zonam soluit diu ligatam* ('which loosed her girdle too long tied'), hence 'saith the poet'.

54. *whether it be to plead, or to praise, or to advise*: Referring to the three kinds or branches ('all three cases') of rhetoric – judicial, epideictic and deliberative.

55. *copious amplification, or enlargement, of language*: On 'copious amplification' see note 28.

56. *whereof the audible is ... as the philosopher saith*: Aristotle, *De sensu* ('On Sense'), 1.437a.

57. *In vain mine eyes ... for fortune keeps my love*: Lines 9–12 of 'Fortune hath taken thee away my love', Ralegh's half of the verse exchange between him and 'his greatest mistress' Queen Elizabeth I (her poem is 'Ah silly pug, wert thou so sore afraid'), which survives in various contemporary manuscripts. (See May, *The Elizabethan Courtier Poets*.) The exchange may date from as late as 1587. Puttenham quotes from the poems three times: see notes 59 and 87.

58. *Fear many must he needs, whom many fear*: The commonplace versified in the second line, often attributed to Publilius Syrus (first century BC comic dramatist), is attributed to Laberius (first-century BC dramatist) by Macrobius (fifth-century AD writer), *Saturnalia*, 2.7.

59. *With wisdom's eyes . . . my love forever been*: 'Fortune hath taken thee away my love', ll. 21–2: see note 57.

60. *The Greeks call him . . . we may call him the underlay*: 'Underlay' has no exactly appropriate meaning, but is chosen because as verb and noun its meanings, including 'lie under', 'subject', 'a support or backing', are relevant and close to the Latin verb *subiungo*.

61. *Yet when I saw myself . . . because myself loved you*: The closing couplet of Ralegh's poem 'Calling to mind mine eye long went about', reproduced by Puttenham from a manuscript source; it was later printed in *The Phoenix Nest* (1593). (See *The Poems of Sir Walter Ralegh*, ed. Michael Rudick [Tempe, Ariz., 1999].)

62. *As Tiberius the Emperor . . . instead of Claudius Tiberius Nero*: Suetonius' *Life of Tiberius*, 42. The nicknames imply, more or less, 'Mulled wine Drunkard Wino'.

63. *And all my life . . . I live the less*: The closing couplet of 'All my sense thy sweetness gained', *Certain Sonnets*, 27, first printed in 1598. (See *Poems of Sidney*, ed. Ringler.)

64. *When wert thou born, Desire . . . In hope devoid of fears*: From manuscript; the poem 'When wert thou born, Desire?' was printed in *Breton's Bower of Delights* (1591). See May, *The Elizabethan Courtier Poets*.

65. *by his Greek and Latin originals*: The Latin term is *gradatio*, 'gradation, staircase'.

66. *Peace makes plenty . . . and war brings peace*: Versions of this proverbial paradox are found in a fifteenth-century manuscript of Lydgate, and in Gascoigne's 'The fruits of war', in *Posies* (1575). (See *A Hundredth Sundrie Flowres*, ed. G. W. Pigman III.)

67. *If poesy be . . . To be a mute poesy*: For this aphorism, attributed by Plutarch to the Greek poet Simonides, see Sidney, note 35. A version of it is used in the account of *antimetabole* (Latin *commutatio*) in the anonymous *Ad Herennium*, 4.28.39. In the last line 'poesy' is pronounced as a trisyllable, and the spelling of 'mute' in 1589 is 'muet', the disyllable needed for the scansion created by the 'misplacing of a letter' discussed by Puttenham in Book 3, chapter 11.

68. *tantae molis erat Romanam condere gentem*: Aeneid, 1.33.

69. *What medicine, then . . . and hate engenders love*: The closing couplet of a sonnet from the manuscript 'old' *Arcadia*, 'The love which is imprinted in my soul' (*Poems of Sidney*, ed. Ringler, OA 61).

NOTES TO PP. 174-9

70. *Then if there be . . . Of your bounty*: *Partheniads*, poem 6, last stanza.

71. *Set me whereas . . . although my chance be naught*: This poem is in fact by the Earl of Surrey, translating Petrarch, *Rime* ('Rhymes'), poem 145, printed in *Songs and Sonnets* ('Tottel's Miscellany', 1557, poem no. 12). (See *Tottel's Miscellany*, ed. H. E. Rollins.)

72. *When faith fails . . . to great confusion*: Based on an apocryphal poem included in the early Chaucer canon. Famously imitated by the Fool in *King Lear*, at the end of Act 3, scene 2.

73. *They called such linking verse . . . the love-burden*: Cf. the treatment in Book 2, p. 129.

74. *My true love hath my heart . . . and I have his*: From the manuscript 'old' *Arcadia* (OA 45), a sonnet which ends by repeating its opening line, but which does not use it as a refrain; Puttenham may be taking *his* text from a musical source, in which lines 1–4 and 5–8 of the sonnet are separated by repetition of the opening line to form a refrain.

75. *If my speech . . . so to say*: Versifying the example given in Susenbrotus' discussion of *parrhesia* in the *Epitome troporum ac schematum*.

76. *Sir Thomas Smith . . . called it 'spite-wed' or 'wed-spite'*: Sir Thomas Smith (1513–77), legal and Greek scholar, Secretary of State under Edward VI and again from 1572–7, author of *De republica anglorum* ('The Commonwealth of England', 1573).

77. *Master Secretary Wilson . . . called it 'Witcraft'*: Thomas Wilson (?1525–81), author of *The Art of Rhetoric* (1553) and *The Rule of Reason, Containing the Art of Logic* (1551), Secretary of State from 1578 until his death. Wilson attacked inkhornisms in *The Art of Rhetoric* but Puttenham has here confused his *Art of Logic* with Ralph Lever's *The Art of Reason, Rightly Termed Witcraft* (1573).

78. *confirmed*: (1589: 'contemned').

79. *We also call him the reason-renderer . . . English word 'tell-cause'*: Both elements of 'reason-renderer' come into English from French in the thirteenth and fourteenth centuries. 'Tell' is Old English ('right English'), but 'cause' comes from the Latin *causa* in the fourteenth century; for Puttenham, though, it sounds Anglo-Saxon because it is a monosyllable.

80. *When fortune . . . both mast and shroud*: Wyatt, 'The lover hopeth of better chance', printed in 'Tottel's Miscellany' (1557), no. 72, 3–6. (See *Tottel's Miscellany*, ed. H. E. Rollins.)

81. *Procatalepsis . . . this figure was called the 'presumptuous'*:

Puttenham expects the reader to recognize the etymological sense of 'presumptuous', from 'presume', 'to take before', so that it carries the meaning both of 'bold' and of 'anticipating'.

82. *comparatio . . . or the figure of comparison*: The opening of the paragraph on *comparatio* seems to be missing from the printed text, as is therefore the usual heading; however, the two English names are both given and the discussion makes clear that this figure is referred to. See *ERLC*, 272 n.174.

83. *So if, by way of fiction . . . or the right reasoner*: After the Norman invasion of 1066 England became part of a state which spanned the channel. This was expanded in the twelfth century when the marriage of Henry II to Eleanor of Aquitaine brought most of south-west France under the control of the English crown. Most of this territory was lost by King John in the early thirteenth century and subsequently contested in the 'Hundred Years' War' of the fourteenth and fifteenth centuries. Despite the dramatic gains of Henry V, most of the French possessions were lost again by 1466, except for Calais, which had been captured by Edward III in 1346. Even in the late sixteenth century there were those who hoped that England would one day reverse this situation. Henry VIII took Boulogne in 1544, but maintaining it proved impossible for the protectorate of Edward VI; Calais remained an English possession until January 1558, the last year of Mary I's reign.

84. *Nature bids us . . . to love another*: From Terence, *Andria* ('The Maid of Andros'), 2.5, probably via Erasmus, *Adagia* ('Adages'), 1.3.91.

85. *The prince that covets . . . full mild and patient to be*: In his discussion of *gnome* Quintilian attributes the saying 'The prince who would know all must needs ignore much' to Domitius Afer (*Institutio oratoria*, 8.5.3).

86. *Nothing sticks faster . . . in our tender years*: From Erasmus, *Adagia*, 2.4.20, though similar statements are found in Quintilian and Susenbrotus.

87. *Never think you . . . to obey*: From Elizabeth's half of the verse exchange with Ralegh ('Ah silly pug, wert thou so sore afraid', 11–12: 'But never think that fortune can bear sway, If virtue watch and will not her obey'), which survives in various contemporary manuscripts. For Puttenham's quotations from Ralegh's half see note 57.

88. *And as for you . . . soon kill a gentle mind*: By the courtier and poet Sir Arthur Gorges (1557–1625), 'But this and then no more',

29–30, from manuscript. (See *Poems*, ed. H. E. Sandison [Oxford, 1953].) Puttenham quotes four times from this poem, once attributing it to Gorges and twice to Dyer.

89. *But, O Phoebus . . . For her cursed heart, etc*: From another lost work. The 'unkind runaway' is Daphne, turned into the laurel tree ('bay') as she fled Apollo.

90. *Prosopographia, or the counterfeit countenance*: (1589: English title omitted): supplied from 1589 table of contents.

91. *And this kind . . . and not by fiction*: It was believed that the *Iliad* was to some extent historical.

92. *And no prettier examples . . . out of French by Chaucer*: Cf. the mention of the work in Book 1, p. 105.

93. *so did Chaucer . . . in his report of the lady Grisild*: I.e. patient Griselda, in 'The Clerk's Tale'.

94. *Lord Nicholas Vaux*: As in Book 1, p. 104, Puttenham means Thomas, Lord Vaux (1509–56).

95. *When Cupid scalèd . . . Each piece discharging a lover's look, etc.*: From 'Tottel's Miscellany' (1557), no. 211, ll. 1–22.

96. *But as the wat'ry showers . . . despair out of my mind*: Surrey, 'Against him that had slandered a gentlewoman with himself', from 'Tottel's Miscellany', no. 265, 47–8.

97. *Then as the stricken deer . . . I may make my moan*: Ibid., 21–2.

98. *Sir Philip Sidney . . . in his book of Arcadia*: The extended *blason* 'What tongue can her perfections tell' from the manuscript 'old' *Arcadia* (OA 62).

99. *Of silver was her forehead high . . . Or else I think a strawberry*: *Partheniads* (see note 49), poem no. 7.5–8, 13–16, 9–12, 25–8.

100. *Such parables were . . . and a number more*: For 'the wise and foolish maidens' see Matthew 25:1–13; for 'the evil steward' see Luke 16:1–8; for 'the labourers in the vineyard' see Matthew 20:1–16.

101. *or resemblance*: (1589: 'or a resemblance').

102. *so did King Edward I . . . Robert le Bruce, no lawful king*: Edward I (1239–1307), King of England from 1272, chose John de Balliol (*c.* 1250–1314) as King of the Scots in 1292, but when Balliol rebelled against English domination he was deposed and Edward took the crown. Robert the Bruce (1274–1329) seized the Scottish throne in 1306, was forced into exile, but recovered the kingdom, defeating Edward II at Bannockburn in 1314 and gaining English recognition of Scottish independence in 1328.

103. *so did King Edward the Third . . . against Henry, bastard and usurper*: The rule of Peter the Cruel (or the Just, 1334–69), King

of Castile and Leon from 1350 was persistently challenged by his half-brother Henry of Trastámara (1333–79), later Henry II, with the help of France. An Anglo-Castilian alliance was concluded with Edward III (1312–77) in 1362 and Edward's son the Black Prince routed Henry's forces at Nájera in 1367.

104. *and why may not the Queen . . . from the Spanish servitude*: From 1566 the Dutch provinces rebelled against Spanish Habsburg rule, leading to a split between the northern Protestant provinces and the southern Catholic provinces. Queen Elizabeth I finally decided to offer military aid to the Dutch cause in 1585 and an English presence continued into the seventeenth century. It was in the Low Countries that Philip Sidney (appointed governor of Flushing, one of the 'cautionary towns' put temporarily into English hands) lost his life in 1586 after being shot in battle. This section originally included a rather different paradigm, in a passage probably written *c.* 1583–85: the Dutch break faith with their lawful sovereigns, so 'what likelihood is there they should be more assured to the Queen of England than they have been to all these princes and governors, longer than the distress continueth and is to be relieved by her goodness and puissance?' And this contribution to the debate leading up to English intervention in 1585 was originally printed, being replaced in press but surviving in some copies.

105. *Exergasia, or the gorgeous . . . our tale or argument*: It is Puttenham's original touch to place this figure where it might seem to belong – at the end. Quintilian (*Institutio oratoria*, 8.3.88) distinguishes between '*exergasia*, or finish, which produces completeness of effect' and '*epexergasia*, an intensified form of the preceding, which reasserts our proofs and clinches the argument by repetition'. Susenbrotus (*Epitome troporum ac schematum*) is close to Puttenham: *exergasia* is 'when we repeat something and amplify it continually by other words, units of discourse, ideas, and figures' (*ERLC*, 279 n. 201). The original spelling in the 1589 text, *exargasia*, associates the figure with the lustre of Puttenham's *enargeia* rather than the active force of *energeia*. Despite Puttenham's clothing images, *expolitio* only carries the sense of 'embellishment, adornment' in rhetorical contexts.

106. *In a work of ours entitled Philocalia . . . to which we refer you*: Another lost work. The Greek word means 'a love of the beautiful'.

107. *Our sovereign Lady . . . evil and undutiful practices*: Forced to

abdicate in favour of her son, James VI, the Catholic Mary, Queen of Scots (1542–87) fled to England and was kept under house arrest because of her claim to the English throne (as the granddaughter of Henry VIII). The focus of a series of plots, Elizabeth I finally agreed to put her on trial for treason and she was executed in 1587.

108. *The doubt of future foes . . . and gape for future joy*: Taken from manuscript, this text differs from others in a number of variants; Puttenham's readings are kept here, but 'future' is supplied in the final line to make up the scansion (1589: 'gape for joy'). The poem employs *hysteron proteron* in 'Their dazzled eyes with pride' (i.e. 'their eyes, dazzled with pride') and 'Our rusty sword with rest' (i.e. 'our sword, rusty with rest'); Puttenham finds such constructions a vice in chapter 22, instancing the phrase 'A coral lip of hew', from George Turberville (*c*.1544–*c*.1597).

109. *It hath been said . . . a virtue in the poetical science*: See above, chapter 7.

110. *the philosopher Heraclitus*: A sixth-century BC Greek philosopher and cosmologist.

111. *leaving no little to the grammarians . . . war and altercations*: It was conventional to refer to grammarians for more detailed discussion of faults: cf. *Ad Herennium*, 4.12.17 and Quintilian, *Institutio oratoria*, 8.1.2.

112. *For ever may my true love . . . crowned a queen*: Imitating an example given by Susenbrotus in his discussion of *pleonasmus* in the *Epitome troporum ac schematum*.

113. *The tenth of March . . . the weather was so fair*: Gascoigne, 'A loving lady, being wounded in the springtime'. See note 50. The reader is intended to think of the narrator what Puttenham thinks of the poet.

114. *These doubtful speeches . . . the Sibyl's prophecies*: Cf. Sidney, note 21.

115. *a scholastical term, 'decency'; our own Saxon English term is 'seemliness'*: 'Decency' is a 'scholastical [i.e. academic] term' because it is modelled on the Latin *decentia*, 'seemliness', from *decens*, 'suitable'. *Decorum* comes from the same root, both words coming into English in the sixteenth century.

116. *we call it also 'comeliness' . . . 'pleasant approach'*: Puttenham's fanciful etymology of 'comely' is unfortunately inaccurate: the word derives from Old English *cymlic*, 'beautiful'.

117. *or sentencer of 'decency'*: Over ten pages of examples from history

and literature of decorous and indecorous speeches follow, and are omitted here.

118. *our book which we have written De Decoro*: Puttenham's *De Decoro* ('On Decorum') is not extant.

119. *with like consideration*: Over seventeen pages of examples of decorum in all aspects of human behaviour, including four pages on dress and hairstyles, follow.

120. *all your figures poetical . . . even by very nature, without discipline*: Cf. Quintilian, *Institutio oratoria*, 3.2.3: 'It was, then, nature that created speech, and observation that originated the art of speaking'. On this point and that of the subsequent chapter, cf. Sidney, p. 51 and note 268.

121. *when he is most artificial . . . to know his art well, and little to use it*: Cf. the popular, post-classical Latin tag *ars est celare artem* ('the art is to hide art'). Puttenham's discussion is also informed by the doctrine of *sprezzatura*, the careless disdain required of the courtier by the influential *Il cortegiano* of Castiglione. See Sidney, note 223.

122. *as Homer of Priamus or Ulysses*: In the *Iliad* (Priam is King of Troy) and the *Odyssey*.

123. *in driving of a prince's chariot, or coach (as your Majesty's might be)*: 1589: 'in driving of a prince's chariot or coach (as your Majesty might be).'

124. *Quoth Plato . . . in studies of more consequence*: Adapted from Aelian's second-century AD *Varia historia* ('Historical Miscellany'), 2.27, which describes Anniceris giving a practical demonstration rather than a discourse. Puttenham's peroration parallels Sidney's exordium: each compares his performance to that of an over-zealous master of a more practical art. Puttenham also implies that he might have served Elizabeth I in a greater capacity if asked.

SAMUEL DANIEL: A DEFENCE OF RHYME

Text: *A panegyrike congratulatory delivered to the Kings most excellent majesty . . . By Samuel Daniel. Also certaine epistles. With a defence of ryme, heeretofore written, and now published by the author.* [1603]

Separate title page: *A defence of ryme: Against a pamphlet entituled: Observations in the Art of English Poesie. Wherein is demonstratively*

*proved, that ryme is the fittest harmonie of words that comportes with
our language. By Sa: D.*

Running title: 'An Apologie for Ryme.'

On Daniel (1562/3–1619), see the Introduction, pp. lxvii–lxxi. The
work was written as a direct riposte to Campion's *Observations.*

1. *a great friend of mine*: Often taken to be the poet Fulke Greville
(1554–1628), to whom Daniel addresses *Musophilus*, as Daniel's
only male poet-patron. However, as Sidney's best friend and
fellow-poet, Greville would long ago have been exposed to arguments about quantitative verses and was not likely to be 'won
from us'.

2. *our sovereign's happy inclination this way*: James VI and I (1566–
1625), whose journey south at his accession to the English throne
in 1603 was the occasion of Daniel's *Panegyric Congratulatory*.
James had already published *The Essays of a Prentice, in the
Divine Art of Poesy* (1584) and *His Majesty's Poetical Exercises
at Vacant Hours* (1591). The former included *An Short Treatise,
Containing Some Rules and Cautels* [precautions] *to be Observed
and Eschewed in Scots Poesy*, a treatise similar in scope to Gascoigne's.

3. *under the patronage of a noble earl*: William Herbert (1580–
1630), Earl of Pembroke since his father's death in 1601. Daniel
had probably lived at Wilton, the Pembrokes' estate, between
1592 and 1595, after dedicating his sonnet sequence *Delia* to
Pembroke's mother, Mary, Countess of Pembroke, in 1592. He
is likely to have acted as William Herbert's tutor and he wrote a
play, *Cleopatra* (1594), as a companion piece to the Countess of
Pembroke's *Antonius* (1592), a translation from the French of
Robert Garnier. The Countess of Pembroke was the sister of Sir
Philip Sidney, and was engaged at this time in editing his *Arcadia*
for publication in 1593. The legacy of Sidney patronage and
Pembroke's own interest in writing poetry is why he 'in blood
and nature is interested'.

4. *Wilton*: The Pembrokes' estate (see above).

5. *my worthy Lord*: Daniel probably means Pembroke's father,
Henry Herbert, second Earl of Pembroke (1534?–1601) rather
than Pembroke himself, although all the patronage Daniel
received seems to have come via Pembroke's mother.

6. *these new measures*: Campion's various quantitative metres and
verse forms.

7. *And the rather ... best notice of his worth*: Campion's published
    verse had been conventionally both rhymed and accentual-
    syllabic. He had written both words and music (including a sole
    example in quantitative metre) for the first part of *A Book of
    Airs* (1601), a collaboration with the lutenist songwriter Philip
    Rosseter. Campion's first published verses had appeared immedi-
    ately after Daniel's in a supplement to the unauthorized first
    printing of Sidney's *Astrophil and Stella* in 1591.

8. *discit enim ... probat et veneratur*: Horace, *Epistles*, 2.1.262–3
    (to Augustus).

9. *Which frame of words ... number or measure*: *Metrum* refers to
    quantitative metres; *rhythmus* had a more open sense, originally
    signifying some pleasing or harmonious regularity in music and
    verse, and coming to be used of medieval accentual-syllabic
    metres. Both 'rhyme' and 'rhythm' (their spelling frequently
    identical in the sixteenth century) come from *rhythmus*.

10. *And these rhythmi ... è naturale et sponte fusa composizione*:
    Poetics, 1448b, paraphrased from an unidentified Italian com-
    mentary.

11. *Which, whether it be derived ... as some Italians hold*: The
    Italian critic Giraldi Cinthio, in his *Discorso al comporre dei
    romanzi* ('Discourse on the Composition of Romances', 1554)
    proposed this spurious etymology of 'romances' from Reims
    (*'Remense'*), a city in north-eastern France.

12. *For as Greek and Latin verse ... English verse of measure and
    accent*: See A Note on English Versification and cf. Sidney, p. 52.

13. *the acute and grave accent*: Cf. Gascoigne, p. 239 for this termin-
    ology: 'acute' = stressed, 'grave' = unstressed.

14. *Georgevicz' De Turcarum moribus*: Bartolomaeus Georgevicz,
    De Turcarum moribus epitome ('A Digest of Turkish Customs',
    1552), translated into English by Hugh Gough (*c.* 1569).

15. *our verse of eleven syllables in feminine rhyme*: A feminine ending
    is an extra unstressed syllable at the end of the line (e.g. 'taken',
    where a masculine ending would be 'take'). In lines of iambic
    pentameter, feminine rhyme begins on the tenth, stressed, syllable
    and extends into the eleventh, extra syllable (e.g. 'taken' /
    'awaken').

16. *Schola Salerna and those Carmina proverbialia*: The *Conservan-
    dae bonae valetudinis praecepta* ('Precepts for the Maintenance
    of Good Health'), produced in 1100 by the 'School of Salerno',
    the first medical school of medieval Europe, was written in

rhymed Latin verse and was often reprinted. The *Carminia prov-erbialia* ('Proverbial Poems') was a popular collection of rhyming proverbs ridiculed by Campion in *Observations*.

17. *Cato, Theognis*: Marcus Porcius Cato Censorius (234–149 BC); his *De agri cultura* ('On Agriculture') included medical recipes. The poems of Theognis, a Greek elegiac poet of the sixth century BC, were celebrated for their moral maxims.

18. *Whereas . . . saith Aristotle*: *Metaphysics*, 10.1.

19. *non ego paucis . . . cavit natura*: Horace, *Ars poetica*, 351–3.

20. *'Ill customs are to be left'*: Paraphrasing Campion's argument, p. 283: 'For custom, I allege that ill uses are to be abolished, and that things naturally imperfect cannot be perfected by use.'

21. *these laboured measures*: That is, Campion's 'laboured' quantitative verses.

22. *like a tedious fancy without a close*: A 'fancy' was a fantasia, an elaborate contrapuntal piece of music; a 'close' is in music a cadence.

23. *form*: This word was 'force' originally, altered at the second 1603 printing.

24. *Scythian*: The Scythians, nomads living across Europe and Asia, were proverbially barbarous (as in *King Lear*, Act 1, scene 1, l. 116, 'The barbarous Scythian'); note, though, that Daniel works throughout the *Defence* to elevate the supposedly barbaric.

25. *scribimus . . . passim*: Horace, *Epistles*, 2.1.117.

26. *mutavit mentem . . . carmina dictant*: Horace, *Epistles*, 2.1.108–10.

27. *servum pecus*: Horace, *Epistles*, 1.19.19.

28. *We admire them not . . . but for their inventions*: We admire them for their content, as opposed to their form. Invention was the first stage of rhetorical composition.

29. *For to say truth . . . what they represent unto us*: As inflected languages both Greek and Latin exercised great flexibility in word order, a useful licence when trying to make a line of verse scan.

30. *that sometimes, unless . . . in their natural sound*: Pronunciation of Latin was until comparatively recently anglicized and paid no attention to the length of syllables; a regular reading of Latin or English verses in quantitative metres would lack the regular pulse of long and short syllables that the theory requires, sounding like 'flat prose' unless the reader chose to emphasize 'their measure'.

31. *licentia poetica*: The term 'poetic licence' seems to have been coined by Quintilian (*Institutio oratoria*, 2.4.3 and 4.1.58; and

cf. 1.8.14 and 10.5.4), although Cicero had almost managed it
(*De oratore*, 3.38.153). Gascoigne's account, p. 244, is in line
with both authors.

32. *The striving to show . . . in the variety of their odes*: Greek and
Latin odes employed a wide variety of metres and verse forms.

33. *And indeed I have wished . . . in sonnets*: Writing after the 1590s
sonnet vogue, initiated with the printing of Sidney's *Astrophil and
Stella* in 1591 and bolstered with Daniel's own *Delia*, included in
part in that volume and printed in full in 1592, Daniel is glancing
at Sidney here. Whilst Sidney experimented endlessly with the
sonnet form in his *Arcadia* as well as in *Astrophil and Stella*,
Daniel is complaining about the 'multiplicity of rhymes' (that is,
the number of lines with the same rhyme) in Sidney's preferred
Italian form, its octave always *abbaabba*, where Daniel preferred
the English form, beginning *ababcdcd*.

34. *Nor is this certain limit . . . any tyrannical bounding of the conceit*:
A response to Campion's conceit of the sonnet as Procrustes' bed,
p. 284.

35. *For the body . . . order and form*: Daniel's language deliberately
echoes Genesis 1.

36. *stanzas consisting of six, seven or eight lines*: The commonest
six-line pentameter stanza, or sexain, was rhymed *ababcc*, as used
in Shakespeare's *Venus and Adonis* (1593). The classic seven-line
stanza was rhyme royal, as used in Shakespeare's *The Rape of
Lucrece* (1594) and Daniel's *The Complaint of Rosamond*
(1592). The commonest eight-line pentameter form was based on
the Italian *ottava rima*, *abababcc*, as used in Daniel's *Panegyric*
and in his *The Civil Wars* (1595). Daniel experimented with
different rhyme schemes in each length of stanza: cf. *Musophilus*.

37. *the apt planting the sentence . . . ever attained unto*: 'sentence':
both the pith of the stanza and a particular *sententia* or aphorism; a 'period' was a unit of prose rhythm equivalent to a
long, balanced sentence, and the word came to be used for the
end of such a sentence; 'is such': the redundant 'is' is one of a
number of features of this sentence which we would find ungram-
matical.

38. *et Catilinam . . . quocumque sub axe*: Juvenal, *Satires*, 14.41–2.

39. *quem penes arbitrium est et vis et norma loquendi*: Horace, *Ars
poetica*, 72, reading *vis* ('power') for *ius* ('right'). Cf. Puttenham,
Book 3, note 10.

40. *yet Pyrrhus . . . manner of proceeding*: Pyrrhus (319–272 BC),
King of Epirus. The whole sentence is adapted from Michel de

Montaigne's essay 'On the Cannibals' (*Essais*, 1.31); Montaigne takes the anecdote from Plutarch's *Life of Pyrrhus*. Daniel's friend John Florio published his translation of Montaigne's *Essais* in 1603, although Daniel had access to the work in manuscript.

41. *anapaestics . . . tribrachs*: metrical feet. See A Note on English Versification, Puttenham, pp. 111–12, and Campion, p. 285.

42. *'all lay pitifully deformed . . . Reuchlin, Erasmus and More'*: Paraphrasing Campion, p. 282, on three of the founding fathers of North European humanism: Johann Reuchlin (1455–1522), German scholar of Greek and Hebrew; Desiderius Erasmus (1469–1536), Dutch humanist scholar, greatly influential in England; and the English scholar and politician Thomas More (1477–1535).

43. *the coming down of Tamburlaine into Europe*: Timur, known as Tamerlane (1336–1405), Mongol conqueror of the area from Mongolia to the Mediterranean; best known to Daniel's readers from Christopher Marlowe's two-part *Tamburlaine the Great* (1590).

44. *Franciscus Petrarca . . . to this day*: Francesco Petrarca, known to the English as Petrarch (1304–74), Italian poet and classical scholar, most famous to Daniel's contemporaries for his *Canzoniere* ('Poems'), the inspiration for the Elizabethan sonnet sequence. He wrote both in Latin and Italian; his 'great volumes written in moral philosophy', in Latin, include *De vita solitaria* ('On the Solitary Life') and *De remediis utriusque fortuna* ('On the Remedies of Both Types of Fortune'), and Daniel mentions his Latin poems, the *Bucolicum carmen* ('Pastoral Song'), the epic *Africa*, and the *Epistolae* ('Letters').

45. *which questionless they will not change . . . our adversary imagines*: Cf. Campion, p. 284.

46. *C. Tolomei*: Claudio Tolomei, whose *Versi, et regole de la nuova poesia toscana* ('Verses, and Rules of the New Tuscan Poetry', 1539) applied quantitative rules to Italian verse.

47. *Tasso*: Torquato Tasso (1544–95), author of the influential epic poem *Gerusalemme liberata* ('Jerusalem Delivered'), translated into English by Edward Fairfax in 1600. It was, like other sixteenth-century Italian epics, in *ottava rima*.

48. *Boccaccius*: Giovanni Boccaccio (1313–75), Italian poet and scholar, best known for his collection of prose stories, the *Decameron*, and other works in Latin and Italian. These and most of the details which follow, up to the mention of Pico della Mirandola, are lifted from Louis Le Roy's *De la vicissitude*

(1575), translated by R. Ashley as *Of the Interchangeable Course, or Variety of Things in the Whole World* (1594).

49. *Johannes Ravenensis*: Either Giovanni de Malpaghini da Ravenna (*c*. 1346–*c*. 1417), pupil of Petrarch and scholar, or Giovanni Conversini da Ravenna (*c*. 1343–*c*. 1408), poet, philosopher and friend of Petrarch.

50. *tanquam ex equo Troiano*: Cicero, *De oratore*, 2.22.94.

51. *Leonardus Aretinus . . . and many others*: A roll call of eminent Italian humanists: Leonardo Bruni Aretino (1370–1444), author of a history of Florence and lives of Dante and Petrarch; Lorenzo Valla (1407–57), historian; Poggio Bracciolini (1380–1459), historian and satirist; Flavio Biondo (1392–1463), historian.

52. *Then Emmanuel Chrysolaras . . . seven hundred years*: Manuel Chrysolaras (*c*. 1353–1415), a Byzantine humanist, was sent by John Paleologus, the Byzantine emperor, from Constantinople to Italy to seek aid against the Turks. Tamerlane's defeat of the Turkish Sultan Bayezid at the Battle of Ankara (1402) delayed the fall of Constantinople by fifty years. Chrysolaras stayed in Florence and Venice and was instrumental in introducing the study of ancient Greek to western Europe.

53. *Bessarion, George Trapezuntius, Theodore Gaza*: Cardinal Johannes Bessarion (1403–72), Georgius Trapezuntius (i.e. of Trebizond) (1396–1486), and Theodorus Gaza (*c*. 1400–75), all Byzantine scholars key to the spread of Greek learning via Italy after the fall of Constantinople in 1453.

54. *the new invented stamp of printing*: Invented in the 1430s, printing with movable type took off in the second half of the fifteenth century.

55. *Pomponius Laetus . . . Johannes Pico de Mirandola*: More Italian humanists: Giulio Pomponio Leto (1428–97), a celebrated teacher; Aeneas Sylvius Piccolomini (1405–64), poet and scholar, later Pope Pius II; Angelo Poliziano (1454–94), poet and scholar; Ermolao Barbaro (1453/4–93), scholar and diplomat; Giovanni Pico della Mirandola (1463–94), philosopher and theologian.

56. *More . . . a great ornament to this land, and a rhymer*: More wrote English verse in his youth.

57. *venerable Bede*: St Bede, known as the Venerable Bede (*c*. 673–735), English monk and historian of England.

58. *Aldelmus Durotelmus*: St Aldhelm of Sherborne (*c*. 639–709); the tribute quoted by Daniel is untraced.

59. *Witness Josephus Devonius . . . one of the ancients*: The *De bello*

Troiano ('On the Trojan War') of Joseph of Exeter (fl. 1190) was not published as his own until 1620, being long ascribed to Cornelius Nepos (*c.* 100–*c.* 24 BC), poet, historian and friend of Catullus and Cicero.

60. *Walterus Map ... Bacon, Ockham*: Walter Map (*c.* 1140–*c.* 1209), Latin poet; Nigel Wireker (fl. 1190), author of a satire on monks, *Speculum stultorum* ('The Mirror of Fools'); Gervase of Tilbury (*c.* 1150–1235), historian; Henry de Bracton (d. 1268), historian of English laws and customs; Roger Bacon (*c.* 1214–*c.* 1294), philosopher and scientist; William of Ockham (1285–1349), philosopher and theologian.

61. *Scipios, Caesars, Catos and Pompeys*: Great Roman statesmen and generals.

62. *mercurium in pectore though not in lingua*: Adapted from a letter of 1485 from Pico della Mirandola to Ermolao Barbaro (see note 55). Mercury was the god of eloquence, which is why 'mercurium' ('mercury') here signifies eloquence.

63. *though they were not Ciceronians*: This could mean great orators and philosophers generally, or specifically, in light of the sixteenth-century Ciceronian controversy, slavish imitators.

64. *Lycurgus' counsel ... ut labores perferrent*: From a Latin translation of Plutarch's *Life of Lycurgus*, 16.6; Lycurgus was the semimythical Spartan lawgiver.

65. *Had not unlearned Rome ... in her greatest skill*: Possibly adapted from Montaigne's 'An Apology for Raymond Sebond' (*Essais*, 2.12).

66. *omnes gentes habent scriptum in cordibus suis*: Adapted from II Corinthians 3:2.

67. *Discretion is the best measure, the rightest foot*: Daniel uses a prosodic vocabulary ('measure' ... 'foot') here.

68. *it bred not ... than Scotus*: St Thomas Aquinas (*c.* 1225–74), the greatest medieval theologian and philosopher; Bartolus (1313–57), an Italian legal scholar; Johannes Duns Scotus (*c.* 1265–1308), influential Scottish theologian.

69. *impexa illa antiquitatis can yet compare with them*: Adapted from Tacitus, *Dialogus de oratoribus* ('Dialogue on Orators'), 20. Just as, in Tacitus' 'Dialogue', the first age of classical oratory is not eclipsed by the moderns of the first centuries BC and AD, so medieval scholarship ('that unpolished antiquity') can still stand comparison to the achievements of Renaissance scholars.

70. *ubi nunc ... simus in nulla*: Adapted from Cicero, *Epistulae ad familiares* ('Familiar Letters'), 9.9.3.

71. *But shall we not tend to perfection*: Daniel picks up on Campion's claim to be engaged in 'a lawful defence of perfection' (p. 282).

72. *non convalescit . . . saepius transfertur*: Seneca, *Epistulae morales* ('Moral Letters'), 2.3.

73. *Stimulos dat emula virtus*: Adapted from Lucan, *Bellum civile* ('The Civil War'), 1.120.

74. *ab optimis . . . dedecus publicum*: Adapted from Tacitus, *Annales* ('Annals'), 1.80.

75. *So that it is . . . to Mount Athos*: During his attemped invasion of Greece, the Persian King Xerxes (486–465 BC) whipped the sea for destroying his bridge of boats across the Hellespont; the previous Persian invasion fleet had been destroyed in a storm under Mount Athos in 492 BC, so Xerxes cut a canal through its isthmus; the anecdote comes from Herodotus via Montaigne (*Essais*, 1.4).

76. *a few loose and uncharitable epigrams*: Most of Campion's examples are indeed facetious epigrams.

77. *constat sibi . . . aliquid sit dictum quod non sit dictum prius*: Adapting respectively Horace, *Ars poetica*, 127 and Terence, *Eunuchus* ('The Eunuch'), prologue, line 41: 'nothing can be said that has not been said before', a popular maxim in Renaissance arguments about the virtues of imitation and originality.

78. *which in conclusion is . . . to be unperfect*: Cf. Campion's closing words, p. 288.

79. *Rhadamanthus*: Cretan hero who for his wisdom was made one of the judges of the dead in the underworld.

80. *theta*: The Greek letter θ, the first letter of *thanatos* [death] was marked on ballots by Athenian judges voting on the execution of a criminal.

81. *in pessima republica plurimae leges*: Adapted from Tacitus, *Annales*, 3.27.

82. *What strange precepts . . . time out of mind*: In the following paragraph, Daniel treats each of Campion's proposed verse forms in order (see Campion, pp. 286–7). His method is to show that they already exist in regular accentual-syllabic prosody. Campion had argued 'that the Latin verses of six feet, as the heroic and iambic, or of five feet, as the trochaic, are in nature all of the same length of sound with our English verses of five feet'. Though the regular Elizabethan pentameter had not been used 'time out of mind', something like it had been in constant use since Chaucer.

83. *'our English march'*: Campion: 'We may term this [the iambic dimeter] our English march, because the verse answers our war-

NOTES TO PP. 226-8

like form of march in similitude of number', *Works of Campion*, ed. W. R. Davis (Garden City, NY, 1967), 301.

84. *we must make a rest . . . saving the monosyllables*: The words are taken from Campion's two examples. Daniel misrepresents the form somewhat. Campion's dimeter is a flexible, two-foot, five-syllable line. Campion tells us that 'It consists of two feet and one odd syllable', with either a trochee, spondee or iamb in the first position, and a trochee or tribrach (three shorts) in the second. The final 'odd syllable' is left 'common' (i.e. either long or short). In theory, then, the line can have between one and four long syllables. The question is how many long syllables will be given further prominence or *ictus* (a sort of emphasis akin to stress in quantitative metrics); since the metre is a march, one must assume only two. Daniel supposes that a line like 'Drēad Ĕlīzăbēth' will have three stresses, as it would if accentual-syllabic (two-and-a-half trochees); Campion may have heard it within a rapid two-beat framework, scanned as above but heard as 'Drēad Ĕlīzăbĕth'.

85. *Then follows the 'English trochaic' . . . at the last*: A simpler form, Campion's 'English trochaic' line has five trochees, with the option of substituting a spondee or iamb in the first position only. With ten syllables, it is indeed similar to an accentual-syllabic pentameter with its first, unstressed syllable detached from the start and stuck on at the end (in accentual-syllabic prosody either a headless iambic pentameter with a feminine ending or trochaic pentameter).

86. *Next comes the 'Elegiac' . . . of the word*: Campion's form, on the model of the classical elegiac couplet (hexameter alternating with pentameter), alternates a line of his iambic verse and a line made from two dimeters, creating a pause in the middle of every second line, as in the classical form.

87. *And as for those . . . free and indifferent in our language*: See A Note on English Versification. Syllables have either been 'free' from determinations of quantity or 'indifferent', long or short.

88. *in nullius verba iurati*: Adapted from Horace, *Epistles*, 1.1.14.

89. *prosodia*: The study of the rules of versification and the quantities of syllables, taught as part of grammar, one of the subjects in the medieval trivium, the lower division of the seven liberal arts (the others being rhetoric and logic). After mastering the trivium, students progressed to the quadrivium of arithmetic, geometry, astronomy and music.

90. *lean numbers instead of fat rhyme*: Cf. Campion, p. 287.

91. *and if Tully . . . to God and man*: Tully is Cicero; Daniel summarizes *De oratore*, 1.6.20: 'no man can be an orator complete in all points of merit, who has not attained a knowledge of all important subjects and arts'.

92. *loose*: (1603: 'less'), but corrected in subsequent editions. English quantitative verses are 'loose' because the rules are arbitrary, and not natural like the 'full course of her accents'.

93. *the reproach of others' idle tongues . . . curse of nature upon us*: Cf. Campion, p. 284.

94. *and that it is not rhyme but our idle arguments*: The sense is: 'and as though it is rhyme and not our idle arguments . . .'.

95. *a quest of enquiry*: Cf. John Florio, in the dedicatory epistle to his Italian dictionary of 1598: 'I in this search or quest of inquiry have spent most of my studies'. Daniel, however, shades towards the legal senses of both words: an inquest or inquiry.

96. *legunt priscos . . . sine invidia*: Adapted from Seneca, *De brevitate vitae* ('On the Shortness of Life'), 15.4; a marginal note in 1603 reads '*simplicius longe posita miramur*' ('we more readily admire things far removed'), the words immediately following the passage adapted.

97. *And let this make us . . . better to our manners*: With the evident double meanings of metrical feet, materials given literary or rhetorical treatment (*res*), and style (*verba*).

98. *scribendi recte . . . principium et fons*: Horace, *Ars poetica*, 309; see Jonson, p. 305.

99. *verba sequi . . . ediscere vitae*: Horace, *Epistles*, 2.2.143 and 144.

100. *recti apud . . . factus est*: Seneca, *Epistulae morales*, 123.6.

101. *And I must confess that . . . rather than entertains it*: Notwithstanding Daniel's apt criticism, the couplet was to become the dominant form of late-seventeenth- and eighteenth-century poetry.

102. *Besides, methinks sometimes . . . in my conceit most happy*: Daniel describes the running on of sense in couplet poems both from line to line (enjambment) and from couplet to couplet. This is now characterized as the difference between the open couplet style preferred by Elizabethan poets like Marlowe and the more epigrammatic closed couplet style used by later poets like Dryden and Pope. The Latin poet Lucan's *Bellum civile* was a key model for Daniel's *Civil Wars* (1595; successively enlarged to 1609). Like Lucan, Daniel preferred to write an epic grounded in recent history rather than in more distant pseudo-history or myth, which is why he is Daniel's 'Homer'; his poetry is of course unrhymed

but Daniel admires the tendency for its sense units to run over line ends.

103. *I think a tragedy … shall require a couplet*: This had in fact become the common practice, and Daniel's *Cleopatra* (1594) follows these ground rules.

104. *And, to avoid this over-glutting … in my affection*: The volume in which Daniel's *Defence* was printed includes the epistles Daniel is talking about. Some are conventional in form (the 'cross rhyme' of *ottava rima* – *ababab cc*), but others are more experimental, e.g. *abcabc*, *abcabcdd* and *terza rima*; the *abcabc* pattern is what Daniel is referring to here.

105. *Master Hugh Sanford*: Hugh Sanford was employed, like Daniel, at Wilton, acting as the previous Earl of Pembroke's secretary. He seems to have done much of the work on the 1593 edition of Sidney's *Arcadia*, and his advice matches the practices of his patron the Countess of Pembroke. He is Daniel's 'countryman' because both come from the West Country.

106. *holding feminine rhymes … or else by themselves*: 'Ditties' are lyric poems rather than epic (like the *Civil Wars*) or dramatic. By 'set certain' Daniel means that feminine rhymes should be in the same position in every stanza in shorter poems: if a poem in a stanza form *abab* begins with the *b* rhyme feminine, it must continue in this way in every stanza; in practice this extended to sonnet quatrains, and Daniel revised his sequence *Delia* to conform to this rule. To put feminine rhymes 'by themselves' means in a stanza form or sonnet in which every line has a feminine ending.

107. *this excellent painter man … in his own affections*: Referring to the practice of grinding pigments to make paints.

108. *Multos puto ad sapientiam … se pervenisse*: From Seneca, *De tranquillitate animi* ('On Tranquillity of Mind'), 1.16, the word order misremembered.

109. *caecus amor sui*: Horace, *Odes*, 1.18.14.

110. *neque idem umquam … se ipse miratur*: Daniel quotes Catullus 22.15–17, on Suffenus, a charming, witty man, but a bad, though prolific and self-satisfied, poet; '*Suffenus est quisque sibi*' is Daniel's own addition.

111. *quem vero arripuit, tenet occiditque legendo*: Horace, *Ars poetica*, 475.

112. *Next to this deformity … novelty can ever do*: Daniel scratches the surface of another issue at the interface of literature and an evolving national identity. Daniel's contemporaries coined many

of the words we now use, but some were excessive in use of neologisms and loan words. Edmund Spenser used many archaisms (often getting their meanings wrong) in pursuit of a more Anglo-Saxon lexicon; according to Ben Jonson, he 'writ no language'. Poetic licence, as described by Gascoigne, p. 244, also allowed extempore word formations. Alexander Gill, in his *Logonomia anglica* ('The Order of the English Language', 1621), even posited a separate, poetic dialect of English. Cf. Puttenham, Book 2, note 33.

SELECTED PASSAGES

GEORGE GASCOIGNE: CERTAIN NOTES OF INSTRUCTION

Text: *The posies of George Gascoigne Esquire* (1575)

On Gascoigne (*c.* 1534–77), see the Introduction, p. lxxii.

1. *Master Eduardo Donati*: The addressee has not been identified and is likely to be a fiction, to allow Gascoigne to pretend that only a non-native speaker might need instruction in English versification.

2. *The first and most necessary point . . . some fine invention*: Invention is the first part of rhetoric and the first stage of the composition of an oration. It involves finding material, both of one's own inventing and in the form of commonplaces and recognizable kinds of argument. Where short poems are concerned it coincides with what we understand by a 'conceit' – the basic argument or paradox upon which the poem is built.

3. *nor yet to thunder . . . (quoth my master Chaucer)*: In *The Canterbury Tales* the Parson is 'a Southern man, / I kan nat geest "rum, ram, ruf"', by lettre' ('The Parson's Prologue', 42–3), parodying the verse of the northern alliterative revival. Cf. note 20.

4. *For that being found . . . fast enough*: A popular rhetorical dictum ('hold to the matter, the words will follow') attributed to the Roman statesman and writer Cato the Elder (234–149 BC) and paraphrased by Horace, *Ars poetica*, 311: 'when matter is in hand words will not be loath to follow'. See Jonson's translation of this passage, p. 306.

5. *indecorum*: On *decorum* cf. Sidney, p. 46 and Puttenham, Book 3, chapters 23–4.

6. *beginning with the measure of twelve ... the common kind of verse*: What Gascoigne later calls 'poulter's measure': alternating lines of hexameter and heptameter. His point is that a poem begun in a certain verse form must continue in that form: in the example, one cannot begin in poulter's measure and then slip into fourteeners. He is not advocating using only one length of line in a poem. Cf. Webbe's first rule, pp. 254–6.

7. *And in your verses ... commonly pronounced or used*: Cf. Webbe's second rule, pp. 255 and 257–8.

8. *we have three manner of accents ... sometimes elevate*: Gascoigne's understanding of English prosody is sophisticated and revolutionary. Although Surrey and Richard Tottel, the editor of *Songs and Sonnets* (also known as 'Tottel's Miscellany', 1557), had recognized that English verse needed to be regulated by a discernible iambic pattern, Gascoigne is the first to spell this out in theoretical terms, and gets further than Puttenham was to do in Book 2 of the *Art*. 'Accent' is now understood to be a matter of pitch, stress and length. Gascoigne knowingly combines terms descriptive of pitch, of stress and of length, but the conciseness of his treatment has led to a great deal of confusion. He adds to the rule that English verse is regulated by patterns of stress the recognition that the length of syllables is also a factor, an observation which is borne out by the best poetic practice of the subsequent centuries. But the relevance of pitch seems strained. Gascoigne's accents are borrowed from the Latin grammarians, but confused: cf. Quintilian, *Institutio oratoria*, 1.5.22–4, where the acute accent marks stress and perhaps a rise in pitch, the grave no stress and a drop in pitch, and the circumflex a slight stress. Terms relating to syllable duration ('drawn out', 'long'; 'snatched up', 'short') allude to quantitative versification, where syllables were either long or short but some metrical positions in the line might be *anceps* or *indifferens*, that is, able to admit either a long or a short syllable indifferently. In Gascoigne's system, the 'grave' accent equates with stress, length and a rise in pitch, and the 'light' accent with a lack of stress, shortness and a depression of pitch. The circumflex, as is suggested in Gascoigne's fifth point (see note 16), accounts for the recognized ability of many monosyllables to be either stressed or unstressed without upsetting 'natural emphasis' or metre (cf. Puttenham, p. 120). It has to be

said that Gascoigne is wrong to group together length, pitch and stress so crisply, to imply an easy correspondence between quantitative and accentual-syllabic systems, and in his understanding of pitch. But he challenges English poets to think about these elements and to experiment with them, and that was an intervention of lasting importance.

9. *(for I dare not call them English verses)*: In common with Sidney, Puttenham, and others, Gascoigne tends to reserve the word 'verse' for classical, quantitative verses and uses the cognate terms 'rhyme' and 'rhythm' (often synonymous – see Puttenham, Book 2, note 10) for accentual-syllabic (and rhyming) verses.

10. *a foot of two syllables . . . elevate or made long*: Gascoigne describes the iambic foot, and makes clear that it is now the only common medium of English verse, confirming in theory the practice that his own poetry had substantially reinforced but which many (e.g. Puttenham) remained unable fully to recognize.

11. *as for example this following*: In the example which follows, the four-stress triple metre alternates iambs (˘ -) and anapaests (˘ ˘ -). The diagram above the first line corresponds to the entire couplet: stressed ('grave', 'drawn out or elevate') syllables occupy the upper of the two vertical positions and unstressed ('light', 'depressed or snatched up') syllables the lower; a double trough corresponds to the two unstressed syllables of the anapaest; the diagonal lines represent the rising or falling movement between syllables. The markings above the second line scan only that line's syllables as 'grave' (/ = stressed) or 'light' (\ = unstressed).

12. *Also, our father Chaucer . . . more syllables of lighter accents*: Cf. Puttenham, Book 2, p. 118 and note 23 for another attempt to account for Chaucer. Gascoigne's view, though misleading in associating Chaucer with quantitative verse, is an improvement on Puttenham's and is not without sense: if Chaucer wrote a four-stress line and if that line was to be perceived as having any regularity, then his lines would need to be spoken with a similar duration, regardless of the number of syllables.

13. *And, surely, I can lament . . . the name of a verse*: See note 9.

14. *In these two verses . . . and not 'ùndérstànd'*: The marks of scansion over the second verse line indicate not its natural pattern of stress but the abstract metrical grid to which both lines are obliged to conform. Gascoigne's explanation would make better sense if he remembered the circumflex accent (˜) and placed it over the first syllable of 'understand' and over 'by', allowing each syllable to bear the stress in the first line but to seem not to require

it in the unmetrical, second version of the line. Perhaps Gascoigne realizes that the symbol is only of use in explaining how prose rhythm ('Ĭ ūndèrstánd yòur méaniṅg bȳ yòur eýe') becomes verse ('Ĭ úndèrstánd yòur méanìng bý yòur éye').

15. *First, the most ancient English words ... of the inkhorn*: Cf. Puttenham, Book 2, p. 123 and note 33.

16. *whereas words of one syllable ... of an indifferent sound*: See note 8. If there is a difference between monosyllables being 'short or long as occasion requireth', or merely being indifferent, it is a subtle one. Gascoigne may just be saying the same thing in two different ways, or he may be saying, on the one hand, that some syllables can be either stressed or unstressed as occasion demands, and, on the other, that some metrical positions in a line need not be either stressed or unstressed but may be occupied by an indifferent syllable. The implications are more for the vocal performance of a line than for its composition.

17. *I would exhort you also to beware of rhyme without reason*: Like Puttenham (p. 115), Gascoigne exploits the proverbial 'neither rhyme nor reason'. Cf. Webbe's third rule, p. 255.

18. *ne quid nimis*: Cf. Puttenham, Book 3, note 21, where the saying is attributed to the Greek philosopher Bias.

19. *crambe bis positum mors est*: From Erasmus, *Adagia* ('Adages'), based on a Greek saying and Juvenal, *Satires*, 7.154: 'served up again and again, the cabbage is the death of the unhappy master'.

20. *repetition of sundry words ... therefore, ne quid nimis*: On alliterative 'hunting' or 'coursing' of letters cf. Sidney, p. 49 and note 256.

21. *Also, as much as may be ... use discretion*: Cf. Daniel, p. 233 and note 112, and Sidney on English as a 'mingled language', p. 51 and note 270. Gabriel Harvey annotates this passage in his copy (Bodleian Library, Malone 792(1), fol. T4ᵛ) as follows: 'Spenser hath revived "uncouth", "whilom", "of yore", "forthy"'.

22. *This poetical licence ... 'heaven' for 'heav'n'*: 'Power' and 'heaven' were pronounced and commonly scanned as monosyllables, though in verse they were often spelled, as in the 1575 edition, 'powre' and 'heavn' to distinguish them from dissyllabic 'power', 'heaven'. Gabriel Harvey annotates this passage in his copy (fol. U1ʳ) as follows: 'all these in Spenser, and many like; but with discretion, and tolerably, though sometime not greatly commendably'. Puttenham deals with these effects in Book 3, chapter 11. Cf. Cicero, *De oratore*, 3.38.152-4 for nonce words

(words coined for single occasions) and archaisms, and Daniel, note 31, for poetic licence.

23. *'cesures'*: The Latin term *caesura* is anglicized, as by Puttenham (Book 2, chapters 4-5).

24. *But yet thus much ... the end of the line*: Puttenham provides similar rules in Book 2, chapter 5. It is interesting that Gascoigne implies a contrast between the 'verse of ten' (i.e. pentameter), where the caesura should fall after the second foot, and 'rhyme royal' (which uses pentameter), where caesural placement is more flexible. Gascoigne's own pentameters are often split with the caesura after four syllables and six following it, but subsequent writers were more likely to follow the practice he outlines for rhyme royal: that caesura can fall at any point, or be lacking altogether. 'Rhyme royal' is spelled 'rithme royall' or 'rhythme royall' in the 1575 edition, implying that Gascoigne thinks of the stanza form in terms of its metre as much as of its rhyme scheme.

25. *Rhyme royal ... grave discourse*: The rhyme scheme of rhyme royal is $ababbcc_{10}$; cf. Puttenham, Book 2, chapter 2, on the staff of seven verses.

26. *There is also another kind called ballad ... light matters*: The ballad was a popular stanzaic poem, often with a refrain, and intended originally for singing. Lines of eight and six syllables ('these two were wont to be most commonly used') in quatrains were the norm; the most usual form (now known as ballad stanza) was $a_8b_6a_8b_6$ (sometimes *abxb*), but, as well as the 'common metre' instanced in this form, 'long metre' (stresses: 4-4-4-4) and 'short metre' (3-3-4-3) were also used. The form Gascoigne describes extends this pattern by adding a couplet, but he then confounds the ballad with the six-line pentameter stanza popular in the period. The word 'ballad' comes from the French but is related to the Italian and late Latin *ballare*, 'to dance', as Gascoigne suggests.

27. *rondelet*: The *rondel*, a French fixed form of determined length with certain lines repeated; its name means 'a little round'.

28. *but yet I can best allow ... do conclude the whole*: Gascoigne describes the 'English sonnet' (*abab cdcd efef gg*), as introduced by Surrey and later used by Shakespeare, and ignores the Italian form (octave *abbaabba* plus sestet, e.g. *cdedce, cdecde*) from which the English sonnet derives. When in his second note (p. 239 above) he talks of 'a pleasant sonnet' he is using the word in the general sense: 'any short lyric poem'. The etymology is correct.

29. *Then is there an old kind of rhyme ... my journey into Holland,*

etc.: The virelay is a French fixed form of three verses with refrains (French *virelai*), nothing like Gascoigne's description (five-line pentameter stanzas rhyming *ababa*). The poem he refers to, 'Gascoigne's Voyage into Holland' (printed in *A Hundred Sundry Flowers*, 1573) is indeed in this form. The etymology is uncertain: the word perhaps comes from 'vireli', a meaningless refrain word, which was then modified to suggest a type of 'lai' or song.

30. *There are also certain poems . . . what name to give them*: Gascoigne describes the base unit of the Italian sonnet, the quatrain *abba*.

31. *And the commonest sort of verse . . . and fourteen for another*: Poulter's measure, the alternation of hexameter and heptameter (the same metrical pattern in long lines as common metre), was overwhelmingly the most popular verse form of the third quarter of the sixteenth century. For an example see the poem by Queen Elizabeth given by Puttenham, p. 190. The fanciful title seems to be Gascoigne's own invention. 'Rhyme royal' is another term which may originate with him, although in this case a previous term, 'ballad royal', did exist.

32. *I had forgotten . . . delectable and light enterprises*: What Gascoigne understands by 'riding rhyme' is unclear. It is now used of the open couplets employed by Chaucer in *The Canterbury Tales*. Puttenham uses the term to refer to the metrically irregular line of 'our ancient rhymers' (Book 2, p. 118 and note 23), but Gascoigne elsewhere refers to one of his own long poems ('Dan Bartholomew's Dolorous Discourses' in pentameter *abab*) as 'this foolish riding rhyme'. Gascoigne may mean (i) (rough) pentameter in open couplets or continuous quatrains; or (ii) a loose four-stress line (see note 12). 'Rhyme' may once again be being used in the sense of 'rhythm' or 'verse'.

33. *Then, to return to my matter . . . psalms and hymns*: There is no great value or thought in these prescriptions, and it is in metre, rather than stanza form, genre, or subject matter, that Gascoigne's influence is felt. Many psalms and hymns were in lines of eight and six syllables; although these usually rhymed *abab*, where the rhyme was only on the second and fourth lines (*abxb*) the form was identical to a long-line rhyming couplet with caesura placed as Gascoigne advises. Cf. the end of Gascoigne's thirteenth note above, and on this phenomenon see Puttenham, p. 116 and Webbe, pp. 255–6.

HENRY PEACHAM:
FROM THE GARDEN OF ELOQUENCE

Texts: (i) *The garden of eloquence. Conteyning the figures of grammer and rhetorick, from whence maye bee gathered all manner of flowers, coulors, ornaments, exornations, formes and fashions of speech, very profitable for all those that be studious of eloquence and that reade most eloquent poets and orators, and also helpeth much for the better understanding of the holy scriptures.* (1577)

(ii) *The garden of eloquence, conteining the most excellent ornaments, exornations, lightes, flowers and formes of speech, commonly called the figures of rhetorike. By which the singular partes of mans mind, are most aptly expressed, and the sundrie affections of his heart most effectuallie uttered. Manifested, and furnished with varietie of fit examples, gathered out of the most eloquent orators, and best approved authors, and chieflie out of the holie scripture. Profitable and necessarie, as wel for private speech, as for publicke orations. Corrected and augmented by the first author.* (1593)

On Peacham, see the Introduction, p. lxxiii.

1. *To the Right Reverend Father ... Lord Bishop of London*: John Aylmer (1521–94), made Bishop of London in 1577.
2. *And to the end ... declare our thoughts to other*: The importance of reason and speech to humanity is a commonplace theme in the classical orators, and is the analogue of the argument repeated by both Sidney and Puttenham (Book 1, chapter 3) that it is to poetry that the first civilizing influence is owed, and where the first learning is to be found. Cf. Cicero, *De officiis* ('On Duties'), 1.16.50, on how reason and speech form the bond essential to human society, and Quintilian, *Institutio oratoria*, 2.16.12–17, on how reason is nothing without speech, the fairest gift from heaven. And behind both, the Greek orator Isocrates, *Nicocles*, 6–9: 'because there has been implanted in us the power to persuade each other and to make clear to each other whatever we desire, not only have we escaped the life of wild beasts, but we have come together and founded cities and made laws and invented arts; and, generally speaking, there is no institution devised by man which the power of speech has not helped us to establish.' The theme receives a classic formulation in the preface to Thomas Wilson's *The Art of Rhetoric* (1553).
3. *Of this sort among the Grecians ... Marcus Antonius, Fabius*

Quintilianus: Plato (*c.* 427–347 BC), the most archly persuasive of philosophers, is fairly branded an orator here, although he initiated the lasting dispute between the sweet-talking orators and sophists on the one hand, and the honest philosophers on the other in *Phaedrus*, *Protagoras* and, especially, *Gorgias*. Demosthenes (384–322 BC) was the greatest Greek orator, and the works of Aristotle (also 384–322 BC) included the important *Rhetoric*, which was revolutionary in concentrating not on style but on types and modes of argument. For Marcus Tullius Cicero (106–43 BC) and Marcus Fabius Quintilianus (*c.* 35–*c.*100 AD) see Puttenham, Book 3, note 23. For Lucius Licinius Crassus (140–91 BC) and Marcus Antonius (143–87 BC) see Sidney, note 266.

4. *such figurative flowers, both of grammar and rhetoric*: The figures 'of grammar and rhetoric' are schemes and tropes respectively (see Puttenham, Book 3, note 26); for the metaphor of flowers which encourages Peacham to create a garden of eloquence see Sidney, note 13, and Puttenham, Book 3, note 2.

5. *the goodly and beautiful colours of elocution*: For colours (figures or types of argument) see Puttenham, Book 3, note 2; 'elocution' means 'style', 'expression', 'eloquence', and in its Latin form (*elocutio*) is the name given to the third branch of rhetorical study and the third stage in the composition of an oration; most English rhetorics, including Peacham's, confined themselves to *elocutio*, and therefore 'rhetoric' came primarily to be identified with rhetorical figures.

6. *no man can read profitably . . . the holy scriptures without them*: It is important to note that rhetoric is here presented as a tool of reading as well as composition. Cf. the work's full title, given in the headnote above, and Puttenham, Book 3, chapter 10, page 148.

7. *For by figures . . . pleasantly poured forth*: Quintilian, in the *Institutio oratoria*, frequently compares eloquence to an irresistible flood. See, e.g., 6.1.51 and 12.10.60–61, on the middle and grand styles: 'its [the middle style's] flow will be gentle, like that of a river whose waters are clear, but overshadowed by the green banks on either side. But he whose eloquence is like to some great torrent that rolls down rocks and "disdains the bridge" [Virgil, *Aeneid*, 8.728] and carves out its own banks for itself, will sweep the judge from his feet, struggle as he may, and force him to go whither he bears him.'

8. *wisdom speaking eloquently*: Classical rhetoric's answer to its

critics was that the orator was 'a good man skilled in speaking' (*vir bonus dicendi peritus*), that the orator would also be a philosopher and was not simply a mercenary happy to make any case persuasive. See Quintilian, *Institutio oratoria*, 1.pr.9 and 12.1, and cf. Isocrates, *Nicocles*, 7: 'the power to speak well is taken as the surest index of a sound understanding, and discourse which is true and lawful and just is the outward image of a good and faithful soul.' Quintilian offers a fine survey of answers to the question 'what is rhetoric?' in *Institutio oratoria*, 2.15.

9. *the strength of apt and eloquent pleading … in these kind of exornations*: Quintilian, *Institutio oratoria*, e.g. 9.1.21, 9.2.2–4.

10. *such as have not the understanding of the Latin tongue*: It was unlikely that anyone coming to this book would not have learned Latin at school, and have used a Latin rhetoric like the *Epitome troporum ac schematum* ('Outline of Schemes and Tropes') of Susenbrotus (*c.* 1541). It has been suggested, however, that the vernacular rhetorics would have been especially valued by older students of oratory whose Latin had grown rusty.

11. *To the Right Honourable Sir John Puckering … Great Seal of England*: Sir John Puckering (1544–96), barrister, Speaker of the House of Commons 1584–5 and 1586–7, knighted and made Lord Keeper in 1592.

12. *as martial instruments both of defence and invasion*: On ornaments as weapons see Puttenham, Book 3, note 1.

WILLIAM WEBBE:
FROM A DISCOURSE OF ENGLISH POETRY

Text: *A discourse of English poetrie. Together, with the authors judgment, touching the reformation of our English verse. By William Webbe. Graduate.* (1586)

On Webbe, see the Introduction, p. lxxiii.

1. *Which rude kind of verse … compiled in that verse*: For the association of rhyme with barbarism and custom, cf. Campion, p. 282, and Daniel's *Defence*, p. 211 and throughout. Webbe belongs to the first wave of experimenters with classical metres, like Sidney, who could see both systems operating side by side (cf. Sidney, p. 52). As a theorist of accentual-syllabic metres he is perceptive and in no way blinded by dogma. At the end of his

treatise he demonstrates his preference for the classical system by translating poems from Spenser's *The Shepheardes Calender* into quantitative verses.

2. *There be three special notes . . . our accustomed English rhyme*: Webbe's three notes are probably derived from Gascoigne's. His first corresponds to Gascoigne's third; his second to Gascoigne's fourth; and his third to Gascoigne's sixth.

3. *proportionable to the tune . . . read or measured*: Many poems were written to the tunes of popular dances and ballads, either to enable performance as song or without any musical performance necessarily being intended. The poet might attempt to match the rhythms of the melody exactly, or might only take the proportions of the tune as the basis for a metrical scheme. Webbe returns to this issue again, p. 256.

4. *The longest verse in length . . . in dangers deep it drowns*: Neither Gascoigne nor Puttenham mentions a line of octameter, both setting the limit at fourteen syllables. That Webbe sees it as theoretically possible is important, as are his clear-headed observations on how lines of six or eight syllables can be connected to make long lines of fourteen and sixteen syllables (twelve also could be generated in the same way). The two observations together align him with a trend in modern prosody which sees the four-stress line as the basic unit of all line lengths except for pentameter: a three-stress line ends with a pause corresponding to the omitted stress, and longer lines are made by running together pairs of short lines, six plus six, six plus eight and eight plus eight, giving twelve-, fourteen- and sixteen-syllabled lines respectively. In a continuous sequence of lines of eight plus eight or sixteen, all metrical positions of the basic four-stress line are filled, making the lines the longest possible. For less developed hints about the relation between long and short lines cf. Gascoigne, note 33 and Puttenham, p. 116.

5. *My mind with fury fierce . . . adorned with laurel bough*: The opening of Barnaby Googe, *The Zodiac of Life* (1561; 1565), a translation from the Latin *Zodaicus vitae* (1531?) of Marcellus Palingenius. The 'fury' is the *furor poeticus* (see Puttenham, Book 1, note 6); Parnassus is the mountain sacred to Apollo and the Muses; the laurel is the tree sacred to Apollo. The 'translators of the Latin poets' who used the fourteener (believing it to be the closest vernacular approximation to the classical hexameter) also included Arthur Golding, whose translation of Ovid's *Metamorphoses* was printed in 1565 (the first four books)

and 1567 (the complete work); Webbe quotes the opening line below.

6.   *Which may be likewise, and so it often is, divided*: (1586: 'Which may likewise and so it often is divided').

7.   *Which may be likewise . . . Adorned with laurel bough*: Webbe simply divides the lines in two and leaves the first and third unrhymed, to show that the $a_8 b_6 x_8 b_6$ scheme common in hymns and ballads is identical to the fourteener couplet. The short line layout is used in *The Zodiac of Life*.

8.   *counter rhyme*: Webbe introduces a sensible term for the envelope pattern *abba*, which Gascoigne could not find a name for (p. 245). For Puttenham the pattern is an instance of 'plain compass' (Book 2, chapter 11, p. 128). The pattern, less used than cross rhyme, was little discussed, and so Webbe's term was not taken up.

9.   *Neither is there any tune . . . I will let them pass*: 'Rogero' and 'Downright Squire' were popular tunes to which ballads in collections like *A Handful of Pleasant Delights* (*c.* 1566) were written; 'Trenchmore' was a popular dance tune in 6/8 with a simple rhythm corresponding readily to iambic tetrameter. The galliard was a triple-time dance, the pavan a dance in duple time, and the two forms were the most popular models for dance and instrumental tunes; the songs of John Dowland include examples of poems written to the music of both pavans and galliards. The jig was a lively dance in triple time, and the 'brawl' (French *branle*) a dance in duple time.

10. *I that my slender oaten pipe in verse was wont to sound*: The first line of the spurious or rejected four-line opening (*Ille ego, qui quondam . . .*) to Virgil's *Aeneid*, which in most editions preceded the famous opening *Arma virumque cano*. Webbe quotes it in Thomas Phaer's translation (1555).

11. *rules of prosodia*: The rules of prosody determined the quantity of syllables. A syllable would be long 'by position' if it was made up of a naturally short vowel followed by two consonants: 'aloud' would therefore be scanned as an iamb (short-long), 'allowed' as a spondee (long-long). Because orthography was flexible, writers of English quantitative verses were able to manipulate spelling to ensure scansion (e.g. 'alowd', iamb).

12. *Of shapes transformed to bodies strange I purpose to entreat*: The opening line of Ovid's *Metamorphoses* in Golding's 1565 translation.

13. *Make the first syllable long . . . to the words*: Webbe's point is that Golding's line may not be written according to quantitative

rules, but it conforms to them to some extent. One cannot perform the unstressed syllables as long (taking twice the time to pronounce) and the stressed syllables as short, which suggests that length is a factor in metrical accent. Cf. Gascoigne on 'natural emphasis', p. 239 and note 8.

14. *some there be of indifferency that will stand in any place*: For the idea that Anglo-Saxon monosyllables are particularly flexible in the matter of scansion – able to be long or short, stressed or unstressed – cf. Gascoigne, p. 241 and Puttenham, Book 2, p. 120.

15. *For though it be tolerable . . . the sense obscure*: Cf. Gascoigne's eleventh note, p. 243.

16. *And sure it is a wonder . . . his speech seem nothing poetical*: Webbe sensibly challenges the doctrine that the study of poetry helps the development of good prose style, one of the reasons for the strong presence of poetry in traditional rhetoric. See for example Quintilian on poetry and prose style, *Institutio oratoria*, 10.1.27–30 and 10.5.4–5.

SIR JOHN HARINGTON:
A BRIEF APOLOGY OF POETRY

Text: 'A preface, or rather a briefe apologie of poetrie, and of the author and translator of this poem', *from* [Ludovico Ariosto,] *Orlando furioso in English heroical verse, by John Harington* (1591)

On Harington (*c.* 1561–1612), see the Introduction, pp. lxxiii–lxxiv. Ariosto's *Orlando furioso* was one of the most influential Italian heroic poems, an important model for both Sidney's *Arcadia* and Spenser's *The Faerie Queene*, both of which were first printed in 1590. Harington's translation is dedicated to Queen Elizabeth I, at whose instigation he is supposed to have undertaken it. His entertaining preface borrows extensively from Sidney's *Defence*, not printed until 1595 and evidently available to Harington in manuscript.

1. *The learned Plutarch, in his Laconical Apothegms . . . who had dispraised Hercules*: Plutarch, *Apothegmata Laconica*, 192c. 'Laconic(al)' means both 'pertaining to Laconia, Lacedaemonia, Sparta' and 'in a Laconian style, i.e. concise, sententious'; 'apothegms' are sayings or maxims.

2. *poesy (the very first nurse . . . of all learning)*: For the 'first nurse' cf. Sidney, p. 4 and note 4.

3. *a squint-eyed Zoilus*: Zoilus was a fourth-century BC Greek critic

and grammarian famous for his severe criticism of Homer; his name became a type for the envious, carping critic.

4. *yea, sure there will be some . . . rapier and dagger*: Hercules is traditionally portrayed with a club; the rapier and dagger method of fighting was fashionable among courtiers and gentlemen.

5. *scientia non habet inimicum . . . but the ignorant*: A popular saying of unknown origin.

6. *But now*: Marginal note: 'The division of this apology into three parts'.

7. *where the hedge is . . . there doth every man go over*: Cf. Sidney, p. 26 for this proverbial saying.

8. *First, therefore, of poetry itself*: Marginal note: 'Of Poetry'.

9. *Alexanders, Caesars, Scipios*: This is borrowed directly from Sidney, pp. 40-41.

10. *Neither do I suppose it . . . their sundry kinds*: This and the preceding paragraph offer a masterly instance of the rhetorical figure *paralepsis* (see Puttenham, pp. 179-80), by which the speaker emphasizes a point by stating that he will not mention it.

11. *that unknown godfather . . . Art of English Poetry*: Since our only contemporary reference to Puttenham as the author of the *Art* comes in a letter from Harington to the printer of both the *Art* and *Orlando Furioso*, it is probable that Harington knows exactly to whom he is referring here and below (see headnote to Puttenham, p. 359). On the poet as maker see Sidney, p. 8 and Puttenham, Book 1, chapter 1.

12. *Plato, Xenophon and Erasmus . . . termeth all translators*: Sidney discusses Plato (who wrote in dialogues), Xenophon (whose fictitious *Cyropaedia* is counted by Sidney as a poem in prose), Erasmus (for his dialogues) and Lucan (whose *Bellum civile* is a historical poem on the civil wars between Caesar and Pompey). Puttenham praises Phaer and Golding in the final chapter of Book 1 (pp. 105 and 107, and notes 89 and 90), and describes the translator as 'a versifier, but not a poet' in the *Art*'s opening paragraph, p. 57 (cf. Sidney, p. 12).

13. *I will refer you to Sir Philip Sidney's Apology*: This remark implies that some of Harington's readers would have had access to Sidney's work in manuscript: it was not to be printed for another four years. As far as we know, Sidney gave the work no title and it had no title in manuscript. It was generically an 'apology' (Greek *apologia*, a speech in defence); that Harington calls it this does not mean that it was its given title.

14. *For though the poor gentleman . . . the most praiseworthy*: For

the *Partheniads* see Puttenham, Book 3, note 49 and examples on pp. 163, 174, and 186; for an example of another poem in praise of Elizabeth I see the quotation from the 'Triumphals' on p. 182. Harington's alliteration subtly associates Puttenham with an outmoded poetic fashion.

15. *it is a gift and not an art*: See Sidney's discussion of the proverb *orator fit, poeta nascitur*, p. 43.

16. *carmina quod scribis . . . hoc Ciceronis habes*: Martial, *Epigrams*, 2.89.3–4.

17. *yea, (as the wise man saith) . . . nothing but vanity*: A conflation of Ecclesiastes 1:2 and 1:14.

18. *So we read how that great Moses . . . with God*: Acts 7:22 (cf. Exodus 2:9–10).

19. *So the notable prophet Daniel . . . to be a prophet*: Daniel 1:4.

20. *Wherefore Plutarch*: Marginal note: 'Plutarch de audiendis poetis'.

21. *Wherefore Plutarch, having written . . . the popular divines*: The essay on Homer (*De Homero*) included in some texts of the *Moralia* is not now believed to be by Plutarch. Harington paraphrases the opening of 'How the Young Man Ought to Study Poetry' (known as 'De audiendis poetis'), *Moralia*, 14d–e; he shares an interest in this essay with Sidney, and borrows another of Sidney's phrases (p. 18): 'But the poet is the food for the tenderest stomachs; the poet is indeed the right popular philosopher'. Cf. Sidney, note 258 for further instances of this gustatory metaphor.

22. *Likewise Tasso*: Marginal note: 'Tasso. Canto 1, staff 3'. (The reference is correct.)

23. *his verse is this . . . a pretty prosopopoeia*: Harington gives the Italian original, omitted here, before his translation. For *prosopopoeia* and *prosopographia* see Puttenham, p. 183; and cf. Sidney, p. 7.

24. *This is then that honest fraud . . . that doth not deceive*: Attributed to Gorgias by Plutarch in *Moralia*, 348d, and also cited in 'How the Young Man Ought to Study Poetry', *Moralia*, 15d. See Sidney, note 165.

25. *that it is a nurse of lies . . . an enticer to wantonness*: Marginal notes: 'Agrippa, *De vanitate scientiarum*, cap. 4'; 'Four objections against poetry'. The arguments are drawn from Cornelius Agrippa's *De vanitate et incertitudine scientiarum* ('On the Vanity and Uncertainty of the Sciences', 1530), chapter 4, and are similar to the four arguments countered by Sidney (see p. 33).

26. *And first for lying*: Marginal note: 'Answer to the first, of lying'.

27. *the rule of poetica licentia ... feign what they list*: See Horace, *Ars poetica*, 1-13, on poetic licence as a matter of fictions rather than word formations (cf. Gascoigne, p. 244). For poetry as an art of imitation according to Aristotle (*Poetics*, 1447a-1448b) see Sidney, p. 10 and note 35.

28. *iuridicis, Erebo, fisco ... pictoribus atque poetis*: Untraced, but 'pictoribus atque poetis' is the famous tag from Horace, *Ars poetica*, 9-10: 'Painters and poets have always had an equal right in venturing to do anything'.

29. *But what if they lie ... though they would*: These sentences are based squarely on Sidney's answer to the charge of lying, p. 34.

30. *the active life of man*: The 'active life' is always coupled with or contrasted to the 'contemplative life'. Compare Sidney's Aristotelian 'it is not *gnōsis* but *praxis* must be the fruit', p. 22, and his parody of philosophers disputing 'whether the contemplative or the active life do excel', p. 24.

31. *Many times also ... by that another is understood*: On allegory (Greek *allēgoria* = 'other speaking') cf. Puttenham, p. 159. The allegorical method stretches back to efforts in the sixth and fifth centuries BC to interpret Homer and Hesiod in such a way as to defend them against charges of immorality, and by the time of Boccaccio had become a means of presenting pagan myth as a precursive Christian theology. The system of meaning which Harington describes is based on the fourfold method of interpretation, which was the dominant system of biblical interpretation in the Middle Ages and Renaissance. It distinguished between the literal or historical level, the allegorical (typological or figural) level, the moral level, and the anagogical (eschatological, spiritual) level. This was helpfully glossed in a popular Latin mnemonic couplet: 'The *letter* teaches the event, the *allegory* what you should believe, the *moral* what you should do, the *anagogy* where you are heading'. Harington's system simply merges the allegorical and the anagogical to give a threefold method. All non-literal senses could be grouped together as allegory in the broad sense of the word, but Harington tends to use it in the narrow sense of one level (encompassing the allegorical and anagogical levels). Harington refers to Plutarch, 'How the Young Man Ought to Study Poetry', *Moralia*, 19e-f, where allegory is discussed but not defined; cf. Quintilian, *Institutio oratoria*, 8.6.44-59, for the classical understanding of allegory.

32. *Perseus, son of Jupiter ... flown up to heaven*: Marginal note:

'Ovid, *Metamorph.[oses]*, 4'. Perseus features in *Metamorphoses*, 4.604–803 and 5.1–249, and Ovid touches briefly on the killing of Medusa the Gorgon, and Perseus' flight through the heavens on the winged sandals given him by Mercury, at 4.769–89.

33. *The historical sense is this . . . the kings of Crete or Athens so called*: On the pagan gods as kings inflated by the power of legend cf. Puttenham, Book 1, chapter 16.

34. *because man one of the chief works of nature*: The text follows 1591, which perhaps omits a word: 'because man [is] one of the chief works of nature'.

35. *the men of greatest learning . . . for sundry causes*: On 'the veil of fables' cf. Sidney, p. 53.

36. *Another cause why . . . in verse than in prose*: On the fitness of poetry for memory see Sidney, p. 32.

37. *Aristotle, though rejecting both . . . studious of philosophy*: See Plutarch, *Life of Alexander*, 7.4. Aristotle (384–322 BC) acted as tutor to the young Alexander the Great (356–323 BC) between 343/2 BC and 340 BC; Alexander later helped to fund Aristotle's Lyceum in Athens, and ordered that interesting phenomena observed in his empire be reported to Aristotle. Cf. Puttenham on the philosopher Heraclitus 'the Obscure', p. 191.

38. *But (as I say) Plato . . . which is fiction and imitation*: On Plato as a poet for his use of dialogue, and on his arguments against poetry in the *Republic*, see Sidney, pp. 5 and 38, and notes 12 and 187.

39. *yet his master Socrates . . . as Plutarch testifieth*: 'How the Young Man Ought to Study Poetry', *Moralia*, 16c. See Sidney, p. 41 and note 207.

40. *Demosthenes . . . to overthrow them*: Philip of Macedonia expanded his power across Greece in the mid-fourth century BC; Demosthenes tried to stir up the Athenians against him in a series of speeches, but Philip won a crushing victory over Athens in 338 BC and Demosthenes' influence waned. Harington's anecdote is based on Plutarch, *Life of Demosthenes*, 23.4, citing the report of Aristobulus.

41. *As that divine parable . . . Dives and Lazarus*: The Sower: Matthew 13:3–23, Mark 4:2–20, Luke 8:4–15; the Prodigal Son: Luke 15:11–32; Dives and Lazarus: Luke 16:19–31. Sidney also uses the parables of Dives and Lazarus and the Prodigal Son as examples (p. 18).

42. *The other part of poetry, which is verse*: Marginal note: 'Two parts of poetry: imitation or invention and verse'.

43. *saepe etiam steriles . . . exsudat inutilis umor*: Georgics, 1.84–8.

44. *Multum adeo . . . iuvat arva*: Georgics, 1.94–5.

45. *the greatest philosophers . . . in their writings*: Socrates, for example, quotes frequently from the poets in Plato's dialogues.

46. *Orpheus, Linus, Hesiodus*: For Orpheus, Linus and Hesiod as among the first writers see Sidney, p. 4, and notes 6 and 7.

47. *that some part of the Scripture . . . they agree not on*: Harington again borrows from Sidney, pp. 10 and 7.

48. *Now, the second objection is pleasing of fools*: Marginal note: 'Answer to the second objection'.

49. *omne tulit punctum qui miscuit utile dulci*: Ars poetica, 343. Cf. the centrality of teaching and delighting to Sidney's *Defence*, and for rhubarb specifically p. 23.

50. *able to keep a child from play . . . from the chimney corner*: Lifted directly from Sidney (p. 23), just above the discussion of sweetening bitter medicines. That Harington at times crosses the line between imitation and plagiarism perhaps suggests that he did not expect the *Defence* to be printed.

51. *Now, for the breeding of errors . . . the third objection*: Marginal note: 'Answer to the third'.

52. *as Sir Philip Sidney confesseth . . . subject to this reproof*: Cf. Sidney, p. 35.

53. *poetry doth not abuse us, but writers have abused poetry*: Cf. Sidney, p. 35.

54. *First, the tragical . . . but pity or detestation*: 'Detestation' is an odd companion for 'pity', and may suggest that Harington's grasp of Aristotle's *Poetics* and its formula of pity and fear was not as strong as Sidney's, whose version of the formula is 'admiration and commiseration': see Sidney, p. 27 and note 135.

55. *laudant illa, sed ista legunt*: Martial, 4.49.10.

56. *erubuit posuitque . . . Brute, recede: leget*: Martial, 11.16.9–10.

57. *Lucretia . . . she will to it again and read it all*: The names are taken bathetically from the important Roman story of the rape of the chaste Lucretia by Sextus, the son of the king Tarquinius Superbus. After her suicide, Brutus led the enraged people in an uprising to expel the Tarquins, and the Roman republic was born.

58. *as Scaliger writeth of Virgil . . . both wiser and honester*: Julius Caesar Scaliger, *Poetices libri septem* (1561), 3.19; and cf. Sidney's peroration, p. 53.

59. *And thus much be said for poesy*: The preface continues with the second and third parts, the apologies of 'the author and translator of this poem'.

SAMUEL DANIEL: *FROM* MUSOPHILUS: CONTAINING A GENERAL DEFENCE OF LEARNING

Text: *The poeticall essayes of Sam. Danyel.* (1599)

On Daniel, see the Introduction, pp. lxvii–lxxi. Dedicated to Fulke Greville, Daniel's poem is an unequal dialogue, but a dialogue all the same. Each character has three speeches, each longer than their last: Philocosmus starts (8 lines; 42; 116), and is answered each time by Musophilus (28 lines; 318; 490), totalling 1002 lines of which Musophilus gets 836 and Philocosmus 166. Musophilus means 'lover of the Muses', Philocosmus 'lover of the world'. The poem is written in continuous six-line stanzas rhyming *ababab*, and occasionally *abababcc*.

1. *Besides, so many . . . to get eternity the while*: For versions of the complaint that the multitude of bad rhymers devalue poetry and cause 'poet' to be a term of abuse cf. Sidney (on 'the laughing stock of children'), p. 4; Puttenham, Book 1, chapter 8 (p. 70); Harington on 'every base rhymer and ballad maker', p. 263; and Campion, p. 283.

2. *Since Chaucer lived . . . but in his last*: The sense is difficult: if Chaucer 'yet shall' live, then these will not be 'his last' days; alternatively, it may mean that his reputation survives only in 'his last' work, *The Canterbury Tales* (both the last he wrote, and the last in worth according to neoclassical criteria of decorum and generic correctness), but *Troilus and Criseyde* (not open to the same critical objections) was if anything more popular.

3. *the speaking picture*: For a poetic representation as a speaking picture see Sidney, p. 10 and note 35.

4. *Soul of the world*: Scansion requires 'world' to be pronounced as a dissyllable, as in Daniel's Somerset accent.

5. *this scarce discernèd isle . . . traffic of our style*: English was at this point in history spoken only in the British Isles. The English were good linguists and no Europeans needed to learn English to communicate with them (Latin, Italian, French or Spanish being the languages widely known and used). There was therefore no audience for vernacular English literature on the Continent and the only British authors with an international reputation wrote in Latin.

6.   *Yet do I not dislike . . . for like glorious parts*: Philocosmus echoes
     Plato's *Republic*, where hymns to the gods and praises of great
     men are the only forms of poetry allowed. See *Republic*, 607a
     and Sidney, note 187.

7.   *And for my part . . . all I am is his*: Cf. Cicero, *Brutus*, 191: 'Once
     Antimachus [the poet] got an audience together and began to
     read them a large volume of his . . . Everyone but Plato walked
     out as he read. "I shall go on reading all the same," he said. "For
     me Plato counts as a hundred thousand." And quite right too; for
     a poem, if abstruse, need move the enthusiasm only of the few.
     But a speech is meant for the people – and must win the approval
     of the crowd.' Cf. Seneca, *Epistulae morales*, 7.11 for a gathering
     of similar maxims.

8.   *Power above powers . . . more than all their swords*: For the
     power of rhetoric cf. Peacham, p. 249 and note 2.

9.   *unmaterial fruits of shades*: This phrase refers back to Philocos-
     mus' 'unmaterial swellings of your pen' (l. 495) which are 'Begot
     in shades' (l. 494), i.e., insubstantial writings which are the prod-
     uct of obscurity; however, there may be a Platonic implication
     too: existence is a mere shadow of the ideal forms or ideas, and
     art a copy of that shadow, and hence doubly worthless (cf. Sidney
     note 30).

10. *And who, in time, knows whither . . . is now ordained*: Daniel's
     apparent prophecy of English as a world language is an extrava-
     gant extrapolation from the English colonization of North
     America; his prediction of a 'great work' (which in retrospect fits
     Shakespeare and Milton well enough) would have seemed equally
     over optimistic in an age when England was a minor European
     power and English a minority language.

11. *And as for poesy (mother of this force)*: For poetry as a mother
     or nurse cf. Sidney, p. 4 and note 4, and Harington, p. 260.

12. *a loose, yet measured, course*: This describes English vernacular
     metre; Daniel's imagery depicts eloquence as a baby helped to its
     (poetic) feet by Mother Poetry.

13. *since it is well approved . . . out of themselves removed*: 'They
     have commerce' with heaven by being 'out of themselves
     removed' through inspiration and the *furor poeticus* (see Putten-
     ham, Book 1, note 6).

THOMAS CAMPION: *FROM* OBSERVATIONS IN THE ART OF ENGLISH POESY

Text: *Observations in the Art of English Poesie. By Thomas Campion. Wherein it is demonstratively prooved, and by example confirmed, that the English toong will receive eight severall kinds of numbers, proper to it selfe, which are all in this booke set forth, and were never before this time by any man attempted.* (1602)

On Campion (1567–1620), see the Introduction, p. lxix. Campion's *Observations* might have been written at any point in the twelve or so years prior to its publication. Although a few writers had continued to compose English verses in classical metres, no contribution to the debate had been made since the death of Sir Philip Sidney, the movement's best ambassador, in 1586. Campion's, then, is a belated and anachronistic intervention, but it is also one which steers a more moderate theoretical course and manages successfully to reconcile classically derived rules and English speech patterns. The treatise was dedicated to Thomas Sackville, Lord Buckhurst (1536–1608), contributor to *A Mirror for Magistrates*, and author of the blank verse tragedy *Gorboduc* with Thomas Norton (on which see Sidney, p. 44).

1. *Number is discreta quantitas*: In mathematics number was understood as being a matter of 'discrete quantity', i.e. numbers and rational numbers (how many), or of 'continuous quantity', i.e. magnitude (how much). Campion perhaps follows Julius Caesar Scaliger, *Poetices libri septem*, 4.45, where the distinction is applied to the difference between the number of syllables or words in a line of verse and their quantities.

2. *when we speak of a poem written in number . . . of their sound*: In classical metrics, that is, we consider not the syllable count of a line but the required pattern of long and short syllables. In many simple metres syllable count would be constant because only one type of foot was used throughout, or respectively in each position in the line. But in other metres there was flexibility. The classical hexameter, for example, could have either a spondee (two syllables, long-long) or a dactyl (three syllables, long-short-short) for each of the first four feet; the fifth had to be a dactyl and the sixth a spondee. Since the dactyl and the spondee were of equivalent quantity (two shorts being equivalent to one long) each line would be of equal temporal length (continuous quantity), but

the syllable count (discrete quantity) could be anything from thirteen to seventeen.

3. *As in music we do not say ... no more notes than semibreves*: Campion was an able composer who later wrote a treatise on harmony. He was unique in the period in writing both words and music for his simple lute airs. Only one of these uses words written in the quantitative system and set in a strictly quantitative fashion. But all achieve a marriage of word and music which could only be achieved by paying attention to the quantity of syllables written in accentual-syllabic metres. His musical explanation here is helpful. In music of distinct phrasal units of predictable length (e.g. dances and the dance-derived song forms favoured by Campion) a strain would be such a unit, e.g. the music setting one of the four lines of verse in each stanza of a strophic song, or the music corresponding to the first of three sets of steps in a galliard (a common triple-time dance). Renaissance music did not employ regular bar lines or time signatures, but the impetus for their introduction came from this type of music rather than from the more complex polyphonic tradition. The 'semibreve' (American 'whole note') unit could be used to measure the length of such a strain. A strain of eight semibreves (equivalent in modern notation to eight bars of 4/4) might have any number of notes, or, as Campion observes, 'no more notes' than eight (although those notes could be of other values, and rests would also be allowed for).

4. *The world is made ... and music to poetry*: Campion alludes to the Pythagorean tradition, whereby the universe is constructed according to the ratios and proportions which govern musical intervals and harmonies. A correspondence existed between the planetary music of the spheres (*musica mundana*) and the harmonic composition of individual men (*musica humana*), which was why different kinds of music (*musica instrumentalis*) could directly affect human moods and dispositions (cf. Puttenham, Book 2, note 39 and Sidney, note 157).

5. *for Terence saith ... confounding music and poetry together*: Terence, *Phormio*, prologue, 17.

6. *both diligent oberservers ... likewise in their prose*: Quantity was not simply a device for measuring syllables in verse but was a fact of grammar. Metrical patterns were recommended by the rhetoricians to heighten the effect of the orator's prose (see for example the lengthy discussion in Quintilian, *Institutio oratoria*, 9.4).

7. *Learning ... and other learned men of that age*: This point is picked up by Daniel, p. 218. Consigning all mediaeval scholarship to the Dark Ages and ignoring the origins of the Renaissance in fourteenth- and fifteenth-century Italy, Campion somewhat blindly gives all the credit to three of the important figures in the early tradition of North European humanism: Johann Reuchlin (1455–1522), German scholar of Greek and Hebrew; Desiderius Erasmus (?1466–1535), Dutch humanist scholar, greatly influential in England; and the English scholar and politician Thomas More (?1477–1535).

8. *Epistolae obscurorum virorum*: A series of satirical letters by Ulrich van Hutten and others published in 1515 and 1516, aimed at the philistinism, pedantry and pomposity of medieval theologians and friars.

9. *which we abusively call ... of rhythmus and metrum*: See Puttenham, Book 2, notes 7 and 10. Campion objects to the use of the word 'rhyme' because *rhythmus* denotes pattern or rhythm, and to the use of 'metre' in modern accentual-syllabic or syllabic systems because it denotes 'measure', which should, as he has earlier indicated, be about both syllable count (discrete quantity) and syllable quantity (continuous quantity) and not only the former.

10. *and those very expert ... rhyme a man to death*: On rhyming to death see Sidney, p. 54 and note 284; and cf. the moderate Webbe's grudging admiration for 'extempore' rhyming, p. 259.

11. *similiter desinentia*: On the figure *similiter desinens* (also *similiter cadens* and Greek *homoioteleuton*) as equivalent to rhyme see Puttenham, Book 2, p. 121 and note 28; cf. Sidney, p. 50.

12. *and that, being but figura verbi ... tedious affectation*: Warnings against the overuse of schemes, or figures of words, are frequent; see, e.g., Quintilian, *Institutio oratoria*, 9.3.4: 'If a speaker use them sparingly and only as occasion demands, they will serve as a seasoning to his style and increase its attraction. If, on the other hand, he strains after them overmuch, he will lose that very charm of variety which they confer.'

13. *Such was that ... now hissed out of Paul's Churchyard*: St Paul's Churchyard was the centre of the London printing and bookselling trade. Excessive alliteration was a feature of early Elizabethan verse and often involved, as in Gascoigne's practice, a marking of stressed syllables in order to realize audibly the iambic pattern which was beginning to be accepted as the basis of English verse (e.g. 'The passing pangs, which they in fancies feign', from

'Gascoigne's Passion'). Cf. Sidney, p. 49 and note 256, and Gascoigne himself, p. 242.

14. *Iambic and trochaic feet . . . unapt drawing of their speech*: The conventions which in retrospect appear to apply to Elizabethan iambic verse include the reversal of some feet (or 'trochaic substitution') in iambic lines: frequently the first foot (e.g. Shakespeare's 'Līliěs that fester smell far worse than weeds', sonnet 94, l. 14); less frequently the third or fourth. Those conventions do not allow for other foot substitutions (e.g. a pyrrhic for an iamb), but, as Campion's example following demonstrates, some stressed syllables were more stressed than others, and some verses might seem to fall short. Cf. Gascoigne on indifferent syllables or accents, pp. 239 and 241 and notes 8 and 14. Because Campion is a musician who favours quantitative verses he cannot see the accentual-syllabic system as an abstract set of rules for generating lines which might sound very unlike each other; he needs to be able to hear the pattern in performance, and therefore understands it as a kind of quantitative system.

15. *Was it my destiny or dismal chance . . . than it ought by nature*: Such lines are in fact frequent, and offer support to those who see a residual four-stress pattern operating beneath the five-foot pentameter grid. In Campion's example the third foot is a pyrrhic instead of an iamb, meaning that the whole line falls short (in 'continuous quantity') by the time value of one-third of an iambic foot or one short syllable. A modern prosodist might say that for 'stiny' to be an iamb it only requires that the second syllable be relatively more stressed than the first, and that temporal value is not an issue.

16. *quot caelum stellas, tot habet tua Roma puellas*: Ovid, *Ars amatoria*, 1.59.

17. *For in quatorzains . . . he would cut them shorter*: Procrustes was a mythical robber killed by Theseus. Ben Jonson repeated this conceit in the table talk recorded by William Drummond of Hawthornden (*Conversations with Drummond*, no. 4, see *Ben Jonson*, ed. Ian Donaldson [Oxford, 1985]): 'He cursed Petrarch for redacting verses to sonnets, which he said were like that tyrant's bed, where some who were too short were racked, others too long cut short.' For Daniel's response in defence of the sonnet, see p. 216.

18. *What divine in his sermon . . . the testimony of a rhyme*: The implication is that such orators might use metre to ornament their prose; see note 6 above.

19. *Galen*: Galen (129–99 AD) was one of the foremost ancient medical authorities. Campion received the degree of M.D. from the University of Caen in France in 1605, and had probably been training since the year the *Observations* was published, 1602. He later practised as a physician in London.

20. *If the Italians . . . would they not answer 'into numbers'*: It is true that Renaissance vernacular poets struggled with an inferiority complex in relation to Greek and Latin literature and language. Some wrote vindications of their vernaculars; the form and content of most poetry (especially evident in the case of Renaissance epics) witnessed an attempt to emulate classical examples. Experiments with classical metres in the vernacular were on the fringes of this culture but stemmed from the same impulse. Whilst most of the great Renaissance writers might have feared that their language and literature would never achieve the lasting permanence of Greek and Latin, they had the options of writing in Latin and of composing poems in quantitative vernacular metres and few took either. See Daniel's response to this point, p. 218.

21. *There are but three feet . . . but to little purpose*: For a fuller, but still incomplete, list, see Puttenham, Book 2, p. 112 and note 8.

22. *For both the concourse . . . unapt to slide*: 'To slide' was a rhetorical virtue. Cf. Thomas Wilson, *The Art of Rhetoric* (1553; 1560), Book 1: 'every orator should earnestly labour to file [i.e. smooth, polish] his tongue, that his words may slide with ease, and that in his deliverance he may have such grace as the sound of a lute, or any such instrument doth give' (*ERLC*, 77); and Quintilian, *Institutio oratoria*, on *pronuntiatio*, 12.3.30–65.

23. *Thence it is that . . . our hardly entreated dactyl*: With the exception of Sidney, most writers of English verse in classical metres had written extended poems in hexameters, e.g. Richard Stanyhurst's translation of *Aeneid* Books 1–4 (1582) and the poems of Abraham Fraunce; for the hexameter see note 2 above. For the nature of English monosyllables cf. Gascoigne, p. 241, Webbe, p. 258, and Puttenham, Book 2, p. 120. Amyntas is a pastoral name used in Thomas Watson's Latin *Amyntas* (1585) and Fraunce's translation *The Lamentations of Amyntas* (1587) and subsequent sequels (1591; 1592); Avernus was a lake at the entrance to the underworld; an Erinys was a Fury. Such words 'supply the defect' of the dactyl because they are of the pattern short-long-long, and thus could terminate a dactyl-spondee sequence at any point in the line (the previous word could then be long-short rather than a whole dactyl); they tended to flock to the ends of lines where

dactyl-spondee was required. Word-foot coincidence was recommended for the last two feet of the line, but this proved difficult to manage because, as Campion observes, few English trisyllables are dactylic. Watson's *Amyntas* uses 'Amyntas', 'Olympus' and 'Avernus' for some line endings, and in Fraunce's translation they proliferate spectacularly: on some pages as many as half of the lines end with 'Amyntas'.

24. *And first for the iambics . . . hereafter more evidently appear*: Cf. Gascoigne, p. 240 and Webbe, p. 257, although both are thinking of a pattern of stresses rather than a quantitative pattern. The proximity of the iambic pattern to speech was a classical commonplace. See Aristotle, *Poetics*, 1449a: 'nature herself found the right metre, the iambic being the most speakable of all metres; this we can see from the fact that it is the one we most often produce accidentally in conversation, where hexameters are rare and only occur when we depart from conversational tone.'

25. *ditties or odes*: 'Ditty' is used of lyric poems, often when referring to the words of songs or to poems which are intended for musical setting. The Greek ode (Greek *ōdē*, 'song') was originally a form of song for public performance and of great metrical complexity, using (in its Pindaric form) different strophic forms for different sections of the whole. The Latin, Horatian, form is metrically simpler, descending from the alternative Greek tradition of Alcaeus and Sappho, and tends also to prefer less grand, and more private, subject matter. Typical of the Horatian odes Campion imitates is a variety of different line structures in each strophe or stanza.

26. *The second kind consists of . . . is made of two trochees*: This form combines different types of line. The dimeter line, described in Campion's fifth chapter, 'consists of two feet and one odd [extra] syllable'; its first foot is a spondee or a trochee, or occasionally an iamb, and its second foot a trochee followed by a final extra syllable which could be long or short; a tribrach (three short syllables) could be substituted for the second trochee. No special observation of the metre is required in performance – if each word is enunciated naturally, the metre will take care of itself. The points of variation are in the first feet of the first three lines of each stanza, where the second syllable may be long or short, and in the last syllable of the initial lines of each stanza, which may be long or short; this means that these lines can vary in temporal length from stanza to stanza, thus avoiding a predictable rhythm. 'Rose-cheeked Laura' is included here as the most cele-

brated of Campion's experimental poems. Most of his other examples, it is agreed, do not justify his claims.

27. *the fatness of rhyme*: Daniel picks up on this image, p. 228.

28. *as the grammarians leave . . . to the authority of poets*: On this category of poetic licence see Gascoigne, p. 244 and note 22 and Daniel, p. 215 and note 31.

29. *there is no art begun and perfected at one enterprise*: Daniel (p. 225) scores a point by connecting this closing remark to Campion's earlier claim to be making 'a lawful defence of perfection'.

FRANCIS BACON:
FROM THE ADVANCEMENT OF LEARNING

Text: *The twoo bookes of Francis Bacon. Of the proficience and advancement of learning, divine and humane.* (1605)

This extract is taken from the second book of *The Advancement of Learning*. On Bacon (1561–1626), see the Introduction, pp. lxxiv–lxxv.

1. *Poesy is a part of learning . . . the imagination*: Bacon follows the traditional tripartite division of the mind into reason, imagination and memory, but innovates, in his discussion of 'the parts of human learning' at the start of Book 2, by attaching a branch of human learning to each: history to the memory, poesy to the imagination and philosophy to reason.

2. *pictoribus atque poetis, etc*: Horace, *Ars poetica*, 9–10.

3. *It is taken in two senses . . . words or matter*: The separation of words (*verba*) and matter (*res*) runs right through rhetorical and literary theory. Bacon, in Book 1 of the *Advancement*, identifies three 'distempers' (sicknesses) which stand in the way of the advancement of learning. The first is 'when men study words and not matter', and a particular target is the slavish Ciceronianism also criticized by Sidney (see p. 49 and note 258).

4. *In the latter . . . in prose as in verse*: For the extension of poetry to fictitious prose see Sidney, p. 12 and note 45, following Aristotle, *Poetics*, 1447b and 1451b.

5. *Therefore, because the acts or events of true history . . . unexpected and alternative variations*: On the relation between poetry and history cf. Sidney, p. 18 and note 76, following Aristotle, *Poetics*, 1451b.

6. *So as it appeareth . . . and to delectation*: Cf. Sidney, pp. 18–21.
7. *it hath had access . . . where other learning stood excluded*:
    For the use of the example of the popularity of poetry among
    barbarians, cf. Cicero, *Pro Archia poeta*, 8.19, Sidney, p. 6 and
    note 15, Puttenham, pp. 64–5 and Daniel, p. 211.

MICHAEL DRAYTON:
'TO HENRY REYNOLDS, OF POETS
AND POESY'

Text: *The battaile of Agincourt.* (1627)

On Drayton (1563–1631), see the Introduction, pp. lxxv–lxxvi.

1. *To my most dearly loved friend, Henry Reynolds, Esquire*: Henry
    Reynolds (1563/4–1632), schoolmaster and poet, author of a
    translation of Tasso's pastoral drama *Aminta* (1628) and a critical
    work, *Mythomystes, wherein a Short Survey is Taken of the
    Nature and Value of True Poesy and Depth of the Ancients above
    our Modern Poets* (1632).
2. *And when that once Pueriles . . . had my Cato construèd*: The
    Sententiae pueriles ('Sentences for Boys', 1544) was a manual of
    Latin sentences by the German pedagogue Leonhard Culmann
    used in Elizabethan schools. The *Distichs* of Dionysius Cato was
    a popular school text from which schoolboys learnt Latin syntax
    as well as proverbial morality. The young Drayton served as a
    page in the household of the Gooderes at Polesworth Hall, and
    this must be the site of the early education described.
3. *first read to me honest Mantuan . . . Virgil's Eclogues*: The Latin
    eclogues of Mantuan (1448–1516) were widely used in Eliza-
    bethan schools, as were those of Virgil.
4. *Methought I straight . . . Parnassus' bicleft top*: Pegasus was the
    winged horse which sprang from the blood of Medusa. He was
    tamed and ridden by the hero Bellerophon. During the singing
    contest to which the nine daughters of Pierus (the Pierides) chal-
    lenged the nine Muses, Mount Helicon, home of the Muses
    and sacred to Apollo, swelled in pleasure, almost touching the
    heavens. Pegasus was ordered by Poseidon to strike the mountain
    with his hoof to order it to return to its proper size. From the site
    of the blow sprang the Hippocrene, the fountain of the Muses.
    Parnassus, which had two peaks ('bicleft'), was also sacred to
    Apollo and the Muses.

5. *And had for Finis, William Elderton*: William Elderton (died *c.* 1592) was a popular ballad writer; ballads printed as broadsides (single sheets) or gathered in popular collections usually ended 'Finis', followed by either the name or the initials of the author.

6. *That noble Chaucer ... honest Gower*: Geoffrey Chaucer (*c.* 1343–1400), author of *The Canterbury Tales* and *Troilus and Criseyde*; John Gower (?1330–1408), author of the *Confessio Amantis*. For this survey of English literature cf. Puttenham, Book 1, chapter 31.

7. *Aganippe's brim*: Aganippe was the fountain on Mount Helicon, sacred to the Muses and giving poetic inspiration.

8. *That princely Surrey ... Wyatt*: Sir Thomas Wyatt (1503–42) and Henry Howard, Earl of Surrey (?1517–47), courtier poets of the later part of Henry VIII's reign.

9. *Amongst our poets, Bryan ... Songs and Sonnets*: Songs and Sonnets (1557, known as 'Tottel's Miscellany') was an influential anthology of Henrician and mid-century poets, and included a substantial body of the work of both Wyatt and Surrey. It is not clear if Drayton indicates that the courtier and diplomat Sir Francis Bryan (died 1550) was also included in Tottel's collection, and the extent of any such contribution is not known.

10. *Gascoigne and Churchyard ... to have buried been*: George Gascoigne (*c.* 1534–77), on whom see the Introduction; Thomas Churchyard (?1520–1604), a prolific author over more than forty years, whose style came to seem very dated by the 1590s, when his publications included a verse paraphrase of Sidney's *Defence of Poesy* (*A Praise of Poetry out of Sir Philip Sidney*, 1595).

11. *Grave moral Spenser ... his Iliads up did make*: Edmund Spenser (?1552–99), author of *The Faerie Queene* (1590; 1596), the heroic poem to which Drayton compares the *Iliad* of Homer (often given in the plural form).

12. *The noble Sidney ... and idle similes*: Sir Philip Sidney (1554–86) is credited by Drayton with firmly establishing the conventions for English versification: 'paced' implies the even feet of accentual-syllabic verse, with a pun on 'peised' (weighed), a common term for measuring (quantitative) verses. He is also credited with setting a model for prose style, principally in the *Arcadia* (printed in 1590), which eclipsed the fashionable euphuistic style of John Lyly (?1554–1606), as developed in *Euphues, the Anatomy of Wit* (1578, with a sequel in 1580). On euphuism cf. Sidney, p. 50 and note 265.

13. *Warner ... so exactly limbed*: The spelling is 'lim'd' in the original

text, punning on 'limned', drawn, painted. William Warner (c. 1558–1609) was the author of *Albion's England* (1586; 1592; 1612), a much-admired poem giving a mythical history of Britain from Noah to the present day.

14. *Neat Marlow ... possess a poet's brain*: Marlowe's association with 'the first poets' (cf. Sidney, p. 4) and the *furor poeticus* (see Puttenham, p. 57 and Daniel, *Musophilus*, ll. 966–7) is due not so much to his drama as to his popular poem *Hero and Leander* (published posthumously in 1598), based on the Greek poem of Musaeus (c. 500 BC), who was consistently identified with his namesake, the mythical pupil of Orpheus.

15. *And surely Nashe ... Sharply satiric was he*: Thomas Nashe (c. 1567–1601) wrote some verse but is given a branch of the poet's laurel by Drayton for such works as *The Unfortunate Traveller* (1594). His brilliant and vicious satirical exchanges with the academic, and friend of Spenser, Gabriel Harvey, led to both writers' works being banned by the Archbishop of Canterbury in 1599.

16. *Shakespeare ... that trafficked with the stage*: The 'sock' referred to is the footwear of the comic actor (see note 18). William Shakespeare (1564–1616) was equally celebrated for his tragedies, histories, comedies and non-dramatic poetry; Drayton praises only his comedies. His 'rage' is the *furor poeticus*, an ability to be inspired, also seen in Marlowe.

17. *Amongst these Samuel Daniel ... his manner better fitted prose*: Drayton's criticism of Samuel Daniel (1563–1619) is often repeated, although it is neither impartial nor just. Both poets had written verse epics based on recent English history – Daniel's *Civil Wars* (1595; 1609) and Drayton's *Mortimeriados* ('The Mortimeriad', 1596), revised as *The Barons' Wars* (1603). That Daniel was by far the better historian, also writing an important prose history of England, may have suggested the criticism.

18. *Next these, learn'd Jonson ... the buskin or the sock away*: Ben Jonson (?1572–1637), poet and playwright, and a man who enjoyed daunting the likes of Drayton with his scholarship. His close relationship with classical models suggests the mention of the Roman tragedian Seneca and comic dramatist Plautus. The 'buskin' was equated with the *cothurnus*, a high thick-soled boot supposedly worn by Greek tragic actors. The 'sock' is the *soccus*, the low-heeled, light shoe worn by comic actors (on both cf. Puttenham, p. 86). This footwear is here turned into the prize for pre-eminence as a dramatist.

19. *As reverent Chapman . . . Out of the Greek*: George Chapman
    (?1559–1634) first published translations from the *Iliad* in 1598;
    1616 saw the publication of a complete *Iliad* and *Odyssey*. His
    translation of Musaeus' *Hero and Leander* (the basis of Mar-
    lowe's poem, which Chapman had completed in 1598) was pub-
    lished in 1616, and *The Georgics of Hesiod* followed in 1618.
    On these three as the first Greek poets whose works we have cf.
    Sidney, p. 4.

20. *And Sylvester . . . in striving to write more*: Joshua Sylvester
    (*c.* 1563–1618) published his *Divine Weeks and Works* between
    1592 and 1608, a translation of *La semaine* ('The Week', 1578),
    an epic account of the creation by the French protestant Guil-
    laume de Salluste, Sieur du Bartas (1544–90). The other works
    which Drayton disparages include *Lachrymae Lachrymarum*
    ('Tears of Tears', 1612).

21. *Then dainty Sandys . . . as though stiff and lame*: George Sandys
    (1578–1644) published the first five books of his translation of
    Ovid's *Metamorphoses* in 1621 and a complete translation in
    1626. Where Arthur Golding's translation (1565–7) had been
    into fourteeners, Sandys reduces Ovid's hexameters to 'the neat-
    ness' of iambic pentameter.

22. *So Scotland sent us hither . . . and Hawthornden*: It is not clear
    why Drayton talks of his Scottish friends in the past tense. The
    works of Sir William Alexander of Menstry (?1567–1640)
    include the poetical collection *Aurora* (1604), various plays, a
    bridging passage for Sidney's incomplete *Arcadia* [1617?], and
    Anacrisis; he was Secretary of State for Scotland from 1626 until
    his death. William Drummond of Hawthornden (1585–1649)
    was a correspondent of Drayton and friend of Alexander who
    played host to Ben Jonson in the winter of 1618/19 and recorded
    Jonson's conversation; much of his poetry was not printed until
    1656.

23. *Then the two Beaumonts and my Browne arose*: Francis Beau-
    mont (1584–1616), playwright and collaborator of John
    Fletcher; his brother Sir John Beaumont (1583–1627), author
    of *The Metamorphosis of Tobacco* (1602) and *Bosworth Field*
    (1629); William Browne (?1590–?1645), author of *Britannia's
    Pastorals* (1616).

24. *For such whose poems . . . I pass not for them*: Such authors as
    John Donne and Fulke Greville were well-known manuscript
    poets of Drayton's generation, the bulk of whose poetry was not
    published until after their deaths. Greville's work was allowed

little circulation beyond his closest friends, but Donne was probably the most copied manuscript poet of the period.

SIR WILLIAM ALEXANDER:
FROM ANACRISIS. OR A CENSURE OF
SOME POETS ANCIENT AND MODERN

Text: *The works of William Drummond, of Hawthornden.* (Edin-
burgh, 1711)

On Alexander (?1567–1640), see the Introduction, pp. lxxvi–lxxvii.
The title *Anacrisis* (Greek *anakrisis* from *anakrinō*) signifies 'inquiry',
'examination', usually in legal contexts, although 'criticism' comes
from the same root. The work was dedicated in manuscript to Alexander's friend William Drummond of Hawthornden, 'as well for a
testimony to after-times of our friendship and love as for that, to my
knowledge, there is not any in our northern country who hath more
diligently perused the authors cited in this censure'. The dedication is
signed 'Stirling', dating the work to between 1633, when Alexander
was created Earl of Stirling, and his death in 1640. On Alexander and
Drummond as friends and the leading figures of Scottish letters see
Drayton, ll. 163–74 and note 22.

1. *Language is but the apparel ... in its own degree*: Alexander
    follows the standard distinction between *res* (matter) and *verba*
    (words), the province in rhetoric of *inventio* and *dispositio* in the
    first case, and *elocutio* in the second. Sidney's theory of the
    'fore-conceit' (see p. 9) lies behind this passage, but Alexander
    introduces an anti-rhetorical perspective.
2. *I value language as a conduit ... it should deliver*: This sentence
    constructs a metaphor just as the following sentence does, with
    such a verb as 'compare' understood in the second and third
    clauses: truth and fiction ('witty inventions') are delivered in
    various styles of language (shaped conduits).
3. *I compare a poem to a garden*: The formal gardens of the Renais-
    sance, with their proportioned and patterned beds and walks,
    must be seen in this image. For the comparison of writing to a
    garden, implicit in the popularity of the term 'flowers' for choice
    passages, cf. Peacham's *The Garden of Eloquence* and note 4.
4. *the decorum kept in descriptions, and representing of persons*:
    For decorum see Sidney, p. 46 and Puttenham, Book 3, chapters
    23–24.

5.   *three sorts do chiefly please me . . . inflamed for great things*: The
     'rapture' (cf. Drayton, l. 107) is either the *furor poeticus* or
     visionary inspiration of the poet, or a transporting of the reader.
     Alexander's 'three sorts' correspond conveniently to the three
     elements of the rhetorical triad made central to Sidney's *Defence*:
     the 'grave sentence' to teaching (*docere*), the 'witty conceit' to
     delighting (*delectare*), and the 'generous rapture' to moving
     (*movere*).

6.   *Many would bound . . . but in a fiction*: Cf. Sidney, p. 12, Putten-
     ham, p. 57, and Harington, p. 262.

7.   *not considering that the ancients . . . inferior unto theirs*: Alex-
     ander's point is that, since a work like Homer's *Iliad* was con-
     sidered by the early Greeks to be both historical and theologically
     sound, those who argue that only fiction belongs to poetry
     demean either Christianity or the Christian's devotion to his faith
     by denying them the resources of poetry. The argument is a little
     confused. The theoretical issue is not the right of poets to write
     versifications of history or Scripture, but whether such works can
     be called 'poetry'. Alexander's own works include a long religious
     poem, *Doomsday* (1614).

8.   *that the poet . . . at his own pleasure*: This point follows the
     central argument of Sidney's *Defence* closely.

9.   *I have heard some . . . virtue to prove miserable*: Alexander again
     summarizes a number of points from Sidney.

10. *leaving the gifts of nature . . . whereof a human mind could be
     capable*: I.e. adding to natural physical beauty (which appeals
     only to the eye) virtues which appeal to the mind.

11. *the accomplishing of that excellent work*: Alexander goes on to
     describe how he wrote a bridging passage (printed in around
     1617 and included in subsequent editions of the *Arcadia*) designed
     to connect the unfinished Book 3 of the revised 'new' *Arcadia* to
     the ending supplied from the last three books of the original 'old'
     Arcadia.

BEN JONSON:
'A FIT OF RHYME AGAINST RHYME'

Text: *Under-woods. Consisting of divers poems*. In *The workes of
Benjamin Jonson* (1640), vol. 2.

On Jonson (1572/3–1637), see the Introduction, pp. lxxvii–lxxviii.

The poems in *The Underwood* mostly date from after 1616, the year in which Jonson's first folio was printed; Jonson died in 1637 and the poems were printed posthumously in the second folio. The poem cannot be dated any more precisely. According to the *Conversations with William Drummond of Hawthornden*, Drummond's record of Jonson's conversation when he visited Drummond in 1618/19, Jonson 'said he had written a discourse of poesy both against Campion and Daniel, especially this last, where he proves couplets to be the bravest sort of verses, especially when they are broken, like hexameters; and that cross rhymes and stanzas – because the purpose would lead him beyond eight lines to conclude – were all forced' (*Ben Jonson*, ed. Ian Donaldson [Oxford, 1985]). Only with Milton's *Paradise Lost* is the case put for accentual-syllabic verse without rhyme. Previous arguments are between quantitative, unrhymed verse (Campion's position) and accentual-syllabic rhymed verse (Daniel's). Jonson was a writer of the latter, preferring couplets but also writing stanzaic verse which includes some highly intricate forms. In this poem he takes up a position with which he had some sympathy as the most neoclassically minded poet of his generation. But he does so to have fun.

1.   *Rhyme, the rack of finest wits . . . To the ground*: For rhyme as a rack (instrument of torture) cf. Campion's conceit of Procrustes' bed as repeated by Jonson (Campion, p. 284 and note 17); there is also a pun on 'wrack', ruin. The 'measure, / But false weight' is accentual-syllabic metre as opposed to the true weight of quantitative metre. For the propping up of verse cf. Puttenham on 'staff' (stanza), p. 109.

2.   *Jointing syllabs . . . They were bound*: Lines 10–12 refer primarily to the poetic licence in word formation, or *metaplasm*, discussed by the rhetoricians and glanced at by Gascoigne and others (see Gascoigne, note 22 and Daniel, note 31). Jonson is speaking in colourful images rather than precise technical terms; the following are among the possible interpretations. Jointed syllables are either separated, perhaps across a line (e.g. 'them- / Selves' in the last two lines of Campion's 'Rose-cheeked Laura', p. 287), or split in two for the sake of metre (e.g. 'bewailèd', l. 21; and the *diaeresis* which separates adjacent vowels in 'heroë', Drayton, 'To Henry Reynolds, of Poets and Poesy', l. 86), or elided, as in 'Fast'ning' (l. 11). Drowned letters are omitted through elision or through such figures as *apocope* ('oft' for 'often'), *aphaeresis* ('twixt' for 'betwixt'), and *syncope* ('syllabs' for 'syllables', ll. 10 and 52). Fastened vowels are elided by *synalepha* when two words meet (e.g. dissyllabic 't'attain' for 'to attain'). Further examples are

given by Puttenham (Book 3, chapter 11, not included in this edition).

3. *Soon as lazy thou wert known*: Probably 'lazy thou' is the subject of 'wert known', rather than the line meaning 'as soon as you were known to be lazy'.

4. *For a thousand years together . . . All light failèd*: The 'thousand years' covers the period between the fall of the Roman Empire and the present. Parnassus is one of the mountains sacred to Apollo, god of poetry and music, and the Muses, and a source and site of poetry and poetic inspiration. Pegasus is associated with the Hippocrene, a fountain on Mount Helicon produced by a strike of his hoof (see Drayton, note 4). The 'wells' (usually emended to 'well') and 'fountain' could include Hippocrene and Aganippe on Mount Helicon, and Castalia on Mount Parnassus. Cf. Drayton for a similarly blurred image.

5. *Worth a-crowning*: In the 1640 edition this line is simply 'Worth crowning': the line thus lacks a syllable. Since many of Jonson's metrical effects in this poem are ironically brash examples of *metaplasm* (e.g. ll. 10–11), the emendation, suggested in the edition of the poem in *Ben Jonson*, ed. Herford and Simpson, vol. 8 (Oxford, 1947), seems apt, making the word an example of *prothesis* (the addition of a prefix). For poetic coronations see Sidney, note 150.

6. *Whilst the Latin . . . But rests foilèd*: Latin remains compromised by having been polluted by rhyme. Cf. Puttenham, Book 1, chapters 6–7 and Campion, chapter 1.

7. *Vulgar languages that want . . . Other cesure*: The quantitative system of long and short syllables ('true measure') was natural to Greek and was grafted successfully on to Latin. 'Cesure', as used by Puttenham and others, is caesura, the break in the middle of a line, but the term was also used of line-ends: Jonson is saying that modern languages will not be governed by patterns of medial or terminal pauses, or the use of specified feet in those positions, but will only follow the rule of ending each line with a rhyme.

8. *May his sense . . . Grow unsounder*: The poetic feet of rhyme's founder are swollen by the 'cold tumour' which is rhyme; the sense which grows unsounder is both the founder's, cursed by Jonson to suffer a dizzy spell, and the meaning of the verse, its reason confused by rhyme.

BEN JONSON:

FROM HORACE, HIS ART OF POETRY

Text: *Horace, his art of poetrie*. In *The workes of Benjamin Jonson* (1640), vol. 2.
Running title: 'Horace, of the Art of Poetry'

On Jonson (1572/3–1637), see the Introduction, pp. lxxvii–lxxviii. Jonson's undated translation of Horace's *Ars poetica* was published posthumously in 1640 in two forms: in an early draft in John Benson's edition of the *Poems*, and in a later revision in the second folio, with facing Latin text; the latter is followed here. In the preface to *Sejanus* (1605), Jonson had promised to discuss dramatic theory 'in my Observations upon Horace his Art of Poetry, which, with the text translated, I intend shortly to publish'. This work never appeared, and the translation may date, at least in its revised form, from as late as the 1630s. This brief selection includes most of the passages quoted and alluded to frequently by Renaissance authors; at the head of each passage is the Latin tag those authors used as a shorthand reference to the larger passage (in some cases, e.g. *in medias res*, these tags enter critical terminology); the notes give line references for the corresponding Latin text, a translation of the tag, and, in some cases, the rest of the phrase from which it is taken.

1.   *si vis me flere*: 'If you would have me weep, you must first feel grief yourself' (*Ars poetica*, ll. 86–107). In Heinsius' 1610 edition of Horace certain passages are reordered to give greater coherence. Jonson's earlier draft follows the order preferred in modern editions, ll. 126–31, ll. 121–5, ll. 132–51, but the later folio version used here follows Heinsius' order.

2.   *Thyestes' feast*: The feast at which Atreus feeds his unwitting brother Thyestes his own sons is the subject of the *Thyestes* of Seneca (who post-dates Horace) and lost plays of the same name by Sophocles and Euripedes.

3.   *the sock*: The 'sock' (the *soccus*, a low-heeled, light shoe worn by comic actors) stands for comedy; cf. Drayton, l. 136, on Jonson.

4.   *angry Chremes*: Chremes is a stock character in Roman comedy.

5.   *Telephus and Peleus*: The subject of various lost plays, Telephus, the son of Hercules, was abandoned as a child; in Euripides' fragmentary *Telephus*, he is disguised as a beggar. Peleus, father of Achilles, was banished by his father for the murder of his half-brother, again went into exile after accidentally killing his

father-in-law, and, as an old man, was driven from his kingdom
by the sons of an enemy; he figures in various lost and surviving
plays by Euripides.

6.   *If thou wouldst have me weep . . . Peleus or Telephus*: This is an
     important fusion of literary decorum and the rhetorical theory of
     convincing performance. See Sidney, note 253.

7.   *in medias res*: 'Ever he hastens to the issue, and hurries his hearer
     into the story's midst' (*Ars poetica*, ll. 143–52).

8.   *He thinks not . . . But light from smoke*: Horace: 'He plans to
     give not smoke from fire but light from smoke' (*Ars poetica*,
     l. 143). Metaphorically the 'smoke' is muddled and over-
     complicated plotlines, but it is also literal: from the burning of
     Troy, included in neither the *Iliad* (which precedes it) nor the
     Odyssey (which succeeds it). The meaning is that it is better not
     to attempt to tell the story of the whole Trojan war, but to tell of
     something consequent on it, in this case Odysseus' efforts to
     return home.

9.   *Antiphates, Scylla, Charybdis, Polypheme*: Antiphates is the king
     of a race of cannibal giants, the Laestrygonians, who destroy
     most of Odysseus' fleet; Scylla and Charybdis are the sea-monsters
     between which Odysseus must sail; Polyphemus is the Cyclops.

10. *Nor from the brand . . . Of Diomede*: Diomedes is one of the
     Greek heroes and a frequent companion of Odysseus in the *Iliad*.
     His return home as recounted in the *Odyssey* is straightforward.
     Meleager is his uncle. At his birth the fates told Meleager's mother
     that his life was bound to that of a log burning on the fire; she
     removed it and kept it safe but when Meleager killed his uncles
     she threw it on the fire.

11. *nor Troy's sad war . . . that did disclose the twins*: The pairs of
     twins, Helen of Troy and Pollux, and Clytemnestra and Castor,
     were born from two eggs, their mother Leda having been raped
     by Zeus in the form of a swan, although Castor and Clytemnestra
     were the issue of Leda's husband Tyndareus. Cf. Sidney's example
     of where to begin a story, p. 46.

12. *Scribendi recte, sapere*: 'Of good writing the source and fount is
     wisdom'. (*Ars poetica*, ll. 309–22).

13. *The very root of writing well . . . not against their will*: 'Socratic'
     means simply 'philosophical', since 'all philosophers claimed . . .
     the title of followers of Socrates' (Cicero, *De oratore*, 3.16.61).
     The necessity of wisdom is a point borrowed from rhetoric. Cf.
     De oratore, 2.2.5 on the need for the orator to have a broad
     education, and 3.15.56–19.73 for a discussion of the relations

between rhetoric and philosophy which includes nostalgia for
the pre-Socratic days before 'the philosophers looked down on
eloquence and the orators on wisdom'. Cf. Quintilian, *Institutio
oratoria*, 2.21 and 12.2, and Peacham, note 8. Cf. Gascoigne's
version of the dictum 'hold to the matter, the words will follow',
attributed to Cato the Elder, p. 239 and note 4.

14. *He that hath studied well ... fitting dues to every man*: Cf.
    Puttenham on decorum, Book 3, chapters 23–4.

15. *Aut prodesse ... utile dulci*: 'Poets aim either to benefit, or to
    amuse ... He has won every vote who has blended profit and
    pleasure' (*Ars poetica*, ll. 333–46). In Heinsius' edition the pass-
    age is interrupted after l. 334 (Jonson's l. 478) by the transposed
    passage ll. 391–407 (Jonson's ll. 479–502, omitted here).
    Jonson's earlier draft gives the passage in the order preferred in
    modern editions and arrived at in this edition by the omission of
    ll. 479–502, but the later version in the folio follows Heinsius.
    This passage lies behind the 'delightful teaching' of Sidney's
    Defence.

16. *Let what thou feign'st ... The truth*: The *Ars poetica* begins by
    considering an imagined picture of a monster composed of parts
    from different animals: ' "Painters and poets," you say, "have
    always had an equal right in hazarding anything." We know it:
    this licence we poets claim and in our turn we grant the like; but
    not so far that savage should mate with tame, or serpents couple
    with birds, lambs with tigers' (ll. 9–13). For the idea of verisimili-
    tude in fiction cf. Aristotle, *Poetics*, 1460a: 'One ought to prefer
    likely impossibilities to unconvincing possibilities'.

17. *when Lamia's dined*: Lamia was a female monster or enchantress
    who stole children, the ancient nurse's equivalent of the
    bogeyman.

18. *our grave men ... Our gallants give them none*: The separation
    of 'grave men' and young 'gallants' is based on the Roman classi-
    fication of men as *seniores* (aged between forty-six and sixty) and
    iuniores.

19. *the Sosii*: Famous Roman booksellers.

20. *dormitat Homerus ... Ut pictura poesis*: 'Homer nods ... A
    poem is like a picture' (*Ars poetica*, ll. 359–65).

Index